THE HORROR THEORY READER

THE HORROR THEORY READER

Jeffrey Andrew Weinstock, Editor

University of Minnesota Press
Minneapolis
London

The Publication History at the end of the book gives original and previous publication history for the writings compiled in this book.

Every effort was made to obtain permission to reproduce material in this book. If any proper acknowledgment has not been included here, we encourage copyright holders to notify the publisher.

Copyright 2026 by the Regents of the University of Minnesota

All rights reserved. No part of this publication may be reproduced, stored in a retrieval system, utilized for purposes of training artificial intelligence technologies, or transmitted in any form or by any means, electronic, mechanical, photocopying, recording, or otherwise, without the prior written permission of the publisher.

Published by the University of Minnesota Press
111 Third Avenue South, Suite 290
Minneapolis, MN 55401-2520
http://www.upress.umn.edu

ISBN 978-1-5179-1781-4 (hc)
ISBN 978-1-5179-1782-1 (pb)

A Cataloging-in-Publication record for this book is available from the Library of Congress.

Printed in the United States of America on acid-free paper

The University of Minnesota is an equal-opportunity educator and employer.

35 34 33 32 31 30 29 28 27 26   10 9 8 7 6 5 4 3 2 1

CONTENTS

Introduction. "Won't Someone Please Think of the Children?!"
Thinking Horror Through the Lens of Moral Panic   1
   Jeffrey Andrew Weinstock

Part I. Early Inquiries and Quick Takes

1. From *Poetics*   35
   Aristotle

2. Of Tragedy   39
   David Hume

3. On the Reason We Take Pleasure in Tragic Subjects   46
   Friedrich Schiller

4. From *A Philosophical Enquiry into the Origin of Our Ideas of the Sublime and the Beautiful*   57
   Edmund Burke

5. From "Why Terrour and Grief Are Pleasing to the Mind When Excited by Descriptions"   63
   Joseph Addison

6. On the Pleasure Derived from Objects of Terror   67
   Anna Laetitia Barbauld

7. On the Supernatural in Poetry   70
   Ann Radcliffe

8. On the Supernatural in Fictitious Composition; and Particularly on the Works of Ernest Theodore William Hoffmann 78
   Walter Scott

9. Introduction to *Supernatural Horror in Literature* 115
   H. P. Lovecraft

10. Introduction to *Uncanny Stories* 119
    Christopher St. John Sprigg

11. The Enjoyment of Fear 122
    Alfred Hitchcock

12. From *Danse Macabre* 127
    Stephen King

Part II. The Paradox of Horror

13. Fearing Fictions 133
    Kendall Walton

14. The Paradox of Horror 153
    Berys Gaut

15. From *The Philosophy of Horror; or, Paradoxes of the Heart* 166
    Noël Carroll

16. Enjoying Negative Emotions in Fictions 171
    John Morreall

17. Fear for Your Life: The Appeals, Functions, and Effects of Horror 179
    Mathias Clasen

18. An Introduction to the American Horror Film 190
    Robin Wood

19. From *Sacred Terror: Religion and Horror on the Silver Screen* 217
    Douglas E. Cowan

20. From "Discipline and Distraction: *Psycho,* Visual Culture, and Postmodern Cinema" 224
    Linda Williams

21. Frightening Fascination: A Phenomenology of Direct Horror 239
    Julian Hanich

22. (Why) Do You Like Scary Movies? A Review of the Empirical Research on Psychological Responses to Horror Films 268
    G. Neil Martin

23. Horror's Long-Lasting Appeal 317
    Nina Nesseth

Part III. Different Voices

24. Displaying Connoisseurship, Recognizing Craftsmanship 329
    Matt Hills

25. My Words to Victor Frankenstein Above the Village of Chamounix: Performing Transgender Rage 349
    Susan Stryker

26. Refusing to Refuse to Look: Female Viewers of the Horror Film 366
    Brigid Cherry

27. From "Horror at the Crossroads: Class, Gender, and Taste at the Rialto" 384
    Mark Jancovich and Tim Snelson

28. Critical Pleasures: Reflections on the Indonesian Horror Genre and Its Anti-Fans 392
    Meghan Downes

29. New Black Gothic 408
    Sheri-Marie Harrison

30. Black Horror Beyond the White Gaze: A Conversation 415
    Dani Bethea and Monika Negra

31. Contemporary Horror and Disability: Adaptations and Active Readers 432
    Petra Kuppers

32. A Demon-Girl's Guide to Life 447
    S. Trimble

Publication History 457

Contributors 461

Index 465

Introduction

"WON'T SOMEONE PLEASE THINK OF THE CHILDREN?!"
Thinking Horror Through the Lens of Moral Panic

Jeffrey Andrew Weinstock

THIS ANTHOLOGY COLLECTS TOGETHER writings from antiquity to the twenty-first century that address the seemingly counterintuitive appeal of horror. "Horror" here is meant primarily in the sense of what philosopher Noël Carroll in *The Philosophy of Horror* (1990) refers to as "art-horror"—a transmedial genre that entertains through displays or representations of violence and gore.[1] Art-horror, for Carroll, refers to fiction, dramatizations, and aestheticized depictions of threatening and gruesome content and includes things like Gothic novels, horror films, theater performances, and even works of fine art (he mentions Francisco Goya and H. R. Giger) that, in his view, seek to evoke fear and disgust from their audiences. In the twenty-first century, we could extend this to podcasts, gaming, and other forms of new media.

The "art" part of "art-horror" is vital for Carroll's consideration. Importantly, art-horror isn't real life but rather the expression of human creative skill and imagination. When consuming art-horror, the audience is aware that they are not watching or listening to someone or something who is really being threatened or harmed. Because the audience knows that it is art rather than real life, they are licensed—although with certain caveats—to consider things like aesthetics (the composition of scenes, the realism of the representations, the eloquence of the language, and so on), themes and symbolism present, the role of such scenes within the work as a whole, and the "message" intended by the work's creator and to derive pleasure from such things. This licensing of analysis and enjoyment extends even to reenactments of violent scenes or artistic depictions of gruesome subject matter. However, as the writings included in this anthology will attest, the question of whether and how horror evokes pleasure is a subject of considerable debate, as is whether and under what conditions it is ethically or morally acceptable to enjoy horrific content.

Carroll distinguishes art-horror from what he calls "natural horror," which includes actual scenes of harm, depictions of actual harm done, or even the contemplation of concepts that evoke psychic distress. To Carroll, there is a commonsense distinction between, on one hand, driving by a gruesome car crash, viewing a photograph of the aftermath of a suicide bombing, or contemplating Nazi gas chambers and, on the other hand, reading Stephen King's *The Shining* (1977), watching Jordan Peele's film *Get Out* (2017), or even looking at a horrifying painting, such as Henry Fuseli's *The Nightmare* (1781). Natural horror is thus excluded from consideration in Carroll's *The Philosophy of Horror*; it isn't art—an expression of human creative skill and imagination (and Carroll isn't interested in taking up the question of if it is ethically acceptable to aestheticize documentation of horrific scenes). Carroll's focus is squarely on what he conceives as the horror genre—a category of artistic expression that, he asserts, originated in the ancient world and then coalesced in the middle part of the eighteenth century with the rise of the Gothic novel[2]—with a focus on explaining the seemingly contradictory enjoyment audiences derive from contributions to the genre. If horror seeks to evoke fear and disgust, and these emotions are unpleasant, why, he asks, would anyone subject themselves voluntarily to art-horror?

The distinction Carroll draws between art-horror and natural horror is, in reality, a little murkier than he acknowledges. This is because human beings have a long history of taking pleasure in witnessing real scenes of violence and gore. From gladiatorial contests and Roman persecution of Christians to public executions to events like bearbaiting and cockfights, things that today many would find brutal and disturbing involving very real violence, gore, and the death of both human beings and animals have often served as forms of human enjoyment. Public hangings in seventeenth-century England, for example, inspired a "carnival-like atmosphere,"[3] while, as Robert Darnton notes, "the torture of animals, especially cats, was a popular amusement throughout early modern Europe."[4]

It is important here to avoid evaluating events and spectacles of earlier time periods in light of modern sensibilities, as understandings of the nature and value of both human and animal life have shifted over time and from place to place. One must also bear in mind context: No doubt the holiday atmosphere that prevailed at early modern public executions had much to do with the pleasures of a public gathering and a break from routine—and certainly attendance was encouraged or, at times, enforced by those in power to reinforce their authority. Of course, one must also remember that so-called blood sports pitting humans against one another, humans against animals, and animals against other animals remain common today, although with varying degrees of legal and social acceptance.

Carroll's consideration of the "paradox of horror" significantly also sidesteps questions of morality. Carroll isn't concerned with whether it is natural or perverse, good or bad, or moral or immoral to consume art-horror (although he implicitly suggests that there is or should be something problematic about enjoying non-art-horror);

his is a more academic exercise: Bracketing off questions of morality, how can we explain the attraction? However, for millennia, very real concerns have been expressed about what the attraction to horror writ large says about human nature and character, and about the possibly pernicious consequences of indulging the taste for horror. The critics, censors, and safeguarders of public morality whose concerns about horror have sometimes fueled the fire of "moral panics," therefore, have all on some level theorized the appeal and effects of horror—often, although not always, focusing on the presumed negative effects of exposure to horror on children. The next section of this introduction surveys some of those critical voices with attention to several key moments in the history of public responses to horror as entertainment and their implicit theorization of its appeal.

"A Cruel Enjoyment": Anxious Voices in Antiquity

As Edmund P. Cueva explains, even in the ancient world, there were individuals who protested against the violence and horror of public entertainments like gladiatorial contests and the persecution of Christians. "These voices," Cueva elaborates, "illustrate that even in a society where such violent entertainment was popular and widely accepted, there were people who found them morally repugnant and spoke out against them. Their critiques often focused on the dehumanizing effects of these spectacles, the moral decay they fostered, and the incompatibility of such practices with ethical and philosophical ideals."[5] Such entertainments were condemned for a variety of reasons ranging from their inherent immorality to their supposed detrimental effects on society.

The early Christian author Tertullian, for example, devotes his *De spectaculis* (*On the Spectacles*, circa 200 CE) to condemning both Circensian games (i.e., those taking place in the Circus in Rome) and the theater as sinful. This is in part because such entertainments derive from pagan ritual and are thus considered by him to be forms of idolatry; more important, though, according to Tertullian, such spectacles evoke "spiritual agitation" and stimulate in us not only lust but "rage, bitterness, wrath and grief."[6] Since, he explains, "passionate excitement is forbidden us [by God], we are debarred from every kind of spectacle, and especially from the circus, where such excitement presides as in its proper element."[7] "May God avert from His people any such passionate eagerness after a cruel enjoyment!" he pleads.

Equally caustic in his condemnation of both Circensian games and the theater is Lactantius—an early Christian author and adviser to Roman emperor Constantine I. In his *Divinae institutiones* (*The Divine Institutes,* 303–11 CE), he cautions the virtuous against surrendering to debased pleasures. Of gladiatorial contests, he writes:

> I ask now whether they can be just and pious men, who, when they see men placed under the stroke of death, and entreating mercy, not only suffer them to be put to

death, but also demand it, and give cruel and inhuman votes for their death, not being satiated with wounds nor contented with bloodshed. Moreover, they order them, even though wounded and prostrate, to be attacked again, and their caresses to be wasted with blows, that no one may delude them by a pretended death. They are even angry with the combatants, unless one of the two is quickly slain; and as though they thirsted for human blood, they hate delays. They demand that other and fresh combatants should be given to them, that they may satisfy their eyes as soon as possible. Being imbued with this practice, they have lost their humanity.[8]

The theater functions similarly to make a spectacle of iniquitous acts and to stimulate lust:

And I am inclined to think that the corrupting influence of the stage is still more contaminating. . . . The stories of the tragedians place before the eyes the parricides and incests of wicked kings, and represent tragic crimes. And what other effect do the immodest gestures of the players produce, but both teach and excite lusts? . . . What can young men or virgins do, when they see that these things are practised without shame, and willingly beheld by all? They are plainly admonished of what they can do, and are inflamed with lust, which is especially excited by seeing; and every one according to his sex forms himself in these representations.[9]

In his commentary, Lactantius condemns violent forms of entertainment as well as stage plays both for evoking base urges—blood lust and sexual desire—and for modeling bad behavior that may negatively affect impressionable youths. These entertainments appeal to audiences, he explains, because we derive pleasure from our senses; however, sensory pleasures are presented as being at odds with virtue, the role of which is to "subdue and conquer pleasure."[10]

St. Augustine then echoes Lactantius in his *Confessions* (397–400 CE) when he discusses the seduction of a young man by gladiatorial games. This young man had previously resisted such displays, "being utterly opposed to and detesting such spectacles." Dragged there, however, by classmates, his scruples fell by the wayside:

For, directly he saw that blood, he therewith imbibed a sort of savageness; nor did he turn away, but fixed his eye, drinking in madness unconsciously, and was delighted with the guilty contest, and drunken with the bloody pastime. Nor was he now the same he came in, but was one of the throng he came unto, and a true companion of those who had brought him there. Why need I say more? He looked, shouted, was excited, carried away with him the madness which would stimulate him to return, not only with those who first enticed him, but also before them, yea, and to draw in others.[11]

For Tertullian, Lactantius, and Augustine, there is a form of debased pleasure that audiences derive from spectacles of violence. Such things appeal to the baser side of human nature—the part of human nature that must be subordinated to please God and achieve salvation. Put simply, they appeal to use because we are lustful, savage creatures and this is the part of our nature that must be repressed if we wish to be rewarded after death. As such, we need to be constantly on guard against such desires and to discipline ourselves to resist illicit temptations.

"Sinfull, Heathenish, Lewde, Ungodly Spectacles": Early Modern Theater

As the Roman Church increased in power, gladiatorial contests and the theater declined in the fifth century. Theatrical performance reemerged in the Middle Ages as part of church life and then expanded during the Renaissance, precipitating a vigorous response from Puritan antitheatrical critics concerned about cross-dressing and that representations of what they construed as immorality could infect audience members—stimulating impure thoughts, provoking immoral behavior, and degrading society as a whole. Jonas Barish in his *The Antitheatrical Prejudice* explains that, for antitheatrical polemicists, enjoying the spectacle of violence makes one complicit in the crimes depicted: "The audience, by attending and enjoying applauding, approves, in effect, what it sees, and so shares in the sins it beholds. It is the element of spectator complicity which makes the experience perilous."[12]

Joel Elliot Slotkin proposes that, for Protestant reformers during the Early Modern period, "works of literature had to demonstrate a moral benefit in order to justify their existence, and pleasure was inherently suspicious—the possibility of pleasure in artistic representations of evil doubly so."[13] The theater in this regard was a particular focus of scorn for early modern critics where "witty and engaging villains upstaged virtuous characters and engaged in baroque acts of sadism and depravity."[14] Slotkin's article, "A Taste for Slaughter: Stephen Gosson, *Titus Andronicus,* and the Appeal of Evil," focuses in particular on the criticisms of sixteenth- and seventeenth-century antitheatrical writer Stephen Gosson, with Shakespeare's play *Titus Andronicus* (composed sometime between 1588 and 1593) as an example of the kinds of entertainment Gosson was targeting. I will attend to the Shakespeare first.

Titus Andronicus is one of Shakespeare's tragedies and is his work that most fully emulates the popular revenge tragedies of the sixteenth and early seventeenth centuries. These works, including Thomas Kyd's *The Spanish Tragedy* (composed between 1582 and 1592), John Webster's *The White Devil* (1612) and *The Dutchess of Malfi* (1613 or 1614), and John Marton's *Antonio's Revenge* (1602), take place, as Andrew Dickson explains, in "a shadowy universe in which sexual and political betrayal combine with incest, insanity, forced marriage and ferocious honour codes that would not disgrace the 19th-century mafia."[15] James A. Knapp notes that the plots of such works are intricate and "move relentlessly toward the dramatic depiction of sensational acts of violence."[16] They sometimes include ghosts and always include torture and blood. Slotkin argues concerning *Titus Andronicus* that "the baroque, gory tortures inflicted and endured by its characters seem calculated to outrage contemporary moralists" and that the "primary effect of the play's exploration of the depths of blood and horror is to aestheticize violence and to articulate and develop a connoisseurship of pain."[17] Revenge tragedies including *Titus Andronicus* certainly can be accommodated within Carroll's category of art-horror.

For critics of the theater like Stephen Gosson and William Prynne, the theater in general and revenge tragedies in particular provoke what Slotkin refers to as "moral perversity": a willingness to embrace wickedness for its own sake and to reject virtue.[18] The theater is figured in Gosson's 1579 treatise, *The Schoole of Abuse*, as seductive. The aesthetic pleasures of the performance serve as a "gateway to immoral behaviour."[19] As Slotkin explains, the idea was widespread in early modern Christian thought that, as a consequence of original sin, human beings have a predisposition toward evil against which we must be continually on guard. Violent tragedies, however, "encourage a kind of perversity that takes pleasure in the experience of sadness and gory, destructive violence, which we ought to repudiate on both moral and aesthetic grounds."[20] Barish notes that Renaissance attacks on the theater culminated in 1632 with William Prynne's mammoth *Histriomastix: The Player's Scourge, or Actor's Tragedy*, "a gargantuan encyclopedia of antitheatrical lore which scourges every form of theater in the most ferocious terms."[21] The work itself leaves little doubt concerning its intentions, as explained in its impressive extended title:

> Wherein it is largely evidenced, by divers arguments, by the concurring authorities and resolutions of sundry texts of Scripture . . . that popular stage-plays . . . are sinfull, heathenish, lewde, ungodly spectacles, and most pernicious corruptions; condemned in all ages, as intolerable mischiefes to churches, to republickes, to the manners, mindes, and soules of men. And that the profession of play-poets, of stage-players; together with the penning, acting, and frequenting of stage-plays, are unlawfull, infamous and misbeseeming Christians.[22]

Barish's humorous commentary on Prynne foregrounds the moral panic at the core of *Histriomastix*. Prynne expresses, explains Barish, "in most agonized form, the fears of impurity, of contamination, of 'mixture,' of the blurring of strict boundaries, which haunted thousands in the Renaissance."[23] Prynne, Barish continues, "is terrified, maddened, by the fear of total breakdown. . . . He conjures up a nightmarish vision of a world itself out of control, a horrendous dystopia ruled by the Prince of Darkness, who has made of the theater his chosen weapon for the overthrow of man and the final establishment of his own empire."[24]

To be fair, early modern antitheatrical writers found many problems with the theater, including its pagan origins, its "feminizing" effect on cross-dressing boys and men, its erosion of class boundaries, and so on.[25] Chief among these concerns, however, was its stimulation of dangerous passions. For Puritan antitheatrical critics, as for early Christian writers, the theater is deeply suspect in large measure because it caters to our baser inclinations, not just sanctioning but eliciting lust and vice. Plays are, in Prynne's overheated rhetoric, "sinfull, heathenish, lewde, ungodly spectacles" that infect and corrupt. This is because of an inherent human tendency toward depravity. We are sensual creatures, lustful and prone to sin, and the theater excites these "baser" urges. We enjoy representations of depravity because we are ourselves, if not depraved, then always perched upon the precarious edge of being so. The censors (at least in their own minds) thus seek to protect us from ourselves by sparing us from temptation. Put simply, we enjoy horror because we ourselves, at least in part, are horrible.

The Distempered Imagination: The Gothic Novel

Early modern concerns about horror on the stage were folded into larger criticisms of the theater in general. Where eighteenth- and early nineteenth-century Gothic novels are concerned, however, the anxiety is focused directly on what Carroll would call art-horror—artistic representations of violence, murder, incest, and gore—with attacks directed not just at particular works but also at their creators, whose imaginations are figured as diseased and debased.

Gothic novels emerged in the middle part of the eighteenth century, with scholars and critics often pointing to Horace Walpole's 1764 novel, *The Castle of Otranto*, as the first work to refer to itself as "Gothic." Ann Radcliffe, Matthew Lewis, and Clara Reeve are among the notable eighteenth-century contributors to the genre and were followed in the nineteenth century by authors including Edgar Allan Poe, Mary Shelley, Charles Maturin, Robert Louis Stevenson, and Bram Stoker. Including themes of rape, incest, and murder, the Gothic genre, in the estimation of critic Fred Botting, is the literature of transgression—and, as such, provoked the ire of those invested in safeguarding existing standards of moral behavior and decorum. "Attacked throughout the second half of the eighteenth century for encouraging excessive emotions and invigorating unlicensed passions," writes Botting, "Gothic texts were also seen to be subverting the mores and manners on which good social behaviour rested."[26] "Gothic fictions," Botting continues, "seemed to promote vice and violence, giving free reign [sic] to selfish ambitions and sexual desires beyond the prescriptions of law or familial duty."[27] As Rictor Norton explains, concerns over the Gothic novel involved three interrelated issues: "the power of fear and the supernatural to stimulate the creative imagination (for both writer and reader); the tendency of the genre to deprave and corrupt its readers; and the subversive or revolutionary political nature of the genre." Norton continues, "These three aesthetic, moral and ideological critiques are linked by the repeated charge that such literature appeals to and is created by 'the distempered imagination.'"[28] Norton's characterization of Gothic anxiety here is notable for highlighting the attack upon not just the work but its creator as well.

An important node in the history of horror-related moral panics is occupied by Matthew Lewis's notorious Gothic novel, *The Monk: A Romance.* Published in 1796,

Lewis's novel focuses on the lascivious monk Ambrosio, who lusts after a young woman named Antonia and is assisted in his seduction of her by a demon named Matilda. The story culminates in rape, murder, the revelation of incest, and a guest appearance by the devil himself. Unsurprising, the lurid content provoked public outrage. Scholar Sarah Cleary opens her study of horror and censorship, *The Myth of Harm: Horror, Censorship, and the Child,* by noting poet Samuel Coleridge's condemnation of *The Monk*. Coleridge wrote in his 1797 review of the book, "Mildness of censure would here be criminally misplaced and silence would make us accomplices. Not without reluctance then, but on full conviction that we are performing a duty, we declare it to be our opinion, that the monk [sic] is a romance, which if a parent saw in the hands of a son or daughter he might reasonably turn pale."[29] Coleridge was followed in his condemnation by British satirist and scholar Thomas James Mathias, who not only "damned Lewis . . . and condemned, in general, lust and blasphemy disguised as literature" but argued that a portion of the novel was, in fact, indictable by law.[30] In his screed against Lewis's novel, Mathias attacks Lewis—who was a member of Parliament—asserting that he "has neither scrupled nor blushed to depict, and to publish to the world, the arts of lewd and systematic seduction, and to thrust upon the nation the most open and unqualified blasphemy against the very code and volume of our religion."[31] Mathias figures the novel as both a poison that harms and a disease that must be suppressed—and its author punished—for the good of the nation. As Irwin details, Coleridge and Mathias were then followed in their condemnations of the novel by many other attacks, "all of them reiterating in one way or another the charges of plagiarism, brutality, indecency, eroticism, and blasphemy."[32] Lewis did have his defenders, and of course, the notoriety surrounding the novel only served to heighten public interest in it (any press is good press, some might say). However, the novel's detractors were very clear: The debased content of the novel sprang from the diseased imagination of its creator and catered to the prurient interest of its audience.

As Cleary observes, the controversy around *The Monk* was intense, but not different in kind from the concerns articulated by critics about other Gothic novels: "Many eighteenth-century critics of the Gothic described it as something akin to a 'venereal disease,' or a 'virus . . . spreading in all directions,' capable of 'impressing young imaginations with gross improbabilities, unnatural horrors, and mysterious nonsense.'"[33] Botting, too, notes that "between 1790 and 1810 critics were almost univocal in their condemnation of what was seen as the unending torrent of popular trashy novels."[34] Botting continues, explaining that "the challenge to aesthetic values was framed in terms of social transgression: virtue, propriety, and domestic order were considered under threat."[35] What's interesting here is that, while critical condemnation was frequently framed as in past centuries in religious terms, such as blasphemy and immorality, these concerns are underwritten by broader anxieties regarding social stability. Nick Groom suggests that "the Gothic novels of 1790s'

Figure I.1. The devil collects his due from the monk Ambrosio in Matthew Lewis's *The Monk*. Frontispiece to volume 4 of the French translation, 1797.

Britain can be seen as a way of addressing the carnage of the [French] Revolution."[36] Their appeal to the masses, therefore, may have inhered—at least in part—in their antiauthoritarian stance. Gothic representations of debased aristocrats and clergy who, with seeming impunity, terrorize, exploit, and prey upon the virtuous and unprotected might have found a receptive audience among those who themselves felt in various ways terrorized, exploited, and preyed upon by cultural elites. That such novels could function to stoke the indignation of the underclasses might also then explain the caustic response from well-heeled critics and public figures. From such a perspective, moral panic is really an alibi obscuring political anxiety associated with class upheaval.

"Penny Packets of Poison": Penny Dreadfuls and Dime Novels

Nineteenth-century social changes and technological advances, including rising literacy rates and improved printing and papermaking technologies, created markets for cheap popular literature and furnished publishers in first the United Kingdom, then the United States with the ability to provide material for public consumption. Among the most popular forms of literature in nineteenth-century Britain were penny dreadfuls—sometimes also referred to as penny bloods or penny horribles—which were cheap forms of serialized narratives telling sensationalistic tales of criminals, detectives, and supernatural entities. Starting in the 1830s, popular penny dreadfuls featured monstrous characters like Varney the Vampire, Sweeney Todd, the highwayman Dick Turpin, and the monstrous Spring-Heeled Jack. Penny dreadfuls also frequently offered reprints or rewritings of Gothic thrillers, such as Walpole's *The Castle of Otranto* and Lewis's *The Monk*. Hephzibah Anderson characterizes penny dreadfuls as a "19th-Century British publishing phenomenon" that by the 1860s and 1870s "papered the nation's newsstands." "At a penny apiece," Anderson explains, "they cost as little as a twelfth of the price of an instalment of a Charles Dickens novel, and historians estimate that there were as many as 100 publishers in the business, paying authors by the line to crank out tales."[37]

As penny dreadfuls became increasingly targeted at and popular with young readers during the second half of the nineteenth century, notes Anderson, they "fanned the flames of moral panic." Anderson details that the journalist James Greenwood referred to them as "penny packets of poison," and as they were increasingly held responsible for juvenile crime and suicides, police began raiding publishers' offices. "According to the moralists," writes Anderson, "young errand boys, sailors and textile workers all were susceptible to stories that left them dissatisfied with their own small lives, making them yearn for wealth and adventure before their station and glamorising the criminal life. . . . The great unwashed had been taught how to read, the argument went, but not what to read."[38]

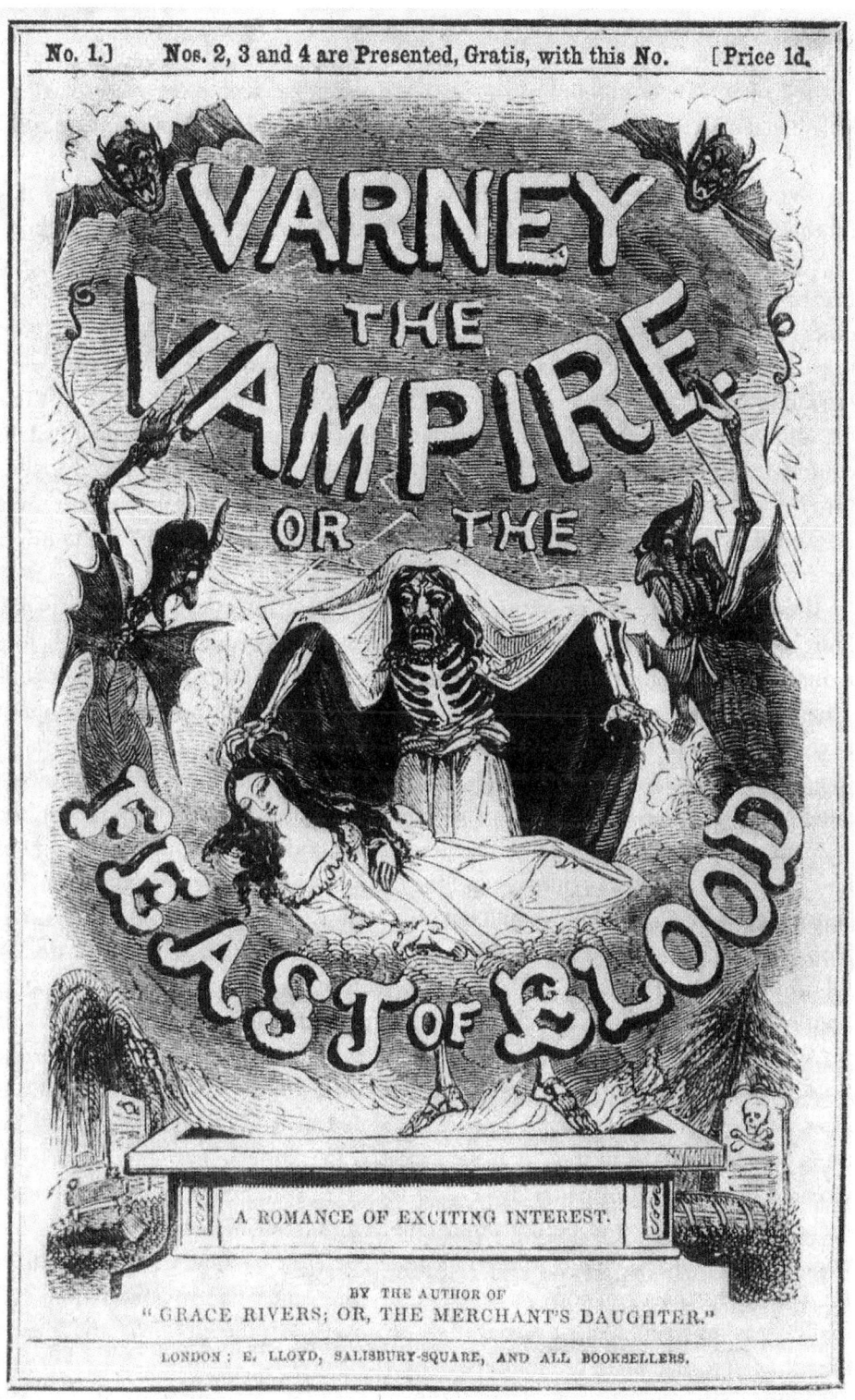

Figure I.2. The cover to the penny dreadful *Varney the Vampire; or, the Feast of Blood*, 1845.

The reading habits of the lower classes became a focus of particular scrutiny in the United Kingdom following several voting reform acts in the second half of the nineteenth century that significantly extended suffrage to both urban and rural working-class men. As Kate Summerscale describes, these new voters—raised on a diet of penny dreadfuls—would be in the position of electing the nation's rulers. It is for this reason that *The Pall Mall Gazette,* a London evening newspaper, announced in 1886 that penny dreadfuls were "the poison which is threatening to destroy the manhood of the democracy."[39] *The Quarterly Review,* a literary and political periodical that often published politically conservative reviews and editorials, amplified this concern in 1890, asserting that penny dreadfuls might transform the laboring class into "agents for the overthrow of society."[40] As Summerscale puts it, "The dreadfuls gave a frightening intimation of the uses to which the labourers of Britain could put their literacy and newly won power: these fantasies of wealth and adventure might foster ambition, discontent, defiance, a spirit of insurgency. There was no knowing the consequences of enlarging the minds and dreams of the lower orders."

It might be more apt to say that the *full extent* of the consequences was unknown, because British society had at least some of the consequences paraded before it on a seemingly daily basis. Summerscale observes that newspaper reports of children being led to commit crimes by such literature were common and that "inquest juries frequently linked suicide to cheap literature." Penny dreadfuls were then implicated in a particularly notorious 1895 murder case in which two children, Robert and Nattie Coombes, ages thirteen and twelve, respectively, were charged with the stabbing death of their mother. Penny dreadfuls found in a search of the Coombes house were submitted as evidence, and the coroner's jury verdict stated baldly, "We consider that the Legislature should take some steps to put a stop to the inflammable and shocking literature that is sold, which in our opinion leads to many a dreadful crime being carried out."[41] Calls to ban such salacious fiction were echoed by politicians and in newspaper editorials, although such measures were resisted.

A similar kind of moral panic took hold in the United States at about the same time in relation to dime novels, which, like penny dreadfuls, were cheap publications often telling lurid, sensationalistic tales marketed to working-class readers—and the American parallel to the Coombes case was that of Jesse Pomeroy, a thirteen-year-old boy found guilty first in 1872 of torturing other children and then subsequently in 1874 of murdering other children. As Dawn Keetley details in her book on the subject, *Making a Monster: Jesse Pomeroy, the Boy Murderer of 1870s Boston,* among the more popular explanations for Pomeroy's atrocious actions was that he was imitating violent scenes in dime novels.[42] In the same way that penny dreadfuls were blamed in the Coombes case, dime novels were brought up at Pomeroy's murder trial when a physician testifying for the prosecution recalled for the jury, "He once told me that he had an uncontrollable desire to commit torture on boys, which he thought might have come from reading cheap novels, which he had done a great many times; he took great delight in reading Indian tales where cruelties were described."[43] Keetley explains that this theory was quickly picked up by the popular press and especially by the well-known Boston publisher James T. Fields, who interviewed Pomeroy in his jail cell after his conviction and "came away from the murderer's cell with the conviction more deeply impressed on my mind than ever that the chief curse of youth in our day is that wide spread degrading, unwatched literature, called 'cheap,' which if unchecked by law is destined to sap the morals of our land and render crime a thing of daily and hourly occurrence."[44]

As Keetley details, Fields's interview with Pomeroy "added fuel to a swelling moral panic about the flood of cheap fiction washing over the nation."[45] As publishers increasingly targeted boys and working-class readers, as in England, "the middle-class arbiters of culture . . . were afraid they were losing their ability to shape the tastes and values of the lower classes."[46] Among the more notable crusaders against the presumed debasing effect of dime novels was Anthony Comstock, the founder of the Society for the Suppression of Vice whose name is reflected in the 1873 Comstock Law prohibiting the mailing of obscene, indecent, and vulgar material. As Michael Denning explains, Comstock became a special agent for the US Post Office to enforce this law, and part of his campaign was directed at dime novels.[47] In his 1883 reflection on his attempts to suppress vice, *Traps for the Young*, Comstock included dime novels together with other forms of salacious fiction as part of Satan's attempt to "advance his kingdom by destroying the young."[48]

In *Mechanic Accents: Dime Novels and Working-Class Culture in America,* Denning situates the controversy over dime novels in relation to "social conflict over the relations between the dominant genteel culture, and the relatively autonomous and 'foreign' working class cultures, and the new commercial culture, the new 'mass culture.'"[49] As with the controversy over penny dreadfuls, moral panic over "corruption" of youths by dime novels had a good deal to do with anxiety on the part of "genteel culture" over challenges to their positions as makers of culture and arbiters of taste. Pronouncing such works as distasteful is an oblique way of saying that they threatened the authority and control of the monied classes through the assertion of a set of values at variance with those held by people in positions of power. The cardinal sin of dime novels and penny dreadfuls both might well be figured as disrespect for authority, which manifested in any number of ways, ranging from the celebration of criminality and vigilantism; the rendering villainous of the upper classes; depictions of vice, violence, and immorality; and the refusal to abide by socially sanctioned standards of "good taste" to the competition they presented in the commercial publishing marketplace to more conservative authors, publishers, and publications. "Corruption of the youth," therefore, is another way to say refusal to respect "one's betters" and to act in accordance with established and socially sanctioned law and custom.

Figure I.3. The intriguing cover to an 1870 dime novel.

The appeal of such works to readers likely stems at least in part from the same source: vicarious liberation from social constraint. One can reasonably ask what attraction representations of "immorality" might have to readers. Of course, financial constraints limited reading options for boys and working-class readers in general in the nineteenth and twentieth centuries, and part of the appeal of penny dreadfuls and dime novels was that they were inexpensive and available; however, no one is obligated to buy something, even if it is cheap, and both children and the working class have options for entertainment other than reading, so the popularity of the works was dictated by factors other than simply price and availability. Penny dreadfuls and dime novels often combined exciting, suspenseful narratives with shocking scenes of violence that, as with horror media today, captivated readers. And, as is developed in some of the inclusions in this anthology, it may also be that such narratives allow for the vicarious expression or "purging" of negative emotions.

The Seduction of the Innocent: Comics

In many respects, a direct line can be drawn from Anthony Comstock's nineteenth-century crusade against salacious dime novels in *Traps for the Young* to psychiatrist Fredric Wertham's twentieth-century attacks on comic books in his 1954 book, *Seduction of the Innocent: The Influence of Comic Books on Today's Youth*[50]—a book that led to US Senate subcommittee hearings that resulted in significant constraints on the comic book industry. Where horror is concerned, however, we need to back up a bit.

The successors to nineteenth-century penny dreadfuls and dime novels were what are called pulp magazines, which emerged at the very end of the nineteenth century and flourished from the end of World War I in 1918 until their decline in the 1950s, doing particularly well during the period of the US Great Depression, which lasted from 1929 until about 1939. "The pulps" were inexpensive magazines printed on cheap wood pulp paper; although the pulps covered a range of genres, including science fiction, adventure stories, and detective tales, and many notable authors wrote for them, they were best known for sensationalistic subject matter and were often marketed with lurid cover art. Horror pulps, including what are referred to as "shudder pulps" and "weird menace" magazines, blossomed in the 1920s and 1930s and included *Weird Tales, Strange Tales of Mystery and Terror, Eerie Stories, Dime Mystery Magazine* (which, attempting to outdo *Weird Tales,* marketed itself as containing "the weirdest stories ever told"), *Terror Tales, Horror Stories, Spicy Mystery Stories, Thrilling Mystery,* and so on. Such magazines presented to the reading public tales of monsters and undead horrors, extraterrestrial invaders, and sadistic villains in stories with titles along the lines of "Little Children of Murder," "They Seek Your Skin!," and "Beware the Returning Dead!"

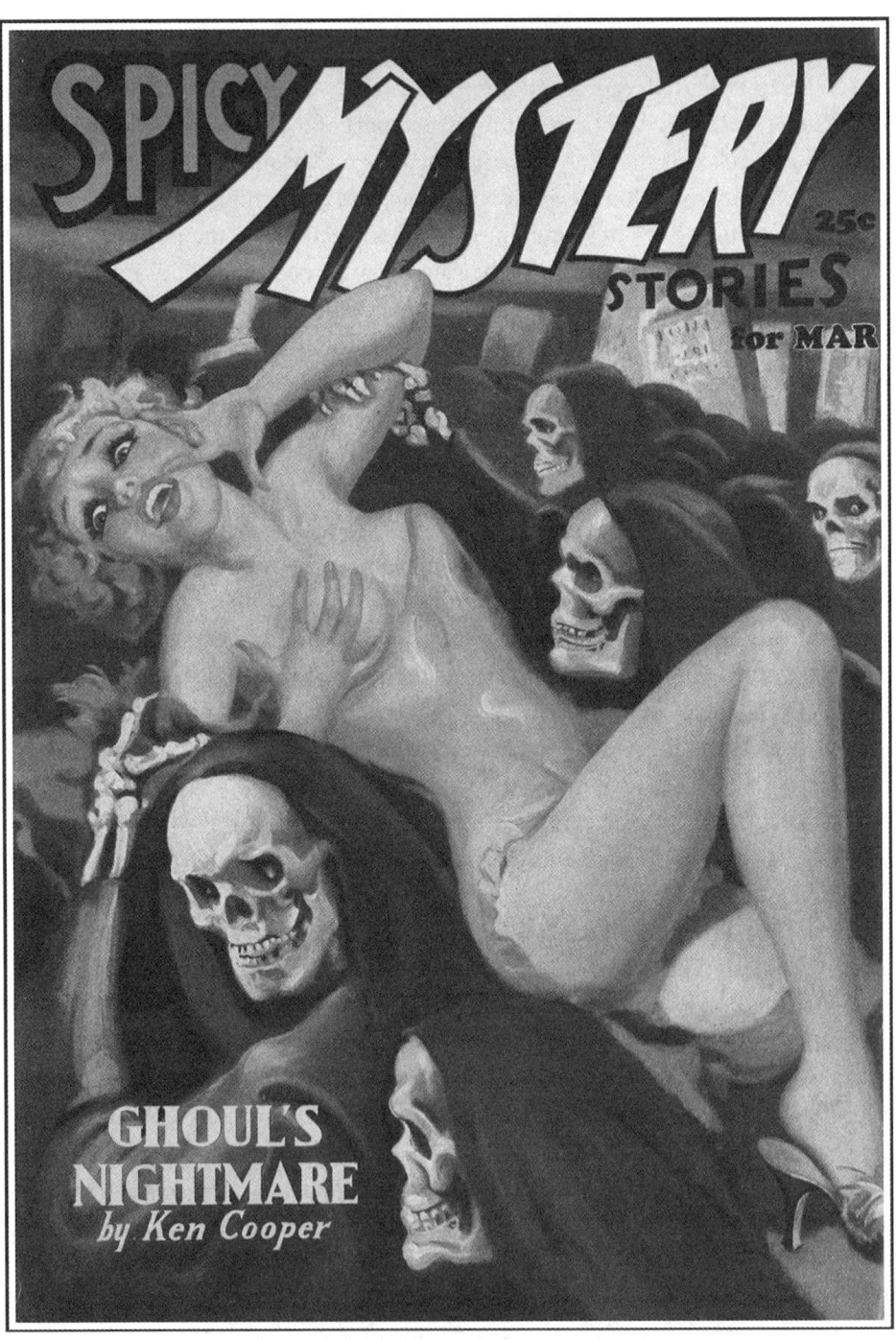

Figure I.4. The lurid cover to an issue of the pulp magazine *Spicy Mystery Stories*, March 1936.

Predictably, the sensationalistic tales and images provoked backlash from those invested in safeguarding conventional standards of public morality. Robert Jones notes in his *The Shudder Pulps: A History of the Weird Menace Magazines of the 1930s* that *The American Mercury*, a magazine with a conservative slant (which later become a very far right and anti-Semitic publication), condemned horror pulps in 1938, writing, "This month, as every month, the 1,508,000 copies of terror magazines, known to the trade as the shudder group, will be sold throughout the nation.... They will contain enough illustrated sex perversion to give Krafft-Ebing the unholy jitters."[51] The attack on the pulps then accelerated in the 1940s when, for example, New York Mayor Fiorello La Guardia, seizing on the 1936 rape and murder of a young woman named Nancy Evans Titterton, sought to clean up "vice" in Manhattan. Burlesque and similar forms of entertainment were demonized, and "decency law" restrictions on newsstands were pushed through, prohibiting what could be displayed.[52] Pulp publishers, concerned about losing both newsstand sales and US postal privileges, began to self-censor.[53]

The moral panic related to the pulps, as well as to comic books, the modern form of which debuted together with Superman in *Action Comics* no. 1 in 1938 and rapidly increased in popularity, culminated in 1954 with Wertham's notorious *Seduction of the Innocent*. Wertham's argument was essentially the same one that cultural critics and moralists had been making for millennia: Exposure to violent images and sexual "perversion" influences behavior in ways considered socially problematic or unacceptable. However, Wertham's conclusions came with the imprimatur of a licensed psychiatrist.

As part of his investigation into juvenile delinquency, Wertham centered his attention on the impact of mass media on children, with a focus on what he referred to as "crime comics"—a term that, for Wertham, covered not only crime and detective comics, but also superhero and horror comics—and his argument was that overt or covert depictions of sex, violence, drug use, and so on encouraged similar behavior in children. As part of his study, Wertham reproduced gruesome images and analyzed their violence and sexual themes and subtexts. His analyses, such as that Batman and Robin are coded as a homosexual couple or Wonder Woman as a lesbian, sometimes depended on a good bit of imaginative "reading between the lines"; more concerning, his conclusions regarding the link between crime comics and juvenile delinquency depended in large measure on anecdotal evidence that tended to focus on crime comic consumption to the exclusion of other factors.

Despite the absence of actual data linking crime comics to so-called juvenile delinquency, Wertham's conclusions found a receptive audience with 1950s politicians and moralists, such as Tennessee Senator Estes Kefauver, who invited Wertham to testify before the Senate Subcommittee on Juvenile Delinquency. Communism and juvenile delinquency were perhaps the top two American concerns of the 1950s, and, as the Toronto Metropolitan University "Crisis of Innocence" project explains,

Children told me what the man was going to do with the red-hot poker.

Outside the forbidden pages of de Sade, you find draining a girl's blood only in children's comics.

Figure I.5. Fredric Wertham's study reproduced comic frames and added commentary highlighting morbid or violent imagery and themes.

"During the 1940s and early 1950s, newspapers and popular magazines regularly carried sensational stories about the 'discovery' of shocking content in children's comic books."[54] Wertham testified that comic book representations of brutality, sadism, and sexual activity or innuendo harmed the development of children and argued that access to such works by children under the age of fifteen must be prohibited. The subcommittee did not, in fact, follow this recommendation; however, it did recommend that the comics industry voluntarily undertake to tone down violent and sexual content, which led the industry to develop the Comics Code Authority (CCA) as a form of self-regulation. As Amy Kiste Nyberg explains, "The 41 provisions [of the Comics Code] purged sex, violence and any other content not in keeping with critics' standards. Respect for government and parental authority was stressed, and censors even became the grammar police, eliminating slang and colloquialisms. Comics books received the Seal of Approval only if they were suitable for the youngest readers."[55] While adherence to the code and submission of works to the Comics Magazine Association of America for vetting was voluntary, in practice wholesalers refused to handle comics without the CCA seal of approval, and, at least in part due to this, EC Comics (publisher notably of *Tales from the Crypt*) and several other smaller comics publishers folded. Summing up the Wertham controversy, comic book writer, editor, and publisher Stan Lee explained that Wertham "said things that impressed the public, and it was like shouting fire in a theater, but there was little scientific validity to it. And yet because he had the name doctor people took what he said seriously, and it started a whole crusade against comics."[56] Ryan Chaloner Winton Hall and Susan Hatters Friedman note that "there was such fervor against comic books that there were even book-burning events focused on them in the late 1940s in many American cities."[57]

Unlike religious critics of horror, Wertham does not assume that horror's attraction inheres in innate human depravity. Indeed, it is rather the opposite; crime comics are a trap for the naive and unwary. His title, *Seduction of the Innocent*, makes plain that he perceives comics as a kind of "forbidden fruit" that tempt children with the allure of the forbidden. Then, through the normalization of violence, the modeling of criminal behavior including sexual deviancy, and the undermining of traditional values and sources of authority, children become confused about what is right and wrong, leading to delinquent behavior. Wertham referred to this process as "moral disarmament."[58] Wertham thus theorizes both the appeal of horror (basic curiosity) and its effect (juvenile delinquency). However, given that comic book consumption overall by children and teenagers in the 1940s and 1950s was exceptionally high—a publishers' survey in 1944 "calculated that 95 percent of boys and 91 percent of girls between the ages of six and eleven were regular comic book readers who read an average of twelve comics a month"[59]—it is unclear why some children succumbed to this alleged pernicious effect of comic books while the vast majority did not.

Horror as Child Abuse: The United Kingdom's "Video Nasties" Controversy

Concerns about the possibly pernicious effects of violence and sex in the movies have gone hand in glove with the development of cinema since its origins in the late nineteenth century. Indeed, Thomas Edison's pioneering twenty-six-second-long film, *The Kiss,* from 1896, was attacked as a threat to morality.

Horror films, however, have always held a special place in the censor's heart—Noel Yaxley writes that, "in all of cinematic history, no other genre has suffered as organized a campaign to ban, edit, and censor it as horror."[60] "Then, as now," notes Wilson, "a moral panic bubbled about the connection between the depravity shown onscreen and what audiences thought, said and did after they left the theater."[61] To address these concerns, in the United States what became known as the Hays Code to govern cinematic content was introduced by the Motion Picture Producers and Distributers of America in 1930 but was not enforced until 1934, permitting films such as James Whale's *Frankenstein* (1931), Tod Browning's *Dracula* (1931), and Browning's infamous *Freaks* (1932) to play uncut on Depression-era screens. The Hays Code was divided into two parts. The "General Principles" section prohibited a film from "lower[ing] the moral standards of those who see it." As such, films must avoid creating sympathy for "the side of crime, wrongdoing, evil or sin"

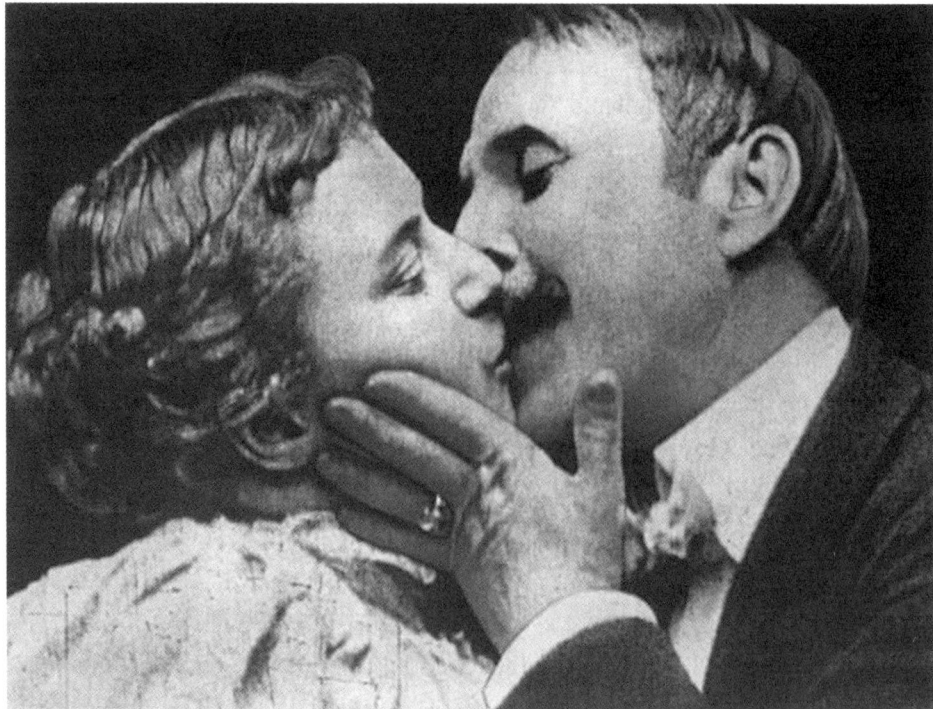

Figure I.6. The on-screen kiss featured in Thomas Edison's 1896 film was criticized as encouraging immorality.

and must avoid ridiculing "natural or human law" or creating sympathy for its violation.[62] The "Particular Applications" section then outlined a specific list of dos and don'ts regarding categories like "repellant subjects" (which, oxymoronically, must somehow "be treated within the careful limits of good taste"), "obscenity" (forbidden entirely), "sex," and "Crimes Against the Law." The Hays Code was subsequently replaced in 1968 by the Motion Picture Association of America film rating system.

In the United Kingdom, the British Board of Film Censors (BBFC) was created in 1912 and rated films (counterintuitively) as either "U," meaning suitable for all, or "A," which signified more adult content. The BBFC also had the power to cut scenes it felt "would be offensive, present a moral danger, or generate political controversy."[63] In response to Whale's *Frankenstein,* the BBFC introduced an "H" designator, meaning "horrific," which classified a film as unsuitable for those under sixteen.[64] Films receiving the "H" designation were often banned by local councils, and as a result, "exhibitors were reluctant to book prints as they might not be able to screen them as advertised—the councils had a nasty habit of waiting until the last minute to announce their ban."[65] Mark Kermode explains that the distribution of horror films was effectively suppressed in the United Kingdom until the end of World War II.[66]

As Yaxley details, however, a legal loophole prevented the BBFC's power of classification from extending to videos, which became a significant issue in the 1980s[67]—but first, we need to back up slightly. The late 1960s and early 1970s witnessed a spate of psychologically disturbing horror films, including *A Clockwork Orange* (Stanley Kubrick, 1971), *The Exorcist* (William Friedkin, 1973), *Last House on the Left* (Wes Craven, 1974), and *The Texas Chainsaw Massacre* (Tobe Hooper, 1974), and, as Cleary explains, films like these inevitably were met with opposition by religious groups, moral crusaders, and, to a certain extent, rank-and-file individuals concerned that such works would degrade morals and inspire acts of violence.[68] Concerns were then amplified by what has been referred to as "extreme cinema," which upped the ante, so to speak, when it came to representations of violence, mutilation, and torture—notable here are Meir Zarchi's 1978 *I Spit on Your Grave* and Ruggero Deodato's 1980 *Cannibal Holocaust*. Such films, however, fell under the purview of the BBFC, which banned or cut them—*Last House on the Left, The Texas Chainsaw Massacre, I Spit on Your Grave,* and *Cannibal Holocaust* were all refused theatrical certification in the United Kingdom.

Despite being banned, however, they nevertheless made their way into the United Kingdom in the 1980s on videotape—a market not under the BBFC's thumb. Kermode details the consequences:

> The anarchic infancy of unregulated video was to prove extremely short lived, as tabloid newspapers mounted a campaign against the new "threat" which they dubbed with the infantile label "video nasties." In a wave of government- and media-promoted

hysteria, horror videos were promptly blamed for everything from inattentiveness at school to muggings and rapes, with teachers, clergymen, politicians and the usual moral entrepreneurs demanding drastic measures to protect the country from video dealers who were bizarrely branded "merchants of menace."[69]

As Kate Egan puts it, the films "became the target of a media panic orchestrated, centrally, by a group of moral campaigners and the right-wing British newspaper, the *Daily Mail*."[70] "For its detractors," writes Cleary, "the video nasty represented a 'veritable cornucopia of sleaze,' specialising in 'sadism, mutilation, and cannibalism,' which allegedly had the 'tendency to deprave and corrupt, or make morally bad, a significant proportion of the *likely* audience.'"[71]

In response to the growing moral panic around "video nasties," in 1983, Great Britain's director of public prosecutions began drawing up a list of prosecutable titles under the United Kingdom's Obscene Publications Act of 1959, and then, in 1984, Parliament passed the Video Recordings Act (VRA), which empowered the BBFC to classify and cut video releases. As Kermode explains, the VRA's emphasis on home viewing assumed that videos might be accessed by children and thus "should be judged more harshly than their cinematic counterparts. [The VRA] also assumed that the malleability of videos would encourage miscreants to enjoy scenes of horror repeatedly and 'out of context.'"[72] "At a single stroke," writes Kermode, "the so-called 'nasties' were removed from British video shelves, and fines of £20,000 enforced on those who transgressed."[73] The consequences of the act, however, went beyond this, as some titles, such as *The Exorcist*, that hadn't originally been labeled a "nasty" were also banned, and many other horror films were extensively cut before being released.

From the horror aficionado's perspective, things then went from bad to worse in the United Kingdom in 1993, when two ten-year-old boys abducted, tortured, and murdered a two-year-old boy named James Bulger. As had been the case in the United Kingdom concerning penny dreadfuls when Robert and Nattie Coombes were found guilty of murdering their mother, and as had been the case in the United States concerning dime novels when Jesse Pomeroy was found guilty of child murder—and in keeping with general claims about the link between horror and juvenile delinquency—fingers were pointed at horror media in the Bulger case, with some British tabloids claiming that the attack on Bulger was inspired by the film *Child's Play 3* (Jack Bender, 1991), featuring the murderous doll Chucky. As Kermode explains, although there was no proof either child had actually seen the film, "Liberal Democrat MP David Alton promptly demanded that new laws should be passed which would effectively have removed *all* horror videos from distribution in the UK."[74] Alton's demand received support in the form of a 1994 report titled *Video Violence and the Protection of Children*, authored by British developmental psychologist Elisabeth Newson, that "alleged a definitive link between fictional representations of violence and violence exhibited by children allegedly 'exposed' to such representations"[75] and asserted that, because parents cannot be relied upon to monitor their children's viewing habits, the onus falls on the government:

> Most of us would prefer to rely on the discretion and responsibility of parents, both in controlling their children's viewing and in giving children clear models of their own distress in witnessing sadistic brutality; however, it is unhappily evident that many children cannot rely on their parents in this respect. By restricting such material from home viewing, society must take on a necessary responsibility in protecting children from this as from other forms of *child abuse*.[76]

Widely hailed, as Cleary observes, as a "victory for common sense,"[77] the *Video Violence* report's characterization of exposure to horror as a form of child abuse is striking, as it implies something actively malicious not only in creating and distributing horror but in permitting children (purposefully or inadvertently) access to such media. Parents and caregivers are thus characterized as not simply negligent in allowing children to view horror deemed age inappropriate but active participants in harm. Such language makes it difficult to contest assertions linking horror and harm because few wish to be perceived as excusing or defending child abuse.

In the wake of the Bulger case, and supported by the conclusions of the *Video Violence* report, language was then added to the VRA in 1994 requiring the BBFC "to have special regard among the other relevant factors to any harm that might be caused to potential viewers or, through their behaviour, to society" by the ways the films represent criminality, drug use, violence, "horrific behaviour," and sex.[78] As Julian Petley addresses in his 2011 *Film and Video Censorship in Modern Britain*, shifting public opinion and changing personnel on the BBFC since 1994 have resulted in some liberalization of attitudes toward horror, even allowing some of the "nasties" to be released uncut.[79]

Although it goes well beyond the purview of this introduction, it is worth mentioning that, on the other side of the pond, the United States experienced its own moral panic in the 1980s and 1990s—one that is generally referred to as the Satanic panic. Although it centered on alleged abuse of children during occult or Satanic rituals, horror films, heavy metal music, and the role-playing game Dungeons and Dragons were all implicated as either Satanic "recruitment tools" or symptoms of moral degradation.[80]

Conclusions and Inclusions

This quick survey of anxious and outraged responses to horror as entertainment is instructive in several respects. To begin, it offers us two models for understanding the appeal of horror: moral turpitude and naive curiosity. Religious moralists in general and Christian evangelizers in particular take as their starting point the assumption that humans are prone to sin and that enjoyment of horror entertainment is sinful for a variety of reasons, including that horror entertainment distracts from contemplation of God and the holy; blunts and degrades our finer sensibilities, including our capacities for sympathy and kindness; and presents sinful actions in an appealing light, thereby encouraging further iniquitous actions. Importantly, because of our debased nature, we are naturally attracted to sin and therefore must be on guard against submitting to our baser inclinations. Horror entertainment is thus akin to "pleasures of the flesh"; it is a snare laid by the devil that caters to our lustful and violent nature, enticing us over to the dark side.

The situation where children are concerned is a bit different. Rather than the assumption that children are ensnared as a consequence of their debased and lustful natures, they are instead figured as innocents who naively consume something for which they are unprepared and which they are ill-equipped to process. The results, however, are the same or perhaps even more dramatic: Children are, to borrow language from the United Kingdom's Obscene Publications Act of 1959, at risk of becoming "depraved and corrupted." Drawing support from "common sense" rather than any actual empirical data, the assumption at work is that precocious consumption of horror media may cloud the ability of children to distinguish right from wrong and good from evil, may "pervert" their sensibilities, and may incline them to imitate the violent actions they see portrayed in literature or on the screen. As was noted, the United Kingdom's 1994 *Video Violence* report figures facilitating or failing to prevent access to horror media by children as a form of child abuse.

In both sets of circumstances—sinful adults attracted to sin and innocent children naively treading on dangerous territory—the operative assumption is the essentially Platonic belief that literature (here extended to film and narrative in general) can mislead, distract, and corrupt our understandings of truth and virtue; evoke strong emotions, clouding rational thought; and inspire acts of imitation. Horror, however, is singled out from among other genres both because of its "bad content" (violence and gore) and because it stimulates "bad emotions" (fear and disgust). It makes evil deeds attractive and elicits from us negative emotions.

Importantly, although those making the case that horror possesses the potential to deprave and corrupt need not be religious, a moral framework is nevertheless inevitably implied—one that differentiates (often with an eye toward the assumed audience's age) between acceptable topics, themes, images, and attitudes and those that are off-limits. Horror texts by their nature explore fear, violence, and suffering and engage with taboo topics. When such depictions are considered acceptable and when they aren't reveals the moral boundaries of a given time and place as determined by those making the evaluations. What a society considers horror and how it responds to artistic representations of horror tell us a lot about what that society values and its openness to self-scrutiny.

The chapters that follow this introduction all attempt to explain the counterintuitive appeal of horror—or to provide frameworks that can be extended to such a consideration. Like Carroll in *The Paradox of Horror*, most academic considerations leave considerations of morality to the moralists—although a handful of inclusions here do explicitly or implicitly champion horror as fulfilling particular positive functions for individuals and groups. This anthology is divided into three parts. Part I, "Early Inquiries and Quick Takes," includes three types of readings that serve as the basis for twentieth- and twenty-first-century efforts to theorize horror enjoyment: analogies to consumption of tragedy; early considerations of horror and its appeal; and brief, twentieth-century meditations on horror from horror creators. Rather than being organized in rigorous chronological order, I have clustered the readings based on shared themes or approaches.

Aristotle, David Hume, and Friedrich Schiller address tragedy and how people can take pleasure in artistic representations of tragic events—Aristotle famously introduces the notion of catharsis, while Hume proposes that one can take pleasure in artistic representations of tragic events. Schiller, for his part, proposes that we can take pleasure in our sympathy and compassion for those afflicted by grief. Somewhat tangential but important here is Edmund Burke's idea of the sublime, which Ann Radcliffe and others will use in their considerations of terror and horror.

Joseph Addison, Anna Laetitia Barbauld, and Ann Radcliffe tackle terror and horror head-on. Addison proposes that we can take pleasure in descriptions of awful things because knowing we are safe transforms them into items of curiosity. Barbauld says something along the same lines, but adds the impetus of narrative suspense: The scene may be horrible, but we can't look away because we want to know how things will turn out (an idea that will be revisited by Carroll in part II). Radcliffe's famous piece proposes a distinction between terror and horror: The former, akin to the sublime, leads to an expansion of self, while the latter (associated with Matthew Lewis's famous Gothic novel, *The Monk*) elicits disgust and causes us to contract into ourselves. Radcliffe, trying to differentiate her own Gothic novels from Lewis's, makes a case for the former as having an intrinsic interest and dignity. For his part, romance writer Walter Scott reflects on the judicious use of the supernatural to evoke "superstitious awe."

The brief selections from H. P. Lovecraft, Alfred Hitchcock, and Stephen King offer commentary from the perspectives of twentieth-century horror creators. Lovecraft compares horror to dreams and proposes that horror appeals to our desire to believe in something more than the circumscribed world of consensus reality. Hitchcock relates cinematic horror to thrill-seeking. King, for his part, famously addresses horror as being "as conservative as an Illinois Republican in a three-piece pinstriped suit." We can enjoy the messy middle to horror narratives, but, in the end, the status quo is generally restored, reaffirming a traditional set of values. Also included here is a short introduction from Christopher St. John Sprigg, better known by his pseudonym Christopher Caldwell, to his edited volume of "uncanny stories," in which he asserts that the supernatural's violation of rationalist principles is what engages the interest of modern consumers.

Part II, "The Paradox of Horror," gathers together general approaches to the appeal of horror, which can be broadly grouped into three categories: denial theories, conversion theories, and competition theories. As in part I, the organization is not rigorously chronological, as the attempt has been made to group readers that build off of or respond to one another. Denial theorists reject the idea that horror actually evokes painful emotions. To a certain extent, this could be referred to as schadenfreude theory. Included under this denial of pain is philosopher Kendall Walton, who argues that our emotional responses to horror are not inherently unpleasant. Walton argues that it makes very little sense to say that we are afraid when watching or reading horror because we know we're safe. Our emotional arousal is real, but it is what Walton refers to as a "quasi-emotion" elicited through a form of make-believe. When we consume horror, we are thus playing an enjoyable kind of game in which we pretend to be afraid. For denial of pain theorists, there is no paradox associated with horror enjoyment because we aren't really ever truly scared or grossed out. Berys Gaut offers a similar approach in proposing that we can in fact enjoy fear and disgust, which reflect our evaluations of objects and situations.

As opposed to denial theories of horror enjoyment that reject the proposition that we are ever actually scared or truly disgusted, conversion theorists propose that unpleasant or painful emotions can certainly be elicited by art but that they are then transformed into something more pleasurable; discomfort is the price paid, so to speak, for the enjoyment or relief that comes afterward—this is the oldest approach to the paradox of horror and is represented primarily in part I through the inclusions from Aristotle and Hume.

Rather than one emotion being converted into another, competition theories of horror enjoyment propose that more than one emotion is aroused by horror but that enjoyment prevails. This is the basis of one of the better-known theories of horror consumption: Carroll's proposition that the negative emotions evoked by what he calls "art-horror" are offset by the enjoyments of narrative and the interest elicited by categorically impure monsters. According to Carroll, while we really do experience fear and disgust when watching horror, we are also fascinated by the monsters and get wrapped up in the plot and want to see how things turn out. If our curiosity prevails, we keep reading or watching. If our disgust or fear wins the competition, we stop. Carroll's approach can and should, I think, be expanded to include aspects of narrative other than plot and its eliciting of curiosity or suspense. Viewer engagement with or appreciation of any other element of a horror narrative may reasonably be considered to compete with negative affect: We may, for example, be disgusted or disturbed by a film but appreciate on an intellectual level its theme or subtext or that it functions as an allegory and therefore keep watching for that reason. The main idea is that two (or more) different responses are simultaneously elicited by horror literature or media and fight it out to determine whether one keeps watching or reading or calls it quits.

Carroll's approach does, however, leave an important question unanswered: If narrative by its nature creates curiosity and a desire to see how things turn out, all things being equal, why wouldn't we just choose stories that don't evoke fear or disgust? An answer to this question is provided by John Morreall, whose "control theory" proposes that we can enjoy even unpleasant things as long as we know we can "start, stop, and direct the experience." This explains, for example, why roller coasters are appealing—they may be frightening, but we can also experience pleasure because we assume that we are safe. The same goes for television or film: We can always turn off the TV or leave the theater.

Mathias Clasen shifts the terms of the debate by arguing from a "biocultural" perspective that human beings are in some ways evolutionarily conditioned to "find pleasure in make-believe that allows them to experience negative emotions at high levels of intensity within a safe context." Horror fictions, which, according to Clasen, toss a "live wire into ancient structures in the audience's central nervous system," thus actually serve some important functions. Among other things, horror, according to Clasen, helps us learn to manage negative emotions, acquire coping skills, and thus learn to negotiate real-world dangers.

A somewhat different form of competition theory is repression theory. Derived from Freudian psychoanalysis, repression theory, especially as developed by Robin Wood, proposes that, like dreams, horror films express tabooed desire in disguised forms. From this perspective, which is, to be fair, difficult to prove or disprove, fear or disgust is the price the viewer pays to be able to secretly enjoy the lifting of repression, which is pleasurable.

Yet another take on competition theory is provided by Douglas E. Cowan's consideration of horror in relation to religion. In *Sacred Terror: Religion and Horror on the Silver Screen*, he proposes—with some connections to Lovecraft's consideration included in part I—that horror expresses a form of "yearning" for a more capacious universe than the one perceived to be offered by materialist theories of existence that dismiss the realms of spirit and the supernatural.

Linda Williams and Julian Hanich move us more fully into the realm of affect theory. Williams, in her piece, explores the "fun" to be had watching *Psycho* (which coordinates with the Hitchcock letter in part I) in relation to the pleasures of surprise. Hanich's approach is, in fact, difficult to summarize or excerpt because his study rejects the idea of horror as a monolithic category and instead explores the appeal of different types of horror. Consistent, though, is his phenomenological approach to the experience of horror, which is exemplified by his third chapter, included here, on "direct horror."

Rounding out part II are G. Neil Martin and Nina Nesseth. Martin's "(Why) Do You Like Scary Movies? A Review of the Empirical Research on Psychological

Responses to Horror Films" covers a lot of ground concisely as it explores "priming," the role of sound, the delights of narrative, sensation seeking, how the enjoyment of horror is inflected by way of sex differences, relations to mental illness, and so on. Nesseth, for her part, summarizes several of the approaches already covered and then develops Clasen's biocultural approach more fully, observing genetic and physiological components that make consuming horror pleasurable.

The third and final part of the book, "Different Voices," brings together approaches to the pleasures of horror that reject the notion that consumers all respond in the same way. The readings here focus instead on particular groups of horror consumers. Part III is organized chronologically for the most part, although it starts with a chapter from Matt Hills's important *The Pleasures of Horror,* which sets the stage for the rest of part III by shifting away from general theories of horror and into the terrain of fan studies, arguing that the pleasure fans take in horror comes, in part, from expressions of connoisseurship. Hills's inclusion is followed by an older but important piece by Susan Stryker that explores the sympathy trans horror consumers feel for Frankenstein's monster. Brigid Cherry's empirical research then disputes the stereotype that women don't like horror or refuse to look.

Class position is an underdeveloped area of horror studies—the excerpt from Mark Jancovich and Tim Snelson provides a starting point. Non-Western explorations of horror consumption (at least in English) are also in short supply. Though increasing attention is being paid to the histories of and themes present in horror from different regions, including South Korea, Japan, India, and the Middle East, considerations of the pleasures viewers find in such works have lagged behind and remain unexplored in such analyses. One notable exception is Meghan Downes's "Critical Pleasures: Reflections on the Indonesian Horror Genre and Its Anti-Fans." Within the essay, Downes examines how young, urban Indonesians enjoy ridiculing the horror genre—they "love to hate it" and, in so doing, reaffirm their own subject positions as urban and comparatively affluent.

The inclusions from Sheri-Marie Harrison and Dani Bethea and Monika Negra, organized back to back, explore the appeal of horror to Black viewers. These essays are followed by Petra Kuppers's meditation on the appeal of horror for disabled consumers, and part III—and the volume—then concludes with a focus on *The Exorcist* and the pleasures of horror for queer viewers by S. Trimble.

All notes included with the chapter inclusions should be presumed to be the author's unless otherwise indicated.

Notes

1. Noël Carroll, *The Philosophy of Horror; or, Paradoxes of the Heart* (Routledge, 1990).
2. Carroll, 13.

3. C.W.S., "The Ridiculous Spectacle of Public Hangings in Old England," *HuntaKiller* (blog), March 25, 2017, https://members.huntakiller.com/blog-articles/2017/3/25/public-hangings-a-fun-day-out-in-17th-century-england.

4. Robert Darnton, *The Great Cat Massacre and Other Episodes in French Cultural History* (Basic Books, 1984), 90.

5. Edmund P. Cueva, email to the author, June 11, 2024.

6. Tertullian, *De spectaculis*, chap. 15, https://www.newadvent.org/fathers/0303.htm.

7. Tertullian, chap. 16.

8. Lactantius, *Divine Institutes* 6.20, https://www.newadvent.org/fathers/07016.htm.

9. Lactantius, 6.20.

10. Lactantius, 6.20.

11. St. Augustine, *Confessions* VI.6.8, https://www.newadvent.org/fathers/110106.htm.

12. Jonas Barish, *The Antitheatrical Prejudice* (University of California Press, 1981), 80.

13. Joel Elliot Slotkin, "A Taste for Slaughter: Stephen Gosson, *Titus Andronicus*, and the Appeal of Evil," in *The Routledge Companion to Shakespeare and Philosophy*, edited by Craig Bourne and Emily Caddick Bourne (Routledge, 2019), 485–86.

14. Slotkin, 485.

15. Andrew Dickson, "Jacobean Tragedy: Of Love and Death," *The Guardian*, January 20, 2012, https://www.theguardian.com/stage/2012/jan/20/jacobean-tragedies-changeling-duchess-malfi.

16. James Knapp, "A. rev. of *Revenge Tragedy and Classical Philosophy on the Early Modern Stage* by Christopher Crosbie," *Modern Philology* 117, no. 4 (2020), https://www.journals.uchicago.edu/doi/10.1086/708344.

17. Slotkin, "Taste for Slaughter," 486.

18. Slotkin, 486.

19. Slotkin, 487.

20. Slotkin, 489.

21. Barish, *Antitheatrical Prejudice*, 83.

22. Ellipses original.

23. Barish, 87.

24. Barish, 87–88.

25. Logan Connors, "The Theater's Many Enemies," *Restoration and Eighteenth-Century Research* (2015): 5–16.

26. Fred Botting, *Gothic* (Routledge, 1996), 4.

27. Botting, 4.

28. Rictor Norton, "Gothic Readings: 1764–1840," http://rictornorton.co.uk/gothic/critics.htm.

29. Quoted in Sarah Cleary, *The Myth of Harm: Horror, Censorship, and the Child* (Bloomsbury Academic, 2022), 1.

30. As cited in Joseph James Irwin, *M. G. "Monk" Lewis* (Twayne, 1976), 46.

31. As quoted in Cleary, *Myth of Harm*, 190.

32. Irwin, *M. G. "Monk" Lewis*, 46.

33. Cleary, *Myth of Harm*, 1.

34. Botting, *Gothic*, 22.

35. Botting, 22.

36. Nick Groom, *The Gothic: A Very Short Introduction* (Oxford University Press, 2012), 86.

37. Hephzibah Anderson, "The Shocking Tale of the Penny Dreadful," BBC, May 2, 2016, https://www.bbc.com/culture/article/20160502-the-shocking-tale-of-the-penny-dreadful.

38. Anderson.

39. Quoted in Kate Summerscale, "Penny Dreadfuls: The Victorian Equivalent of Video Games," *The Guardian*, April 30, 2016, https://www.theguardian.com/books/2016/apr/30/penny-dreadfuls-victorian-equivalent-video-games-kate-summerscale-wicked-boy.

40. Quoted in Summerscale.

41. Quoted in Summerscale.

42. Dawn Keetley, *Making a Monster: Jesse Pomeroy, the Boy Murderer of 1870s Boston* (University of Massachusetts Press, 2017), 106.

43. Quoted in Keetley, 107.

44. Quoted in Keetley, 110.

45. Keetley, 110.

46. Keetley, 110.

47. Michael Denning, *Mechanic Accents: Dime Novels and Working-Class Culture in America* (Verso Books, 1987), 50–51.

48. Quoted in Denning, 51.

49. Denning, 47.

50. Fredric Wertham, *Seduction of the Innocent: The Influence of Comic Books on Today's Youth* (1954; repr., Main Road Books, 2004).

51. Robert Jones, *The Shudder Pulps: A History of the Weird Menace Magazines of the 1930s* (FAX Collector's Editions, 1975), 138–39.

52. See Jonathan Kay, "The Complicated Legacy of Paul Moss, La Guardia's Infamous 'Gutter-Cleaner,'" Gotham Center for New York City History, January 18, 2022, https://www.gothamcenter.org/blog/the-complicated-legacy-of-paul-moss-la-guardias-infamous-gutter-cleaner.

53. Mike Chomko, "Weird Menaces: The Shudder Pulps," *Pulpfest: Celebrating Mystery, Adventure, Science Fiction, and More* (blog), July 6, 2014, https://pulpfest.com/2014/07/06/weird-menaces-the-shudder-pulps/.

54. "Crime! Horror!" A Crisis of Innocence: Comic Books and Children's Culture, 1940–1954, https://crisisofinnocence.library.torontomu.ca/exhibits/show/a-crisis-of-innocence/crime-horror.

55. Amy Kiste Nyberg, "Comics Code History: The Seal of Approval," CBLDF, 2024, https://cbldf.org/comics-code-history-the-seal-of-approval/.

56. "Interview with Stan Lee," in *David Kraft's Comics Interviews*, no. 64 (Fictioneer Books, 1988), 17.

57. Ryan Chaloner Winton Hall and Susan Hatters Friedman, "Comic Books, Dr. Wertham, and the Villains of Forensic Psychiatry," *Journal of the American Academy of Psychiatry and Law Online* 53, no. 1 (2020), https://jaapl.org/content/early/2020/10/06/jaapl.200041-20.

58. Wertham, *Seduction of the Innocent*, 91.

59. "The Child Readers of Comics: Concerns and Numbers," A Crisis of Innocence: Comic Books and Children's Culture, 1940–1954, https://crisisofinnocence.library.torontomu.ca/exhibits/show/a-crisis-of-innocence/child-readers-of-comics.

60. Noel Yaxley, "The Horror of Censorship," *Washington Examiner,* April 25, 2024, https://www.washingtonexaminer.com/magazine-life-arts/2976114/the-horror-of-censorship/.

61. Karina Wilson, "Horror Movie Censorship in the 1930s," Horror Film History: A Decade by Decade Guide to the Horror Film Genre, November 27, 2018, https://horrorfilmhistory.com/wp/horror-movie-censorship-in-the-1930s/.

62. "'Complete Nudity Is Never Permitted': The Motion Picture Production Code of 1930," History Matters: The U.S. Survey Course on the Web, https://historymatters.gmu.edu/d/5099/.

63. Wilson, "Horror Movie Censorship in the 1930s."

64. Wilson.

65. Wilson.

66. Mark Kermode, "The British Censors and Horror Cinema," in *British Horror Cinema,* edited by Steve Chibnall and Julian Petley (Routledge, 2001), 11.

67. Yaxley, "Horror of Censorship."

68. See Cleary, *Myth of Harm,* 141–50.

69. Kermode, "British Censors and Horror Cinema," 17.

70. Kate Egan, *Trash or Treasure? Censorship and the Changing Meanings of the Video Nasties* (Manchester University Press, 2007), 1.

71. Cleary, *Myth of Harm,* 138, emphasis original.

72. Kermode, "British Censors and Horror Cinema," 18.

73. Kermode, 18.

74. Kermode, 20.

75. Cleary, *Myth of Harm,* 135.

76. Newson, quoted in Cleary, 136, emphasis added.

77. Cleary, 182.

78. Kermode, "British Censors and Horror Cinema," 20.

79. Julian Petley, *Film and Video Censorship in Modern Britain* (Edinburgh University Press, 2011), 161–62.

80. For a particularly good study of the moral panic related to gaming, see Joseph P. Laycock, *Dangerous Games: What the Moral Panic over Role-Playing Games Says About Play, Religion, and Imagined Worlds* (University of California Press, 2015).

I
Early Inquiries and Quick Takes

Chapter 1

FROM *POETICS*

Aristotle

> Despite not addressing horror directly, Aristotle's consideration of tragedy provides a useful framework for thinking about the appeal of horror via the concept of *catharsis*. As Aristotle explains in the *Poetics*, tragedy aims to elicit pity and fear from the audience. The experiencing of these emotions then leads to the purgation of negative affect akin to the way someone might feel better after having a good cry. By extension, the negative affect elicited by horror could lead to a similar kind of "detoxification."
>
> As mentioned in the introduction, this is an example of a "conversion" explanation for how horror functions as negative emotions are subsequently replaced by more positive ones. The application of the idea of catharsis to horror also has some interesting parallels with Robin Wood's argument that horror allows for the expression of repressed fears and anxieties, relieving psychic pressure in a salutary way.

Reserving hexameter poetry and comedy for consideration hereafter, let us proceed now to the discussion of tragedy; before doing so, however, we must gather up the definition resulting from what has been said. A tragedy, then, is the imitation of an action that is serious and also, as having magnitude, complete in itself; in language with pleasurable accessories, each kind brought in separately in the parts of the work; in a dramatic, not in a narrative form; with incidents arousing pity and fear, wherewith to accomplish its catharsis of such emotions[.] Here by "language with pleasurable accessories" I mean that with rhythm and harmony; and by "the kinds separately" I mean that some portions are worked out with verse only, and others in turn with song.

As they act the stories, it follows that in the first place the spectacle must be some part of the whole; and in the second melody and diction, these two being the means of their imitation. Here by diction I mean merely this, the composition of the verses; and by melody, what is too completely understood to require explanation.

But further: the subject represented also is an action; and the action involves agents, who must necessarily have their distinctive qualities both of character and thought, since it is from these that we ascribe certain qualities to their actions, and in virtue of these that they all succeed or fail. Now the action is represented in the play by the plot. The plot, in our present sense of the term, is simply this, the combination of the incidents, or things done in the story; whereas character is what makes us ascribe certain qualities to the agents; and thought is shown in all they say when proving a particular point or, it may be, enunciating a general truth. There are six parts consequently of every tragedy, that make it the sort of tragedy it is, viz. a plot, characters, diction, thought, spectacle, and melody; two of them arising from the means, one from the manner, and three from the objects of the dramatic imitation; and there is nothing else besides these six. Of these, its formative elements, then, not a few of the dramatists have made due use, as every play, one may say, admits of spectacle, character, plot, diction, melody, and thought.[1]

The most important of the six is the combination of the incidents of the story. Tragedy is essentially an imitation not of persons but of action and life. [All human happiness or misery takes the form of action; the end for which we live is a certain kind of activity, not a quality. Character gives us qualities, but it is in our actions that we are happy or the reverse.][2] In a play accordingly they do not act in order to portray the characters; they include the characters for the sake of the action. So that it is the action in it, i.e., its plot, that is the end and purpose of the tragedy; and the end is everywhere the chief thing. Besides this, a tragedy is impossible without action, but there might be one without Character. The tragedies of most of the moderns are characterless—a characteristic common among poets of all kinds, and with its counterpart in painting in Zeuxis as compared with Polygnotus; for whereas the latter is strong in character, the work of Zeuxis is devoid of it. And again: one may string together a series of characteristic speeches of the utmost finish as regards diction and thought, and yet fail to produce the true tragic effect; but one will have much better success with a tragedy which, however inferior in these respects, has a plot, a combination of incidents, in it. And again: the most powerful elements of attraction in Tragedy, the peripeties and discoveries, are parts of the plot. A further proof is in the fact that beginners succeed earlier with the diction and characters than with the construction of a story; and the same may be said of nearly all the early dramatists. We maintain, therefore, that the first essential, the life and soul, so to speak, of tragedy is the plot; and that the characters come second—compare the parallel in painting, where the most beautiful colors laid on without order will not give one the same pleasure as a simple black-and-white sketch of a portrait. We maintain that tragedy is primarily an imitation of action, and that it is mainly for the sake of the action that it imitates the personal agents. Third comes the element of thought, i.e., the power of saying whatever can be said, or what is appropriate to the occasion. This is what, in the speeches in tragedy, falls under the arts of politics and rhetoric; for the older poets make their personages discourse like statesmen, and the moderns like orators. One must not confuse it with character. Character in a play is that which reveals the choice of the agents—hence there is no room for character in a speech on a purely indifferent subject. Thought, on the other hand, is shown in all they say when proving or disproving some particular point, or enunciating some universal proposition. Fourth among the literary elements[3] is the diction of the personages, i.e., as before explained, the expression of their thoughts in words, which is practically the same thing with verse as with prose. As for the two remaining parts, the Melody is the greatest of the pleasurable accessories of Tragedy. The spectacle, though an attraction, is the least artistic of all the parts, and has least to do with the art of poetry. The tragic effect is quite possible without a public performance and actors; and besides, the getting-up of the spectacle is more a matter for the designer than the poet. . . .

The tragic fear and pity may be aroused by the spectacle; but they may also be aroused by the very structure and incidents of the play—which is the better way and shows the better poet. The plot in fact should be so framed that, even without seeing the things take place, he who simply hears the account of them shall be filled with horror and pity at the incidents; which is just the effect that the mere recital of the story in *Oedipus* would have on one. To produce this same effect by means of the spectacle is less artistic, and requires extraneous aid. Those, however, who make use of the spectacle to put before us that which is merely monstrous and not productive of fear, are wholly out of touch with tragedy; not every kind of pleasure should be required of a tragedy, but only its own proper pleasure.

The tragic pleasure is that of pity and fear, and the poet has to produce it by a work of imitation; it is clear, therefore, that the causes should be included in the incidents of his story. Let us see, then, what kinds of incident strike one as horrible, or rather as piteous. In a deed of this description the parties must necessarily be either friends, or enemies, or indifferent to one another. Now when enemy does it on enemy, there is nothing to move us to pity either in his doing or in his meditating the deed, except so far as the actual pain of the sufferer is concerned; and the same is true when the parties are indifferent to one another. Whenever the tragic deed, however, is done among friends—when murder or the like is done or meditated by brother on brother, by son on father, by mother on son, or son on mother—these are the situations the poet should seek after. The traditional stories, accordingly, must be kept as they are, e.g., the murder of Clytaemnestra by Orestes and of Eriphyle by Alcmeon. At the same time even with these there is something left to the poet himself; it is for him to devise the right way of treating them. Let us explain more clearly what we mean by "the right way." The deed of horror may be done by the doer knowingly and consciously, as in the old poets, and in Medea's murder of her children in Euripides. Or he may do it, but in ignorance of his relationship, and discover that afterward, as does the Oedipus in Sophocles. Here the deed is outside the play; but it may be within it, like the act of the Alcmeon in Astydamas, or that of the Telegonus in *Ulysses Wounded*. A third possibility is for one meditating some deadly injury to another, in ignorance of his relationship, to make the discovery in time to draw back. These exhaust the possibilities, since the deed must necessarily be either done or not done, and either knowingly or unknowingly.

The worst situation is when the personage is with full knowledge on the point of doing the deed, and leaves it undone. It is odious and also (through the absence of suffering) untragic; hence it is that no one is made to act thus except in some few instances, e.g., Haemon and Creon in *Antigone*. Next after this comes the actual perpetration of the deed meditated. A better situation than that, however, is for the deed to be done in ignorance, and the relationship discovered afterward, since there is nothing odious in it, and the discovery will serve to astound us. But the best of all is the last; what we have in *Cresphontes,* for example, where Merope, on the point of slaying her son, recognizes him in time; in *Iphigenia,* where sister and brother are in a like position; and in *Helle,* where the son recognizes his mother, when on the point of giving her up to her enemy.

This will explain why our tragedies are restricted (as we said just now) to such a small number of families. It was accident rather than art that led the poets in quest of subjects to embody this kind of incident in their plots. They are still obliged, accordingly, to have recourse to the families in which such honors have occurred.

On the construction of the plot, and the kind of plot required for tragedy, enough has now been said.

Notes

All notes are from Jonathan Barnes, editor of the Princeton University Press edition.
1. The text of this sentence is uncertain.
2. Excised by Kassel.
3. Text uncertain.

Chapter 2

OF TRAGEDY

David Hume

> Like Aristotle, the eighteenth-century Scottish philosopher David Hume focuses on tragedy rather than horror, and his approach, too, involves the conversion of negative affect into more positive emotion. However, rather than focusing on purgation via catharsis, Hume argues instead that we can derive pleasure from intense emotions like fear, sorrow, and pity when they are experienced within the controlled context of the aesthetic experience of the performance. This allows the audience to confront these emotions in a safe space as aesthetic pleasure and intellectual engagement work together to transform negative emotions into a satisfying emotional experience. Applied to horror, this might suggest that the aesthetic qualities of the work, together with its engagement of our intellect, transform feelings of fear and disgust into pleasurable appreciation.

IT SEEMS AN UNACCOUNTABLE PLEASURE, which the spectators of a well-written tragedy receive from sorrow, terror, anxiety, and other passions, that are in themselves disagreeable and uneasy.[1] The more they are touched and affected, the more are they delighted with the spectacle; and as soon as the uneasy passions cease to operate, the piece is at an end. One scene of full joy and contentment and security is the utmost, that any composition of this kind can bear; and it is sure always to be the concluding one. If, in the texture of the piece, there be interwoven any scenes of satisfaction, they afford only faint gleams of pleasure, which are thrown in by way of variety, and in order to plunge the actors into deeper distress, by means of that contrast and disappointment. The whole heart of the poet is employed, in rouzing and supporting the compassion and indignation, the anxiety and resentment of his audience. They are pleased in proportion as they are afflicted, and never are so happy as when they employ tears, sobs, and cries to give vent to their sorrow, and relieve their heart, swoln with the tenderest sympathy and compassion.

The few critics who have had some tincture of philosophy, have remarked this singular phænomenon, and have endeavoured to account for it.

L'Abbe DUBOS, in his reflections on poetry and painting, asserts, that nothing is in general so disagreeable to the mind as the languid, listless state of indolence, into which it falls upon the removal of all passion and occupation. To get rid of this painful situation, it seeks every amusement and pursuit; business, gaming, shews, executions; whatever will rouze the passions, and take its attention from itself. No matter what the passion is: Let it be disagreeable, afflicting, melancholy, disordered; it is still better than that insipid languor, which arises from perfect tranquillity and repose.

It is impossible not to admit this account, as being, at least in part, satisfactory. You may observe, when there are several tables of gaming, that all the company run to those, where the deepest play is, even though they find not there the best players. The view, or, at least, imagination of high passions, arising from great loss or gain, affects the spectator by sympathy, gives him some touches of the same passions, and serves him for a momentary entertainment. It makes the time pass the easier with him, and is some relief to that oppression, under which men commonly labour, when left entirely to their own thoughts and meditations.

We find that common liars always magnify, in their narrations, all kinds of danger, pain, distress, sickness, deaths, murders, and cruelties; as well as joy, beauty, mirth, and magnificence. It is an absurd secret, which they have for pleasing their company, fixing their attention, and attaching them to such marvellous relations, by the passions and emotions, which they excite.

There is, however, a difficulty in applying to the present subject, in its full extent, this solution, however ingenious and satisfactory it may appear. It is certain, that the same object of distress, which pleases in a tragedy, were it really set before us, would give the most unfeigned uneasiness; though it be then the most effectual cure to languor and indolence. Monsieur FONTENELLE seems to have been sensible of this difficulty; and accordingly attempts another solution of the phenomenon; at least makes some addition to the theory above mentioned.[2]

"Pleasure and pain," says he, "which are two sentiments so different in themselves, differ not so much in their cause. From the instance of tickling, it appears, that the movement of pleasure, pushed a little too far, becomes pain; and that the movement of pain, a little moderated, becomes pleasure. Hence it proceeds, that there is such a thing as a sorrow, soft and agreeable: It is a pain weakened and diminished. The heart likes naturally to be moved and affected. Melancholy objects suit it, and even disastrous and sorrowful, provided they are softened by some circumstance. It is certain, that, on the theatre, the representation has almost the effect of reality; yet it has not altogether that effect. However we may be hurried away by the spectacle; whatever dominion the senses and imagination may usurp over the reason, there still lurks at the bottom a certain idea of falsehood in the whole of what we see. This idea, though weak and disguised, suffices to diminish the pain which we suffer from the misfortunes of those whom we love, and to reduce that affliction to such a pitch as converts it into a pleasure. We weep for the misfortune of a hero, to whom we are attached. In the same instant we comfort ourselves, by reflecting, that it is nothing but a fiction: And it is precisely that mixture of sentiments, which composes an agreeable sorrow, and tears that delight us. But as that affliction, which is caused by exterior and sensible objects, is stronger than the consolation which arises from an internal reflection, they are the effects and symptoms of sorrow, that ought to predominate in the composition."

This solution seems just and convincing; but perhaps it wants still some new addition, in order to make it answer fully the phænomenon, which we here examine. All the passions, excited by eloquence, are agreeable in the highest degree, as well as those which are moved by painting and the theatre. The epilogues of CICERO are, on this account chiefly, the delight of every reader of taste; and it is difficult to read some of them without the deepest sympathy and sorrow. His merit as an orator, no doubt, depends much on his success in this particular. When he had raised tears in his judges and all his audience, they were then the most highly delighted, and expressed the greatest satisfaction with the pleader. The pathetic description of the butchery, made by VERRES of the SICILIAN captains, is a masterpiece of this kind: But I believe none will affirm, that the being present at a melancholy scene of that nature would afford any entertainment. Neither is the sorrow here softened by fiction: For the audience were convinced of the reality of every circumstance. What is it then, which in this case raises a pleasure from the bosom of uneasiness, so to speak; and a pleasure, which still retains all the features and outward symptoms of distress and sorrow?

I answer: This extraordinary effect proceeds from that very eloquence, with which the melancholy scene is represented. The genius required to paint objects in a lively manner, the art employed in collecting all the pathetic circumstances, the judgment displayed in disposing them: the exercise, I say, of these noble talents, together with the force of expression, and beauty of oratorial numbers, diffuse the highest satisfaction on the audience, and excite the most delightful movements. By this means, the uneasiness of the melancholy passions is not only overpowered and effaced by something stronger of an opposite kind; but the whole impulse of those passions is converted into pleasure, and swells the delight which the eloquence raises in us. The same force of oratory, employed on an uninteresting subject, would not please half so much, or rather would appear altogether ridiculous; and the mind, being left in absolute calmness and indifference, would relish none of those beauties of imagination or expression, which, if joined to passion, give it such exquisite entertainment. The impulse or vehemence, arising from sorrow, compassion, indignation, receives a new direction from the sentiments of beauty. The latter, being the predominant emotion, seize the whole mind, and convert the former into themselves, at least tincture them so strongly as totally to alter their nature. And the soul, being, at the same time, rouzed by passion, and charmed by eloquence, feels on the whole a strong movement, which is altogether delightful.

The same principle takes place in tragedy; with this addition, that tragedy is an imitation; and imitation is always of itself agreeable. This circumstance serves still farther to smooth the motions of passion, and convert the whole feeling into one uniform and strong enjoyment. Objects of the greatest terror and distress please in painting, and please more than the most beautiful objects, that appear calm and indifferent.[3] The affection, rouzing the mind, excites a large stock of spirit and vehemence; which is all transformed into pleasure by the force of the prevailing movement. It is thus the fiction of tragedy softens the passion, by an infusion of a new feeling, not merely by weakening or diminishing the sorrow. You may by degrees weaken a real sorrow, till it totally disappears; yet in none of its graduations will it ever give pleasure; except, perhaps, by accident, to a man sunk under lethargic indolence, whom it rouzes from that languid state.

To confirm this theory, it will be sufficient to produce other instances, where the subordinate movement is converted into the predominant, and gives force to it, though of a different, and even sometimes though of a contrary nature.

Novelty naturally rouzes the mind, and attracts our attention; and the movements, which it causes, are always converted into any passion, belonging to the object, and join their force to it. Whether an event excite joy or sorrow, pride or shame, anger or good-will, it is sure to produce a stronger affection, when new or unusual. And though novelty of itself be agreeable, it fortifies the painful, as well as agreeable passions.

Had you any intention to move a person extremely by the narration of any event, the best method of encreasing its effect would be artfully to delay informing him of it, and first to excite his curiosity and impatience before you let him into the secret. This is the artifice practised by IAGO in the famous scene of SHAKESPEARE; and every spectator is sensible, that OTHELLO's jealousy acquires additional force from his preceding impatience, and that the subordinate passion is here readily transformed into the predominant one.

Difficulties encrease passions of every kind; and by rouzing our attention, and exciting our active powers, they produce an emotion, which nourishes the prevailing affection.

Parents commonly love that child most, whose sickly infirm frame of body has occasioned them the greatest pains, trouble, and anxiety in rearing him. The agreeable sentiment of affection here acquires force from sentiments of uneasiness.

Nothing endears so much a friend as sorrow for his death. The pleasure of his company has not so powerful an influence.

Jealousy is a painful passion; yet without some share of it, the agreeable affection of love has difficulty to subsist in its full force and violence. Absence is also a great source of complaint among lovers, and gives them the greatest uneasiness: Yet nothing is more favourable to their mutual passion than short intervals of that kind. And if long intervals often prove fatal, it is only because, through time, men are accustomed to them, and they cease to give uneasiness. Jealousy and absence in love compose the *dolce peccante* of the ITALIANS, which they suppose so essential to all pleasure.

There is a fine observation of the elder PLINY, which illustrates the principle here insisted on. *It is very remarkable,* says he, *that the last works of celebrated artists, which they left imperfect, are always the most prized, such as the* IRIS *of* ARISTIDES, *the* TYNDARIDES *of* NICOMACHUS, *the* MEDEA *of* TIMOMACHUS, *and the* VENUS *of* APELLES. *These are valued even above their finished productions: The broken lineaments of the piece, and the half-formed idea of the painter are carefully studied; and our very grief for that curious hand, which had been stopped by death, is an additional encrease to our pleasure.*[4]

These instances (and many more might be collected) are sufficient to afford us some insight into the analogy of nature, and to show us, that the pleasure, which poets, orators, and musicians give us, by exciting grief, sorrow, indignation, compassion, is not so extraordinary or paradoxical, as it may at first sight appear. The force of imagination, the energy of expression, the power of numbers, the charms of imitation; all these are naturally, of themselves, delightful to the mind: And when the object presented lays also hold of some affection, the pleasure still rises upon us, by the conversion of this subordinate movement into that which is predominant. The passion, though, perhaps, naturally, and when excited by the simple appearance of a real object, it may be painful; yet is so smoothed, and softened, and mollified, when raised by the finer arts, that it affords the highest entertainment.

To confirm this reasoning, we may observe, that if the movements of the imagination be not predominant above those of the passion, a contrary effect follows; and the former, being now subordinate, is converted into the latter, and still farther encreases the pain and affliction of the sufferer.

Who could ever think of it as a good expedient for comforting an afflicted parent, to exaggerate, with all the force of elocution, the irreparable loss, which he has met with by the death of a favourite child? The more power of imagination and expression you here employ, the more you encrease his despair and affliction.

The shame, confusion, and terror of VERRES, no doubt, rose in proportion to the noble eloquence and vehemence of CICERO: So also did his pain and uneasiness. These former passions were too strong for the pleasure arising from the beauties of elocution; and operated, though from the same principle, yet in a contrary manner, to the sympathy, compassion, and indignation of the audience.

Lord CLARENDON, when he approaches towards the catastrophe of the royal party, supposes, that his narration must then become infinitely disagreeable; and he hurries over the king's death, without giving us one circumstance of it. He considers it as too horrid a scene to be contemplated with any satisfaction, or even without the utmost pain and aversion. He himself, as well as the readers of that age, were too deeply concerned in the events, and felt a pain from subjects, which an historian and a reader of another age would regard as the most pathetic and most interesting, and, by consequence, the most agreeable.

An action, represented in tragedy, may be too bloody and atrocious. It may excite such movements of horror as will not soften into pleasure; and the greatest energy of expression, bestowed on descriptions of that nature, serves only to augment our uneasiness. Such is that action represented in the *Ambitious Stepmother,* where a venerable old man, raised to the height of fury and despair, rushes against a pillar, and striking his head upon it, besmears it all over with mingled brains and gore. The ENGLISH theatre abounds too much with such shocking images.

Even the common sentiments of compassion require to be softened by some agreeable affection, in order to give a thorough satisfaction to the audience. The mere suffering of plaintive virtue, under the triumphant tyranny and oppression of vice, forms a disagreeable spectacle, and is carefully avoided by all masters of the drama. In order to dismiss the audience with entire satisfaction and contentment, the virtue must either convert itself into a noble courageous despair, or the vice receive its proper punishment.

Most painters appear in this light to have been very unhappy in their subjects. As they wrought much for churches and convents, they have chiefly represented such horrible subjects as crucifixions and martyrdoms, where nothing appears but tortures, wounds, executions, and passive suffering, without any action or affection. When they turned their pencil from this ghastly mythology, they had commonly recourse to OVID, whose fictions, though passionate and agreeable, are scarcely natural or probable enough for painting.

The same inversion of that principle, which is here insisted on, displays itself in common life, as in the effects of oratory and poetry. Raise so the subordinate passion that it becomes the predominant, it swallows up that affection which it before nourished and encreased. Too much jealousy extinguishes love: Too much difficulty renders us indifferent: Too much sickness and infirmity disgusts a selfish and unkind parent.

What so disagreeable as the dismal, gloomy, disastrous stories, with which melancholy people entertain their companions? The uneasy passion being there raised alone, unaccompanied with any spirit, genius, or eloquence, conveys a pure uneasiness, and is attended with nothing that can soften it into pleasure or satisfaction.

Notes

1. This Essay was first published in Edition L.
2. *Reflexions sur la poetique,* sec. 36.

3. Painters make no scruple of representing distress and sorrow as well as any other passion: But they seem not to dwell so much on these melancholy affections as the poets, who, tho' they copy every emotion of the human breast, yet pass very quickly over the agreeable sentiments. A painter represents only one instant; and if that be passionate enough, it is sure to affect and delight the spectator: But nothing can furnish to the poet a variety of scenes and incidents and sentiments, except distress, terror, or anxiety. Compleat joy and satisfaction is attended with security, and leaves no farther room for action.

4. Illud vero perquam rarum ac memoria dignum, etiam supreme opera artificum, imperfectasque tabulas, sicut, IRIN ARISTIDIS, TYNDARINAS NICOMACHI, MEDEAM TIMOMACHI, & quam diximus VENERAM APELLIS, in majori admiratione esse quam perfecta. Quippe in üs lineamenta reliqua, ipsæque cogitationes artiflcum spectantur, atque in lenocinio commendationis dolor est manus, cum id ageret, extinctæ. Lib. xxxv. cap. 11.

Chapter 3

ON THE REASON WE TAKE PLEASURE IN TRAGIC SUBJECTS

Friedrich Schiller

Translated by George W. Gregory

> Friedrich Schiller was a late eighteenth-century playwright, poet, philosopher, and historian. In his "On the Reason We Take Pleasure in Tragic Subjects," he echoes and expands on ideas introduced by Aristotle and Hume and leads us into Edmund Burke in the next chapter. Schiller, like Aristotle, understands tragedy to have a purgative function. Tragedy, for Schiller, explores profound philosophical and moral questions as it leads the audience to feel awe and admiration for the protagonist's resolve in the face of suffering. Fear and pity then evoke a kind of expansion of the self as the audience, witness to suffering, emerges with a deeper understanding of the human condition. The experience in this way touches on the idea of the sublime, explored in the next chapter. One could easily extend Schiller's consideration of tragedy to the horror genre, with special attention, perhaps, to the "final girl" character who persists in the face of horror and ultimately prevails, although her victory is tempered by the loss of her friends and family, as well as by her own suffering.

As much as some of the more recent aestheticians make it their business to defend the arts of imagination and emotion against the general belief, that they aim at enjoyment, as if this were a pejorative accusation, nevertheless, this belief will remain standing upon its firm ground, and the fine arts will not gladly exchange their traditional, incontestable, and beneficial vocation for a new one to which one intends to elevate them. Unconcerned that their vocation, aimed at our enjoyment, might degrade them, they will instead be proud of the prerogative of achieving directly what all other directions and activities of the human mind bring about only indirectly. Certainly no one who concedes that nature has any purpose at all, will doubt that nature's purpose with human beings is to achieve their happiness, even if the individual human being wants to know nothing about this purpose in his moral actions. Thus, the fine arts have their purpose in common with nature, or actually with her Author. They playfully grant what their more serious sister allows us to obtain only with labor; they make a gift of what is usually the bitterly won prize of much effort.

We must purchase enjoyments of the mind with straining diligence, the sanction of reason with painful sacrifice, the pleasures of the senses with austere abstinence, or atone for the excesses of these with a train of suffering; only art affords us pleasures which need not first be earned, which demand no sacrifice, and need not be purchased with repentance. But who will put the merit of bringing pleasure in this way into one category with the paltry merits of amusement? Who could conceive of denying the former purpose to the fine arts merely for the reason that they are elevated over the latter purpose?

The well-meant intention of seeking the morally good everywhere as the highest purpose, which has yielded no few mediocre products in art, and also taken them under its protection, has wrought similar damage to theory. In order to assign to the arts a quite high rank, in order to obtain for them the favor of the state, the respect of all people, one bans them from their proper sphere in order to impose upon them a vocation which is foreign and utterly unnatural to them. One believes one is doing the arts a great service by imputing to them a moral purpose instead of the frivolous purpose of bringing pleasure, and their quite apparent influence upon morality necessarily supports this claim. It is thought to be contradictory, that the same art which promotes the supreme purpose of humanity to such a great extent, accomplishes this effect only incidentally, and actually has its attention ultimately directed to the vulgar purpose which pleasure is thought to be. But a cogent theory of pleasure and a complete philosophy of art would be able to easily resolve this contradiction, if it existed. It would thus be demonstrated, that a free pleasure, such as art brings it forth, is absolutely founded upon moral conditions, that the entire moral nature of a person is active in its production. It would be demonstrated, furthermore, that the production of this pleasure is a purpose which can be achieved solely by moral means; that art, therefore, in order to perfectly achieve pleasure as its true purpose, must make its way through morality. But it is entirely irrelevant for the appreciation of art, whether its purpose is a moral one or whether it can achieve its purpose only with moral means, because art has to do with morality in both cases, and must act in most intimate concord with moral sentiment; but, for perfection in art, it is irrelevant which of the two is purpose, and which the means. If the purpose is itself moral, art loses that, on account of which alone it is powerful, its freedom, as well as that, on account of which it is so universally effective, the allure of pleasure. The play becomes transformed into a serious business; and yet it is just the play on account of which it can best execute its business. Only by achieving its highest aesthetic effect will art have a beneficial influence upon morality; but only by fully exercising its authority, can it fulfill its highest aesthetic effect.

Moreover, it is certain that every enjoyment, insofar as it flows from a moral source, improves a person morally, and that here the effect once more becomes a cause. Enjoyment in the beautiful, the moving, the exalted, strengthens our moral consciousness, just as enjoyment of doing good, of love, etc., strengthens these inclinations. Just as a cheerful mind is the certain lot of a morally excellent person, moral excellence is the glad attendant of a cheerful spirit. Thus, art has a moral effect not only because it gives pleasure by moral means, but also because the pleasure itself, which art provides, becomes a means to morality.

The means by which art achieves its purpose, are as manifold as there are sources of free pleasure. But I call that pleasure free, in which the intellectual powers, reason and the power of imagination, are active, and where the feeling is produced by the idea, contrary to physical or sensuous pleasure, whereby the soul is subjugated to a blind natural necessity, and the sensation follows directly upon its physical cause. Sensuous desire is the only desire excluded from the field of fine art, and an aptitude for awakening sensuous desire can either never elevate itself to art, or only if the sensuous impressions are ordered according to an artful plan, strengthened or moderated, and this plan is recognized in the performance. But even then, only that would be art in it, which is the object of a free pleasure, i.e., the taste for the ordering, which gives pleasure to our mind, not the physical attraction itself, which gives pleasure only to our sensuousness.

The general source of all pleasure, including the sensuous, is purposiveness. Pleasure is sensuous if purposiveness is not recognized by the powers of imagination, but merely effected by the law of necessity which has the sensation of pleasure as a physical consequence. Thus, a purposive movement of the blood and the life spirits in individual organs or in the whole machine produces bodily desire with all of its forms and modifications; we feel this purposiveness through the medium of the pleasant sensation, but we do not obtain any idea of it, neither clear nor confused.

Pleasure is free when we prefigure the purposiveness, and the general sensation accompanies the prefiguration; all prefiguration, therefore, through which we experience agreement and purposiveness, are sources of a free pleasure, and insofar capable of employment by art to this end. They comprise the following classes, exhaustively: good, true, perfect, beautiful, moving, exalted. The good occupies our intellect, the true and perfect, the understanding, the moving and the exalted, intellect together with the power of imagination. The attraction or the force summoning to activity indeed pleases, but art employs attraction only to accompany the higher feeling of purposiveness; considered on its own, it looses itself among the life-forces, and art shuns it as it does all sensuous desire.

The diversity of sources from which art draws the pleasure which it obtains for us, can not justify a classification of the arts on its own, since many, often all kinds of pleasure may flow together in the same class of art. But insofar as a certain kind of pleasure is pursued as the chief purpose, it may, nonetheless, be the basis for a particular view of the artwork, but not of a class of its own. One might, for example, comprehend those arts which primarily satisfy the understanding and the power of imagination, those, therefore, which make the true, the perfect, the beautiful their chief purpose, under the name of the fine arts (arts of taste, arts of understanding); those, on the other hand, which occupy the power of imagination together with intellect, which thus have the good, the exalted, and the moving as their chief subject, we might comprehend under the moving arts (arts of feeling, of the heart) in a particular class. It is, indeed, impossible to completely separate the moving from the beautiful, but the beautiful can exist quite well without the moving. Although this diversity of views does not justify a complete differentiation of the free arts, it at least serves to identify the principles of judgment more closely, and to prevent the confusion which must unavoidably arise if one intermingles the entirely different fields of the moving and the beautiful in a legislation on aesthetic matters.

The moving and the exalted are commensurate with each other in that they elicit desire by way of aversion, that they give us the sensation of a purposiveness (since desire ensues from purposiveness, anguish from the contrary), which presumes a counter-purposiveness.

The feeling of the exalted consists, on the one hand, in the feeling of our impotence and limitedness to encompass an object, on the other hand, however, in the feeling of our supremacy which shudders at no limits, and intellectually subjugates that to which our sensuous forces succumb. The object of the exalted thus clashes with our sensuous capacity, and this counter-purposiveness necessarily awakens our aversion. But at the same time, it is an inducement to bring another capacity to consciousness, which is superior to that in the face of which the power of imagination is vanquished. An exalted object, therefore, for the very reason that it is in conflict with sensuousness, is purposeful for the intellect, and gives pleasure by way of the higher capacity by causing anguish to the lower.

Being moved, in the proper sense, signifies the mixed sensation of suffering and the desire for suffering. One can thus feel moved at one's own misfortune, only if the anguish is sufficiently moderate to leave room for the desire which a compassionate observer feels for it. The loss of a great good smites us to the ground today, and our anguish moves the observer; after one year, we ourselves recall this anguish, and are moved by it. The weak person is always but the prey of his anguish; the hero and the wise man are only moved by the greatest of their own misfortunes.

Being moved, like the feeling of the exalted, has two constituent parts, anguish and pleasure; in both cases, the foundation of the purposiveness is a counter-purposiveness. It thus appears to be a counter-purposiveness in nature, that the human being suffers, who is not fated to suffer, and this counter-purposiveness causes us anguish. But this anguish of counter-purposiveness is purposeful for our intellectual nature as such, and insofar as it summons us to activity, it is purposeful for human society. We must, therefore, necessarily perceive desire for the very aversion which the counter-purposeful awakens in us, because that aversion is purposeful. In order to determine whether desire or aversion will predominate when we are moved, the chief point at issue is whether the prefiguration of counter-purposiveness or purposefulness maintains the upper hand. This may depend either upon the number of purposes achieved or violated, or upon their relationship to the ultimate purpose of all purposes.

The anguish of the virtuous person moves us more painfully than the anguish of the wicked person, because there it is not only the universal end of human beings to be happy, but also the particular end, that the virtuous should be happy, which is contradicted, whereas, in the latter case, it is only the first which is contradicted. The good fortune of the wicked person, to the contrary, causes us far more anguish than the misfortune of the virtuous, because, first of all, vice itself, and secondly, the reward for a vice contains a counter-purposiveness.

Furthermore, virtue is far more suited to rewarding itself than the successful vice is in punishing itself; for just that reason, the righteous person is far more likely to remain true to his virtue in misfortune than the wicked person is to turn virtuous in his success.

Chiefly, however, the determination of the relationship of desire to aversion when we are moved depends upon whether the violated purpose surpasses the obtained purpose in importance, or the obtained purpose surpasses the violated one. There is no purposiveness more important to us than that which is moral, and nothing surpasses the desire which we feel for this. Natural purposiveness may always be problematic, moral purposiveness is certain. It alone is founded upon our intellectual nature and upon inner necessity. It is the most proximate to us, the most important, and at once the most knowable, because it is determined by nothing from the outside, but only by an inner principle of our intellect. It is the Palladium of our freedom.

This moral purposiveness is recognized most vividly when it maintains the upper hand in conflict with other purposes; only then is the entire power of the moral law demonstrated, when it is displayed in conflict with all other forces of nature, and these lose their power over a human heart in this conflict. Among these forces of nature, everything is embraced which is not moral, everything which does not stand under the supreme legislation of the intellect; sensations, instincts, affects, passions, as well as physical necessity and fate. The more fearsome the opponent, the more glorious the victory; resistance alone can make power visible. From this it follows, that the highest consciousness of our moral nature can be maintained only in a violent condition, in struggle, and that the highest moral pleasure will always be accompanied by anguish.

That form of art, therefore, which provides us moral desire to a preeminent degree must, just for that reason, employ these mixed sensations, and please us with anguish. This is done preeminently in tragedy, and its field encompasses all possible cases in which some natural purposiveness is sacrificed to amoral purposiveness, or even one moral purposiveness sacrificed to another, which is higher. It were, perhaps, not impossible to demonstrate an upward gradation from the lowest to the highest, according to the relationship in which moral purposiveness is recognized and perceived in contradiction with another, and to stipulate the intensity of being pleasantly or painfully moved a priori, out of the principle of purposiveness. Indeed, it might be possible to derive a certain ordering of tragedy from this principle, and to exhaust all possible classes of it a priori in a complete table, so that one would be able to assign any given tragedy its place, and calculate the intensity as well as the type of being moved in advance, above which any given tragedy cannot ascend, on account of its species. But this subject is reserved for a separate treatment.

How much the prefiguration of moral purposiveness is preferred to natural purposiveness in our mind, will be easily recognizable in particular examples.

When we see Hüon and Amanda bound to the stake, both willing, out of free choice, rather to die a horrible death in the fire than to obtain a throne by being unfaithful.—What makes this performance a subject of such heavenly pleasure for us? The contradiction of their present condition with laughing fate, which scorns them, the apparent counter-purposiveness of nature, which recompenses virtue with misery, the unnatural relinquishment of self-love, etc., ought to fill us with the most excruciating agony, since it calls up so many ideas of counter-purposiveness in our soul—but what do we care about nature with all of her purposes and laws, when, through her counter-purposiveness, she becomes the inducement to demonstrate the moral purposiveness in ourselves to us in the fullest light? The experience of the victorious power of the moral law, which we have when we look upon this performance, is such a high, such an essential good, that we are even tempted to reconcile ourselves with the evil to which we are grateful for it. Accord in the realm of freedom gives us infinitely more pleasure than all the contradictions in the world of nature are capable of dissipating.

When Coriolanus, vanquished by spousal, filial, and citizen's duties, quits Rome, as good as already conquered, suppresses his vengeance, withdraws his army, and surrenders himself to the hatred of a jealous rival, his deed is clearly quite counter-purposive; with this step he loses not only the fruits of all previous victories, but dashes deliberately to his ruin—but how fitting, how unspeakably great it is, on the other hand, to prefer the crassest contradiction to a tendency for a contradiction with moral feeling, and in such a way, contrary to the supreme interest of sensuousness, to violate the rules of prudence, only in order to act in accordance with higher moral responsibility? Every sacrifice of life is counter-purposive, for life is the condition of all things good; but sacrifice of life in moral intent is purposive to a high degree, for life is never important for itself, never as an end, but only as a means to morality. If, therefore, there is a case where surrendering life becomes a means of morality, life must be subordinated to morality. "It is not necessary that I live, but it is necessary that I save Rome from starvation," says the great Pompey, who should sail to Africa, and his friends implore him to postpone his voyage until the storm has abated.

But the life of a criminal is no less tragically pleasant than the anguish of the virtuous person; and yet here we obtain the prefiguration of something morally counter-purposive. The contradiction of his deed with the moral law ought to fill us with aversion, the moral imperfection, which acting in such a way presupposes, fills us with anguish, even were we to leave out of consideration the misfortune of the innocent persons who become its victim. Here, there is no satisfaction with the morality of the persons, which might be capable of recompensing us for the anguish which we feel over their action and suffering—and yet, both are a very fruitful subject for art, at which we tarry with great pleasure. It will not be difficult to demonstrate the agreement of this phenomenon with what has been said previously.

It is not solely obedience to the moral law which gives us the prefiguration of moral purposiveness; anguish over the violation of this law does also. The sadness which consciousness of moral imperfection produces, is purposeful, because it contrasts with the satisfaction which accompanies morally righteous action. Contrition, self-condemnation, even in its highest degree, in desperation, are morally exalted, because they could never be felt if an incorruptible sense of right and wrong did not stand guard, deep in the breast of the criminal, staking its claim even against the most fierce interests of self-love. Contrition over a deed issues from the comparison of the deed with the moral law, and constitutes disapproval of this deed, because it is in conflict with the moral law. Thus, in the moment of contrition, the moral law must be the highest tribunal in the heart of such a person; it must be more important to him than the prize of the crime itself, because the consciousness of the offended moral law sours his enjoyment of this prize. The condition of a mind, however, in which the moral law is recognized as the highest tribunal, is morally purposeful, and therefore a source of moral desire. And what can be more exalted than that heroic desperation which casts all the goods of life, life itself, into the dust, because it cannot bear the disapproving voice of its inner judge, and cannot drown it out? Whether the virtuous person freely sacrifices his life in order to act in accordance with the moral law, or whether the criminal destroys his life with his own hand under the compulsion of his conscience, in order thus to punish the trespassing of that law upon himself, our esteem for the moral law is intensified to an equally high degree; and, if there is still a difference, it would turn out to the advantage of the latter, for the gladdening consciousness of doing right may have made the decision of the virtuous person somewhat easier, and thus reduced the moral merit of a deed in just that measure as inclination and desire partake of it. Contrition and desperation over a committed crime demonstrate the power of the moral law only later, but not weaker; these are portraits of the most exalted morality, but sketched in a condition of violence. A person who is desperate on account of a violated moral duty, reverts to obedience to the same in that very desperation, and the more horribly his self-condemnation expresses itself, the more powerfully do we see the moral law rule over him.

But there are cases where moral pleasure is purchased only at the price of moral anguish, and this comes to pass when a moral duty must be violated in order to act more in accord with a higher and more universal duty. Had Coriolanus stood with his Roman army before Antium or Carioli, instead of before his own home city, had his mother been a Volkser, and if her entreaties had had the same effect upon him, the victory of filial duty had had the contrary effect upon us. The reverence for his mother would then have been in conflict with the far higher obligation of the citizen, which deserves priority in case of a collision. That commander who is left a choice of either surrendering a city or seeing his imprisoned son impaled before his eyes, will choose the latter without reservation, because his duty to his child is fittingly subordinate to that toward his country. It is, indeed, at first sight, an outrage to our heart, that a father acts so contrary to natural instinct and the duty of a father, but soon we are drawn into sweet admiration, that a moral motivation, even when it is paired with inclination, cannot confuse reason in its legislation. When the Corinthian Timoleon lets a beloved, but ambitious brother, Timophanes, be killed, because his opinion of patriotic duty binds him to eliminate everything which puts the republic in danger, we thus see him, indeed, not without horror and abhorrence, commit this deed, so unnatural, much contrary to moral sentiment, but our abhorrence is quickly resolved in the highest esteem for the heroic virtue which maintains its verdict against any foreign influence of inclination, and, in the stormy conflict of emotions, decides as freely as correctly, as if in a condition of greatest calm. Our view of republican duty may be quite different from Timoleon's; but that changes nothing of our pleasure. Instead, it is in just such cases, where our understanding is not on the side of the person acting, in which one recognizes how much we give preference to acting according to duty over acting according to purposefulness, how much we exalt concord with reason over concord with the understanding.

There will be no greater diversity of judgments, however, about a moral phenomenon than about this one, and we need not seek very far for the reason for this diversity. All people are, indeed, endowed with the moral sense, but it is not present in everyone in that strength and freedom which must be presumed in the judgment of these cases. For most, it is sufficient to approve of one action, because its agreement with the moral law is easily grasped, and to condemn another, because its conflict with this law is evident. But a clear mind and a reason independent of any force of nature, and thus of moral instinct (insofar as it takes effect instinctively), is required for determining the relationship of moral duties to the highest principle of morality correctly. The same act, therefore, in which some few recognize the highest purposiveness, will appear to the larger majority as an outrageous contradiction, although both make a moral judgment; that is why the emotion of being moved felt at such an action cannot be communicated in the universality which the unity of human nature and the necessity of the moral law would lead one to expect. But to many, as we know, the most true and the most exalted is exaggeration and nonsense, because the measure of reason which recognizes what is exalted is not the same in everyone. A small soul vanishes under the burden of such great prefigurations, or feels itself torn asunder over its moral radius. Does not the common crowd often enough see the most detestable chaos, where the thinking spirit admires the most exquisite order?

So much about the feeling of moral purposiveness, insofar as it is the foundation of being moved tragically and our pleasure in the anguish. But, nonetheless, there are cases enough where natural purposiveness itself seems to please us at the cost of moral purposiveness. The greatest tenacity of the scoundrel in ordering his plot clearly pleases us, although his plot and its purpose conflict with our moral feeling. Such a person is capable of awakening our most vivid sympathy, and we shudder at the miscarriage of the very plans, where, if it really came down to our referring everything to moral purposiveness, we ought to wish to thwart them most fiercely. But even this phenomenon does not annul what has been claimed heretofore concerning the sense of moral purposiveness and its influence upon our pleasure in being moved tragically.

Purposiveness gives us pleasure under all circumstances, be it related either not at all to what is moral, or even in conflict with it. We enjoy this pleasure pure, as long as we do not recall a moral purpose contradicted by it. Just as we take pleasure in the instinct of animals, which is similar to human understanding, in the industriousness of bees, and the like, without relating this natural purposiveness to a will possessed of understanding, and even less to a moral purpose, the purposiveness of every human undertaking gives us enjoyment in itself, as soon as we do not think of anything else than the relationship of the means to their purpose. But if it occurs to us that it is the action of a moral being, profound indignation takes the place of the first pleasure, and no purposiveness of the understanding is capable of reconciling us with the prefiguration of what is morally counter-purposive. It must never become vividly evident to us that this Richard III, this Iago, this Lovelace, are human beings, for otherwise our sympathy will inevitably turn into its opposite. That we have a capacity, however, and exercise it often enough, to divert our attention from a certain aspect of things, and direct it to another, that the pleasure itself, which is possible for us only by means of this segregation, invites us to do so, and does not relent, is confirmed by daily experience.

It not seldom happens, that an ingenious act of malice wins our favor preeminently, because it is a means to provide us the enjoyment of moral purposiveness. The more perilous the snares which Klarissa's virtue lay for Lovelace, the more severe the ordeal to which the inventive cruelty of a despot puts the intransigence of his innocent victim, we see moral purposiveness triumph in all the more supreme glory. We delight in the power of the feeling of moral duty which can so trouble the inventiveness of a seducer. On the other hand, we account the victory of the tenacious scoundrel over the moral sense, of which we know that it necessarily stirs in him, as a kind of merit, because it testifies to a certain strength of soul and a great purposiveness of the understanding that he not permit himself to be led astray by any stirring of morality.

It is otherwise incontrovertible that a purposeful malice can only become the object of a perfect pleasure if it is foiled by moral purposiveness. In that case, it is even an essential condition of supreme delight, because it alone is capable of making the predominance of the moral sense evident. There is no more persuasive proof of this than the last impression with which the author of Clarissa releases us. The highest purposiveness of understanding, which we necessarily admire in Lovelace's plan of seduction, is gloriously surpassed by the purposiveness of reason, which Clarissa counterposes to this fearsome enemy of her innocence, and we see ourselves made thus capable of unifying the enjoyment of both to a high degree.

To the degree that the tragic poet sets himself the goal of bringing the feeling of moral purposiveness to living consciousness, to the degree, therefore, that he skilfully selects the means to this purpose, and employs them, he must please the connoisseur in a double way, by means of the moral and the natural purposiveness. With the former he will satisfy the heart, with the latter, the understanding. The general run of people suffers blindly, as it were, the effect the artist intends upon the heart, without seeing through the magic by means of which art exerts this power over them. But there is a certain class of connoisseur, among whom, to the contrary, the artist loses the effect he intends upon the heart, whose taste, however, he can win with the purposiveness of the means employed to that end. Often the most refined culture of taste degenerates into this peculiar contradiction, particularly where moral ennoblement lags behind the education of the mind. This kind of connoisseur seeks only what is understandable in what is moving and exalted; this he perceives and tests with the most correct taste, but one must beware of appealing to his heart. Age and culture lead us to this reef, and to successfully vanquish this deleterious influence of both is the highest claim to fame of the refined man. Among the nations of Europe, our neighbors, the French, have been led closest to this extreme, and we, as in everything else, hasten to imitate this model.

Note

This essay arose in connection with lectures Schiller gave on his Theory of Tragedy in Jena in the summer of 1790. He began to work out his views in the spring of 1791, after a severe illness. The sources studied by Schiller included the writings of Lessing and Mendelssohn, and Kant's *Critique of Judgment,* which he began to study in February 1791. The essay, written in late 1791, first appeared in January 1792, in the first installment of *The New Thalia.*
—George W. Gregory, translator

Chapter 4

FROM *A PHILOSOPHICAL ENQUIRY INTO THE ORIGIN OF OUR IDEAS OF THE SUBLIME AND THE BEAUTIFUL*

Edmund Burke

> The consideration of the sublime from eighteenth-century Anglo-Irish philosopher and statesman Edmund Burke is included here because it is often referenced either implicitly or explicitly in considerations of the appeal and effect of both tragedy and horror, including in works by Schiller, Barbauld, and Radcliffe. For Burke, the sublime is a powerful emotional response mixing terror and delight elicited by things that are vast, powerful, and obscure. The sublime is both overwhelming and exhilarating. Ann Radcliffe in particular, in her essay included in this volume, draws on Burke in her considerations of the Gothic horror genre, aligning it with "terror."

Part I

Section VII. Of the Sublime

Whatever is fitted in any sort to excite the ideas of pain, and danger, that is to say, whatever is in any sort terrible, or is conversant about terrible objects, or operates in a manner analogous to terror, is a source of the *sublime*; that is, it is productive of the strongest emotion which the mind is capable of feeling. I say the strongest emotion, because I am satisfied the ideas of pain are much more powerful than those which enter on the part of pleasure. Without all doubt, the torments which we may be made to suffer, are much greater in their effect on the body and mind, than any pleasures which the most learned voluptuary could suggest, or than the liveliest imagination, and the most sound and exquisitely sensible body could enjoy. Nay I am in great doubt, whether any man could be found who would earn a life of the most perfect satisfaction, at the price of ending it in the torments, which justice inflicted in a few hours on the late unfortunate regicide in France.[1] But as pain is stronger in its operation than pleasure, so death is in general a much more affecting idea than pain; because there are very few pains, however exquisite, which are not preferred to death; nay, what generally makes pain itself, if I may say so, more painful, is, that it is considered as an emissary of this king of terrors. When danger or pain press too nearly, they are incapable of giving any delight, and are simply terrible; But at certain distance, and with certain modifications, they may be, and they are delightful, as we every day experience. The cause of this I shall endeavour to investigate hereafter. . . .

Part II

Section III. Obscurity

To make any thing very terrible, obscurity[2] seems in general to be necessary. When we know the full extent of any danger, when we can accustom our eyes to it, a great deal of the apprehension vanishes. Every one will be sensible of this, who considers how greatly night adds to our dread, in all cases of danger, and how much the notions of ghosts and goblins, of which none can form clear ideas, affect minds, which give credit to the popular tales concerning such-sorts of beings. Those despotic governments, which are founded on the passions of men, and principally upon the passion of fear, keep their chief as much as may be from the public eye. The policy has been the same in many cases of religion. Almost all the heathen temples were dark. Even in the barbarous temples of the Americans at this day, they keep their idol in a dark part of the hut, which is consecrated to his worship. For this purpose too the druids performed all their ceremonies in the bosom of the darkest woods, and in the shade of the oldest and most spreading oaks. No person seems better to have understood the secret of heightening, or of setting terrible things, if I may use the expression, in their strongest light by the force of a judicious obscurity, than Milton. His description of Death in the second book is admirably studied; it is astonishing with what a gloomy pomp, with what a significant and expressive uncertainty of strokes and colouring he has finished the portrait of the king of terrors.

> The other shape,
> If shape it might be called that shape had none
> Distinguishable, in member, joint, or limb;
> Or substance might be called that shadow seemed,
> For each seemed either; black he stood as night;
> Fierce as ten furies; terrible as hell;
> And shook a deadly dart. What seemed his head
> The likeness of a kingly crown had on.[3]

In this description all is dark, uncertain, confused, terrible, and sublime to the last degree.

Section IV. Of the Difference Between Clearness and Obscurity with Regard to the Passions

It is one thing to make an idea clear, and another to make it *affecting* to the imagination. If I make a drawing of a palace, or a temple, or a landscape, I present a very clear idea of those objects; but then (allowing for the effect of imitation which is something) my picture can at most affect only as the palace, temple, or landscape would have affected in the reality. On the other hand, the most lively and spirited verbal description I can give, raises a very obscure and imperfect *idea* of such objects; but then it is in my power to raise a stronger *emotion* by the description than I could do by the best painting. This experience constantly evinces. The proper manner of conveying the *affections* of the mind from one to another, is by words; there is a great insufficiency in all other methods of communication; and so far is a clearness of imagery from being absolutely necessary to an influence upon the passions, that they may be considerably operated upon without presenting any image at all, by certain sounds adapted to that purpose; of which we have a sufficient proof in the acknowledged and powerful effects of instrumental music. In reality a great clearness helps but little towards affecting the passions, as it is in some sort an enemy to all enthusiasms whatsoever.

... There are two verses in Horace's art of poetry that seem to contradict this opinion, for which reason I shall take a little more pains in clearing it up. The verses are,

*Segnius inritant animos demissa per aurem
Quam quæ sunt oculis subjecta fidelibus.*[4]

On this the abbe du Bos founds a criticism,[5] wherein he gives painting the preference to poetry in the article of moving the passions; principally on account of the greater *clearness* of the ideas it represents. I believe this excellent judge was led into this mistake (if it be a mistake) by his system, to which he found it more conformable than I imagine it will be found to experience. I know several who admire and love painting, and yet who regard the objects of their admiration in that art, with coolness enough, in comparison of that warmth with which they are animated by affecting pieces of poetry or rhetoric. Among the common sort of people, I never could perceive that painting had much influence on their passions. It is true that the best sorts of painting, as well as the best sorts of poetry, are not much understood in that sphere. But it is most certain, that their passions are very strongly roused by a fanatic preacher, or by the ballads of Chevy-Chase,[6] or the children in the wood, and by other little popular poems and tales that are current in that rank of life. I do not know of any paintings, bad or good, that produce the same effect. So that poetry with all its obscurity, has a more general as well as a more powerful dominion over the passions than the other art. And I think there are reasons in nature why the obscure idea, when properly conveyed, should be more affecting than the clear. It is our ignorance of things that causes all our admiration, and chiefly excites our passions. Knowledge and acquaintance make the most striking causes affect but little. It is thus with the vulgar, and all men are as the vulgar in what they do not understand. The ideas of eternity, and infinity, are among the most affecting we have, and yet perhaps there is nothing of which we really understand so little, as of infinity and eternity. We do not any where meet a more sublime description than this justly celebrated one of Milton, wherein he gives the portrait of Satan with a dignity so suitable to the subject.

> He above the rest
> In shape and gesture proudly eminent
> Stood like a tower; his form had yet not lost
> All her original brightness, nor appeared
> Less than archangel ruin'd, and th' excess
> Of glory obscured: as when the sun new ris'n
> Looks through the horizontal misty air
> Shorn of his beams; or from behind the moon
> In dim eclipse disastrous twilight sheds
> On half the nations; and with fear of change
> Perplexes monarchs.[7]

Here is a very noble picture; and in what does this poetical picture consist? in images of a tower, an archangel, the sun rising through mists, or in an eclipse, the ruin of monarchs, and the revolutions of kingdoms. The mind is hurried out of itself, by a croud of great and confused images; which affect because they are crouded and confused. For separate them, and you lose much of the greatness, and join them, and you infallibly lose the clearness. The images raised by poetry are always of this obscure kind; though in general the effects of poetry, are by no means to be attributed to the images it raises; which point we shall examine more at large hereafter.[8] But painting, when we have allowed for the pleasure of imitation, can only affect simply by the images it presents; and even in painting a judicious obscurity in some things contributes to the effect of the picture; because the images in painting are exactly similar to those in nature; and in nature dark, confused, uncertain images have a greater power on the fancy to form the grander passions than those have which are more clear and determinate. But where and when this observation may be applied to practice, and how far it shall be extended, will be better deduced from the nature of the subject, and from the occasion, than from any rules that can be given.

I am sensible that this idea has met with opposition, and is likely still to be rejected by several.[9] But let it be considered that hardly any thing can strike the mind with its greatness, which does not make some sort of approach towards infinity; which nothing can do whilst we are able to perceive its bounds; but to see an object distinctly, and to perceive its bounds, is one and the same thing. A clear idea is therefore another name for a little idea. There is a passage in the book of Job amazingly sublime, and this sublimity is principally due to the terrible uncertainty of the thing described. *In thoughts from the visions of the night, when deep sleep falleth upon men, fear came upon me and trembling, which made all my bones to shake. Then a spirit passed before my face. The hair of my flesh stood up. It stood still,* but I could not discern the form thereof; *an image was before mine eyes; there was silence; and I heard a voice,—Shall mortal man be more just than God?*[10] We are first prepared with the utmost solemnity for the vision; we are first terrified, before we are let even into the obscure cause of our emotion; but when this grand cause of terror makes its appearance, what is it? is it not, wrapt up in the shades of its own incomprehensible darkness, more aweful, more striking, more terrible, than the liveliest description, than the clearest painting could possibly represent it? When painters have attempted to give us clear representations of these very fanciful and terrible ideas, they have I think almost always failed; insomuch that I have been at a loss, in all the pictures I have seen of hell, whether the painter did not intend something ludicrous. Several painters have handled a subject of this kind, with a view of assembling as many horrid phantoms as their imagination could suggest; but all the designs I have chanced to meet of the temptations of St. Anthony,[11] were rather a sort of odd, wild grotesques, than any thing capable of producing a serious passion. In all these subjects poetry is very happy. Its apparitions, its chimeras, its harpies, its allegorical figures, are grand and affecting; and though Virgil's Fame,[12] and Homer's Discord,[13] are obscure, they are magnificent figures. These figures in painting would be clear enough, but I fear they might become ridiculous.

Notes

1. On January 5, 1757, Robert Francis Damiens (1714–57) attempted to kill Louis XV and was put to death, after being viciously tortured, on March 28.

2. Part 4, secs. 14, 15, 16.

3. Milton, *Paradise Lost,* 666–73; line 5 should read "For each seemd either; black it stood as night"; and in the penultimate line Milton has "a dreadful dart."

4. "Slowly, through the news put before the eyes of a good man, the fate of those downcast arouses pity." *De arte poetica* 180–81.

5. Burke is referring here to *Reflexions critiques sur la poesie et sur la peinture* (Paris, 1755), I. 416.

6. Addison referred to Chevy-Chase in *The Spectator,* 70 and 74. "The old song of Chevy-Chase," Addison writes in 70, "is the favourite Ballad of the common People of England; and Ben Jonson used to say he had rather have been the Author of it than of all his Works."

7. *Paradise Lost,* 589–99.

8. Part 5.

9. For the opposition Burke refers to, see contemporary reviews in *Monthly Review* 16 (1757) and *Literary Magazine* 2 (1757).

10. Job 4:13–17.

11. A popular subject for European painters in the sixteenth and seventeenth centuries, with examples by Salvator Rosa, Breughel, Teniers, and Ribera, among others. For an interesting account of the subject, see the introduction to Kitty Mrosovsky's edition of *The Temptation of St. Anthony,* by Flaubert (Penguin, 1983).

12. *Aeneid* iv. 173.

13. *Il* iv. 440–45.

Chapter 5

FROM "WHY TERROUR AND GRIEF ARE PLEASING TO THE MIND WHEN EXCITED BY DESCRIPTIONS"

Joseph Addison

> Joseph Addison was a late seventeenth-century/early eighteenth-century British essayist, poet, playwright, and politician, notable for having cofounded the British magazine *The Spectator*. Addison's speculations here further develop ideas contributed by Aristotle and Hume concerning our ability to derive pleasure from intense and often unpleasurable emotions within the context of a safe space. Addison asserts that, while watching a performance, when the audience knows it is not in danger, intense emotions may be experienced without fear of real harm. He emphasizes the role of the imagination in transforming terror and grief into pleasure as fear is blended with admiration in a satisfying way. That terror can lead to wonder has obvious applications to the horror genre.

THE PLEASURES OF THESE SECONDARY VIEWS of the Imagination, are of a wider and more universal Nature than those it has when joined with Sight; for not only what is Great, Strange or Beautiful, but any Thing that is Disagreeable when looked upon, pleases us in an apt Description. Here, therefore, we must enquire after a new Principle of Pleasure, which is nothing else but the Action of the Mind, which *compares* the Ideas that arise from Words, with the Ideas that arise from the Objects themselves; and why this Operation of the Mind is attended with so much Pleasure, we have before considered. For this Reason therefore, the Description of a Dunghill is pleasing to the Imagination, if the Image be represented to our Minds by suitable Expressions; tho', perhaps, this may be more properly called the Pleasure of the Understanding than of the Fancy, because we are not so much delighted with the Image that is contained in the Description, as with the Aptness of the Description to excite the Image.

But if the Description of what is Little, Common or Deformed, be acceptable to the Imagination, the Description of what is Great, Surprising or Beautiful, is much more so; because here we are not only delighted with *comparing* the Representation with the Original, but are highly pleased with the Original it self. Most Readers, I believe, are more charmed with *Milton*'s Description of Paradise, than of Hell; they are both, perhaps, equally perfect in their Kind, but in the one the Brimstone and Sulphur are not so refreshing to the Imagination, as the Beds of Flowers and the Wilderness of Sweets in the other.

There is yet another Circumstance which recommends a Description more than all the rest, and that is, if it represents to us such Objects as are apt to raise a secret Ferment in the Mind of the Reader, and to work, with Violence, upon his Passions. For, in this Case, we are at once warmed and enlightened, so that the Pleasure becomes more Universal, and is several ways qualified to entertain us. Thus, in Painting, it is pleasant to look on the Picture of any Face, where the Resemblance is hit, but the Pleasure increases, if it be the Picture of a Face that is beautiful, and is still greater, if the Beauty be softened with an Air of Melancholy or Sorrow. The two leading Passions which the more serious Parts of Poetry endeavour to stir up in us, are Terror and Pity. And here, by the way, one would wonder how it comes to pass, that such Passions as are very unpleasant at all other times, are very agreeable when excited by proper Descriptions. It is not strange, that we should take Delight in such Passages as are apt to produce Hope, Joy, Admiration, Love, or the like Emotions in us, because they never rise in the Mind without an inward Pleasure which attends them. But how comes it to pass, that we should take delight in being terrified or dejected by a Description, when we find so much Uneasiness in the Fear or Grief which we receive from any other Occasion?

If we consider, therefore, the Nature of this Pleasure, we shall find that it does not arise so properly from the Description of what is Terrible, as from the Reflection we make on our selves at the time of reading it. When we look on such hideous Objects, we are not a little pleased to think we are in no Danger of them. We consider them at the same time, as Dreadful and Harmless; so that the more frightful Appearance they make, the greater is the Pleasure we receive from the Sense of our own Safety. In short, we look upon the Terrors of a Description, with the same Curiosity and Satisfaction that we survey a dead Monster.

> . . . *Informe cadaver*
> *Protrahitur: nequeunt expleri corda tuendo*
> *Terribiles oculos, vultum, villosaque setis*
> *Pectora semiferi, atque extinctos faucibus ignes.* —Virg.[1]

It is for the same Reason that we are delighted with the reflecting upon Dangers that are past, or in looking on a Precipice at a distance, which would fill us with a different kind of Horrour, if we saw it hanging over our Heads.

In the like manner, when we read of Torments, Wounds, Deaths, and the like dismal Accidents, our Pleasure does not flow so properly from the Grief which such melancholy Descriptions give us, as from the secret Comparison which we make between our selves and the Person who suffers. Such Representations teach us to set a just Value upon our own Condition, and make us prize our good Fortune, which exempts us from the like Calamities. This is, however, such a kind of Pleasure as we are not capable of receiving, when we see a Person actually lying under the Tortures that we meet with in a Description; because, in this Case, the Object presses too close upon our Senses, and bears so hard upon us, that it does not give us Time or Leisure to reflect on our selves. Our Thoughts are so intent upon the Miseries of the Sufferer, that we cannot turn them upon our own Happiness. Whereas, on the contrary, we consider the Misfortunes we read in History or Poetry, either as past, or as fictitious, so that the Reflection upon our selves rises in us insensibly, and over-bears the Sorrow we conceive for the Sufferings of the Afflicted.

But because the Mind of Man requires something more perfect in Matter, than what it finds there, and can never meet with any Sight in Nature which sufficiently answers its highest Ideas of Pleasantness; or, in other Words, because the Imagination can fancy to it self Things more Great, Strange, or Beautiful, than the Eye ever saw, and is still sensible of some Defect in what it has seen; on this account it is the part of a Poet to humour the Imagination in its own Notions, by mending and perfecting Nature where he describes a Reality, and by adding greater Beauties than are put together in Nature, where he describes a Fiction.

He is not obliged to attend her in the slow Advances which she makes from one Season to another, or to observe her Conduct in the successive Production of Plants and Flowers. He may draw into his Description all the Beauties of the Spring and Autumn, and make the whole Year contribute something to render it the more agreeable. His Rose-trees, Wood-bines and Jessamines may flower together, and his Beds be covered at the same time with Lilies, Violets, and Amaranths. His Soil is not restrained to any particular Sett of Plants, but is proper either for Oaks or Mirtles, and adapts it self to the Products of every Climate. Oranges may grow wild in it; Myrrh may be met with in every Hedge, and if he thinks it proper to have a Grove of Spices, he can quickly command Sun enough to raise it. If all this will not furnish out an agreeable Scene, he can make several new Species of Flowers, with richer Scents and higher Colours than any that grow in the Gardens of Nature. His Consorts of Birds may be as full and harmonious, and his Woods as thick and gloomy as he pleases. He is at no more Expence in a long Vista, than a short one, and can as easily throw his Cascades from a Precipice of half a Mile high, as from one of twenty Yards. He has his Choice of the Winds, and can turn the Course of his Rivers in all the variety of *Meanders*, that are most delightful to the Reader's Imagination. In a Word, he has the modelling of Nature in his own Hands, and may give her what Charms he pleases, provided he does not reform her too much, and run into Absurdities, by endeavouring to excel.

Note

1. The wond'ring neighborhood, with glad surprise,
   Behold his shagged breast, his giant size,
   His mouth that flames no more, and his extinguish'd eyes.

   —Virgil, *The Aeneid*

   Note from Gregory Smith, editor of *The Spectator*.

Chapter 6

ON THE PLEASURE DERIVED FROM OBJECTS OF TERROR

Anna Laetitia Barbauld

> Anna Laetitia Barbauld was a prominent late-eighteenth/early nineteenth-century British poet, author, editor, teacher, and literary critic. Barbauld's consideration of the transformation of terror into pleasure brings together ideas contributed by the authors of the preceding chapters. However, hers is the first voice here to address literature rather than theater. Barbauld explains that people are drawn to representations of fear and danger because there is pleasure in exploring intense emotions without risk and explorations of the supernatural and extraordinary delight the imagination. Suspense, in particular, creates a heightened emotional state that is exciting and pleasurable.

THAT THE EXERCISE OF OUR benevolent feelings, as called forth by the view of human afflictions, should be a source of pleasure, cannot appear wonderful to one who considers that relation between the moral and natural system of man, which has connected a degree of satisfaction with every action or emotion productive of the general welfare. The painful sensation immediately arising from a scene of misery, is so much softened and alleviated by the reflex sense of self-approbation attending virtuous sympathy, that we find, on the whole, a very exquisite and refined pleasure remaining, which makes us desirous of again being witnesses to such scenes, instead of flying from them with disgust and horror. It is obvious how greatly such a provision must conduce to the ends of mutual support and assistance. But the apparent delight with which we dwell upon objects of pure terror, where our moral feelings are not in the least concerned, and no passion seems to be excited but the depressing one of fear, is a paradox of the heart, much more difficult of solution.

The reality of this source of pleasure seems evident from daily observation. The greediness with which the tales of ghosts and goblins, of murders, earthquakes, fires, shipwrecks, and all the most terrible disasters attending human life, are devoured by every ear, must have been generally remarked. Tragedy, the most favourite work of fiction, has taken a full share of those scenes; "it has supt full with horrors"—and has, perhaps, been more indebted to them for public admiration than to its tender and pathetic parts. The ghost of Hamlet, Macbeth descending into the witches' cave, and the tent scene in *Richard,* command as forcibly the attention of our souls as the parting of Jaffeir and Belvidera, the fall of Wolsey, or the death of Shore. The inspiration of terror was by the antient critics assigned as the peculiar province of tragedy; and the Greek and Roman tragedians have introduce[d] some extraordinary personages for this purpose: not only the shades of the dead, but the furies, and other fabulous inhabitants of the infernal regions. Collins, in his most poetical ode to Fear, has finely enforced this idea.

> Tho' gentle Pity claim her mingled part,
>   Yet all the thunders of the scene are thine.

The old Gothic romance and the Eastern tale, with their genii, giants, enchantments, and transformations, however a refined critic may censure them as absurd and extravagant, will ever retain a most powerful influence on the mind, and interest the reader independently of all peculiarity of taste. Thus the great Milton, who had a strong bias to these wildnesses of the imagination, has with striking effect made the stories "of forests and enchantments drear," a favourite subject with his *Penseroso*; and had undoubtedly their awakening images strong upon his mind when he breaks out,

> Call up him that left half-told
> The story of Cambuscan bold; &c.

How are we then to account for the pleasure derived from such objects? I have often been led to imagine that there is a deception in these cases; and that the avidity with which we attend is not a proof of our receiving real pleasure. The pain of suspense, and the irresistible desire of satisfying curiosity, when once raised, will account for our eagerness to go quite through an adventure though we suffer actual pain during the whole course of it. We rather chuse to suffer the smart pang of a violent emotion than the uneasy craving of an unsatisfied desire. That this principle, in many instances, may involuntarily carry us through what we dislike, I am convinced from experience. This is the impulse which renders the poorest and most insipid narrative interesting when once we get fairly into it; and I have frequently felt it with regard to our modern novels, which, if lying on my table, and taken up in an idle hour, have led me through the most tedious and disgusting pages, while, like Pistol eating his leek, I have swallowed and execrated to the end. And it will not only force us through dullness, but through actual torture—through the relation of a Damien's execution, or an inquisitor's act of faith. When children, therefore, listen with pale and mute attention to the frightful stories of apparitions, we are not, perhaps, to imagine that they are in a state of enjoyment, any more than the poor bird which is dropping into the mouth of the rattlesnake—they are chained by the ears, and fascinated by curiosity. This solution, however, does not satisfy me with respect to the well-wrought scenes of artificial terror which are formed by a sublime and vigorous imagination. Here, though we know before-hand what to expect, we enter into them with eagerness, in quest of a pleasure already experienced. This is the pleasure constantly attached to the excitement of surprise from new and wonderful objects. A strange and unexpected event awakens the mind, and keeps it on the stretch; and where the agency of invisible beings is introduced, of "forms unseen, and mightier far than we," our imagination, darting forth, explores with rapture the new world which is laid open to its view, and rejoices in the expansion of its powers. Passion and fancy co-operating elevate the soul to its highest pitch; and the pain of terror is lost in amazement.

Hence, the more wild, fanciful, and extraordinary are the circumstances of a scene of horror, the more pleasure we receive from it; and where they are too near common nature, though violently borne by curiosity through the adventure, we cannot repeat it or reflect on it, without an over-balance of pain. In the Arabian nights are many most striking examples of the terrible joined with the marvellous: the story of Aladdin and the travels of Sinbad are particularly excellent. *The Castle of Otranto* is a very spirited modern attempt upon the same plan of mixed terror, adapted to the model of Gothic romance. The best conceived, and most strongly worked-up scene of mere natural horror that I recollect, is in Smollett's *Ferdinand Count Fathom*; where the hero, entertained in a lone house in a forest, finds a corpse just slaughtered in the room where he is sent to sleep, and the door of which is locked upon him. It may be amusing for the reader to compare his feelings upon these, and from thence form his opinion of the justness of my theory.

Chapter 7

ON THE SUPERNATURAL IN POETRY

Ann Radcliffe

> Ann Radcliffe numbers among the most famous of Gothic novelists. Her major works, including *The Mysteries of Udolpho* (1794) and *The Italian* (1797), follow a pattern of introducing apparently supernatural phenomena, only later to provide rational explanations for them. Radcliffe's essay is notable for the distinction she draws between terror and horror. Terror, according to Radcliffe, is evoked by a fear of the unknown and expands the mind by engaging the imagination, mixing fear with wonder. She relates it to the idea of the sublime. Horror, in contrast, is the experience of revulsion and shock elicited by confronting something gruesome or grotesque. Horror, according to Radcliffe, freezes and contracts the mind. Radcliffe argues for terror as the proper goal for the Gothic novel.

ONE OF OUR TRAVELLERS BEGAN a grave dissertation on the illusions of the imagination. "And not only on frivolous occasions," said he, "but in the most important pursuits of life, an object often flatters and charms at a distance, which vanishes into nothing as we approach it; and 'tis well if it leave only disappointment in our hearts. Sometimes a severer monitor is left there."

These truisms, delivered with an air of discovery by Mr. S——, who seldom troubled himself to think upon any subject, except that of a good dinner, were lost upon his companion, who, pursuing the airy conjectures which the present scene, however humbled, had called up, was following Shakespeare into unknown regions. "Where is now the undying spirit," said he, "that could so exquisitely perceive and feel? that could inspire itself with the various characters of this world, and create worlds of its own; to which the grand and the beautiful, the gloomy and the sublime of visible Nature, up-called not only corresponding feelings, but passions; which seemed to perceive a soul in everything: and thus, in the secret workings of its own characters, and in the combinations of its incidents, kept the elements and local scenery always in unison with them, heightening their effect."

So the conspirators at Rome pass under the fiery showers and sheeted lightning of the thunder-storm, to meet, at midnight, in the porch of Pompey's theatre. The streets being then deserted by the affrighted multitude, that place, open as it was, was convenient for their council; and, as to the storm, they felt it not; it was not more terrible to them than their own passions, nor so terrible to others as the dauntless spirit that makes them, almost unconsciously, brave its fury. These appalling circumstances, with others of supernatural import, attended the fall of the conqueror of the world—a man, whose power Cassius represents to be dreadful as this night, when the sheeted dead were seen in the lightning to glide along the streets of Rome. How much does the sublimity of these attendant circumstances heighten our idea of the power of Caesar, of the terrific grandeur of his character, and prepare and interest us for his fate. The whole soul is roused and fixed, in the full energy of attention, upon the progress of the conspiracy against him; and, had not Shakespeare wisely withdrawn him from our view, there would have been no balance of our passions. —"Caesar was a tyrant," said Mr. S——. W—— looked at him for a moment, and smiled, and then silently resumed the course of his own thoughts. No master ever knew how to touch the accordant springs of sympathy by small circumstances like our own Shakespeare. In Cymbeline, for instance, how finely such circumstances are made use of, to awaken, at once, solemn expectation and tenderness, and, by recalling the softened remembrance of a sorrow long past, to prepare the mind to melt at one that was approaching, mingling at the same time, by means of a mysterious occurrence, a slight tremour of awe with our pity. Thus, when Belarius and Arviragus return to the cave where they had left the unhappy and worn-out Imogen to repose, while they are yet standing before it, and Arviragus, speaking of her with tenderest pity, as "the poor sick Fidele," goes out to enquire for her,—solemn music is heard from the cave, sounded by that harp of which Guiderius says, "*Since the death of my dearest mother, it did not speak before. All solemn things should answer solemn accidents.*" Immediately Arviragus enters with Fidele senseless in his arms:

> "The bird is dead, that we have made so much of.
> —How found you him? Stark, as you see, thus smiling.
> —I thought he slept, and put My clouted brogues from off my feet, whose rudeness
> Answered my steps too loud."—"Why he but sleeps!"
> "With fairest flowers
> While summer lasts, AND I LIVE HERE, FIDELE, I'll sweeten thy sad grave–."

Tears alone can speak the touching simplicity of the whole scene. Macbeth shows, by many instances, how much Shakespeare delighted to heighten the effect of his characters and his story by correspondent scenery: there the desolate heath, the troubled elements, assist the mischief of his malignant beings. But who, after hearing Macbeth's thrilling question—

> —What are these,
> So withered and so wild in their attire,
> That look not like the inhabitants o' the earth,
> And yet are on't?

Who would have thought of reducing them to mere human beings, by attiring them not only like the inhabitants of the earth, but in the dress of a particular country, and making them downright Scotch-women? Thus not only contradicting the very words of Macbeth, but withdrawing from these cruel agents of the passions all that strange and supernatural air which had made them so affecting to the imagination, and which was entirely suitable to the solemn and important events they were foretelling and accomplishing. Another *improvement* on Shakespeare is the introducing a crowd of witches thus arrayed, instead of the three beings "so withered and so wild in their attire." About the latter part of this sentence, W——, as he was apt to do, thought aloud, and Mr. S—— said, "*I*, now, have sometimes considered, that it was quite sensible to make Scotch witches on the stage, appear like Scotch-women. You must recollect that, in the superstition concerning witches, they lived familiarly upon the earth, mortal sorcerers, and were not always known from mere old women; consequently they must have appeared in the dress of the country where they happened to live, or they would have been more than suspected of witchcraft, which we find was not always the case."

"You are speaking of old women, and not of witches," said W—— laughing, "and I must more than suspect you of crediting that obsolete superstition which destroyed so many wretched, yet guiltless persons, if I allow your argument to have any force. I am speaking of the only real witch—the witch of the poet; and all our notions and feelings connected with terror accord with his. The wild attire, the look *not of this earth,* are essential traits of supernatural agents, working evil in the darkness of mystery. Whenever the poet's witch condescends, according to the vulgar notion, to mingle mere ordinary mischief with her malignity, and to become familiar, she is ludicrous, and loses her power over the imagination; the illusion vanishes. So vexatious is the effect of the stage-witches upon my mind, that I should probably have left the theatre when they appeared, had not the fascination of Mrs. Siddons's influence so spread itself over the whole play, as to overcome my disgust, and to make me forget even Shakespeare himself; while all consciousness of fiction was lost, and his thoughts lived and breathed before me in the very form of truth. Mrs. Siddons, like Shakespeare, always disappears in the character she represents, and throws an illusion over the whole scene around her, that conceals many defects in the arrangements of the theatre. I should suppose she would be the finest Hamlet that ever appeared, excelling even her own brother in that character; she would more fully preserve the tender and refined melancholy, the deep sensibility, which are the peculiar charm of Hamlet, and which appear not only in the ardour, but in the occasional irresolution and weakness of his character—the secret spring that reconciles all his inconsistencies. A sensibility so profound can with difficulty be justly imagined, and therefore can very rarely be assumed. Her brother's firmness, incapable of being always subdued, does not so fully enhance, as her tenderness would, this part of the character. The strong light which shows the mountains of a landscape in all their greatness, and with all their rugged sharpness, gives them nothing of the interest with which a more gloomy tint would invest their grandeur; dignifying, though it softens, and magnifying, while it obscures."

"I still think," said Mr. S——, without attending to these remarks, "that, in a popular superstition, it is right to go with the popular notions, and dress your witches like the old women of the place where they are supposed to have appeared."

"As far as these notions prepare us for the awe which the poet designs to excite, I agree with you that he is right in availing himself of them; but, for this purpose, everything familiar and common should be carefully avoided. In nothing has Shakespeare been more successful than in this; and in another case somewhat more difficult—that of selecting circumstances of manners and appearance for his supernatural beings, which, though wild and remote, in the highest degree, from common apprehension, never shock the understanding by incompatibility with themselves—never compel us, for an instant, to recollect that he has a license for extravagance. Above every ideal being is the ghost of Hamlet, with all its attendant incidents of time and place. The dark watch upon the remote platform, the dreary aspect of the night, the very expression of the office on guard, 'the air bites shrewdly; it is very cold'; the recollection of a star, an unknown world, are all circumstances which excite forlorn, melancholy, and solemn feelings, and dispose us to welcome, with trembling curiosity, the awful being that draws near; and to indulge in that strange mixture of horror, pity, and indignation, produced by the tale it reveals. Every minute circumstance of the scene between those watching on the platform, and of that between them and Horatio, preceding the entrance of the apparition, contributes to excite some feeling of dreariness, or melancholy, or solemnity, or expectation, in unison with, and leading on toward that high curiosity and thrilling awe with which we witness the conclusion of the scene. So the first question of Bernardo, and the words in reply, 'Stand and unfold yourself.' But there is not a single circumstance in either dialogue, not even in this short one, with which the play opens, that does not take its secret effect upon the imagination. It ends with Bernardo desiring his brother-officer, after having asked whether he has had 'quiet watch,' to hasten the guard, if he should chance to meet them; and we immediately feel ourselves alone on this dreary ground.

"When Horatio enters, the challenge—the dignified answers, 'Friends to this ground, and liegemen to the Dane,'—the question of Horatio to Bernardo, touching the apparition—the unfolding of the reason why 'Horatio has consented to watch with them the minutes of this night'—the sitting down together, while Bernardo relates the particulars of what they had seen for two nights; and, above all, the few lines with which he begins his story, 'Last night of all,' and the distinguishing, by the situation of 'yon same star,' the very point of time when the spirit had appeared—the abruptness with which he breaks off, 'the bell then beating one'—the instant appearance of the ghost, as though ratifying the story for the very truth itself—all these are circumstances which the deepest sensibility only could have suggested, and which, if you read them a thousand times, still continue to affect you almost as much as the first. I thrill with delighted awe, even while I recollect and mention them, as instances of the exquisite art of the poet."

"Certainly you must be very superstitious," said Mr. S——, "or such things could not interest you thus."

"There are few people less so than I am," replied W——, "or I understand myself and the meaning of superstition very ill."

"That is quite paradoxical."

"It appears so, but so it is not. If I cannot explain this, take it as a mystery of the human mind."

"If it were possible for me to believe the appearance of ghosts at all," replied Mr. S——, "it would certainly be the ghost of Hamlet; but I never can suppose such things; they are out of all reason and probability."

"You would believe the immortality of the soul," said W——, with solemnity, "even without the aid of revelation; yet our confined faculties cannot comprehend *how* the soul may exist after separation from the body. I do not absolutely know that spirits are permitted to become visible to us on earth; yet that they may be permitted to appear for very rare and important purposes, such as could scarcely have been accomplished without an equal suspension, or a momentary change, of the laws prescribed to what we call *Nature*—that is, without one more exercise of the same CREATIVE POWER of which we must acknowledge so many millions of existing instances, and by which alone we ourselves at this moment breathe, think, or disquisite at all, cannot be impossible, and, I think, is probable. Now, probability is enough for the poet's justification, the ghost being supposed to have come for an important purpose. Oh, I should never be weary of dwelling on the perfection of Shakespeare, in his management of every scene connected with that most solemn and mysterious being, which takes such entire possession of the imagination, that we hardly seem conscious we are beings of this world while we contemplate 'the extravagant and erring spirit.' The spectre departs, accompanied by natural circumstances as touching as those with which he had approached. It is by the strange light of the glow-worm, which 'gins to pale his Ineffectual fire'; it is at the first scent of the morning air—the living breath, that the apparition retires. There is, however, no little vexation in seeing the ghost of Hamlet *played*. The finest imagination is requisite to give the due colouring to such a character on the stage; and yet almost any actor is thought capable of performing it. In the scene where Horatio breaks his secret to Hamlet, Shakespeare, still true to the touch of circumstances, makes the time evening, and marks it by the very words of Hamlet, 'Good even, sir,' which Hanmer and Warburton changed, without any reason, to 'good morning,' thus making Horatio relate his most interesting and solemn story by the clear light of the cheerfullest part of the day; when busy sounds are stirring, and the sun itself seems to contradict every doubtful tale, and lessen every feeling of terror. The discord of this must immediately be understood by those who have bowed the willing soul to the poet."

"How happens it then," said Mr. S——, "that objects of terror sometimes strike us very forcibly, when introduced into scenes of gaiety and splendour, as, for instance, in the Banquet scene in Macbeth?"

"They strike, then, chiefly by the force of contrast," said W——; "but the effect, though sudden and strong, is also transient; it is the thrill of horror and surprise, which they then communicate, rather than the deep and solemn feelings excited under more accordant circumstances, and left long upon the mind. Who ever suffered for the ghost of Banquo, the gloomy and sublime kind of terror, which that of Hamlet calls forth? Though the appearance of Banquo, at the high festival of Macbeth, not only tells us that he is murdered, but recalls to our minds the fate of the gracious Duncan, laid in silence and death by those who, in this very scene, are revelling in his spoils. There, though deep pity mingles with our surprise and horror, we experience a far less degree of interest, and that interest too of an inferior kind. The union of grandeur and obscurity, which Mr. Burke describes as a sort of tranquility tinged with terror, and which causes the sublime, is to be found only in Hamlet; or in scenes where circumstances of the same kind prevail."

"That may be," said Mr. S——, "and I perceive you are not one of those who contend that obscurity does not make any part of the sublime." "They must be men of very cold imaginations," said W——, "with whom certainty is more terrible than surmise. Terror and horror are so far opposite, that the first expands the soul, and awakens the faculties to a high degree of life; the other contracts, freezes, and nearly annihilates them. I apprehend, that neither Shakespeare nor Milton by their fictions, nor Mr. Burke by his reasoning, anywhere looked to positive horror as a source of the sublime, though they all agree that terror is a very high one; and where lies the great difference between horror and terror, but in the uncertainty and obscurity, that accompany the first, respecting the dreaded evil?"

"But what say you to Milton's image—'On his brow sat horror plumed.'"

"As an image, it certainly is sublime; it fills the mind with an idea of power, but it does not follow that Milton intended to declare the feeling of horror to be sublime; and after all, his image imparts more of terror than of horror; for it is not distinctly pictured forth, but is seen in glimpses through obscuring shades, the great outlines only appearing, which excite the imagination to complete the rest; he only says, 'sat horror plumed'; you will observe, that the look of horror and the other characteristics are left to the imagination of the reader; and according to the strength of that, he will feel Milton's image to be either sublime or otherwise. Milton, when he sketched it, probably felt, that not even his art could fill up the outline, and present to other eyes the countenance which his 'mind's eye' gave to him. Now, if obscurity has so much effect on fiction, what must it have in real life, when to ascertain the object of our terror, is frequently to acquire the means of escaping it. You will observe, that this image, though indistinct or obscure, is not confused."

"How can anything be indistinct and not confused?" said Mr. S——.

"Ay, that question is from the new school," replied W——; "but recollect, that obscurity, or indistinctness, is only a negative, which leaves the imagination to act upon the few hints that truth reveals to it; confusion is a thing as positive as distinctness, though not necessarily so palpable; and it may, by mingling and confounding one image with another, absolutely counteract the imagination, instead of exciting it. Obscurity leaves something for the imagination to exaggerate; confusion, by blurring one image into another, leaves only a chaos in which the mind can find nothing to be magnificent, nothing to nourish its fears or doubts, or to act upon in any way; yet confusion and obscurity are terms used indiscriminately by those, who would prove, that Shakespeare and Milton were wrong when they employed obscurity as a cause of the sublime, that Mr. Burke was equally mistaken in his reasoning upon the subject, and that mankind have been equally in error, as to the nature of their own feelings, when they were acted upon by the illusions of those great masters of the imagination, at whose so potent bidding, the passions have been awakened from their sleep, and by whose magic a crowded Theatre has been changed to a lonely shore, to a witch's cave, to an enchanted island, to a murderer's castle, to the ramparts of an usurper, to the battle, to the midnight carousal of the camp or the tavern, to every various scene of the living world."

"Yet there are poets, and great ones too," said Mr. S——, "whose minds do not appear to have been very susceptible of those circumstances of time and space—of what you, perhaps, would call the picturesque in feeling—which you seem to think so necessary to the attainment of any powerful effect on the imagination. What say you to Dryden?"

"That he had a very strong imagination, a fertile wit, a mind well prepared by education, and great promptness of feeling; but he had not—at least not in good proportion to his other qualifications—that delicacy of feeling, which we call taste; moreover, that his genius was overpowered by the prevailing taste of the court, and by an intercourse with the world, too often humiliating to his morals, and destructive of his sensibility. Milton's better morals protected his genius, and his imagination was not lowered by the world."

"Then you seem to think there may be great poets, without a full perception of the picturesque; I mean by picturesque, the beautiful and grand in nature and art—and with little susceptibility to what you would call the accordant circumstances, the harmony of which is essential to any powerful effect upon your feelings."

"No; I cannot allow that. Such men may have high talents, wit, genius, judgment, but not the soul of poetry, which is the spirit of all these, and also something wonderfully higher—something too fine for definition. It certainly includes an instantaneous perception, and an exquisite love of whatever is graceful, grand, and sublime, with the power of seizing and combining such circumstances of them, as to strike and interest a reader by the representation, even more than a general view of the real scene itself could do. Whatever this may be called, which crowns the mind of a poet, and distinguishes it from every other mind, our whole heart instantly acknowledges it in Shakespeare, Milton, Gray, Collins, Beattie, and a very few others, not excepting Thomson, to whose powers the sudden tear of delight and admiration bears at once both testimony and tribute. How deficient Dryden was of a poet's feelings in the fine province of the beautiful and the graceful, is apparent from his alteration of the Tempest, by which he has not only lessened the interest by incumbering the plot, but has absolutely disfigured the character of Miranda, whose simplicity, whose tenderness and innocent affections, might, to use Shakespeare's own words in another play, 'be shrined in crystal.' A love of moral beauty is as essential in the mind of a poet, as a love of picturesque beauty. There is as much difference between the tone of Dryden's moral feelings and those of Milton, as there is between their perceptions of the grand and the beautiful in nature. Yet, when I recollect the 'Alexander's Feast,' I am astonished at the powers of Dryden, and at my own daring opinions upon them; and should be ready to unsay much that I have said, did I not consider this particular instance of the power of music upon Dryden's mind, to be as wonderful as any instance he has exhibited of the effect of that enchanting art in his sublime ode. I cannot, however, allow it to be the finest ode in the English language, so long as I remember Gray's Bard, and Collins's Ode on the Passions.—But, to return to Shakespeare, I have sometimes thought, as I walked in the deep shade of the North Terrace of Windsor Castle, when the moon shone on all beyond, that the scene must have been present in Shakespeare's mind, when he drew the night-scenes in Hamlet; and, as I have stood on the platform, which there projects over the precipice, and have heard only the measured step of a sentinel or the clink of his arms, and have seen his shadow passing by moonlight, at the foot of the high Eastern tower, I have almost expected to see the royal shade armed cap-a-pee standing still on the lonely platform before me. The very star—'yon same star that's westward from the pole'—seemed to watch over the Western towers of the Terrace, whose high dark lines marked themselves upon the heavens. All has been so still and shadowy, so great and solemn, that the scene appeared fit for 'no mortal business nor any sounds that the earth owns.' Did you ever observe the fine effect of the Eastern tower, when you stand near the Western end of the North terrace, and its tall profile rears itself upon the sky, from nearly the base to the battled top, the lowness of the parapet permitting this? It is most striking at night, when the stars appear, at different heights, upon its tall dark line, and when the sentinel on watch moves a shadowy figure at its foot."

Chapter 8

ON THE SUPERNATURAL IN FICTITIOUS COMPOSITION; AND PARTICULARLY ON THE WORKS OF ERNEST THEODORE WILLIAM HOFFMANN

Walter Scott

> Although little read today, Sir Walter Scott was among the most popular and influential authors of the early nineteenth century, and, although his literary fictions certainly wouldn't be classified as works of horror, the supernatural nevertheless is occasionally suggested, if not confirmed, in his fiction. In this reflection on the role of the supernatural, Scott cautions that, to evoke "superstitious awe" from the reader, such instances should be "rare, brief, [and] indistinct." E. T. A. Hoffmann (the pen name of Ernest Theodore William Hoffmann) was a German Romanticist who is perhaps best known today for his short story "The Sandman" ("Der Sandmann"), which is referenced by Freud in his famous essay, "The Uncanny."

NO SOURCE OF ROMANTIC FICTION, and no mode of exciting the feelings of interest which the authors in that description of literature desire to produce, seems more directly accessible than the love of the super-natural. It is common to all classes of mankind, and perhaps is to none so familiar as to those who assume a certain degree of scepticism on the subject; since the reader may have often observed in conversation, that the person who professes himself most incredulous on the subject of marvellous stories, often ends his remarks by indulging the company with some well-attested anecdote, which it is difficult or impossible to account for on the narrator's own principles of absolute scepticism. The belief itself, though easily capable of being pushed into superstition and absurdity, has its origin not only in the facts upon which our holy religion is founded, but upon the principles of our nature, which teach us that while we are probationers in this sublunary state, we are neighbours to, and encompassed by the shadowy world, of which our mental faculties are too obscure to comprehend the laws, our corporeal organs too coarse and gross to perceive the inhabitants.

All professors of the Christian Religion believe that there was a time when the Divine Power showed itself more visibly on earth than in these our latter days; controlling and suspending, for its own purposes, the ordinary laws of the universe; and the Roman Catholic Church, at least, holds it as an article of faith, that miracles descend to the present time. Without entering into that controversy, it is enough that a firm belief in the great truths of our religion has induced wise and good men, even in Protestant countries, to subscribe to Dr. Johnson's doubts respecting supernatural appearances.

> That the dead are seen no more, said Imlac, I will not undertake to maintain against the concurrent and unvaried testimony of all ages, and of all nations. There is no people, rude or learned, among whom apparitions of the dead are not related and believed. This opinion, which perhaps prevails as far as human nature is diffused, could become universal only by its truth; those that never heard of one another could not have agreed in a tale which nothing but experience can make credible. That it is doubted by single cavillers, can very little weaken the general evidence; and some who deny it with their tongues, confess it by their fears.[1]

Upon such principles as these there lingers in the breasts even of philosophers, a reluctance to decide dogmatically upon a point where they do not and cannot possess any, save negative, evidence. Yet this inclination to believe in the marvellous gradually becomes weaker. Men cannot but remark that (since the scriptural miracles have ceased), the belief in prodigies and supernatural events has gradually declined in proportion to the advancement of human knowledge; and that since the age has become enlightened, the occurrence of tolerably well-attested anecdotes of the supernatural character are so few, as to render it more probable that the witnesses have laboured under some strange and temporary delusion, rather than that the laws of nature have been altered or suspended. At this period of human knowledge, the marvellous is so much identified with fabulous, as to be considered generally as belonging to the same class.

It is not so in early history, which is full of supernatural incidents; and although we now use the word *romance* as synonymous with fictitious composition, yet as it originally only meant a poem, or prose work contained in the Romance language, there is little doubt that the doughty chivalry who listened to the songs of the minstrel, "held each strange tale devoutly true,"[2] and that the feats of knighthood which he recounted, mingled with tales of magic and supernatural interference, were esteemed as veracious as the legends of the monks, to which they bore a strong resemblance. This period of society, however, must have long past before the Romancer began to select and arrange with care, the nature of the materials out of which he constructed his story. It was not when society, however differing in degree and station, was levelled and confounded by one dark cloud of ignorance, involving the noble as well as the mean, that it need be scrupulously considered to what class of persons the author addressed himself, or with what species of decoration he ornamented his story. "Homo was then a common name for all men,"[3] and all were equally pleased with the same style of composition. This, however, was gradually altered. As the knowledge to which we have before alluded made more general progress, it became impossible to detain the attention of the better instructed class by the simple and gross fables to which the present generation would only listen in childhood, though they had been held in honour by their fathers during youth, manhood, and old age.

It was also discovered that the supernatural in fictitious composition requires to be managed with considerable delicacy, as criticism begins to be more on the alert. The interest which it excites is indeed a powerful spring; but it is one which is peculiarly subject to be exhausted by coarse handling and repeated pressure. It is also of a character which it is extremely difficult to sustain, and of which a very small proportion may be said to be better than the whole. The marvellous, more than any other attribute of fictitious narrative, loses its effect by being brought much into view. The imagination of the reader is to be excited if possible, without being gratified. If once, like Macbeth, we "sup full with horrors," our taste for the banquet is ended, and the thrill of terror with which we hear or read of a night-shriek, becomes lost in that sated indifference with which the tyrant came at length to listen to the most deep catastrophes that could affect his house. The incidents of a supernatural character are usually those of a dark and undefinable nature, such as arise in the mind of the Lady in the Mask of Comus,—incidents to which our fears attach more consequence, as we cannot exactly tell what it is we behold, or what is to be apprehended from it:—

>   A thousand fantasies
> Begin to throng into my memory,
> Of calling shapes and beck'ning shadows dire,
> And aery tongues that syllable men's names
> On sands, and shores, and desert wildernesses.[4]

Burke observes upon obscurity, that it is necessary to make any thing terrible, and notices "how much the notions of ghosts and goblins, of which none can form clear ideas, affect minds which give credit to the popular tales concerning such sorts of beings." He represents also, that no person "seems better to have understood the secret of heightening, or of setting terrible things in their strongest light, by the force of a judicious obscurity, than Milton. His description of Death, in the second book, is admirably studied; it is astonishing with what a gloomy pomp, with what a significant and expressive uncertainty of strokes and colouring, he has finished the portrait of the king of terrors.

> The other shape,—
> If shape it might be called, which shape had none
> Distinguishable in member, joint, or limb:
> Or substance might be called that shadow seemed,—
> For each seemed either; black he stood as night;
> Fierce as ten furies; terrible as hell;
> And shook a deadly dart. What seemed his head
> The likeness of a kingly crown had on.[5]

In this description all is dark, uncertain, confused, terrible and sublime to the last degree."[6]

The only quotation worthy to be mentioned along with the passage we have just taken down, is the well-known apparition introduced with circumstances of terrific obscurity in the book of Job:

> Now a thing was secretly brought to me, and mine ears received a little thereof. In thoughts from the visions of the night, when deep sleep falleth on men, fear came upon me, and trembling which made all my bones to shake. Then a spirit passed before my face; the hair of my flesh stood up. It stood still, but I could not discern the form thereof: an image was before mine eyes; there was silence, and I heard a voice.[7]

From these sublime and decisive authorities, it is evident that the exhibition of supernatural appearances in fictitious narrative ought to be rare, brief, indistinct, and such as may become a being to us so incomprehensible, and so different from ourselves, of whom we cannot justly conjecture whence he comes, or for what purpose, and of whose attributes we can have no regular or distinct perception. Hence it usually happens, that the first touch of the supernatural is always the most effective, and is rather weakened and defaced, than strengthened by the subsequent recurrence of similar incidents. Even in *Hamlet,* the second entrance of the ghost is not nearly so impressive as the first; and in many romances to which we could refer, the supernatural being forfeits all claim, both to our terror and veneration, by condescending to appear too often; to mingle too much in the events of the story, and above all, to become loquacious, or, as it is familiarly called, *chatty.* We have, indeed, great doubts whether an author acts wisely in permitting his goblin to speak at all, if at the same time he renders him subject to human sight. Shakespeare, indeed, has contrived to put such language in the mouth of the buried majesty of Denmark as befits a supernatural being, and is [sic] by the style distinctly different from that of the living persons in the drama. In another passage he has had the boldness to intimate, by two expressions of similar force, in what manner and with what tone supernatural beings would find utterance:

> And the sheeted dead
> Did *squeak* and *gibber* in the Roman streets.[8]

But the attempt in which the genius of Shakespeare has succeeded would probably have been ridiculous in any meaner hand; and hence it is, that, in many of our modern tales of terror, our feelings of fear have, long before the conclusion, given way under the influence of that familiarity which begets contempt.

A sense that the effect of the supernatural in its more obvious application is easily exhausted, has occasioned the efforts of modern authors to cut new walks and avenues through the enchanted wood, and to revive, if possible, by some means or other, the fading impression of its horrors.

The most obvious and inartificial mode of attaining this end is, by adding to, and exaggerating the supernatural incidents of the tale. But far from increasing its effect, the principles which we have laid down, incline us to consider the impression as usually weakened by exaggerated and laborious description. Elegance is in such cases thrown away, and the accumulation of superlatives, with which the narrative is encumbered, renders it tedious, or perhaps ludicrous, instead of becoming impressive or grand.

There is indeed one style of composition, of which the supernatural forms an appropriate part, which applies itself rather to the fancy than to the imagination, and aims more at amusing than at affecting or interesting the reader. To this species of composition belong the eastern tales, which contribute so much to the amusement of our youth, and which are recollected, if not re-perused, with so much pleasure in our more advanced life. There are but few readers of any imagination who have not at one time or other in their life sympathized with the poet Collins, "who," says Dr. Johnson, "was eminently delighted with those flights of imagination, which pass the bounds of nature, and to which the mind is reconciled only by a passive acquiescence in popular traditions. He loved fairies, genii, giants, and monsters; he delighted to rove through the meadows of enchantment, to gaze on the magnificence of golden palaces, to repose by the waterfalls of Elysian gardens."[9] It is chiefly the young and the indolent who love to be soothed by works of this character, which require little attention in the perusal. In our riper age we remember them as we do the joys of our infancy, rather because we loved them once, than that they still continue to afford us amusement. The extravagance of fiction loses its charms for our riper judgment; and notwithstanding that these wild fictions contain much that is beautiful and full of fancy, yet still, unconnected as they are with each other, and conveying no result to the understanding, we pass them by as the championess Britomart rode along the rich strand.

> Which as she overwent,
> She saw bestrewed all with rich array
> Of pearls and precious stones of great assay,
> And all the gravel mixt with golden ore:
> Whereat she wondered much, but would not stay
> For gold, or pearls, or precious stones, one hour;
> But them despised all, for all was in her power.[10]

With this class of supernatural composition may be ranked, though inferior in interest, what the French call *Contes des Fées*; meaning, by that title, to distinguish them from the ordinary popular tales of fairy folks which are current in most countries. The *Conte des Fées* is itself a very different composition, and the fairies engaged are of a separate class from those whose amusement is to dance round the mushroom in the moonlight, and mislead the belated peasant. The French *Fée* more nearly resembles the Peri of Eastern or the Fata of Italian poetry. She is a superior being, having the nature of an elementary spirit, and possessing magical powers enabling her, to a considerable extent, to work either good or evil. But whatever merit this species of writing may have attained in some dexterous hands, it has, under the management of others, become one of the most absurd, flat, and insipid possible. Out of the whole *Cabinet des Fées*, when we get beyond our old acquaintances of the nursery, we can hardly select five volumes, from nearly fifty, with any probability of receiving pleasure from them.[11]

It often happens that when any particular style becomes somewhat antiquated and obsolete, some caricature, or satirical imitation of it, gives rise to a new species of composition. Thus the English Opera arose from the parody upon the Italian stage, designed by Gay, in *The Beggar's Opera*. In like manner, when the public had been inundated, ad nauseam, with Arabian tales, Persian tales, Turkish tales, Mogul tales, and legends of every nation cast of the Bosphorus, and were equally annoyed by the increasing publication of all sorts of fairy tales,—Count Anthony Hamilton, like a second Cervantes, came forth with his satirical tales, destined to overturn the empire of Dives, of Genii, of Peris, *et hoc genus omne*.[12]

Something too licentious for a more refined age, the Tales of Count Hamilton subsist as a beautiful illustration, showing that literary subjects, as well as the fields of the husbandman, may, when they seem most worn out and effete, be renewed and again brought into successful cultivation by a new course of management. The wit of Count Hamilton, like manure applied to an exhausted field, rendered the eastern tale more piquant, if not more edifying, than it was before. Much was written in imitation of Count Hamilton's style; and it was followed by Voltaire in particular, who in this way rendered the super-natural romance one of the most apt vehicles for circulating his satire. This, therefore, may be termed the comic side of the supernatural, in which the author plainly declares his purpose to turn into jest the miracles which he relates, and aspires to awaken ludicrous sensations without affecting the fancy—far less exciting the passions of the reader. By this species of delineation the reader will perceive that the super-natural style of writing is entirely travestied and held up to laughter, instead of being made the subject of respectful attention, or heard with at least that sort of imperfect excitement with which we listened to a marvellous tale of fairy-land. This species of satire—for it is often converted to satirical purposes—has never been more happily executed than by the French authors, although Wieland, and several other German writers, treading in the steps of Hamilton, have added the grace of poetry to the wit and to the wonders with which they have adorned this species of composition. Oberon, in particular, has been identified with our literature by the excellent translation of Mr. Sotheby, and is nearly as well known in England as in Germany.[13] It would, however, carry us far too wide from our present purpose, were we to consider the comiheroic poetry which belongs to this class, and which includes the well-known works of Pulci, Berni[14]—perhaps, in a certain degree, of Ariosto himself, who, in some passages at least, lifts his knightly vizor so far as to give a momentary glimpse of the smile which mantles upon his countenance.

One general glance at the geography of this most pleasing "Londe of Faery," leads us into another province, rough as it may seem and uncultivated, but which, perhaps, on that very account, has some scenes abounding in interest. There are a species of antiquarians who, while others laboured to re-unite and ornament highly the ancient traditions of their country, have made it their business, *antiquos accedere fontes,* to visit the ancient springs and sources of those popular legends which cherished by the grey and superstitious Elde, had been long forgotten in the higher circles, but are again brought forward and claim, like the old ballads of a country, a degree of interest even from their rugged simplicity. The *Deutsche Sagen* of the brothers Grimm, is an admiral work of this kind;[15] assembling, without any affectation either of ornamental diction or improved incident, the various traditions existing in different parts of Germany respecting popular superstitions and the events ascribed to supernatural agency. There are other works of the same kind, in the same language, collected with great care and apparent fidelity. Sometimes trite, sometimes tiresome, sometimes childish, the legends which these authors have collected with such indefatigable zeal form nevertheless a step in the history of the human race; and, when compared with similar collections in other countries, seem to infer traces of a common descent which has placed one general stock of superstition within reach of the various tribes of mankind. What are we to think when we find the Jutt and the Fin telling their children the same traditions which are to be found in the nurseries of the Spaniard and Italian; or when we recognize in our own instance the traditions of Ireland or Scotland as corresponding with those of Russia? Are we to suppose that their similarity arises from the limited nature of human invention, and that the same species of fiction occurs to the imaginations of different authors in remote countries as the same species of plants are found in different regions without the possibility of their having been propagated by transportation from the one to others? Or ought we, rather, to refer them to a common source, when mankind formed but the same great family, and suppose that as philologists trace through various dialects the broken fragments of one general language, so antiquaries may recognize in distant countries parts of what was once a common stock of tradition? We will not pause on this inquiry, nor observe more than generally that, in collecting these traditions, the industrious editors have been throwing light, not only on the history of their own country in particular, but on that of mankind in general. There is generally some truth mingled with the abundant falsehood, and still more abundant exaggeration of the oral legend; and it may be frequently and unexpectedly found to confirm or confute the meagre statement of some ancient chronicle. Often, too, the legend of the common people, by assigning peculiar features, localities, and specialities to the incidents which it holds in memory, gives life and spirit to the frigid and dry narrative which tells the fact alone, without the particulars which render it memorable or interesting.

It is, however, in another point of view, that we wish to consider those popular traditions in their collected state: namely, as a peculiar mode of exhibiting the marvellous and supernatural in composition. And here we must acknowledge, that he who peruses a large collection of stories of fiends, ghosts, and prodigies, in hopes of exciting in his mind that degree of shuddering interest approaching to fear, which is the most valuable triumph of the supernatural, is likely to be disappointed. A whole collection of ghost stories inclines us as little to fear as a jest book moves us to laughter. Many narratives, turning upon the same interest, are apt to exhaust it: as in a large collection of pictures an ordinary eye is so dazzled with the variety of brilliant or glowing colours as to become less able to distinguish the merit of those pieces which are possessed of any.

But notwithstanding this great disadvantage, which is inseparable from the species of publication we are considering, a reader of imagination, who has the power to emancipate himself from the chains of reality, and to produce in his own mind the accompaniments with which the simple or rude popular legend ought to be attended, will often find that it possesses points of interest, of nature, and of effect, which, though irreconcilable to sober truth, carry with them something that the mind is not averse to believe, something in short of plausibility, which, let poet or romancer do their very best, they find it impossible to attain to. An example may, in a case of this sort, be more amusing to the reader than mere disquisition, and we select one from a letter received many years since from an amiable and accomplished nobleman some time deceased, not more distinguished for his love of science, than his attachment to literature in all its branches:—

> It was in the night of, I think, the 14th of February, 1799, that there came on a dreadful storm of wind and drifting snow from the south-east, which was felt very severely in most parts of Scotland. On the preceding day a Captain M——, attended by three other men, had gone out a deer-shooting in that extensive tract of mountains which lies to the west of Dalnacardoch. As they did not return in the evening, nothing was heard of them. The next day, people were sent out in quest of them, as soon as the storm abated. After a long search, the bodies were found, in a lifeless state, lying among the ruins of a *bothy*, (a temporary hut,) in which it would seem Captain M—— and his party had taken refuge. The bothy had been destroyed by the tempest, and in a very astonishing manner. It had been built partly of stone, and partly of

strong wooden uprights driven into the ground; it was not merely blown down, but quite torn to pieces. Large stones, which had formed part of the walls, were found lying at the distance of one or two hundred yards from the site of the building, and the wooden uprights appeared to have been rent asunder by a force that had twisted them off as in breaking a tough stick. From the circumstances in which the bodies were found, it appeared that the men were retiring to rest at the time the calamity came upon them. One of the bodies, indeed, was found at a distance of many yards from the bothy; another of the men was found upon the place where the bothy had stood, with one stocking off, as if he had been undressing; Captain M—— was lying without his clothes, upon the wretched bed which the bothy had afforded, his face to the ground, and his knees drawn up. To all appearance the destruction had been quite sudden: yet the situation of the building was such as promised security against the utmost violence of the wind. It stood in a narrow recess, at the foot of a mountain, whose precipitous and lofty declivities sheltered it on every side, except in the front, and here, too, a hill rose before it, though with a more gradual slope. This extraordinary wreck of a building so situated, led the common people to ascribe it to a supernatural power. It was recollected by some who had been out shooting with Captain M—— about a month before, that while they were resting at this bothy, a shepherd lad had come to the door and inquired for Captain M——, and that the captain went out with the shepherd, and they walked away together, leaving the rest of the party in the bothy. After a time, Captain M—— returned alone; he said nothing of what had passed between him and the lad, but looked very grave and thoughtful, and from that time there was observed to be a mysterious anxiety hanging about him. It was remembered, that one evening after dusk, when Captain M—— was in the bothy, some of his party that were standing before the door saw a fire blazing on the top of the hill which rises in front of it. They were much surprised to see a fire in such a solitary place, and at such a time, and set out to inquire into the cause of it, but when they reached the top of the hill, there was no fire to be seen! It was remembered, too, that on the day before the fatal night, Captain M—— had shown a singular obstinacy in going forth upon his expedition. No representations of the inclemency of the weather, and of the dangers he would be exposed to, could restrain him. He said he *must* go, and was resolved to go. Captain M——'s character was likewise remembered; that he was popularly reported to be a man of no principles, rapacious, and cruel; that he had got money by procuring recruits from the highlands,—an unpopular mode of acquiring wealth; and that, amongst other base measures for this purpose, he had gone so far as to leave a purse upon the road, and to threaten the man who had picked it up with an indictment for robbery, if he did not enlist.[16] Our informer added nothing more; he neither told us his own opinion nor that of the country; but left it to our own notions of the manner in which good and evil is rewarded in this life, to suggest the Author of the miserable event. He seemed impressed with superstitious awe on the subject, and said, "There was na' the like seen in a' Scotland." The man is far advanced in years, and is a schoolmaster in the neighbourhood of Rannoch. He was employed by us as a guide upon Schehallion; and he told us the story one day as we walked before our horses, while we slowly wound up the road on the northern declivity of Rannoch. From this elevated ground we commanded an extensive prospect over the dreary mountains to the north, and amongst them our guide pointed out that at the foot of which was the scene of his dreadful tale. The account is, to the best of my recollection, just what I received from my guide. In some trifling particulars, from defect of memory, I may have misrepresented or added a little, in order to connect the leading circumstances; and I fear, also, that something may have been forgotten. Will you ask Mr. P——whether Captain M——, on leaving the bothy after his conversation with the shepherd lad, did not say that he must return there in a month after? I have a faint idea that it was so; and, if true, it would be a pity to lose it. Mr. P—— may, perhaps, be able to correct or enlarge my account for you in other instances.

The reader will, we believe, be of our opinion, that the feeling of superstitious awe annexed to the catastrophe contained in this interesting narrative, could not have been improved by any circumstances of additional horror which a poet could have invented; that the incidents and the gloomy simplicity of the narrative are much more striking than they could have been rendered by the most glowing description; and that the old highland schoolmaster, the outline of whose tale is so judiciously preserved by the narrator, was a better medium for communicating such a tale than would have been the form of Ossian, could he have arisen from the dead on purpose. It may however be truly said of the muse of romantic fiction,

Mille habet ornatus.[17]

The Professor Musaeus,[18] and others of what we may call his school, conceiving, perhaps, that the simplicity of the unadorned popular legend was like to obstruct its popularity, and feeling, as we formerly observed, that though individual stories are sometimes exquisitely impressive, yet collections of this kind were apt to be rather bald and heavy, employed their talents in ornamenting them with incident, in ascribing to the principal agents a peculiar character, and rendering the marvellous more interesting by the individuality of those in whose history it occurs. Two volumes were transcribed from the *Volksmärchen* of Musaeus by the late Dr. Beddoes, and published under the title of *Popular Tales of the Germans,* which may afford the English reader a good idea of the stile of that interesting work.[19] It may, indeed, be likened to the Tales of Count Anthony Hamilton already mentioned, but there is great room for distinction. *Le Belier,* and *Fleur d'Epine,* are mere parodies arising out of the fancy; but indebted for their interest to his wit. Musaeus, on the other hand, takes the narration of the common legend, dresses it up after his own fashion, and describes, according to his own pleasure, the personages of his drama. Hamilton is a cook who compounds his whole banquet out of materials used for the first time; Musaeus brings forward ancient traditions, like yesterday's cold meat from the larder, and, by dint of skill and seasoning, gives it a new relish for the meal of today. Of course the merit of the *rifaciamento* will fall to be divided in this case betwixt the effect attained by the ground-work of the story, and that which is added by the art of the narrator. In the tale, for example, of the *Child of Wonder,* what may be termed the raw material is short, simple, and scarce rising beyond the wonders of a nursery tale, but it is so much enlivened by the vivid sketch of the selfish, old father who barters his four daughters against golden eggs and sacks of pearls, as to give an interest and zest to the whole story. *The Spectre Barber* is another of these popular tales, which, in itself singular and fantastic, becomes lively and interesting from the character of a good-humoured, well-meaning, thick-sculled burgher of Bremen, whose wit becomes sharpened by adversity, till he learns gradually to improve circumstances as they occur, and at length recovers his lost prosperity by dint of courage, joined with some degree of acquired sagacity.

A still different management of the wonderful and supernatural has, in our days, revived the romance of the earlier age with its history and its antiquities. The Baron de la Motte Fouqué has distinguished himself in Germany by a species of writing which requires at once the industry of the scholar, and the talents of the man of genius.[20] The efforts of this accomplished author aim at a higher mood of composition than the more popular romancer. He endeavours to recall the history, the mythology, the manners of former ages, and to offer to the present time a graphic description of those which have passed away. The travels of Thioldolf, for example, initiate the reader into that immense storehouse of Gothic superstition which is to be found in the Edda and the Sagas of northern nations; and to render the bold, honest, courageous character of his gallant young Scandinavian the more striking, the author has contrasted it forcibly with the chivalry of the south, over which he asserts its superiority. In some of his works the baron has, perhaps, been somewhat profuse of his historical and antiquarian lore; he wanders where the reader has not skill to follow him; and we lose interest in the piece because we do not comprehend the scenes through which we are conducted. This is the case with some of the volumes where the interest turns on the ancient German history, to understand which, a much deeper acquaintance with the antiquities of that dark period is required than is like to be found in most readers. It would, we think, be a good rule in this stile of composition, were the author to confine his historical materials to such as are either generally understood as soon as mentioned, or at least can be explained with brief trouble in such a degree as to make a reader comprehend the story. Of such happy and well-chosen subjects, the Baron de la Motte Fouqué has also shown great command on other occasions. His story of "Sintram and His Followers" is in this respect admirable; and the tale of his Naiad, Nixie, or Water-Nymph, is exquisitely beautiful. The distress of the tale—and, though relating to a fantastic being, it is *real distress*—arises thus. An elementary spirit renounces her right of freedom from human passion to become the spouse of a gallant young knight, who requites her with infidelity and ingratitude. The story is the contrast at once, and the *pendant* to the *Diable amoureux* of Cazotte, but is entirely free from a tone of *polissonnerie* which shocks good taste in its very lively prototype.[21]

The range of the romance, as it has been written by this profusely inventive author, extends through the half-illumined ages of ancient history into the Cimmerian frontiers of vague tradition; and, when traced with a pencil of so much truth and spirit as that of Fouqué, affords scenes of high interest, and forms, it cannot be doubted, the most legitimate species of romantic fiction, approaching in some measure to the epic in poetry, and capable in a high degree of exhibiting similar beauties.

We have thus slightly traced the various modes in which the wonderful and supernatural may be introduced into fictitious narrative; yet the attachment of the Germans to the mysterious has invented another species of composition, which, perhaps, could hardly have made its way in any other country or language. This may be called the FANTASTIC mode of writing,—in which the most wild and unbounded license is given to an irregular fancy, and all species of combination, however ludicrous, or however shocking, are attempted and executed without scruple. In the other modes of treating the supernatural, even that mystic region is subjected to some laws, however slight; and fancy, in wandering through it, is regulated by some probabilities in the wildest flight. Not so in the fantastic style of composition, which has no restraint save that which it may ultimately find in the exhausted imagination of the author. This style bears the same proportion to the more regular romance, whether ludicrous or serious, which Farce, or rather Pantomime, maintains to Tragedy and Comedy. Sudden transformations are introduced of the most extraordinary kind, and wrought by the most inadequate means; no attempt is made to soften their absurdity, or to reconcile their inconsistencies; the reader must be contented to look upon the gambols of the author as he would behold the flying leaps and incongruous transmutations of Harlequin, without seeking to discover either meaning or end further than the surprise of the moment.

Our English severity of taste will not easily adopt this wild and fantastic tone into our own literature; nay, perhaps will scarce tolerate it in translations. The only composition which approaches to it is the powerful romance of *Frankenstein,* and there, although the formation of a thinking and sentient being by scientific skill is an incident of the fantastic character, still the interest of the work does not turn upon the marvellous creation of Frankenstein's monster, but upon the feelings and sentiments which that creature is supposed to express as most natural—if we may use the phrase—to his unnatural condition and origin. In other words, the miracle is not wrought for the mere wonder, but is designed to give rise to a train of acting and reasoning in itself just and probable, although the *postulatum* on which it is grounded is in the highest degree extravagant. So far *Frankenstein,* therefore, resembles the *Travels of Gulliver,* which suppose the existence of the most extravagant fictions, in order to extract from them philosophical reasoning and moral truth. In such cases the admission of the marvellous expressly resembles a sort of entry-money paid at the door of a lecture-room,—it is a concession which must be made to the author, and for which the reader is to receive value in moral instruction. But the *fantastic* of which we are now treating encumbers itself with no such conditions, and claims no further object than to surprise the public by the wonder itself. The reader is led astray by a freakish goblin, who has neither end nor purpose in the gambols which he exhibits, and the oddity of which must constitute their own reward. The only instance we know of this species of writing in the English language, is the ludicrous sketch in Mr. Geoffrey Crayon's tale of *The Bold Dragoon,* in which the furniture dances to the music of a ghostly fiddler.[22] The other ghost stories of this well-known and admired author come within the legitimate bounds which Glanvill[23] and other grave and established authors, ascribe to the shadowy realms of spirits; but we suppose Mr. Crayon to have exchanged his pencil in the following scene, in order to prove that the pandours, as well as the regular forces of the ghostly world, were alike under his command:—

> By the light of the fire he saw a pale, weazon-faced fellow, in a long flannel gown, and a tall white night-cap with a tassel to it, who sat by the fire with a bellows under his arm by the way of bagpipe, from which he forced the asthmatical music that had bothered my grandfather. As he played too, he kept twitching about with a thousand queer contortions, nodding his head, and bobbing about his tasselled night-cap.
>
> From the opposite side of the room, a long-backed, bandy-legged chair, covered with leather, and studded all over in a coxcombical fashion with little brass nails, got suddenly into motion, thrust out first a claw-foot, then a crooked arm, and at length making a leg, slid gracefully up to an easy chair of tarnished brocade, with a hole in its bottom, and led it gallantly out in a ghostly minuet about the floor.
>
> The musician now played fiercer and fiercer, and bobbed his head and his night-cap about like mad. By degrees, the dancing mania seemed to seize upon all the other pieces of furniture. The antique long-bodied chairs paired off in couples and led down a country-dance; a three-legged stool danced a hornpipe, though horribly puzzled by its supernumerary leg; while the amorous tongs seized the shovel round the waist, and whirled it about the room in a German waltz. In short, all the moveables got in motion, pirouetting, hands across, right and left, like so many devils: all except a great clothes-press, which kept curtseying and curtseying in a corner like a dowager, in exquisite time to the music; being rather too corpulent to dance, or, perhaps, at a loss for a partner.[24]

This slight sketch, from the hand of a master, is all that we possess in England corresponding to the Fantastic style of composition which we are now treating of. *Peter Schlemil*,[25] *The Devil's Elixir,* and other German works of the same character, have made it known to us through the medium of translation. The author who led the way in this department of literature was Ernest Theodore William Hoffmann; the peculiarity of whose genius, temper, and habits, fitted him to distinguish himself where imagination was to be strained to the pitch of oddity and bizarrerie. He appears to have been a man of rare talent,—a poet, an artist, and a musician, but unhappily of a hypochondriac and whimsical disposition, which carried him to extremes in all his undertakings; so his music became capricious,—his drawings caricatures,—and his tales, as he himself termed them, fantastic extravagances. Bred originally to the law, he at different times enjoyed, under the Prussian and other governments, the small appointments of a subordinate magistrate; at other times he was left entirely to his own exertions, and supported himself as a musical composer for the stage, as an author, or as a draughtsman. The shifts, the uncertainty, the precarious nature of this kind of existence, had its effect, doubtless, upon a mind which nature had rendered peculiarly susceptible of elation and depression; and a temper, in itself variable, was rendered more so by frequent change of place and of occupation, as well as by the uncertainty of his affairs. He cherished his fantastic genius also with wine in considerable quantity, and indulged liberally in the use of tobacco. Even his outward appearance bespoke the state of his nervous system: a very little man with a quantity of dark-brown hair, and eyes looking through his elf-locks, that

> E'en like grey goss-hawk's stared wild.[26]

indicated that touch of mental derangement, of which he seems to have been himself conscious, when entering the following fearful memorandum in his diary:—

> Why, in sleeping and in waking, do I, in my thoughts, dwell upon the subject of insanity? The out-pouring of the wild ideas that arise in my mind may perhaps operate like the breathing of a vein.[27]

Circumstances arose also in the course of Hoffmann's unsettled and wandering life, which seemed to his own apprehension to mark him as one who "was not in the roll of common men." These circumstances had not so much of the extraordinary as his fancy attributed to them. For example; he was present at deep play in a watering-place, in company with a friend, who was desirous to venture for some of the gold which lay upon the table. Betwixt hope of gain and fear of loss, distrusting at the same time his own luck, he at length thrust into Hoffmann's hand six gold pieces, and requested him to stake for him. Fortune was propitious to the young visionary, though he was totally inexperienced in the game, and he gained for his friend about thirty Fredericks d'or. The next evening Hoffmann resolved to try fortune on his own account. This purpose, he remarks, was not a previous determination, but one which was suddenly suggested by a request of his friend to undertake the charge of staking a second time on his behalf. He advanced to the table on his own account, and deposited on one of the cards the only two Fredericks d'or of which he was possessed. If Hoffmann's luck had been remarkable on the former occasion, it now seemed as if some supernatural power stood in alliance with him. Every attempt which he made succeeded—every card turned up propitiously.—

"My senses," he says, "became unmanageable, and as more and more gold streamed in upon me, it seemed as I were in a dream, out of which I only awaked to pocket the money. The play was given up, as is usual, at two in the morning. In the moment when I was about to leave the room, an old officer laid his hand upon my shoulder, and regarding me with a fixed and severe look, said: 'Young man, if you understand this business so well, the bank, which maintains free table, is ruined; but if you do so understand the game, reckon upon it securely that the devil will be as sure of you as of all the rest of them.' Without waiting an answer, he turned away. The morning was dawning when I came home, and emptied from every pocket heaps of gold on the table. Imagine the feelings of a lad in a state of absolute dependance, and restricted to a small sum of pocket-money, who finds himself, as if by a thunder-clap, placed in possession of a sum enough to be esteemed absolute wealth, at least for the moment! But while I gazed on the treasure, my state of mind was entirely changed by a sudden and singular agony so severe, as to force the cold sweat-drops from my brow. The words of the old officer now, for the first time, rushed upon my mind in their fullest and most terrible acceptation. It seemed to me as if the gold, which glittered upon the table, was the earnest of a bargain by which the Prince of Darkness had obtained possession of my soul, which never more could escape eternal destruction. It seemed as if some poisonous reptile was sucking my heart's blood, and I felt myself fall into an abyss of despair."[28]

Then the ruddy dawn began to gleam through the window, wood and plain were illuminated by its beams, and the visionary begun to experience the blessed feeling of returning strength, to combat with temptations, and to protect himself against the infernal propensity, which must have been attended with total destruction. Under the influence of such feelings Hoffmann formed a vow never again to touch a card, which he kept till the end of his life. "The lesson of the officer," says Hoffmann, "was good, and its effect excellent." But the peculiar disposition of Hoffmann made it work upon his mind more like an empiric's remedy than that of a regular physician. He renounced play less from the conviction of the wretched moral consequences of such a habit, than because he was actually afraid of the Evil Spirit in person.

In another part of his life Hoffmann had occasion to show, that his singularly wild and inflated fancy was not accessible to that degree of timidity connected with insanity, and to which poets, as being of "imagination all compact," are sometimes supposed to be peculiarly accessible. The author was in Dresden during the eventful period when the city was nearly taken by the allies, but preserved by the sudden return of Buonaparte and his guards from the frontiers of Silesia. He then saw the work of war closely carried on, venturing within fifty paces of the French sharp-shooters while skirmishing with those of the allies in front of Dresden. He had experience of a bombardment: one of the shells exploding before the house in which Hoffmann and Keller, the comedian, with bumpers in their hands to keep up their spirits watched the progress of the attack from an upper window. The explosion killed three persons; Keller let his glass fall,[29]—Hoffmann had more philosophy; he tossed off his bumper and moralized: "What is life!" said he, "and how frail the human frame that cannot withstand a splinter of heated iron!"[30] He saw the field of battle when they were cramming with naked corpses the immense fosses which form the soldier's grave; the field covered with the dead and the wounded,—with horses and men; powder-waggons which had exploded, broken weapons, schakos, sabres, cartridge-boxes, and all the relics of a desperate fight. He saw, too, Napoleon in the midst of his triumph, and heard him ejaculate to an adjutant, with the look and the deep voice of the lion, the single word "Voyons." It is much to be regretted that Hoffmann preserved but few memoranda of the eventful weeks which he spent at Dresden during this period, and of which his turn for remark and powerful description would have enabled him to give so accurate a picture. In general, it may be remarked of descriptions concerning warlike affairs, that they resemble plans rather than paintings; and that, however calculated to instruct the tactician, they are little qualified to interest the general reader. A soldier, particularly, if interrogated upon the actions which he has seen, is much more disposed to tell them in the dry and abstracted style of a gazette, than to adorn them with the remarkable and picturesque circumstances which attract the general ear. This arises from the natural feeling, that, in speaking of what they have witnessed in any other than a dry and affected professional tone, they may be suspected of a desire to exaggerate their own dangers,—a suspicion which, of all others, a brave man is most afraid of incurring, and which, besides, the present spirit of the military profession holds as amounting to bad taste. It is, therefore, peculiarly unfortunate, that when a person unconnected with the trade of war, yet well qualified to describe its terrible peculiarities, chances to witness events so remarkable as those to which Dresden was exposed in the memorable 1813, he should not have made a register of what could not have failed to be deeply interesting. The battle of Leipsig, which ensued shortly after, as given to the public by an eye-witness—M. Shoberl,[31] if we recollect the name aright—is an example of what we might have expected from a person of Hoffmann's talents, giving an account of his personal experience respecting the dreadful events which he witnessed. We could willingly have spared some of his grotesque works of *diablerie*, if we had been furnished, in their place, with the genuine description of the attack upon, and the retreat from Dresden, by the allied army, in the month of August, 1813. It was the last decisive advantage which was obtained by Napoleon, and being rapidly succeeded by the defeat of Vandamme,[32] and the loss of his whole *corps d'armée*, was the point from which his visible declension might be correctly dated. Hoffmann was also a high-spirited patriot,—a true, honest, thoroughbred German, who had set his heart upon the liberation of his country, and would have narrated with genuine feeling the advantages which she obtained over her oppressor. It was not, however, his fortune to attempt any work, however slight, of an historical character, and the retreat of the French army soon left him to his usual habits of literary industry and convivial enjoyment.

It may, however, be supposed, that an imagination which was always upon the stretch received a new impulse from the scenes of difficulty and danger through which our author had so lately passed. Another calamity of a domestic nature must also have tended to the increase of Hoffmann's morbid sensibility. During a journey in a public carriage, it chanced to be overturned, and the author's wife sustained a formidable injury on the head, by which she was a sufferer for a length of time.

All these circumstances, joined to the natural nervousness of his own temper, tended to throw Hoffmann into a state of mind very favourable, perhaps, to the attainment of success in his own peculiar mode of composition, but far from being such as could consist with that right and well-balanced state of human existence, in which philosophers have been disposed to rest the attainment of the highest possible degree of human happiness. Nerves which are accessible to that morbid degree of acuteness, by which the mind is incited, not only without the consent of our reason, but even contrary to its dictates, fall under the condition deprecated in the beautiful Ode to Indifference:

> Nor peace, nor joy, the heart can know,
>   Which, like the needle, true,
> Turns at the touch of joy or woe,
>   But, turning, trembles too.[33]

The pain which in one case is inflicted by an undue degree of bodily sensitiveness, is in the other the consequence of our own excited imagination; nor is it easy to determine in which the penalty of too much acuteness or vividness of perception is most severely exacted. The nerves of Hoffmann in particular were strung to the most painful pitch which can be supposed. A severe nervous fever, about the year 1807, had greatly increased the fatal sensibility under which he laboured, which acting primarily on the body speedily affected the mind. He had himself noted a sort of graduated scale concerning the state of his imagination, which, like that of a thermometer, indicated the exaltation of his feelings up to a state not far distant, probably, from that of actual mental derangement. It is not, perhaps, easy to find expressions corresponding in English to the peculiar words under which Hoffmann classified his perceptions: but we may observe that he records, as the humour of one day, a deep disposition towards the romantic and religious; of a second, the perception of the exalted or excited humourous; of a third, that of the satirical humourous; of a fourth, that of the excited or extravagant musical sense; of a fifth, a romantic mood turned towards the unpleasing and the horrible; on a sixth, bitter satirical propensities excited to the most romantic, capricious, and exotic degree; of a seventh, a state of quietism of mind open to receive the most beautiful, chaste, pleasing, and imaginative impressions of a poetical character; of an eighth, a mood equally excited, but accessible only to ideas the most unpleasing, the most horrible, the most unrestrained at once and most tormenting. At other times, the feelings which are registered by this unfortunate man of genius, are of a tendency exactly the opposite to those which he marks as characteristic of his state of nervous excitement. They indicate a depression of spirits, a mental callousness to those sensations to which the mind is at other times most alive, accompanied with that melancholy and helpless feeling which always attends the condition of one who recollects former enjoyments in which he is no longer capable of taking pleasure. This species of moral palsy is, we believe, a disease which more or less affects every one, from the poor mechanic who finds that his *hand,* as he expresses it, *is out,* that he cannot discharge his usual task with his usual alacrity, to the poet whose muse deserts him when perhaps he most desires her assistance. In such cases wise men have recourse to exercise or change of study; the ignorant and infatuated seek grosser means of diverting the paroxysm. But that which is to the person whose mind is in a healthy state, but a transitory though disagreeable feeling, becomes an actual disease in such minds as that of Hoffmann, which are doomed to experience in too vivid perceptions in alternate excess, but far most often and longest in that which is painful,—the influence of an over-excited fancy. It is minds so conformed to which Burton applies his abstract of Melancholy, giving alternately the joys and the pains which arise from the influence of the imagination. The verses are so much to the present purpose, that we cannot better describe this changeful and hypochondriac system of mind than by inserting them:

> When to myself I act and smile,
> With pleasing thoughts the time beguile,
> By a brook-side or wood so green,
> Unheard, unsought for, and unseen,
> A thousand pleasures do me bless,
> And crown my soul with happiness;
>   All my joys besides are folly,
>   None so sweet as Melancholy.
>
> When I lye, sit, or walk alone,
> I sigh, I grieve, making great moan,
> In a dark grove, or irksome den,
> With discontents and furies; then
> A thousand miseries at once
> Mine heavy heart and soul ensconce;
>   All my griefs to this are jolly,
>   None so sour as Melancholy.
>
> Methinks I hear, methinks I see,
> Sweet musick, wonderous melody,

Towns, palaces, and cities fine;
Here now, then, then, the world is mine,
Rare beauties, gallant ladies shine,
Whate'er is lovely or divine;
    All other joys to this are folly,
    None so sweet as Melancholy.

Methinks I hear, methinks I see
Ghosts, goblins, fiends; my phantasie
Presents a thousand ugly shapes,
Headless bears, black men and apes,
Doleful outcries and fearful sights
My sad and dismal soul affrights;
    All my griefs to this are jolly,
    None so damn'd as Melancholy.[34]

In the transcendental state of excitation described in these verses, the painful and gloomy mood of the mind is, generally speaking, of much more common occurrence than that which is genial, pleasing, or delightful. Every one who chooses attentively to consider the workings of his own bosom, may easily ascertain the truth of this assertion, which indeed appears a necessary accompaniment of the imperfect state of humanity, which usually presents to us, in regard to anticipation of the future, so much more that is unpleasing than is desirable; in other words, where fear has a far less limited reign than the opposite feeling of hope. It was Hoffmann's misfortune to be peculiarly sensible of the former passion, and almost instantly to combine with any pleasing sensation, as it arose, the idea of mischievous or dangerous consequences. His biographer has given a singular example of this unhappy disposition, not only to apprehend the worst when there was real ground for expecting evil, but also to mingle such apprehension capriciously and unseasonably, with incidents which were in themselves harmless and agreeable. "The devil," he was wont to say, "will put his hoof into every thing, how good soever in the outset."[35] A trifling but whimsical instance will best ascertain the nature of this unhappy propensity to expect the worst. Hoffmann, a close observer of nature, chanced one day to see a little girl apply to a market-woman's stall to purchase some fruit which had caught her eye and excited her desire. The wary trader wished first to know what she was able to expend on the purchase; and when the poor girl, a beautiful creature, produced with exultation and pride a very small piece of money, the market-woman gave her to understand that there was nothing upon her stall which fell within the compass of her customer's purse. The poor little maiden, mortified and affronted, as well as disappointed, was retiring with tears in her eyes, when Hoffmann called her back, and arranging matters with the dealer filled the child's lap with the most beautiful fruit. Yet he had hardly time to enjoy the idea that he had altered the whole expression of the juvenile countenance from mortification to extreme delight and happiness, than he became tortured with the idea that he might be the cause of the child's death, since the fruit he had bestowed upon it might occasion a surfeit or some other fatal disease. This presentiment haunted him until he reached the house of a friend, and it was akin to many which persecuted him during life, never leaving him to enjoy the satisfaction of a kind or benevolent action, and poisoning with the vague prospect of imaginary evil whatever was in its immediate tendency productive of present pleasure or promising future happiness.

We cannot here avoid contrasting the character of Hoffmann with that of the highly imaginative poet Wordsworth, many of whose smaller poems turn upon a sensibility affected by such small incidents as that abovementioned, with this remarkable difference—that the virtuous, and manly, and well-regulated disposition of the author leads him to derive pleasing, tender and consoling reflections from those circumstances which induced Hoffmann to anticipate consequences of a different character. Such petty incidents are passed noteless over by men of ordinary minds. Observers of poetical imagination, like Wordsworth and Hoffmann, are the chemists who can distil them into cordials or poisons.

We do not mean to say that the imagination of Hoffmann was either wicked or corrupt, but only that it was ill-regulated and had an undue tendency to the horrible and the distressing. Thus he was followed, especially in his hours of solitude and study, by the apprehension of mysterious danger to which he conceived himself exposed; and the whole tribe of demi-gorgons, apparitions, and fanciful spectres and goblins of all kinds with which he has filled his pages, although in fact the children of his own imagination, were no less discomposing to him than if they had had a real existence and actual influence upon him. The visions which his fancy excited are stated often to be so lively, that he was unable to endure them; and in the night, which was often his time of study, he was accustomed frequently to call his wife up from bed, that she might sit by him while he was writing, and protect him by her presence from the phantoms conjured up by his own excited imagination.

Thus was the inventor, or at least the first distinguished artist who exhibited the fantastic or supernatural grotesque in his compositions, so nearly on the verge of actual insanity, as to be afraid of the beings his own fancy created. It is no wonder that to a mind so vividly accessible to the influence of the imagination, so little under the dominion of sober reason, such a numerous train of ideas should occur in which fancy had a large share and reason none at all. In fact, the grotesque in his compositions partly resembles the arabesque in painting in which is introduced the most strange and complicated monsters, resembling centaurs, griffins, sphinxes, chimeras, rocs, and all other creatures of romantic imagination, dazzling the beholder as it were by the unbounded fertility of the author's imagination, and sating it by the rich contrast of all the varieties of shape and colouring, while there is in reality nothing to satisfy the understanding or inform the judgment. Hoffmann spent his life, which could not be a happy one, in weaving webs of this wild and imaginative character, for which after all he obtained much less credit with the public, than his talents must have gained if exercised under the restraint of a better taste or a more solid judgment. There is much reason to think that his life was shortened not only by his mental malady, of which it is the appropriate quality to impede digestion and destroy the healthful exercise of the powers of the stomach, but also by the indulgences to which he had recourse in order to secure himself against the melancholy, which operated so deeply upon the constitution of his mind. This was the more to be regretted, as, notwithstanding the dreams of an overheated imagination, by which his taste appears to have been so strangely misled, Hoffmann seems to have been a man of excellent disposition, a close observer of nature, and one who, if this sickly and disturbed train of thought had not led him to confound the supernatural with the absurd, would have distinguished himself as a painter of human nature, of which in its realities he was an observer and an admirer.

Hoffmann was particularly skilful in depicting characters arising in his own country of Germany. Nor is there any of her numerous authors who have better and more faithfully designed the upright honesty and firm integrity which is to be met with in all classes which come from the ancient Teutonic stock. There is one character in particular in the tale called *Der Majorat*—the Entail,—which is perhaps peculiar to Germany, and which makes a magnificent contrast to the same class of persons as described in romances, and as existing perhaps in real life in other countries. The justiciary B—— bears about the same office in the family of the Baron Roderick von R——, a nobleman possessed of vast estates in Courland, which the generally-known Baillie Macwheeble occupied on the land of the baron of Bradwardine.[36] The justiciary, for example, was the representative of the Seigneur in his feudal courts of justice; he superintended his revenues, regulated and controlled his household, and, from his long acquaintance with the affairs of the family, was entitled to interfere both with advice and assistance in any case of peculiar necessity. In such a character, the Scottish author has permitted himself to introduce a strain of the roguery supposed to be incidental to the inferior classes of the law,—may be no unnatural ingredient. The Baillie is mean, sordid, a trickster, and a coward, redeemed only from our dislike and contempt by the ludicrous qualities of his character, by a considerable degree of shrewdness, and by the species of almost instinctive attachment to his master and his family which seem to overbalance in quality the natural selfishness of his disposition. The justiciary of R—— is the very reverse of this character. He is indeed an original: having the peculiarities of age and some of its satirical peevishness; but in his moral qualities he is well described by la Motte Fouqué, as a hero of ancient days in the night-gown and slippers of an old lawyer of the present age. The innate worth, independence, and resolute courage of the justiciary seem to be rather enhanced than diminished by his education and profession, which naturally infers an accurate knowledge of mankind, and which, if practised without honour and honesty, is the basest and most dangerous fraud which an individual can put upon the public. Perhaps a few lines of Crabbe may describe the general tendency of the justiciary's mind, although marked, as we shall show, by loftier traits of character than those which the English poet has assigned to the worthy attorney of his borough:

> He, roughly honest, has been long a guide
> In borough business on the conquering side;
> And seen so much of both sides and so long,
> He thinks the bias of man's mind goes wrong:
> Thus, though he's friendly, he is still severe,
> Surly, though kind, suspiciously sincere:
> So much he's seen of baseness in the mind,
> That while a friend to man, he scorns mankind;
> He knows the human heart and sees with dread
> By slight temptation how the strong are led;
> He knows how interest can asunder rend
> The bond of parent, master, guardian, friend,
> To form a new and a degrading tie
> 'Twixt needy vice and tempting villainy.[37]

The justiciary of Hoffmann, however, is of a higher character than the person distinguished by Crabbe. Having known two generations of the baronial house to which he is attached, he has become possessed of their family secrets, some of which are of a mysterious and terrible nature. This confidential situation, but much more the nobleness and energy of his own character, gives the old man a species of authority even over his patron himself, although the baron is a person of stately manners, and occasionally manifests a fierce and haughty temper. It would detain us too long to communicate a sketch of the story, though it is, in our opinion, the most interesting contained in the reveries of the author. Something, however, we must say to render intelligible the brief extracts which it is our purpose to make, chiefly to illustrate the character of the justiciary.

The principal part of the estate of the baron consisted in the castle of R——sitten, a majorat, or entailed property, which gives name to the story, and which, as being such, the baron was under the necessity of making his place of residence for a certain number of weeks in every year, although it had nothing inviting in its aspect or inhabitants. It was a huge old pile overhanging the Baltic Sea, silent, dismal, almost uninhabited, and surrounded, instead of gardens and pleasure-grounds, by forests of black pines and firs which came up to its very walls. The principal amusement of the baron and his guests was to hunt the wolves and bears which tenanted these woods during the day, and to conclude the evening with a boisterous sort of festivity, in which the efforts made at passionate mirth and hilarity showed that, on the baron's side at least, they did not actually exist. Part of the castle was in ruins; a tower built for the purpose of astrology by one of its old possessors, the founder of the majorat in question, had fallen down, and by its fall made a deep chasm, which extended from the highest turret down to the dungeon of the castle. The fall of the tower had proved fatal to the unfortunate astrologer; the abyss which it occasioned was no less so to his eldest son. There was a mystery about the fate of the last, and all the facts known or conjectured respecting the cause of his fatal end were the following.

The baron had been persuaded by some expressions of an old steward, that treasures belonging to the deceased astrologer lay buried in the gulf which the tower had created by its fall. The entrance to this horrible abyss lay from the knightly hall of the castle, and the door, which still remained there, had once given access to the stair of the tower, but since its fall only opened on a yawning gulf full of stones. At the bottom of this gulf the second baron, of whom we speak, was found crushed to death, holding a wax-light fast in his hand. It was imagined he had risen to seek a book from a library which also opened from the hall, and, mistaking the one door for the other, had met his fate by falling into the yawning gulf. Of this, however, there could be no certainty.

This double accident, and the natural melancholy attached to the place, occasioned the present Baron Roderick residing so little there; but the title under which he held the estate laid him under the necessity of making it his residence for a few weeks every year. About the same time when he took up his abode there, the justiciary was accustomed to go thither for the purpose of holding baronial courts, and transacting his other official business. When the tale opens he sets out upon his journey to R——sitten, accompanied by a nephew, the narrator of the tale, a young man, entirely new to the world, trained somewhat in the school of Werter,—romantic, enthusiastic, with some disposition to vanity,—a musician, a poet, and a coxcomb; upon the whole, however, a very well-disposed lad, with great respect for his grand uncle, the justiciary, by whom he is regarded with kindness, but also as a subject of raillery. The old man carries him along with him partly to assist in his professional task, partly that he might get somewhat casehardened by feeling the cold wind of the north whistle about his ears, and undergoing the fatigue and dangers of a wolf-hunt.

They reach the old castle in the midst of a snow-storm, which added to the dismal character of the place, and which lay piled thick up the very gate by which they should enter. All knocking of the postilion was in vain; and here we shall let Hoffmann tell his own story.

> The old man then raised his powerful voice: "Francis! Francis! where are you then? be moving; we freeze here at the door: the snow is peeling our faces raw; be stirring;—the devil!" A watch-dog at length began to bark, and a wandering light was seen in the lower story of the building,—keys rattled, and at length the heavy folding-doors

opened with difficulty. "A fair welcome t'ye in this foul weather!" said old Francis, holding the lantern so high as to throw the whole light upon his shrivelled countenance, the features of which were twisted into a smile of welcome; the carriage drove into the court, we left it, and I was then for the first time aware that the ancient domestic was dressed in an old-fashioned Iägger-livery, adorned with various loops and braids of lace. Only one pair of grey locks now remained upon his broad white forehead; the lower part of his face retained the colouring proper to the hardy huntsman; and, in spite of the crumpled muscles which writhed the countenance into something resembling a fantastic mask, there was an air of stupid yet honest kindness and good-humour, which glanced from his eyes, played around his mouth, and reconciled you to his physiognomy.

"Well, old Frank!" said my great uncle, as entering the anti-chamber he shook the snow from his pelisse, "well, old man, is all ready in my apartments? Have the carpets been brushed,—the beds properly arranged,—and good fires kept in my room yesterday and today?" "No!" answered Frank with great composure, "no, worthy sir! not a bit of all that has been done." "Good God!" said my uncle, "did not I write in good time,—and do I not come at the exact day? Was ever such a piece of stupidity? And now I must sleep in rooms as cold as ice!" "Indeed, worthy Mr. Justiciary," said Francis with great solemnity, while he removed carefully with the snuffers a glowing waster from the candle, flung it on the floor, and trod cautiously upon it, "you must know that the airing would have been to no purpose, for the wind and snow have driven in, in such quantities through the broken window-frames: so—" "What!" said my uncle, interrupting him, throwing open his pelisse, and placing both arms on his sides, "what! the windows are broken, and you, who have charge of the castle, have not had them repaired?" "That would have been done, worthy sir," answered Francis, with the same indifference, "but people could not get rightly at them on account of the heaps of rubbish and stone that are lying in the apartment." "And how, in a thousand devils' names," said my great uncle, "came rubbish and stones into my chamber?" "God bless you, my young master," said the old man, episodically to me, who happened at the moment to sneeze, then proceeded gravely to answer the justiciary, that the stones and rubbish were those of a partition-wall which had fallen in the last great tempest. "What, the devil! have you had an earthquake?" said my uncle, angrily. "No, worthy sir," replied the old man, "but three days ago the heavy paved roof of the justice-hall fell in with a tremendous crash." "May the devil—" said my uncle, breaking out in a passion, and about to let fly a heavy oath; but suddenly checking himself, he lifted submissively his right hand towards heaven, while he moved with his left his fur cap from his forehead, was silent for an instant, then turned to me and spoke cheerfully: "In good truth, kinsman, we had better hold our tongues and ask no further questions, else we shall only learn greater mishaps, or perhaps the whole castle may come down upon our heads. But Frank," said he, "how could you be so stupid as not to get another apartment arranged and aired for me and this youth? Why did you not put some large room in the upper-story of the castle in order for the court-day?" "That is already done," said the old man, pointing kindly to the stairs, and beginning to ascend with the light. "Now, only think of the old houlet, that could not say this at once," said my uncle, while we followed the domestic. We passed through many long, high, vaulted corridors,—the flickering light carried by Francis throwing irregular gleams on the thick darkness; pillars, capitals, and arches of various shapes appeared to totter as we passed them; our own shadows followed us with giant steps, and the singular pictures on the wall, across which these shadows passed, seemed to waver and to tremble, and their voices to whisper amongst the heavy echoes of our footsteps, saying—"Wake us not, wake us not, the enchanted inhabitants of this ancient fabric!" At length, after we had passed along the range of cold and dark apartments, Francis opened a saloon in which a large blazing fire received us with a merry crackling, resembling a hospitable welcome. I felt myself cheered on the instant I entered the apartment; but my great uncle remained standing in the middle of the hall, looked round him, and spoke with a very serious and almost solemn tone: "This, then, must be our hall of justice!" Francis raising the light so that it fell upon an oblong whitish patch of the large dark wall, which patch had exactly the size and form of a walled-up or condemned door, said in a low and sorrowful tone, "Justice has been executed here before now." "How came you to say that, old man?" said my uncle, hastily throwing the pelisse from his shoulders. "The word escaped me," said Francis, as he lighted the candles on the table, and opened the door of a neighbouring apartment where two beds were comfortably prepared for the reception of the guests. In a short time a good supper smoked before us in the hall, to which succeeded a bowl of punch, mixed according to the right northern fashion, and it may therefore be presumed none of the weakest. Tired with his journey, my uncle betook himself to bed; but the novelty and strangeness of the situation, and even the excitement of the liquor I had drank, prevented me from thinking of sleep. The old domestic removed the supper-table, made up the fire in the chimney, and took leave of me after his manner with many a courteous bow.

And now I was left alone in the wide high hall of chivalry; the hail-storm had ceased to patter, and the wind to howl; the sky was become clear without-doors, and the full moon streamed through the broad transome windows, illumining, as if by magic, all those dark corners of the singular apartment into which the imperfect light of the wax candles and the chimney-fire could not penetrate. As frequently happens in old castles, the walls and roof of the apartment were ornamented,—the former with heavy pannelling, the latter with fantastic carving gilded and painted of different colours. The subjects chiefly presented the desperate hunting matches with bears and wolves, and the heads of the animals, being in many cases carved, projected strangely from the painted bodies, and even, betwixt the fluttering and uncertain light of the moon and of the fire, gave a grisly degree of reality. Amidst these pieces were hung portraits, as large as life, of knights striding forth in hunting-dresses, probably the chase-loving ancestors of the present baron. Every thing, whether of painting or of carving, showed the dark and decayed colours of times long passed, and rendered more conspicuous the blank and light-coloured part of the wall before noticed. It was in the middle space betwixt two doors which led off through the hall into side-apartments, and I could now see that it must itself have been a door, built up at a later period, but not made to correspond with the rest of the apartment, either by being painted over or covered with carved work. Who knows not that an unwonted and somewhat extraordinary situation possesses a mysterious power over the human spirit? Even the dullest fancy will awake in a secluded valley surrounded with rocks, or within the walls of a gloomy church, and will be taught to expect in such a situation things different from those encountered in the ordinary course of human life. Conceive too that I was only a lad of twenty years of age, and that I had drunk several glasses of strong liquor, and it may easily be believed that the knight's hall in which I sat made a singular impression on my spirit. The stillness of the night is also to be remembered,—broken, as it was, only by the heavy waving of the billows of the sea, and the solemn piping of the wind, resembling the tones of a mighty organ touched by some passing spirit; the clouds wandering across the moon, drifted along the arched windows, and seemed giant shapes gazing through the rattling casements; in short, in the slight shuddering which crept over me I felt as if an unknown world was about to expand itself visibly before me. This feeling, however silly, only resembled the slight and not unpleasing shudder with which we read or hear a well-told ghost story. It occurred to me in consequence that I could find no more favourable opportunity for reading the work to which, like most young men of a romantic bias, I was peculiarly partial, and which I happened to have in my pocket. It was "the Ghost Seer" of Schiller:[38] I read—and read, and in doing so excited my fancy more and more, until I came to that part of the tale which seizes on the imagination with so much fervour, viz. the wedding feast in the house of the Count von B——. Just at the very moment when I arrived at the passage where the bloody spectre of Gironimo entered the wedding apartment, the door of the knights' hall, which led into an antichamber, burst open with a violent shock;—I started up with astonishment and the book dropped from my hand; but, as in the same moment all was again still, I became ashamed of my childish terror;—it might be by the impulse of the rushing night-wind, or by some other natural cause that the door was flung open. "It is nothing," I said aloud, "my overheated fancy turns the most natural accidents into the supernatural." Having thus re-assured myself, I picked up the book and again sat down in the elbow-chair; but then I heard something move in the apartment with measured steps, sighing at the same time, and sobbing in a manner which seemed to express at once the extremity of inconsolable sorrow, and the most agonising pain which the human bosom could feel. I tried to believe that this could only be the moans of some animal enclosed somewhere near our part of the house, I reflected upon the mysterious power of the night, which makes distant sounds appear as if they were close beside us, and I expostulated with myself for suffering the sounds to affect me with terror. But as I thus debated the point, a sound like that of scratching mixed with louder and deeper sighs, such as could only be extracted by the most acute mental agony, or during the parting pang of life, was indisputably heard upon the very spot where the door appeared to have been built up: "Yet it *can* only be some poor animal in confinement,—I shall call out aloud, or I shall stamp with my foot upon the ground, and then either every thing will be silent or the animal will make itself be known"; so I purposed, but the blood stopped in my veins,—a cold sweat stood upon my forehead,—I remained fixed in my chair, not daring to rise, far less to call out. The hateful sounds at last ceased,—the steps were again distinguished,—it seemed as if life and the power of motion returned to me,—I started up and walked two paces forward, but in that moment an ice-cold night-breeze whistled through the hall, and at the same time the moon threw a bright light upon the picture of a very grave, well-nigh terrible looking man, and it seemed to me as if I plainly heard a warning voice amid the deep roar of the sea and the shriller whistle of the night-wind speaking the warning—"No farther! No farther! Lest thou encounter the terrors of the spiritual world!" The door now shut with the same violent clash with which it had burst open; I heard the sound of steps retiring along the anti-room and descending the staircase: the principal door of the castle was opened and shut with violence; then it seemed as if a horse was led out of the stable, and, after a short time, as if it was again conducted back to its stall. After this, all was still, at the same time I became aware that my uncle in the neighbouring apartment was struggling in his sleep and groaned like a man afflicted with a heavy dream. I hastened to awake him, and when I had succeeded, I received his thanks for the service. "Thou hast done well, kinsman, to awake me," he said; "I have had a detestable dream, the cause of which is this apartment and the hall, which set me a thinking upon past times and upon many extraordinary events which have here happened. But now we shall sleep sound till morning."

With morning the business of the justiciary's office began. But, abridging the young lawyer's prolonged account of what took place, the mystic terror of the preceding evening retained so much effect on his imagination, that he was disposed to find out traces of the supernatural in every thing which met his eyes; even two respectable old ladies, aunts of Baron Roderick von R——, and the sole old-fashioned inhabitants of the old-fashioned castle, had in their French caps and furbelows a ghostly and phantom-like appearance in his prejudiced eyes. The justiciary becomes disturbed by the strange behaviour of his assistant; he enters into expostulation upon the subject so soon as they were in private:

"What is the matter with you?" he said; "thou speakest not; thou eatest not; thou drinkest not;—art thou sick; or dost thou lack any thing? in short, what a fiend ails thee?" I embraced the opportunity to communicate all the horrible scenes of the preceding night; not even concealing from my grand uncle that I had drunk a good deal of punch, and had been reading "the Ghost Seer" of Schiller. "This, I must allow," I added, "because it is possible, that my toiling and overheated fancy might have created circumstances which had no other existence." I now expected that my kinsman would read me a sharp lecture on my folly, or treat me with some bitter jibes: but he did neither; he became very grave, looked long on the ground, then suddenly fixed a bold and glowing look upon me. "Kinsman," said he, "I am unacquainted with your book; but you have neither it nor the liquor to thank for the ghostly exhibition you have described. Know, that I had a dream to the self-same purpose. I thought I sat in the hall as thou didst; but whereas *thou* only heardst sounds, *I* beheld, with the eyes of my spirit, the appearances which these voices announced. Yes! I beheld the inhuman monster as he entered,—saw him glide to the condemned door,—saw him scratch on the wall in comfortless despair until the blood burst from under his wounded nails; then I beheld him lead a horse from the stable and again conduct it back;—didst thou not hear the cock crow in the distant village? it was then that thou didst awake me, and I soon got the better of the terrors by which this departed sinner is permitted to disturb the peace of human life." The old man stopped, and I dared not ask further questions, well knowing he would explain the whole to me when it was proper to do so. After a space, during which he appeared wrapt in thought, my uncle proceeded: "Kinsman, now that thou knowest the nature of this disturbance, hast thou the courage once more to encounter it, having me in thy company?" It was natural that I should answer in the affirmative, the rather as I found myself mentally strengthened to the task: "Then will we," proceeded the old man, "watch together this ensuing night. There is an inward voice which tells me this wicked spirit must give way, not so much to the force of my understanding, as to my courage, which is built upon a firm confidence in God. I feel, too, that it is no rash or criminal undertaking, but a bold and pious duty that I am about to discharge. When I risk body and life to banish the evil spirit who would drive the sons from the ancient inheritance of their fathers, it is in no spirit of presumption or vain curiosity: since, in the firm integrity of mind, and the pious confidence which lives within me, the most ordinary man is and remains a victorious hero. But should it be God's will that the wicked spirit shall have power over me, then shalt thou, kinsman, make it known that I died in honourable Christian combat with the hellish spectre which haunts this place. For thee, thou must keep thyself at a distance, and no ill will befall thee."

The evening was spent in various kinds of employment; the supper was set as before in the knights' hall; the full moon shone clear through the glimmering clouds; the billows of the sea roared; and the night-wind shook the rattling casements. However inwardly excited, we compelled ourselves to maintain an indifferent conversation. The old man had laid his repeating watch on the table; it struck twelve,—then the door flew open with a heavy crash, and, as on the former night, slow and light footsteps traversed the hall, and the sighs and groans were heard as before. My uncle was pale as death; but his eyes streamed with unwonted fire, and as he stood upright, his left arm dropped by his side and his right uplifted toward heaven, he had the air of a hero in the act of devotion. The sighs and groans became louder and more distinguishable, and the hateful sounds of scratching upon the wall were again heard more odiously than on the former night. The old man then strode forward right towards the condemned door, with a step so bold and firm that the hall echoed back his tread. He stopped close before the spot where the ghostly sounds were heard yet more and more wildly, and spoke with a strong and solemn tone such as I never heard him before use: "Daniel! Daniel!" he said, "what makest thou here at this hour?" A dismal screech was the reply, and a sullen heavy sound was heard, as when a weighty burden is cast down upon the floor. "Seek grace and mercy before the throne of the Highest!" continued my uncle, with a voice even more authoritative than before, "there is thy only place of appeal! Hence with thee out of the living world in which thou hast no longer a portion!" It seemed as if a low wailing was heard to glide through the sky and to die away in the roaring of the storm which began now to awaken. Then the old man stepped to the door of the hall and closed it with such vehemence that the whole place echoed. In his speech, in his gestures, there seemed something almost superhuman which filled me with a species of holy fear. As he placed himself in the arm chair, the fixed sternness of his rigid brow began to relax; his look appeared more clear; he folded his hands, and prayed internally. Some minutes passed away ere he said, with that mild tone which penetrates so deeply into the heart, the simple words, "Now, kinsman?" Overcome by horror, anxiety, holy reverence and love, I threw myself on my knees, and moistened with warm tears the hand which he stretched out to me; the old man folded me in his arms, and, after he had pressed me to his bosom with heartfelt affection, said, with a feeble and exhausted voice, "Now, kinsman, shall we sleep soft and undisturbed!"

The spirit returned no more. It was the ghost—as may have been anticipated—of a false domestic, by whose hand the former baron had been precipitated into the gulf which yawned behind the new wall so often mentioned in the narrative.

The other adventures in the castle of R——sitten are of a different cast, but strongly mark the power of delineating human character which Hoffmann possessed. Baron Roderick and his lady arrive at the castle with a train of guests. The lady is young, beautiful, nervous, and full of sensibility,—fond of soft music, pathetic poetry, and walks by moonlight; the rude company of huntsmen by which the baron is surrounded, their boisterous sports in the morning, and their no less boisterous mirth in the evening, is wholly foreign to the disposition of the Baroness Seraphina, who is led to seek relief in the society of the nephew of the justiciary, who can make sonnets, repair harpsichords, sustain a part in an Italian duet, or in a sentimental conversation. In short, the two young persons, without positively designing any thing wrong, are in a fair way of rendering themselves guilty and miserable, were they not saved from the snare which their passion was preparing by the calm observation, strong sense, and satirical hints of our friend the justiciary.

It may therefore be said of this personage, that he possesses that true and honourable character which we may conceive entitling a mortal as well to overcome the malevolent attacks of evil beings from the other world as to stop and control the course of moral evil in that we inhabit, and the sentiment is of the highest order by which Hoffmann ascribes to unsullied masculine honour and integrity that same indemnity from the power of evil which the poet claims for female purity:

> Some say no evil thing that walks by night
> In fog, or fire, by lake or moorish fen,
> Blue meagre hag, or stubborn unlaid ghost
> That breaks his magic chain at curfew time,
> No goblin, nor swart faery of the mine,
> Hath hurtful power o'er true virginity.[39]

What we admire, therefore, in the extracts which we have given is not the mere wonderful or terrible part of the story, though the circumstances are well narrated; it is the advantageous light in which it places the human character as capable of being armed with a strong sense of duty, and of opposing itself, without presumption but with confidence, to a power of which it cannot estimate the force, of which it hath every reason to doubt the purpose, and at the idea of confronting which our nature recoils.

Before we leave the story of *The Entail*, we must notice the conclusion, which is beautifully told, and will recal [sic] to most readers who are passed the prime of life, feelings which they themselves must occasionally have experienced. Many, many years after the baronial race if R—— had become extinguished, accident brought the young nephew, now a man in advanced age, to the shores of the Baltic. It was night, and his eye was attracted by a strong light which spread itself along the horizon.

> "What fire is that before us, postilion?" said I; "It is no fire," answered he, "it is the beacon light of R——sitten." "Of R——sitten!" He had scarce uttered the words, when the picture of the remarkable days which I had passed in that place arose in clear light in my memory. I saw the baron,—I saw Seraphina,—I saw the strange-looking old aunts,—I saw myself, with a fair boyish countenance, out of which the mother's milk seemed not yet to have been pressed, my frock of delicate azure blue, my hair curled and powdered with the utmost accuracy, the very image of the lover sighing like a furnace, who tunes his sonnets to his mistress's eye-brows. Amidst a feeling of deep melancholy, fluttered like sparkles of light the recollection of the justiciary's rough jests, which appeared to me now much more pleasant than when I was the subject of them. Next morning I visited the village, and made some inquiries after the baronial steward: "With your favour, Sir," said the postilion, taking the pipe out of his mouth, and touching his night-cap, "there is here no baronial steward; the place belongs to his majesty, and the royal superintendent is still in bed." On farther questions, I learned that the Baron Roderick von R—— having died without descendants, the entailed estate, according to the terms of the grant, had been vested in the crown. I walked up to the castle which lay now in a heap of ruins. An old peasant, who came out of the pine wood, informed me that a great part of the stones had been used to build the beacontower; he told me too of the spectre which in former times had haunted the spot, and asserted that when the moon was at the full, the voice of lamentation was still heard among the ruins.

If the reader has, in a declining period of his life, revisited the scenes of youthful interest, and received from the mouth of strangers an account of the changes which have taken place, he will not be indifferent to the simplicity of this conclusion.

The passage which we have quoted, while it shows the wildness of Hoffmann's fancy, evinces also that he possessed power which ought to have mitigated and allayed it. Unfortunately, his taste and temperament directed him too strongly to the grotesque and fantastic,—carried him too far "extra mœnia flammantia mundi,"[40] too much beyond the circle not only of probability but even of possibility, to admit of his composing much in the better style which he might easily have attained. The popular romance, no doubt, has many walks, nor are we at all inclined to halloo the dogs of criticism against those whose object is merely to amuse a passing hour. It may be repeated with truth, that in this path of light literature, "tout genre est permis hors les genres ennuyeux,"[41] and of course, an error in taste ought not to be followed up and hunted down as if it were a false maxim in morality, a delusive hypothesis in science, or a heresy in religion itself. Genius too, is, we are aware, capricious, and must be allowed to take its own flights, however eccentric, were it but for the sake of experiment. Sometimes, also, it may be eminently pleasing to look at the wildness of an Arabesque painting executed by a man of rich fancy. But we do not desire to see genius expand or rather exhaust itself upon themes which cannot be reconciled to taste; and the utmost length in which we can indulge a turn to the fantastic is, where it tends to excite agreeable and pleasing ideas.

We are not called upon to be equally tolerant of such capriccios as are not only startling by their extravagance, but disgusting by their horrible import. Moments there are, and must have been, in the author's life, of pleasing as well as painful excitation; and the Champagne which sparkled in his glass must have lost its benevolent influence if did not sometimes wake his fancy to emotions which were pleasant as well as whimsical. But as repeatedly the tendency of all overstrained feelings is directed towards the painful, and the fits of lunacy, and the crises of very undue excitement which approaches to it, are much more frequently of a disagreeable than of a pleasant character, it is too certain, that we possess in a much greater degree the power of exciting in our minds what is fearful, melancholy, or horrible, than of commanding thoughts of a lively and pleasing character. The grotesque, also, has a natural alliance with the horrible; for that which is out of nature can be with difficulty reconciled to the beautiful. Nothing, for instance, could be more displeasing to the eye than the palace of that crack-brained Italian prince, which was decorated with every species of monstrous sculptures which a depraved imagination could suggest to the artist. The works of Callot, though evincing a wonderful fertility of mind, are in like manner regarded with surprise rather than pleasure.[42] If we compare his fertility with that of Hogarth, they resemble each other in extent; but in that of the satisfaction afforded by a close examination the English artist has wonderfully the advantage. Every new touch which the observer detects amid the rich superfluities of Hogarth is an article in the history of human manners, if not of the human heart; while, on the contrary, in examining microscopically the diablerie of Callot's pieces, we only discover fresh instances of ingenuity thrown away, and of fancy pushed into the regions of absurdity. The works of the one painter resemble a garden carefully cultivated, each nook of which contains something agreeable or useful; while those of the other are like the garden of the sluggard, where a soil equally fertile produces nothing but wild and fantastic weeds.

Hoffmann has in some measure identified himself with the ingenious artist upon whom we have just passed a censure by his title of "Night Pieces *After the Manner of Callot,*" and in order to write such a tale, for example, as that called *The Sandman,* he must have been deep in the mysteries of that fanciful artist, with whom he might certainly boast a kindred spirit. We have given an instance of a tale in which the wonderful is, in our opinion, happily introduced, because it is connected with and applied to human interest and human feeling, and illustrates with no ordinary force the elevation to which circumstances may raise the power and dignity of the human mind. The following narrative is of a different class:

half horror and half whim,
Like fiends in glee, ridiculously grim.[43]

Nathaniel, the hero of the story, acquaints us with the circumstances of his life in a letter addressed to Lothair, the brother of Clara; the one being his friend, the other his betrothed bride. The writer is a young man of a fanciful and hypochondriac temperament, poetical and metaphysical in an excessive degree, with precisely that state of nerves which is most accessible to the influence of imagination. He communicates to his friend and his mistress an adventure of his childhood. It was, it seems, the custom of his father, an honest watchmaker, to send his family to bed upon certain days earlier in the evening than usual, and the mother in enforcing this observance used to say, "To-bed, children, *the Sandman* is coming!" In fact, on such occasions, Nathaniel observed that after their hour of retiring, a knock was heard at the door, a heavy step echoed on the staircase, some person entered his father's apartments, and occasionally a disagreeable and suffocating vapour was perceptible through the house. This then was the Sandman; but what was his occupation, and what was his purpose? The nursery-maid being applied to, gave a nursery-maid's explanation, that the Sandman was a bad man, who flung sand in the eyes of little children who did not go to bed. This increased the terror of the boy, but at the same time raised his curiosity. He determined to conceal himself in his father's apartment and wait the arrival of the nocturnal visitor; he did so, and the Sandman proved to be no other than the lawyer Copelius, whom he had often seen in his father's company. He was a huge left-handed, splay-footed sort of personage, with a large nose, great ears, exaggerated features, and a sort of ogre-like aspect, which had often struck terror into the children before this ungainly limb of the law was identified with the terrible Sandman. Hoffmann has given a pencil sketch of this uncouth figure, in which he has certainly contrived to represent something as revolting to adults as it might be terrible to children. He was received by the father with a sort of humble observance; a secret stove was opened and lighted, and they instantly commenced chemical operations of a strange and mysterious description, but which immediately accounted for that species of vapour which had been perceptible on other occasions. The gestures of the chemists grew fantastic, their faces, even that of the father, seemed to become wild and terrific as they prosecuted their labours; the boy became terrified, screamed and left his hiding-place;—was detected by the alchemist, for such Copelius was, who threatened to pull out his eyes, and was with some difficulty prevented by the father's interference from putting hot ashes in the child's face. Nathaniel's imagination was deeply impressed by the terror he had undergone, and a nervous fever was the consequence, during which the horrible figure of the disciple of Paracelsus[44] was the spectre which tormented his imagination.

After a long interval, and when Nathaniel was recovered, the nightly visits of Copelius to his pupil were renewed, but the latter promised his wife that it should be for the last time. It proved so, but not in the manner which the old watchmaker meant. An explosion took place in the chemical laboratory which cost Nathaniel's father his life; his instructor in the fatal art, to which he had fallen a victim, was nowhere to be seen. It followed from these incidents, calculated to make so strong an impression upon a lively imagination, that Nathaniel was haunted through life by the recollections of this horrible personage, and Copelius became in his mind identified with the evil principle.

When introduced to the reader, the young man is studying at the university, where he is suddenly surprised by the appearance of his old enemy, who now personates an Italian or Tyrolese pedlar, dealing in optical glasses and such trinkets, and, although dressed according to his new profession, continuing under the Italianized name of Giuseppe Coppola to be identified with the ancient adversary. Nathaniel is greatly distressed at finding himself unable to persuade either his friend or his mistress of the justice of the horrible apprehensions which he conceives ought to be entertained from the supposed identity of this terrible jurisconsult with his double-ganger the dealer in barometers. He is also displeased with Clara, because her clear and sound good sense rejects not only his metaphysical terrors, but also his inflated and affected strain of poetry. His mind gradually becomes alienated from the frank, sensible, and affectionate companion of his childhood, and he grows in the same proportion attached to the daughter of a professor called Spalanzani, whose house is opposite to the windows of his lodging. He has thus an opportunity of frequently remarking Olympia as she sits in her apartment; and although she remains there for hours without reading, working, or even stirring, he yet becomes enamoured of her extreme beauty in despite of the insipidity of so inactive a person. But much more rapidly does this fatal passion proceed when he is induced to purchase a perspective glass from the pedlar, whose resemblance was so perfect to his old object of detestation. Deceived by the secret influence of the medium of vision, he becomes indifferent to what was visible to all others who approach Olympia,—to a certain stiffness of manner which made her walk as if by the impulse of machinery,—to a paucity of ideas which induced her to express herself only in a few short but reiterated phrases,—in short, to all that indicated Olympia to be what she ultimately proved, a mere literal puppet, or automaton, created by the mechanical skill of Spalanzani, and inspired with an appearance of life by the devilish arts we may suppose of the alchemist, advocate, and weather-glass seller Copelius, alias Coppola. At this extraordinary and melancholy truth the enamoured Nathaniel arrives by witnessing a dreadful quarrel between the two imitators of Prometheus, while disputing their respective interests in the subject of their creative power. They uttered the wildest imprecations, and tearing the beautiful automaton limb from limb, belaboured each other with the fragments of their clock-work figure. Nathaniel, not much distant from lunacy before, became frantic on witnessing this horrible spectacle.

But we should be mad ourselves were we to trace these ravings any farther. The tale concludes with the moon-struck scholar attempting to murder Clara by precipitating her from a tower. The poor girl being rescued by her brother, the lunatic remains alone on the battlements, gesticulating violently and reciting the gibberish which he had acquired from Copelius and Spalanzani. At this moment, and while the crowd below are devising means to secure the maniac, Copelius suddenly appears among them, assures them that Nathaniel will presently come down of his own accord, and realizes his prophecy by fixing on the latter a look of fascination, the effect of which is instantly to compel the unfortunate young man to cast himself headlong from the battlements.

This wild and absurd story is in some measure redeemed by some traits in the character of Clara, whose firmness, plain good sense, and frank affection are placed in agreeable contrast with the wild imagination, fanciful apprehensions, and extravagant affection of her crazy-pated admirer.

It is impossible to subject tales of this nature to criticism. They are not the visions of a poetical mind, they have scarcely even the seeming authenticity which the hallucinations of lunacy convey to the patient; they are the feverish dreams of a light-headed patient, to which, though they may sometimes excite by their peculiarity, or surprise by their oddity, we never feel disposed to yield more than momentary attention. In fact, the inspirations of Hoffmann so often resemble the ideas produced by the immoderate use of opium, that we cannot help considering his case as one requiring the assistance of medicine rather than of criticism; and while we acknowledge that with a steadier command of his imagination he might have been an author of the first distinction, yet situated as he was, and indulging the diseased state of his own system, he appears to have been subject to that undue vividness of thought and perception of which the celebrated Nicolai became at once the victim and the conqueror.[45] Phlebotomy and cathartics, joined to sound philosophy and deliberate observation, might, as in the case of that celebrated philosopher, have brought to a healthy state, a mind which we cannot help regarding as diseased, and his imagination soaring with an equal and steady flight might have reached the highest pitch of the poetical profession.

The death of this extraordinary person took place in 1822. He became affected with the disabling complaint called *tabes dorsalis,* which gradually deprived him of the power of his limbs. Even in this melancholy condition he dictated several compositions, which indicate the force of his fancy, particularly one fragment entitled *The Recovery,* in which are many affecting allusions to the state of his own mental feelings at this period; and a novel called *The Adversary,* on which he had employed himself even shortly before his last moments. Neither was the strength of his courage in any respect abated; he could endure bodily agony with firmness, though he could not bear the visionary terrors of his own mind. The medical persons made the severe experiment whether by applying the actual cautery to his back by means of glowing iron, the activity of the nervous system might not be restored. He was so far from being cast down by the torture of this medical martyrdom, that he asked a friend who entered the apartment after he had undergone it, whether he did not smell the roasted meat. The same heroic spirit marked his expressions, that "he would be perfectly contented to lose the use of his limbs, if he could but retain the power of working constantly by the help of an amanuensis." Hoffmann died at Berlin, upon the 25th June, 1822, leaving the reputation of a remarkable man, whose temperament and health alone prevented his arriving at a great height of reputation, and whose works as they now exist ought to be considered less as models for imitation than as affording a warning how the most fertile fancy may be exhausted by the lavish prodigality of its possessor.

Notes

Notes are from Ioan Williams, editor of the Routledge edition, except for those designated with an "S," which are Scott's.

1. S. Johnson, *The History of Rasselas, Prince of Abyssinia* (1759), chap. xxxi.
2. Compare Johnson, 89n7.
3. *1 Henry IV* II. ii; "Go to; 'homo' is a name common to all men."
4. *Comus,* 205–9.
5. *Paradise Lost,* ii. 666–73.
6. E. Burke, *On the Sublime and Beautiful* (1756), ii. 3.
7. Job 4:12–16.
8. *Hamlet* I. i.
9. *Life of Collins.*
10. *Faery Queene* III. iii. 18.
11. *Cabinet des Fees, or Collection choisie des Contes des Fees, et autres Contes Merveilleux,* compiled by C. J. Mayer (1751–1825), published between 1785 and 1786, contained the work of English, French and German authors, in forty-one volumes. Scott had this in his library.
12. Count Anthony Hamilton's satirical tales, published together in 1730, were *Le Belier, Histoire de Fleur d'epine,* and *Les Quatres Facardins.*
13. The *Oberon* (1780), of Cristophe Martin Wieland (1733–1813), was translated by William Southeby in 1798. Wieland's *Don Sylvia de Rosalva* (1764) is a more appropriate example of this kind.

14. Luigi Pulci (1432–84), author of *Morgante Maggiore, an Epic Romance* (1481). Francesco Berni (1490–1536), author of *Orlando Innamorato* (1541), a recast of Boiardo's *Orlando Innamorato*.

15. Jacob Ludwig Carl Grimm (1785–1863) and Wilhelm Carl Grimm (1786–1859) published their *Deutsche Sagen* between 1816 and 1818.

16. It is needless to say that this was a mere popular report, which might greatly misrepresent the character of the unfortunate sufferer. S.

17. *Tibullus* III. viii. 14 (wears a thousand garbs).

18. Johann Karl August Musaeus (1735–87).

19. A translation of the *Volksmärchen* of Musaeus was the first of the translations of German tales into English. It appeared in 1791 without the name of the translator, which the British Museum Catalogue gives as J. Beresford. There is no record of a translation by Beddoes.

20. Friedrich, Baron de la Motte Fouque (1777–1843), officer of the German cuirassiers and author of *Undine* (1811).

21. Jacques Cazotte (1719–92), author of *Le Diable amoureux* (1772), also wrote *Les Milles et une fadaises* (1742) and *Le Lord Impromptu* (1767).

22. Geoffrey Crayon was the pseudonym of Washington Irving (1783–1859), who wrote *Tales of a Traveller* (1824), *The Sketch-Book* (1820), and *Bracebridge Hall* (1822). He visited Scott at Abbotsford in 1817 and left an account of the visit.

23. Joseph Glanvill (1636–80), author of *Saducismus Triumphatis* (1681), in which he defended belief in witchcraft.

24. *Tales of a Traveller,* i. S.

25. *Peter Schlemil* (1814) was by Adalbert von Chamisso (1781–1838). It was translated by Sir John Bowring in 1824, with illustrations by George Cruickshank, and was widely thought to be by de la Motte Fouque.

26. Untraced.

27. *E. T. A. Hoffmanns ausgewahlte Schriften,* ed. J. E. Hitzig (Berlin, 1817–23). *Leben und Nachlass,* xiv, 46. All references to Hoffmann's work are to this edition (referred to hereafter as "Hitzig"), which is the one which Scott used himself.

28. Hitzig, xiii. 113–18.

29. "Schauspieler Keller," a frequent companion of Hoffmann's while he was in Dresden (1813). He is referred to in Hitzig (xiv. 52) as "ein in Leipzig durchaus geschatzter Mann" (a man very highly thought of in Leipzig).

30. Hitzig, xiv. 67–68.

31. F. Schoeberl's account of the battle of Leipzig appears in *Relations militaires de la bataille de Waterloo* (1814).

32. Dominique Rene Vandamme (1770–1830), Comte d'Unebourg, was defeated at Kulm on August 12, 1813, and forced to surrender with ten thousand men.

33. *A Prayer for Indifference* (not Ode) was by Frances Macartney (1772?–89).

34. Robert Burton, "The Author's Abstract of Melancholy," in *The Anatomy of Melancholy* (1621).

35. Hitzig, xv. 28.

36. Baillie Macwheeble appears in *Waverley* (1814).

37. G. Crabbe, *The Borough* (1810), vi.

38. *The Ghost Seer* of Johann Cristoph Friedrich von Schiller (1759–1805) was published between 1785 and 1789 in the magazine *Thalia*.

39. *Comus*, 432–37.

40. Lucretius, i. 73 (beyond the flaming ramparts of the world).

41. Voltaire, *L'Enfant prodigue* (1736), preface.

42. Jacques Callot (1592–1635), artist and engraver of his own drawings.

43. Untraced.

44. Aureole Philippe Theophrastus Bombastus von Hohenheim (1493–1541), alchemist, scholar, and doctor. A convenient source of information is the note to Browning's poem *Paracelsus* (1835).

45. Cristophe Friedrich Nicolai (1733–1811) was author of a novel called *Sebaldus Nothanker* (1773–76).

Chapter 9

INTRODUCTION TO
SUPERNATURAL HORROR IN LITERATURE

H. P. Lovecraft

> H. P. Lovecraft was an early twentieth-century American author of "weird tales." Little known during his lifetime, his reputation has grown steadily since his death in 1937, and his influence is now central to twenty-first-century horror. His influence on authors and filmmakers, including Stephen King, John Carpenter, and Guillermo del Toro, is clear. Lovecraft's treatise *Supernatural Horror in Literature* focuses for the most part on the history of the Gothic novel, horror, and the weird tale. However, in his introduction, he advances a concept of what he refers to as "cosmic fear"—a particular species of horror evoked by the suspicion that the universe is a hostile place. Lovecraft's idea of cosmic fear has direct connections to Burke's notion of the sublime as readers experience wonder and dread simultaneously, leading to a pleasurable emotional intensity.

THE OLDEST AND STRONGEST EMOTION of mankind is fear, and the oldest and strongest kind of fear is fear of the unknown. These facts few psychologists will dispute, and their admitted truth must establish for all time the genuineness and dignity of the weirdly horrible tales as a literary form. Against it are discharged all the shafts of a materialistic sophistication which clings to frequently felt emotions and external events, and of a naively inspired idealism which deprecates the aesthetic motive and calls for a didactic literature to "uplift" the reader toward a suitable degree of smirking optimism. But in spite of all this opposition the weird tale has survived, developed, and attained remarkable heights of perfection; founded as it is on a profound and elementary principle whose appeal, if not always universal, must necessarily be poignant and permanent to minds of the requisite sensitiveness.

The appeal of the spectrally macabre is generally narrow because it demands from the reader a certain degree of imagination and a capacity for detachment from everyday life. Relatively few are free enough from the spell of the daily routine to respond to rappings from outside, and tales of ordinary feelings and events, or of common sentimental distortions of such feelings and events, will always take first place in the taste of the majority; rightly, perhaps, since of course these ordinary matters make up the greater part of human experience. But the sensitive are always with us, and sometimes a curious streak of fancy invades an obscure corner of the very hardest head; so that no amount of rationalisation, reform, or Freudian analysis can quite annul the thrill of the chimney-corner whisper or the lonely wood. There is here involved psychological pattern or tradition as real and as deeply grounded in mental experience as any other pattern or tradition of mankind; coeval with the religious feeling and closely related to many aspects of it, and too much a part of our innermost biological heritage to lose keen potency over a very important, though not numerically great, minority of our species.

Man's first instincts and emotions formed his response to the environment in which he found himself. Definite feelings based on pleasure and pain grew up around the phenomena whose causes and effects he understood, whilst around those which he did not understand—and the universe teemed with them in the early days—were naturally woven such personifications, marvelous interpretations, and sensations of awe and fear as would be hit upon by a race having few and simple ideas and limited experience. The unknown, being likewise the unpredictable, became for our primitive forefathers a terrible and omnipotent source of boons and calamities visited upon mankind for cryptic and wholly extra-terrestrial reasons, and thus clearly belonging to spheres of existence whereof we know nothing and wherein we have no part. The phenomenon of dreaming likewise helped to build up the notion of an unreal or spiritual world; and in general, all the conditions of savage dawn-life so strongly conducted toward a feeling of the supernatural, that we need not wonder at the thoroughness with which man's very hereditary essence has become saturated with religion and superstition. That saturation must, as a matter of plain scientific fact, be regarded as virtually permanent so far as the subconscious mind and inner instincts are concerned; for though the area of the unknown has been steadily contracting for thousands of years, an infinite reservoir of mystery still engulfs most of the outer cosmos, whilst a vast residuum of powerful inherited associations clings round all the objects and processes that were once mysterious, however well they may now be explained. And more than this, there is an actual physiological fixation of the old instincts in our nervous tissue, which would make them obscurely operative even were the conscious mind to be purged of all sources of wonder.

Because we remember pain and the menace of death more vividly than pleasure, and because our feelings toward the beneficent aspects of the unknown have from the first been captured and formalised by conventional religious rituals, it has fallen to the lot of the darker and more maleficent side of cosmic mystery to figure chiefly in our popular supernatural folklore. This tendency, too, is naturally enhanced by the fact that uncertainty and danger are always closely allied; thus making any kind of an unknown world a world of peril and evil possibilities. When to this sense of fear and evil the inevitable fascination of wonder and curiosity is superadded, there is born a composite body of keen emotion and imaginative provocation whose vitality must of necessity endure as long as the human race itself. Children will always be afraid of the dark, and men with minds sensitive to hereditary impulse will always tremble at the thought of the hidden and fathomless worlds of strange life which may pulsate in the gulfs beyond the stars, or press hideously upon our own globe in unholy dimensions which only the dead and the moonstruck can glimpse.

With this foundation, no one need wonder at the existence of a literature of cosmic fear. It has always existed, and always will exist; and no better evidence of its tenacious vigour can be cited than the impulse which now and then drives writers of totally opposite leanings to try their hands at it in isolated tales, as if to discharge from their minds certain phantasmal shapes which would otherwise haunt them. Thus Dickens wrote several eerie narratives; Browning, the hideous poem *Childe Roland*; Henry James, *The Turn of the Screw*; Dr. Holmes, the subtle novel *Elsie Venner*; F. Marion Crawford, *The Upper Berth* and a number of other examples; Mrs. Charlotte Perkins Gilman, social worker, *The Yellow Wall Paper*; whilst the humorist, W. W. Jacobs, produced that able melodramatic bit called *The Monkey's Paw*.

This type of fear-literature must not be confounded with a type externally similar but psychologically widely different; the literature of mere physical fear and the mundanely gruesome. Such writing, to be sure, has its place, as has the conventional or even whimsical or humorous ghost story where formalism or the author's knowing wink removes the true sense of the morbidly unnatural; but these things are not the literature of cosmic fear in its purest sense. The true weird tale has something more than secret murder, bloody bones, or a sheeted form clanking chains according to rule. A certain atmosphere of breathless and unexplainable dread of outer, unknown forces must be present; and there must be a hint, expressed with a seriousness and portentousness becoming its subject, of that most terrible conception of the human brain—a malign and particular suspension or defeat of those fixed laws of Nature which are our only safeguard against the assaults of chaos and the daemons of unplumbed space.

Naturally we cannot expect all weird tales to conform absolutely to any theoretical model. Creative minds are uneven, and the best of fabrics have their dull spots. Moreover, much of the choicest weird work is unconscious; appearing in memorable fragments scattered through material whose massed effect may be of a very different cast. Atmosphere is the all-important thing, for the final criterion of authenticity is not the dovetailing of a plot but the creation of a given sensation. We may say, as a general thing, that a weird story whose intent is to teach or produce a social effect, or one in which the horrors are finally explained away by natural means, is not a genuine tale of cosmic fear; but it remains a fact that such narratives often possess, in isolated sections, atmospheric touches which fulfill every condition of true supernatural horror-literature. Therefore we must judge a weird tale not by the author's intent, or by the mere mechanics of the plot; but by the emotional level which it attains at its least mundane point. If the proper sensations are excited, such a "high spot" must be admitted on its own merits as weird literature, no matter how prosaically it is later dragged down. The one test of the really weird is simply this—whether or not there be excited in the reader a profound sense of dread, land of contact with unknown spheres and powers; a subtle attitude of awed listening, as if for the beating of black wings or the scratching of outside shapes and entities on the known universe's utmost rim. And of course, the more completely and unifiedly a story conveys this atmosphere, better it is as a work of art in the given medium.

Chapter 10

INTRODUCTION TO *UNCANNY STORIES*

Christopher St. John Sprigg

> Christopher St. John Sprigg, better known by his pseudonym Christopher Caldwell, was a British intellectual, writer, critic, and activist. He also appears to have had a penchant for the supernatural, as attested to by the existence of his edited collection of ghostly tales. In his brief introduction to the volume, he argues that the "uncanny tale"—stories that seem to affirm premodern beliefs about monsters and magic—is a modern invention because "people must be rational to be thrilled by the irrational." Suggested here, although not developed fully, is the argument that supernatural horror is appealing because it feeds the desire for a more capacious universe than modern rationalist perspectives permit.

THE UNCANNY STORY, as a self-conscious, highly developed art-form, is a typically modern product. Its father is Edgar Allan Poe, whose stories are so well-known to all connoisseurs of the *macabre* that it has been considered unnecessary to include them in this anthology. It may seem at first illogical that the uncanny story should be a modern development, when it is precisely in modern times that supernatural apparitions and miraculous interventions are treated with the greatest scepticism. But in fact the one follows the other as effect follows cause.

If you believe whole-heartedly and simply in vampires, ghosts, and were-wolves, as do primitive folk, they are as real people to you as your next-door neighbour. Hence in folk-tales these beings are treated in the same simple, matter-of-fact style as flesh-and-blood characters. Even such a sophisticated art as Hellenistic literature deals with magic in a straightforward way, as readers of Apuleius' "Golden Ass" will remember. With the dawn of the "age of Reason" in the eighteenth century, supernatural apparitions were at first frowned upon in literature, although the stir created by the "Cock-Lane Ghost" showed that belief in the world of phantoms was by no means completely extinguished. Then, towards the end of the eighteenth century, a new thrill was discovered—the thrill of the irrational. Walpole's "Castle of Otranto" and Mrs. Radcliffe's novels were the precursors of a whole host of "Gothic" horrors; but these ghosts still remained rational in the last analysis—there was always some mechanical or human explanation of the screaming skulls and hooded apparitions.

It was left to Poe to lift the ghost story to its present plane. Just as he created the story of horror with an entirely rational interest, the ancestor of the modern detective story, so he created the story of horror with an entirely irrational interest, ancestor of the modern ghost story.

This reveals the real cause of the development of the uncanny story in a rational age. People must be rational to be thrilled by the irrational. If you believe wholeheartedly in the world of matter-of-fact event, then, when for a moment all this concrete reality seems to quiver and the Impossible peeps through, the effect is shattering. This also explains the peculiar technique of the "ghost story"—its simple "reasonable" style, its dealing in half-hints and evasions, its insinuating approach to the reader so as to enlist his confidence. Once gained, this confidence is slowly undermined by the development of the inexplicable. The writer of the uncanny story must therefore be an expert in the creation of this feeling of "the uneasy," of impossible things glimpsed in the half-light, of unexpected possibilities of horror latent in the commonplace. There are several good specimens of this subtle treatment in the present collection—W. F. Harvey's "Beast with Five Fingers," for example, or John Metcalfe's "The Guards," or Walter de la Mare's "A Recluse."

M. R. James, himself a master of the uncanny technique, has discussed the problem of whether the writer of ghost stories should himself "believe in ghosts." Our analysis of the cause of the specific "thrill" given by the uncanny story answers this question. The writer of the ghost story should be a rational man, otherwise he cannot build up the matter-of-fact framework which is so horrifyingly shattered by the incursion of the Impossible. Any credulity would make his readers sceptical from the start; and he would underestimate the amount of preliminary mining and sapping of their confidence in the rational which it is necessary to undertake before he shows his hand. But though he must be by habit a materialist, he must be one with chinks in his armour. He must be devoid of simple faith and also of completely honest doubt—in other words, he must be a typically modern writer.

Connoisseurs of the uncanny recognize certain conventions. These bar a rational explanation of an apparently supernatural phenomenon, which only irritates the reader by suggesting that he was a fool to be taken in at first. The type of ghost story in which there is a real haunting, at first completely arbitrary and inexplicable and only later explained by some dead and forgotten crime or tragedy, is a legitimate treatment, but is now so stereotyped that the expert avoids it. He prefers to make the possibility of the haunting grow out of the story as he tells it until, when the horror finally materializes, it seems so much the more credible and upsetting. Certain "stock apparitions," such as the vampire, are now avoided by most of the masters, but the skilled writer can make something new and vivid even of these, as is shown in "An Episode of Cathedral History," which is really a "vampire" story. "The Book," by Margaret Irwin, is also an example of how, under an expert hand, even such ancient beliefs as that in demoniac possession can become terrifyingly new, while "Saki," in his little masterpiece "Sredni Vashtar," gave a bizarre twist to another old superstition, that of totem-worship. Even modern science can bring grist to the *macabre* mill, for John Buchan's "Space" could hardly have been written without Einstein or Gauss, and le Fanu's "Green Tea" derives most of its effect from its medical atmosphere. W. W. Jacobs on the other hand is a writer who, in all his ghost stories has a knack of breaking completely new territory, remote both from new science and old superstition.

Within its convention, therefore, the ghost story gives room for the very widest range of treatment, and can number in its ranks such stylists as Stevenson, de la Mare, Hawthorne, and Henry James. There is a wide gulf between the strange poetry of de la Mare's "Recluse" and the convincingly historical setting of Stevenson's "Body-Snatcher," yet both are real ghost stories.

Even so, the ghost story's resources have by no means been exhausted. Modern psychiatry has given scientific recognition to the world of the uncanny by its revelation of a whole universe of the irrational, solid *façade* of the conscious mind. Obsessions and archaic presences quite as weird and eerie as those of ghost stories are to be found here, if we are to credit Jung and his followers. Indeed, in such stories as "The Double Admiral" and "The Best with Five Fingers," this psychiatric lore has already been drawn upon.

The field of the English ghost story is so rich that the anthologist is saved the usual apology for omissions. It is quite obvious that only a small selection can be made out of so large a total. The editor's chief concern has been to make the selection as representative and varied as is possible within the limits of one anthology.

Chapter 11

THE ENJOYMENT OF FEAR

Alfred Hitchcock

> Alfred Hitchcock sought throughout his long cinematic career to evoke pleasurable fear from his audiences. In the short piece included here, the "master of suspense" reflects—with affinities to the Barbauld piece included earlier in this part—on the difference between terror and suspense. The former has to do with surprise, while the latter—for which Hitchcock expresses a preference—is a continuing experience that is easier to savor.

I SUPPOSE THE PROPER WAY TO BEGIN a piece on the enjoyment of fear would be to prove that such a thing exists. Can fear be enjoyable? Or even pleasant? I was discussing this point with an old friend not long ago.

"Fear," he said, "is the least pleasant of all emotions. I experienced it when I was a boy, and again during both wars. I never want my children to experience it. I think it entirely possible, if I have anything to say about it, that they'll live their entire lives and never know the meaning of the word."

"Oh," I said, "what a dreadful prospect!" My friend looked at me quizzically. "I mean it," I went on. "The boys will never be able to ride a roller coaster, or climb a mountain, or take a midnight stroll through a graveyard. And when they're older"—my friend is a champion motorboat racer—"there'll be no speedboating for them."

"What do you mean?" he asked, obviously offended.

"Well, now, let's take the speedboat racing, for instance. Can you honestly tell me that the sensation you get when you cut close to a pylon, or rough water, with a boat riding close on one side and another skidding across in front of you, is anything but fear? Can you deny that a day on the water without fear, without that prickly sensation as the short hairs on your neck rise, would be an utter dead failure? It seems to me that you pay lots of money a year for fear. Why do you want to deny it to your sons?"

"I'd never thought of it quite that way," he said. And he hadn't.

Few people have. That's why my statement, made in all sincerity, that millions of people every day pay huge sums of money and go to great hardship merely to *enjoy* fear seems paradoxical. Yet it is no exaggeration. Any carnival man will tell you the rides that attract the greatest clientele are those that inspire the greatest fear. It is self-evident that the poloist, the steeplechaser, the speedboat racer, and the fox hunter ride for the thrill that comes only from danger. The boy who walks a tightrope or tiptoes along the top of a picket fence is looking for fear, as are the auto racer, the mountain climber, and the big-game hunter.

And that is only the beginning. For every person who seeks fear in the real or personal sense, millions seek it vicariously, in the theater and in the cinema. In darkened auditoriums they identify themselves with fictitious characters who are experiencing fear, and experience, themselves, the same fear sensations (the quickened pulse, the alternately dry and damp palm, etc.), but without paying the price. That the price need not be paid—indeed, must not be paid—is the important factor. Take, for example, one of the classic fear situations: the legendary, though now sadly obsolete, circular bandsaw approaching the bound and gagged heroine. If this distressing contretemps were to exist in real life, the emotional experience of the helpless young woman as the saw approached would be anything but pleasant. Even if one merely viewed a real person thus jeopardized, it would be most displeasing. The suburban matron whose eyes all but pop out of her head with ecstatic excitement as she watches the cinematic blade approach the cinematic neck would no doubt faint dead away if she encountered a similar problem in her home. Why, then, does she enjoy it in the movies?

Precisely because the price will not be paid and she knows it. The saw will never reach its intended target. The plot may, and indeed should, indicate that the heroine's rescue is totally impossible. But deep in the subconscious mind of the spectator is the certainty, engendered by attendance at similar dramatic works, that the totally impossible will occur. The hero, though we have just been made aware that he lies unconscious at the bottom of a pit, surrounded by rattlesnakes, boiling oil, and the smell of bitter almonds, will appear in time to reverse the action of the saw and trap the villain. Or the saw will break down. Or it will appear that the villain has carelessly neglected to sharpen it—or, if it is an electric saw, to pay his electric bill. Fear and fear not, that is the essence of melodrama. Fear: the saw may dismember the ingénue. Fear not: it won't.

Fear in the cinema is my special field, and I have, perhaps dogmatically, but I think with good cause, split cinematic fear into two broad categories—terror and suspense. The difference is comparable to the difference between a buzz bomb and a V-2.

To anyone who has experienced attacks by both bombs, the distinction will be clear. The buzz bomb made a noise like an outboard motor, and its chugging in the air above served as notice of its impending arrival. When the motor stopped, the bomb was beginning its descent and would shortly explode. The moments between the time the motor was first heard and the final explosion were moments of *suspense*. The V-2, on the other hand, was noiseless until the moment of its explosion. Anyone who heard a V-2 explode, and lived, had experienced *terror*.

Another example, one that has been experienced by most of us, may make the distinction more definite. Walking down a dimly lighted street in the late hours of the night, with no other people about, a person may find his mind playing strange tricks. The silence, the loneliness, and the gloom may set the scene for fear.

Suddenly a dark form thrusts itself before the lonely walker. *Terror*. It does not matter that the form was a waving branch, a newspaper picked up by a gust of wind, or simply an oddly shaped shadow unexpectedly coming into view. Whatever it was, it produced its moment of terror.

The same walker, on the same dark street, might have no inclination toward fear. The sound of footsteps coming from somewhere behind might cause the late stroller to become curious, then uneasy, then fearful. The walker stops, the footsteps are not heard; the pace is increased, so also the tempo of the thin sounds coming out of the night. *Suspense.* The echo of his own steps? Probably. But suspense.

On the screen, terror is induced by surprise; suspense, by forewarning. Let us suppose, to make all this clear, that our plot is concerned with a married woman residing in Manhattan and engaged in amorous dalliance with a young cad.

The young cad learns that his inamorata's husband is in Detroit on business and immediately proceeds to the lady's apartment. The two are there engaged in activity as compromising as the censors will permit. Suddenly the door is flung open. There stands the enraged spouse, gun in hand. Net result: terror. There is no suspense whatsoever in the sequence, for the possibility that the husband might be in the vicinity was never hinted by the lovers, and the audience, identifying itself with them, must share their shock at the husband's entrance.

Now, how could we play that incident if we wished to create, not terror, but suspense? Remember our rule: terror by surprise, suspense by forewarning. Very well, we begin with the two lovers in the hotel room. The husband, we learn from the less personal fragments of their conversation, is presumed by them to be in Detroit. Then we see the husband alighting from an airplane. But what is this? This is not Detroit, but New York! For the benefit of those who are not familiar with the two airports, we incorporate a significant glance at an identifying sign at the airport or, perhaps better, at the license plate of the cab as the husband gives the address of the hotel.

Now back to the two lovers. Note that, in this telling, the audience cannot identify itself with the lovers, because the audience knows what the lovers do not, that the husband is on his way and may trap them. But the audience cannot identify itself with the husband either, for the audience knows what he, poor fellow, only suspects: his wife is unfaithful. Now we go back and forth between the lovers and the husband. They continue their lovemaking. The husband alights from his cab. The cad straightens his tie and prepares to depart. The husband begins to mount the stairs. Will he arrive in time? Will the cad make good his escape? What will happen if he does not? These are the questions that the audience asks itself, and whether or not the husband arrives in time, a suspenseful situation has been created.

It is obvious from the above that suspense and terror cannot coexist. To the extent that the audience is aware of the menace or danger to the people it is watching—that is, to the extent that suspense is created—so is its surprise (or terror) at the eventual materialization of the indicated danger diminished. This poses a pretty problem for the director and for the writer of a motion picture. Shall the terror be diminished to enhance the suspense; or shall all suspense be eliminated by making the surprise complete and the terror as shocking to the audience as to the fictional participants?

The terror-suspense dilemma is normally resolved by compromise. There are several situations in a motion picture; the ordinary, and I think best, practice is to play most of the situations for suspense and a few for terror. Suspense is more enjoyable than terror, actually, because it is a continuing experience and attains a peak crescendo fashion; while terror, to be truly effective, must come all at once, like a bolt of lightning, and is more difficult, therefore, to savor.

However, one conflict in making pictures in which fear is a major element cannot be compromised. That is the conflict between the validity of the plot and situations and the implied guarantee given the audience that it shall not "pay the price" for its fear. To the roller-coaster operator that is a simple problem; it means that, although in appearance the ride must be as terrifying as possible, it must, in reality, be completely safe. The pleasant fear sensation experienced by a roller-coaster rider as the car approached a sharp curve would cease to exist if he seriously thought for one moment that the car might really fail to negotiate the curve. The audience at a motion picture is, of course, entirely safe from that point of view. Though knives and guns may be used on the screen, the audience is aware that no one out front is going to be shot or stabbed. But the audience must also be aware that the characters in the picture, with whom they strongly identify themselves, are not to pay the price of fear. This awareness must be entirely subconscious; the spectator must *know* that the spy ring will never succeed in pitching Madeleine Carroll off London Bridge, and the spectator must be induced to *forget* what he knows. If he didn't *know*, he would be genuinely worried; if he didn't *forget*, he would be bored.

What all this amounts to is this: as the audience sympathy for a character is built up, the audience assumes that a sort of invisible cloak to protect the wearer from harm is being fitted. Once the sympathies are fully established and the cloak is finished, it is not—in the audience opinion, and in the opinion of many critics—fair play to violate the cloak and bring its wearer to a disastrous end. I did it once, in a picture called *Sabotage*. One of the characters was a small boy, with whom the audience was encouraged to fall in love. I sent the boy wandering about London with what he supposed was a can of film under his arm, but what the audience knew full well contained a time bomb. Under this set of circumstance, the lad is protected by his cloak from premature explosion of the bomb. I blew him up anyway, along with several other passengers on a bus he happened to be riding.

Now, that episode in *Sabotage* was a direct negation of the invisible cloak of protection worn by sympathetic characters in motion pictures. In addition, because the audience knew the film can contained a bomb and the boy did not, to permit the bomb to explode was a violation of the rule forbidding a direct combination of suspense and terror, or forewarning and surprise. Had the audience not been informed of the real contents of the can, the explosion would have come as a complete surprise. As a result of a sort of emotional numbness induced by a shock of this kind, I believe their sensibilities might not have been so thoroughly outraged. As it was, the audiences—and the critics, too—were unanimously of the opinion that I should have been riding in the seat next to the lad, preferably the seat he set the bomb on.

Chapter 12

FROM *DANSE MACABRE*

Stephen King

> Stephen King is not only among the world's most popular horror writers but, in works including *Danse Macabre* (1981) and *On Writing: A Memoir of the Craft* (2020), has reflected deeply on the horror genre. *Danse Macabre* is in some ways like Lovecraft's *Supernatural Horror in Literature*—a survey of and commentary on the genre. In the brief selection included here, King offers a rejoinder to the aggrieved moralists surveyed in the introduction to this anthology: Horror in large measure reaffirms the status quo by expunging the monster and reestablishing equilibrium. We may enjoy the messy middle, which King figures in Dionysian terms—but, in the end, virtue triumphs, and vice is punished.

WITH ITS DISGUISE OF SEMANTICS carefully removed and laid aside, what those who criticize the tale of horror (or who simply feel uneasy about it and their liking for it) seem to be saying is this: You are selling death and disfigurement and monstrosity; you are trading upon hate and violence, morbidity and loathing; you are just another representative of those forces of chaos which so endanger the world today.

You are, in short, immoral.

A critic asked George Romero, following the release of *Dawn of the Dead* (1978), if he felt such a movie, with its scenes of gore, cannibalism, and gaudy pop violence, was a sign of a healthy society. Romero's reply, worthy of the Hitchcock anecdote related earlier, was to ask the critic if he felt the DC-10 engine-mount assembly was a healthy thing for society. His response was dismissed as a quibble ("You get the impression Romero likes this kind of sparring," I can almost hear the critic thinking).

Well, let's see if the quibble really is a quibble—and let's go one layer deeper than we have yet gone. The hour has grown late, the last waltz is playing, and if we don't say certain things now, I suppose we never will.

I've tried to suggest throughout this book that the horror story, beneath its fangs and fright wig, is really as conservative as an Illinois Republican in a three-piece pinstriped suit; that its main purpose is to reaffirm the virtues of the norm by showing us what awful things happen to people who venture into taboo lands. Within the framework of most horror tales we find a moral code so strong it would make a Puritan smile. In the old E.C. comics, adulterers inevitably came to bad ends and murderers suffered fates that would make the rack and the boot look like kiddy rides at the carnival.[1] Modern horror stories are not much different from the morality plays of the fifteenth, sixteenth, and seventeenth centuries, when we get right down to it. The horror story most generally not only stands foursquare for the Ten Commandments, it blows them up to tabloid size. We have the comforting knowledge when the lights go down in the theater or when we open the book that the evildoers will almost certainly be punished, and measure will be returned for measure.

Further, I've used one pompously academic metaphor, suggesting that the horror tale generally details the outbreak of some Dionysian madness in an Apollonian existence, and that the horror will continue until the Dionysian forces have been repelled and the Apollonian norm restored again. Excluding a powerful if puzzling prologue set in Iraq, William Friedkin's film *The Exorcist* (1973) actually begins in Georgetown, an Apollonian suburb if ever there was one. In the first scene, Ellen Burstyn is awakened by a crashing, roaring sound in the attic—it sounds like maybe someone let a lion loose up there. It is the first crack in the Apollonian world; soon everything else will pour through in a nightmare torrent. But this disturbing crack between our normal world and a chaos where demons are allowed to prey on innocent children is finally closed again at the end of the film. When Burstyn leads the pallid but obviously okay Linda Blair to the car in the film's final scene, we understand that the nightmare is over. Steady state has been restored. We have watched for the mutant and repulsed it. Equilibrium never felt so good.

Those are some of the things we've talked about in this book . . . but suppose all of that is only a sham and a false front? I don't say that it is, but perhaps (since this *is* the last dance) we ought to discuss the possibility, at least.

In our discussion of archetypes, we've had occasion to discuss the Werewolf, that fellow who is sometimes hairy and who is sometimes deceptively smooth. Suppose there was a double werewolf? Suppose that the creator of the horror story was, under his or her fright wig and plastic fangs, a Republican in a three-button suit, as we have said . . . ah, but suppose below *that* there is a *real* monster, with real fangs and a squirming Medusa-tangle of snakes for hair? Suppose it's all a self-serving lie and that when the creator of horror is finally stripped all the way to his or her core of being we find not an agent of the norm but a friend—a capering, gleeful, red-eyed agent of chaos?

What about *that* possibility, friends and neighbors?

Note

1. My all-time favorite (he said affectionately): A crazed husband stuffs the hose of an air compressor down his skinny wife's throat and blows her up like a balloon until she bursts. "Fat at last," he tells her happily just moments before the pop. But later on the husband, who is roughly the size of Jackie Gleason, trips a booby-trap she has set for him and is squashed to a shadow when a huge safe falls on him. This ingenious reworking of the old story of Jack Sprat and his wife is not only gruesomely funny; it offers us a delicious example of the Old Testament eye-for-an-eye theory. Or, as the Spanish say, revenge is a dish best eaten cold.

II
The Paradox of Horror

Chapter 13

FEARING FICTIONS

Kendall Walton

> Several of the chapter inclusions in part I subscribe to or suggest what we may refer to as the "conversion theory" of horror, whereby negative emotions are transformed into positive ones. In contrast, Walton here is the first example of a "denialist theory" of horror: Simply put, when we consume horror, we aren't really scared because we know we are safe. Our emotional arousal is real, but our fear is simulated (what Walton refers to as a "quasi-emotion")—and, because it isn't real fear, we are able to enjoy it.

The plot [of a tragedy] must be structured ... that the one who is hearing the events unroll shudders with fear and feels pity at what happens: which is what one would experience on hearing the plot of the Oedipus.

Aristotle, *Poetics*

I

Charles is watching a horror movie about a terrible green slime. He cringes in his seat as the slime oozes slowly but relentlessly over the earth, destroying everything in its path. Soon a greasy head emerges from the undulating mass, and two beady eyes roll around, finally fixing on the camera. The slime, picking up speed, oozes on a new course straight toward the viewers. Charles emits a shriek and clutches desperately at his chair. Afterward, still shaken, Charles confesses that he was "terrified" of the slime. *Was* he?

This question is part of the larger issue of how "remote" fictional worlds are from the real world. There is a definite barrier against *physical* interactions between fictional worlds and the real world. Spectators at a play are prevented from rendering aid to a heroine in distress. There is no way that Charles can dam up the slime, or take a sample for laboratory analysis.[1] But, as Charles's case dramatically illustrates, this barrier appears to be psychologically transparent. It would seem that real people can, and frequently do, have psychological attitudes toward merely fictional entities, despite the impossibility of physical intervention. Readers or spectators detest Iago, worry about Tom Sawyer and Becky lost in the cave, pity Willy Loman, envy Superman—and Charles fears the slime.

But I am skeptical. We do indeed get "caught up" in stories; we often become "emotionally involved" when we read novels or watch plays or films. But to construe this involvement as consisting of our having psychological attitudes toward fictional entities is, I think, to tolerate mystery and court confusion. I shall offer a different and, in my opinion, much more illuminating account of it.

This issue is of fundamental importance. It is crucially related to the basic question of why and how fiction is important, why we find it valuable, why we do not dismiss novels, films, and plays as "mere fiction" and hence unworthy of serious attention. My conclusions in this chapter will lead to some tentative suggestions about this basic question.

II

Physical interaction is possible only with what actually exists. That is why Charles cannot dam up the slime, and why in general real people cannot have physical contact with mere fictions. But the nonexistence of the slime does not prevent Charles from fearing it. One may fear a ghost or a burglar even if there is none; one may be afraid of an earthquake that is destined never to occur.

But a person who fears a nonexistent burglar *believes* that there is, or at least might be, one. He believes that he is in danger, that there is a possibility of his being harmed by a burglar. It is *conceivable* that Charles should believe himself to be endangered by the green slime. He might take the film to be a live documentary, a news flash. If he does, naturally he is afraid.

But the situation I have in mind is the more usual and more interesting one in which Charles is not deceived in this straightforward way. Charles knows perfectly well that the slime is not real and that he is in no danger. Is he afraid even so? He says that he is afraid, and he is in a state that is undeniably similar, in some respects, to that of a person who is frightened of a pending real-world disaster. His muscles are tensed, he clutches his chair, his pulse quickens, his adrenaline flows. Let us call this physiological/psychological state "quasi-fear." Whether it is actual fear (or a component of actual fear) is the question at issue.

Charles's state is crucially different from that of a person with an ordinary case of fear. The fact that Charles is fully aware that the slime is fictional is, I think, good reason to deny that what he feels is fear. It seems a principle of common sense, one that ought not to be abandoned if there is any reasonable alternative, that fear[2] must be accompanied by, or must involve, a belief that one is in danger. Charles does not believe that he is in danger; so he is not afraid.

Charles might try to convince us that he was afraid by shuddering and declaring dramatically that he was "*really terrified.*" This emphasizes the intensity of his experience. But we need not deny that he had an intense experience. The question is whether his experience, however intense, was one of fear of the slime. The fact that Charles, and others, call it "fear" is not conclusive, even if we grant that in doing so they express a truth. For we need to know whether the statement that Charles was afraid is to be taken literally or not.

More sophisticated defenders of the claim that Charles is afraid may argue that Charles *does* believe that the green slime is real and is a real threat to him. There are, to be sure, strong reasons for allowing that Charles realizes that the slime is only fictional and poses no danger. If he didn't, we should expect him to flee the theater, call the police, warn his family. But perhaps it is *also* true that Charles believes, in some way or "on some level," that the slime is real and really threatens him. It has been said that in cases like this one "suspends one's disbelief," or that "part" of a person believes something that another part of him disbelieves, or that one finds oneself (almost?) believing something one nevertheless knows to be false. We must see what can be made of these notions.

One possibility is that Charles *half* believes that there is a real danger, and that he is, literally, at least half afraid. To half believe something is to be not quite sure that it is true, but also not quite sure that it is not true. But Charles has *no* doubts about whether he is in the presence of an actual slime. If he half believed, and were half afraid, we would expect him to have *some* inclination to act on his fear in the normal ways. Even a hesitant belief, a mere suspicion, that the slime is real would induce any normal person seriously to consider calling the police and warning his family. Charles gives no thought whatever to such courses of action. He is not *uncertain* whether the slime is real; he is perfectly sure that it is not.

Moreover, the fear symptoms that Charles does exhibit are not symptoms of a mere suspicion that the slime is real and a queasy feeling of half fear. They are symptoms of the certainty of grave and immediate danger and of sheer terror. Charles's heart pounds violently, he gasps for breath, he grasps the chair until his knuckles are white. This is not the behavior of a man who realizes basically that he is safe but suffers flickers of doubt. If it indicates fear at all, it indicates acute and overwhelming terror. Thus, to compromise on this issue, to say that Charles half believes he is in danger and is half afraid, is not a reasonable alternative.

One might claim that Charles believes he is in danger, but that this is not a hesitant or weak or half belief, but rather a belief of a special kind—a "gut" belief as opposed to an "intellectual" one. Compare a person who hates flying. He realizes, in one sense, that airplanes are (relatively) safe. He says, honestly, that they are, and can quote statistics to prove it. Nevertheless, he avoids traveling by air whenever possible. He is brilliant at devising excuses. And if he must board a plane, he becomes nervous and upset. I grant that this person believes at a "gut" level that flying is dangerous, despite his "intellectual" belief to the contrary. I grant also that he is really afraid of flying.

But Charles is different. The air traveler performs *deliberate* actions that one would expect of someone who thinks flying is dangerous, or at least he is strongly inclined to perform such actions. If he does not actually decide against traveling by air, he has a strong inclination to do so. But Charles does not have even an inclination to leave the theater or call the police. The only signs that he might really believe he is endangered are his more or less automatic, nondeliberate reactions: his pulse rate, his sweaty palms, his knotted stomach, his spontaneous shriek.[3] This justifies us in treating the two cases differently.

Deliberate actions are done for reasons; they are done because of what the agent wants and what he thinks will bring about what he wants. There is a presumption that such actions are reasonable in light of the agent's beliefs and desires (however unreasonable the beliefs and desires may be). So we postulate beliefs or desires to make sense of them. People also have reasons for doing things that they are inclined to do but, for other reasons, refrain from doing. If the air traveler thinks that flying is dangerous, then, assuming that he wants to live, his actions or tendencies thereto are reasonable. Otherwise, they probably are not. So we legitimately infer that he does believe, at least on a "gut" level, that flying is dangerous. But we don't have to make the same kind of sense of Charles's automatic responses. One doesn't have reasons for things one doesn't *do*, like sweating, increasing one's pulse rate, knotting one's stomach (involuntarily). So there is no need to attribute beliefs (or desires) to Charles that will render these responses reasonable.[4] Thus, we can justifiably infer the air passenger's ("gut") belief in the danger of flying from his deliberate behavior or inclinations, and yet refuse to infer from Charles's automatic responses that he thinks he is in danger.

Someone might reply that at moments of special crisis during the movie—for example, when the slime first spots Charles—Charles "loses hold of reality" and, *momentarily,* takes the slime to be real and really fears it. These moments are too short for Charles to think about doing anything; so (one might claim) it isn't surprising that his belief and fear are not accompanied by the normal inclinations to act.

This move is unconvincing. In the first place, Charles's quasi-fear responses are not merely momentary; he may have his heart in his throat throughout most of the movie, yet without experiencing the slightest inclination to flee or call the police. These long-term responses, and Charles's propensity to describe them afterward in terms of "fear," need to be understood even if it is allowed that there are moments of real fear interspersed among them. Furthermore, however tempting the momentary-fear idea might be, comparable views of other psychological states are much less appealing. When we say that someone "pitied" Willy Loman or "admired" Superman, it is unlikely that we have in mind special moments during his experience of the work when he forgot, momentarily, that he was dealing with fiction and felt flashes of actual pity or admiration. The person's "sense of reality" may well have been robust and healthy throughout his experience of the work, uninterrupted by anything like the special moments of crisis Charles experiences during the horror movie. Moreover, it may be appropriate to say that someone "pities" Willy or "admires" Superman even when he is not watching the play or reading the cartoon. The momentary-*fear* theory, even if it were plausible, would not throw much light on cases in which we apparently have other psychological attitudes toward fictions.

Although Charles is not really afraid of the fictional slime depicted in the movie, the movie might nevertheless produce real fear in him. It might cause him to be afraid of something other than the slime it depicts. If Charles is a child, the movie may make him wonder whether there might not be real slimes or other "exotic horrors" *like* the one depicted in the movie, even if he fully realizes that the movie-slime itself is not real. Charles may well fear these suspected actual dangers; he might have nightmares about them for days afterward. (*Jaws* caused a lot of people to fear sharks that they thought might really exist. But whether they were afraid of the fictional sharks in the movie is another question.)

If Charles is an older moviegoer with a heart condition, he may be afraid of the movie itself. Perhaps he knows that any excitement could trigger a heart attack and fears that the movie will cause excitement, for example, by depicting the slime as being especially aggressive or threatening. This is real fear. But it is fear of the depiction of the slime, not fear of the slime that is depicted.

Why is it so natural to describe Charles as afraid of the slime, if he is not, and how *is* his experience to be characterized? In what follows I shall develop a theory to answer these questions.

III

Propositions that are, as we say, "true in (the world of)" a novel or painting or film are *fictional*. Thus it is fictional that there is a society of tiny people called "Lilliputians." And in the example discussed earlier it is fictional that a terrible green slime is on the loose. Other fictional propositions are associated not with works of art but with games of make-believe, dreams, and imaginings. If it is "true in a game of make-believe" that Johnnie is a pirate, then fictionally Johnnie is a pirate. If someone dreams or imagines that he is a hero, then it is fictional that he is a hero.

Fictional truths[5] come in groups, and each of these groups constitutes a "fictional world." The fact that fictionally there was a society of tiny people and the fact that fictionally a man named "Gulliver" was a ship's physician belong to the same fictional world. The fact that fictionally a green slime is on the loose belongs to a different one. There is, roughly, a distinct fictional world corresponding to each novel, painting, film, game of make-believe, dream, or daydream.

All fictional truths are in one way or another man-made. But there are two importantly different ways of making them, and two corresponding kinds of fictional truths. One way to make a proposition fictional is simply to imagine that it is true. If it is fictional that a person is a hero because he imagines himself to be a hero, then this fictional truth is an *imaginary* one. Imagining is not always a deliberate, self-conscious act. We sometimes find ourselves imagining things more or less spontaneously, without having decided to do so. Thoughts pop into our heads unbidden. Dreams can be understood as simply very spontaneous imaginings.

Fictional truths of the second kind are established in a less direct manner. Participants in a game of mud pies may decide to recognize a principle to the effect that whenever there is a glob of mud in a certain orange crate, it is "true in the game of make-believe," that is, it is fictional, that there is a pie in the oven. This fictional truth is a *make-believe* one. The principles in force in a given game of make-believe are, of course, just those principles that participants in the game recognize or accept, or understand to be in force.

It can be make-believe that there is a pie in the oven without anyone's imagining that there is. This will be so if there is a glob in the crate that no one knows about. (Later, after discovering the glob, a child might say, "There was a pie in the oven all along, but we didn't know it.") But propositions that are known to be make-believe are usually imaginary as well. When kids playing mud pies do know about a glob in the crate by virtue of which it is make-believe that a pie is in the oven, they imagine that there is a pie in the oven.

Principles of make-believe that are in force in a game need not have been formulated explicitly or deliberately adopted. When children agree to let globs of mud "be" pies, they are in effect establishing a great many unstated principles linking make-believe properties of pies to properties of globs. It is implicitly understood that the size and shape of globs determine the make-believe size and shape of pies; it is understood, for example, that make-believedly a pie is one handspan across just in case that is the size of the appropriate glob. It is understood also that if Johnnie throws a glob at Mary, then make-believedly Johnnie throws a pie at Mary. (It is *not* understood that if a glob is 40 percent clay, then make-believedly a pie is 40 percent clay.)

It is not always easy to say whether or not someone does accept, implicitly, a given principle of make-believe. But we should notice that much of the plausibility of attributing to children implicit acceptance of a principle linking the make-believe size and shape of pies to the size and shape of globs rests on the dispositional fact that if the children should discover a glob to have a certain size or shape, they would imagine, more or less automatically, that a pie has that size or shape. The children are disposed to imagine pies as having whatever size and shape properties they think the relevant globs have. In general, nondeliberate, spontaneous imagining, prompted in a systematic way by beliefs about the real world, is an important indication of implicit acceptance of principles of make-believe. I do not claim that a person disposed to imagine, nondeliberately, that p when he believes that q *necessarily* recognizes a principle of make-believe whereby if q, then it is make-believe that p. It must be his understanding that whenever it is true that q, *whether he knows it or not*, it will be fictional that p. It may be difficult to ascertain whether this is his understanding, especially since his understanding may be entirely implicit. But the spontaneity of a person's imagining that p on learning that q strongly suggests that he thinks of p as having been fictional even before he realized that q.

A game of make-believe and its constituent principles need not be shared publicly. One might set up one's own personal game, adopting principles that no one else recognizes. And at least some of the principles constituting a personal game of make-believe may be implicit, principles that the person simply takes for granted.

Representational works of art generate make-believe truths. *Gulliver's Travels* generates the truth that make-believedly there is a society of six-inch-tall people. It is make-believe that a green slime is on the loose in virtue of the images on the screen of Charles's horror movie. These make-believe truths are generated because the relevant principles of make-believe are understood to be in force. But few such principles are ever formulated, and our recognition of most of them is implicit. Some probably seem so natural that we assume them to be in force almost automatically. Others we pick up easily through unreflective experience with the arts.[6]

IV

> [The actor] on a stage plays at being another before a gathering of people who play at taking him for that other person.
>
> Jorge Luis Borges, "Everything and Nothing"

Compare Charles with a child playing an ordinary game of make-believe with his father. The father, pretending to be a ferocious monster, cunningly stalks the child and, at a crucial moment, lunges viciously at him. The child flees, screaming, to the next room. The scream is more or less involuntary, and so is the flight. But the child has a delighted grin on his face even while he runs, and he unhesitatingly comes back for more. He is perfectly aware that his father is only "playing," that the whole thing is "just a game," and that only make-believedly is there a vicious monster after him. He is not really afraid.

The child obviously belongs to the fictional world of the game of make-believe. It is make-believe that the monster lunges, not into thin air, but at the child. Make-believedly the child is in grave and mortal danger. And when the child screams and runs, make-believedly he knows he is in danger and is afraid. The game is a sort of theatrical event in which the father is an actor portraying a monster and the child is an actor playing himself.

I propose to regard Charles similarly. When the slime raises its head, spies the camera, and begins oozing toward it, it is make-believe that Charles is threatened.

And when as a result Charles gasps and grips his chair, make-believedly he is afraid. Charles is playing a game of make-believe in which he uses the images on the screen as props. He too is an actor impersonating himself. In this section I shall explain this proposal in detail. My main arguments for it will come later.

Charles differs in some important respects from an ordinary onstage, self-portraying actor. One difference has to do with what makes it make-believe that Charles is afraid. Facts about Charles generate *(de re)* make-believe truths about him; in this respect he is like an actor portraying himself onstage. But the sorts of facts about Charles that do the generating are different. Make-believe truths about Charles are generated at least partly by what he thinks and feels, not just by how he acts. It is partly the fact that Charles is in a state of quasi-fear, the fact that he feels his heart pounding, his muscles tensed, and so on, which makes it make-believe that he is afraid. It would not be appropriate to describe him as "afraid" if he were not in some such state.[7]

Charles's quasi-fear is not responsible, by itself, for the fact that make-believedly it is the *slime* he fears, nor even for the fact that make-believedly he is afraid rather than angry or excited or merely upset. Here Charles's (actual) beliefs come into play. Charles believes (he knows) that make-believedly the green slime is bearing down on him and he is in danger of being destroyed by it. His quasi-fear results from this belief.[8] What makes it make-believe that Charles is afraid rather than angry or excited or upset is the fact that his quasi-fear is caused by the belief that make-believedly he is in danger. And his belief that make-believedly it is the slime that endangers him is what makes it make-believe that the slime is the object of his fear. In short, my suggestion is this: The fact that Charles is quasi-afraid as a result of realizing that make-believedly the slime threatens him generates the truth that make-believedly he is afraid of the slime.[9]

An onstage actor, by contrast, generates make-believe truths solely by his acting, by his behavior. Whether it is make-believe that the character portrayed is afraid or not depends just on what the actor says and does and how he contorts his face, regardless of what he actually thinks or feels. It makes no difference whether his actual emotional state is anything like fear. This is just as true when the actor is playing himself as it is when he is portraying some other character. The actor may find that putting himself into a certain frame of mind makes it easier to act in the appropriate ways. Nevertheless, it is how he acts, not his state of mind, that determines whether make-believedly he is afraid.

This is how our conventions for theater work, and it is entirely reasonable that they should work this way. Audiences cannot be expected to have a clear idea of an actor's personal thoughts and feelings while he is performing. That would require knowledge of his offstage personality and of recent events that may have affected his mood (e.g., an argument with his director or his wife). Moreover, acting involves a certain amount of dissembling; actors hide some aspects of their mental states from the audience. If make-believe truths depended on actors' private thoughts and feelings, it would be awkward and unreasonably difficult for spectators to ascertain what is going on in the fictional world. It is not surprising that the make-believe truths for which actors on stage are responsible are understood to be generated by just what is visible from the galleries.

But Charles is not performing for an audience. It is not his job to get across to anyone else what make-believedly is true of himself. Probably no one but he much cares whether or not make-believedly he is afraid. So there is no reason why his actual state of mind should not have a role in generating make-believe truths about himself.

It is not so clear in the monster game what makes it make-believe that the child is afraid of a monster. The child *might* be performing for the benefit of an audience; he might be *showing* someone, an onlooker, or just his father, that make-believedly he is afraid. If so, perhaps he is like an onstage actor. Perhaps we should regard his observable behavior as responsible for the fact that make-believedly he is afraid. But there is room for doubt here. The child experiences quasi-fear sensations as Charles does. And his audience probably has much surer access to his mental state than theater audiences have to those of actors. The audience may know him well, and the child does not try so hard or so skillfully to hide his actual mental state as actors do. It may be perfectly evident to the audience that the child has a case of quasi-fear, and also that this is a result of his realization that make-believedly a monster is after him. So it is not unreasonable to regard the child's mental state as helping to generate make-believe truths.

A more definite account of the situation is possible if the child is participating in the game solely for his own amusement, with no thought of an audience. In this case the child himself, at least, almost certainly understands his make-believe fear to depend on his mental state rather than (just) his behavior.[10] In fact, let us suppose that the child is an undemonstrative sort who does not scream or run or betray his "fear" in any other especially overt way. His participation in the game is purely passive. Nevertheless the child does experience quasi-fear when make-believedly the monster attacks him, and he still would describe himself as being "afraid" (although he knows that there is no danger and that his "fear" isn't real). Certainly in this case it is (partly) his quasi-fear that generates the make-believe truth he expresses when he says he is "afraid."

My proposal is to construe Charles on the model of this undemonstrative child. Charles may, of course, exhibit his "fear" in certain observable ways. But his observable behavior is not meant to show anyone else that make-believedly he is afraid. It is likely to go unnoticed by others, and even Charles himself may be unaware of it. No one, least of all Charles, regards his observable behavior as generating the truth that make-believedly he is afraid.

V

It is clear enough now what makes it make-believe that Charles fears the slime, assuming that make-believedly he does fear the slime. But more needs to be said in support of my claim that this is a make-believe truth. What needs to be established is that the relevant principle of make-believe is accepted or recognized by someone, that someone understands it to be in force. I contend that Charles, at least, does so understand it.

It is clear that Charles imagines himself to be afraid of the slime (though he knows he is not). He thinks of himself as being afraid of it; he readily describes his experience as one of "fear"—once he has a chance to catch his breath. So it is at least imaginary (and hence fictional) that he fears the slime.

Charles's act of imagining himself afraid of the slime is hardly a deliberate or reflective act. It is triggered more or less automatically by his awareness of his quasi-fear sensations. He is simply disposed to think of himself as fearing the slime, without deciding to do so, when during the movie he feels his heart racing, his muscles tensed, and so forth. It is just such a disposition as this, we recall, that goes with implicit recognition of a principle of make-believe. If a child is disposed to imagine a pie to be six inches across when he discovers that that is the size of a glob of mud, this makes it reasonable to regard him as recognizing a principle whereby the glob's being that size makes it make-believe that the pie is also. Similarly, Charles's tendency to imagine himself afraid of the slime when he finds himself in the relevant mental state constitutes persuasive grounds for attributing to him acceptance of a principle whereby his experience makes it make-believe that he is afraid.[11]

Several further considerations will increase the plausibility of this conclusion. First, I have claimed only that Charles recognizes the principle of make-believe. There is no particular reason why anyone else should recognize it, since ordinarily only Charles is in a position to apply it and only he is interested in the make-believe truth that results. Others might know about it and realize how important it is to Charles. But even so, the principle clearly is in important respects a personal one. It differs in this regard from the principles whereby an onstage actor's behavior generates make-believe truths, and also from those whereby images on the movie screen generate make-believe truths about the activities of the green slime. *These* principles are fully public; they are clearly (even if implicitly) recognized by everyone watching the play or movie. Everyone in the audience applies them and is interested in the resulting make-believe truths.

This makes it reasonable to recognize two distinct games of make-believe connected with the horror movie—a public game and Charles's personal game—and two corresponding fictional worlds. The situation is analogous to that of an illustrated edition of a novel. Consider an edition of Dostoyevsky's *Crime and Punishment* that includes a drawing of Raskolnikov. The text of the novel, considered alone, establishes a fictional world comprising the make-believe truths that it generates, for example, the truth that make-believedly a man named "Raskolnikov" killed an old lady. The illustration is normally understood not as establishing its own separate fictional world, but as combining with the novel to form a "larger" world. This larger world contains the make-believe truths generated by the text alone, plus those generated by the illustration (e.g., that make-believedly Raskolnikov has wavy hair and a receding chin), and also those generated by both together (e.g., that make-believedly a man with wavy hair killed an old lady). So we have two fictional worlds, one included within the other: the world of the novel and the world of the novel-plus-illustration.

Charles's state of mind supplements the movie he is watching in the way an illustration supplements what it illustrates. The movie considered alone establishes a fictional world consisting only of the make-believe truths that it generates (e.g., that make-believedly there is a green slime on the loose). But Charles recognizes, in addition, a larger world in which these make-believe truths are joined by truths generated by Charles's experience as he watches the movie, and also by truths generated by the images on the screen and Charles's experience together. It is only in this more inclusive world that make-believedly Charles fears the slime. (And it is the larger world that occupies Charles's attention when he is caught up in the movie.)

The analogy between Charles's case and the illustrated novel is not perfect. The novel-plus-illustration world is publicly recognized, whereas the fictional world established by the movie plus Charles's experience of it probably is not. Dolls provide an analogy that is better in this respect. Anyone who sees a doll of a certain sort will recognize that it generates the truth that make-believedly there is a blonde baby girl. The doll, regarded simply as a sculpture to be observed from a distance, generates make-believe truths such as this. But a child playing with the doll is playing a more personal game of make-believe, one in which she herself is a self-portraying actor and the doll serves as a prop. What she does with the doll generates make-believe truths, for example, the truth that make-believedly she is dressing the baby for a trip to town. Similarly, Charles uses the screen images as props in a personal game of make-believe in which he himself is a character. He plays his own game with the images. The screen images, of course, do not lend themselves to being "dressed" or manipulated in all the ways that dolls do, and this limits the extent of Charles's participation in the game. But the relations and interactions between Charles and the images do generate a number of important make-believe truths: that make-believedly Charles notices the slime and stares apprehensively at it, that make-believedly it turns toward him and attacks, and that make-believedly he is scared out of his wits.[12]

One source of uneasiness about my claim that make-believedly Charles fears the slime may have been the impression that this can be so only if Charles belongs to the fictional world of the *movie*. (The movie itself doesn't depict Charles, nor does it make any reference to him, so he doesn't belong to the movie-world.) My two-worlds theory shows that this impression is mistaken and hence that the uneasiness based on it is out of place.

I have portrayed Charles so far as participating rather automatically in his game of make-believe. But he might easily slip into participating deliberately. The naturalness of his doing so gives added support to my claim that Charles does recognize a make-believe world that he and the slime share, even when his participation is not deliberate. Suppose that during the movie Charles exclaims, deliberately, to a companion or to himself, "Yikes, here it comes! Watch out!" How are we to understand this verbal action? Certainly Charles is not seriously asserting that a slime is coming and warning himself or his companion of it. Presumably he is asserting that it is *make-believe* that a slime is coming. But the indexical "here" carries an implicit reference to the speaker. So Charles's exclamation shows that he takes it to be make-believe that the slime is headed toward *him*; it shows that he regards himself as coexisting with the slime in a make-believe world.

But this does not take us to the bottom of the matter. "Yikes!" and "Watch out!" are not assertions, and so not assertions of what make-believedly is the case. Moreover, if in saying "Here it comes" Charles were merely making an assertion about what make-believedly is the case, he could well have made this explicit and exclaimed instead, "Make-believedly the slime is coming!" or "The slime is coming, in the fictional world!" But these variants lack the flavor of the original. Charles's exclamatory tone is absurdly out of place when the make-believe status of the danger is made explicit. Compare how ridiculous it would be for an actor playing Horatio in a performance of *Hamlet* to exclaim, when the ghost appears, "Look, my lord, it comes, in the fictional world of the play!"

The comparison is apt. For Charles is doing just what actors do, *pretending* to make an assertion. He is pretending to assert (seriously) that the slime is headed his way. (Pretending to assert this is not incompatible with actually asserting that make-believedly the slime is coming. Charles might be doing both at once.) In my terms, Charles understands his utterance of "Here it comes!" to generate the truth that make-believedly he asserts (seriously) that the slime is coming. He is playing along with the fiction of the movie, incorporating it into a game of make-believe of his own. This makes it obvious why it would not do to say "Here it comes, in the fictional world!" Saying that is simply not (normally) how one would pretend to assert that a slime is (really) coming. The rest of Charles's verbal behavior is now easily explainable as well. In saying "Yikes!" and "Watch out!" he is pretending to express amazement or terror and pretending to issue a (serious) warning; make-believedly he is doing these things.

We have now arrived at the solution to a pair of puzzles. Why is it that in everyday conversation we regularly omit phrases like "in the fictional world" and "in the novel," whereas we rarely omit other intensional operators such as "It is believed that," "Jones wished that," "Jones denies that"? Why do we so naturally say just "Tom and Becky were lost in a cave" rather than "In the novel Tom and Becky were lost in a cave," whereas it would be almost unheard of to shorten "Jones wishes that a golden mountain would appear on the horizon" to simply "A golden mountain will appear on the horizon" (even if the context makes it clear that Jones's wishes are the subject of conversation)?

The explanation lies in our habit of playing along with fictions, of make-believedly asserting, pretending to assert, what we know to be only make-believedly the case. We mustn't be too quick to assume that an utterance of "p" is merely an ellipsis for "make-believedly p" (or for "in the novel p"). This assumption is wrong if the speaker make-believedly is asserting that p, rather than (or in addition to) asserting that make-believedly p. Charles's frantic "Yikes, here it comes!" is an obvious case in point. A case only slightly less obvious is that of a person reading *The Adventures of Tom Sawyer* who remarks, gravely and with an expression of deep concern, that Tom and Becky are lost in a cave.

I do not suggest that the omission of "in the novel" is *never* a mere ellipsis. "Tom and Becky were lost in a cave" uttered by a critic analyzing the novel could easily have been expanded to "In the novel Tom and Becky were lost in a cave" without altering the character of the remark. The critic probably is not pretending to assert that Tom and Becky were (actually) lost in a cave. But our habit of dropping fictional operators persists even in sober criticism, and testifies to the ease with which we can be induced to play along, deliberately, with a work of fiction.

In German the indicative mood is used ordinarily only when the speaker is committed to the truth of the sentence or clause in question. But fictional statements constitute a striking exception to this generalization; the indicative is used in fictional statements even though the speaker is *not* committed to their truth. (One says, for example, "Robinson Crusoe hat einen Schiffbruch überlebt," which is indicative, even though one is not claiming that there actually was a person named "Robinson Crusoe" who survived a shipwreck.) The explanation is that speakers are often pretending to express their commitment to the truth of sentences or clauses in fictional contexts. So naturally they use the indicative mood in these cases; they speak as they would if they were not pretending. And the habit of using the indicative persists even when there is little or no such pretense.

VI

The treatment of Charles's "fear of the slime" suggested earlier can serve as a model for understanding other psychological attitudes ostensibly directed toward fictional things. When it is said that someone pities Willy Loman, or worries about Tom and Becky, or detests Iago, or envies Superman, what is said is probably not literally true.[13] But the person is, actually, in a distinctive psychological (emotional?) state, even if that state is not pity or worry or hate or envy. And his being in this state is a result of his awareness of certain make-believe truths: that make-believedly Willy is an innocent victim of cruel circumstances, that make-believedly Tom and Becky might perish in the cave, that make-believedly Iago deceived Othello about Desdemona, that make-believedly Superman can do almost anything. The fact that the person's psychological state is as it is, and is caused by such beliefs, makes it make-believe that he pities Willy, worries about Tom and Becky, hates Iago, or envies Superman.

We have here a particularly intimate relation between the real world and fictional worlds. Insofar as make-believe truths are generated by a spectator's or reader's state of mind, he is no mere "external observer" of the fictional world. Ascertaining what make-believedly is true of himself is to a large extent a matter of introspection (or of whatever sort of "privileged access" one has to one's own beliefs and sensations). In fact, when Charles watches the horror movie, for example, introspection is involved in ascertaining not merely that make-believedly he is afraid of the slime, but also make-believe truths about the nature and progress of his fear. If it is make-believe that his fear is overwhelming, or that it is only momentary, this is so because his quasi-fear sensations are overwhelming or are only momentary. Make-believedly his fear grows more or less intense, or becomes almost unbearable, or finally subsides, and so on, as his quasi-fear feelings change in these ways. So it is by attention to the nature of his own actual experience that Charles is aware of make-believe truths about the nature of his fear. He follows the progress of his make-believe fear by introspection, much as one who is literally afraid follows the progress of his actual fear.

It would not be too far wrong to say that Charles actually experiences his make-believe fear. I don't mean that there is a special kind of fear, make-believe fear, that Charles experiences. What he actually experiences, his quasi-fear feelings, are not feelings of fear. But it is true *of them* that *make-believedly* they are feelings of fear. They generate *de re* make-believe truths about themselves and so belong to the fictional world just as Charles himself does. What Charles actually experiences is such that make-believedly it is (an experience of) fear.

Cases like that of Charles contrast strikingly with others in which an actual person belongs to a fictional world. Consider a performance of William Luce's play about Emily Dickinson, *The Belle of Amherst,* in which Julie Harris plays Emily Dickinson. Suppose that Emily Dickinson herself, with the help of a time machine or a fortuitous reincarnation, is in the audience. In order to discover make-believe truths about herself, including what make-believedly she thinks and feels, Dickinson must observe Julie Harris's actions, just as any spectator must. It is as though she is watching another person, despite the fact that that "person," the character, is herself. Dickinson has no special intimacy with make-believe truths about her own mental state.[14] The situation is basically the same if Dickinson should replace Julie Harris in the lead role and act the part herself. She still must judge from her external behavior, from what spectators could observe, whether or not it is make-believe that she is afraid or worried or whatever—and she might easily be mistaken about how she looks to spectators. It is still as though she considers herself "from the outside," from the perspective of another person.

This is clearly not true of Charles. It is not as though Charles were confronting another person, a fictional version of himself, but rather as though he himself actually fears the slime. (Nevertheless, he does not.) Make-believe facts about his fear, especially the fact that make-believedly it is his, are portrayed to Charles in an extraordinarily realistic manner. And make-believe facts about our pity for Willy, our dislike of Iago, and so forth, are similarly vivid to us. We and Charles feel ourselves to be part of fictional worlds, to be intimately involved with the slime, or Willy, or with whatever constituents of fictional worlds are, make-believedly, objects of our feelings and attitudes.

We see, now, how fictional worlds can seem to us almost as "real" as the real world is, even though we know perfectly well that they are not. We have begun to understand what happens when we get emotionally "involved" in a novel or play or film, when we are "caught up in the story."

The theory I have presented is designed to capture intuitions lying behind the traditional ideas that the normal or desired attitude toward fiction involves a *"suspension of disbelief"* or a *"decrease of distance."* These phrases are unfortunate. They strongly suggest that people do not (completely) disbelieve what they read in novels and see on the stage or screen; that, for example, we somehow accept it as fact that a boy named "Huckleberry Finn" floated down the Mississippi River—at least while we are engrossed in the novel. The normal reader does not accept this as fact, nor should he. Our disbelief is "suspended" only in the sense that it is, in some ways, set aside or ignored. We don't believe that there was a Huck Finn, but what interests us is the fact that *make-believedly* there was one, and that make-believedly he floated down the Mississippi and did various other things. But this hardly accounts for the sense of "decreased distance" between us and fictions. It still has us peering down on fictional worlds from reality above, however fascinated we might be, for some mysterious reason, by what we see.

On my theory we accomplish the "decrease of distance" not by promoting fictions to our level but by descending to theirs. (More accurately, we *extend* ourselves to their level, since we do not stop actually existing when it becomes fictional that we exist.) *Make-believedly* we do believe, we know, that Huck Finn floated down the Mississippi. And make-believedly we have various feelings and attitudes about him and his adventures. Rather than somehow fooling ourselves into thinking fictions are real, we become fictional. So we end up "on the same level" with fictions. And our presence there is accomplished in the extraordinarily realistic manner that I described. This enables us to comprehend our sense of closeness to fictions, without attributing to ourselves patently false beliefs.

We are now in a position to expect progress on the fundamental question of why and how fiction is important. Why don't we dismiss novels, plays, and films as "mere fiction" and hence as unworthy of serious attention?

Much has been said about the value and importance of dreams, fantasy, and children's games of make-believe.[15] It has been suggested, variously, that such activities serve to clarify one's feelings, help one to work out conflicts, provide an outlet for the expression of repressed or socially unacceptable feelings, and prepare one emotionally for possible future crises by providing "practice" in facing imaginary crises. It is natural to presume that our experience of representational works of art is valuable for similar reasons. But this presumption is not very plausible, I think, unless something like the theory I have presented is correct.

It is my impression that people are usually, perhaps always, characters in their own dreams and daydreams. We dream and fantasize about ourselves. Sometimes one's role in one's dream-world or fantasy-world is limited to that of observing other goings-on. But to have even this role *is* to belong to the fictional world. (We must distinguish between being, in one's dream, an observer of certain events and merely "observing," having, a dream about those events.) Similarly, children are nearly always characters in their games of make-believe. To play dolls or school, hobby horses or mud pies, is to be an actor portraying oneself.

I suggest that much of the value of dreaming, fantasizing, and making-believe depends crucially on one's thinking of oneself as belonging to a fictional world. It is chiefly by fictionally facing certain situations, engaging in certain activities, and having or expressing certain feelings, I think, that a dreamer, fantasizer, or game player comes to terms with his actual feelings—that he discovers them, learns to accept them, purges himself of them, or whatever exactly it is that he does.

If I am right about this, people can be expected to derive similar benefits from novels, plays, and films only if it is fictional that they themselves exist and participate (if only as observers) in the events portrayed in the works, that is, only if my theory is on the right track.

I find encouragement for these speculations in the deliberate use of role-playing in educational simulation games, and as a therapeutic technique in certain kinds of psychotherapy (e.g., Gestalt therapy). A therapist may ask his patient to pretend that his mother is present, or that some inanimate object is his mother, and to "talk to her." He may then be asked to "be" the mother and to say how he feels (when he "is" the mother), how he acts, what he looks like, and so on. I will not venture an explanation of how such therapeutic techniques are effective, nor of why simulation games work. But whatever explanation is appropriate will, I suspect, go a long way toward explaining why we are as interested in works of fiction as we are and clarifying what we get from them. The important place that novels, plays, and films have in our lives appears mysterious only on the supposition that we merely stand outside fictional worlds and look in, pressing our noses against an inviolable barrier. Once our presence within fictional worlds is recognized, suitable explanations seem within reach.

VII

A more immediate benefit of my theory is its capacity to handle puzzles. I conclude with the resolution of two more. First, consider a playgoer who finds happy endings asinine or dull, and hopes that the play he is watching will end tragically. He "wants the heroine to suffer a cruel fate," for only if she does, he thinks, will the play be worth watching. But at the same time he is caught up in the story and "sympathizes with the heroine"; he "wants her to escape." It is obvious that these two apparent desires may perfectly well coexist. Are we to say that the spectator is *torn* between opposite interests, that he wants the heroine to survive and also wants her not to? This does not ring true. Both of the playgoer's "conflicting desires" may be wholehearted. He may hope unreservedly that the work will end with disaster for the heroine, and he may, with equal singlemindedness, "want her to escape such an undeserved fate." Moreover, he may be entirely aware of both "desires," and yet feel no particular conflict between them.

My theory provides a neat explanation. It is merely make-believe that the spectator sympathizes with the heroine and wants her to escape. And he (really) wants it to be make-believe that she suffers a cruel end. He does not have conflicting desires. Nor, for that matter, is it make-believe that he does.

The second puzzle concerns why it is that works last as well as they do, how they can survive multiple readings or viewings without losing their effectiveness.[16]

Suspense of one kind or another is an important ingredient in our experience of most works: Will Jack, of "Jack and the Beanstalk," succeed in ripping off the giant without being caught? Will Tom and Becky find their way out of the cave? Will Hamlet ever get around to avenging the murder of his father? What is in store for Julius Caesar on the Ides of March? Will Godot come?

But how can there be suspense if we already know how things will turn out? Why, for example, should Tom and Becky's plight concern or even interest a reader who knows, from reading the novel previously, that eventually they will escape from the cave? One might have supposed that, once we have experienced a work often enough to learn thoroughly the relevant features of the plot, it would lose its capacity to create suspense, and that future readings or viewings of it would lack the excitement of the first one. But this frequently is not what happens. *Some* works, to be sure, fade quickly from exposure, and familiarity does alter our experience in certain ways. But the power of many works is remarkably permanent, and the nature of their effectiveness remarkably consistent. In particular, suspense may remain a crucial element in our response to a work almost no matter how familiar we are with it. One may "worry" just as intensely about Tom and Becky while rereading *The Adventures of Tom Sawyer*, despite one's knowledge of the outcome, as would a person reading it for the first time. A child listening to "Jack and the Beanstalk" for the umpteenth time, long after she has memorized it word for word, may feel much the same excitement when the giant discovers Jack and goes after him, the same gripping suspense that she felt when she first heard the story. Children, far from being bored by familiar stories, often beg to hear the same ones over and over again.

None of this is surprising on my theory. The child hearing "Jack and the Beanstalk" knows that make-believedly Jack will escape, but make-believedly she does *not* know that he will—until the reading of the passage describing his escape. She is engaged in her own game of make-believe during the reading, a game in which make-believedly she learns for the first time about Jack and the giant as she hears about them.[17] It is her make-believe uncertainty (the fact that make-believedly she is uncertain), not any actual uncertainty, that is responsible for the excitement and suspense that she feels. The point of hearing the story is not, or not merely, to learn about Jack's confrontation with the giant, but to play a game of make-believe. One cannot learn, each time one hears the story, what make-believedly Jack and the giant do unless one always forgets in between times. But one can and does participate each time in a game of make-believe. The point of hearing "Jack and the Beanstalk" is to have the experience of being such that, *make-believedly,* one realizes with trepidation the danger Jack faces, waits breathlessly to see whether the giant will awake, feels sudden terror when he does awake, and finally learns with admiration and relief how Jack chops down the beanstalk, killing the giant.

Why play the same game over and over? In the first place, the game may not be exactly the same each time, even if the readings are the same. On one occasion it may be make-believe that the child is paralyzed by fear for Jack, overwhelmed by the gravity of the situation, and emotionally drained when Jack finally bests the giant. On another occasion it may be make-believe that the child is not very seriously concerned about Jack's safety and that her dominant feelings are admiration for Jack's exploits, the thrill of adventure, and a sense of exhilaration at the final outcome. But even if the game is much the same from reading to reading, one's emotional needs may require the therapy of several or many repetitions.

Notes

1. I examine this barrier in a companion piece to the present paper, "How Remote Are Fictional Worlds from the Real World?," *Journal of Aesthetics and Art Criticism* 37, no. 1 (1978): 11–23.

2. By "fear" I mean fear for oneself. Obviously a person can be afraid for someone else without believing that he himself is in danger. One must believe that the person for whom one fears is in danger.

3. Charles *might* scream *deliberately*. But insofar as he does, it is probably clear that he is only pretending to take the slime seriously. (See section V.)

4. Charles's responses are *caused* partly by a belief, though not the belief that he is in danger. (See section IV.) This belief is not a *reason* for responding as he does, and it doesn't make it "reasonable," in the relevant sense, to respond in those ways.

5. A "fictional truth" is the fact that a certain proposition is fictional.

6. I have developed the notion of make-believe truths and other ideas presented in this section more fully elsewhere, especially in "Pictures and Make-Believe," *Philosophical Review* 81, no. 3 (1973): 283–319. Compare also "Are Representations Symbols?," *The Monist* 58, no. 2 (1974): 236–54. I should indicate that, in my view, there are no propositions "about" mere fictions, and hence none that are make-believe. It is make-believe not that Gulliver visited Lilliput, but that a man named "Gulliver" visited a place called "Lilliput." I shall occasionally ignore this point in the interest of simplicity, for example, when I write in section V as though the same slime resides in two different fictional worlds. Compare Walton, "How Remote Are Fictional Worlds?," note 22.

7. It is arguable that the purely physiological aspects of quasi-fear, such as the increase of adrenalin in the blood, which Charles could ascertain only by clinical tests, are not part of what makes it make-believe that he is afraid. Thus one might want to understand "quasi-fear" as referring only to the more psychological aspects of Charles's condition: the feelings or sensations that go with increased adrenalin, faster pulse rate, muscular tension, etc.

8. One can't help wondering why Charles's realization that make-believedly he is in danger produces quasi-fear in him, why it brings about a state similar to real fear, even though he knows he is not really in danger. This question is important, but we need not speculate about it here. For now we need only note that Charles's belief does result in quasi-fear, however this fact is to be explained.

9. This, I think, is at least approximately right. It is perhaps equally plausible, however, to say that the fact that Charles *believes* his quasi-fear to be caused by his realization that the slime endangers him is what makes it make-believe that his state is one of fear of the slime. There is no need to choose now between my suggestion and this variant.

10. Observers might, at the same time, understand his behavior alone to be responsible for his make-believe fear. The child and the observers might recognize somewhat different principles of make-believe.

11. These grounds are not conclusive. But the question of whether Charles accepts this principle is especially tricky, and there is reason to doubt that it can be settled conclusively. One would have to determine whether it is Charles's understanding that, if he were to have the quasi-fear sensations, etc., without realizing that he does and hence without imagining that he is afraid, it would still be fictional that he is afraid. If so, the fictional truth depends not on his imagining but on his quasi-fear, etc. It is hard to decide whether this is Charles's understanding, mainly because it is hard to conceive of his being ignorant of his quasi-fear sensations, etc. But insofar as I can get a grip on the question I think that the answer is affirmative.

12. One important difference between dolls and the screen images is that the dolls generate *de re* make-believe truths about themselves and the images do not. The doll is such that make-believedly *it* is a baby that is being dressed for a trip to town. But a screen image is not such that make-believedly it (the image itself) is a green slime.

13. Assuming of course that the person realizes that he is dealing with a work of fiction. Even so, arguments are needed to show that such statements are not literally true, and I shall not provide them here. But it is plausible that pity, worry about, hate, and envy are such that one cannot have them without believing that their objects exist, just as one cannot fear something without believing that it threatens one. Yet even if one can, and does, envy a character, for example, it may *also* be make-believe that one does so, and this make-believe truth may be generated by facts of the sort my theory indicates.

14. I have in mind those make-believe truths about her mental state which are generated by what happens on stage. Dickinson is not only a character in the play, but also a spectator. In the latter capacity she is like Charles; her actual mental state generates make-believe truths about herself. Dickinson is in a curiously ambiguous position. But it is not an uncommon one; people frequently have dreams in which they watch themselves ("from the outside") doing things.

15. A good source concerning make-believe games is Jerome L. Singer, *The Child's World of Make-Believe* (Academic Press, 1973).

16. David Lewis pointed out to me the relevance of my theory to this puzzle.

17. It is probably make-believe that someone (the narrator), whose word the child can trust, is giving her a serious report about a confrontation between a boy named "Jack" and a giant. Compare my "Points of View in Narrative and Depictive Representation," *Noûs* 10, no. 1 (1976): 49–61.

Chapter 14

THE PARADOX OF HORROR

Berys Gaut

> After a useful summary of other theories of pleasurable fear, Gaut offers his own contribution in this short piece: There is no actual paradox to horror, he maintains, because we can enjoy being afraid or disgusted under certain controlled conditions.

"IT SEEMS AN UNACCOUNTABLE PLEASURE, which the spectators of a well-written tragedy receive from sorrow, terror, anxiety, and other passions, that are in themselves disagreeable and uneasy."[1] Thus did Hume open his classic discussion of the paradox of tragedy, and it can properly serve as a statement of the kernel of the puzzle found in the closely related paradox of horror. We can approach this paradox by reflecting on the following statements, all of which seem to be true. (1) Some of us enjoy horror fictions. (2) Horror fictions characteristically produce fear and disgust in their audience. (3) Fear and disgust are intrinsically unpleasant emotions. The most straightforward explanation of these facts seems to be that we enjoy the fear and disgust the fictions produce in us. But to assert this yields the apparently paradoxical view that we enjoy intrinsically unpleasant emotions. So the paradox of horror rests on what might be termed the paradox of the enjoyment of negative emotions. However, there is another explanation of the phenomena available: We are enjoying not negative emotions, but rather some other feature of the situation, such as the curiosity we feel about what is going to happen. This is, roughly, the solution to the paradox that Noël Carroll defends in a recent book.[2] I will criticize this solution, as well as an expressivist solution. I then examine several recent claims that there is nothing paradoxical about our enjoyment of negative emotions and will show that a variation of this view can be defended against apparently decisive objections. Thus, it transpires that we can enjoy fear and disgust, so there is nothing paradoxical about our enjoyment of negative emotions, nor about our enjoyment of horror fictions.

I

Carroll provides a cognitivist solution to the paradox of horror. Drawing on the work of the anthropologist Mary Douglas, he argues that monsters, such as werewolves or a man with a fly's head, are violations of our categorial schemes. Douglas argues that such violations are seen as threatening and impure, and this is Carroll's explanation of why works of horror generate fear and disgust. But because monsters are categorial violations, being physically impossible according to our conceptual scheme, we are also curious about them and find them fascinating. This curiosity is heightened in the case of novels and films by the process of narration, which entices us to wonder whether the monster exists and what it looks like, involves us in the question of whether the characters in the fiction will come to believe in its existence and can destroy it, and so on. Hence our enjoyment of horror arises from its exploitation and satisfaction of our curiosity about monsters and the narrational process of their discovery, monsters being peculiarly suited to elicit our interest because of their status as categorial violations. But this status also explains why monsters produce fear and disgust in us. So we cannot have the enjoyment without the negative emotions: "The disgust that such beings [monsters] evince might be seen as part of the price to be paid for the pleasure of their disclosure" (184). Moreover, because we know that the monsters are only fictional, the fear and disgust they arose in us are muted in comparison with what they would be if we were to meet such monsters in real life, which allows the pleasures of curiosity more easily to outweigh the displeasures of fear and disgust.

Though Carroll demonstrates considerable skill in defending his solution, it is, I believe, unsatisfactory. He view depends crucially on claims about monsters, defined as beings not believed to exist now according to contemporary science (27). Yet not all horror fictions involve monsters: An important and popular subgenre of the modern horror film is the "slasher" movie, which deals with psychopathic serial killers.[3] Psychopaths are not monsters; they are instances of an all-too-real phenomenon. Carroll's response to this sort of objection is that some of these psychopaths are presented as having supernatural powers, and so are really monsters (37); if the characters are human, but are akin to monsters, then fictions involving them are borderline cases of horror (39); and otherwise we should regard the fictions as tales of terror (15). But to take the latter course is simply to transform the paradox of horror into a paradox of terror, where the solution involving appeal to monsters cannot work. On the other hand, to treat certain clearly human psychopaths as akin to monsters depends on a metaphorical extension of the term "monster," and to talk of psychopaths as categorial violations extends the notion of a categorial violation to the point where what begins simply with unexpected or unusual traits will be counted as categorial violations: Yet we clearly need not feel disgust at the unusual. Moreover, to hold a position from which it follows that films such as Demme's *The Silence of the Lambs* (1991) are borderline cases of horror marginalizes what look like paradigm examples of the modern horror film. Carroll's appeal to monsters disguises the simple point that we can be disgusted by and afraid of human beings because they do evil and awful things, and no mention of monsters or of categorical violations is needed to explain our reactions.

It might be thought that Carroll should drop his talk of monsters and his definition of horror in terms of them, and simply appeal to our curiosity about the extraordinary characters in horror fictions as overcoming the fear and disgust they produce in us. He is doubtless correct in holding that such fear and disgust are less intense than they would be if we thought these beings were real, but, even so, as his many examples and common observation show, we can feel great fear and disgust during horror films. The problem with Carroll's solution is that most horror films are so formulaic in their plots, and their monsters and killers so stereotypical, that it is difficult to believe that our curiosity could very often be sufficiently stimulated to overcome the purported disadvantages such works incur in producing disagreeable emotional states in us. The conventions of genre weigh too heavily on most horror fictions for Carroll's solution to be a plausible one.

Finally, and most simply, consider Norman, a disappointed spectator who comes out of a horror film and complains that it wasn't scary enough. He wanted to be really frightened, but the film hardly raised a mild tremor of apprehension in him. On Carroll's view Norman must really be complaining that his curiosity wasn't heightened enough. But that is not what he says, and indeed, he might say the film was quite interesting. The problem was, he avers, that it wasn't *frightening*. We are back to the core of the paradox of horror again: People seem to enjoy experiencing negative emotions.

II

It is worth briefly exploring an expressivist solution to the paradox. This holds that we do not enjoy the negative emotions that horror engenders, but, rather, we enjoy the expression of these emotions, by which we relieve ourselves of them, or lighten the grip they have on us.[4] Collingwood usefully distinguishes two versions of expressivism: The simpler holds that the process is akin to unburdening oneself of emotions by engaging in acts of make-believe (for instance, getting rid of one's anger by imagining kicking someone); the more sophisticated overlaps with the cognitivist view, holding that one lightens one's emotion by coming to understand what was before an unknown perturbation.[5]

Carroll rejects expressivist solutions for horror, claiming that we cannot gain satisfaction from the expression of our fear of monsters, for there are none, so we have no antecedently felt fear of them (246). However, this objection is too swift, for it fails to recognize that monsters can serve as metaphors for our fears. Interpretations of horror fictions as expressing convert sexual fears, or fear of death and the physicality of the body, or loss of sexual identity, are legion, and are, in many cases, quite plausible. Carroll does acknowledge that the horror film cycle correlates quite well with periods of social tension (e.g., the 1930s cycle with the Great Depression), but he objects that horror had its *aficionados* even at times when there were no social anxieties, and that mere expression of social anxieties is not appealing, for otherwise public lecturers on these topics would have mass appeal. Hence expressivism cannot provide a general solution to the problem of horror (206–14, 248). But this reply, too, succumbs to the objection that horror can express perennial personal anxieties, as well as social ones, and do so in a powerfully metaphorical form.

However, I believe that Carroll is correct in rejecting the expressivist position, for, even as adumbrated earlier, it suffers from severe shortcomings. If we are attracted to horror for its cathartic effect, so that watching a horror film is the equivalent of "talking out" one's fears, it is odd that these films are least attractive if one is in an uneasy or fearful mood. One doesn't say "I'm scared, so I think I'll go to see a horror film." Rather, one needs to be in a fairly robust psychological state in order to enjoy these fictions at all. Further, these films not infrequently leave (and are designed to leave) a lingering sense of fearfulness in their audience: One may feel scared as one walks home, and uneasy going to sleep. This is precisely the opposite effect one would expect if one's fear had been "lightened." Instead, these fears have been induced and exacerbated, and then one is frequently left in a state of disquiet. Even if one has been given metaphors for the objects of one's fears, this has not resulted in a lightening of one's emotions, but rather provides new materials with which to produce these emotions at will. Finally, if the expressivist doctrine were correct, we should expect to dislike the arousal of our emotion of fear when watching a film, and then only start to enjoy ourselves when the emotion was dissipated at the end of the film, assuming that it has an end that did not further enhance our fear. But horror audiences can enjoy themselves throughout the film, and hence they cannot enjoy merely the "lightening" of the emotion.

III

It would be a Herculean task to examine the many possible variations of cognitivist and expressivist accounts of the paradox of horror. But I have shown that some simple versions of both are incorrect. However, the motivation to think that some version of these theories must be correct is presumably that otherwise we are left with the apparent paradox that audiences are enjoying the negative emotions of fear and disgust. If we can show that this is not paradoxical, then cognitivist and expressivist theories will be less compelling. Instead, we can endorse the enjoyment theory: Horror attracts because people can enjoy being scared and disgusted. This thesis has the merit of simplicity, and it accounts for the intelligibility of Norman's complaint. It can also explain a salient fact about horror, of which it is easy to lose sight. The genre has as its self-conscious aim the production of fear and disgust in its audience, and it has become increasingly sophisticated and successful in achieving this effect. Moreover, the majority of horror works lack any serious artistic worth. They are pure entertainment: They aim simply at providing their audiences with enjoyable experiences. Taking these points together, the simplest, most straightforward explanation of the phenomenon of horror is that sometimes people enjoy being scared.

Consider Suzy, a mountaineering enthusiast. She enjoys putting herself into dangerous situations, feeling the thrill of fear as she dangles over the edge, knowing that it is only her skill and equipment that save her from certain death. She finds life simpler, more elemental in such situations; her fear gives an acuteness and "edge" to her experience that is lacking in everyday life. She appreciates many aspects of the experience, and her fear is an inextricable part of the composite whole that she enjoys. Her motivations are not the stuff of psychopathology, still less are they unintelligible: The existence of many activities from skydiving to motor racing testifies to the enduring attractions of danger. On a humbler level, even the pleasures of riding roller coasters depend partly on the fear one feels as the car careens around the bend, and one is not entirely convinced that it will stay on the tracks.

Nor are such phenomena confined to fear alone. One can also enjoy other "negative" emotions. One can enjoy disgusting stories, and there is a minor genre, popular on college campuses, of "disgust" movies, preeminent among which is John Waters's *Pink Flamingos* (1972). The negative emotion of anger can also be enjoyed: Irascible individuals sometimes seek out situations in which they will have an opportunity to get angry. Likewise, it is possible to relish a feeling of quiet melancholy, dwelling on the sorrows and disappointments of life, and weeping for the sadness of the world.

Phenomena of this sort have been noted by several philosophers in the last decade, and have been seen as key ingredients in the solution of the paradoxes.[6] It would be tempting simply to cite such cases without explanation of how they are possible, and think that this would decisively show that one can enjoy negative emotions, and so dissolve the paradox of horror. But to do so merely opens one to the objection that they are not really possible at all, for they would involve the enjoyment of intrinsically unpleasant emotions. Hence, the objection continues, such cases are misdescribed, and what is enjoyed in them is something other than the presence of a negative emotion. For instance, Susan Feagin in her critique of Carroll's solution to the paradox discusses several examples, including the rollercoaster case, of the enjoyment of negative emotions and their associated sensations.[7] Carroll's response is that she simply ignores the paradoxicality of negative emotions, and what he enjoys about roller coasting is not the queasiness, but the "novel way of moving through space" and the "overall thrill" of the ride.[8] This redescription strategy will be attractive only as long as we are unable to explain away the apparent paradoxicality of the enjoyment of these emotions.

Two kinds of theories have been advanced to explain how the enjoyment of negative emotions is possible, but neither is entirely satisfactory as it stands. The first is the "control thesis," developed by Marcia Eaton, and refined by John Morreall, on whose version I shall focus.[9] Morreall holds that one can enjoy negative emotions when one is "in control" of the situation that produces the emotions, where control is understood in terms of an ability to direct one's thoughts and actions. So Suzy can enjoy her mountaineering escapades because she knows that she is skillful enough to avoid coming to harm. It is peculiarly easy to enjoy negative emotions in the case of fiction, since the fiction has no practical consequences for its audience. In this case it is sufficient in order to be in control that one be able to direct one's attention and thoughts. However, if one loses this control, perhaps because the fiction depicts violence and suffering so graphically that one's negative emotions become too strong, then one will not enjoy the emotions.[10] Thus there is a ready explanation for how one can enjoy negative emotions, both in fiction and in real life.

This solution is ingenious, but inadequate. The paradox of negative emotions arises because, apparently, we are able to enjoy intrinsically unpleasant emotions. But the control thesis leaves it utterly mysterious how the mere fact that I can choose to attend or not to an otherwise unpleasant emotion, such as fear, could render that emotion pleasant. Further, the believer in the intrinsicality claim will hold that it is a necessary, conceptual condition on an emotion being fear that it is experienced as unpleasant, so that the psychic mechanism of hedonic transformation, to which the control theorist gestures, is a conceptual impossibility. There is thus a lacuna in the control theory, which owes us an account of how the apparent conceptual connection between fear and displeasure can be explained away, or how the connection can be construed so that it does not undermine the theory. But, in any case, the theory's linkage of the enjoyment of such emotions with the control of them seems straightforwardly false. People vary greatly and unpredictably as to whether or not they enjoy horror films. If Morag does not enjoy them, that need not be because she cannot adequately control her attention with respect to them. Rather, her reason for not enjoying the film is that when she does direct her attention to the bloody corpse, she does not like what she experiences. Conversely, Norman may believe that the very height of enjoyable fear is when his gaze is riveted to the gruesome spectacle, when he "cannot take his eyes off" the unfolding carnage. For, after all, if one is enjoying something, then one's attention tends to be drawn irresistibly to it.

IV

The second, more promising view of how it is possible to enjoy negative emotions has been developed by both Kendall Walton and Alex Neill. They deny that these emotional responses are intrinsically unpleasant. They both speak as if it is a purely contingent matter whether or not people enjoy the emotions themselves. It is not the emotions themselves that are intrinsically unpleasant, they hold, but, rather, it is the *objects* of the emotions that are unpleasant or disvaluable. Walton argues that Hume was wrong to think that sorrow is in itself disagreeable. Rather: "What is clearly disagreeable, what we regret, are the things we are sorrowful *about*—the loss of an opportunity, the death of a friend—not the feeling or experience of sorrow itself."[11] Neill, in a critique of Carroll's theory, similarly points out that the emotions of pity or fear aren't painful in the way that stepping on a thumbtack is. Instead, he says, "In describing an emotion as 'painful' or 'negative' or 'unpleasant,' I suggest, we are in fact saying something about the situations in response to which we typically experience those emotions. That is, it's the situations rather than the emotions which are distasteful or undesirable, which we (metaphorically?) describe as painful or unpleasant."[12]

However, this view encounters two serious objections as thus formulated. First, the defender of the claim that negative emotions are intrinsically unpleasant will properly protest that it can't be a purely contingent matter that these emotions are felt as unpleasant. For imagine we came across a tribe who said that they felt a certain emotion at the death of their loved ones, and that this emotion was the most enjoyable one to be had. We would, I take it, be justifiably reluctant to translate the word they used to name this emotion as "grief." This suggests that there is a conceptual constraint on negative emotions being felt as unpleasant. Second, both Walton and Neill have a problem insofar as they appeal to a contrast between the unpleasantness of the emotion and the unpleasantness of the object of the emotion. For to say that something is unpleasant is to attribute to that thing a dispositional property, namely, the property of producing unpleasant experiences in people, and the salient experiences in the cases under discussion are those of sorrow and fear. Neill tries to counter his objection in a footnote by claiming that the unpleasantness may be in the situation itself rather than in the feelings I have toward the object. He gives the example of pity, which is an emotion directed toward others' suffering. So the painfulness figures here as something that the people whom I pity suffer, rather than as something that I experience.[13] As he admits, the suggestion needs further work, but it does not seem promising. For it is not sufficient for me to pity others that I think are suffering: The sadist may believe the latter without feeling any pity at all for them. If we have to appeal to unpleasantness here, it must be an unpleasantness that I also feel.

There is a more promising way to meet this second objection. Neill explicitly disavows a hedonistic theory of value,[14] and in the passage that I quoted, he says that the situations toward which negative emotions are directed are distasteful *or undesirable*. Walton would doubtless take this position as well, and both he and Neill endorse versions of the evaluative theory of the emotions, to be discussed in the next section. I suggest, then, that we drop talk of the pleasant and unpleasant here and speak purely in general evaluative terms. This move would allow us to counter the objection I raised about the dispositionality of the unpleasant. Hence we could allow that when people are enjoying negative emotions, it is not because they regard the objects of the emotions as unpleasant, even though they enjoy the emotions, but because they regard the objects of the emotions as undesirable, and to believe that something is undesirable is not *ipso facto* to find it unpleasant. However, it will be replied, to drop the reference to pleasure, and merely to speak of the objects of the emotions as disvaluable, seems to make the first objection I considered even more devastating, for now the contingency of the link between the negativity of emotions and their unpleasantness is even more salient. But I will argue that one can meet this objection in a way that neither Walton nor Neill considers, by showing that there are conceptual connections between evaluations, desire, and pleasure, but that these noncontingent links are of a sort that do not threaten the solution to the paradoxes defended here.

V

Hume was puzzled by how it is that the spectators of a tragedy can enjoy sorrow, terror, and anxiety, since he held that such emotions essentially involve feelings of pain.[15] As Walton notes, we can dissolve the paradox by disputing Hume's analysis of the emotions. In fact, as I will now argue, the correct view of the emotions *entails* that negative emotions are such, not in respect of unpleasant feelings, nor even in respect of the unpleasantness of their objects, but, rather, in respect of the negative evaluative thoughts they incorporate.

Hume's theory is an instance of the "traditional" view of the emotions as phenomenologically characterized feelings. The dominant modern theory of the emotions, however, holds that emotions are cognitive, essentially incorporating evaluations.[16] Thus to fear something involves evaluating it as threatening, to be angry with someone involves evaluating her actions as wrong, to be sorrowful involves thinking that a loss has been suffered, and so on. What other factors must be present for an emotion to exist is a matter of dispute, but plausibly they include the requirement that the subject be in an abnormal physiological state caused by the evaluation. However, one emotion is to be individuated from another in terms of the evaluations involved, rather than by the particular features of the physiological state or of the associated bodily sensations, for there is no pattern of physiological changes or set of sensations peculiar to each emotion, and an emotion may be associated with different sensations in different people.[17] Now, if the emotions are to be individuated by the evaluations, then the difference between "positive" and "negative" emotions must consist in the difference between the evaluative thoughts. But there is no phenomenal character to a thought *per se*. So the difference between positive and negative emotions can only consist in the fact that the *evaluations* incorporated into the former are positive and those in the latter are negative. That is, what makes negative emotions negative is not the painfulness of either the emotional response or the object. Rather, it consists in the fact that objects to which these emotions are directed are brought under negative evaluative concepts: the dangerous, the wrongful, the shameful, and so on. Since we can disvalue something without finding it unpleasant, it follows that it is possible to find both negative emotional responses *and* their objects pleasant. Hence, by appeal to an evaluative theory of the emotions, we can show that there is nothing paradoxical about the enjoyment of negative emotions, for it is only required that one *disvalue* the *objects* of these emotions. Hence one can dissolve the paradoxes of horror and tragedy.

There is a certain irony in this solution, since Carroll is fully aware of the evaluative theory of the emotions. Indeed, his account of the emotions is based on the version of the evaluative theory due to William Lyons, which I have drawn upon in the preceding paragraph, and he elaborates his definition of the emotion of art-horror so as to conform to an evaluative analysis of the emotions (24–27). But he does not see in his book that the "abnormal, physically felt agitation" (27), which he requires for fear to be present, need not be an intrinsically unpleasant state, for the negativity of the emotion can be explained in terms of the object of the emotion being negatively evaluated, rather than the emotion itself being unpleasant. Indeed, Carroll himself argues that what the agitation feels like can vary massively from person to person and from time to time in one person, so it is doubly puzzling why he assumes that the agitation must be experienced as unpleasant.

We now have to answer the objection that his solution allows it to be a contingent matter that we generally experience negative emotions as unpleasant. I am going to argue that the view of the emotions as evaluative does allow for the existence of a conceptual connection, but a conceptual connection of a sort that still allows it to dissolve the paradoxes. I will consider the connection in two stages: first, the conceptual link between evaluations and desire, and second, that between desire and pleasure.

Internalists about evaluation hold that there is a necessary connection between judging a situation to be good and having a motivating reason to bring it about (the reason need be only prima facie, and so may be overridden by other, conflicting reasons). This is so, because evaluations give us reasons for action: For someone to hold that an action is good, but that he has no reason to bring it about, shows that he has not grasped the meaning of the word "good." Further, people can be deceived about the contents of their beliefs, and if someone claims to believe that something is good, but it is apparent that he has no motivating reason to bring it about, that is defeasible evidence that he is mistaken about the content of his belief. Now internalism of this sort is too strong, for it is possible to be in a state of *anomie* or despair in which one can recognize that a course of action is a good one, yet not be motivated to pursue it. Further, it is at least conceivable that a moral pervert should be motivated by a course of action just because it is evil. But both sorts of cases are motivational deviations, which are specifiable as such only against a background of motivational normality. Hence a more modest internalism will claim that necessarily *typically*, if someone believes that something is good, then he will have a motivating reason to promote it.[18]

Second, there is a conceptual connection between having a motivating reason (a desire, in the broad sense in which philosophers use that term) and finding something pleasant. Hedonists try to capture this connection by claiming that the only thing desired for its own sake is pleasure. As many philosophers have argued, this is false, since I can, for instance, rationally choose to forego a life of pleasure if it is based on systematic deception.[19] But a more promising conceptual connection is captured by Mill's dictum that "to desire anything, except in proportion as the idea of it is pleasant, is a physical and metaphysical impossibility."[20] This is compatible with holding that we desire for their own sakes things other than pleasure, for instance, knowledge. For even if I desire knowledge for its own sake, I will find the idea of acquiring it pleasant. As J. C. Gosling has argued, Mill's dictum captures the characteristically human way of desiring things, one might say, passionately: If we really want something, we will be joyful at the prospect of achieving it, and downcast if we cannot obtain it.[21] This is supported by the fact that if one thinks that one desires something, yet feels no pleasure at the prospect of getting it, then that is strong, though defeasible, evidence that one does not desire it after all. So there is a conceptual connection between desire and pleasure. However, Mill, in holding that we always find the idea of the desired thing pleasant, makes the connection too strong, for one may, for instance, do one's duty without enjoyment. So we should adopt the same strategy as we used earlier and hold that necessarily *typically*, if someone desires something, then the idea of achieving it gives her pleasure.

Putting together these two conceptual connections, we have the conclusion that there is a conceptual connection between evaluation and pleasure: Necessarily, typically if someone positively evaluates a state of affairs, then she will feel pleasure at the idea of achieving it. Now, if the individual has the relevant knowledge about the state of affairs concerned—if the state of affairs is as her idea represents it to be—then the state of affairs will be pleasant. Conversely, necessarily typically, if someone negatively evaluates a state of affairs and she is relevantly informed about it, she will find that state of affairs unpleasant. So it follows that, given that the agent is adequately informed, the view of the emotions as evaluative does place conceptual constraints on whether it is typically possible to enjoy being in the situations that are the objects of the emotions. Further, since the pleasant is a dispositional property, if the object is unpleasant, the experience of it (including one's affective experience of it) is unpleasant. Hence, in the case of negative emotions, the view of the emotions as evaluative entails that informed agents will typically experience the objects of their emotions and the emotions themselves as unpleasant.

So the evaluative theory of the emotions is not susceptible to the counterexample based on the unintelligibility of the tribal people who feel sorrow, yet find the emotion pleasant. For, we can note that the emotion concerned is not typically unpleasant for them, and therefore is not sorrow. But have we not now reproduced the paradox of horror, by showing that one cannot feel fear, and hence evaluate something as threatening, without experiencing the emotion as unpleasant? However, this is not so, for it was crucial to the conceptual connections discussed earlier that they were of the form "necessarily *typically*." This being so, there is plenty of scope for the enjoyment of these emotions in atypical situations or by atypical people. This allows Suzy to enjoy her fear, and it allows the *aficionados* of horror to enjoy their fear and disgust. The latter are helped by the fact that they know the film is fictional and that neither they nor the actors depicted are in real danger. But these atypical cases are only possible against a background in which people do not enjoy these negative emotions. The background of typical unpleasant responses is necessary for these emotions to be negative.

This itself might seem a paradoxical result, but it is not. It is, in fact, a perfectly familiar result of holistic theories about the mental. The position I defend here does not assume, or entail, the truth of functionalism. But like functionalism, it is a holistic view, and functionalists similarly define mental states by means of a "typical" operator, in order to respect the holism of the mental. Functionalists seek to define mental concepts in terms of their functional role, and so hold, for instance, that pain is (roughly) that state which typically results from bodily damage, typically produces the desire to escape the source of the damage, and typically produces avoidance-behavior. As David Lewis has pointed out, this allows for cases where atypical people may not be motivated to avoid pain (or, we can add, may even enjoy it); but it is only pain that they can enjoy because of the background of normal aversive reactions to that state in the (human) community of which they are members.[22] So the full solution to the paradoxes depends both on a view of the emotions as evaluative and on the recognition of how mental holism presents itself in respect of emotions, desires, and enjoyment.

Hence, we can dissolve the paradox of horror. That paradox rests on the claim that the enjoyment of negative emotions, understood as intrinsically unpleasant emotions, is impossible. The paradox seems to arise only because we construe the negativity in terms of these emotions being intrinsically unpleasant, whereas we should really construe their negativity in terms of the fact that the emotions essentially incorporate negative evaluations. But this entails that typically people will find the objects of these emotions unpleasant and that the emotions themselves are typically unpleasant. Thus, it is wrong to hold that whether people enjoy these emotions or not is a merely contingent, nonconceptual matter. But because there is only a conceptual requirement that people *typically* don't enjoy them, that allows room for some individuals on some occasions to enjoy them. Moreover, this solution explains why it can seem so plausible to hold that these emotions are intrinsically unpleasant. For, while it is false that necessarily, if someone feels fear, she does not enjoy the experience, it *is* true that necessarily she or others of her community *typically* feel fear. It should be clear that this solution, being entirely general, also solves the paradox of tragedy.

Of course, why any particular individual enjoys feeling fear, and another doesn't, or why some horror films are enjoyable and others not, is an interesting and no doubt complex matter. But it is the proper subject of empirical, psychological investigation, and it would be unproductive to engage in armchair speculation about why this is so. What I have shown here is that this empirical investigation is possible. For I have argued that there is no a priori, conceptual problem about the enjoyment of negative emotions in real life, or in fiction. There is no paradox of horror.

Notes

I am grateful to John Haldane for his comments on this chapter (Berys Gaut note).

1. David Hume, "Of Tragedy," in *Essays: Moral, Political, and Literary*, ed. T. H. Green and T. H. Grose (Longmans, Green, 1907), 258.

2. Noël Carroll, *The Philosophy of Horror; or, Paradoxes of the Heart* (Routledge, 1990), esp. 178–95. Page references in the text are to this work. In chapter 1, he defends the view, recorded in section II of this chapter, that the horror genre produces not just fear but also disgust in its audience.

3. See Carol J. Clover, "Her Body, Himself: Gender in the Slasher Film," in *Fantasy and the Cinema*, ed. James Donald (BFI, 1989), for some evidence of how widespread such films are.

4. This is, of course, a common, though perhaps incorrect, way of interpreting Aristotle's doctrine of katharsis. For a welcome skepticism about the possibility of establishing precisely what Aristotle meant by this term, see K. Bennett, "The Purging of Catharsis," *British Journal of Aesthetics* 21 (1981): 204–13.

5. R. G. Collingwood, *The Principles of Art* (Oxford University Press, 1938), 109–11.

6. See the later references to Feagin, Eaton, Morreall, Walton, and Neill.

7. Susan L. Feagin, "Monsters, Disgust and Fascination," *Philosophical Studies* 65 (1992): 81.

8. Noël Carroll, "Disgust or Fascination: A Response to Susan Feagin," *Philosophical Studies* 65 (1992): 87–88.

9. Marcia Eaton, "A Strange Kind of Sadness," *Journal of Aesthetics and Art Criticism* 41 (1982): 51–64; John Morreall, "Enjoying Negative Emotions in Fictions," *Philosophy and Literature* 9 (1985): 95–102.

10. Morreall, "Enjoying Negative Emotions," 99, 101.

11. Kendall Walton, *Mimesis as Make-Believe: On the Foundations of the Representational Arts* (Havard University Press, 1990), 257.

12. Alex Neill, "On a Paradox of the Heart," *Philosophical Studies* 65 (1992): 62.

13. Neill, 65n15.

14. Neill, 61.

15. See Hume's discussion of the passions in *A Treatise of Human Nature,* book 2, ed. L. A. Selby-Bigge and P. H. Nidditch (Oxford University Press, 1978), esp. 438–48.

16. For an extremely useful overview of the modern debate, see Daniel Farrell, "Recent Work on the Emotions," *Analyse und Kritik* 10 (1988): 71–102.

17. See William Lyons, *Emotion* (Cambridge University Press, 1980), esp. chaps. 3, 7, and 8. Lyons also thinks that the concepts of some, though not all, emotions involve reference to desires. But the internalism I argue for later will show that the concepts of all emotions implicitly incorporate reference to desires that are typically possessed by those experiencing the emotion.

18. The argument of this paragraph is that of James Dreier, "Internalism and Speaker Relativism," *Ethics* 101 (1991): 9–14, though I have substituted "typically" for his "normally."

19. Robert Nozick, *Anarchy, State, and Utopia* (Basil Blackwell, 1974), 42–45.

20. J. S. Mill, *Utilitarianism,* ed. Mary Warnock (Fontana, 1962), 293. Mill, of course, endorses the dictum in the context of his defense of hedonism, but the dictum itself does not entail hedonism as formulated earlier.

21. J. C. Gosling, "Pleasure and Enjoyment," in *The Business of Reason,* ed. J. J. Macintosh and S. Coval (Routledge and Kegan Paul, 1969), 111–13.

22. David Lewis, "Mad Pain and Martian Pain," in *Readings in Philosophy of Psychology,* ed. Ned Block (Havard University Press, 1980), 1:216–22.

Chapter 15

FROM *THE PHILOSOPHY OF HORROR; OR, PARADOXES OF THE HEART*

Noël Carroll

> Noël Carroll's study of what he refers to as "art-horror" has been influential and is often cited. It is also our first example in this volume of what we might refer to as a *competition theory* of horror enjoyment. With a focus on monsters, Carroll argues that horror elicits fear and disgust; however, these negative emotions are in competition with our curiosity regarding how the story will turn out. If our curiosity prevails, we see the story through to the end; if our disgust wins out, we abandon the story.

On the Impact of Characteristic Horror Narratives

I begin by noting that many of the art forms that practice horror are narrative. Horror, it seems, flourishes most notably in narrative art forms. This is not to say that horror cannot exist in nonnarrative forms—such as nonnarrative painting—but only that when we think of horror what comes to mind paradigmatically are narratives as those are embodied in novels, short stories, plays, movies, radio shows, TV programs, and so on. Thus, it seems reasonable to hypothesize that a major source of pleasure with respect to the horror genre is related to narrative. Perhaps Stephen King would appear to subscribe to some such view when he writes in the preface to his collection of short stories *Night Shift* (1978) that "All my life as a writer, I have been committed to the idea that in fiction the story value holds dominance over every other facet of the writer's craft." But, in any case, narrative would seem to be crucial to most of the essential works of horror. Consequently, if horror narratives have some saliently recurring features, they may help to explain the appeal of the genre.

Looking at the field of plot structures recounted so far, one is struck by one theme that cuts across the majority of these examples. That theme is discovery. In the overreacher plot, the overreacher discovers some secret of the universe, often to the dismay of the rest of humanity. And, in most of the plot structures derived from the complex discovery story, the discovery of that which heretofore was denied existence is foregrounded.

Admittedly, these two plot families make different points about our relation to the unknown. The overreacher plot warns against wanting to know too much while many of the plots in the complex discovery family chide humanity for being too complacent about the unknown. One family of plots chastens the desire to know everything while the other is an attack on rigid, commonplace, myopic thinking—that is, one plot constellation says there are things better left unknown, while the other implies that to refuse to admit the existence of the hitherto unknown is a deep flaw. However, though the themes, here, at one level of analysis, appear incompatible, they nevertheless share a basic subject matter—viz., knowing the unknown—which subject matter serves to motivate not only Basic plot movements but also those interludes, beloved to the genre, which I have referred to as the play of ratiocination and the drama of proof.

Even in those plots that do not involve fully developed discovery and/or confirmation functions, in the vast majority of cases we nevertheless still tend to find some play of ratiocination. There is usually some conjecture about the nature and origin of the monster, if only to discuss the best way to destroy it. Plots comprising confrontation completely unalloyed with ratiocination about the nature of the monster are rare, as are completely unexplained onsets. This is not to say that there are no examples of such plots; but only that they are the exception rather than the rule. Moreover, the most frequently recurring horror plots, it seems to me, tend to involve either discovery, confirmation, or both, while plots lacking these functions nevertheless contain residues of these functions that abet some play of ratiocination. Often, this play of ratiocination concerns the nature or pertinent aspects of the monster in order to figure out how it is best opposed.[1]

Likewise, turning to the overreacher family, experiments or incantations without explanations and/or justifications, no matter how silly, are hard to come by, indicating again that some sort of imitation of reasoning, proof, and demonstration is generally important to the narrative engine that drives the horror story.

Undoubtedly there can be horror stories that simply stage the struggle between humanity and some monster. One would not refuse to categorize a story as horrific simply because it had no element of discovery or ratiocination. The conflict between humanity and the inhuman, or between the normal and the abnormal, is fundamental to horror. Nor is much theoretical advantage to be gained by saying that simple, unadorned conflicts between humanity and the inhuman are likely to be rather impoverished examples of the genre, though that may be empirically accurate. Nevertheless, admitting that there can be such horror stories should not preclude the insight that most horror stories, including the most distinguished ones, tend to be elaborated in such a way that the discovery of the unknown (voluntarily or otherwise), the play of ratiocination, and the drama of proof are sustaining sources of narrative pleasure in the horror genre.

There are, of course, crime stories that involve no discovery or ratiocination—that propose nothing more than extended fisticuffs and shoot-outs with bad guys. But this would not lead us to deny that being engaged in or caught up by the play of reasoning by the detective or private eye is not one of the major narratological calling cards of the crime genre. Similarly, though the drama of discovery may sometimes be absent in horror stories, it remains a central, characteristic source of pleasure in the genre.

Moreover, there is a certain fit between our findings about horror narration and about the nature of horror. The emotion of art-horror is generated in part by the apprehension of something that defies categorization in virtue of our standing or commonplace ways of conceptualizing the order of things. That this subject matter should be wedded to narrative structures that enact and expatiate upon the discovery of the unknown seems perfectly appropriate. The point of the horror genre, if the first part of this book is correct, is to exhibit, disclose, and manifest that which is, putatively in principle, unknown and unknowable. It can be no accident that the plots that are characteristically mobilized to motivate this moment of unavoidable recognition are concerned to show that, within the fiction, what is unknown is *known* or has become, as the plotting would have it, undeniable. Rendering the unknown known is, in fact, the point of such plots, as well as the source of their seductiveness.

That is, horror stories are predominantly concerned with knowledge as a theme. The two most frequent families of plot structures are those of the complex discovery cluster and the overreacher cluster. In one variant of the complex discovery example, the monster arrives, unbeknownst to anyone, and sets about its gruesome work. Gradually the protagonist, or a group of protagonists, discovers that a monster is responsible for all those unexplained deaths. However, when the protagonists approach the authorities with this information, the authorities dismiss the very possibility of the monster. The energies of the narrative are then devoted to *proving* the monster's existence. Such a plot celebrates the existence of things beyond the boundaries of common knowledge.

Plots in this family, concerned with discovery and confirmation, are concerned at the level of narrative with the process of disclosure and revelation—specifically the disclosure and revelation of that which is excluded from our standing conceptual categories. Given that the object of emotional focus in horror stories is that which is unknown, that many of the plot structures revolve around disclosure, revelation, discovery, and confirmation seems quite appropriate. That revelation should be accompanied by the play of ratiocination about the unknown and horrific monster also appears eminently natural, since the presentation of the unknown calls forth the desire to know more about it.

In a variation of the theme of the unknown, the overreacher plot proposes a central figure embarked on the pursuit of hidden, unholy, or forbidden knowledge. Once the scientist, alchemist, priest, or magus acts on this forbidden knowledge—for example, brings a golem to life—inestimable, maleficent power is released and the consequent destruction becomes the stuff of the story. Whereas the protagonists in the complex discovery family of plots generally must go beyond the bounds of common knowledge, overreachers are warned not to exceed them. But both major plot families characteristically take the compass of common knowledge as their basic donnée and explore it, albeit for different thematic effects. This, of course, fits very nicely with a theory that regards cognitive threat as a major factor in the generation of art-horror.

At the level of narrative effect, the introduction of processes of proof and discovery is a way of securing and holding the audience's attention. This is not to deny that, in the fiction, these discoveries are not celebrations of the exercise of pure thought, since these discoveries are usually connected to the question of the survival of the human race, an issue to be resolved or at least frequently alluded to in the confrontation movements of the subtending fabulae. Nevertheless, a great deal of the sustaining interest in horror stories concerns the discovery of the unknown. The majority of horror stories are, to a significant extent, representations of processes of discovery, as well as often occasions for hypothesis formation on the part of the audience, and, as such, these stories engage us in the drama of proof....

Thus, to a large extent, the horror story is driven explicitly by curiosity. It engages its audience by being involved in processes of disclosure, discovery, proof, explanation, hypothesis, and confirmation. Doubt, skepticism, and the fear that belief in the existence of the monster is a form of insanity are predictable foils to the revelation (to the audience or to the characters or both) of the existence of the monster.

Horror stories, in a significant number of cases, are dramas of proving the existence of the monster and disclosing (most often gradually) the origin, identity, purposes, and powers of the monster. Monsters, as well, are obviously a perfect vehicle for engendering this kind of curiosity and for supporting the drama of proof, because monsters are (physically, though generally not logically) impossible beings. They arouse interest and attention through being putatively inexplicable or highly unusual vis-à-vis our standing cultural categories, thereby instilling a desire to learn and to know about them. And since they are also outside of (justifiably) prevailing definitions of what is, they understandably prompt a need for proof (or the fiction of a proof) in the face of skepticism. Monsters are, then, natural subjects for curiosity, and they straightforwardly warrant the ratiocinative energies the plot lavishes upon them.

All narratives might be thought to involve the desire to know—the desire to know at least the outcome of the interaction of the forces made salient in the plot. However, the horror fiction is a special variation on this general narrative motivation, because it has at the center of it something which is given as in principle *unknowable*—something which, *ex hypothesi,* cannot, given the structure of our conceptual scheme, exist and that cannot have the properties it has. This is why, so often, the real drama in a horror story resides in establishing the existence of the monster and in disclosing its horrific properties. Once this is established, the monster, generally, has to be confronted, and the narrative is driven by the question of whether the creature can be destroyed. However, even at this point, the drama of ratiocination can continue as further discoveries—accompanied by arguments, explanations, and hypotheses—reveal features of the monster that will facilitate or impede the destruction of the creature.

Note

1. Sometimes elements of this "figuring out" are left up to the reader, as in Clive Barker's "Rawhead Rex," where we understand more about the significance of the stone Venus than the protagonist does (although he does do some on-the-spot ratiocination in the heart of confrontation).

Chapter 16

ENJOYING NEGATIVE EMOTIONS IN FICTIONS

John Morreall

> Like Gaut, Morreall maintains that we can enjoy fear under certain conditions. He relates fear to novelty, which is something from which we can derive satisfaction provided we are in control of the situation. He differentiates fear, which can be pleasurable, from both terror and anxiety, over which we have no control and, as a consequence, cannot enjoy.

THERE IS A PUZZLE GOING BACK to Aristotle and Augustine that has sometimes been called the "paradox of tragedy": How is it that nonmasochistic, nonsadistic people are able to enjoy watching or reading about fictional situations that are filled with suffering? The problem here actually extends beyond tragedy to our enjoyment of horror films and other fictional depictions of situations that we would not enjoy in real life. What is it about fiction that turns intensely unpleasant situations into situations we can enjoy?

Of the many solutions proposed to this puzzle, I shall mention just four. Aristotle held that in viewing tragedy we experience negative emotions—pity and fear—but get pleasure from the experience nonetheless because we are thereby purged of excess pity and fear. For Aristotle, too, there is a pleasure that tragedy shares with fiction in general, the delight we take in representations.[1] Hume put more weight on this latter delight. Our pleasure in tragedy, he said, is based on our appreciation of the skill with which the literary or other artist has depicted the unpleasant scenes.[2] Susan Feagin has recently located the pleasure we take in tragic art not in our direct responses to the work, which are "unpleasant experiences," she says, but in our meta-response of moral self-congratulation at these responses.[3] The fourth solution to our puzzle is really a dissolution: It consists of denying that we actually feel fear, pity, and other negative emotions in our experience of fiction. The guiding principle here is that in order to have some emotion toward a situation, we must believe that it is a real situation. This principle is articulated in an influential article by Kendall Walton, though he does not apply it to our puzzle.[4]

I believe that this last solution is no solution at all because we do in fact feel emotions in our appreciation of fiction (a point I will develop later). The other three solutions address the puzzle, and the pleasures they appeal to all have some explanatory power. But these solutions seem to me to overlook perhaps the most basic pleasure we take in tragedy, horror films, and the like—the direct pleasure of feeling fear, pity, and similar emotions.

The idea of enjoying negative emotions seems counterintuitive at first; indeed it may seem analytically false. But let us look more closely at those emotions to see what there might be to enjoy in them. Because the idea that we experience real emotions in response to fiction is controversial, we will begin not with fiction but with real life. After seeing how negative emotions can be enjoyed in real life, we can then consider their enjoyment in response to fiction.

Fear is perhaps the most basic negative emotion, and at first glance one of the least likely to be enjoyed. To feel fear, many have claimed, we have to judge that we are in danger, and danger is disturbing to us. And so it is natural that in fear there is the motivation to eliminate the danger, by fleeing, protecting ourselves, or attacking. Changes in the autonomic nervous system and the endocrine system equip us for just such actions. They produce an increase in alertness and muscle tension, a faster and stronger heartbeat, a redistribution of the blood from the skin and internal organs to the voluntary muscles and brain, and a release of stored sugar from the liver into the bloodstream. Now although we may not be able to identify all these changes when we are in a state of fear, we can feel many of them directly, and we certainly feel the overall excitement that they produce. It is this excitement, I think, that makes fear potentially enjoyable. Especially for someone who leads a relatively dull life, the stimulation provided by fear can be pleasurable by contrast with the ordinary lack of stimulation. Many people, indeed, go to considerable trouble to put themselves into dangerous situations, in part, at least, for the thrill of fear that the danger will provide. Consider mountain climbers and skydivers, for instance. Now there are many sources of pleasure in these sports—the scenery, pride in one's skills, the camaraderie, and so on. But a major part of the pleasure, the "rush," comes from activating the innate human fear of falling. Putting oneself in danger for the pleasure of it even has a name—"adventure"—and it is a powerful motivating force for many people, including soldiers, police officers, and criminals. The danger in an adventurous activity need not be the risk of losing one's life, of course. In gambling for high stakes, for example, it may be the risk of losing all one's savings. But even here the possible loss must be the kind of thing we can fear—which explains why there is no adventure in penny poker.

Having considered a few cases of enjoyable fear, then, let us look at what distinguishes them from the more common case in which fear is not enjoyed. First of all, as Hume pointed out in "Of Tragedy," the emotion must not be too strong. If a skydiver, say, pulls the rip cord and the main parachute fails to open, and then the reserve parachute also does not open, what may have been an exhilarating kind of fear will turn into an utterly unenjoyable terror. This need for fear to remain within certain limits applies also to other negative emotions, and it can be explained by appealing to a more general principle, that we can enjoy negative emotions only when we retain our overall control of our situation.[5]

Being in control in any situation is a function of our desires and of what we are doing in that situation. Control is usually easiest to maintain when we are merely attending to something that has no practical consequences for us, as when we watch from a distance some event unrelated to us. Here our control requires our ability to pay attention when we want, to stop paying attention when we want, and to direct our attention to those features of the event that interest us. When we have this ability to start, stop, and direct the experience, we can enjoy a wide range of experiences, even "unpleasant" ones. We may enjoy watching a car crash at a race. We can even enjoy mild pain, as when we probe a sore spot in our mouth with our tongue or stretch a sore muscle just for the sensation it produces.[6] Even with stronger pains, the kind we cannot actually enjoy, we are less disturbed by them to the extent that we have some kind of control over them, as when we have signals worked out with our dentist for when to start and stop drilling.

In activities like mountain climbing where we are doing more than just attending to something, our being in control will often involve special skills and so challenges, and pride in those skills is often added to the thrill of fear. The accomplished climber may enjoy climbing a particularly dangerous rock face all the more knowing that the average climber would not be in control in that situation, and so would not enjoy it.

Intense fear—terror—is not enjoyable because in such a state we lose control over our attention, our bodies, and our total situation. We can no longer even flee as we can in milder fear; instead we freeze in our tracks, are "petrified," or we go limp, perhaps even faint. Objectless fear, or general anxiety, is also not enjoyable because, not knowing its source, we feel unable to control it and our situation generally.

Let us now turn our attention from fear to other negative emotions that can be enjoyed. As representative examples we can consider anger, sadness, and pity. Anger is an emotion we have all taken pleasure in. When we are angry, some situation is upsetting us—an action of ours has been frustrated, perhaps harm has come to us or those we care about, or our rights and concerns have not been respected. If we are the kind of persons who picture ourselves as unappreciated, long-suffering heroes or heroines, the mere contemplation of whatever is upsetting us will give us a certain satisfaction by reinforcing our self-image as martyr. But even if we are not that kind of person, there can be considerable pleasure in the arousal and excitement of getting angry. Physiologically, this arousal is much like that in fear, but it seems potentially more enjoyable than that in fear, because it accompanies our asserting and expressing ourselves: In anger we are telling whoever has offended us, and perhaps the whole world, who we are, what our rights and interests are, and what we expect—nay, demand—from other people. As young children, we develop our concept of ourselves as beings separate from the world, largely by running into opposition—something we want is not forthcoming, something we try to do fails or is not permitted. This frustration is disturbing, of course, and that disturbance is our anger, but it helps us define who we are. As adults, too, we are seldom more conscious of who we are than in those situations that evoke our anger. The pleasure we take in "giving someone a piece of our mind" is largely the pleasure of defining and expressing our self-image.

The pleasure possible in sadness is somewhat different from that in fear and anger, most importantly in that sadness is not a form of arousal. In sadness, there is no excitement or thrill; on the contrary, our activity and in general our liveliness are diminished. But this slowing down and withdrawal can itself be pleasurable, much as staying in bed nursing a cold can be. When we withdraw in sadness, too, we withdraw into our thoughts about ourselves and what we have experienced or lost. The concentrating on self here can be pleasant, much as it is in anger: We get to devote all our thoughts, often over an extended period of time, to what is important to us. Indeed, people sometimes intentionally put themselves into a melancholy mood, and even exaggerate their sad memories, just to savor the bittersweet thoughts that will arise. There can also be pleasure in expressing our sadness. Besides the mostly physical pleasure of "having a nice cry," there is the pleasure, similar to that in anger, of asserting who we are and what our interests are, to ourselves and to others. When others are present, too, expressing sadness will usually evoke their sympathy, and we will have the added pleasure of their comforting us, a lesson children learn very early.

If there is pleasure in receiving comfort from others, there is also a certain pleasure in feeling pity for and giving comfort to others. Indeed, we seem to have a general capacity for getting satisfaction from reverberating to the emotions of other human beings whether positive or negative. This pleasure of sympathy probably evolved in our species, as in social species generally, as a way to increase cooperative behavior.

In anger, sadness, pity, and other negative emotions that can be enjoyed, the element of control mentioned earlier is important. Control is most often lost when the emotion gets too strong. When anger becomes blind rage, for example, we lose the control that makes moderate anger potentially enjoyable. In extreme anger our higher rational functions are suspended—we cannot see beyond the immediate situation disturbing us, nor can we reflect on ourselves and what we are doing. We no longer direct our thoughts or actions: As so many primitive descriptions put it, it is as if a demon has taken control over us. And with this loss of control, the pleasure found in moderate anger, of focusing on ourselves and telling the world who we are, is also lost. Extreme sadness or pity also takes us out of control so that the emotion cannot be enjoyed. Unlike the person who cultivates melancholy, retaining some control over the flow of bittersweet thoughts, the person overcome by numbing sadness has lost his or her higher functions, especially self-reflection, and so has lost the capacity for savoring memories and for enjoying the expression of sadness. Because deep sadness involves such great psychological withdrawal, too, this person is not even able to enjoy the comfort that other people might offer. Pity is not as likely as sadness to overcome us, because, after all, the suffering is that of the other person. But where we reverberate with such fellow-feeling that we feel a distress or sadness equal to, or even surpassing, that of the other person, we may lose control and be unable to find any satisfaction in what we are feeling.

Having seen, then, how negative emotions can be enjoyed in real life, we can now return to the puzzle with which we began, to see how the enjoyment of negative emotions fits into our appreciation of fiction. First, however, it is necessary to say something in defense of the view that we actually experience negative emotions in fiction, against the claim of Kendall Walton that we cannot really feel fear and pity toward what we know to be fictional, and the claim of Colin Radford that such emotions are possible but incoherent. There have been many replies to these claims, most of them arguing against the principle that one must believe that x exists before being able to coherently feel emotions toward x.[7] Here I will not rehearse all these arguments, but simply stress one element mentioned in many of them, the role of imagination in reacting to fiction.

Walton and Radford get off the track in focusing on the role of belief in emotion. What is important to our feeling emotion toward a situation is not whether we believe that the situation exists, but rather how vividly and engagingly that situation is presented to our consciousness, in either perception, memory, or imagination. It may in general be easier for situations we perceive to move us, because what we are now seeing and hearing is potentially the most vivid in our consciousness. But memories can also evoke emotions when they are sufficiently vivid. And though situations we imagine may frequently not have the vividness and engaging quality of situations perceived or remembered, when they do, they can also evoke emotions. Notice here that what is *imagined* need not be *imaginary*: We imagine not only fictional situations, but situations existing now and those that once existed but no longer do. We use imagination, that is, just as much in reading a newspaper story or a biography as in reading a novel. And whenever any of these—the present situation, the past situation, or the fictional situation—is vivid and engaging enough in our imagination, we can feel emotion in response to it, regardless of whether we believe that it exists. If it were true that we have to believe that x exists in order to (coherently) feel emotions toward x, then it would be just as problematic to say that we now feel admiration for Helen Keller when we read her biography as it would be to say that we feel pity for Anna Karenina when we read *Anna Karenina*. In reality, neither Helen's nor Anna's nonexistence prevents us from vividly imagining them, getting interested in their lives, and feeling emotions toward them.

This is not to say, of course, that there are no differences between our reactions to a current situation, a past situation, and a fictional one. The major difference here lies in the presence or absence of practical motivation toward the events in the story. If we read in today's newspaper about a mother of five going blind, for instance, we may well contact her to offer our help; if the story is in an old newspaper we find in the attic, or in a book of short stories, we would have no such motivation.

The lack of a practical orientation not only distinguishes our emotion toward fiction and toward the past from emotion toward current situations, but also helps to explain why we enjoy negative emotions toward fiction and toward the past far more often than we enjoy negative emotions toward present situations. The most important factor in enjoying negative emotions, as we saw earlier, is our maintaining control, and being in control is a function of our desires and what we are doing in a particular situation. It is usually easiest to maintain control, I suggested, when we are merely attending to something that has no practical consequences for us. Then being in control requires only the abilities to start, stop, and direct our attention and thought. By contrast, when the situation evoking the negative emotion has practical consequences, especially when it requires action from us, it is unlikely that we will feel in control. In most cases, if we were in control, the undesirable situation would not have arisen in the first place. The exceptions here are cases like mountain climbing in which we put ourselves into a fear-evoking situation, say, knowing that we have the skills to remain in control; and cases like cultivated sadness or anger in which, though we may not have initiated the emotion, we know that we could "snap out of it" if we chose. Now most of the time when we feel negative emotions toward fiction, and much of the time when we feel such emotions toward the past, we experience the control mentioned, of attending to something that has no practical consequences for us, and being able to start, stop, and direct this attending. And maintaining this control, we are able to enjoy these negative emotions, as we are frequently not able to enjoy negative emotions toward real-life situations.

The lack of a practical dimension in a fictional or past situation is not enough to ensure our control in feeling negative emotions toward that situation. As we saw earlier, control can also be lost if the emotion gets too strong. In real life our emotions often get too strong to be enjoyable, but in fiction this is far less likely, because there is someone—the dramatist, novelist, painter, or other artist—who has created the situation we are responding to for our appreciation. Part of the artist's job is to present that situation in such a way that we can stay in control while feeling negative emotions, so that we can get satisfaction from the experience, rather than being overwhelmed and utterly distressed by it. We feel that the artist has slipped up if the fictional work is, say, so graphic in its depiction of violence or suffering that most of the audience is disgusted and has to stop reading the book or watching the movie screen. We even have aesthetic categories like "grotesque" and "macabre" for those works that walk the line separating enjoyable from unenjoyable negative emotions.

Besides allowing us to remain in control, the artist has other ways to make our negative emotions in fiction more enjoyable than such emotions usually are in real life. The most important lies in the organization and coherence the artist gives the work. Because a story, for instance, typically has a structure in which each part contributes to the whole, the emotions we feel in response to the story will have a structure, and usually a progression and resolution, that emotions in real life often lack.

There are other differences, too, between our enjoyment of negative emotions in fiction and in real life. A significant one, in light of our discussion of anger and sadness, is that we are far less likely to concentrate on ourselves in our appreciation of fiction than in real life. A character's plight could remind us of a similar situation that we were or are in, so that the anger or sadness evoked involved our thinking about ourselves. But more often the plight of fictional characters evokes our emotions in a way that does not take our attention off those characters. Rather, we identify with them and feel what they are feeling in their situation. And to the extent that we can "enter into" the characters, we can vicariously feel their pleasure in focusing on themselves when they feel emotions like anger and sadness, just as we can when they feel positive emotions like pride.

To go into more detail about what is special in our enjoyment of negative emotions in fiction, we would have to examine the relation of emotion in fiction to such things as character development and plot, and enter into a wider discussion of our enjoyment of fiction generally. I am not ambitious enough to do either here. My purpose has been the more modest one of making room for such discussions by showing the coherence of the idea that part of our enjoyment of fiction is our enjoyment of negative emotions.

Notes

An earlier version of this paper was presented at the Western Division of the American Philosophical Association in 1984. I am grateful to Susan Feagin, John Deigh, and Paul Teller for their comments on that paper.

1. Aristotle, *Poetics* chap. 6.

2. David Hume, "Of Tragedy," in *Of the Standard of Taste and Other Essays* (Bobbs-Merrill, 1965).

3. Susan Feagin, "The Pleasures of Tragedy," *American Philosophical Quarterly* 20 (1983): 95–104.

4. Kendall Walton, "Fearing Fictions," *Journal of Philosophy* 75 (1978): 5–27. In conversation Walton says that he does not hold what most critics have taken him to hold—that emotions presuppose beliefs—and that he does think that "quasi-fear" (toward fictions) *is* an emotion, though a different one from fear. See also Colin Radford, "How Can We Be Moved by the Fate of Anna Karenina?," *Proceedings of the Aristotelian Society* 49 (suppl.) (1975): 81–93.

5. For many of my ideas about control I am indebted to Marcia Eaton's essay "A Strange Kind of Sadness," *Journal of Aesthetics and Art Criticism* 41 (1982): 51–63.

6. I am grateful to Virginia Warren for these examples.

7. See Ralph Clark, "Fictional Entities: Talking About Them and Having Feelings About Them," *Philosophical Studies* 38 (1980): 341–50; Peter Lamarque, "How Can We Fear and Pity Fictions?," *British Journal of Aesthetics* 21 (1981): 291–304; H. O. Mounce, "Art and Real Life," *Philosophy* 55 (1980): 183–92; David Novitz, "Fiction, Imagination and Emotion," *Journal of Aesthetics and Art Criticism* 38 (1980): 279–88; and Harold Skulsky, "On Being Moved by Fiction," *Journal of Aesthetics and Art Criticism* 39 (1980): 5–14. Mike Martin's "Imaginative Emotions," presented at the American Philosophical Association, Pacific Division, 1983, also helped me here.

Chapter 17

FEAR FOR YOUR LIFE

The Appeals, Functions, and Effects of Horror

Mathias Clasen

> Among horror's more ardent advocates is Mathias Clasen, who argues in *Why Horror Seduces* that our enjoyment of horror is in some ways "hardwired" into us. Clasen advances what he refers to as a "biocultural" explanation for the appeal of horror, arguing that experiencing strong emotions in a safe context lets us practice at dealing with those emotions so we are better equipped to manage them when we encounter danger in the real world. We thus possess an evolutionary predisposition toward enjoying horror stories.

WHY ARE SO MANY PEOPLE attracted to horror in literature, film, and video games? The horror writer Peter Straub rightly says that there are many answers to the question. "One would be that people desire extremity of circumstance in perfect safety, so that they can feel all sorts of dangerous and despairing and frightening moments without in the least being in danger." But that can be only part of the answer, according to Straub—and, I'd add, it just begs the question of *why* people would want to feel "dangerous and despairing and frightening moments" while in perfect safety. Straub thinks that a more adequate answer to the question is this: "Horror stories are about engagement. About actual experience, instead of simulated, false experience.... It's about discovering one's ability to feel in certain ways, and deepening and widening one's emotional experience by that means" (Clasen 2009, 40). I think that is true, and I will argue that an evolutionary analysis can help us understand how the genre works to widen one's emotional experience and why many of us are attracted to such mediated experience—and to the elicitation of negative emotion in safe contexts generally.

Straub's "extremity of circumstance in perfect safety" brings to mind the activities offered by roller coasters and extreme sports, and such activities surely share some appeal with horror in different media. The pleasures afforded by roller coasters and skydiving are primarily the elicitation of strong emotions and physiological arousal within a safe context (Kerr 2015). As Rush W. Dozier Jr. (1998) argues, people manipulate fear to produce pleasure. When we step on a roller coaster, we "increase our fears artificially and then enjoy the sensation of our body pushing the fear back down to normal levels through the secretion of natural opiates and other fear-suppressing chemicals" (165). We artificially provoke—and enjoy—a release of endogenous morphine-like substances produced in the brain. Such an explanation cannot exhaustively account for the appeal of horror, though. If all we wanted from horror stories was the relief of the film, the novel, or the game to be over, we'd be better off not seeking it out in the first place. And if all we wanted was a kick of adrenaline and a jolt to the nervous system, there are quicker and easier ways to get such stimulation than to wade through 1,095 pages of *It* (King 1981), sit through two hours of *Alien* (Scott 1979), or spend eight or nine hours completing *Amnesia: The Dark Descent* (Frictional Games 2010). A thirty-second internet screamer gets the job done admirably. But the experience of being absorbed in a fictional universe and made to feel afraid as a result of this mediated experience has value and appeal in and of itself. There's bound to be a neurochemical payoff—what we call "pleasure"—but it is not the pleasure of the termination of the experience, it is the pleasure of experiencing strong and rich emotions in a safe context. That is a primary and irreducible appeal of horror.

Horror, of course, is a many-headed beast, difficult to pin down and to make stay down. Different works of horror may offer somewhat different pleasures: The epic scope and postapocalyptic grandeur of Stephen King's *The Stand* ([1978] 1980) are different from the creeping terror provided by a short story such as King's "The Raft" (1986), a story about teenagers caught on a raft on a lake, preyed upon by a weird monster. Both works, however, engage our attention and encourage emotional involvement by inviting us to share the perspective of plausible and sympathetic protagonists in highly dangerous situations, faced with hostile monsters and adverse supernatural forces. Both works stimulate negative emotion such as anxiety and dread. They both target evolved cognitive and emotional mechanisms. More pointedly, the pleasure afforded by a simple survival horror computer game, such as *Slender: The Eight Pages* (Parsec Productions 2012), is much less rich than the pleasure afforded by an accomplished and complex horror novel such as Peter Straub's *Ghost Story* (1979)—simple survival horror games have almost no narrative content, hardly anything in the way of symbolic figuration, no profound character depiction, and very little in the way of meaning, though both target evolved cognitive and emotional mechanisms. Narrative horror—stories and films—offer the same appeals as do simple survival horror games, but they offer much more than that. They offer the appeals of story generally: the opportunity to see the world through another person's eyes, to see different worlds, to peer inside fictional people's heads, to engage with interesting characters, to model hypothetical scenarios in imaginatively engaging and emotionally compelling ways.

Fiction is a human universal, found in all documented cultures (Brown 1991; Carroll 2006). Normally developing children spontaneously and with delight construct imaginary worlds, and adults spend vast amounts of time in lands of make-believe (Gottschall 2012). We seem to be hardwired with a penchant for fiction. Is this because fiction is biologically adaptive, that our appetite for fiction helps us survive and reproduce, or is our love affair with fiction an evolutionary by-product? This is a live debate in evolutionary literary study (Carroll 2012a). Some evolutionary social scientists claim that our appetite for fiction is an evolutionary by-product, a functionless biological accident—that our appetite for fiction serves no adaptive purpose, but that we cook up and consume stories as a means of artificially stimulating evolved pleasure circuits (Carroll 2012b; Pinker 2007). As the psychologists Eric Youngstrom and Carroll E. Izard (2008, 376) claim, "Horror films, sad songs, elegiac poetry—all of these serve no obvious biological function in terms of survival or sexual selection. Instead, these are 'junk food of the mind'—things that achieve their popularity by pandering to evolved preferences for approach and avoidance."

Other scholars and scientists, however, have argued that our appetite for fiction is biologically adaptive (Carroll 2011; Dutton 2009; Gottschall 2012; Tooby and Cosmides 2001). According to these theorists, our involvement in fictional worlds is not a frivolous waste of time; it's a crucial way in which we make sense of the world, ourselves, and each other. Imagine a new species of *Homo* that because of a genetic mutation has absolutely no appetite for fiction (Gottschall 2012). In contrast to *Homo sapiens*, who spends vast amounts of time in made-up worlds—we daydream, night-dream, read and listen to stories, attend plays and movies, watch television, listen to jokes and tall tales—our story-less cousins care only about the factual world. They have no time for the Crusoes or the Simpsons. Would they be better adapted than us, undistracted by "junk food of the mind" as they are; would they survive and reproduce at greater rates than us and eventually outcompete us? Probably not. Fiction is not just "junk food of the mind." Fiction helps us make sense of the world, including our inner, mental world; it helps us assign value to behavioral alternatives and intelligently choose between such alternatives; it helps us gain a better understanding of what makes people, groups, and societies tick (Gottschall 2012). Fiction is condensed and engaging simulation of social and psychological interactions (Mar and Oatley 2008). Fiction allows us to vicariously lead countless lives, it frees us from the phenomenological present and throws us into possible and impossible futures, pasts, and parallel universes. Horror fiction can do all of those things and is particularly well equipped to allow readers and viewers to vicariously live through the worst, to model threatening scenarios, and to get imaginatively compelling experience with extreme situations and intense negative emotion. In video games, players get experience with their own reactions to extreme situations; in literature and film, readers and viewers get experience with their own reactions as well as characters' reactions to extreme situations. This is all part of what Straub calls "deepening and widening one's emotional experience."

Stephen King (1981, 7) says that "fiction is the truth inside the lie." That observation works on several levels. A story about fictional characters engaged in fictional events may contain profound moral or existential or psychological truths. Also, on a literal level, made-up stories can contain true factual information; readers learn about chaos theory and paleoarchaeology from Michael Crichton's *Jurassic Park* (1990), and about working-class conditions in nineteenth-century England from Dickens's *Hard Times* ([1854] 2003). Stories engage our emotions, and emotional engagement enhances recall—when an event is drenched in emotion, it is more effectively stored in our memory (Gottschall 2012). Historically, narratives such as those found in myth and folklore have served the function of transmitting information about adaptively crucial issues such as hazards in the physical and social environment in an emotionally compelling way (Scalise Sugiyama 2001; Scalise Sugiyama and Scalise Sugiyama 2011)—information about dangerous animals, information about risky social interactions, information about local norms, information about features of the landscape that may present opportunities or dangers, and so on. Learning about danger in one's environment via narrative is preferable to learning about danger by personal experience and direct observation, because such direct learning can be extremely risky. As Arne Öhman and Susan Mineka (2001, 487) observe, "if effortful trial-and-error learning was the only learning mechanism available, most animals would be dead before they knew which predators and circumstances to avoid." Thus, if a child grows up in an environment in which wolves pose a threat, it is better to tell the child an engaging and memorable story about a dangerous wolf and a careless girl in a red hood than it is to let the child wander off and figure out on its own what happens when you stray from the path. The biologist Hans Kruuk (2002, 179) makes a similar argument, saying about the overrepresentation of deadly carnivores in imaginative culture—there are more dangerous monsters and predators in our art than there are in our actual surroundings—that "there may be a survival value in this aspect of our culture. We are teaching others what is lethal in the environment, how its deadly forces work, and one might call it a cultural alarm system." People evolved to be curious about danger, and fictional stories about danger prime, satisfy, and even exploit that curiosity.

If fictional horror stories can teach us about real-world danger, what kinds of lessons do we draw from such stories? Do modern-day horror stories transmit adaptively useful information? Surely there is no great need for us to be educated on the perils of demonic possession, furious poltergeists, or chainsaw-wielding rednecks. Nonetheless, the writer Joe Hill (2014) suggests in an essay on the usefulness of horror that "while the vast catalog of horrific fantasies may not be able to offer us simple answers to our biggest questions, it does occasionally remind us of small yet undeniably useful truisms: always look in the back seat before you get in the car; don't insult hillbillies with more power tools than teeth; whatever was making that awful noise out in the woods, you can check it out in the morning." That may sound like a stretch. Very few people get disemboweled by murderers hiding in the back seats of their cars, and let's be honest, how many hillbillies with power tools are actually out to get us? Yet as Hill also says in the essay, "I suggest to you that the compulsion to peer into the darkness, and wonder about what's there, is a distinctly useful and adaptive trait. And as it happens, the fiction of the horrific is unusually well tuned to address the most frightening and fascinating unknowns"—such as the meaning of life and death and of being human. This statement rings true. Yes, horror can offer practical advice that could, conceivably, be useful in the real world. Don't go alone to investigate a strange sound in the basement when it's dark. Stay away from psychos with knives. Avoid clowns in the moonlight, sure. Horror reinforces our intuitions that such situations and individuals are to be avoided, horror makes those intuitions ring true with vivid emotional force. But the truths of horror, the genre's truly valuable lessons, tend to be psychological and existential ones. As Stephen King (2011, 366–67) writes in an afterword to a short story collection, "I have tried my best [in these stories] to record what people might do, and how they might behave, under certain dire circumstances." King, in other words, aims at psychological realism even as he employs supernatural elements. Horror fiction, particularly supernatural horror fiction, can be outrageously outlandish and implausible in terms of the monsters or monstrous events depicted—corpses rising from graves because of space radiation? A haunted car? Really?—but good horror fiction is psychologically realistic, and it engages with substantial issues that are relevant to people. It depicts in plausible and careful detail the responses of characters to monsters and monstrous events. Only thus can horror fiction become "one of the vital ways in which we try to make sense of our lives, and the often terrible world we see around us," as King puts it in that same afterword (365). Only thus can horror become "a lamp that can guide you through your own eventual nighttime journeys" (Hill 2014).

The appetite for horror, I argue, is an adaptation that functions to give us experience with negative emotion at levels of intensity not safely come by in real life, and to allow us to incorporate danger into our total imaginative universe. As philosophers like to point out, we may never know what it feels like to be a bat, and we might not even care. But if we seek out horror entertainment, we can learn what it feels like to be genuinely afraid, what it feels like to be hunted prey, what it feels like to face and maybe overcome great danger, what it feels like when the world breaks into pieces—and that, surely, is valuable to know. As the psychologist Paul Bloom (2010, 193–94) has pointed out, even unrealistic stories about the zombie apocalypse can serve as "useful practice for bad times, exercising our psyches for when life goes to hell." If we follow *The Walking Dead* (Darabont 2010–22) on television, we'll be reassured that perseverance in the face of adversity often pays off, we'll learn to cultivate some caution toward strangers in case of disaster or massive upheaval, we'll be reminded of the value of meaningful, dependable social relations when times are tough. More specifically, we will learn what it *feels like* to be in the midst of such disaster, to combat hostile conspecifics and survive and thrive, to find meaning in a hostile environment. That kind of vicarious experience, or experiential expansion, is generalizable to real life, even if the zombies aren't. The zombies become catalysts for social and psychological dramas, and they work well as catalysts because they are inherently fascinating and salient. Moreover, the series prompts us to reflect on the meaning of life in an environment that is stripped of many of the structures that sustain meaningful activities in the modern world. Most people find such imaginative, vicarious experience stimulating and rewarding.

When we read a novel, watch a film, or play a video game, we are engaged in "structured experience," in David Bordwell and Kristin Thompson's (2013, 51) phrase. We are prompted to imaginatively entertain hypothetical scenarios and are (ideally) emotionally invested in, and cognitively stimulated by, those scenarios. Such involvement and stimulation can be regarded as a form of mental play behavior (Boyd 2009; Steen and Owens 2001; Vorderer, Steen, and Chan 2006), and the biological study of the functions of play can help us pinpoint possible biological functions for the structured experience offered by fiction across media. Play behavior—inherently rewarding but apparently nonfunctional behavior—has been observed in many species, especially among mammals and birds, but also among reptiles and fish, for example (Burghardt 2014). Play behavior has been somewhat of an evolutionary puzzle. Given the harsh realities of existence for all species, the often vicious struggle to survive and the fierce competition for mates, why would organisms expend time and energy on less-than-crucial activities such as play fighting? The answer is that such activities are, in fact, crucial. Play researchers have suggested that mammalian play functions as "training for the unexpected" (Špinka, Newberry, and Bekoff 2001). When kittens play fight, they gain skills and capacities at low cost and relatively little risk, skills and capacities that may become critically useful later in life when they face a hostile opponent. If one meets a hungry predator for the first time in one's life, it is desirable to have a store of surrogate experience with predator evasion to draw from rather than proceed by trial and error. Francis Steen and Stephanie Owens (2001) argue that human chase play simulates predator–prey interactions; children evolved to find great pleasure in chase play because such play gives them experience with strategies for predator avoidance and lets them build muscle tone and locomotor dexterity. Play behavior lets children explore and push the limits of their abilities—it allows them to practice hunting behavior, evasion strategies, hiding maneuvers, and simple as well as complex social exchanges. There is a functional parallel in the way that the air force trains fighter pilots, as Peter Vorderer,

Francis Steen, and Elaine Chan (2006, 18) point out: "An F16 flight simulator . . . allows a novice to acquire experience and practical skills in manipulating a single-seat airplane without risking the loss of life and a multi-million-dollar fighter jet." In a similar manner, fiction provides a framework for emotionally and cognitively engaging simulation, at little cost and with almost no risk.

Horror fiction can help us build coping skills, both by giving us personal experience with negative emotion, and with our reactions to negative emotion, and by letting us witness the coping behavior of fictional characters—whether such behavior is efficient or not; theater audiences invariably cry out in frustration when the heroine faces certain death in deciding to check out the weird sound coming from the basement. In narrative media we can observe fictional characters' behavior and the consequences of their behavior; in interactive media such as video games, we can let our avatar try out such behaviors in the game world. All of this works toward the kind of experiential expansion that I mentioned earlier. When we cognitively model the experience of being in great danger, most of us probably draw on imagery provided to us by horror stories, and on remembered emotions induced in us by horror stories.

The hypothesis that horror stories can function as simulation of and rehearsal for the nastier sides of life is corroborated by research on the biological function of nightmares. The neuroscientist Antti Revonsuo (2000) has suggested that the biological function of dreaming is to provide offline simulations of adaptively critical scenarios. Nightmares, according to Revonsuo's "threat simulation theory," serve the function of providing opportunities for "rehearsal of the neurocognitive mechanisms that are essential for threat recognition and avoidance behavior while awake" (Valli and Revonsuo 2009, 17). To back this idea, Katja Valli and Revonsuo provide evidence that mental training or within-mind simulation improves real-world task performance in several domains, and that nightmares are extremely common across cultures. In fact, the "most typical dream theme around the world is that of the dream self being chased or attacked" (31). Valli and Revonsuo conservatively estimate that young adults have dreams featuring "threat simulations" on average 5.1 times per week (26). The threats of such dreams need not be realistic representations of actual, ecologically valid threats; fantasy-based threats play a substantial role in nightmares because "in the modern world, the input concerning extremely threatening agents comes largely from horror movies and similar fictitious sources." But as Valli and Revonsuo note, "rehearsing how to escape from the jaws of a werewolf or a vampire might be just as efficient as running away from a human character or a wild animal" (35).

Horror, then, can help us get better at negotiating real dangers in the real world. But most horror probably does not have such functions. I would argue that most commercial horror stories and games function as forgettable and adaptively useless pleasure-via-displeasure technologies—"junk food of the mind"—that leave behind no more than an ephemeral buzz and perhaps a vague sense of dread. However, some works—the best ones—allow for emotional simulation and prompt us to reflect on important themes; they offer insight into the mechanics of social interactions and psychological processes and give us valuable vicarious experience with the terrifying....

I have focused so far on the positive functions of horror, arguing that horror can serve adaptive functions via its stimulation of evolved psychological danger-management adaptations. But of course such stimulation can come at a cost, and sometimes the genre's effects are more deleterious than benevolent. Horror by definition aims at making us fearful and paranoid. As the horror critic Kim Newman (2011, 5) has wryly pointed out, "The central thesis of horror in film and literature is that the world is a more frightening place than is generally assumed." That is not necessarily a bad lesson, nor a wrong one, but it may come with psychological costs. Who hasn't spent an uneasy night with the bedside lamp on because of a stupid horror film? Who hasn't double-checked under the bed because of stupid Stephen King? Horror may teach us coping skills and make us better adapted to a dangerous world in the long term, but it can also cripple us with anxiety and traumatize us. The negative psychological effects of horror are much better documented in the research literature than are the positive effects.

The communications scientist Joanne Cantor (2004, 283) has spent decades investigating the "lingering effects of frightening media." In her recent study, she collected and quantified 530 reports from individuals whom she had asked to write about fright reactions to media presentations. Strikingly, 91 percent of respondents described negative reactions to fictional media, rather than to news or documentary presentations. One respondent describes how he watched the horror film *Poltergeist* (Hooper 1982) at a young age and refused to sleep with an open closet door in the room for several months (Cantor 2004, 289). Many other respondents reported suffering from nightmares and other sleep disturbances for months after seeing the film (290). Another respondent, after watching *The Blair Witch Project* (Sánchez and Myrick 1999), described how she felt compelled to leave all the lights on in her apartment for several days after seeing the film. Several respondents say they refused to go camping or be in the woods after seeing that film, which depicts a group of young people lost and preyed upon in dark and strange woods (293).

In another study, Cantor and her colleague Becky Omdahl (1991) exposed children (kindergarten through sixth grade) to "scary media presentations" to see whether fictional presentations of realistic life-threatening events would influence the children's risk assessment. They found that children who had been exposed to a "dramatized depiction of a deadly house fire from *Little House on the Prairie* increased their self-reports of worry about similar events in their own lives." Moreover, the children "were also less interested in learning to build a fire in a fireplace" than were children who had not seen the scene, or who had seen a nondramatic scene involving fire (Cantor 2002, 289)—they were more sensitized to this particular source of danger.

Most of the negative psychological consequences identified by Cantor and her colleagues are the result of premature exposure—that is, kids watching or reading stuff they shouldn't be watching or reading. Children find it much harder to disassociate frightening fictional agents from real-world dangers (Cantor and Oliver 1996) and to distinguish fiction from reality; moreover, in terms of neurobiology, they lack the prefrontal maturation necessary for keeping the primitive fear system on a leash. The prefrontal cortex reaches maturation only in a person's early twenties and is one of the last brain structures to mature (Choudhury, Blakemore, and Charman 2006). That is why we have to remind children that "It's just ketchup" or "It's just acting"—to support prefrontal control of the primitive fear system. All the same, even grown-ups can experience sleep disruptions, hypervigilance, and increased anxiety as a result of exposure to horror fiction. As we get older, we find it more difficult to handle stress. This explains why the typical horror audience is composed of fairly young people (Weaver and Tamborini 1996)—not children, who are overwhelmed by the terrifying presence and apparent actuality of fear-inducing depictions, not the elderly, who are easily distressed, but the fairly young, who are eager to test and push their own limits, and eager to achieve and exhibit mastery over their own reactions.

We know, then, that horror fiction can have short-term effects of making us more fearful and vigilant. But we know very little about the long-term psychological consequences of horror consumption. As I argued earlier, it is likely that sustained horror consumption can give audiences tools with which to handle negative emotions and threat situations. Horror fiction can be much more than escapist entertainment—like all fiction, horror can function as an instrument of psychological calibration, as a means of understanding and making sense of the world.

References

Bloom, Paul. 2010. *How Pleasure Works: The New Science of Why We Like What We Like.* W. W. Norton.

Bordwell, David, and Kristin Thompson. 2013. *Film Art: An Introduction.* 10th ed. McGraw-Hill.

Boyd, Brian. 2009. *On the Origin of Stories: Evolution, Cognition, and Fiction.* Belknap Press of Harvard University Press.

Brown, Donald E. 1991. *Human Universals.* McGraw-Hill.

Burghardt, Gordon M. 2014. "A Brief Glimpse at the Long Evolutionary History of Play." *Animal Behavior and Cognition* 1, no. 2: 90–98. https://doi.org/10.12966/abc.05.01.2014.

Cantor, Joanne. 2002. "Fright Reactions to Mass Media." In *Media Effects: Advances in Theory and Research,* edited by Jennings Bryant and Dolf Zillman, 287–306. Lawrence Erlbaum.

Cantor, Joanne. 2004. "'I'll Never Have a Clown in My House': Why Movie Horror Lives On." *Poetics Today* 25, no. 2: 283–304. https://doi.org/10.1215/03335372-25-2-283.

Cantor, Joanne, and Mary Beth Oliver. 1996. "Developmental Differences in Responses to Horror." In *Horror Films: Current Research on Audience Preference and Reactions*, edited by J. B. Weaver and R. Tamborini, 63–80. Lawrence Erlbaum.

Cantor, Joanne, and Becky L. Omdahl. 1991. "Effects of Fictional Media Depictions of Realistic Threats on Children's Emotional Responses, Expectations, Worries, and Liking for Related Activities." *Communications Monographs* 58, no. 4: 384–401.

Carroll, Joseph. 2006. "The Human Revolution and the Adaptive Function of Literature." *Philosophy and Literature* 30, no. 1: 33–49.

Carroll, Joseph. 2011. *Reading Human Nature: Literary Darwinism in Theory and Practice*. SUNY Press.

Carroll, Joseph. 2012a. "The Adaptive Function of the Arts: Alternative Evolutionary Hypotheses." In *Telling Stories: Literature and Evolution*, edited by Carsten Gansel and Dirk Vanderbeke, 50–63. De Gruyter.

Carroll, Joseph. 2012b. "The Truth About Fiction: Biological Reality and Imaginary Lives." *Style* 46, no. 2: 129–160.

Choudhury, Supama, Sarah-Jayne Blakemore, and Tony Charman. 2006. "Social Cognitive Development During Adolescence." *Social Cognitive and Affective Neuroscience* 1, no. 3: 165–74. https://doi.org/10.1093/scan/nsl024.

Clasen, Mathias. 2009. "A Conversation with Peter Straub." *Cemetery Dance* 61: 40–48.

Crichton, Michael. 1990. *Jurassic Park: A Novel*. Knopf.

Darabont, Frank, dir. 2010–22. *The Walking Dead*. AMC Studios.

Dickens, Charles. (1854) 2003. *Hard Times for These Times*. Edited by Kate Flint. Penguin.

Dozier, Rush W., Jr. 1998. *Fear Itself: The Origin and Nature of the Powerful Emotion That Shapes Our Lives and Our World*. St. Martin's Press.

Dutton, Denis. 2009. *The Art Instinct: Beauty, Pleasure, and Human Evolution*. Bloomsbury.

Frictional Games. 2010. *Amnesia: The Dark Descent*. Microsoft Windows, Mac OS X, and Linux.

Gottschall, Jonathan. 2012. *The Storytelling Animal: How Stories Make Us Human*. Houghton Mifflin Harcourt.

Hill, Joe. 2014. "Peering into the Darkness." *The New York Times*, October 30.

Hooper, Tobe, dir. 1982. *Poltergeist*. DVD. SLM Entertainment/Metro-Goldwyn-Mayer.

Kerr, Margee. 2015. *Scream: Chilling Adventures in the Science of Fear*. PublicAffairs.

King, Stephen. (1978) 1980. *The Stand*. New English Library.

King, Stephen. 1981. *It*. New American Library.

King, Stephen. 1986. "The Raft." In *Skeleton Crew*, 278–306. New American Library.

King, Stephen. 2011. Afterword to *Full Dark, No Stars*, 365–68. Gallery Books.

Kruuk, H. 2002. *Hunter and Hunted: Relationships Between Carnivores and People*. Cambridge University Press.

Mar, Raymond A., and Keith Oatley. 2008. "The Function of Fiction Is the Abstraction and Simulation of Social Experience." *Perspectives on Psychological Science* 3, no. 3: 173–92.

Newman, Kim. 2011. *Nightmare Movies: Horror on Screen Since the 1960s*. Rev. and updated ed. Bloomsbury.

Öhman, Arne, and Susan Mineka. 2001. "Fears, Phobias, and Preparedness: Toward an Evolved Module of Fear and Fear Learning." *Psychological Review* 108, no. 3: 483–522. https://doi.org/10.1037/0033-295X.108.3.483.

Parsec Productions. 2012. *Slender: The Eight Pages*. Unity.

Pinker, Steven. 2007. "Toward a Consilient Study of Literature." *Philosophy and Literature* 31, no. 1: 162–78. https://doi.org/10.1353/phl.2007.0016.

Revonsuo, Antti. 2000. "The Reinterpretation of Dreams: An Evolutionary Hypothesis of the Function of Dreaming." *Behavioral and Brain Sciences* 23, no. 6: 877–901. Discussion, 904–1121. https://doi.org/10.1017/S0140525X00004015.

Sánchez, Eduardo, and Daniel Myrick, dirs. 1999. *The Blair Witch Project*. DVD. Haxan Films.

Scalise Sugiyama, Michelle. 2001. "Food, Foragers, and Folklore: The Role of Narrative in Human Subsistence." *Evolution and Human Behavior* 22, no. 4: 221–40.

Scalise Sugiyama, Michelle, and Larry Scalise Sugiyama. 2011. "'Once a Child Is Lost, He Dies': Monster Stories Vis-à-Vis the Problem of Errant Children." In *Creating Consilience: Integrating the Sciences and the Humanities*, edited by Ted Slingerland and Mark Collard, 351–71. Oxford University Press.

Scott, Ridley, dir. 1979. *Alien*. DVD. Brandywine Productions/Twentieth Century-Fox.

Špinka, Marek, Ruth C. Newberry, and Marc Bekoff. 2001. "Mammalian Play: Training for the Unexpected." *Quarterly Review of Biology* 76, no. 2: 141–68. https://doi.org/10.1086/393866.

Steen, Francis F., and Stephanie A. Owens. 2001. "Evolution's Pedagogy: An Adaptationist Model of Pretense and Entertainment." *Journal of Cognition and Culture* 1, no. 4: 289–321. https://doi.org/10.1163/156853701753678305.

Straub, Peter. 1979. *Ghost Story*. Coward, McCann, and Geoghegan.

Tooby, John, and Leda Cosmides. 2001. "Does Beauty Build Adapted Minds? Toward an Evolutionary Theory of Aesthetics, Fiction, and the Arts." *SubStance* 30, no. 1–2: 6–27.

Valli, Katja, and Antti Revonsuo. 2009. "The Threat Simulation Theory in Light of Recent Empirical Evidence: A Review." *American Journal of Psychology* 122, no. 1: 17–38.

Vorderer, Peter, Francis F. Steen, and Elaine Chan. 2006. "Motivation." In *Psychology of Entertainment*, edited by Jennings Bryant and Peter Vorderer, 3–17. Taylor and Francis.

Weaver, James B., and Ronald C. Tamborini, eds. 1996. *Horror Films: Current Research on Audience Preferences and Reactions*. Lawrence Erlbaum.

Youngstrom, Eric, and Carroll E. Izard. 2008. "Functions of Emotions and Emotion-Related Dysfunction." In *Handbook of Approach and Avoidance Motivation*, edited by Andrew J. Elliot, 367–84. Psychology Press.

Chapter 18

AN INTRODUCTION TO THE AMERICAN HORROR FILM

Robin Wood

> In this oft-cited piece, Wood presents a psychoanalytic explanation for the appeal of horror. Horror, according to Wood, confronts the audience with repressed fears and desires that often reflect broader cultural anxieties and tensions related to things like sex and death. Consuming horror, therefore, permits the audience a safe space to explore taboo subjects in ways that offer emotional and psychological relief from the "pressure" exerted by repression.

I. Repression, the Other, the Monster

The most significant development—in film criticism, and in progressive ideas generally—of the last few decades has clearly been the increasing confluence of Marx and Freud, or more precisely of the traditions of thought arising from them: the recognition that social revolution and sexual revolution are inseparably linked and necessary to each other. From Marx we derive our awareness of the dominant ideology—the ideology of bourgeois capitalism—as an insidious all-pervasive force capable of concealment behind the most protean disguises, and the necessity of exposing its operation whenever and wherever possible. It is psychoanalytic theory that has provided (without Freud's awareness of the full revolutionary potential of what he was unleashing) the most effective means of examining the ways in which that ideology is transmitted and perpetuated, centrally through the institutionalization of the patriarchal nuclear family. The battle for liberation, the battle against oppression (whether economic, legal, or ideological), gains enormous extra significance through the addition of that term "patriarchal," since patriarchy long *precedes* and far *exceeds* what we call capitalism. It is here, through the medium of psychoanalytic theory, that feminism and gay liberation join forces with Marxism in their progress toward a common aim, the overthrow of patriarchal capitalist ideology and the structures and institutions that sustain it and are sustained by it.

Psychoanalytic theory, like Marxism, now provides various models, inflecting basic premises in significantly different ways. It is not certain that the Lacanian model promoted by (among others) *Screen* magazine is the most satisfactory. On the evidence so far it seems certainly not the most potentially *effective*, leading either to paralysis or to a new academicism perhaps more sterile than the old, and driving its students into monastic cells rather than the streets. I want to indicate briefly a possible alternative model, developed out of Freud by Marcuse and given definitive formulation in a recent book by Gad Horowitz, *Repression* (1977): a model that enables us to connect theory closely with the ways we actually think and feel and conduct our lives—those daily practicalities from which the theorizing of *Screen* seems often so remote. The book's subtitle is "Basic and Surplus Repression in Psychoanalytic Theory: Freud, Reich, Marcuse." It is the crucial distinction between basic and surplus repression that is so useful in relation to direct political militancy and so suggestive in relation to the reading of our cultural artifacts (among them our horror films), and through them, our culture itself. Horowitz has devoted a dense, often difficult and closely argued book to the subject; in the space at my disposal I can offer only a bald and simplified account.

Basic repression is universal, necessary, and inescapable. It is what makes possible our development from an uncoordinated animal capable of little beyond screaming and convulsions into a human being; it is bound up with the ability to accept the postponement of gratification, with the development of our thought and memory processes, of our capacity for self-control, of our recognition of and consideration for other people. Surplus repression, on the other hand, is specific to a particular culture and is the process whereby people are conditioned from earliest infancy to take on predetermined roles within that culture. In terms of our own culture, then: *basic* repression makes us distinctively human, capable of directing our own lives and coexisting with others; *surplus* repression makes us (if it works) into monogamous heterosexual bourgeois patriarchal capitalists ("bourgeois" even if we are born into the proletariat, for we are talking here of ideological norms rather than material status). *If* it works: If it doesn't, the result is either a neurotic or a revolutionary (or both), and if revolutionaries account for a very small proportion of the population, neurotics account for a very large one. Hardly surprising. All known existing societies are to some degree surplus-repressive, but the degree varies enormously, from the trivial to the overwhelming. Freud saw long ago that our own civilization had reached a point where the burden of repression was becoming all but insupportable, an insight Horowitz (following Marcuse) brilliantly relates to Marx's theory of alienated labor: The most immediately obvious characteristics of life in our culture are frustration, dissatisfaction, anxiety, greed, possessiveness, jealousy, neuroticism—no more than what psychoanalytic theory shows to be the logical product of patriarchal capitalism. What needs to be stressed is that the kind of challenges now being made to the system—and the kind of perceptions and recognitions that structure those challenges and give them impetus—become possible (become in the literal sense *thinkable*) only in the circumstances of the system's imminent disintegration. While the system retained sufficient conviction, credibility, and show of coherence to suppress them, it did so. The struggle for liberation is not utopian, but a practical necessity.

Given that our culture offers an extreme example of surplus repressiveness, one can ask what, exactly, in the interests of alienated labor and the patriarchal family, is repressed. One needs here both to distinguish between the concepts of *repres*sion and *op*pression, and to suggest the continuity between them. In psychoanalytic terms, what is *re*pressed is not accessible to the conscious mind (except through analysis or, if one can penetrate their disguises, in dreams). We may also not be conscious of ways in which we are *op*pressed, but it is much easier to become so: We are oppressed by something "out there." One might perhaps define repression as fully internalized Oppression (while reminding ourselves that all the groundwork of repression is laid in infancy), thereby suggesting both the difference and the connection. A specific example may make this clearer: Our social structure demands the *re*pression of the bisexuality that psychoanalysis shows to be the natural heritage of every human individual, and the *op*pression of homosexuals—obviously, the two phenomena are not identical, but equally obviously, they are closely connected. What escapes *re*pression has to be dealt with by *op*pression.

What, then, is repressed in our culture? First, sexual energy itself, together with its possible successful sublimation into nonsexual creativity—sexuality being the source of creative energy in general. The "ideal" inhabitant of our culture will be the individual whose sexuality is sufficiently fulfilled by the monogamous heterosexual union necessary for the reproduction of future ideal inhabitants, and whose sublimated sexuality (creativity) is sufficiently fulfilled in the totally noncreative and nonfulfilling labor (whether in factory or office) to which our society dooms the overwhelming majority of its members. The "ideal," in other words, is as close as possible to an automaton in whom both sexual and intellectual energy has been reduced to a minimum. Otherwise, the "ideal" is a contradiction in terms and a logical impossibility, hence the *necessary* frustration, anxiety, and neuroticism of our culture.

Second, bisexuality—which should be understood both literally (in terms of possible sexual orientation and practice) and in a more general sense. Bisexuality represents the most obvious and direct affront to the principle of monogamy and its supportive romantic myth of "the one right person"; the homosexual impulse in both men and women represents the most obvious threat to the "norm" of sexuality as reproductive and restricted by the "ideal" of family. But more generally we confront here the whole edifice of clear-cut sexual differentiation that bourgeois-capitalist ideology erects on the flimsy and dubious foundations of biological difference: the social norms of masculinity and femininity, the social definitions of manliness and womanliness, the whole vast apparatus of oppressive male/female myths, the systematic repression from infancy ("blue for a boy . . .") of the man's "femininity" and the woman's "masculinity," in the interests of forming human beings for specific predetermined social roles.

Third, the particularly severe repression of female sexuality/creativity; the attribution to the female of passivity, her preparation for her subordinate and dependent role in our culture. Clearly, a crucial aspect of the repression of bisexuality is the denial to women of drives culturally associated with masculinity: activeness, aggression, self-assertion, organizational power, creativity itself.

Fourth—and fundamentally—the repression of the sexuality of children, taking different forms from infancy, through "latency" and puberty, and into adolescence—the process moving, indeed, from *re*pression to *op*pression, from the denial of the infant's nature as sexual being to the veto on the expression of sexuality before marriage.

None of these forms of repression is necessary for the existence of civilization in some form (i.e., none is "basic")—for the development of our human-ness. Indeed, they impose limitations and restrictions on that development, stunting human potential. All are the outcome of the requirements of the particular, surplus-repressive civilization in which we live.

Closely linked to the concept of repression—indeed, truly inseparable from it—is another concept necessary to an understanding of ideology on which psychoanalysis throws much light, the concept of "the Other": that which bourgeois ideology cannot recognize or accept but must deal with (as Barthes suggests in *Mythologies* [1957]) in one of two ways: either by rejecting and if possible annihilating it, or by rendering it safe and assimilating it, converting it as far as possible into a replica of itself. The concept of Otherness can be theorized in many ways and on many levels. Its psychoanalytic significance resides in the fact that it functions not simply as something external to the culture or to the self, but also as what is repressed (but never destroyed) in the self and projected outward in order to be hated and disowned. A particularly vivid example—and one that throws light on a great many classical Westerns—is the relationship of the Puritan settlers to the Indians in the early days of America. The Puritans rejected any perception that the Indians had a culture, a civilization, of their own; they perceived them not merely as savage but, literally, as devils or the spawn of the devil; and, since the devil and sexuality are inextricably linked in the Puritan consciousness, they perceived them as sexually promiscuous, creatures of unbridled libido. The connection between this view of the Indian and Puritan repression is obvious: a classic and extreme case of the projection onto the Other of what is repressed within the Self, in order that it can be discredited, disowned, and if possible annihilated. It is repression, in other words, that makes impossible the healthy alternative: the full recognition and acceptance of the Other's autonomy and right to exist.

Some versions then, of the figure of the Other as it operates within our culture, of its relation to repression and oppression, and of how it is characteristically dealt with:

1. Quite simply, other people. It is logical and probable that under capitalism all human relations will be characterized by power, dominance, possessiveness, manipulation: the extension into relationships of the property principle. Given the subordinate and dependent position of women, this is especially true of the culture's central relationship, the male/female, and explains why marriage as we have it is characteristically a kind of mutual imperialism/colonization, an exchange of different forms of possession and dependence, both economic and emotional. In theory, relations between people of the same sex stand more chance of evading this contamination, but in practice most gay and lesbian relationships tend to rely on heterosexual models. The "otherness," the autonomy, of the partner, her/his right to freedom and independence of being, is perceived as a threat to the possession/dependence principle and denied.
2. Woman. In a male-dominated culture, where power, money, law, and social institutions are controlled by past, present, and future patriarchs, woman as the Other assumes particular significance. The dominant images of women in our culture are entirely male created and male controlled. Woman's autonomy and independence are denied; onto women men project their own innate, repressed femininity in order to disown it as inferior (to be called "unmanly"—i.e., like a woman—is the supreme insult).
3. The proletariat—insofar as it still has any autonomous existence, escaping its colonization by bourgeois ideology. It remains, at least, a conveniently available object for projection: the bourgeois obsession with cleanliness, which psychoanalysis shows to be closely associated, as outward symptom, with sexual repression, and bourgeois sexual repression itself, find their inverse reflections in the myths of working-class squalor and sexuality.
4. Other cultures. If they are sufficiently remote, no problem: They can be simultaneously deprived of their true character and exoticized (e.g., Polynesian cultures as embodied by Dorothy Lamour). If they are inconveniently close, we already have the example of the American Indian: The procedure is very precisely represented in Ford's *Drums Along the Mohawk* (1939), with its double vision of the Indians as "sons of Belial" fit only for extermination, or the Christianized, domesticated, servile, and (hopefully) comic Blueback.
5. Ethnic groups within the culture. Again, an easily available projection-object (myths of Black sexuality, "animality," etc.). Acceptable in either of two ways: either they keep to their ghettoes and don't trouble us with their "otherness," or they behave as we do and become replicas of the good bourgeois, their otherness reduced to the one unfortunate difference of color. We are more likely to invite a Pakistani to dinner if he dresses in a business suit.
6. Alternative ideologies or political systems. The exemplary case is of course Marxism, the strategy that of parody. Still almost totally repressed within our preuniversity education system (despite the key importance of Marx—whatever way you look at

it—in the development of twentieth-century thought), Marxism exists generally in our culture only in the form of bourgeois myth that renders it indistinguishable from Stalinism (rather like confusing the teachings of Christ with the Spanish Inquisition).

7. Deviations from ideological sexual norms—notably bisexuality and homosexuality. One of the clearest instances of the operation of the repression/projection mechanism: Homophobia (the irrational hatred and fear of homosexuals) is only explicable as the outcome of the unsuccessful repression of bisexual tendencies—what is hated in others is what is rejected (but nonetheless continues to exist) within the self.

8. Children. When we have worked our way through all the other liberation movements, we may discover that children are the most oppressed section of the population (unfortunately, we cannot expect to liberate our children until we have successfully liberated ourselves). Most clearly of all, the "otherness" of children (see Freudian theories of infantile sexuality) is that which is repressed within ourselves, its expression therefore hated in others: what the previous generation repressed in us, and what we, in turn, repress in our children, seeking to mold them into replicas of ourselves, perpetuators of a discredited tradition.

All this may seem to have taken us rather far from our immediate subject. In fact, I have been laying the foundations, stone by stone, for a theory of the American horror film that (without being exhaustive) should provide us with a means of approaching the films seriously and responsibly. One could, I think, approach any of the genres from the same starting point; it is the horror film that responds in the most clear-cut and direct way, because central to it is the actual dramatization of the dual concept of the repressed/the other, in the figure of the Monster. One might say that the true subject of the horror genre is the struggle for recognition of all that our civilization *re*presses or *op*presses: its reemergence dramatized, as in our nightmares, as an object of horror, a matter for terror, the "happy ending" (when it exists) typically signifying the restoration of repression. I think my analysis of what is repressed, combined with my account of the Other as it functions within our culture, will be found to offer a comprehensive survey of horror film monsters from German Expressionism on. It is possible to produce "monstrous" embodiments of virtually every item in the list. Let me preface this by saying that the general sexual content of the horror film has long been recognized, and the list of monsters representing a generalized sexual threat would be interminable; also, the generalized concept of "otherness" offered by the first item on my list cannot be represented by specific films.

Female sexuality. Earlier examples are the panther-woman of *Island of Lost Souls* (1932) and the heroine of *Cat People* (1982) (the association of women with cats runs right through and beyond the Hollywood cinema, cutting across periods and genres from *Bringing Up Baby* [1938] to *Alien* [1979]); but the definitive feminist horror film is clearly De Palma's *Sisters* (co-scripted by the director and Louisa Rose; 1972), among the most complete and rigorous analyses of the oppression of women under patriarchal culture in the whole popular cinema.

The proletariat. I would claim here Whale's *Frankenstein* (1931), partly on the strength of its pervasive class references, more on the strength of Karloff's costume: Frankenstein *could* have dressed his creature in top hat, white tie, and tails, but in fact chose laborer's clothes. Less disputable, in recent years we have *The Texas Chainsaw Massacre* (1988), with its monstrous family of retired, but still practicing, slaughterhouse workers; the underprivileged devil worshippers of *Race with the Devil* (1975); and the revolutionary army of *Assault on Precinct 13* (1976).

Other cultures. In the 1930s the monster was almost invariably foreign; the rebellious animal-humans of *Island of Lost Souls* (though created by the white man's science) on one level clearly signify a "savage," unsuccessfully colonized culture. Recently, one horror film, *The Manitou* (1978), identified the monster with the American Indian (*Prophecy* [1979] plays tantalizingly with this possibility—also linking it to urban Blacks—before opting for the altogether safer and less interesting explanation of industrial pollution).

Ethnic groups. *The Possession of Joel Delaney* (1972) links diabolic possession with Puerto Ricans; Blacks (and a leader clad as an Indian) are prominent, again, in *Assault on Precinct 13*'s monstrous army.

Alternative ideologies. The 1950s science fiction cycle of invasion movies are generally regarded as being concerned with the Communist threat.

Homosexuality and bisexuality. Both Murnau's *Nosferatu* (1922) and Whale's *Frankenstein* can be claimed as implicitly (on certain levels) identifying their monsters with repressed homosexuality. Recent, less arguable instances are Dr. Frank 'n' Furter of *The Rocky Horror Picture Show* (1975) (he, not his creation, is clearly the film's real monster) and, more impressively, the bisexual god of Larry Cohen's *Demon* (1976).

Children. Since *Rosemary's Baby* (1968), children have figured prominently in horror films as the monster or its medium: *The Exorcist* (1973), *The Omen* (1976), and so on. Cohen's two *It's Alive* films again offer perhaps the most interesting and impressive example. There is also the Michael of *Halloween*'s (1978) remarkable opening.

This offers us no more than a beginning, from which one might proceed to interpret specific horror films in detail as well as further exploring the genre's social significance, the insights it offers into our culture. I shall add here simply that these notions of repression and the Other afford us not merely a means of access but a rudimentary categorization of horror films in social/political terms, distinguishing the progressive from the reactionary; the criterion being the way in which the monster is presented and defined.

II. Return of the Repressed

I want first to offer a series of general propositions about the American horror film, then attempt to define the particular nature of its evolution in the 1960s and 1970s.

1. Popularity and Disreputability

The horror film has consistently been one of the most popular and, at the same time, the most disreputable of Hollywood genres. The popularity itself has a peculiar characteristic that sets the horror film apart from other genres: It is restricted to aficionados and complemented by total rejection, people tending to go to horror films either obsessively or not at all. They are dismissed with contempt by the majority of reviewer-critics, or simply ignored. (The situation has changed somewhat since *Psycho* [1960], which conferred on the horror film something of the dignity that *Stagecoach* [1939] conferred on the Western, but the disdain still largely continues. I have read no serious or illuminating accounts of, for example, *Raw Meat* [1972], *It's Alive* [1974], or *The Hills Have Eyes* [1977].) The popularity, however, also continues. Most horror films make money; the ones that don't are those with overt intellectual pretensions, obviously "difficult" works like *God Told Me To (Demon)* (1976) and *Exorcist II* (1977). Another psychologically interesting aspect of this popularity is that many people who go regularly to horror films profess to ridicule them and go in order to laugh—which is not true, generally speaking, of the Western or the gangster movie.

2. Dreams and Nightmares

The analogy frequently invoked between films and dreams is usually concerned with the experience of the audience. The spectator sits in darkness, and the sort of involvement the entertainment film invites necessitates a certain switching off of consciousness, a losing of oneself in a fantasy experience. But the analogy is also useful from the point of view of the filmmakers. Dreams—the embodiment of repressed desires, tensions, fears that our conscious mind rejects—become possible when the "censor" that guards our subconscious relaxes in sleep, though even then the desires can only emerge in disguise, as fantasies that are "innocent" or apparently meaningless.

One of the functions of the concept of "entertainment"—by definition, that which we don't take seriously, or think about much ("It's only entertainment")—is to act as a kind of partial sleep of consciousness. For the filmmakers as well as for the audience, full awareness stops at the level of plot, action, and character, in which the most dangerous and subversive implications can disguise themselves and escape detection. This is why seemingly innocuous genre movies can be far more radical and fundamentally undermining than works of conscious social criticism, which must always concern themselves with the possibility of reforming aspects of a social system whose basic rightness must not be challenged. The old tendency to dismiss the Hollywood cinema as escapist always defined escape merely negatively as escape *from*, but escape logically must also be escape *to*. Dreams are also escapes, from the unresolved tensions of our lives into fantasies. Yet the fantasies are not meaningless;

they can represent attempts to resolve those tensions in more radical ways than our consciousness can countenance.

Popular films, then, respond to interpretation as at once the personal dreams of their makers and the collective dreams of their audiences—the fusion made possible by the shared structures of a common ideology. It becomes easy, if this is granted, to offer a simple definition of horror films: They are our collective nightmares. The conditions under which a dream becomes a nightmare are (1) that the repressed wish is, from the point of view of consciousness, so terrible that it must be repudiated as loathsome; and (2) that it is so strong and powerful as to constitute a serious threat. The disreputability noted earlier—the general agreement that horror films are not to be taken seriously—works clearly *for* the genre viewed from this position. The censor (in both the common *and* the Freudian sense) is lulled into sleep and relaxes vigilance.

3. The Surrealists

It is worth noting here that one group of intellectuals *did* take American horror movies very seriously indeed: the writers, painters, and filmmakers of the surrealist movement. Luis Buñuel numbers *The Beast with Five Fingers* (1946) among his favorite films and paid homage to it in *The Exterminating Angel* (1962); and Georges Franju, an heir of the surrealists, numbers *The Fly* (1958) among *his*. The association is highly significant, given the commitment of the surrealists to Freud, the unconscious, dreams, and the overthrow of repression.

4. Basic Formula

At this stage it is necessary to offer a simple and obvious basic formula for the horror film: Normality is threatened by the Monster. I use "normality" here in a strictly nonevaluative sense, to mean simply "conformity to the dominant social norms"; one must firmly resist the common tendency to treat the word as if it were more or less synonymous with "health."

The very simplicity of this formula has a number of advantages:

1. It covers the entire range of horror films, being applicable whether the Monster is a vampire, a giant gorilla, an extraterrestrial invader, an amorphous gooey mass, or a child possessed by the devil, and this makes it possible to connect the most seemingly heterogeneous movies.
2. It suggests the possibility of extension to other genres: Substitute for "Monster" the term "Indians," for example, and one has a formula for a large number of classical Westerns.
3. Although so simple, the formula provides three variables: normality, the Monster, and, crucially, the relationship between the two. The definition of normality in horror films is in general boringly constant: the heterosexual monogamous couple, the family, and the social institutions (police, church, armed forces) that support and defend them.

The Monster is, of course, much more protean, changing from period to period as society's basic fears clothe themselves in fashionable or immediately accessible garments—rather as dreams use material from recent memory to express conflicts or desires that may go back to early childhood.

It is the third variable, the relationship between normality and the Monster, that constitutes the essential subject of the horror film. It, too, changes and develops, the development taking the form of a long process of clarification or revelation. The relationship has one privileged form: the figure of the doppelgänger, alter ego, or double, a figure that has recurred constantly in Western culture, especially during the past hundred years. The locus classicus is Stevenson's Dr. Jekyll and Mr. Hyde, where normality and Monster are two aspects of the same person. The figure recurs throughout two major sources of the American horror film, German Expressionist cinema (the two Marias of *Metropolis* [1927], the presentation of protagonist and vampire as mirror reflections in *Nosferatu,* the very title of F. W. Murnau's lost Jekyll-and-Hyde film *Der Januskopf* [1920]), and the tales of Poe. Variants can be traced in such oppositions as Ahab/the white whale in *Moby-Dick* (1851) and Ethan/Scar in *The Searchers* (1956). The Westerns of Anthony Mann are rich in doubles, often contained within families or family patterns; *Man of the West* (1958), a film that relates very suggestively to the horror genre, represents the fullest elaboration.

I shall limit myself for the moment to one example from the horror film, choosing it partly because it is so central, partly because the motif is there less obvious, partially disguised, partly because it points forward to Larry Cohen and *It's Alive*: the relationship of Monster to creator in the Frankenstein films. Their identity is made explicit in *Son of Frankenstein* (1939), the most intelligent of the Universal series, near the start of which the title figure (Basil Rathbone) complains bitterly that everyone believes "Frankenstein" to be the name of the monster. (We discover subsequently that the town has also come to be called Frankenstein, the symbiosis of Monster and creator spreading over the entire environment.) But we should be alerted to the relationship's true significance from the moment in the James Whale original when Frankenstein's decision to create his monster is juxtaposed very precisely with his decision to become engaged. The doppelgänger motif reveals the Monster as normality's shadow.

5. Ambivalence

The principle of ambivalence is most eloquently elaborated in A. P. Rossiter's *Angel with Horns* (1989), among the most brilliant of all books on Shakespeare. Rossiter first expounds it with reference to Richard III. Richard, the "angel with horns," both horrifies us with his evil and delights us with his intellect, his art, his audacity; while our moral sense is appalled by his outrages, another part of us gleefully identifies with him. The application of this to the horror film is clear. Few horror films have totally unsympathetic Monsters (*The Thing* [1982] is a significant exception); in many (notably the Frankenstein films) the Monster is clearly the emotional center, and much more human than the cardboard representatives of normality. The Frankenstein monster suffers, weeps, responds to music, longs to relate to people; Henry and Elizabeth merely declaim histrionically. Even in *Son of Frankenstein*—the film in which the restructured monster is explicitly designated evil and superhuman—the monster's emotional commitment to Ygor and grief over his death carry far greater weight than any of the other relationships in the film.

But the principle goes far beyond the Monster's being sympathetic. Ambivalence extends to our attitude to normality. Central to the effect and fascination of horror films is their fulfillment of our nightmare wish to smash the norms that oppress us and that our moral conditioning teaches us to revere. The overwhelming commercial success of *The Omen* cannot possibly be explained in terms of a simple, unequivocal *horror* at the devil's progress.

6. Freudian Theses

Finally, one can simply state the two elementary (and closely interconnected) Freudian theses that structure this article: That in a society built on monogamy and family there will be an enormous surplus of sexual energy that will have to be repressed; and that what is repressed must always strive to return.

Before considering how the horror film has developed in the past decade, I want to test the validity of the preceding ideas by applying them to a classical horror film. I have chosen Robert Florey's *Murders in the Rue Morgue* (1932)—because it is a highly distinguished example, and generally neglected; because its images suggest surrealism as much as expressionism; and because it occupies a particularly interesting place in the genre's evolution, linking two of the most famous, though most disparate, horror films ever made. On one hand it looks back very clearly to *The Cabinet of Dr. Caligari* (1948): the expressionist sets and lighting, with Karl Freund as cinematographer; the fairground that provides the starting point for the action; the figure of the diabolical doctor, who shows off his exhibit and later sends it to kidnap the heroine; the flight over the rooftops. On the other hand it looks forward, equally clearly, to *King Kong* (1933): instead of *Caligari*'s sleepwalker, a gorilla, which falls in love with the heroine, abducts her at night, and is shot down from a roof. It is as important to notice the basic motifs that recur obstinately throughout the evolution of the horror film in Western culture as it is to be aware of the detailed particularities of individual films. *Murders in the Rue Morgue* responds well to the application of my formula.

> 1. *Normality*. The film is quite obsessive about its heterosexual couples. At the opening, we have two couples responding to the various spectacles of the fairground; there is a

scene in the middle where numerous carefree couples disport themselves picturesquely amid nature. Crucial to the film, however, is Pierre's love speech to Camille on her balcony, with its exaggerated emphasis on purity: She is both a "flower" and a "star"; she is told not to be curious about what goes on in the houses of the city around them ("Better not to know"); she is also prevented from obtaining knowledge of the nature of Pierre's activities in the morgue (a "horrid old place"). Even the usual gay stereotype, Pierre's plump and effeminate friend, fits very well into the pattern. He is provided with a girlfriend, to recuperate him into the heterosexual coupling of normality. His relationship with Pierre (they share an apartment, he wears an apron, cooks the dinner, and fusses) is a parody of bourgeois marriage, the incongruity underlining the relationship's repressive sexlessness. And he underlines the attempts at separating "pure" normality from the pervasive contamination of outside forces by complaining that Pierre "brings the morgue into their home."

2. *The Monster. Murders in the Rue Morgue* has a divided Monster, a phenomenon not uncommon in the horror film. (In *The Cabinet of Dr. Caligari* the Monster is both Caligari and Cesar; in *Island of Lost Souls* both Dr. Moreau and his creatures.) Here the division is tripartite: Dr. Mirakle (Bela Lugosi), his servant-assistant, and Erik, "the beast with a human soul." The servant's role is small, but important because of his appearance: half human, half animal, he bridges the gap between Mirakle and Erik. Scientist and ape are linked, however, in another way: Mirakle himself lusts after Camille, and Erik (the animal extension of himself) represents the instrument for the satisfaction of that lust. Together, they combine the two great, apparently contradictory dreads of American culture as expressed in its cinema: intellectuality and eroticism.

3. *Relationship.* The film's superficial project is to insist that purity-normality can be separated from contaminating eroticism-degradation; its deeper project is to demonstrate the impossibility of such a separation. In the opening sequence, the couples view a series of fairground acts as spectacles (the separation of stage from audience seeming to guarantee safety): an erotic dance by "Arabian" girls, a Wild Red Indian show, and finally Erik the ape. The association of the three is suggestive of the link between the horror film and the Western—the link of horror, Indians, and released libido. In each case the separation of show and audience is shown to be precarious: Pierre's sidekick asks his girl if she "could learn to do that dance" for him; two spectators adopt the name "apache" to apply to the savages of Paris; the audience enters the third booth between the legs of an enormous painted ape, where its phallus would be. Dr. Mirakle's introduction uses evolutionary theory to deny separation: Erik is "the darkness at the dawn of Man." His subsequent experiments are carried out to prove that Erik's blood can be "mixed with the blood of man"—and as the experiments all involve women, the sexual connotations are plain.

Though not obvious, the "double" motif subtly structures the film. It comes nearest to explicitness in the effeminate friend's remark that Pierre is becoming fanatical, "like that Dr. Mirakle." But Pierre and Mirakle are paralleled repeatedly, both in the construction of the scenario and through the mise-en-scène. At the end of the balcony love scene Florey cuts from the lovers' kiss to Mirakle and Erik watching from their carriage. Later, the juxtaposition is reversed, the camera panning from Mirakle–Erik lurking in the shadows to Pierre–Camille embracing on the balcony; it is as if the Monster were waiting to be released by the kiss. Mirakle sends Camille a bonnet; she assumes it is from Pierre. After Pierre leaves her at night, there is a knock at her door. She assumes it is Pierre come back and opens; it is Mirakle. Bearing in mind that Mirakle and Erik are not really distinct from one another, one must see Pierre and this composite Monster paralleled throughout as rival mates for Camille, like Jonathan and Nosferatu, or like David Ladd and the underworld man of *Raw Meat*. (The motif's recurrence across different periods and different continents testifies to its importance.) At the climax, Pierre and Erik confront each other like mirror images on the rooftop, and Erik is shot down by Pierre: The hero's drive is to destroy the doppelgänger who embodies his repressed self.

Murders in the Rue Morgue is fascinating for its unresolved self-contradiction. In the fairground, Mirakle is denounced as a heretic, in the name of the biblical/Christian tradition of God's creation of man; the whole notion of purity/normality clearly associates with this—explicitly, in the very prominent, carefully lit crucifix above Camille's bed. Yet Mirakle's Darwinian theories are also obviously meant to be correct. Erik and humanity are *not* separable; the ape exists in all of us; the "morgue" cannot be excluded from the "home."

The horror film since the 1960s has been dominated by five recurrent motifs. The list of examples offered in each case begins with what I take to be the decisive source film of each trend—not necessarily the first, but the film that, because of its distinction or popularity, can be thought of as responsible for the ensuing cycle. I have included a few British films that seem to me American derived (*Raw Meat*, arguably the finest British horror film, was directed by an American, Gary Sherman); they lie outside the main British tradition represented by Hammer Productions, a tradition very intelligently treated in David Pirie's book *A Heritage of Horror* (1973). The lists are not, of course, meant to be exhaustive.

1. The Monster as human psychotic or schizophrenic: *Psycho, Homicidal* (1961), *Repulsion* (1965), *Sisters, Schizo* (1976).
2. The revenge of Nature: *The Birds* (1963), *Frogs* (1972), *Night of the Lepus* (1972), *Day of the Animals* (1977), *Squirm* (1976).
3. Satanism, diabolic possession, the Antichrist: *Rosemary's Baby, The Exorcist, The Omen, The Possession of Joel Delaney* (1972), *The Car* (1977), *God Told Me To (Demon), Race with the Devil,* which, along with *High Plains Drifter* (1973), interestingly connects this motif with the Western.
4. The Terrible Child (often closely connected to the preceding). To the first three films in (3) add *Night of the Living Dead* (1968), *Hands of the Ripper* (1971), *It's Alive, Cathy's Curse* (1977); also, although here the "children" are older, *Carrie* (1976) and *The Fury* (1978).

5. Cannibalism: *Night of the Living Dead, Raw Meat, Frightmare* (1974), *The Texas Chainsaw Massacre, The Hills Have Eyes.*

These apparently heterogeneous motifs are drawn deeper together by a single unifying master-figure: the Family. The connection is most tenuous and intermittent in what has proved, on the whole, the least interesting and productive of these concurrent cycles, the "revenge of Nature" films; but even there, in the more distinguished examples (outstandingly, of course, *The Birds* [1963], but also in *Squirm*), the attacks are linked to, or seem triggered off by, familial or sexual tensions. Elsewhere, the connection of the Family to horror has become overwhelmingly consistent: the psychotic/schizophrenic, the Antichrist, and the child-monster are all shown as products of the family, whether the family itself is regarded as guilty (the "psychotic" films) or innocent *(The Omen)*.

The "cannibalism" motif functions in two ways. Occasionally members of a family devour each other *(Night of the Living Dead,* and *Psycho*'s Mrs. Bates is a metaphorical cannibal who swallows up her son). More frequently, cannibalism is the family's means of sustaining or nourishing itself *(The Texas Chainsaw Massacre, The Hills Have Eyes)*. Pete Walker's revoltingly gruesome and ugly British horror film *Frightmare* deserves a note here, its central figure being a sweet and gentle old mother who has the one unfortunate flaw that she can't survive without eating human flesh, a craving guiltily indulged by her devoted husband.

If we see the evolution of the horror film in terms of an inexorable "return of the repressed," we will not be surprised by this final emergence of the genre's real significance—together with a sense that it is currently the most important of all American genres and perhaps the most progressive, even in its overt nihilism—in a period of extreme cultural crisis and disintegration, which alone offers the possibility of radical change and rebuilding. To do justice to the lengthy process of that emergence would involve a dual investigation too complex for the framework of this article: into the evolution of the horror film, and into the changing treatment of the family in the Hollywood cinema. I shall content myself here with a few further propositions.

1. The family (or marital) comedy, in which the 1930s and 1940s are so rich, turns sour (*Father of the Bride* [1950], *The Long, Long Trailer* [1954]) in the 1950s and peters out; the family horror film starts (not, of course, without precedents) with *Psycho* in 1960, and gains impetus with *Rosemary's Baby* and *Night of the Living Dead* toward the end of the decade.
2. As the horror film enters into its apocalyptic phase, so does the Western. *The Wild Bunch* appeared in 1969, the year after *Rosemary's Baby*. And *High Plains Drifter* fused their basic elements in a Western in which the Hero from the Wilderness turns out to be the devil (or his emissary) and burns the town (American civilization) to the ground after revealing it as fundamentally corrupt and renaming it Hell.

3. The family comedies that seemed so innocent and celebratory in the 1930s and 1940s appear much less so in retrospect from the 1970s. In my book *Personal Views* (1976) I pointed to the remarkable anticipation in *Meet Me in St. Louis* (1944) of the Terrible Child of the 1970s horror film, especially in the two scenes (*Halloween,* and the destruction of the snow people) in which Margaret O'Brien symbolically kills parent-figures. What is symbolic in 1944 becomes literal in *Night of the Living Dead,* where a little girl kills and devours her parents—just as the implications of another anticipatory family film of the early 1940s, *Shadow of a Doubt* (1943), becomes literally enacted in *It's Alive* (the monster as product of the family).
4. The process whereby horror becomes associated with its true milieu, the family, is reflected in its steady *geographical* progress toward America.

a. In the 1930s, horror is always foreign. The films are set in Paris *(Murders in the Rue Morgue),* in Middle Europe (*Frankenstein, Dracula* [1931]), or on uncharted islands *(Island of Lost Souls, King Kong)*; it is always external to Americans, who may be attacked by it physically but remain (superficially, that is) uncontaminated by it morally. The designation of horror as foreign stands even when the "normal" characters are Europeans. In *Murders in the Rue Morgue,* for example, the young couples, though nominally French, are to all intents and purposes nice, clean-living Americans (with American accents); the foreignness of the horror characters is strongly underlined, both by Lugosi's accent and by the fact that nobody knows where he comes from. The foreignness of horror in the 1930s can be interpreted in two ways: simply, as a means of disavowal (horror exists, but is un-American), and, more interestingly and unconsciously, as a means of locating horror as a "country of the mind," as a psychological state—the films set on uncharted (and usually nameless) islands lend themselves particularly to interpretation of this kind.

b. The Val Lewton films of the 1940s are in some ways outside the mainstream development of the horror film. They seem to have had little direct influence on its evolution (certain occasional haunted-house movies like *The Uninvited* [1944] and *The Haunting* [1963] may owe something to them), though they strikingly anticipate, by at least two decades, some of the features of the modern horror film. *Cat People* is centered on the repression of female sexuality, in a period when the Monster is almost invariably male and phallic. (Other rare exceptions are the panther-woman of *Island of Lost Souls* and, presumably, *Dracula's Daughter* [1936], which I have not seen.) *The Seventh Victim* (1943) has strong undertones of sibling envy and sexual jealousy (the structure and editing of the last scene suggesting that Jacqueline's suicide is willed by her "nice" husband and sister rather than by the "evil" devil worshippers), as well as containing striking anticipations of *Psycho* and *Rosemary's Baby*; it is also set firmly in America, with no attempt to disown evil as foreign.

Above all, *I Walked with a Zombie* (1943) explicitly locates horror at the heart of the family, identifying it with sexual repressiveness in the cause of preserving family unity. *The Seventh Victim* apart, horror is still associated with foreignness; Irena in *Cat People* is from Serbia, [*I Walked with a*] *Zombie* is set in the West Indies, *The Leopard Man* (1943) in Mexico, and so on. Yet the best of the series are concerned with the undermining of such distinctions—with the idea that no one escapes contamination. Accordingly, the concept of the Monster becomes diffused through the film (closely linked to the celebrated Lewton emphasis on atmosphere, rather than overt shock), no longer identified with a single figure.

Zombie, one of the finest of all American horror films, carries this furthest. It is built on an elaborate set of apparently clear-cut structural oppositions—Canada–West Indies, white–Black, light–darkness, life–death, science–black magic, Christianity–voodoo, conscious–unconscious, and so on—and it proceeds systematically to blur all of them. Jessica is both living and dead; Mrs. Rand mixes medicine, Christianity, and voodoo; the figurehead is both St. Sebastian and a Black slave; the Black–white opposition is poetically undercut in a complex patterning of dresses and voodoo patches; the motivation of *all* the characters is called into question; the messenger-zombie Carrefour can't be kept out of the white domain.

c. The 1950s science fiction cycles project horror onto either extraterrestrial invaders or mutations from the insect world, but they are usually set in America; even when they are not *(The Thing),* the human characters are American. The films, apparently simple, prove on inspection often very difficult to "read." The basic narrative patterns of the horror film repeat themselves obstinately and continue to carry their traditional meanings, but they are encrusted with layers of more transient, topical material. *Them!* (1954), for example, seems to offer three layers of meaning. Explicitly, it sets out to cope with the fear of nuclear energy and atomic experiment: The giant ants are mutants produced by the radioactive aftermath of a bomb explosion; they are eventually destroyed under the guidance of a humane and benevolent science embodied in the comfortingly paternal figure of Edmund Gwenn. The fear of Communist infiltration also seems present, in the emphasis on the ants as a subversive subterranean army and on their elaborate communications system. Yet the film continues to respond convincingly to the application of my basic formula and its Freudian implications. The ants rise up from underground (the unconscious); they kill by holding their victims and injecting into them huge (excessive) quantities of formic acid (the release of repressed phallic energy); and both the opening and final climax of the film are centered on the destruction (respectively actual and potential) of family groups.

Since *Psycho,* the Hollywood cinema has implicitly recognized horror as both American and familial. I want to conclude this section by briefly examining two key works of recent years that offer particularly illuminating and suggestive contrasts and comparisons: *The Omen* and *The Texas Chainsaw Massacre.*

One can partly define the nature of each by means of a chart of oppositions:

The Omen	*The Texas Chainsaw Massacre*
big budget	low budget
glossy production values	raw, unpolished
stars	unknown actors
bourgeois entertainment	nonbourgeois "exploitation"
Good Taste	Bad Taste
"good" family	"bad" family
the Monster	the Monster
imported from Europe	indigenously American
child destroys parents	parent figures destroy "children"
traditional values reaffirmed	traditional values negated

I don't wish to make any claims for *The Omen* as a work of art: The most one could say is that it achieves a sufficient level of impersonal professional efficiency to ensure that the "kicks" inherent in its scenario are not dulled. (I would add here that my earlier description of *Massacre* as "raw, unpolished" refers to the overall effect of the film, as it seems to be generally experienced.) Its mise-en-scène is, without question, everywhere more intelligent, more inventive, more cinematically educated and sophisticated, than that of *The Omen*. Hooper's cinematic intelligence, indeed, becomes more apparent on every viewing, as one gets over the initial traumatizing impact and learns to respect the pervasive felicities of camera placement and movement.

In obvious ways *The Omen* is old-fashioned, traditional, reactionary: The "goodness" of the family unit isn't questioned, "horror" is disowned by having the devil-child a product of the Old World, unwittingly *adopted* into the American family, the devil-child and his independent-female guardian (loosely interpretable in "mythic" terms as representing child liberation and women's liberation) are regarded as purely evil (oh for a cinematic Blake to reverse all the terms).

Yet the film remains of great interest. It is about the end of the world, but the "world" the film envisages ending is very particularly defined within it: the bourgeois-capitalist patriarchal Establishment. Here "normality" is not merely threatened by the monster, but totally annihilated: the state, the church, the family. The principle of ambivalence must once again be invoked: With a film so shrewdly calculated for box-office response, it is legitimate to ask what general satisfaction it offers its audience.

Superficially, the satisfaction of finding traditional values reaffirmed (even if "our" world is ending, it was still the good, right, true one); more deeply, and far more powerfully, under cover of this, the satisfaction of the ruthless logic with which the premise is carried through—the supreme satisfaction (masquerading as the final horror) being the revelation, as the camera cranes down in the last shot, that the devil has been adopted by the president and first lady of the United States. The translation of the film into Blakean terms is not in fact that difficult: The devil-child is its implicit hero, whose systematic destruction of the bourgeois Establishment the audience follows with a secret relish. *The Omen* would make no sense in a society that was not prepared to enjoy and surreptitiously condone the working out of its own destruction.

As Andrew Britton pointed out to me, *The Omen* and *The Texas Chainsaw Massacre* (together with numerous other recent horror films) have one premise disturbingly in common: The annihilation is inevitable, humanity is now completely powerless, there is nothing anyone can do to arrest the process. (Ideology, that is, can encompass despair, but not the imagining of constructive radical alternatives.) *The Omen* invokes ancient prophecy and shows it inexorably fulfilling itself despite all efforts at intervention; we infer near the opening of *Massacre* that the Age of Aquarius whose advent was so recently celebrated in *Hair* (1979) has already passed, giving way to the Age of Saturn and universal malevolence. Uncontrol is emphasized throughout the film: Not only have the five young victims no control over their destiny, their slaughterers (variously psychotic and degenerate) keep losing control of themselves and each other.

This is partly (in conjunction with the film's relentless and unremitting intensity) what gives *Massacre* to such a degree (beyond any other film in my experience) the authentic quality of nightmare. I have had since childhood a recurring nightmare whose pattern seems to be shared by a very large number of people within our culture: I am running away from some vaguely terrible oppressors who are going to do dreadful things to me; I run to a house or a car, and so on, for help; I discover its occupants to be precisely the people I am fleeing. This pattern is repeated twice in *Massacre,* where Sally "escapes" from Leatherface first to his own home, then to the service station run by his father.

The application of my formula to *Massacre* produces interesting results: The pattern is still there, as is the significant relationship between the terms, but the definitions of "normality" and "monster" have become partly reversed. Here "normality" is clearly represented by the quasi-liberated, permissive young (though still forming two couples and a brother/sister family unit, hence reproducing the patterns of the past); the monster is the family, one of the great composite monsters of the American cinema, incorporating four characters and three generations, and imagined with an intensity and audacity that far transcend the connotations of the term "exploitation movie." It has a number of important aspects:

1. The image of the "Terrible House" stems from a long tradition in American (and Western capitalist) culture. Traditionally, it represents an extension or "objectification" of the personalities of the inhabitants. *Massacre* offers two complementary "terrible houses": the once imposing, now totally decayed house of Franklyn's and Sally's parents (where we keep *expecting* something appalling to happen), and the more modest, outwardly spruce, inwardly macabre villa of the monstrous family in which every item of decor is an expression of the characters' degeneracy. The borderline between home

and slaughterhouse (between work and leisure) has disappeared—the slaughterhouse has invaded the home, humanity has begun literally to "prey upon itself, like monsters of the deep." Finally, what the "terrible house" (whether in Poe's "Fall of the House of Usher," in *Psycho,* in *Mandingo* [1975], or here) signifies is the dead weight of the past crushing the life of the younger generation, the future—an idea beautifully realized in the shot that starts on the ominous gray, decayed Franklyn house and tilts down to show Kirk and Pam, dwarfed in long shot, playing and laughing as they run to the swimming hole, and to their doom.

2. The contrast between the two houses underlines the distinction the film makes between the affluent young and the psychotic family, representatives of an exploited and degraded proletariat. Sally's father used to send his cattle to the slaughterhouse of which the family are products.

3. The all-male family (the grandmother exists only as a decomposing corpse) also derives from a long American tradition, with notable antecedents in Ford's Westerns (the Clantons of *My Darling Clementine* [1946], the Cleggses of *Wagon Master* [1950]) and in *Man of the West* (1958). The absence of Woman (conceived of as a civilizing, humanizing influence) deprives the family of its social sense and social meaning while leaving its strength of primitive loyalties largely untouched. In *Massacre,* Woman becomes the ultimate object of the characters' animus (and, I think, the film's, since the sadistic torments visited on Sally go far beyond what is necessary to the narrative).

4. The release of sexuality in the horror film is always presented as perverted, monstrous, and excessive (whether it takes the form of vampires, giant ants, or Mrs. Bates), both the perversion and the excess being the logical outcome of repression. Nowhere is this carried further than in *Massacre.* Here sexuality is totally perverted from its functions, into sadism, violence, and cannibalism. It is striking that there is no suggestion anywhere that Sally is the object of an overtly sexual threat: She is to be tormented, killed, dismembered, eaten, but not raped. Ultimately, the most terrifying thing about the film is its total negativity; the repressed energies—represented most unforgettably by Leatherface and his continuously whirring phallic chainsaw—are presented as irredeemably debased and distorted. It is no accident that the four most intense horror films of the 1970s at "exploitation" level (*Night of the Living Dead, Raw Meat,* and *The Hills Have Eyes* are the other three) are all centered on cannibalism, and on the specific notion of present and future (the younger generation) being devoured by the past. Cannibalism represents the ultimate in possessiveness, hence the logical end of human relations under capitalism. The implication is that "liberation" and "permissiveness," as defined within our culture, are at once inadequate and too late—too feeble, too unaware, too undirected to withstand the legacy of long repression.

5. This connects closely with the recurrence of the "double" motif in *Massacre.* The young people are, on the whole, uncharacterized and undifferentiated (the film's energies are mainly with its monsters—as usual in the horror film, the characteristic here surviving the reversal of definitions), but in their midst is Franklyn, who is as grotesque, and almost as psychotic, as his nemesis Leatherface. (The film's refusal to sentimentalize the fact that he is crippled may remind one of the blind beggars of Buñuel.) Franklyn associates himself with the slaughterers by imitating the actions of Leatherface's

brother the hitchhiker: wondering whether he, too, could slice open his own hand, and toying with the idea of actually doing so. (Kirk remarks, "You're as crazy as he is.") Insofar as the other young people are characterized, it is in terms of a pervasive petty malice. Just before Kirk enters the house to meet his death, he teases Pam by dropping into her hand a human tooth he has found on the doorstep; later, Jerry torments Franklyn to the verge of hysteria by playing on his fears that the hitchhiker will pursue and kill him. Franklyn resents being neglected by the others, Sally resents being burdened with him on her vacation. The monstrous cruelties of the slaughterhouse family have their more pallid reflection within "normality." (The reflection pattern here is more fully worked out in *The Hills Have Eyes,* with its stranded "normal" family besieged by its dark mirror-image, the terrible shadow-family from the hills, who want to kill the men, rape the women, and eat the baby.)

6. Despite the family's monstrousness, a degree of ambivalence is still present in the response they evoke. Partly, this is rooted in our sense of them as a *family.* They are held together—and torn apart—by bonds and tensions with which we are all familiar—with which, indeed, we are likely to have grown up. We cannot cleanly dissociate ourselves from them. Then there is the sense that *they* are victims too—of the slaughterhouse environment, of capitalism—*our* victims, in fact. Finally, they manifest a degraded but impressive creativity. The news reporter at the start describes the tableau of decomposing corpses in the graveyard (presumably the work of the hitchhiker, and perhaps a homage to his grandparents: a female corpse is posed in the lap of a male corpse in a hideous parody of domesticity) as "a grisly work of art." The phrase, apt for the film itself, also describes the artworks among which the family live, some of which achieve a kind of hideous aesthetic beauty: the lightbulb held up by a human hand, the sofa constructed out of human and animal bones, surmounted by ornamental skulls, the hanging lamp over the dining table that appears to be a shrunken human head. The film's monsters do not lack that characteristically human quality, an aesthetic sense, however perverted its form; also, they waste nothing, a lesson we are all taught as children.

7. Central to the film—and centered on its monstrous family—is the sense of grotesque comedy, which in no way diminishes (but rather intensifies) its nightmare horror: Leatherface chasing Sally with the chainsaw, unable to stop and turn, skidding, wheeling, like an animated character in a cartoon; the father's response to Leatherface's devastations, which by that time include four murders and the prolonged terrorization of the heroine ("Look what your brother did to that door"); Leatherface dressed up in jacket and tie and fresh black wig for formal dinner with Grandpa; the macabre farce of Grandpa's repeated failures to kill Sally with the hammer. The film's sense of fundamental horror is closely allied to a sense of the fundamentally absurd. The family, after all, only carries to its logical conclusion the basic (though unstated) tenet of capitalism, that people have the right to live off other people. In twentieth-century art, the sense of the absurd is always closely linked to total despair (Beckett, Ionesco . . .). The fusion of nightmare and absurdity is carried even further in *Death Trap* (1962), a film that confirms that the creative impulse in Hooper's work is centered in his monsters (here, the grotesque and pathetic Neville Brand) and is essentially nihilistic.

The Texas Chainsaw Massacre, unlike *The Omen,* achieves the force of authentic art, profoundly disturbing, intensely personal, yet at the same time far more than personal, as the general response it has evoked demonstrates. As a "collective nightmare," it brings to a focus a spirit of negativity, an undifferentiated lust for destruction, that seems to lie not far below the surface of the modern collective consciousness. Watching it recently with a large, half-stoned youth audience who cheered and applauded every one of Leatherface's outrages against their representatives on the screen was a terrifying experience. It must not be seen as an isolated phenomenon: It expresses, with unique force and intensity, at least one important aspect of what the horror film has come to signify: the sense of a civilization condemning itself, through its popular culture, to ultimate disintegration, and ambivalently (with the simultaneous horror/wish fulfillment of nightmare) celebrating the fact. We must not, of course, see that as the last word.

III. The Reactionary Wing

I suggested earlier that the theory of repression offers us a means toward a political categorization of horror movies. Such a categorization, however, can never be rigid or clear-cut. While I have stressed the genre's progressive or radical elements, its potential for the subversion of bourgeois patriarchal norms, it is obvious enough that this potential is never free from ambiguity. The genre carries within itself the capability of reactionary inflection, and perhaps no horror film is entirely immune from its operations. It need not surprise us that there is a powerful reactionary tradition to be acknowledged—so powerful it may at times appear the dominant one. Its characteristics are, in extreme cases, very strongly marked.

Before noting them, however, it is important to make one major distinction, between the reactionary horror film and the "apocalyptic" horror film. The latter expresses, obviously, despair and negativity, yet its very negation can be claimed as progressive: The "apocalypse," even when presented in metaphysical terms (the end of the world), is generally reinterpretable in social/political ones (the end of the highly specific world of patriarchal capitalism). The majority of the most distinguished American horror films (especially in the 1970s) are concerned with this particular apocalypse; they are progressive insofar as their negativity is not recuperable into the dominant ideology, but constitutes (on the contrary) the recognition of that ideology's disintegration, its untenability, as all it has repressed explodes and blows it apart. *The Texas Chainsaw Massacre, Sisters,* and *Demon* are all apocalyptic in this sense; so are Romero's two Living Dead movies. (Having said that, it must be added that important distinctions remain to be made between these works.)

Some of the characteristics, then, that have contributed to the genre's reactionary wing:

1. The designation of the monster as *simply* evil. Insofar as horror films are typical manifestations of our culture, the *dominant* designation of the monster must necessarily be "evil": What is repressed (in the individual, in the culture) must always return as a threat, perceived by the consciousness as ugly, terrible, obscene. Horror films, it might be said, are progressive precisely to the degree that they refuse to be satisfied with this simple designation—to the degree that, whether explicitly or implicitly, consciously or unconsciously, they modify, question, challenge, seek to invert it. All monsters are by definition destructive, but their destructiveness is capable of being variously explained, excused, and justified. To identify what is repressed with "evil incarnate" (a metaphysical, rather than a social, definition) is automatically to suggest that there is nothing to be done but strive to *keep* it repressed. Films in which the "monster" is identified as the devil clearly occupy a privileged place in this group; though even the devil can be presented with varying degrees of (deliberate or inadvertent) sympathy and fascination—*The Omen* should not simply be bracketed with *The Sentinel* (1977) for consignment to merited oblivion.
2. The presence of Christianity (insofar as it is given weight or presented as a positive force) is in general a portent of reaction. (This is a comment less on Christianity itself than on what it signifies within the Hollywood cinema and the dominant ideology.) *The Exorcist* is an instructive instance—its validity is in direct proportion to its failure convincingly to impose its theology.
3. The presentation of the monster as totally nonhuman. The "progressiveness" of the horror film depends partly on the monster's capacity to arouse sympathy; one can feel little for a mass of viscous black slime. The political (McCarthyite) level of 1950s science fiction films—the myth of communism as total dehumanization—accounts for the prevalence of this kind of monster in that period.
4. The confusion (in terms of what the film wishes to regard as "monstrous") of *repressed* sexuality with sexuality itself. The distinction is not always clear-cut; perhaps it never can be, in a culture whose attitudes to sexuality remain largely negative and where a fear of sex is implanted from infancy. One can, however, isolate a few extreme examples where the sense of horror is motivated by sexual disgust.

A very common generic pattern plays on the ambiguity of the monster as the "return of the repressed" and the monster as punishment for sexual promiscuity (or, in the more extreme puritanical cases, for *any* sexual expression whatever: two teenagers kiss; enter, immediately, the Blob). Both Jaws films (their sources in both 1950s McCarthyite science fiction and all those beach-party/monster movies that disappeared with the B feature) are obvious recent examples, Spielberg's film being somewhat more complex, less blatant, than Szwarc's, though the difference is chiefly one of ideological sophistication.

I want to examine briefly here some examples of the "reactionary" horror film in the 1970s, of widely differing distinction but considerable interest in clarifying these tendencies.

David Cronenberg's *Shivers* (1975; formerly *The Parasite Murders*) is, indeed, of very special interest here, as it is a film single-mindedly about sexual liberation, a prospect it views with unmitigated horror. The entire film is premised on and motivated by sexual disgust. The release of sexuality is linked inseparably with the spreading of venereal disease (VD), the scientist responsible for the experiments having seen fit (for reasons never made clear) to include a VD component in his aphrodisiac parasite. The parasites themselves are modeled very obviously on phalluses, but with strong excremental overtones (their color) and continual associations with blood; the point is underlined when one enters the Barbara Steele character through her vagina. If the film presents sexuality in general as the object of loathing, it has a very special animus reserved for female sexuality (a theme repeated, if scarcely developed, in Cronenberg's subsequent *Rabid* [1977]). The parasites are spread initially by a young girl (the original subject of the scientist's experiments), the film's Pandora whose released eroticism precipitates general cataclysm; throughout, sexually aroused preying women are presented with a particular intensity of horror and disgust. *Shivers* systematically chronicles the breaking of every sexual-social taboo—promiscuity, lesbianism, homosexuality, age difference, and, finally, incest—but each step is presented as merely one more addition to the accumulation of horrors. At the same time, the film shows absolutely no feeling for traditional relationships (or for human beings, for that matter): With its unremitting ugliness and crudity, it is very rare in its achievement of *total* negation.

The Brood (1979), again, is thematically central to the concept of the horror film proposed here (its subject being the transmission of neurosis through the family structure) and the precise antithesis of the genre's progressive potential. It carries over all the major structural components of its two predecessors (as an auteur, Cronenberg is nothing if not consistent): the figure of the Scientist (here psychotherapist) who, attempting to promote social progress, precipitates disaster; the expression of unqualified horror at the idea of releasing what has been repressed; the projection of horror and evil onto women and their sexuality, the ultimate dread being of women usurping the active, aggressive role that patriarchal ideology assigns to the male. The film is remarkable for its literal enactment, at its climax, of the Freudian perception that, under patriarchy, the child becomes the woman's penis-substitute—Samantha Eggar's latest offspring representing, unmistakably, a monstrous phallus. The film is laboriously explicit about its meaning: The terrible children are the physical embodiments of the woman's rage. But that rage is never seen as the logical product of woman's situation within patriarchal culture; it is blamed entirely on the woman's mother (the father being culpable only in his weakness and ineffectuality). The film is useful for offering an extremely instructive comparison with *Sisters* on one hand and *It's Alive* on the other.

In turning from Cronenberg's films to *Halloween* I do not want to suggest that I am bracketing them together. John Carpenter's films reveal in many ways an engaging artistic personality: They communicate, at the very least, a delight in skill and craftsmanship, a pleasure in play with the medium, that is one of the essential expressions of true creativity. Yet the film buff innocence that accounts for much of the charm of *Dark Star* (1974) can go on to combine (in *Assault on Precinct 13*) *Rio Bravo* (1959) and *Night of the Living Dead* without any apparent awareness of the ideological consequences of converting Hawks's fascists (or Romero's ghouls, for that matter) into an army of revolutionaries. The film buff is very much to the fore again in *Halloween,* covering the film's confusions, its lack of real *thinking,* with a formal/stylistic inventiveness that is initially irresistible. If nothing in the film is new, everything testifies to Carpenter's powers of assimilation (as opposed to mere imitation): As a resourceful amalgam of *Psycho, The Texas Chainsaw Massacre, The Exorcist,* and *Black Christmas* (1974), *Halloween* is cunning in the extreme.

The confusions, however, are present at its very foundation, in the conception of the monster. The opening is quite stunning both in its virtuosity and in its resonances. The long killer's-point-of-view tracking shot with which the film begins establishes the basis for the first murder as sexual repression: The girl is killed because she arouses in the voyeur-murderer feelings he has simultaneously to deny and enact in the form of violent assault. The second shot reveals the murderer as the victim's bewildered six-year-old brother. Crammed into those first two shots (in which *Psycho* unites with the Halloween sequence of *Meet Me in St. Louis*) are the implications for the definitive family horror film: the child-monster, product of the nuclear family and the small-town environment; the sexual repression of children; the incest taboo that denies sexual feeling precisely where the proximities of family life most encourage it. Not only are those implications not realized in the succeeding film, their trace is obscured and all but obliterated. The film identifies the killer with "the Bogeyman," as the embodiment of an eternal and unchanging evil that, by definition, can't be understood; and with the devil ("those eyes . . . the devil's eyes"), by none other than his own psychoanalyst (Donald Pleasence)—surely the most extreme instance of Hollywood's perversion of psychoanalysis into an instrument of repression.

The film proceeds to lay itself wide open to the reading Jonathan Rosenbaum offered in *Take One*: The killer's victims are all sexually promiscuous, the one survivor a virgin; the monster becomes (in the tradition of all those beach-party monster movies of the late 1950s to early 1960s) simply the instrument of Puritan vengeance and repression rather than the embodiment of what Puritanism repressed.

Halloween is more interesting than that—if only because more confused. The basic premise of the action is that Laurie is the killer's real quarry throughout (the other girls merely distractions en route), because she is for him the reincarnation of the sister he murdered as a child (he first sees her in relation to a little boy who resembles him as he was then, and becomes fixated on her from that moment). This compulsion to reenact the childhood crime keeps Michael tied at least to the *possibility* of psychoanalytical explanation, thereby suggesting that Donald Pleasence may be wrong. If we accept that, then one tantalizing unresolved detail becomes crucial: the question of how Michael learned to drive a car. There are only two possible explanations: Either he *is* the devil, possessed of supernatural powers; or he has *not* spent the last nine years (as Pleasence would have us believe) sitting staring blankly at a wall meditating further horrors. (It is to Carpenter's credit that the issue is raised in the dialogue, not glossed over as an unfortunate plot necessity we aren't supposed to notice; but he appears to use it merely as another tease, a bit of meaningless mystification.) The possibility this opens up is that of reading the whole film against the Pleasence character: Michael's "evil" is what his analyst has been projecting onto him for the past nine years. Unfortunately, this remains merely a possibility in the material that Carpenter chose not to take up: It does not constitute a legitimate (let alone a coherent) reading of the actual film. Carpenter's interviews suggest that he strongly resists examining the connotative level of his own work; it remains to be seen how long this very talented filmmaker can preserve this false innocence.

At first glance, *Alien* seems little more than *Halloween*-in-outer-space: more expensive, less personal, but made with similar professional skill and flair for manipulating its audiences. Yet it has several distinctive features that give it a limited interest in its own right: It clearly wants to be taken, on a fairly simple level, as a "progressive" movie, notably in its depiction of women. What it offers on this level amounts in fact to no more than a "pop" feminism that reduces the whole involved question of sexual difference and thousands of years of patriarchal oppression to the bright suggestion that a woman can do anything a man can do (almost). This masks (not very effectively) its fundamentally reactionary nature.

Besides its resemblance to *Halloween* in general narrative pattern and suspense strategies (Where is the monster hiding? Who will be killed next? When? How? etc.), *Alien* has more precise parallels with *The Thing*. There is the enclosed space, cut off from outside help; the definition of the monster as both non- and superhuman; the fact that it feeds on human beings; its apparent indestructibility. Most clearly of all, the relationship of Ash, the robot science officer, to the alien is very close to that of Professor Carrington to the Thing; in both films, science regards the alien as a superior form of life to which human life must therefore be subordinate; in both films, science is initially responsible for bringing the monster into the community and thereby endangering the latter's existence.

What strikingly distinguishes *Alien* from both *Halloween* and *The Thing* (and virtually every other horror movie) is the apparently total absence of sexuality. Although there are two women among the spaceship's crew of seven, there is no "love interest," not even any sexual banter—in fact, with the characters restricted exclusively to the use of surnames, no recognition anywhere of sexual difference (unless we see Parker's ironic resentment of Ripley's domineeringness as motivated partly by the fact that she is a woman; but he reacts like that to all displays of authority in the film, and his actual phrase for her is "son of a bitch"). Only at the end of the film, after all the men have been killed, is female sexuality allowed to become a presence (as Ripley undresses, not knowing that the alien is still alive and in the compartment). The film constructs a new "normality" in which sexual differentiation ceases to have effective existence—on condition that sexuality be obliterated altogether.

The term "son of a bitch" is applied (by Ripley herself) to one other character in the film: the alien. The cinematic confrontation of its two "sons of bitches" is the film's logical culmination. Its resolution of ideological contradictions is clear in the presentation of Ripley herself: She is a "safe threat," set against the real threat of the alien. On one hand, she is the film's myth of the "emancipated woman": "Masculine," aggressive, self-assertive, she takes over the ship after the deaths of Kane and Dallas, rebelling against and dethroning both "Mother" (the computer) and father (Ash, the robot). On the other hand, the film is careful to supply her with "feminine," quasi-maternal characteristics (her care for Jones the cat) and gives her, vis-à-vis the alien, the most reactionary position of the entire crew (it is she who is opposed to letting it on board, even to save Kane's life). She is, of course, in the film's terms, quite right; but that merely confirms the ideologically reactionary nature of the film, in its attitude to the Other.

If male and female are superficially and trendily united in Ripley, they are completely fused in the alien (whose most striking characteristic is its ability to transform itself). The sexuality so rigorously repressed in the film returns grotesquely and terrifyingly in its monster (the more extreme the repression, the more excessive the monster). At first associated with femaleness (it begins as an egg in a vast womb), it attaches itself to the most "feminine" of the crew's males (John Hurt, most famous for his portrayal of Quentin Crisp) and enters him through the mouth as a preliminary to being "born" out of his stomach. The alien's phallic identity is strongly marked (the long reptilian neck); but so is its large, expandable mouth, armed with tiers of sharp metallic teeth. As a composite image of archetypal sexual dread, it could scarcely be bettered: the monstrous phallus combined with *vagina dentata*. Throughout the film, the alien and the cat are repeatedly paralleled or juxtaposed, an association that may remind us of the panther–domestic cat opposition in *Cat People* (the cats even have the same surname, the John Paul Jones of Tourneur's movie reduced here to a mere "Jones" or "Jonesey"). The film creates its image of the emancipated woman only to subject her to massive terrorization (the use of flashing lights throughout *Alien*'s climactic scenes strikingly recalls the finale of *Looking for Mr. Goodbar* [1977]) and enlist her in the battle for patriarchal repression. Having destroyed the alien, Ripley can become completely "feminine"—soft and passive, her domesticated pussy safely asleep.

It is not surprising, though disturbing and sad, that at present it is the reactionary horror film that dominates the genre. This is entirely in keeping with the overall movement of Hollywood in the past five years. Vietnam, Nixon, and Watergate produced a crisis in ideological confidence that the Carter administration has temporarily resolved; *Rocky* (1976), *Star Wars* (1977), and *Heaven Can Wait* (1978) (all overwhelming popular successes) are but the echoes of a national sigh of relief. *Sisters, Demon, Night of the Living Dead,* and *The Texas Chainsaw Massacre* in their various ways reflect ideological disintegration and lay bare the possibility of social revolution; *Halloween* and *Alien,* while deliberately evoking maximum terror and panic, variously seal it over again.

Note

This article owes a considerable debt to the work of Tony Williams. Tony has been writing an MA thesis on the horror film under my supervision, and in the last two years we have exchanged so many ideas that it would no longer be possible to sort out whose was which (Wood's note).

Chapter 19

FROM *SACRED TERROR:*
RELIGION AND HORROR ON THE SILVER SCREEN

Douglas E. Cowan

> In *Sacred Terror*, religious studies scholar Douglas E. Cowan proposes that the horror genre in some ways puts us in touch with the sacred. That is, it often explicitly and implicitly proposes the existence of a world beyond that of the senses. As such, it responds to what Cowan proposes is a "yearning" for what we might consider a transcendental plane beyond what we can see, feel, taste, touch, and hear.

The Ubiquity of Horror and the Persistence of Belief

"Human acquiescence," intones the demonic Pinhead (Doug Bradley) in *Hellraiser: Bloodline* (1996), "is as easily obtained by terror as by temptation." And how true this has proven to be in the religious history of humankind. While it may be overstating the case to argue that all religion is rooted in fear of the dark, of disease, of drought or flood, of the myriad terrors that threaten from the forest's edge, and, ultimately, of death, there are certainly significant cross-cultural instances in which this is manifestly the case. On his way up Mount Sinai to meet Yahweh, for example, Moses is cautioned not to look on the face of the Divine if he wants to come down from the mountain alive (Exodus 33:18–23). When the Ark of the Covenant was completed, the Israelites learned not to touch it if they wanted to live (see Exodus 25:12–15; Numbers 4:15; 2 Samuel 6:1–7). When the Tabernacle was erected in the wilderness, and later the Temple in Jerusalem, only the High Priest could enter the Holy of Holies—and that only on one particular day of the year. The penalty for transgression? Death (Leviticus 16:2; Hebrews 9:7). Thousands of years later, the world of the Kwaio, who inhabit the island of Malaita in the Solomon Islands, is still bounded on all sides by a host of "unseen presences" (Keesing 1982, 33), both benevolent and malevolent, and the taboos associated with these beings form the framework of socialization for Kwaio children and of behavior for Kwaio adults.

Jeanette Southgate, a young woman in Norfolk, England, has seen ghosts for most of her life and lives in a house with a variety of haunting spirits. Moved by a range of poltergeist activities, she now keeps an online diary as part of her attempt to understand her experiences and those of the spirits with whom she believes she shares her life (Southgate 2007).

It matters little whether we believe in the ancestral spirits of the Kwaio or the noisy ghosts that disrupt Southgate's life. They believe, and they structure their worlds and their behaviors accordingly. Similarly, it matters little whether Moses really met with Yahweh, whether the Ark really destroyed all who touched it, or whether sudden death came to those who entered the Holy of Holies unbidden by the Divine. The point is that they are remembered in the sacred narratives as though they really happened, and for hundreds of millions of Jews and Christians worldwide, they have behind them the power of memory, mythistory, and, for some, literal truth.

Whether terror is the mechanism by which the gods ensure compliance or the bedrock of belief upon which compliance is built—and whether the gods invoked want such compliance, need it, or exist at all—a common denominator in the negotiation of the unseen order is *fear*. All this is part and parcel of the *mysterium tremendum et fascinans* (Otto [1923] 1950)—*fear* of the Lord as the beginning of wisdom, despite the fact that generations of Christian preachers have glossed the passage, insisting that it means "awe" not "fear," "worship" not "terror," and "reverence" not death, destruction, and sundry mayhem as the inevitable price for transgressing the boundaries between the sacred and the profane. The fact of the matter, however, is that fear (insert *terror*) is the thread that often holds the cloth of religion together. And we have good, solid, empirical (if mythistorical) reasons to fear the Divine—just ask the assembled residents of Sodom and Gomorrah or Noah's neighbors. Oh, wait, that's right. We can't. They're dead, riven from the earth by fire and flood at the hands of an angry, some might argue capricious and arbitrary deity. So Pinhead's comment is not without merit. Indeed, a 2006 national survey found that more than 30 percent of Americans believe in what the researchers called an "Authoritarian God," one who "is highly involved in their daily lives," but who "is quite angry and is capable of meting out punishment to those who are unfaithful or ungodly" (Baylor Religion Survey 2006, 27).

Belief in the unseen order persists in other ways, as well. In a fascinating look at the plight of minority faiths in a largely Christian America, Carol Barner-Barry (2005) recounts several instances in which public school officials have disciplined children for allegedly casting spells on teachers and classmates. In Oklahoma, for example, a high school student "was suspended for 15 days when school officials accused her of hexing a teacher who fell ill" (131). Despite exemplary attendance and performance records, she had been suspended a year earlier when Wiccan literature was discovered in her book bag. In Baltimore, a student received a day-long suspension for spellcasting, and numerous Pagan students have been suspended, sent home, or forced to remove religious symbols, such as pentagrams (see Barner-Barry 2005, 129–35). Indeed, in an incident reminiscent of a scene from Andrew Fleming's *The Craft* (1996), a student was suspended for writing a poem—which was interpreted as a spell—in which she wanted a rival's hair to fall out. "The interesting thing about such cases," writes Barner-Barry, "is the readiness of school authorities to take seriously the ability of a student to cast effective spells or hex others" (132). What is important to note is that these are not historical cases—all occurred within the last decade. Unsurprising, really, since the persistence of belief in the supernatural, coupled with a growing ambivalence toward established religious institutions, has marked American society for decades.

According to the Gallup organization, 68 percent of respondents to a 2001 survey told researchers that "they believe in the Devil," and, while such belief is slightly higher in rural areas, the study concluded that "majorities of Americans of every political inclination, region, education level, and age group said they believe in the Devil" (Robison 2003). The importance of a finding like this cannot be overstated, for if belief in the devil cuts across every demographic boundary, it also cuts across both the viewing audiences for cinema horror and the cultural stocks of knowledge on which the sociophobics of demonic attack and possession draw. Put simply, they are not limited to one type of religious believer. Moreover, a 2004 Gallup report indicated that 70 percent of Americans believe in hell, including 92 percent of those who declared that they attend church at least weekly and 50 percent "of those who attend church seldom or never" (Winseman 2004). While the first breakdown here should not surprise anyone, the author of the report editorializes the second breakdown as "just half." "Just half," however, is hardly insignificant. Half of the people surveyed who said that they attend church rarely or never also reported that they still believe in hell! Although precisely what either Gallup or the respondents mean by "hell" is not made clear, it is not unlikely that their conception is based in this instance on a three-tiered Christian cosmology, an "unseen order" in which one's transgressions on earth are punished for eternity in the pit.

In his discussion of the nature of "superstition" in the twentieth century Gustav Jahoda (1969, 19) notes that, very often, when "talk comes around to the supernatural, the chances are that several persons will tell stories of occult occurrences that allegedly happened either to themselves or their relatives and friends; such stories are apt to range all the way from vague premonitions to seeing ghosts." What this points out is that, however many rationalist, empirical, positivist, naturalist, or secularist explanations are offered for belief in the supernatural, nearly a generation ago (i.e., at the height of the secularization hypothesis's explanatory power), Jahoda's comments were right on the mark. "Enough has been said," Jahoda continues, "to indicate that under the seemingly rational surface of modern society there is an unexpectedly widespread yearning for the mysterious and occult we are supposed to have outgrown" (23).

The keyword is *yearning*. That is, there is not only an ongoing *belief* in supernatural phenomena, but an equally strong inclination *to believe*, an equally powerful desire that these things be true, that, however frightening they are, the "things that go bump in the night" really do reside outside our minds. People want near-death experiences to bear out their belief in life after death; they want spiritualists, mediums, channels, and EVP (electronic voice phenomena, the belief that the unseen order can communicate through the white noise of televisions and radios) to confirm for them the ongoing existence of their loved ones, and, by extension, themselves. Borne out by recent polling data, Jahoda's (1969) words are almost prescient. "Superstition," he argues, "is still very much with us, and it is even possible that some forms of it may be on the increase" (26). And, while "the dominant intellectual temper of nineteenth-century Europe was rationalistic, the same period saw the spectacular rise of occultism, by no means confined to the vulgar and ignorant" (33).

From 1993 to 2002, one of the most popular series on television was Chris Carter's *The X-Files*. Each week, audiences from Sweden to Singapore tuned in to watch FBI agents Dana Scully (Gillian Anderson) and Fox Mulder (David Duchovny) face the improbable and investigate the inexplicable. Though a variety of conspiracy theories and an alien abduction subplot anchored the overall *X-Files* narrative, numerous individual episodes dealt either explicitly or implicitly with supernatural or paranormal phenomena. Though it would be too much to argue for a direct correlation—and they do not try—Gallup researchers did note an increase in popular belief in psychic phenomena over the course of the series. Between 1990 and 2001, American belief in psychic or spiritual healing, for example, went from 44 to 54 percent, while belief in ghosts or haunting spirits rose from 25 to 38 percent, and a more general belief in human ability to communicate with the dead from 18 to 28 percent (Newport and Strausberg 2001). Moreover, while belief in demonic possession fell from 49 to 41 percent, belief in haunted houses rose from 29 to 42 percent and in witches (presumably of the "wicked" variety, though the study does not specify) from 14 to 26 percent.

Clearly, we know more now than we did once. Explanations for what have turned out to be natural phenomena; causal frameworks into which events as disparate as infant deaths, cattle disease, and volcanic eruptions; theoretical positions that claim to have the answer for everything from Vegas card counting to flightless waterfowl—all these may have shifted belief away from the supernatural in the past couple of hundred years, and shifted even more rapidly in the past few decades, but for a great many people a frightening darkness still exists just beyond the range and sweep of our cultural headlights. However bright our beams, the dark is still the dark.

Exploring Our Fear: The Sociophobics of Cinema Horror

In his book *Monsters and Mad Scientists* (1989), Andrew Tudor notes that the most enduring narrative schema in the films he considered—990 British horror films released from the 1930s to the 1970s—is what he calls "supernature," a threat that comes from beyond the bounds of accepted "natural" reality, that is, the "unseen order" to which participants must adapt themselves in one way or another. Tudor divides this broader category into a "manipulative supernature," populated by wizards, witches, and magicians (which he lumps together with Satanists) who inhabit no larger religious tradition and who use their access to the supernatural for personal, often malevolent gain, and "nonmanipulative supernature"—vampires, demons, werewolves, and other preternatural creatures that simply "invade" the natural order. The problem with this categorization is that it ignores precisely those larger dimensions of religious belief and practice in which many of these cinematic examples are (and are very easily) embedded, as well as the particular religious beliefs, practices, histories, and cultural stocks of knowledge on which each draws or to which it adverts. If, as I am suggesting, religiously oriented horror films are much more than the simple pornography of violence implied by such critics as Medved and Stone, and not simply the infantilistic regression or adolescent identity play argued by such scholars as Wexman, Zillman, and Weaver, what then are they?

They are sociophobic artifacts, the artistic traces of a wide variety of fears that continue to haunt us. In his introduction to *The Horror People* (1976), journalist and novelist John Brosnan notes what a number of commentators have pointed out—that horror cinema has often been denigrated as a kind of second-rate celluloid home for faded actors and failed directors. It's the place where washed-up filmmakers go to die (again and again and again). This is, of course, not to say that there are not bad horror films out there. There are, measured by any standard one cares to name. But lousy movies are hardly the sole provenance of horror cinema. Brosnan continues, however, that horror has been "picked up" by cultural critics as a reflection of the popular fears extant at the time of production. He suggests, though, that this interpretive hand has often been overplayed by academics who insist on finding meaningful symbolism in films that are simply exploitation.

> Horror films have come to be regarded by this critical "new wave" as important works that more accurately reflect the obsessions and tensions of society than their more serious, and respectable, counterparts. In some cases such claims are justifiable, but too often it becomes ludicrous when all manner of complicated symbolism is read into a film that has obviously been designed as pure exploitation. (1–2)

The problem with this—or, rather, the shortsightedness of this approach (which may have something to do with a fan's entirely reasonable desire not to have his enjoyment of horror ruined by an excess of scholarly dissection, analysis, and commentary)—is that the cultural dynamic of *exploitation* is a direct function of the audience for whom a particular film is produced. There must be something within the audience that the filmmaker can exploit. In the case of cinema horror, there must be some fear a director can tap into and bring to life on the screen, if only for a moment. The mistake made by Brosnan and other critics who critique films for their exploitative character is that they tend to stop with exploitation and neglect to ask the more significant questions: With all the potential scary things around, why do horror filmmakers return over and over to an identifiable pattern of topics, themes, and treatments? Why do we fear the dead, for example? Why do we fear that the church is not the pristine sanctuary it pretends to be or presents itself as? Why do we fear the chaogonic invasion/inversion of our world, and the apparent powerlessness (or capriciousness) of God in the face of it? In this sense, it is possible that cinema horror is one cultural means by which we confront the classic theological problem of evil. Because it speaks to the social construction of fear and fearing, it is this pool of potential exploitation that interests me.

Rather than simply the product of individual psychology, for more than two decades now, sociologists, anthropologists, and cultural critics have thought about fear as a social phenomenon, an affect as conditioned by culture as it is established by personality. In his introduction to sociophobics, David Scruton (1986, 9) writes:

> Fearing is an event that takes place in a social setting; it is performed by social animals whose lives and experiences are dominated by culture. . . . It is impossible to understand fully what human fearing is, how fears happen in the individual, how they are expressed both to self and to others, how they are received and reacted to by others in the community, and what their function in our lives is unless we treat fearing as a function of cultural experience, which people participate in because they are members of specific societies at particular times. Fearing is thus a dimension of human social life.

Put differently, our culture teaches us in a variety of ways what to fear, and through a variety of culture products reflects and reinforces the fears we have been taught. What, then, are the religiously oriented fears that cinema horror reveals to us? Though they are hardly discrete categories, and while many films contain more than one sociophobic element, there are six basic themes . . . : fear of change in the sacred order; fear of sacred places; fear of death, of dying badly, and of not remaining dead; fear of evil that is both externalized and internalized; fear of fanaticism and the power of religion; and, finally, fear of the flesh and the powerlessness of religion. Exploiting these fears, filmmakers make us shiver, scream, and seek comfort beneath the bedclothes.

References

Barner-Barry, Carol. 2005. *Contemporary Paganism: Minority Religions in a Majoritarian America*. Palgrave Macmillan.

Baylor Religion Survey. 2006. *American Piety in the 21st Century: New Insights into the Depth and Complexity of Religion in the US*. Baylor Institute for Studies of Religion.

Brosnan, John. 1976. *The Horror People*. St. Martin's Press.

Jahoda, Gustav. 1969. *The Psychology of Superstition.* Penguin Books.
Keesing, Roger M. 1982. *Kwaio Religion: The Living and the Dead in a Solomon Island Society.* Columbia University Press.
Newport, Frank, and Maura Strausberg. 2001. "Americans' Belief in Psychic and Paranormal Phenomena Is Up over Last Decade." Gallup, June 8.
Otto, Rudolf. (1923) 1950. *The Idea of the Holy.* Translated by John W. Harvey. Oxford University Press.
Robison, Jennifer. 2003. "The Devil and the Demographic Details." Gallup, February 25.
Scruton, David L. 1986. "The Anthropology of an Emotion." In *Sociophobics: The Anthropology of Fear,* edited by David L. Scruton, 7–49. Westview Press.
Southgate, Jeanette. 2007. "I Live with a Ghost in My House." *Beyond Magazine*, June 6, 56–57.
Tudor, Andrew. 1989. *Monsters and Mad Scientists: A Cultural History of the Horror Movie.* Basil Blackwell.
Winseman, Albert L. 2004. "Eternal Destinations: Americans Believe in Heaven, Hell." Gallup, May 25.

Chapter 20

FROM "DISCIPLINE AND DISTRACTION: *PSYCHO*, VISUAL CULTURE, AND POSTMODERN CINEMA"

Linda Williams

> Having heard from Hitchcock himself in part I, Linda Williams's analysis of the pleasures of *Psycho* seems apropos and starts to push us toward the kinds of reception models developed by Matt Hills and the authors included in part III. Eschewing traditional approaches to film, Williams considers the visceral experience of "going to the movies," likening the film to an amusement park thrill ride.

Disciplining Fear: "The Care and Handling of *Psycho*"

From the very first screenings of the film, audience reaction, in the form of gasps, screams, yells, and even running up and down the aisles, was unprecedented. Although Hitchcock later claimed to have calculated all this, saying he could hear the screams when planning the shower montage, screenwriter Joseph Stefano claims, "He was lying.... We had no idea. We thought people would gasp or be silent, but screaming? Never" (cited in Rebello 1990, 117).

No contemporary review of the film ignored the fact that audiences were screaming as never before. Here are some typical reviews:

> Scream! It's a good way to let off steam in this Alfred Hitchcock shockeroo, ... so scream, shiver and shake and have yourself a ball. (Delaplane 1960)

> So well is the picture made ... that it can lead audiences to do something they hardly ever do any more—cry out to the characters, in hopes of dissuading them from going to the doom that has been cleverly established as awaiting them. (Callenbach 1960, 48)

And on the negative side:

> Director Hitchcock bears down too heavily in this one, and the delicate illusion of reality necessary for a creak-and-shriek movie becomes, instead, a spectacle of stomach-churning horror. (*Time*, June 27, 1960, 51)

> *Psycho* is being advertised as more a shocker than a thriller, and that is right—I am shocked, in the sense that I am offended and disgusted. . . . The clinical details of psychopathology are not material for trivial entertainment; when they are used so they are an offense against taste and an assault upon the sensibilities of the audience . . . it makes you feel unclean. (Hatch 1960, 39)

Having unleashed such powerful reactions, the problem now was how to handle them. According to Anthony Perkins, the entire scene in the hardware store following the shower-murder, the mopping up and disposal of Marion's body in the swamp, were inaudible due to leftover howls from the previous scene. Hitchcock even asked [Universal] Studio[s] head Lew Wasserman to allow him to remix the sound to allow for the audience's vocal reaction. Permission was denied (Rebello 1990, 163).

Hitchcock's unprecedented "special policy" of admitting no one to the theater after the film had begun was certainly a successful publicity stunt, but it had lasting repercussions in its transformation of the previously casual act of going to the movies into a much more *disciplined* activity of arriving on time and waiting in an orderly line. As Peter Bogdanovich (1963) has noted, it is because of *Psycho* that audiences now go to movies at the beginning. One popular critic wrote in a Sunday arts and leisure section about the new policy, "At any other entertainment from ice show to baseball games, the bulk of the patrons arrive before the performance begins. Not so at the movies which have followed the policy of grabbing customers in any time they arrive, no matter how it may impair the story for those who come in midway" (*View*: 1).[1] This reviewer then takes it upon himself to advocate the exhibition policy so important to *Psycho*'s success and impact on audiences: that no one be admitted late to the film. Hitchcock (1960) defended this policy in an article published in *The Motion Picture Herald*, saying that the idea came to him one afternoon in the cutting room: "I suddenly startled my fellow-workers with a noisy vow that my frontwards-backwards-sidewards-and-inside-out labors on *Psycho* would not be in vain—that everyone else in the world would have to enjoy the fruits of my labor to the full by seeing the picture from beginning to end. This was the way the picture was conceived—and this was how it had to be seen" (17–18).

This "policy," unheard of in the United States at the time, necessitated important changes in the public's moviegoing habits: Audiences had to be trained to learn the times of each show; if they were late, they had to wait for the next screening; and, once they bought their tickets, they had to be induced to stand patiently in ticket holder lines. The theater managers' new buzzwords were to "fill and spill" theaters efficiently at precise intervals, thus affording more screenings. The unprecedented discipline required to "fill and spill" the theater was in paradoxical contrast to the equally unprecedented thrills of the show itself.

Here is how another columnist described the discipline and thrill of seeing the film over a month after its release:

There was a long line of people at the show—they will only seat you at the beginning and I don't think they let you out while it's going on. . . . A loudspeaker was carrying a sound track made by Mr. Hitchcock. He said it was absolutely necessary—he gave it the British pronunciation like "nessary." He said you absolutely could not go in at the beginning. The loudspeaker then let out a couple of female shrieks that would turn your blood to ice. And the ticket taker began letting us all in. A few months ago, I was reading the London review of this picture. The British critics rapped it. "Contrived," they said. "Not up to the Hitchcock standards." I do not know what standards they were talking about. But I must say that Hitchcock . . . did not seem to be that kind of person at all. Hitchcock turned us all on. Of all the shrieking and screaming! We were all limp. And, after drying my palms on the mink coat next to me, we went out to have hamburgers. And let the next line of people go in and die. Well, if you are reading the trade papers, you must know that *Psycho is* making a mint of money. This means we are in for a whole series of such pictures. (Delaplane 1960)

How shall we construe this new disciplining of audiences to wait in line? Michel Foucault (1978, 138) writes that "discipline produces subjected and practiced bodies, 'docile' bodies." He means that what we experience as autonomy is actually a subtle form of power. Obviously the bodies of the *Psycho* audience were docile. Indeed, the fun of the film was dependent upon the ability of these bodies to wait patiently in line in order to catch the thrills described. No one coerced them to arrive on time and wait in line. This discipline is for fun. And the fun derives partly from the exhilaration of a group submitting itself, as a group, to a thrilling sensation of fear and release from fear. In this highly ritualized masochistic submission to a familiar "master," blood turns to ice, shrieking and screaming are understood frankly as a "turn on," followed by climax, detumescence, and the final recovery and renewal of (literal and metaphorical) appetite.

The passage also offers a rich mix of allusions to gender, class, and nationality: The mink coat next to the columnist is clear indication that these pleasures were not for men only, as well as evidence that a wide variety of the public participated. Hamburger counters mink; snooty English "standards" are foils to America's favorite fantasy of the leveling democratic entertainment of "the movies." What we see here is a conception of the audience as a group with a common solidarity—that of submitting to an experience of mixed arousal and fear and of recognizing those reactions in one another and perhaps even performing them for one another.[2]

This audience, surveilled and policed with unprecedented rigor outside the theater, responding with unprecedented vocalized terror inside the theater, is certainly disciplined in the sense of Foucault's term. But it is also an audience with a newfound sense of itself as bonded around the revelation of certain terrifying visual secrets. The shock of learning these secrets produces a camaraderie, a pleasure of the group, that was, I think, quite new to motion pictures. A certain community was created around *Psycho*'s secret that gender is often not what it seems. The shock of learning this secret helped produce an ironic sadomasochistic discipline of master and slave with Hitchcock hamming up his role as sadistic master and with audiences enjoying their role as submissive victims.

An important tool in disciplining the *Psycho* audience were three promotional trailers, two quite short and one six-minute affair that has become a classic. All hinted at but, unlike most "coming attractions," refrained from showing too much of the film's secret. In the most famous of these, Hitchcock acts as a kind of house-of-horrors tour guide at the Universal International Studio set of the Bates Motel and adjacent house (now the Universal Studios Theme Park featuring the *Psycho* house and motel). Each trailer stressed either the importance of special discipline—"please don't tell the ending, it's the only one we have"—or the importance of arriving on time. But there was also another trailer, not seen by the general public but even more crucial in inculcating audience discipline. Called "The Care and Handling of *Psycho*," this was not a preview of the film but a filmed "press book" teaching theater exhibitors how properly to exhibit the film and police the audience.[3]

The black-and-white trailer begins with a scene outside the DeMille Theater in New York, where *Psycho* began a limited engagement before being released nationwide. To the accompaniment of Bernard Herrmann's driving violin score, we see crowds in line for the film. A man in a tuxedo is a theater manager, the narrator urgently informs us, in charge of implementing the new policy, which the trailer then explains. The sly voice of Alfred Hitchcock is heard over a loudspeaker explaining to the waiting audience that "This queuing up is good for you, it will make you appreciate the seats inside. It will also make you appreciate *Psycho*." The mixture of polite inducement backed up by the presence of Pinkerton guards, and a life-size lobby card cutout of Hitchcock pointing to his watch, adds up to a rather theatrical, sadomasochistic display of coercion. We hear Hitchcock induce the audience to keep the "tiny, little horrifying secrets" of the story while insisting on the democracy of a policy that will not even make exceptions for the Queen of England or the manager's brother.

Perhaps the most striking thing about this trailer is that it worked; not only did audiences learn to arrive on time but they eagerly joined the visible crowds on the sidewalks waiting to see the film. When shaken spectators left the theater, they were grilled by those waiting in line but never gave away the secret (Rebello 1990, 161). By exploiting his popular television persona as the man who loves to scare you, and the man audiences love to be scared by, Hitchcock achieved the kind of rapt audience attention, prompt arrival, and departure that would have been the envy of a symphony orchestra. Yet, he achieved this attention with the casual, general audience more used to the distractions of amusement parks than the discipline of high culture.

On July 17, 1955, Disneyland had already opened its doors to large numbers of visitors taking in the total visual attraction of a variety of film-oriented "fantasy lands." In August 1964, Universal Studios began offering tram ride tours of its movie sets and would eventually expand to a more movie-related and thrill-inducing competitor to Disneyland, including the *Psycho* set and a presentation of how certain scenes from the film were shot.[4] Clearly, the sort of discipline that Hitchcock was teaching was more like that of the crowds at these theme parks than any kind of simple audience taming. Lawrence Levine (1988) has written compellingly about the taming of American audiences during the latter part of the nineteenth century. He argues that while American theater audiences had in the first half of the nineteenth century been a highly participatory and unruly lot, spitting tobacco, talking back to actors, arriving late, leaving early, stamping feet, applauding promiscuously, they were gradually tamed by the arbiters of culture to "submit to creators and become mere instruments of their will, mere auditors of the productions of the artist" (183). Levine tells, for example, of an orchestra conductor in Cincinnati in 1873 who ordered the doors to be closed when he began to play, admitting no one until the first part was finished. When he was resisted, his argument was "When you play Offenbach or Yankee Doodle, you can keep your doors open. When I play Handel . . . they must be shut. Those who appreciate music will be here on time" (188). Levine argues that this late nineteenth-century American audience lost a sense of itself as an active force, a "public," and became instead a passive "mute receptor" of the will of the artist through this discipline. New divisions between high and low meant that it was more and more difficult to find audiences who could serve as microcosms of society, who felt like participants in a general culture, and who could articulate their opinions and feelings vocally (195).

With Hitchcock's policy trailer we certainly see some elements of Levine's tamed audience: Pinkerton guards, loudspeakers, "docile bodies" waiting patiently in line, not to mention Hitchcock's disembodied voice insisting that seeing the film from the beginning is "required." Certainly, Hitchcock asserts "the will of the artist" over the audience. However, this will is in the service of producing visceral thrills and ear-splitting screams that are a far cry from the politely suppressed coughs of the concert hall. It seems that the efficiency and discipline demonstrated outside the theater need to be viewed in tandem with the unprecedented patterns of fear and release unleashed inside. Hitchcock's discipline, like that of the emerging theme parks, was not based on the stratification of audiences into high and low, nor, as would later occur in the ratings system, was it based on the stratification of different age groups. Nor was it based on the acquisition of the same kind of passivity and silence that Levine traces in late nineteenth-century America. In Hitchcock's assumption of the persona of the sadist who expects his submissive audience to trust him to provide a devious form of pleasure, we see a new bargain struck between filmmaker and audience: If you want me to make you scream in a new way and about these new sexually destabilized secrets, the impresario seems to say, then you must line up patiently to receive this thrill.

Hitchcock is, of course, only doing what he often did in his trailers: teasing the audience with their paradoxical love of fear, shock, surprise, and suspense—all emotions that he can rely upon audiences to know that he will manipulate for maximum pleasure. His famous cameos in the early parts of most of his films are another way of teasing the audience, though also of disciplining them to pay close attention. Like the patient crowds standing in line at Disneyland, or the crowds that would eventually stand in line to see the *Psycho* house and motel at Universal Studios,[5] these disciplined audiences were a far cry either from 1970s film theory's notion of distanced, voyeuristic mastery or Levine's passive, mute receptors.

Psycho is popularly remembered as the film that violated spectatorial identification with a main character by an unprecedented killing off of that character in the first third of the film. But in order for audiences to experience the full force of that violation, Hitchcock required the kind of rapt entrance into the spell of a unified space and time that the so-called classical theories of spectatorship assume but that the popular Hollywood cinema, with its distracted viewers wandering into theaters at any old time, had perhaps only rarely delivered. *Psycho* thus needs to be viewed as a film in which disciplined audiences arrived on time in order to be attentively absorbed into the filmic world and narrative, and in which distracted "attractions" of the amusement park variety are equally important. The more rapt viewers' initial attention, the more acute the shock when the rug was pulled out from under them.

Lawrence Levine's analysis of the nineteenth-century taming of the audience argues a singular process of repressing unruly body functions. Theaters, opera houses, and large movie houses were, for him, agents in teaching audiences to adjust to new social imperatives, training them to keep strict control of emotional and physical processes. Levine may be right that bodily repression was necessary to concert- and theatergoers. But the (mostly unwritten) history of cinema reception will require more than a concept of bodily repression to understand the various disciplines of filmgoing that have taken place in this century.[6] It will certainly require a more Foucauldian concept of discipline as productive of certain precise bodily regimes of pleasure rather than the mere repression of the physical. For, as we have seen, *Psycho* simultaneously elicits more bodily reaction along with greater bodily discipline.[7]

The lesson of the "care and handling" of *Psycho* is thus how first Hitchcock, then Hollywood learned how greater spectatorial discipline could pay off in the distracted attractions of a postmodern cinema. *Psycho* needs to be seen as a historical marker of a moment when popular American movies, facing the threat of television, in competition and cooperation with new kinds of amusement parks, began to invent new scopic regimes of visual and visceral "attraction." In this moment, visual culture can be seen getting a tighter grip on the visual pleasures of film spectators through the reinstitution of a postmodern cinema of attractions.

Figure 20.1, a photograph of a Taiwanese audience in thrall to a projection of what is purported to be Alfred Hitchcock's *Psycho,* might be taken as a dramatic example of a large, international audience caught up in the roller-coaster ride of horror that is the film. This picture, taken with the infrared film in Taipei and published in the trade publication *Paramount World* (July–August 1960), could be taken as evidence of Hitchcock's successful emotional engineering, proof that, as he put it, "if you designed a picture correctly, in terms of its emotional impact, the Japanese audience would scream at the same time as the Indian audience" (Houston 1980, 448). Here is a spectacle of spectatorship itself—of spectators in thrall to what W. J. T. Mitchell (1992) calls the most "vulgar productions of the mass media." But as this chapter has tried to show, the spectacle of spectatorship cannot be reduced to a single, or a simple, image. And it is not really clear that Hitchcock was ever correct in assuming an identity of audience response. Note, for example, how much more crowded together this Taiwanese audience is compared to the London audience pictured in the subsequent photos. To reduce spectatorial audience reactions to, in this case, a singular response of fear is to fail see the different regimes and disciplines that may be observed by different viewers.

One way of picturing the variety of these regimes and this perhaps unique moment of discipline and distraction that was *Psycho* is to consider an entire series of publicity photos of audiences watching *Psycho* published in the same trade publication. These photos were taken at the Plaza Theatre, London, during the film's first run in Britain. Figure 20.2 shows a fragment of a very intense-looking audience, jaws set, watching hard except for two people with averted eyes. We can note here the somewhat defensive postures indicating moments of anticipation—arms crossed; one person holding ears, suggesting the importance sound has in cueing the anticipation of terror. Figure 20.3 shows closer detail of what may be the same audience. Here we begin to note significant gender differences. While the men look intently, the women cringe, refusing to look at the screen, as I had once suggested women do at horror films (Williams 1984). In fact, Figure 20.4 shows just how dramatically male viewers seem to assert their masculinity by looking (note the "cool" man who both looks and strokes his tie).

Let's suppose, for the sake of argument, that these scared women in the audience are looking at one of the following: the "scary woman" at the moment of attack ("Mrs. Bates"; Figure 20.5) or a terrified woman being attacked (Marion; Figure 20.6). What is the best way to describe the specifically gendered reactions of these women spectators to terror? Consider the experience of watching the first attack on Marion in the shower. At this point in the film all viewers can be assumed to be somewhat identified with Marion and to be relatively, though not completely, unprepared for the attack—after all, the film is called *Psycho*. They are taken by surprise by this first irrational irruption of violence, mystified by the lack of a distinct view of the attacker, shocked by the eerie sound and rhythms of screaming violins blending with screaming victim, and energized by the rapid cutting of the scene. This much is true for all spectators. Why then do women appear so much more moved,

Figure 20.1

Figure 20.2

often to the point of smiling, grabbing ears, averting and covering eyes? The question, it seems, is whether female viewers can be said to more closely identify with Marion, especially at the height of her fear and pain, than males. Do we identify more, and thus find ourselves more terrorized, because we are insufficiently distanced from the image in general and from this tortured image of our like in particular?

Men, in contrast, may identify with Marion but forcefully limit their correspondence to her. Since terror is itself, as Clover so aptly notes, "gendered feminine," the more controlled masculine reaction immediately distances itself from the scared woman on the screen. It more quickly gets a grip on itself (as does the man with his tie) and checks its expression. Yet at the same time that it exercises this control, this masculine reaction fully *opens up* to the image to, as Clover (1992, 202) puts it, "take it in the eye." If, as she argues, all forms of contemporary horror involve the masochistic and feminine thrill of "opening up" to, of being "assaulted" by, penetrating images, we might say that the men can be seen to open up more because they feel they "correspond" less to the gender of the primary victims (and to the femininity of fear itself).

For the woman viewer, however, this "taking it in the eye" pleasures her less, initially, than it does the man. Because women already perceive themselves as more vulnerable to penetration, as corresponding more to the assaulted, wide-eyed, and opened-up female victim all too readily penetrated by knife or penis, women's response is more likely to *close down,* at least initially, to such images. This is to say that the mix of pleasure and pain common to all horror viewing, and aligned with a feminine subject position, is negotiated differently by men than by women. Thus all viewers experience a second degree of vicarious pain that is felt as feminizing. But in their greater vulnerability, some women viewers react by acting to filter out some of the painful images. In my earlier essays on *Psycho,* I took the woman's refusal to look at the screen as a sensible resistance to pain. Now I am more inclined to suggest that, as with the general audiences who were disciplined to arrive on time, a much more complex and disciplined negotiation of pleasure is taking place, and that this negotiation takes place over time, as we watch first this film and then its host of imitators—something these instantaneous photos cannot register. By involuntarily averting our eyes, for example, we women viewers partially rupture our connection with the female victim. In the process, we may also establish a new connection with the other women in the audience whose screams we hear. This new connection then itself becomes a source of highly ritualized feminine pleasure. We enjoy being scared *with one another*—a camaraderie that also allows us to measure our difference from Marion. Notice, for example, the smile on the half-hidden mouth of the woman in Figure 20.7.

Thus, while our first reactive, introjective experience of fear may elicit almost involuntary screams and the "closing down" response of not looking, we do not stop feeling the film because we stop looking. In fact, our reliance on musical cues may even induce us to feel more at this juncture. What are the violins saying about the

Figure 20.3

Figure 20.4

Figure 20.5

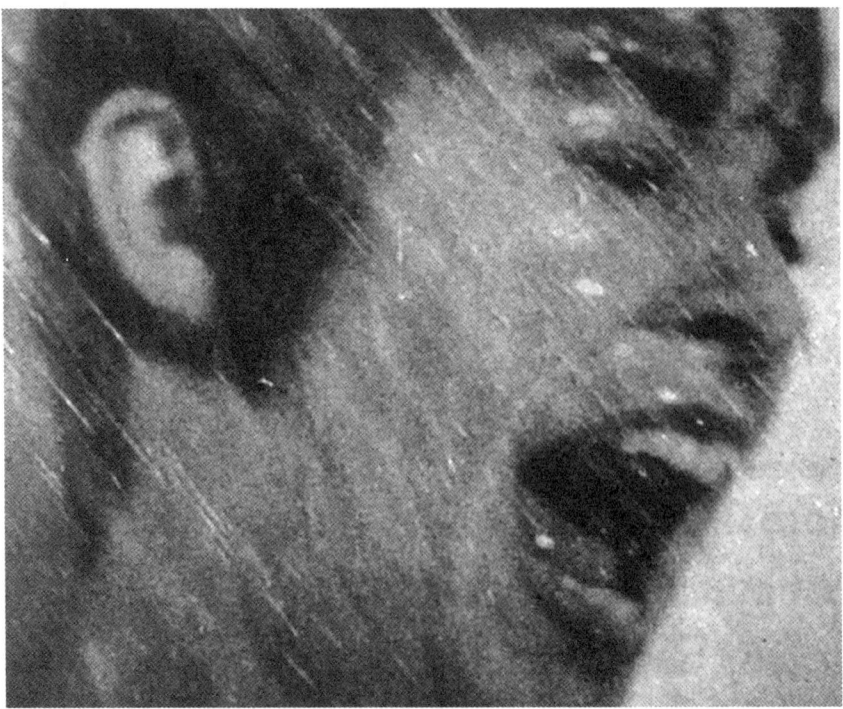

Figure 20.6

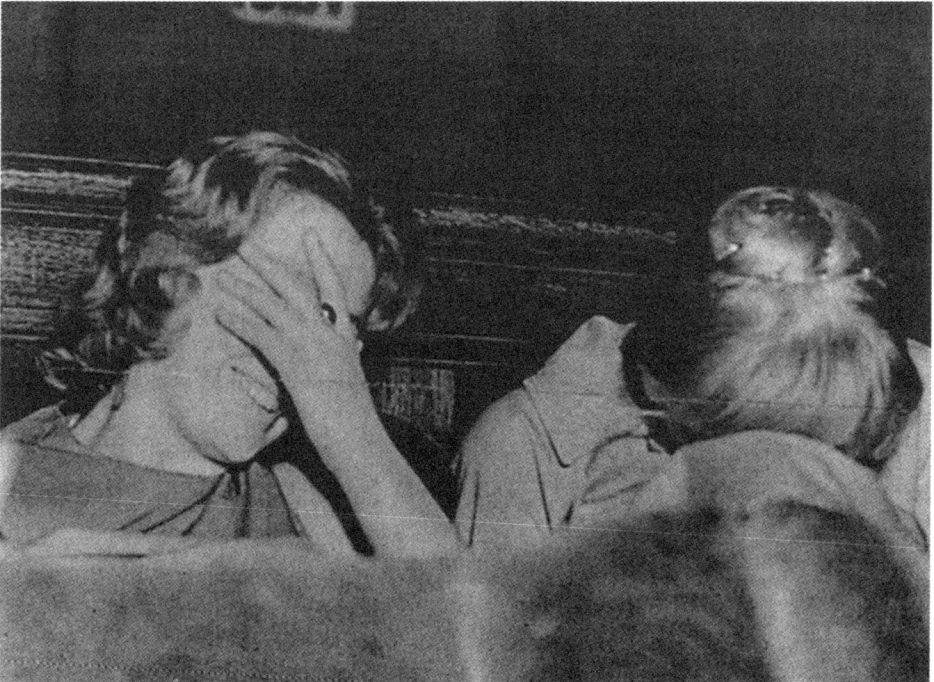

Figure 20.7

danger of looking again? What is my girlfriend's posture telling me about how I might respond? Eventually, however, through the familiarity afforded by the film's repeated attacks, we begin to discipline ourselves to the experience of this reactive, introjective gaze. At this point some women may discipline themselves to keep their eyes more open. Of course, these pictures do not really tell what audiences felt, and like all still images, these are frozen moments, a few hundredths of seconds out of a 109-minute film. They could also have been faked. Nevertheless they dramatize, in acute body language, some general points about the changing distractions and disciplines of film spectatorship inaugurated by *Psycho*.

The first point is that however much we speak about the disembodied and virtual nature of cinematic, and all postmodern, forms of spectatorship, these are still real bodies in the theater, bodies that acutely feel what they see and that, even when visually "assaulted," experience various mixes of vulnerability and pleasure. These people *are* on a kind of roller coaster. They are both disciplined and distracted. "Rapt, mindless fascination" is an inadequate formulation of the engagement with these moving images.

A second point is that this discipline may involve the audience in a new level of performativity. While learning to enjoy the roller-coaster ride of a new kind of thrill, the audience may begin to perceive its own performances of fear as part of the show.

As we also saw in the extended description of seeing *Psycho* by the columnist, these performances—screaming, hiding eyes, clutching the self as well as neighbors—may be important to the pleasures audiences take, as a group, in the film. Such spectatorial performances are certainly not new with *Psycho*. However, the self-consciously ironic manipulations of "the master" eliciting these performances from audiences in a film that is itself about the performance of masculinity and femininity represents a new level of gender play and destabilization. Though this destabilization may have shaken those of us who saw the film on initial release out of some conventional expectations about gender, I would not argue that the experience was necessarily good or bad. It simply was a founding moment of the greater awareness of the performativity of gender roles increasingly ushered in by a postmodern, postclassical reception of cinema.

A final point is that the discipline involved here—both inside and outside the theater—takes place over time. Spectators who clutched themselves, covered eyes or ears, and recoiled in fear at the shower-murder may have been responding involuntarily, the first time, to an unexpected assault. But by the film's second assault this audience was already beginning to play the game of anticipation and to repeat its response in increasingly performed and gender-based gestures and cries. By the time the game of slasher-assault became an actual genre in the mid- and late 1970s, this disciplined and distracted, this attentive, performing audience, will give way to the equivalent of the kids who raise their hands in roller-coaster rides and call out "Look, Ma, no hands!"

Film critics and historians need to investigate the histories of these particular pictorial turns. To find the experience of the popular, fun *Psycho* beneath the layers of ocularphobic high modernist critique is to denigrate neither the film's intelligence nor the intelligence of the audiences who have enjoyed it. It is, rather, to recognize how important the visual and visceral experiences of narrativized roller coasters have become and how assiduously audiences have applied themselves to the disciplines of distraction.

References

Berenstein, Rhona. 1996. *Attack of the Leading Ladies: Gender and Performance in Classic Horror Cinema*. Columbia University Press.

Bogdanovich, Peter. 1963. *The Cinema of Alfred Hitchcock*. Doubleday.

Bukatman, Scott. 1991. "There's Always Tomorrowland: Disney and the Hypercinematic Experience." *October* 57: 55–78.

Callenbach, Ernest. 1960. "Review: *Psycho* by Alfred Hitchcock." *Film Quarterly* 14, no. 1: 47–49.

Clover, Carol. 1992. *Men, Women and Chain Saws: Gender in the Modern Horror Film*. Princeton University Press.

Delaplane, Stan. 1960. *Los Angeles Examiner,* August 12.
Foucault, Michel. 1978. *Discipline and Punish: The Birth of the Prison.* Translated by Alan Sheridan. Vintage.
Hatch, Robert. 1960. *The Nation,* July 2, 39.
Hitchcock, Alfred. 1960. *Motion Picture Herald,* August 8, 17–18.
Houston, Penelope. 1980. "Alfred Hitchcock: I." In *Cinema: A Critical Dictionary,* vol. 1, edited by Richard Roud. Martin Secker and Warburg.
Levine, Lawrence. 1988. *Highbrow/Lowbrow: The Emergence of Cultural Hierarchy in America.* Harvard University Press.
Mitchell, W. J. T. 1992. "The Pictoral Turn." *Art Forum* 30, no. 3: 89–94.
Pechter, William S. 1971. *Twenty-Four Times a Second.* Harper and Row.
Rebello, Stephen. 1990. *Alfred Hitchcock and the Making of "Psycho."* HarperCollins.
Spoto, Donald. 1983. *The Dark Side of Genius: The Life of Alfred Hitchcock.* Ballantine.
Staiger, Janet. 1991. *Interpreting Films: Studies in the Historical Reception of American Cinema.* Princeton University Press.
Williams, Linda. 1984. "When the Woman Looks." In *Re-Vision: Essays in Feminist Film Criticism,* edited by Mary Ann Doane, Patricia Mellencamp, and Linda Williams. American Film Institute Monograph Series 3. University Publications of America.

Notes

1. Source referenced here uncertain. (Editor's note)

2. In 1971, film critic William Pechter (1971, 181) pinpoints this camaraderie of the audience in his own description of how it felt to watch *Psycho*: "The atmosphere . . . was deeply charged with apprehension. Something awful is always about to happen. One could sense that the audience was constantly aware of this; indeed it had the solidarity of a convention assembled on the common understanding of some unspoken *entente terrible*; it was, in the fullest sense, an audience; not merely the random gathering of discrete individuals attendant at most plays and movies."

3. I thank Michael Friend and the Margaret Herrick Library for allowing me to screen this fascinating trailer.

4. The recent Universal Studios "rides"—with the possible exception of the fanciful flight on E.T.'s bicycle, or the more jolting experiences of catastrophic earthquake *(Earthquake)* and fire *(Backdraft)*—seem to operate in the more sensationalizing, blockbuster, Hitchcock tradition of catastrophe and terror, to move audiences quite seriously. In April 1992, the guide on the tram ride portion of the tour showed how thoroughly the Hitchcockian model of assault on the body had been absorbed: "At Universal Studios we not only like to show you the movies, we like you to feel them too." For an excellent discussion of the "hypercinematic" nature of the Disney experience, see Scott Bukatman (1991).

5. It is worth noting that Hitchcock's next project was to have been a film set against the background of Disneyland with Jimmy Stewart as a blind pianist whose sight is restored in operation and who goes to Disneyland in celebration. While there, he discovers that the eyes he has been given are those of a murdered man. He thus begins to hunt down "his" killer.

After the manifest perversions of *Psycho,* the then child- and family-centered Disney claimed that not only would he not permit Hitchcock to shoot in his park, he would not permit his own children to see *Psycho* (Spoto 471).

Hitchcock was greatly disappointed. Yet he may have had at least partial revenge. In a filmed address made sometime later to a British film society, we can see Hitchcock inventing the rudiments of what would one day become the Universal Studios Tour. Called the Westcliffe Address—basically a filmed speech overlaid with documentary shots of the Universal Studio backlots featuring, of course, as the movie-centered amusement park now does, the *Psycho* house as one of its main attractions—the speech is fascinating for its anticipation of the Hollywood rival to Disneyland that would include a most catastrophic, Hitchcockian, assaultive approach to its attractions. As we have already seen, what Hitchcock anticipated, not only in this address but in *Psycho* itself, was the process whereby amusement parks would become more like movies and movies would become more like the new amusement parks. The Westcliffe Address is in the archives of the Margaret Herrick Library.

    6. Janet Staiger offers an impressive theorization and practice of cinematic reception study in her recent *Interpreting Films* (1992).

    7. Berenstein (1996) argues that such performances were a common feature of classic horror cinema. She cites the publicity stunt of a woman planted in the audience of each screening of *Mark of the Vampire* as an extreme example. The woman's task was to scream and faint at predetermined moments so that ushers would whisk her away in a waiting ambulance.

Chapter 21

FRIGHTENING FASCINATION
A Phenomenology of Direct Horror

Julian Hanich

> Julian Hanich in his important study does not paint horror in broad strokes but rather sensibly considers that different types of horror films have different appeals. In the chapter reproduced here, he considers what he refers to as "direct horror"—horror that confronts the audience with acts of violence and monsters directly. With some connections to Noël Carroll's considerations earlier in this part, Hanich claims that the allure of direct horror is its revelation of what usually remains unseen and unheard within the context of a safe viewing space. Emotional immersion and physiological excitation result in what Hanich refers to as "pleasurable fear."

Since time immemorial people have craved spectacles permitting vicariously to experience the fury of conflagrations, the excesses of cruelty and suffering, and unspeakable lusts—spectacles which shock the shuddering and delighted onlooker.

—Siegfried Kracauer

The strongest emotion is fear. The oldest emotion is fear. We all have it, and it is a very deep pool inside every human on the planet. So there are some of us who dive into that pool because we are both repelled and attracted by it.

—John Carpenter

Direct Horror: The Definition

- After being raped and almost strangled by her brother, a young woman is rescued in the nick of time by a friend. The two men start a violent, fatal fight. When the brother smashes a bottle over his opponent's head and sets out to finish him off with the words "Adios, motherfucker!" the woman grabs a metallic comb and pierces it into her brother's eye. He recoils heavily, winces, and screams in pain.

The friend takes the comb and stabs it several times into the brother's stomach. Soon both men are soaked in blood.

- A man walks through a graveyard at night. Suddenly he is surrounded by two monsters. One of them keeps him in check with a knife. The other one threatens him by its sheer monstrosity: piercing, at times blinking eyes, metallic teeth, skin from which snake-like hair emanates, a deep, dark, distorted voice, and a self-assured, highly aggressive demeanor. The monster laughs at the man, threatens him, "You came to die," and calls him an "asshole." At one point, it starts roaring like a deadly, werewolf-like beast, shakes the snake-hair, and suddenly transforms, now flashing sharp, pointed teeth, a drooling mouth, and rotten skin. It roars loudly and screams: "I want meat!" Eventually it attacks the man.
- It is night. A girl clad in a grotesque Halloween bunny costume flees from a murderous, knife-wielding, blonde woman into a dark graveyard. Her escape is in vain. The woman overwhelms her and stabs the screaming girl several times aggressively and with hysterical laughter in the chest until both are splattered with blood. The woman licks her bloody lips and smiles.

The sample scenes are taken from *Henry: Portrait of a Serial Killer* (1986), *Nightbreed* (1990), and *House of 1000 Corpses* (2003), respectively. They exemplify an aesthetic strategy I call "direct horror." The viewer experiences direct horror—the first type of cinematic fear—as a frightening, engrossing, and potentially overwhelming confrontation with vivid *sound-supported moving-images* of threatening acts of *violence* or a dangerous *monster*. In the face of the perceptible violent event and/or monstrous object the viewer is both frightened and fascinated. In contrast to suggested horror, direct horror presents the threatening violent event or monstrous object in full vision and thus as directly as possible.

When he or she experiences direct horror, the viewer is involved in a balancing act between the luring pull *toward* the frightening object of fascination and the threatening push *away* from the fascinating object of fright. The experience vacillates between pleasurably frightening, fascinated *immersion,* and displeasing, overly frightened *extrication.* The former turns into the latter when the frightening aspect obliterates the fascinating side, when pleasurable fear turns into displeasing fear, and when all pleasure components are gone and fear is experienced pure and simple. Moreover, we are horrified by an *instantaneous* event or object: It is what we perceive right now that scares us, not what has happened in the story's past or what might occur in the immediate future. Although we often draw on preceding information or perceptions, the present threatening moving-images are the causes for our horror. Hence remembering and anticipating are subordinate to the concrete event. Since we *are in the face of* the horrific there is a high degree of intentionality and no uncertainty about its coming-into-being. These aspects distinguish horror from anticipatory types of suspenseful fear like dread and terror; the latter are rooted in the present *and* the future; both are dominated by uncertainty and a more complicated kind of intentionality.

But what is it that connects threatening *acts* of violence and the dangerous *object* of the monster? Why do I subsume both under the category of cinematic horror and why, for instance, do natural disasters not qualify? In contrast to the latter, violent events and monstrous entities indicate *intentional* and *disproportional immorality* in combination with *disturbing brutality*. It is precisely this combination of intentional immorality and brutality that we experience as horrifying and that we usually do not ascribe to natural disasters or other threatening events. (Note that I include the adjectives "disproportional" and "disturbing," because they allow for idiosyncratic differences among viewers: What some consider disproportionally immoral and disturbingly cruel, others might regard as tolerable and hence not horrifying.) While we might consider a greedy character delivering nuclear arms to a terrorist group in a political thriller disproportionally immoral, we do not experience this act as cinematic horror because of a lack of disturbing brutality. The disturbingly brutal depictions of a devastating hurricane killing dozens of people in a disaster movie cannot be considered horror either, since a natural disaster cannot be judged in moral terms (unless it is anthropomorphized). And when in a movie like *The Descent* (2005) a female character breaks her leg and we get to see the bloody bone sticking out, this might cause disgust or feelings of pain via somatic empathy. But we do not experience the type of fear I call cinematic horror since no one behaves immorally here. In order to qualify as cinematic horror it does not suffice that a lot of blood is spilled.

Surely, immoral and cruel *acts of violence* should not pose a problem for my definition. But what about moving-images of a monster, say, wandering through the streets of Houston? While such a scene need not *necessarily* evoke horror, the monster often hints at horror so strongly and lets it shine through so vividly that it starts to personify horror: We are frightened by the sheer presence of the monster either because it reminds us forcefully of an act of violence we have already witnessed or have inferred from the plot, or because it points toward an impending cruelty indicated by the monster's aggressive behavior and/or dangerous appearance. Think of the example from *Nightbreed*; although the monster in the graveyard has not attacked the man yet, its menacing looks, its aggressive demeanor, and its hostile comments reveal so much immoral and cruel intention *already*, that many viewers might experience it as horrifying *before* the act of violence has begun. Yet if the definition of the monster hinges on a disproportional intentional immorality combined with disturbing cruelty, the monster does not need to be an ontologically impossible being. This is the reason why we do not call anomalous, supernaturally powerful but likable characters like Yoda or Albus Dumbledore monsters, whereas vicious animals can become horrifying creatures—that is, monsters. Consider *The*

Birds (1963), *Anaconda* (1997), or the killer shark in *Jaws* (1975). Most viewers probably find their intentional attacks on innocent human beings unjustified, overly brutal, and hence horrifying. This definition also helps to explain why human characters can be regarded as (realist) monsters. Just think of Norman Bates, Henry, or Hannibal Lecter. To be sure, they evoke cinematic horror only during threatening moments, that is, in most cases when an act of violence takes place or is at least imminent.

Horror is easily intensified. Two strategies come to mind. First, the victim has to be a character for whom we have developed a strong allegiance and whom we like. This might happen because a star plays the victim, because the actor is attractive, because the character has features or preferences similar to ours, or because he shares an affiliation along race, class, ethnicity, gender, age, or religious lines.[1] More important, an act of violence can horrify us because we strongly approve of the victim on moral grounds, particularly if he or she is sympathetic and innocent. Second, horror can be intensified through an increase in immorality and cruelty. When a bank robber takes great pleasure in cutting off a policeman's ear while dancing rhythmically to a pop song (as in *Reservoir Dogs,* 1992) or a serial killer deeply enjoys eating from a victim's open brain (as in *Hannibal* [2013]), these heinous acts of violence are particularly horrifying.

To be sure, the film cannot merely show an act of violence or a monster, but must present the filmic content in such a vivid and impressive way that the content comes across as *threatening*. That is, in order to be effective, cinematic horror must seamlessly combine content and form, semantics and aesthetics. If one component lags behind, there will be no horror. Hence a vivid, impressive presentation of a ripe banana will create just as little horror as a barely audible monster crossing a cornfield in the far-away distance. Aesthetic choices like proximity through close-ups, precision, and volume of the soundtrack, but also the inconspicuousness of the special effects that draw our attention toward the artifact and away from the scary object, play a fundamental role when it comes to threatening the audience.

Threat is crucial for my definition of horror, insofar as there are funny presentations of violence and the monster as well. Let us look at *violence* first. Stephen Prince has suggested a broad distinction between dominant forms of what he calls "ultra-violence": (1) the aestheticized, balletic violence of Arthur Penn, Sam Peckinpah, John Woo, and the likes relying on slow motion, multicamera filming, and montage editing; and (2) graphic imagery of bodily mutilation exemplified by horror movies of the 1970s and 1980s that employed new makeup special effects to convincingly portray the destruction and dismemberment of the body.[2] According to Prince, both forms of "ultraviolence" are horrifying, if to varying degrees. However, Prince does not take into account that ultraviolence can be hilarious. Think of a funny, violent splatter movie like *Evil Dead II* (1987). The film would clearly fall into Prince's second category, even though it does not have the same horrifying effect as the first

Evil Dead installment simply because, due to various aesthetic strategies, it does not want to and cannot be taken seriously. Similarly, for most people the violence in Quentin Tarantino's *Pulp Fiction* (1994) does not come across as horror, since it is clad in distancing humor and irony and therefore loses its threatening character. Hence one could argue that a "violent" movie is only experientially violent as long as it affects the viewer in a menacing way. It not only matters *what* is presented, but also *how* it is presented.

The same goes for the monster. Depending on the context, the same creature can be a horrifying monster or a funny creature. In *House of Frankenstein* (1944) and *Abbott & Costello Meet Frankenstein* (1948) the creature looks the same and is even played by the same actor (Glenn Strange), but evokes very different reactions.[3] Displaying the monster is not enough to convince us that it is dangerous. The monster must be characterized as a menace by presenting its capabilities and the consequences of its actions. If the monster is not frightening, it might cause all kinds of responses—ranging from laughter to disinterest and even boredom. What is at stake in horror is not violence or the monster per se but their threatening side.

Incidentally, these violent and monstrous moving-images need not be repulsive. My definition of horror rests on a separation between *horrifying* and *disgusting* moving-images and sounds. A frightening film like *Cape Fear* (1991) uses horrifying imagery but works almost completely without disgust, while a splatter parody like *Braindead* (1992) is predominantly revolting without being scary. Obviously, the line between horror and disgust can be quite thin. On one hand, images of cruel acts of torturing mean pure *horror,* and a rotting body full of pus evokes *disgust* and nothing else. On the other hand, a scene in which a character's stomach is sliced open and the intestines can subsequently be seen gushing forth seamlessly blends horror and disgust. Sometimes both emotions occur simultaneously: for instance, when a disgusting monster violently kills a character. Despite the frequent coexistence of these various responses, however, I see no need for a new emotional category. In Noël Carroll's account, fear and disgust are welded together and constitute an emotion he terms "art-horror."[4] His prime instance of art-horror is the monster: It is both threatening and disgustingly impure. But why introduce a new emotion, when the viewer simply feels fear and disgust simultaneously?

The Fascination for Violence and Monsters

Cinematic horror clearly casts an attractive spell. It thrives on a similar kind of fascination that makes people flock around the site of a murder, causes traffic jams at scenes of an accident due to slow-driving gapers, and made people stare at the TV images of the collapsing World Trade Center on 9/11. The snake-headed Gorgo Medusa might be seen as a mythological precursor of today's monsters: a horrible entity highly tempting to look at. The popularity of movies containing violence and monsters clearly points to a high acceptance among viewers. It is hard to deny that graphic violence has generally increased over the last decades. Since the late 1960s, when the Production Code was revised and the Code and Rating Administration introduced its new classification scheme, Hollywood has drastically changed its stance toward violence. At the same time the craft of special effects (makeup) enabling highly graphic depictions of monsters has made considerable progress. Stephen Prince even goes so far as to describe the history of American cinema as a history of ever-more explicit presentational techniques of violence and monstrosity.[5]

Horror movies and thrillers deliberately put the viewer into contact with moving-images that normal life—fortunately—withholds to a large degree, making them both alluring and threatening. This goes in terms of *violence*: the immoral shooting, burning, stabbing, raping, piercing, slicing, smashing, torturing, opening-up, tearing-apart, fragmenting, mutilating, exploding of the body; the cruel disclosure and exposure of the human insides; the death and destruction of the flesh. But it is also true in terms of the *monster*. In most cases monsters are unseen and unheard of entities, often transcending the limits of the human: extremely cunning aliens; deadly living deads; lethal ghouls; mutated, slime-spitting bugs; abnormally intelligent serial killers; haunted, vengeful houses; indestructible slashers; beastly werewolves; outrageously aggressive snakes, dogs, or sharks . . . Noël Carroll explains: "[Monsters] arouse interest and attention through being putatively inexplicable or highly unusual vis-à-vis our standing cultural categories, thereby instilling a desire to learn and to know more about them."[6]

Direct horror is, then, a particularly forceful example of what Mirjam Schaub dubs the cinema of visibility *(Kino der Sichtbarkeit)*.[7] It is a type of cinema that focuses on everything potentially visible and audible. It wants to present what cannot be seen and heard: the more precise, more lasting, more explicit, the better. The depictions of monsters lay bare the cinematic wish—*and* capability—to make visible and audible even nonexistent entities. Schaub calls this the "logic of optical omnipresence." Seen from a reception perspective, the *cinema of visibility* manifests the disposition of its viewers: an urge to see and hear as much as possible.

The extent of this urge can be gauged from our reactions to scenes that deliberately *withhold* the horrific—and thus lure and titillate us. In such scenes of blocked or deferred visual access, there is often a *longing* for a better view: We almost bend to look from a different angle—we are all eyes. David Fincher's *Seven* (1995) belongs to those movies that incessantly play with the viewer's wish to confront the horrific. It variously uses photographs that cannot be seen properly or are glimpsed only shortly. In a crucial scene a policeman urges Detectives Somerset (Morgan Freeman) and Mills (Brad Pitt): "You better see this!"—only to keep back what *they* get to see from our view. In this scene the two detectives enter the bedroom of the prostitute who has become the serial killer's fourth victim. The policeman withdraws a blanket from her corpse like a curtain, as if to say "*Voilà*, here you go!" When the victim is revealed, however, Detective Mills blocks our view. What we see are her legs, slightly covered with blood. However, the fatal wound is—frustratingly?—kept back. Another baiting strategy involves the reaction shot of a horrified character confronting a monster or watching an act of violence. In order to heighten our curiosity for the monster or the effects of violence (and thus to maximize the impact of their presentation), the horror movie often turns around the logical cause-and-effect sequence of storytelling, in which the *re*-action shot *follows* the action, by offering the reaction shot *first* and thus creating heightened curiosity.[8]

The terms *curiosity, interest,* and *fascination* explain—at least in part—our strong attention: We are drawn to violence and the monster because we can see and hear things usually unseen and unheard.

Minding the Ontological Distance, or the Viewer's Relative Safety

This strong attention would not be possible, however, if a certain precondition was inexistent: the viewer's relative safety. In *Seven,* Detective Somerset tells an anecdote that can function as a parable about our fascination with violence and the monster: "First thing they teach women in rape prevention is: Never cry for help. Always yell: 'Fire.' Nobody answers to 'Help.' You holler 'Fire,' they come running." What Somerset bleakly points out is not only our *fascination* with death and destruction, but also the *safety* aspect. No one comes to rescue if there is a demand for active involvement, as implied in the imperative "Help!" If they can take a distanced position, people gather. As a particularly salient part of the cinematic experience, this crucial form of distance enables the vicarious experiences of horror films and thrillers in the first place. I call this detachment *ontological distance* since the movie theater's Here and the filmic world's There are of different existential orders: They are, literally, worlds apart.[9] In Stanley Cavell's reflections on the ontology of film as a *succession of automatic world projections* the fact that the world of the film is present to us, while we are absent from it, that we are safe from it by way of the ontological boundary that is the screen, plays an essential role: "A screen is a barrier. What does the silver screen screen? It screens me from the world it holds—that is, makes me invisible. And it screens that world from me—that is, screens its existence from me," Cavell notes.[10] The ontological distance implies the viewer's physical absence from the scene of action, and thus provides us with a form of safety: We are not threatened by the serial killer Henry or the monster Freddy Krueger *in the same way* as their victims are. This physical absence has important ramifications.

First, we do not have to take action in terms of *geographical* flight from the diegetic threat. When the devil sets about his work of destruction in *The End of Days* (1999), we do not run out of the theater; when all hell breaks loose during the dinosaur attacks in *The Lost World: Jurassic Park* (1997), we do not call 911. Without this sense of safety the emotional experience of the movies would be unbearable.

The idea of a crucial nexus between safety, fear, and pleasure goes back, at least, to the discussions of the sublime in Burke, Kant, and Rousseau.[11] Since then it has resurfaced, among various other places, in the classical film theories of Balázs and Kracauer.[12] A more recent theory that underscores the importance of the ontological (or, as he calls it, "safe") distance is Ed Tan's description of him as an "emotion machine." Tan notes, "A terrifying situation is entertaining precisely because you can do no more than watch; if you were in a position to intervene, in order to protect yourself and others, then you would feel responsible and would no longer be able to enjoy the fictional events on the screen."[13]

Tan points out the second important aspect implied by the notion of ontological distance: It excuses us from action also in the sense of practical *intervention*. In the movie theater we feel no ethical or legal obligation to step in. We cannot cross the film's ontological boundary to heroically throw ourselves in front of the woman and thus prevent her from being stabbed in the shower. And rushing to our cars and heading for Texas to stop the local chainsaw massacre would be utterly in vain. Being relieved from the burden of intervention is closely tied to narrative determinacy. Since in the movie theater the film unrolls without mercy and we cannot stop it, the relieving helplessness is mechanically assured. Hence we could replace Laura Mulvey's aforementioned argument for the viewer's "desire for mastery and will to power [over the movie]" with Stanley Cavell's argument for the viewer's "wish not to need power, not to have to bear its burdens."[14] In terms of frightening movies, being exempted from practical intervention is a blessing—but, as we shall see, it is sometimes a blessing in disguise: Precisely because we have no options to intervene, we can only hope and fear. In other words, the viewer's passivity is also one of the reasons for the frightening power of moving-images.

Third, when the ontological distance is coupled with the *fictional* distance, we are also granted a certain leeway in terms of *moral evaluation*. Since we know that the filmic events are neither live and real *right now* nor have they ever taken place *in the past,* we do not have to be morally outraged as much as in real life when we watch the burying of two well and alive innocents (as in *House of 1000 Corpses*) or the hideous rape of a female protagonist (as in *The Hills Have Eyes II* [2007]). Indeed, projecting ethical norms onto the fiction film might well reduce the intensity of aesthetic experience by drawing us away from the filmic world. This fact becomes quite obvious in cases when the real shines through the irreal and the fiction film unwittingly develops a documentary quality due to its indexical character. All of a sudden we are not interested in what *is taking* place in the fictional filmic world at this moment anymore, but what *has taken* place in front of the camera in the pro-filmic past of the real world. When in Andrej Tarkovsky's *Andrej Rubljov* (1969) a *real* horse really falls from a staircase or in Jean Renoir's *La règle du jeu* (1939) as well as in Robert Bresson's *Mouchette* (1967) a *real* rabbit is really shot, chances are good that we are morally upset.[15]

The uncoupling of perceiving from active participation and moral outrage has an important consequence: Since there is nothing we can do, we are free to watch and listen in order to satisfy our curiosity. Even more important, we can dwell more deeply in our immersive experience. If the disengagement of the practical did not exist and we were to witness a scene of violence in reality, we would act practically, evaluate morally, and be captivated more *strongly* by our emotions—but we would be *less* aware of the whole experience. We would be absorbed completely, whereas in the movie theater the experience is always partial. It is partially there, but simultaneously here, in our body, as well. Hence we need the ontological distance as a prerequisite to devote our awareness more strongly to the fascinating-perceptual and the frightening-emotional experience of violence and monstrosity. Last but not least, add the fact that we know from the outset that this experience is not going to be an endless one: The cinematic experience is a prepackaged, finite, bounded encounter with fear after which we can always return to our everyday life.

Glaring Images, Striking Sounds: The Impressiveness of the Movies

But are we that safe after all? I think we have to answer this question with both yes and no. *Yes,* we are safe insofar as we can always rely on the ontological distance between cinematic surroundings and filmic world. However, just because we are not subjected to the *same* danger as the characters does not imply that we confront *no* danger at all. Readers might have noticed that I have talked about *relative* safety. In fact, some films can have such strong emotional and corporeal effects that we consider them a literal threat to our well-being. They make us feel psychologically mistreated and even physically harmed.[16] Consider the numerous viewers who couldn't cope with *Henry: Portrait of a Serial Killer* and had to leave the theater. Or take the spectators who got sick and even vomited because of *The Exorcist* (1973). These examples do not represent run-of-the-mill horror or thriller experiences. Yet they accentuate quite spectacularly that fear and shock are *real*.

The fact that films *do* sometimes have these overwhelming effects is—implicitly or explicitly—conceded by the existence of four discourses or classificatory systems. First of all, *censorship*: In this case a powerful political or religious group decides to put a ban on a film (or parts of it), because it deems the respective film too harmful for society as a whole. The idea is that some films might harm the moral order of a society or trigger dangerous acts of imitation so that these films need to be concealed from view. Second, *the rating system*: the Motion Picture Association of America judges films according to the well-known rating system that classifies films from G to NC-17. The goal of the rating system is to protect a part of society, namely, children and adolescents, from psychological disturbances or the danger of imitation. Obviously, people judge these media effects quite differently. Hence there are often fierce controversies about censorship and ratings. Third, *academic ideology critique and criticism of the politics of representation*: By exposing films and their representations of women, African Americans, homosexuals, and other minority groups (but also the representations of animals and nature) as agents of ideological manipulation, this form of intellectual iconoclasm also ascribes a harmful effect to movies.[17] Fourth, there is the *genre* as the last, but certainly not the least important classificatory system. The genre as a communicative tool guarantees that the individual knows by and large what to expect from a movie. It thus functions as a means of self-protection. Many people frankly admit that they are not able to bear horror movies, because these films are too frightening—be it because their personal constitution *in general* or their personal phobias vis-à-vis particular presentations *in specific* do not allow for such intense experiences.

But how can something as fleeting as the cinema have such strong effects? Phenomenologists of perception tell us that sight and sound per se have pathic affective quality. The pathic is always a necessary part of perception—we cannot disconnect perception *(Wahrnehmung)* from feeling and affect *(Empfindung)*.[18] To be sure, there are differences between the "higher" and the "lower" senses in terms of what Erwin Straus calls *gnostic* and *pathic* moments of experience: The gnostic (recognition) dominates in a sense like sight; the pathic (feeling) prevails in a sense like touch. Hence the change from one prevailing sense modality to another implies a change in dominance of the gnostic to the pathic moment (or vice versa). However, it would be wrong to understand seeing merely as a *distance sense* that relates the perceiving subject to the perceived object via distance and thus keeps the object at bay. "In seeing, too, we not only experience the seen but also ourselves as someone who sees," Straus notes.[19] What I see is not excluded and distant from me—simply *out there*—but always stands in a pathic relation to me. While we might not be aware of this in everyday circumstances, it becomes all the more obvious in extraordinary cases in which the pathic is so strong that we experience it as affective.[20] Think of visual objects that glare or strike: the sun, the putrefying corpse of a dog at the roadside, the gaze of a beautiful passer-by. The third stanza of Baudelaire's famous poem "To a Woman Passing By" is apposite here. At the sight of a beautiful woman the thunderstruck poetic "I" exclaims, "A gleam . . . then night! O fleeting beauty, / Your glance has given me sudden rebirth."[21] While the glaring of the sun might be explained (away) physiologically, the strong effects of the disgusting dead animal and the female gaze (or male, for that matter) cannot. Seeing is a form of touching at a distance, as is exemplified in the notion *eye contact*.[22]

In what way does this relate to the violent and monstrous moving-images of the cinema? The answer is as simple as it is obvious: The pathic moment or seeing does not stop in front of moving-images in which the object is not *really* there but merely *artificially* present. We cannot deny that we are affected by reality *and* images (which does obviously not imply that both experiences are identical phenomenologically). In his book *The Power of Images,* David Freedberg marvels about the effectiveness, efficacy, and vitality of images and the unrefined, basic, preintellectual, raw responses they entail: "People are sexually aroused by pictures and sculptures; they break pictures and sculptures; they mutilate them, kiss them, cry before them, and go on journeys to them; they are calmed by them, stirred by them, and incited to revolt."[23] And they are, of course, afraid of them. Where does this power of dead material come from, Freedberg wonders? His provocative answer veers in two directions. First, his elaborate cross-cultural research implies that approaching images from the perspective of response means giving up the belief that our response to pictures must be radically different from the way we respond to the world around us: "To respond to a picture or sculpture 'as if' it were real is little different from responding to reality as real," he writes.[24] It would certainly be wrong to deduce from Freedberg's empirical argument that we experience images and reality *identically*. He simply states that we respond *intensely* in both cases. Nor does he argue that images *represent* reality—the second direction he moves in. "I do not wish to suggest that response should be based on the perception of representation as the more or less successful imitation or illusion of nature," he writes.[25] Here lies the simple but important lesson to learn from Freedberg's empirical intervention: We are able to respond vividly to something that is not really there.

As a consequence, we should abandon the third-person standpoint of comparing images to reality. Otherwise we will always and necessarily notice an essential lack. If we expect images to imitate or represent reality, we cannot help but see them as deficient and hampered illusions.[26] Which would take us back to the point where we began: How do we explain the strong effects of a deficient illusion? The same is true for the cinema. One of the traditional ways to explain its strong effects was precisely to invoke the "reality effect" of illusion. As my discussion of the differences between immersion and illusion has shown, in the movie theater we do not respond to an illusion—we respond to a fictional filmic world evoked by sound-supported moving-images. Phenomenologically, this implies a crucial difference: We are not tricked into experiencing the onscreen action as real, but always experience it as a film. This has troubled illusion theorists a great deal. They couldn't cope with the problem how a deficient illusion might result in such intense responses. Since its inception phenomenological aesthetics has rejected the idea of illusion or *Schein*.[27] Hence it suggests itself to go back to the things themselves and describe the filmic image not as a (deficient) illusion but as a phenomenon in its own right.

We should think of images not as acts of *representation* but as acts of *presentation*.[28] To show something via image does not mean that the image has to *refer* to something, but that something is presented artificially.[29] What images present are visible entities with specific ontological features: quasi-things present even if they are not real and cannot be seen outside the image. Lambert Wiesing calls them *phantoms* in order to indicate their ontological ambiguity and to distinguish them from real things and illusions. W. J. T. Mitchell treats images quite similarly when he talks about the "living image" or the "image-as-organism," when he calls images "ghostly semblances" or "pseudo-life-forms," when he speaks about our double consciousness toward images torn between "magical beliefs and sceptical doubts, naive animism and hardheaded materialism, mystical and critical attitudes."[30] This double consciousness is not something one could safely ascribe to primitives, children, the uneducated, or illiterate masses, but it is a deep and abiding feature of human responses to images in general: "It is not something we 'get over' when we grow up, become modern, or acquire critical consciousness," Mitchell notes.[31] Hence what might sound mysterious from a naturalist-objectivist point of view is recognized as an actual phenomenon from a phenomenological standpoint: consciousness of something that has no real and material substance, that does not follow the laws of physics, that cannot be analyzed and measured scientifically—the phantoms of imagery.[32]

Since they are actual, perceptible phenomena, the phantoms of imagery are not exempt from the pathic quality of seeing. Their pathic element is even more striking when we confront *moving*-images supported by *sound*. Before this account becomes too iconocentric, let me hasten to add the pathic quality of sound. Sound is always present: Once we hear it, it has already pressed in upon us, taken hold of us, captivated us.[33] We can only avert it *after* it has had an effect on us. The strong pathic aspect of sound, in fact, propels the pathic moment of the image, as can be seen when both are fused into the single gestalt of sound film.[34]

Searching for a solution to the intricate "paradox of fiction," a number of scholars from the field of philosophical aesthetics have recently argued that the quality, vividness, and impressiveness of a filmic presentation are responsible for the viewer's feelings—not the *beliefs* in the reality of the filmic world and its fictional characters. The vivid appearance of a visually and aurally present cinematic object is sufficient for real feelings. It all depends on the concrete presentational qualities; it needs to be presented vividly enough.[35]

Hence we are neither tricked by a literal illusion nor do we foster the *belief* that what is presented *re*-presents something real in documentary fashion. While the question of *illusion* implies the problem that what we perceive *is* real right *now*, the question of *belief* implies the problem that what we perceive *was* real in the *past*. As to the latter, we rarely lose knowledge of the fact that what we see is fictional (who could forget that slime-spitting giant bugs or rampaging dinosaurs are not really out there?). However, there is a difference: In contrast to illusion, *belief* can be added—and this clearly influences our response. Think of the shocked early audiences who thought that *The Blair Witch Project* (1999) was a documentary and not a fiction film. And remember the response to the harmed animals in the Tarkovsky, Renoir, and Bresson movies mentioned previously. When we assume a documentary consciousness—that is, when we believe that the film not only presents but also *re*-presents what *was* once real and thus loses the fictional distance—the quality of the ontological distance changes. We are, at the very least, more strongly challenged on moral grounds. But the cases under consideration in this study do not presuppose a belief in the reality status of the images and sounds in order to be affective. What the images and sounds *present* artificially makes us respond vividly.

To repeat, the question of a literal illusion is not at stake when we watch a frightening film. Instead, how strongly we respond is a matter of the vividness and impressiveness of the filmic presentation—and the cinema of fear offers some prime examples of highly effective and affective presentations. We are not afraid of the monster and the violent act as if they were real, but of the vivid presentation of the monster and violent act via moving-image and sound. The easiest and most obvious proof is the fact that we do not jump up and run out of the theater in order to escape the *monster,* but simply avoid looking and listening to the images and sounds of the *film.* Thus fear in the face of a nonexistent filmic object or event should be far from astonishing. A tacit assumption of the illusion thesis is that we can only fear the *real* things of *perception.* But this is clearly not the case. There are numerous modes of consciousness in which we are afraid but do not confront the real things of perception: dreams, hallucinations, and memories come to mind. The same goes for images. David Freedberg's search for psychological invariants in response to images suggests that human beings throughout history and across cultures have reacted powerfully: The affective quality of images seems to be an anthropological constant.[36] Why, then, should we *not* be afraid of something that is felt as vividly and impressively as the presentation of the filmic world (even if it is simultaneously irreal)? Even though they are immaterial, cinematic images and sounds literally affect the viewer.

Reducing the Phenomenological Distance, or a Real Threat to the Viewer

When the images and sounds of a frightening movie become literally impressive, when they press in upon us and leave an affective trace, when we stop feeling safe from what we see and hear, we get the feeling that something has broken away or has been extremely diminished: We experience a dangerous *proximity* of the threatening movie. The ontological distance might be the movie's safety net. But a safety net presupposes some kind of risk. Even if we might cut the intertwinement with the horrifying film at any time, the fact that we *are* intertwined implicates a possible exposure to and contact with the unbearable. In fact, the moment we turn away often comes too late: We have already crossed the boundary between the fascinating still-watchable and the abhorrent un-watchable. While the *ontological* distance cannot be bridged, we often face the vanishing (or dwindling) of what I call the *phenomenological* distance. The viewer experiences the phenomenological distance to the film as *vacillating* on a continuum from *growing* to *decreasing,* depending on the relative position beforehand. When the film really closes in on us with all its frightening potential, we can grasp what Carol Clover might have had in mind when she wrote that the "horror movie is somehow more than the sum of its monsters; it is itself monstrous."[37] Hence ascribing a genuine threat to the movies is no rhetorical exaggeration.

But what if the phenomenological distance shrinks radically? In her famous essay *On Photography,* Susan Sontag underscores an important precondition for the frightening impact of (moving) images: "One is vulnerable to disturbing events in the form of photographic images in a way that one is not to the real thing. That vulnerability is part of the *distinctive passivity* of someone who is a spectator twice over, spectator of events already shaped, first by the participants and second by the image maker."[38] Sontag develops her argument with Michelangelo Antonioni's China documentary *Chung Kuo* (1972) in mind, but her remarks are valid for the experience of fiction films as well. When we watch a gruesome thriller in the multiplex, we are also forced to follow events with a double passivity: The events onscreen are determined, first, by the fictional narrative (*what* is presented) and, second, by the aesthetic choices of the filmmaker (*how* it is presented). As real-life spectators of the gruesome events, we would have modest possibilities for—potentially relieving—participation, whereas in the movie theater we are bound to our seats, motor activity largely inhibited, with little else to do but look.

Moreover, while in reality we would be able to direct our attention according to our own will (hence choosing the details we consider appropriate), in the movie theater we are forced to confront what the filmmaker has preselected for us. Furthermore, the film also condenses the temporal extension of the event—the interesting parts presented in an interesting way—generally with regard to maximum effect. Hence what I have described as an essential blessing is simultaneously a curse: our passivity and ontological absence from the scene of action. However, only because the viewer is forced into this ambiguous passivity, he or she can enjoy fear in the first place. Without the restrained viewing position vis-à-vis the horrifying film, the viewer would simply not be afraid (or, at least, be afraid in a very different way). This ambiguity is essential: We do *not have* to do anything against what happens inside the filmic world, but we also *cannot* do anything. As Sontag puts it: "The camera looks for me—and obliges me to look, leaving as my only option not to look."[39]

The last part of the sentence points to a potential way out of the movie theater's distinctive passivity. When all classificatory measures of protection are ineffectual and we are faced with a film that threatens to approach, overwhelm, and harm us despite the barriers of censorship, rating system, and genre, we can still keep the cinematic experience an endurable one. Despite the passivity that the cinematic dispositive forces on us, we often *do* take very specific actions—even though we neither run away nor intervene in the filmic world. When we look away, close our eyes, or cover our ears, we *literally* try to escape from the filmic threat. This is not meant in a metaphoric sense. Depending on what we consider more threatening—the visible or the audible—we might proceed by first looking at the exit sign and then covering our ears, or vice versa, creating a sort of hierarchy of the horrific aspects and thus a hierarchy of different levels of flight. I have talked about *geographical* flight in the sense of running out of the theater. These geographical flight reactions would imply that we took the diegetic of threat literally. Obviously, we are not that naive. To be sure, there are viewers who *do* leave the theater. However, this is less a direct flight reaction to a certain scene—viewers do not *run* out of the theater in panic—rather than the avoidance of an overall, accumulated unpleasant experience.[40]

This does not entail, however, that covering our eyes and ears is not an actual flight from a real threat. As phenomenologist Aurel Kolnai notes, "Flight need not literally mean running away, traveling to a distant place, or going into hiding. It is not the spatial proximity of the feared object but the agent's being actually or virtually exposed to its *impact* that matters."[41] You don't have to *duck* away from gruesome images; it is sufficient to *look* away. You don't have to *run* out of the theater; it's enough if you *cover* your ears. These are *active* decisions. We have to let loose and purposely untangle ourselves from the tight grip of the movie. But why try to escape if not for the sake of our endangered well-being? The film may be fictional; the threat to the well-being of our lived bodies and psyches is not. The danger to the characters might occur at a safe *ontological* distance; what we see, hear, and feel can easily bridge the *phenomenological* distance. Stanley Kubrick has illustrated this difference quite appositely. In a highly self-reflexive sequence in his horror masterpiece *The Shining* (1980) the young boy Danny Torrance (Danny Lloyd) stands in a hallway of the huge Overlook Hotel in which he spends the winter with his family. Suddenly he sees bloody images of mutilated bodies flash up in front of him. Rather than trying to escape, the shocked boy raises his hands in front of his eyes. After a while he hesitantly dares to peek through his fingers. A voice soothes him: "It's just like pictures in a book, Danny. It isn't real." The wise boy does not trust the voice, however. He knows that even if the images are of a different order than reality, they nevertheless have a real effect on him. The boy acknowledges it by raising his hands protectively.

Our various aversive reactions do not have to involve physical movement, though. There are other—albeit less secure—strategies of temporary avoidance (or flight, if you will). The first is looking *at* rather than *into* the movie: By withdrawing from immersion into appreciation—that is, by stressing the film-as-artifice rather than the filmic world—the filmic phantoms might disappear and lose their power to haunt us. Second, one can also look *onto* the movie by either focusing on the material basis of the film through foregrounding an awareness of the screen and the flickering dance of lights and shadows (which is not the same as appreciating the style and technique of the movie) or by taking an elevated, distanced position by emphasizing the film's fictional status. Rather than looking *into* the movie, the viewer looks *away,* looks *at* it or looks *onto* it. Annette Hill usefully distinguishes between "*physical*

Figure 21.1. Daring a fearful look: Danny Torrance (Danny Lloyd) in *The Shining*.

barriers, where participants use their body to withdraw from viewing violence, and *mental* barriers, where participants [focus] on anything other than violent depictions on screen."[42]

What distinguishes looking-at and looking-onto from looking-away (or even covering one's eyes and ears) is the degree of conspicuousness and security. While the activity of the latter is characterized by treacherous movements, other avoidance strategies remain more inconspicuous. This is an advantage for those who are not supposed to reveal fearfulness. Not astonishingly, then, flight reactions seem to be separated roughly along gender lines. While men are supposed to display fearlessness, women are expected to cower and look away. Hence men might more often look for ruptures in realism or try to admire the quality of the special effects as counterparts to looking away. Yet there is a downside to it: Looking-at and looking-onto the movie is risky business, since the horrifying phantoms of imagery return easily; or we might not be able to get rid of them in the first place, because they sturdily occupy a central position in our field of consciousness and thus defy straightforward cognitive detachment. It takes an effort to resist the initial urge to look into rather than at or onto the film.[43] Once my *active* decision to admire, say, special effects artist Tom Savini's ingenuous design of the monster is ruptured—either because the fictional content crosses the threshold of attention or because I am tempted by curiosity—I end up back in the filmic world after all.

Note that these various degrees of control are possible only because the *ontological* distance between reality and filmic world exists. The ontological distance relieves us from deeply involved action in terms of ethical or legal interventions even if the phenomenological distance breaks down momentarily. Once we have looked away, covered our ears, or concentrated on the formal aspects, the phenomenological distance jumps back into place. Since the ontological distance is always present as background knowledge, what would in real life consume our whole attention, in the cinema becomes a cause of pleasure: the foregrounding of the body due to a diminished phenomenological distance. To be sure, even if the impressive and vivid presentation of violence and monstrosity poses a genuine threat, to perceive extreme violence and a powerful monster by way of a *film* does not endanger us identically as *real* violence and monstrosity would—precisely because it endangers us like a *film*. Comparing the resulting forms of fear would be a category mistake—as if I said "I am more afraid of bungee-jumping than losing my job." Being afraid of a film and being afraid of a murderer are two kinds of fear.

True Fright: Afraid of the Horrific

If a genuine threat exists, it is not astonishing that there is also some kind of fear. To put it differently, if we are frightened, we assume a real danger. People are generally frightened only if they consider a situation dangerous. Think of the behavior in front of a cage containing a lethal animal: There is little trace of fear. Of course, there are situations that are—statistically speaking—not dangerous, and we are frightened anyway. These fears are often judged irrational. The fear of flying is a classic case in point. But calling this form of fear irrational implies a third-person perspective: someone waving a statistic and arguing for the safety of flying. For the person *experiencing* fear, however, the danger of flying is very *real*. Trying to convince the scared person with statistics—that is, *rational* arguments—is often futile. This is, by the way, another argument against the central position of beliefs in emotions.

The same goes for the movies. If we find a film frightening, its threat is indisputable. Attempts to soothe us with the argument that this is only a movie might be convincing—often they do not succeed. This is the case precisely because I am afraid of the vivid and impressive presentation of the movie *itself* and not by its status as a failed illusion referring to the extra-filmic world. And even if these arguments *are* successful, it takes an active step to create a distance from the filmic world and look *at* or *onto* it. Being afraid of a movie therefore does not imply that we actively suspend *disbelief*. Far from it. Just as the person afraid of flying does not willingly suspend disbelief in something he or she is rationally aware of (namely, the safety of flying), the viewer in the movie theater does not suspend disbelief in the movie's irreality. He or she is simply afraid, even though the awareness that the movie is irreal does not disappear. In fact, a conscious act of volition would be counterproductive for any emotion. Volition is involved only in our readiness to enter the reception process and our effort to concentrate.[44] Insofar, the talk of a "willing suspension of disbelief" does not make sense in terms of frightening movies. But Coleridge's famous phrase is doubtful also because we do not suspend our disbelief and then consider the fictional world as though it were real: This is precisely the reason why we do not *run* away from the *monster* but *look* away from the *images* of its evil conduct.

What are we afraid of then? The cause of fear is nothing more and nothing less than the onscreen appearance of the *disproportional immorality* and *disturbing brutality* of the violent act or monster, forced on us through the *vividness* and *impressiveness* of threateningly close cinematic images and sounds. Its emotional impact is clearly rooted in the *present*: in our momentary confrontation with dangerous moving-images and sounds. However, we must also take into account the possibility that we are instinctively and unconsciously afraid of a *future* effect. The *episodic* appraisal ("This is threatening to my well-being right now!") might be interlinked with a *long-standing* appraisal ("This can harm my psychical integrity for a long time!"). It is always possible that we fear that we will have to remember these perceptions. They might haunt us in our dreams and daydreams. They can turn into lasting threats. The film critic Pauline Kael once commented on the effects the famous shower scene in *Psycho* (1960) had on her: "The shock stayed with me to a degree that I remember it whenever I'm in a motel shower."[45] Or consider this quote from a participant in Annette Hill's empirical study: "I went to see *The Shining* when I was quite young and this film scared me so much I just decided never to go and see another horror movie. The thrill while you're in the cinema isn't worth the risk when you get home, when you can't sleep."[46] Hence in the face of cinematic horror we also look away, because it can pose a long-term threat to our psychical well-being. We intuitively know that once the frightening film haunts us, hardly any flight reaction will help: We cannot look, let alone run away from our fearful memories.

Cinematic horror does not need to take a detour via characters, then, but affects us *directly*. The directness of horror would help to explain why horror movies are so effective despite our notoriously low allegiance with their—often—unpleasant cardboard characters. It is me who is *directly* frightened by the violent onslaught onscreen, and it is me who is *directly* afraid of the threatening appearance of the monster. Neither a *personal* character involvement nor his or her *observational* facial and bodily responses are *necessary* for our reaction (even if they certainly help to increase it).

This becomes quite clear when we are confronted with the *result* of a violent act that has already occurred unseen earlier in the film. Take the scene in *The Silence of the Lambs* (1991) in which a dead lieutenant (Charles Napier) is revealed slit open and crucified against Hannibal Lecter's cage. The fact that this disclosure frightens (rather than disgusts) me cannot be explained by *empathy* since I do not feel fright together *with* (let alone identical to) the policeman—who is dead after all. Nor can *sympathy* account for my frightened reaction, because I am not afraid *for* the lifeless character.[47] I might feel pity or sorrow for him, but that wouldn't explain the frightening aspect. In terms of the monster, let me note that in direct horror proper we are not afraid of what the monster might do to the characters in the *immediate* future—in this case we would experience the anticipatory fright that I call *terror*. It is the monster's immoral and brutal intention that appears threatening to us. This is not to deny that terror and horror often occur simultaneously, thus reinforcing each other. However, there are instances in which we are afraid of the monster's presence itself even when no character is around. Think, again, of *The Silence of the Lambs*, when the weirdly dressed, makeup- and wig-wearing serial killer James "Buffalo Bill" Gumb (Ted Levine) tells himself "I'd fuck me. I'd fuck me so hard" and dances in front of a video camera, facing us directly. This scene still scares me after numerous viewings even though no character is threatened by the strange demeanor.

The Pleasure of Direct Horror

If the threat wasn't real and the potentiality of being overwhelmed was nonexistent, we would follow the film emotionless. Only because a genuine danger lurks are we frightened at all. The emotional captivation, on the other hand, has ramifications for our intertwinement with the horrific: It is fright that immerses us and thus creates an *emotional* fascination beyond the simple curious *cognitive* fascination that I have talked about at the beginning. The *interest* in violence and the monster itself couldn't explain this immersive effect. If curiosity were the whole story, we would merely pay remote attention to the horrific as something unusual, comparable to a visit to a botanical garden or a zoo. But we do not only confront these sound-supported moving-images in order to satisfy a quasi-scientific curiosity. We are fascinated and drawn to the filmic world because of the very emotional, corporeal effect these exposures entail—namely, fear. Even if correct in one sense, Carroll's overly rational terms "interest" and "curiosity" are therefore too limited.

Instead, what we enjoy in horror is precisely the emotional immersion of *Angst-Lust*, that is, pleasurable fear.[48] Coexistentialist versions of pleasure in horror such as Carroll's—in which the cognitive pleasure of interest and the emotional displeasure of fear exist *next to each other*—have to be replaced by an integrationist one. Moritz Geiger is right when he argues, "When aesthetic pleasure is mixed with moments of displeasure, pleasure acquires a different character. It might become bitterer, more ambivalent, less uniform, but displeasure does not exist next to pleasure. In pleasurable pain, in enjoyable anguish these feelings merge with pleasure.

And pleasurable horror is . . . not simply pleasure plus horror."[49] Hence pleasurable fear *(Angst-Lust)* does not consist of two components that stand next to each other (like the two emotions horror and disgust in many horror scenes). Instead, pleasure is a quality of the emotion *itself*—its positive valence, as psychologists say. What is more, it might be misleading if we associate pleasure exclusively with words like *happy, blissful, glad, joyful,* and so on. The Geiger quote underscores that an emotion like cinematic fear can be experienced positively, even if the pleasure it yields does not make you straightforwardly happy, but comes across as somewhat mixed and with a slightly bitter flavor. Pleasurable fear is described more accurately as satisfying or gratifying rather than pure bliss, joy, and delight.

This also helps to explain why we enjoy the moment of relief after the scene is over. If pleasurable fear were pure bliss, the relief could not stand out. A narrative of unmixed joy soon means utter boredom. It is the slightly more bitter—but still pleasurable—experience of horror, shock, dread, and terror that makes the straightforwardly enjoyable moments of relief all the more noticeable. But this is obviously not to say that we enjoy relief alone; moments of cinematic fear are not a price to be paid but enable a very specific gratifying form of pleasure—one flavored with a grain of ambivalence.

The emotional fascination characteristic of pleasurable fear entails that our phenomenological distance from the filmic world decreases. I have indicated that the viewer experiences the phenomenological distance as vacillating between decreasing and growing. The first type of distance reduction is immersion proper—an experience particularly accentuated in the immersive environment of the multiplex theater. In cinematic horror we seem to be *pulled in,* because we show *interest* in the object, but also and foremost because we are *emotionally captivated*. We acknowledge this phenomenological movement toward the film in ordinary language when we ascribe the movie a "magnetizing" potential or talk about being "glued to the screen." Cinematic horror, at first, draws us near.

However, the direction is reversed once we reach the tipping point where we consider it necessary to untangle ourselves from the film. This tipping point changes, of course, from viewer to viewer. Hence it is impossible to gauge the precise starting point beyond which something objectively or universally becomes unbearable. If it happens and we are overwhelmed and overly frightened by the horrific, we experience a second type of distance variation: a radical reduction in which the film seems to close in on, jump at, or even attack us. This breakdown of the phenomenological distance—the opposite of immersion—happens precisely during those instances when we have turned away too late and have glimpsed and heard too much. The fact that the film is experienced as suddenly and powerfully *coming near* can be judged from the various *receding* activities described previously. During the most intense moments the viewer responds by raising the hands in front of the eyes or covering the ears as if to escape the overwhelming proximity and threat of the film. Hard-pressed by the film, the viewer retreats and reacts with bodily defense reactions, thus putting a literal barrier between him or her and the film. These protective responses against the distance reduction of the film are attempts to renew the previous phenomenological distance. As such, they can lead to the biggest detachment possible: The viewer *extricates* him- or herself from the closeness of the movie by cutting the intertwinement with the filmic world. Even if this happens in most cases only briefly, the viewer leaves the film experience temporarily behind. Immersion makes way for extrication.

The pleasurable-fear experience is therefore characterized by a balancing act between the strong intertwinement of immersion and the loosened or even cut entanglement of extrication. When the viewer decides to watch a thriller or a horror movie, he or she turns into a sensation seeker walking the tightrope of a *still*-pleasurable experience that could easily entail a plunge into the depth of an *already*-unpleasant experience. The pleasure would not be possible, however, if the balancing act did not include the very danger of stumbling into the abyss. Hence direct horror is dominated by the simultaneity of a strong curious and emotional fascination and the fear of being overwhelmed. We want to see it all—but not see *too much*. We wish to hear everything—yet not hear *too much*. We long for a strong emotional experience— but dread an experience that overwhelms. In short, we enjoy pleasurable fear but shy away from displeasing fear. Direct horror can therefore imply a push–pull experience: quick back-and-forth movements between a strong engagement with the pleasurably dangerous filmic There and a receding into the safe shelter of the cinematic Here.

The Lived-Body Experience: A Dense Frightening Moment

No matter what the experiential differences between the two types of distance reduction might be, in *both* cases the viewer is strongly affected *bodily*. But how exactly do we experience the bodily stimulation of direct horror? So far I have talked predominantly about the relation between viewer and film in terms of distance variation, leaving out the bodily experience proper. The frightening confrontation with violence or monstrosity is, above all, a *wholesale* emotional captivation that has to be distinguished from more *localized* reactions such as nausea caused by cinematic disgust (which is focused around the stomach and/or the gorge) or crying in the face of a melodramatic scene (which converges foremost around the eyes). Our experiences of the lived-body have various shadings: sometimes as a fully integrated, close part of the self, at other times as a loosely attached, somewhat distanced part of the self. The less clearly it can be localized and the less qualitatively circumscribed it seems, the more embracing and encompassing it is. Think of extreme fear versus strong pain in your fingertip. The pain in the fingertip is certainly part of you, but it is also somewhat externalized. The (physiological) body that I *have*, not the (lived) body that I *am,* is foregrounded. In contrast, fear colors the whole self with a different hue; hence the lived-body that I *am* pushes to the fore. Aurel Kolnai notes, "Fear never singles out . . . particular spheres of interest in one's own self: for in every genuine case of fear it is somehow the *whole* self, or the very existence of the self, that is put into question. . . . Even if fear be particularly weak because of the distance or uncertain effectiveness of what provokes it, still its intentional directedness always somehow 'permeates through' to the most ultimate and vital interests which appear to be endangered."[50]

This wholesale emotional captivation is characterized by a peculiar *constriction* of the viewer's lived-body caused precisely by the importunate threat of the film. According to Hermann Schmitz, the lived-body experience generally shifts on a continuum between *constriction* and *expansion*. For instance, the emotions of guilt and sorrow amount to a negative constrictive experience, whereas joy and yearning have strong expansive tendencies. Think of the phenomenological—not physical!—heaviness that pulls you down in sorrow or the strong feeling of guilt that leaves you little air to breathe. In joy, on the other hand, we have a tendency to jump into the air or embrace the whole world, and yearning reaches out for the spatial or temporal distance. Hence both are expansive.[51] What about fear? Just as disgust, it is located very much on the constrictive end of the spectrum. In the face of an act of violence or monstrous object the threatening film appears (overly) close phenomenologically: The viewer experiences the fright vis-à-vis the importunate, threatening object's proximity as a constriction of the lived-body. The etymology of the French, German, and English words *angoisse, Angst,* and *anxious* retains this constrictive tendency. The Latin word *angor* has the same roots as *ango,* which implies choking and suffocating.[52]

The notion of constriction will play a crucial role throughout this study: It describes a recurring, if differently shaded experience of *all* forms of cinematic fear discussed here. But constriction is not the whole story. Fear is also characterized by an expansive, if hampered *Away!*-tendency: an ultimately futile impulse to escape the lived-body's constriction. In order to understand what Schmitz means by this expansive *Away!*-tendency, one has to grasp his distinction between *relative* and *absolute* location.[53] In fear, one can escape the *physical* body's *relative* location, that is, the subject's position in geometrical space vis-à-vis the threatening object. This is what we do when we look away or cover our ears: We leave the relative location. However, one cannot flee one's *absolute* location, that is, the *lived*-body's phenomenological Here. It is precisely this absolute phenomenological location right here that we experience as constricted in moments of fear. We desperately want to escape our skin, as it were, by expanding *Away* somewhere, but cannot flee the lived-body's constriction. As a consequence, there is a pulsating *tension* between dominant constriction and attempted expansion—a characteristic experience not unlike the one that defines erotic lust. According to Schmitz, it is this pulsating game of lived-body constriction and expansion that can turn fear into a source of pleasure—if handled properly.

Since our bodies in tension are so intensely engaged by the threatening—and threateningly close—film, moments of horror stand out from the temporal flux of mundane life. What is usually lived transparently and implicitly becomes densely compressed—like a slow river that is suddenly caught by a wild and ferocious current. Horror has a decidedly temporal component that deeply underscores the present here and now. In the face of frightening violence or monstrosity, the body in tension is caught by the gravity of time. As Vivian Sobchack reminds us, it has often been noted that we tend "to feel this intense sense of presence, to feel most alive, when we are most at bodily (and psychic) risk. Faced with a present threat to our being, we have no time to think about past or future, but this could also be reversed: it is the past and future that have 'no time' because the extended 'now' excludes them as it encloses us. Thus, this sense of aliveness—of being just here, just now—emerges both from and as the simultaneous extension of our present and the heightening of our presence."[54]

Somatic Empathy: Painful Acts of Violence

While this intense, engrossing bodily and temporal experience can be recuperated through phenomenological reflection, during the film it does not enter the viewer's *focal* awareness (even if it is much less *peripheral* than in real-life situations of danger). Yet cinematic horror often entails another form of bodily stimulation—one that is *restricted* to a limited corporeal area rather than being *fully* engrossing and is therefore able to force its way into awareness more centrally. I am talking about somatic empathy in its varieties of *sensation, affective,* and *motor* mimicry.[55] Somatic empathy is a form of *Einfühlung* that describes a more or less automatic, but no more than *partial* parallelism between a character's and my own body's sensations, affects, or motions. Think of the muscular urge to support a character who is untangling the cables of a ticking time bomb (motor mimicry); the itchiness experienced when looking at a character wearing coarse cotton on bare skin (sensation mimicry); the disgust one experiences upon seeing a fully grossed-out character waking up in a freezer full of putrefying body parts, as in the 2006 remake of *The Hills Have Eyes* (affective mimicry). Or take the impression that one is short of breath when a character drowns, gets strangled, or has to fight against the breathtaking impact of lethal nerve gas, as in *Saw II* (2005). Having argued that the *frightening* aspect of cinematic horror does not depend on character engagement, I do not want to exclude this important form of empathy, a recurrent corollary of our confrontation with the horrific. However, somatic empathy does not demand strong character allegiance either. In fact, it works in connection with figures never encountered before in the film; even animals or cartoon characters can be objects of somatic empathy.

I have mentioned that the ontological distance allows us to become partly aware of our bodily experience. This is particularly true for cases like shock. But it also goes for somatic empathy, a particular carnal response that makes us feel ourselves feeling and thus enables a strong awareness-of-oneself as an embodied viewer. In horror movies and thrillers a typical form of somatic empathy is the vague and diffuse, yet intense sensation one feels while exposed to graphic moving-images of *pain*. A classic example is the dentist scene in *Marathon Man* (1976), in which Dr. Szell (Laurence Olivier) tortures Babe Levy (Dustin Hoffman) by drilling holes into his teeth. Or the moment in *Misery* (1990) when the mad aficionado Annie Wilkes (Kathy Bates) smashes the ankles of her beloved author Paul Sheldon (James Caan) with a sledgehammer. One could also take a drastic imagination evoked by the description of tubes inserted into a male character's genitals in *Seven*.

In these cases we obviously do not suffer from toothache or a piercing pain in our ankles; nor do we feel a hellish anguish in our genitals. Insofar, the feeling is clearly reduced and changed. Still, one cannot deny that we experience a peculiar, intense foregrounding of the lived-body. In contrast to fear, which overwhelms us completely and therefore cannot be localized directly, painful somatic empathy often affects more distinct *local regions* of the body and thus touches us merely partially. Even in cases in which somatic empathy cannot be pinpointed and seems to be spread out over the lived-body somewhat diffusely, it is less engrossing than fear. What is true for the spatial structure also counts for the temporal side. The wholesale emotional captivation of fearful cinematic horror is comparatively *gradual* and *continual*: The beginning and end are not clearly marked. The *abrupt* transformation of empathic pain, on the other hand, has a much more *episodic* structure. Similar to moments of shock, it stands out as a *discrete puncturing gestalt* with a clear beginning and end. The lived-body speaks up shortly, as it were, but does not keep its voice up for long. Moreover, since it is such an abrupt and reflex-like response, somatic empathy has a *compulsory* quality: We can hardly avoid it. This coercive aspect of empathic pain makes it so effective, yet it is also one of the reasons why some viewers despise it. While I have a certain freedom of avoidance in looking away from the monster, in abrupt cases of empathic pain I have to concede the initiative largely to the film.

Fear appears close to the self, overwhelms us completely, comes into being gradually and lasts. Painful somatic empathy, on the other hand, is a somewhat distanced, localized, and abrupt feeling. These differences are mirrored in the psychological longevity. Fear can haunt us for hours and even weeks. The spectrum ranges from avoiding dark alleys on the way home to the abiding fear of swimming in the ocean (think of Spielberg's *Jaws*) or taking showers (a phobia sparked by

Hitchcock's *Psycho*). Long-lasting effects are rare in connection to somatic empathy. Unlike dread and much like shock, somatic empathy tends to vanish quickly after the scene has ended. When we leave the theater, we might feel a bit unpleasant, but we usually recover quickly.

But how is somatic empathy possible in the first place? Precisely because I am in a position *different* from the character onscreen, the only thing left to balance this experiential disproportion is my own body. Vivian Sobchack explains how the viewer autonomously responds to the solicitation of the graphically violent scene: "My body's intentional trajectory, seeking a sensible object to fulfill this sensual solicitation, will reverse its direction to locate its partially frustrated sensual grasp on something more literally accessible. That more literally accessible sensual object is my own subjectively felt lived-body. Thus, 'on the rebound' from the screen—and *without a reflective thought*—I will *reflexively* turn toward my own carnal, sensual, and sensible being."[56] We experience and comprehend movies not just *cognitively* but with our entire *bodily* being—a body that is always informed by the history and carnal knowledge of our acculturated sensorium. Since the viewer is dependent on the personal *carnal knowledge* of the object and the pain it inflicts, *familiar* weapons and affected body parts tend to cause stronger somatic empathy. Hence knife cuts are more effective than gunshots; needles stabbed in the eye are more

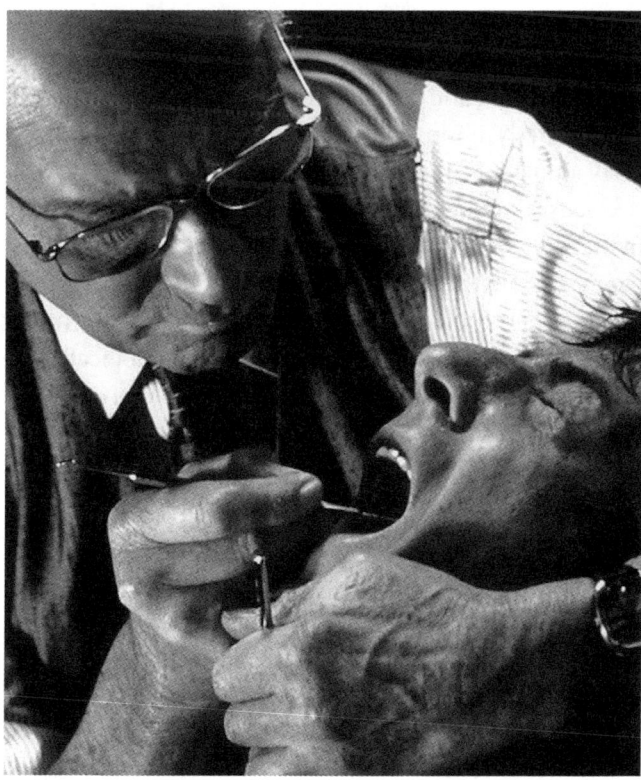

Figure 21.2. Painful somatic empathy: Szell (Laurence Olivier) tortures Babe Levy (Dustin Hoffman) in *Marathon Man*.

somatically painful than the sight and sound of a body torn apart by a bomb.[57] What is more, precisely because the former weapons are familiar, they enhance the likelihood of a collective response: While the great majority of viewers can draw on the carnal knowledge of a knife cut, the spectators who were ripped apart by a bomb must, I gladly assume, be few and far between.

The reflexive turn toward the body in somatic empathy certainly depends on the primacy of seeing and hearing as the two primary cinematic senses. But when we go to the cinema, we do not leave our culturally shaped senses of touch, smell, and taste at the entrance door just because the film privileges seeing and hearing. There might be a sense hierarchy, but the cinema uses dominant vision and hearing to speak comprehensibly to the other senses as well—or better, to the lived-body as a whole. The experiencing body sees and hears always *in cooperation* and *exchange* with other sensorial accesses to the world. A centralizing self always synthesizes the empirically discrete perceptions. Sobchack therefore describes the viewer as a cinesthetic subject—a portmanteau expression that combines the words *cinema* and *synaesthetic*. She notes that "even if the intentional objects of my experience at the movies are not wholly realized by me and are grasped in a sensual distribution that would be differently structured were I outside the theater, I nonetheless do have a *real* sensual experience that is not reducible either to the satisfaction of merely two of my senses or to sensual analogies and metaphors constructed only 'after the fact' through the cognitive operations of conscious thought."[58] Harking back to my examples of painful somatic empathy, despite the fact that my feeling of toothache or genital pain is clearly reduced and transformed, I still have a *partially* fulfilled sensory experience.

Obviously, filmmakers can manipulate the carnal intensity of somatic empathy. They simply need to optimize our sensual access of seeing and hearing so that the two senses can be cross-modally translated more easily. Think of the torture scene in *Marathon Man*: If it was shown in long shot with a distant soundtrack, we would barely feel anything. This is why the film literally brings us closer to the *pain*-ful site. In order to affect us deeply and painfully, close-ups and loud, horrifying sounds reduce the sensual and thus the phenomenological distance. Even if it is primarily an object of vision and not touch, the close-up nevertheless provokes a sense of the intimate and tangible.[59]

Notes

1. Carl Plantinga, *Moving Viewers: American Film and the Spectator's Experience* (University of California Press, 2009), 106.

2. Stephen Prince, "Graphic Violence in the Cinema: Origins, Aesthetic Design, and Social Effects," in *Screening Violence,* ed. Stephen Prince, 1–44 (Athlone, 2000), 10–19.

3. The example comes from Noël Carroll, "Horror and Humor," *Journal of Aesthetics and Art Criticism* 57, no. 2 (1996): 147.

4. Noël Carroll, *The Philosophy of Horror; or, Paradoxes of the Heart* (Routledge, 1990), 24 and 27–35.

5. Prince, "Graphic Violence in the Cinema," 18.

6. Carroll (1990), 182.

7. Mirjam Schaub, *Bilder aus dem Off: Zum philosophischen Stand der Kinotheorie* (VDG, 2005), esp. 48–56.

8. Carroll (1990), 243/245. Or take this example from *The Silence of the Lambs*: An autopsy is performed on a corpse found in water. We can study the grossed-out, horrified faces of the attendant characters. We get to hear detailed descriptions of the wounds. We can see the unfocused contours of the victim at the lower edge of the frame. But it takes roughly eighty seconds from the moment the characters first confront the victim until the camera discloses *parts* of the bloated body, and another hundred seconds until the corpse is fully revealed.

9. I introduce the new terms *ontological* as well as *phenomenological* distance because the previous use of notions like "aesthetic," "psychic," or "psychological" distance seems too muddled. These expressions were often not clearly set apart and were used interchangeably.

10. Stanley Cavell, *The World Viewed: Reflections on the Ontology of Film,* Enlarged ed. (Harvard University Press, 1979), 24. It is precisely this ontological boundary that films like Woody Allen's *The Purple Rose of Cairo* (1985) and *Last Action Hero* (1993) with Arnold Schwarzenegger explored.

11. Edmund Burke, *A Philosophical Enquiry into the Origin of Our Ideas of the Sublime and the Beautiful* (Routledge, 1958), 40; Immanuel Kant, *Critique of the Power of Judgment* (Cambridge University Press, 2001), 144; Jean-Jacques Rousseau, *Confessions* (Oxford University Press, 2000), 168.

12. Bela Balázs, *Der sichtbare Mensch oder die Kultur des Films* (Suhrkamp, 2001), 82; Siegfried Kracauer, *Theory of Film: The Redemption of Physical Reality* (Princeton University Press, 1997), 58.

13. Ed S. Tan, *Emotion and Structure of Narrative Film: Film as Emotion Machine* (Lawrence Erlbaum, 1996), 77.

14. Laura Mulvey, "Visual Pleasure and Narrative Cinema," in *Narrative, Apparatus, Ideology,* edited by Philip Rosen (Columbia University Press, 1986), 198–209, 171; Cavell, *World Viewed,* 40.

15. See the discussion of Renoir in Vivian Sobchack, *The Address of the Eye: A Phenomenology of Film Experience* (Princeton University Press, 1992), 268–75.

16. In his book *Offensive Films,* Mikal Brottman introduces a category called *cinema vomitif* that includes films like *Blood Feast* (1963), *The Texas Chainsaw Massacre,* and *Death Scenes* (1989). These movies aim at the arousal of "strong sensations in the lower body—nausea, repulsion, weakness, faintness, and loosening of bowel or bladder control—normally by way of graphic scenes featuring the by-products of bodily detritus: vomit, excrement, viscera, brain tissue and so on." Brottman, *Offensive Films: Toward an Anthropology of Cinema Vomitif* (Greenwood, 2997), 11.

17. W. J. T. Mitchell, *What Do Pictures Want? The Lives and Loves of Images* (University of Chicago Press, 2005), 8 and 32/33.

18. Erwin Straus, "Die Formen des Raumlichen," *Der Nervenarzt* 3, no. 11 (1930): 641.

19. Erwin Straus, *Vom Sinn der Sinne: Ein Beitrag zur Grundlegung der Psychologie*, 2nd ed. (Springer, 1956), 393 (my translation). Similar to Erwin Straus, Laura Marks underscores that instances of visuality mark a continuum between the distant and the embodied, the optical and the haptic. Marks, *The Skin of the Film: Intercultural Cinema, Embodiment, and the Senses* (Duke University Press, 2000), 132.

20. Straus, "Die Formen des Raumlichen," 640. In German the expression "ins Auge stechen" exists: something is so striking that it stabs the eye.

21. Charles Baudelaire, *Selected Poems of Charles Baudelaire* (Grove Press, 1974).

22. Sue L. Cataldi, *Emotion, Depth, and Flesh: A Study of Sensitive Space* (SUNY Press, 1993), 139.

23. David Freedberg, *The Power of Images: Studies in the History of Response* (University of Chicago Press, 1989), xxii and 1.

24. Freedberg, 438.

25. Freedberg, 438.

26. Lambert Wiesing, "Von der defekten Illusion zum perfekten Phantom: Über phänomenologische Bildtheorien," in *Kraft der Illusion*, edited by Gertrud Koch and Christiane Voss, 89–101 (Fink, 2006).

27. Moritz Geiger, *Zugiinge zur Asthetik* (Der Neue Geist, 1928), 140.

28. Wiesing (2006), 98.

29. Lambert Wiesing, *Artifizielle Präsenz: Studien zur Philosophie des Bildes* (Suhrkamp, 2005), 36.

30. Mitchell, *What Do Pictures Want?*, 11, 10, 55, 93, and 7.

31. Mitchell, 8.

32. Wiesing (2006), 100.

33. Straus, "Die Formen des Raumlichen," 642.

34. Straus, 645.

35. Oswald Hanfling, "Fact, Fiction and Feeling," *British Journal of Aesthetics* 36, no. 4 (1996): 356–66; Malcolm Turvey, "Imagination, Simulation, and Fiction," *Film Studies* 8 (2006): 125.

36. Needless to say, not everybody everywhere at every time responds identically. Freedberg, *Power of Images*, 445. W. J. T. Mitchell argues in a similar direction when he notes the universal tendency to ascribe a magical, lifelike quality to images: "The phenomenon of the living image or animated icon is an anthropological universal, a feature of the fundamental ontology of images as such." Mitchell, *What Do Pictures Want?*, 11.

37. Carol J. Clover, *Men, Women, and Chain Saws: Gender in the Modern Horror Film* (Princeton University Press, 1992), 168.

38. Susan Sontag, *On Photography* (Farrar, Straus, and Giroux, 1977), 168/169 (emphasis added).

39. Sontag, 169.

40. Incidentally, this points to another discrepancy between the cinema and home-viewing: The social pressure of the movie theater keeps audiences much longer in their seats, whereas home-viewers can turn off their video recorders or DVD players quite easily. As a consequence, some viewers choose specific films to be watched at home, because there

is more opportunity for permanent avoidance. Annette Hill, *Shocking Entertainment: Viewer Response to Movie Violence* (University of Luton Press, 1997), 61, 65.

41. Aurel Kolnai, *On Disgust* (Open Court, 2004), 97 (emphasis added).

42. Hill, 47 (emphasis added).

43. See Jean-Paul Sartre, *The Imaginary: A Phenomenological Psychology of the Imagination* (Routledge, 2004).

44. Menachem Brinker, "Aesthetic Illusion," *Journal of Aesthetics and Art Criticism* 36, no. 2 (1977): 195.

45. Pauline Kael, *For Keeps* (Dutton, 1994), 783.

46. Quoted from Hill, 70.

47. See Alex Neill, "Empathy and (Film) Fiction," in *Post-Theory: Reconstructing Film Studies,* ed. David Bordwell and Noël Carroll, 175–94 (University of Wisconsin Press, 1996).

48. For a psychoanalytic account of Angst-Lust, see Michael Balint, *Thrills and Regressions* (International Universities Press, 1959).

49. Moritz Geiger, "Beirrage zur Phanomenologie des asrherischen Genusses." *Jahrbuch für Philosophie und phanomenologische Forschung* 1, no. 2 (1913): 625 (my translation).

50. Kolnai, *On Disgust,* 38 (emphasis added).

51. See Hermann Schmitz, *Der Gefühlsraum* (Bouvier, 1969).

52. Max Pages, *Das affektive Leben der Gruppen: Eine Theorie der menschltchen Beziehung* (Klett, 1974), 172.

53. Hermann Schmitz, *Der Leib* (Bouvier, 1965).

54. Vivian Sobchack, "Peek-a-BOO! Thoughts on Seeing (Most of) *The Descent and Isolation.*" *Film Comment* 42, no. 4 (2006): 41.

55. See Murray Smith, *Engaging Characters: Fiction, Emotion, and the Cinema* (Clarendon Press, 1995), 98–102. Christine Noll Brinckmann, "Somarische Emparhie bei Hitchcock: Eine Skizze," in *Der Körper im Bild: Schauspielen-Darstellen-Erscheinen,* ed. Heinz-B. Heller, Karl Prümm, and Birgit Peulings, 111–20 (Schüren, 1999). I introduce the term *sensation mimicry,* because the expressions *motor* and *affective mimicry* do not capture all of the empathizing experiences described later.

56. Sobchack (2004), 76/77 (emphasis added).

57. This is confirmed by empirical audience research. Hill, 36.

58. Sobchack (2004), 76.

59. Mary Ann Doane, "The Close-Up: Scale and Derail in the Cinema," *Differences: A Journal of Feminist Cultural Studies* 14, no. 3 (2003): 109.

Chapter 22

(WHY) DO YOU LIKE SCARY MOVIES?
A Review of the Empirical Research on Psychological Responses to Horror Films

G. Neil Martin

> Rather than taking a philosophical or literary critical approach to horror, Martin's survey of psychological research summarizes what the psychological data say about the appeal of horror, noting differences between men and women, as well as among different personality types.

WHY DO WE WATCH AND LIKE HORROR FILMS? Despite a century of horror film making and entertainment, little research has examined the human motivation to watch fictional horror and how horror film influences individuals' behavioral, cognitive, and emotional responses. This review provides the first synthesis of the empirical literature on the psychology of horror film using multidisciplinary research from psychology, psychotherapy, communication studies, development studies, clinical psychology, and media studies. The chapter considers the motivations for people's decision to watch horror; why people enjoy horror; how individual differences influence responses to, and preference for, horror film; how exposure to horror film changes behavior; how horror film is designed to achieve its effects; why we fear and why we fear specific classes of stimuli; and how liking for horror develops during childhood and adolescence. The literature suggests that (1) low empathy and fearfulness are associated with more enjoyment and desire to watch horror film but that specific dimensions of empathy are better predictors of people's responses than are others; (2) there is a positive relationship between sensation seeking and horror enjoyment/preference, but this relationship is not consistent; (3) men and boys prefer to watch, enjoy, and seek out horror more than do women and girls; (4) women are more prone to disgust sensitivity or anxiety than are men, and this may mediate the sex difference in the enjoyment of horror; (5) younger children are afraid of symbolic stimuli, whereas older children become afraid of concrete or realistic stimuli; and (6) in terms of coping with horror, physical coping strategies are more successful in younger children; priming with information about the feared object reduces fear and increases children's enjoyment of frightening television and film. A number of limitations in the literature are identified, including the multifarious range of horror stimuli used in studies, disparities in methods, small sample sizes, and a lack of research on cross-cultural differences and similarities. Ideas for future research are explored.

Horror: An Introduction

> It seems an unaccountable pleasure which the spectators of a well-written tragedy receive from sorrow, terror, anxiety and other passions, that are in themselves disagreeable and uneasy. (Hume 1889, 258)

Why do people watch, and enjoy watching, horror films, and why is this an important or useful question to ask? The primary aims of the horror film are to frighten, shock, horrify, and disgust using a variety of visual and auditory leitmotifs and devices including reference to the supernatural, the abnormal, mutilation, blood, gore, the infliction of pain, death, deformity, putrefaction, darkness, invasion, mutation, extreme instability, and the unknown (Cherry 2009; Newman 2011). It is the emphasis on these characteristics that tends to distinguish horror from the related genre of thriller or psychological thriller (Hanich 2011). Thrillers are designed to create suspense and terror, but the creation of these feelings is dependent not on the presence of mutilation, gore, or the supernatural but via more human devices. These boundaries, however, can be fuzzy. If these features are utilized in thrillers, they are not the principal focus of the film but are incidental to it (an example would be the ear-cutting scene in *Reservoir Dogs* [1992], which is bloody and brutal but is contained within a film that has a nonhorror theme). Together with Westerns, science fiction, comedy, musicals, documentaries, and other film genres, which are characterized by particular tropes, styles, themes, characters, and visual leitmotifs, horror sets itself apart from other film types via its distinctive characteristics.

Although commercially successful, the cinematic reputation of horror film has been less than stellar. It has been frequently regarded (if it is regarded at all) as the runt of the cinema family and held in lower esteem than other film categories (Stone 2016). Etchison (2011, 8) observed that "the horror film occupies a position in popular culture roughly comparable to that of horror literature. That is to say, it is generally ignored, sometimes acknowledged with bemused tolerance, and viewed with alarm when it irritates authority beyond a certain point—rather like a child too spirited to follow the rules that tradition has deemed acceptable for proper acculturation," a view that is echoed elsewhere. For example, Tudor (1997, 446) noted that "a taste of horror is a taste for something seemingly abnormal and is therefore deemed to require special attention." Part of the reason for the disdain, apart from the broad and base nature of the content, may be the relative cheapness of horror film: These are often much less expensive to create than are other genre films, such as Westerns, comedies, or science fiction. The first horror film can probably be dated to 1855/1856. The Lumiere Brothers' *L'Arrivée d'un train en gare de La Ciotat* depicts the arrival of a train into a station, the appearance of which, if anecdotal although possibly apocryphal accounts are to be believed, resulted in the audience becoming consumed with a fear that the train would emerge from the screen, such was the novelty of such a depiction at the time.

In terms of industry regard, the reputation of horror has not been high. The American Academy of Motion Picture Arts, which awards the Oscars, has nominated only six horror/supernatural films for Best Picture, and only one has won the award (*The Silence of the Lambs* in 1992, which also won the awards for Best Actress, Actor, and Director). Other horror films to have been nominated include *The Exorcist* (1973), *Jaws* (1975), *The Sixth Sense* (1999), *Black Swan* (2010), and *Get Out* (2017). The latter was also nominated for best comedy/musical at the Golden Globes and was winner of the Oscar for Best Screenplay. Industry recognition for horror film has tended to be reserved for technical achievements; hence, the Oscars awarded for Best Art Direction and Cinematography for *Phantom of the Opera* (1943), Best Score for *The Omen* (1976), Best Visual Effects for *Alien* (1979), and Best Makeup for *An American Werewolf in London* (1981) and *The Fly* (1986). The number of actors to have won an Oscar nomination for horror roles is low—Frederic March (*Dr. Jekyll and Mr. Hyde,* 1931), Ruth Gordon (*Rosemary's Baby,* 1968), Kathy Bates (*Misery,* 1990), Natalie Portman (*Black Swan,* 2010), and Hopkins are exceptions.

Despite the relative lack of formal industry recognition and professional respect, horror thrives. In 2017, the second cinema adaptation of the Stephen King novel *It* generated $700.4 million in global ticket sales, making this the most financially successful horror film of all time based on recorded box-office sales (its production budget was $35 million). The success led to a sequel released in 2019 (*It: Chapter 2*), which has achieved global ticket sales of $185 million in its first week of release. In 1989, two horror films had grossed over $38 million (*The Fly II* and *The Abyss,* earning $38.9 million and $89.8 million, respectively). In 2017, this number was fifteen, with *It* leading and occupying thirteenth place in box-office revenue. *The Mummy* occupied the twenty-third position, *Resident Evil: Final Chapter* the thirtieth position, *Annabelle: Creation* the thirty-second, and *Get Out* the thirty-seventh ($255 million). Nine horror films earned more than $100 million in 2017. These numbers illustrate how successful and popular the horror film has become and that viewers' appetite for it is rapacious.

This commercial enthusiasm exists against a backdrop of considerable fan enthusiasm for the genre, as evidenced by the number of major, significant genre-specific international film festivals that exist. These include the United Kingdom's three Frightfest events, the Sitges International Fantastic Film Festival in Catalonia, Toronto's After Dark Film Festival, Screamfest and Fantasticfest in the United States, the Brussels International Fantastic Film Festival, Australia's A Night of Horror International Film Festival, Amsterdam's Imagine Festival, Argentina's Rojo Sangre, Italy's Ravena Nightmare Film Festival, Wales's Abertoir, and several others. A number of print magazines devoted to horror are available (such as *Rue Morgue, Diabolique, Scream,* and *The Dark Side*), as are various horror websites, online film streaming services (such as Shudder and Screambox), and specialist satellite/freeview TV channels such as the Horror Channel and SyFy. The TV company AMC airs and produces original horror content (and created Shudder), and an Asian-based pay-TV horror channel is available called Thrill. Given the popularity of horror film, a useful question to explore is why people are attracted to this genre of film, given its distinctive nature, and why people are attracted to horror in the first instance, a question addressed in this review.

Historically, horror has formed a significant part of "Western" literary tradition since the Babylonian *Gilgamesh* and the English *Beowulf*. The gothic tradition, a period that covers 1760–1820, features fiction in which the omphalos is their archaic themes, haunted castles, stylized period settings, a supernatural element in the storytelling, suspense, and chaos (Punter 2014). Examples include Walpole's *The Castle of Otranto* (1764), Radcliffe's *The Mysteries of Udolpho* (1794) and *The Italian* (1797), and Lewis's *The Monk* (1795), among others. Although modern horror clearly has its roots and traditions in gothic horror (and castles, spirits, and ghosts are well-documented tropes of horror films), very little modern horror film has been directly inspired by, or has adapted, these works. Victorian literature has exerted a much greater and direct influence, as evidenced by the reimaginings and remakes of films based on literary characters from this period, such as Dracula, Frankenstein (doctor and creation), Dr. Jekyll and Mr. Hyde, the hunchback of Notre Dame, the phantom of the opera, Dr. Moreau, Dorian Gray, the monsters and protagonists in Grimms' fairy tales, and the trolls of Nordic literature. These figures have been interpreted and reinterpreted throughout the twentieth and twenty-first centuries in different fictionalized forms—in theater, drama, radio, television, short stories, novels, and, especially, film.

Given the longevity of horror as a genre and its history in cinema, what is it that draws people to this particular genre, and how does the genre create the psychological effects that it does? The study of individuals' response to horror can be illuminating for several reasons. It may help us understand why people are attracted to a very commercially successful genre of filmmaking but one that is seen as very distinctive and highly specialized. It may also help us to explain why some material that is perceived as being unpleasant and disgusting is appealing to some people more than it is to others. The study of horror film may also help us understand how emotions are generated and processed and may help us understand elements of fear (and the attraction of fear).

The current chapter sets out to review the literature regarding the appeal of horror and why and how horror cinema exerts the effects that it does. Specifically, it will consider whether there are personality types or other individual differences associated with preference for, and enjoyment of, horror films; whether sex differences exist in the preference for, and enjoyment of, horror film; how fear of horror film develops and how coping strategies are recruited to manage the fear elicited by horror; the psychological and emotional consequences of watching horror and whether watching horror is associated with any adverse, short-term, or long-term psychological consequences; the behavioral responses reliably elicited by exposure to horror film; and the use of auditory stimulation to manipulate our response to horror. A number of texts exist that have discussed and addressed various aspects of horror and horror film, including the cinematic portrayal of the "mad scientist" (Tudor 1989; Frayling 2013), the aesthetics of horror film (Sipos 2010), the philosophy of horror (Carroll 2003), the process of horror fiction writing (King 2010), the use of sound and music in horror (Hayward 2009), and the marketing of horror films (Hantke 2004), among others. To the author's knowledge, this is the first attempt to assimilate the psychology and related literature in a comprehensive review of our understanding of the enjoyment of horror film, the motivation to watch horror film, and the effects of watching horror film. This review was based on keyword searches made via Google Scholar and PsychInfo between 2018 and August 2019 and included combinations of the words and terms "horror," "terror," "film," "movie," "cinema," "fear," "thriller," "slasher," "fright," "gore," "anxiety," "the unknown," "the uncanny," "gothic," "blood," "guts," "scream/screaming," "shudder," "shivering," "trauma," and "disgust/disgusting." Material was also sourced from the reference sections of the papers obtained and of books where the topic was horror. The review begins with a definition of horror.

What Is "Horror"?

The word *horror* derives from the Greek *phryke* (meaning "shudder") and describes the physical manifestations of shivering, shuddering, and piloerection. In the fourth stasimon of Sophocles's *Oedipus tyrannus,* the chorus says after the protagonist blinds himself, "Alas, poor man, I cannot ever look at you . . . such is the shiver [*phryke*] you cause in me" (Cairns 2015). An exact and precise modern definition of horror, however, is difficult to determine. Horror has been defined as a "spontaneous response to shocking visual stimulus" (Cairns 2015) and as "a compound of terror and revulsion" (Kawin 2012). In Kawin's interpretation, "imagined horror provides entry to the made-up world where fears are heightened but can be mastered. . . . It accesses a core of fears we may share as humans, such as the fear of being attacked in the dark. . . . It provides a way to conceptualize, give shape to and deal with the evil and frightening." Horror, Stone (2016) argues, "confronts us with the disgusting and the fascinating simultaneously," two aspects of horror returned to later. Horror, according to Marriott (2012), is "the madwoman in the attic."

One view of horror considers it to be of two types: horror, which is genuine and is designed to make us afraid because it is advantageous to our survival (e.g., fear arising from attack and being motivated to fight or flee), and "art-horror," which describes the imagined horror found in horror films (Carroll 1987). Carroll also argues that "horror novels, stories, films, plays and so on are marked by the presence of monsters of either a supernatural or sci-fi origin" (52). In Carroll's definition, it is the presence of a monster that defines the essence of a horror film, as monsters do not exist within our conventional realm of understanding or reason; they defy science; they should not exist. Carroll views films that are typically classed as horror (e.g., *Psycho*) to be of a different type (tales of terror) because "though eerie and scary, [they] achieve their hair-raising effect by explaining extreme psychological phenomena that are all too human." This definition, of course, would exclude a significant number of obviously horrific horror films, such as *The Silence of the Lambs, Henry: Portrait of a Serial Killer* (1986), the Saw and Hostel franchises, and other exemplars of the "torture porn" horror subgenre and the cannibal films of the 1970s (e.g., *Cannibal Holocaust* [1980] and *Cannibal Ferox* [1981]). The view has also been challenged (Gaut 1993). "Slasher" movies, for example, are clearly horror films but do not necessarily contain monsters as described by Carroll (although some, such as Freddie Kruger, Jason Voorhees, and Michael Myers, possess supernatural elements, and Freddie Kruger is an oneiric fiction). Also, Chewbacca and the Force defy the conventions of science, but *Star Wars* (1977) would not be classed a horror film.

Horror invariably includes an element of evil, channeled via a human, a creature, or a supernatural force, which has the power to change events, causing disruption and instability, and which must be challenged and defeated (Kjeldgaard-Christiansen 2016). If this force is not human or supernatural (ghostly, spectral), it is natural—plants, monkeys, ants, leeches, sharks, birds, dogs, bats, rats, bees, fish, earthworms, alligators, spiders, snakes, cockroaches, and dinosaurs have all been employed to create chaos and instability in horror films. Freud ([1919] 2003) referred to horror as the uncanny (a peculiar translation of *unheimlich*, meaning "unhomely"): "the name for everything that ought to have remained secret and hidden but has come to light." Horror films also invariably present a Manichean view of the world, where good battles evil (as is literally the case in films such as *Dracula* [1931], *The Exorcist,* and *The Omen*). There is a driving motivation to overcome "a pure and unmotivated desire to inflict suffering" (Clasen 2014). But horror film, despite the features that the genre shares, is not a unitary cinematic phenomenon, and distinct subgenres or branches exist that are characterized by similar features or styles of filmmaking and storytelling. Often, these are post hoc classifications of films that seem to share core features, and the classification can seem like an exercise in pattern recognition. There are films that do not easily lend themselves to these classifications (and some may straddle boundaries). However, the most common and typical subgenres include gothic, supernatural/occult/paranormal, psychological horror, monster movies, slasher films, body horror/horror typified by extreme gore, exploitation cinema (Cherry 2009), and found footage, which has a very specific technical filmmaking approach and its own identifiable tropes bequeathed from such films as *Cannibal Holocaust* but more demonstrably from *The Blair Witch Project* (1999).

Horror film is the only fictional genre that is specifically created to elicit fear consistently and deliberately rather than sporadically or incidentally. Behaviorally, horror film can create shivering, closing of the eyes, startle, shielding of the eyes, trembling, paralysis, piloerection, withdrawal, heaving, and screaming (Harris et al. 2000). It can produce changes in psychophysiology, specifically increasing heart rate and galvanic skin response (see later). Mentally, it can create anxiety, fear, empathy, and thoughts of disgust (Cantor 2004). One of the earliest empirical studies to examine the effect of watching horror or suspenseful cinema on behavior asked participants to watch three programs that varied in suspense (high and low) and in outcome—where the film had a resolved ending or an unresolved ending (Zillmann, Hay, and Bryant 1975). The suspenseful programs with the resolved endings were better appreciated than were those with unresolved endings. However, similar—but smaller—results were also found for the unresolved endings (i.e., appreciation levels were high if the program was suspenseful). Cantor (2004) asked students to write about their experiences of horror films and analyzed three years' worth of the students' papers (530 in total). Approximately 46 percent of the sample reported experiencing sleep disturbances after the event, and 75 percent reported having experienced anxiety. The four most frequently cited causes of frightening experiences were the films *Poltergeist* (1982) (5.5 percent), *Jaws* (4.3 percent), *The Blair Witch Project* (4.2 percent), and *Scream* (1996) (3.2 percent). There were some film-specific anxieties—respondents would express fear of swimming in lakes and oceans, uneasiness around clowns and televisions, and avoidance of camping and woods.

Behavioral change has also been examined experimentally. Hagenaars, Roelofs, and Stins (2014), for example, asked fifty participants to watch neutral, pleasant, or unpleasant film clips while "standing on a stabilometric platform." This device measures a person's motoric behavior as the participant engages in some exercise or task. They found that when participants watched unpleasant films, the participants would freeze, showing reduced body sway and heart rate deceleration. The reduced body sway was found early on in the viewing of the unpleasant material (one to two seconds after stimulus onset), suggesting that the behavioral effects of watching horror are immediate. The study is one of the few, methodologically well-controlled studies of behavioral response to films designed to elicit strong emotions (pleasant or unpleasant) and demonstrated empirically how exposure to certain types of film affects physical behavior and, in this specific example, how certain types of film inhibit motor behavior.

People's enjoyment of horror can also be affected by priming. Cantor, Ziemke, and Sparks (1984) found that providing adults with information about the types of events they were about to see in four horror films increased the degree of fright and upset that the participants experienced. Neuendorf and Sparks (1988) extended Cantor et al.'s study by presenting 121 attendees of two horror films (*The Texas Chainsaw Massacre* [1974] and *Night of the Living Dead* [1968]) at a US cinema with three levels of warning—the low warning involved the transmission of basic information, such as the film's name, the release date, and its R rating; the moderate warning involved all of the low information plus a description of the film's content; the high warning included both of these plus a statement about a graphic scene in the film (e.g., a paraplegic being sawn in half by a saw-wielding maniac). If individuals reported being previously afraid of the specific types of content mentioned by the experimenters, these "cues" significantly predicted overall fear when prior experience of the film and anxiety were controlled for (fear was measured via questionnaire rather than behaviorally). There was no significant correlation between a trait known as sensation seeking (see later) and liking and enjoyment of either film. There was a correlation between prior experience and enjoyment for *The Texas Chainsaw Massacre,* suggesting that viewers repeated their viewing because they enjoyed it the first time. Viewers' anxiety levels predicted the fright generated by *Night of the Living Dead,* as did fear cues. The greater the experienced anxiety and the fear cues, the greater the experienced fright. The availability of spoilers—the reveal of key scenes and plot points in a work of fiction in advance of viewing—appears to have little effect on the positive enjoyment of horror film or the experience of suspense (Johnson et al. 2019).

Our behavioral reaction to horror tends to be consistent, although there is not much research that has explicitly investigated this response. The next section considers some of the reasons why people watch horror film and some of the dominant theories and models in interdisciplinary research that have been proposed to explain our enjoyment of horror film. It considers first some of the most salient ways in which horror film sets out to frighten viewers, including sound.

Sound in Horror

In addition to the visual and verbal (dialogue) impact of horror, perhaps one of the most significant elements of horror film is auditory. To this end, some authors have argued that "horror is primarily a sound-based medium" (Kawin 2012): The creaking door, the scream, the shriek of an owl, the hiss of a cat, the squelching of a head as it meets a sledgehammer, the ringing of a phone, the bang of a falling object, and the crack of a branch in an otherwise quiet forest at night are all auditory devices deigned to make viewers and listeners afraid and to create suspense.

One of the most successful, and the most common, auditory tropes in horror is the use of a loud sound after a prolonged period of silence—the so-called jump scare. Often the sound is unconnected with what is onscreen, but a loud noise might accompany a reveal, such as a face (an example from the genre would be a character opening a mirrored bathroom cupboard door, then closing to discover the reflection of another person standing behind them, with accompanying loud noise or musical note). A distinction is sometimes made between diegetic sound (which the characters can hear) and nondiegetic sound (which is external to the characters, such as incidental music). Famous examples of the latter are the stabbing and screeching sound of Bernard Herrmann's violins during the shower scene in *Psycho*, John Williams's double bass that precedes the appearance of the shark in *Jaws*, John Carpenter's "stings" and soundtrack in *Halloween* (1978), and the foreboding chorus in *The Omen*. Carpenter has noted that when his film was screened without a soundtrack to a film executive, "she wasn't scared at all. I then became determined to 'save it with music'" (Hayward 2009). The high strings and low bass of *Psycho* were influences on Carpenter and Dan Wyman's score and its 4/5 signature leitmotif, as was the use of Mike Oldfield's tubular bells from the opening of *The Exorcist*.

Some examples of diegetic sounds in horror film include the bangs and creaks caused by entities that are invisible to the actors on screen; one horror film that relies less on gore and blood and more on the potency of audition to increase suspense is *The Blair Witch Project*, with its use of nocturnal wails, screams, and creaking branches. The use of sound to amplify horror can be identified in many early horror films—Ruben Mamoulian's *Dr. Jekyll and Mr. Hyde* (1931), for example, which includes the first use of the sound of a human heartbeat in film, is familiar for the creation of the "Mamoulian sound stew" of noise, and sound used to generate suspense and excitement in the film.

The second most common auditory influence in horror cinema is the use of music and soundtrack. Research suggests that different styles of music can affect the emotional perception of what is seen in film, regardless of the content (Bullerjahn and Güldenring 1994), and this accompaniment allows us to interpret what we see in the context of this music (Gorbman 1987). In horror film, music even has its own trope or leitmotif—the tritone or diabolus in musica ("the devil in music") otherwise known as the devil's tritone (Lerner 2010) can be heard in *Beetlejuice* (1988), *Hocus Pocus* (1993), and *The 'Burbs* (1989).

Some types of music are designed to be unpleasant, to be perceived negatively, and to create tension, and there are many examples of this design in horror film, as discussed earlier. Discordant music has been associated with activity in different brain regions to those found when listening to harmonic or pleasant music; these regions include the right parahippocampal gyrus and precuneus and bilateral orbitofrontal cortex (Blood et al. 1999), and research suggests that these regions are involved in mediating our auditory response to some aspects of horror film. Frightening music has been associated with changes in monoamine receptor activity in the caudate nucleus and right amygdala (decreases) and in the neocortex (increases) in ten men (Zhang et al. 2012). This study did not include a comparison film clip, however, so the conclusion that can be drawn from it is limited.

The most well-used auditory (and visual) device in horror film is the startle reflex (SR), and this tends to be provoked by the jump scare referred to earlier—the sound of a bump, a sudden burst of noise, some dialogue, or music (Baird 2000). The first known example of a startle effect in horror film is seen and heard in *The Cat People* (1942) when the sound of a bus door opening occurs just when the viewer is expecting an attack, but the film cuts to this noise and the shot of the door opening. A more recent example can be found in *Fatal Attraction* (1987), where a child's scream and the whistling of the kettle in the reveal of the boiled rabbit overlap. In the same film, Glenn Close's character's resurrection in the bath provides another example of the jump scare that employs an auditory device.

Under laboratory conditions, an SR is produced by delivering fifty milliseconds of ninety-five decibels of white noise at unpredictable intervals, while eyeblink is measured. The stimulation is not always auditory and can be visual or tactile. The acoustic SR describes an involuntary eyeblink, measured at the orbicularis oculi muscle via EMG, in response to this noise. The SR can be potentiated when individuals anticipate danger (Grillon et al. 1993a, 1993b; Bublatzky et al. 2013; Bradley, Zlatar, and Lang 2018) and when pleasant stimuli signal threat (via conditioning) (Bradley, Moulder, and Lang 2005). This is called affective modulation of the SR, and the startle potentiation is thought to reflect a person's emotional reactivity to threat. When people watch fear-related or violent films, the blink magnitude (SR) is larger than when people watch films with sexual content (Jansen and Frijda 1994), neutral content (Koukounas and McCabe 2001), or sad content (Kreibig et al. 2011). The SR is also greater when people watch unpleasant slides—and smallest when people watch pleasant slides (Vrana, Spence, and Lang 1988)—and when people listen to unpleasant music (Roy et al. 2009). Roy et al.'s study, however, includes a very small sample of sixteen participants.

The SR is higher when people recall fear-related sentences than when they recall neutral sentences (Vrana and Lang 1990) and is higher when people are exposed to negative stimuli than positive or neutral stimuli (Cook et al. 1991), and this is referred to as fear-potentiated startle (Grillon et al. 1993a, 1993b). Women's SR tends to be higher than men's when stimuli are disgusting (Yartz and Hawk 2002). Fear, however, is the stimulus that creates the greatest SR (Bradley, Cuthbert, and Lang 1999), and people with specific phobias show potentiated SR when phobia-related stimuli are viewed. Some studies find that an SR does not occur to some types of negative stimuli such as mutilation or surgery (Stanley and Knight 2004).

The startle effect is a highly replicable behavioral phenomenon and can be reduced with the administration of anxiolytics and when lesions are made to the amygdala (Hitchcock and Davis 1986; Angrilli et al. 1996; Davis 2006). It would be instructive to study whether those high and low in empathy or sensation seeking (see later) and whether individuals who like horror film and those who dislike horror film would generate different SRs.

Why Do People Watch Horror?

Suspense and resolution of suspense are two important components of horror and our response to horror film. Suspense refers to the build up to threat, the tension created prior to the manifestation of threat, and the resolution/elimination of threat. It has been defined as "acute, fearful apprehension about deplorable events that threatens liked protagonists" and "an experience of uncertainty whose hedonic properties can vary from noxious to pleasant" (Zillmann 1996, 108). The tension created during the feeling of suspense can arise from events that signify conflict, dissonance, and instability (Lehne and Koelsch 2015). One theory of horror enjoyment, Zillmann's (1980, 1996) excitation transfer theory, argues that we derive our enjoyment of horror film from this feeling of suspense (this theory might also explain the enjoyment of nonhorror film that involves the invocation of suspense). When a threat is resolved, our negative affect converts to euphoria and suspense ends. The vital aspect of the theory is that enjoyment is derived from the degree of negative affect built up during exposure to the horror film and from the positive affect/reaction that results from the resolution of the threat. If the resolution does not occur, then residual negative affect will lead to increased dysphoria. If there is no suspense but a complete certainty about what will happen, suspense is replaced by dread (Oliver 1993a, 1993b). Very few studies have tested the theory, although limited reviews provide some support for the model (Hoffner and Levine 2005). Zillmann, Hay, and Bryant (1975) showed children animated cartoons that varied in suspense and measured participants' facial expressions, physiological arousal, and cognitive responses. They found that liking of the film increased as suspense increased. Liking was especially great when the threat was overcome, but the relationship between fear and liking was not examined in the study.

Individuals high in empathy will express more negative affect regardless of a successful resolution to the threat in the film (Zillmann et al. 1986; Hoffner and Cantor 1991; Sparks 1991). Zillmann's model has some difficulty accounting for the motivation to watch and for the enjoyment derived from horror films in which the sympathetic characters are (1) dispatched and (2) where the story does not end happily (Hoffner and Levine 2005). There is also evidence that enjoyment of horror may not be affected by the availability of resolution and that unresolved horror is perceived as just as enjoyable as resolved horror (Hoffner and Cantor 1991).

An alternative model to Zillmann's suggests that enjoyment is associated with the presence of destruction, excitement, and unpredictability in films (Sparks 1986a, 1986b; Tamborini, Stiff, and Zillmann 1987; Tamborini and Stiff 1987). This model, the uses and gratification theory of film consumption (Katz, Blumler, and Gurevitch 1973; Palmgreen 1984), argues that the enjoyment and seeking out of material are determined by the specific need for stimulation and the satisfaction one derives following the achievement of gratification. Some research suggests that certain personality types and individuals who are high or low on some psychological traits may seek out horror or violent material for gratification but that the material itself may not always provide this satisfaction (see the "Individual Differences" section). Sensation seeking, verbal aggression, and argumentativeness, for example, have been found to be positively correlated with enjoyment of horror and violent films, but these are not consistent predictors of liking for horror/violent material (Greene and Krcmar 2005).

Zillmann (1980) has argued that a positive outcome for the protagonist and a poor one for the antagonist are the key predictors of satisfaction with a film. If neither occurs but a threat is removed, this would also lead to a satisfactory experience, but the experience would be diluted. A positive outcome is, however, necessary for the "cognitive switch from dysphoria to euphoria" (148). There is no consistent evidence to support this view, and the success of films where the threat is still very much present in some way at the end of a horror film (e.g., *The Exorcist, The Omen, Friday the 13th* [1980]) and even in thrillers such as *Basic Instinct* (1992) and *Presumed Innocent* (1990) suggests that this explanation may not account fully for why we watch and enjoy horror.

It has been proposed that arousal itself might be self-rewarding—the act of watching horror provides us with a thrill regardless of the resolution, and we like and enjoy the film for this reason (Tamborini 1991). The pleasurable experience of arousal motivates us to continue watching in order to sustain that level of arousal, as Berlyne (1967) suggests. Sparks and Spirek (1988), for example, found a positive correlation between skin conductance (a physiological measure of emotional arousal) and self-reported arousal in people who watched a clip of *A Nightmare on Elm Street* (1984), suggesting that the arousal we report also correlates at the physiological level, although whether the psychophysiological changes determine the arousal or the cognitive and emotional arousals (the interpretation of the material) determine the psychophysiological changes is an argument that dates back to James.

Individual Differences in Response to Horror

Carroll (2003) asked, "How can horror audiences find pleasure in what by nature is distressful and unpleasant?" Some research has attempted to answer this question by studying the type of individual who enjoys and likes horror. Some of the personality traits and cognitive/affective traits that have been implicated in horror preference and/or enjoyment of horror include sensation seeking, empathy, theory of mind, need for affect, the dark tetrad, and personality. Other individual differences include age and sex (considered later). Unless a person expresses an interest and liking of horror, the response to graphic violence tends not to be positive. Weaver and Wilson (2009), for example, assigned four hundred people to one of three groups who watched either clips from five television programs showing graphic violence, clips with the violence sanitized, or clips with the violence removed. The nonviolent programs were regarded as more enjoyable than the violent versions, a finding that is consistent with earlier research indicating that removing the violent content from a film does not reduce the film's enjoyment (Sparks, Sherry, and Lubsen 2005). A meta-analysis of the enjoyment of media violence (not horror film specifically) found that greater selective exposure to violence (i.e., choosing to watch violent media) leads to a reduction in the enjoyment of its content (Weaver 2011). The implication of this finding appears to be that even though individuals may seek out exposure to violent media, they do not often enjoy what they find. In addition, participants may vary according to the degree of material they are routinely exposed to. When graduate nursing students and psychology students were shown videos of graphic medical procedures, for example, the nurses expressed less disgust and fear but more sadness (Vlahou, Vanman, and Morris 2011). Both groups, however, showed evidence of psychophysiological arousal (measured via galvanic skin response) in response to watching the procedures.

Sensation Seeking

The most widely studied trait in the research on horror is sensation seeking. According to Zuckerman (1994, 27), sensation seeking is the "seeking of varied, novel, complex and intense sensations and experiences, and the willingness to take physical, social, legal and financial risks for the sake of such experiences." It peaks in the teenage years and declines thereafter (Zuckerman 1988). Zuckerman's measure of sensation seeking describes four related but different factors: (1) thrill and adventure seeking; (2) experience seeking; (3) disinhibition; and (4) boredom susceptibility. In the original conception of the model (Zuckerman 1979), individuals thought to be high sensation seekers would experience much more positive emotion when highly aroused and stimulated and would seek negative stimulation to maximize their arousal because this stimulation was intense. A negative stimulus (such as a horror film) might, therefore, be interpreted by a person high in sensation seeking as being very positive; but a person low in sensation seeking would find the stimulus unpleasant. High-sensation-seeking individuals would also be less vulnerable to the experience of threat in these films (Franken, Gibson, and Rowland 1992).

All four factors of the sensation-seeking scale have been found to predict enjoyment of horror film to some extent, but some factors are better predictors than others. For example, disinhibition was found by Edwards (1984) to be the strongest predictor, followed by experience seeking, thrill and adventure seeking, and boredom susceptibility. Edwards reported a positive correlation between high sensation seeking (in general) and interest in horror film. Tamborini and Stiff (1987) found a positive correlation between liking for horror and a combination of the sensation-seeking factors. Zuckerman and Litle (1986) found that frequency of horror film attendance correlated with disinhibition, thrill and adventure seeking, and boredom susceptibility, but in men only. The sex difference in this study highlights an important constraint on the model, and that is, individual differences (such as sex) may interact with sensation-seeking type to predict viewing, preference for, or enjoyment of horror film (see later). Cantor and Sparks (1984) found that sensation seeking was positively correlated with the enjoyment of frightening films in men and women. However, components of sensation seeking predicted enjoyment differently—thrill and adventure seeking were the best predictor for men, whereas disinhibition was the best predictor for women.

Other studies have reported no positive correlation between sensation seeking and liking and enjoyment for horror films (Neuendorf and Sparks 1988). Aluja-Fabregat (2000) found that disinhibition and psychopathy—a personality trait that describes a charming, remorseless, callous, and manipulative personality type—correlated with curiosity about morbid events in 470 eighth graders in Catalan. Sensation seeking correlated with consumption of violent films, and consumption was associated with psychopathy, specifically in boys.

In a study of the enjoyment of fear experiences in video gaming, Lynch and Martins (2015) found that in their sample of 269 eighteen- to twenty-four-year-old players, men reported more enjoyment of violent video games, played more games, and played more often. Sensation seeking and enjoyment were positively correlated, with high sensation seekers reporting less frequent fear (although $p = 0.05$) and low empathizers enjoying the violent games more. Low empathizers also played more but did not play more frequently. *Resident Evil* was the most commonly played game, and the game's inclusion of zombies and surprises was cited as a cause of fear and fright. Agency in such games, however, appears to be important to the experience of the medium. When players were either asked to watch or to play a horror computer game (Konami's *PT*), players showed increased heart rate and galvanic skin response (emotional arousal) compared to participants who watched (Madsen 2016). There were no differences between the two groups in self-reported fear.

While sensation seeking might be strongly associated with enjoyment of horror, it may not be the strongest predictor of attendance at horror films. Tamborini and Stiff's (1987) study of 155 people (seventy-eight men; average age twenty-one years) attending a horror film in a US Midwestern city reported that men and younger participants scored the highest on the sensation-seeking scale, but that men and women attended for different reasons: Men attended because they sought sensation and to experience the destructive nature of the horror while women attended because they wanted to experience a just ending. More important than sensation seeking appeared to be participants' expectations of the film: The greatest predictor of film attendance was not sensation seeking but a desire to experience a satisfying resolution (especially by women) and to see destruction (men).

Also of note is that there is evidence that sensation seeking is related to the startle potentiation described earlier. Lissek and Powers (2003) found that people low in sensation seeking (as measured via the thrill- and adventure-seeking subscale) produced the typical startle potentiation during the viewing of threatening (vs. neutral) images but that those high in sensation seeking showed equal levels of startle to neutral and threatening images. One explanation for this finding is that high levels of sensation seeking are related to low levels of reactivity to threatening images. Because high sensation seeking involves a degree of sensory overload, less stimulation is required for a startle potentiation to occur, and those scoring high in sensation seeking show less fear startle potentiation.

The literature on sensation seeking, therefore, suggests that this trait and specific components of it, especially disinhibition, may predict enjoyment of horror film, but this prediction does not apply to men and women consistently (a conclusion considered in more detail in the section on sex differences). The literature also highlights a limitation in this—and other areas—of the horror research literature in that samples are often heterogeneous, the film selections are heterogeneous, and sample sizes tend to be small. These limitations are returned to at the end of the review.

Empathy

Empathy is a multidimensional concept whose components have been defined in different ways but which in general are reflected in two types: a cognitive component (e.g., perspective taking) and an affective/emotional component (sympathy and concern for others and sharing of negative affect). One model suggests that empathy comprises a wandering imagination (a tendency to fantasize and daydream about fictional situations), fictional involvement (transposition of oneself into a story), humanistic mentation (a sensitivity to the emotional welfare of others), and emotional contagion (a susceptibility to be influenced by the emotions around oneself) (Tamborini, Stiff, and Heidel 1990). Zillmann[1] has proposed a three-factor model of empathy in which emotional behavior arises from the interaction between these factors: dispositional (a "response-guiding" mechanism that results in motor reactions to a stimulus), excitatory (a "response-energizing" mechanism that enables immediate arousal), and experiential (the conscious experience of the first two). Davis (1983), who originally developed the Interpersonal Reactivity Index, argued that empathy was not a unitary or binary concept but was best considered as a set of constructs that involve our reactions to others but are distinct from each other. These constructs included perspective taking, a fantasy scale (which measures the degree to which a person transposes themselves into the feelings or actions of fictional characters), empathetic concern (which measures the degree of sympathy felt for others), and personal distress (a description of unease or distress experienced in interpersonal relationships).

There is evidence that each component can predict enjoyment of horror film, with low empathy consistently associated with greater enjoyment. In one study (Tamborini, Stiff, and Heidel 1990), ninety-five young people in same-sex pairs watched clips from two one-hour documentaries or two full-length horror films (*A Nightmare on Elm Street* and *The Boogens* [1981]). The study found that tendency to daydream and fantasize predicted the ability to sense the feelings and actions of the films' characters. Those scoring high on the wandering item, fictional involvement, humanistic mentation, and contagion scales described earlier found graphic horror less appealing. Those scoring low in empathy preferred graphic horror. People low in fearfulness also preferred graphic horror (Mundorf, Weaver, and Zillmann 1989). Hall and Bracken's (2011) study of 199 undergraduates found that fantasy empathy (but no other type) predicted narrative transportation (immersion in a text/film or "getting lost" in a story) and was associated with increased enjoyment of the film, although not necessarily horror film exclusively.

In a variant of this procedure, Tamborini, Salomonson, and Bahk (1993) asked participants to watch a pleasant (a comedy) or an unpleasant (*Videodrome* [1983]) film, with a confederate. To evoke empathy, after the film, the confederate said they were distressed because they thought they were going to be thrown out of school and asked "What am I going to do?" If there was no reply, the confederate left. If they received a reply, the responses would be rejected. Those participants scoring high in fictional involvement and empathetic concern provided more comfort and more social support. Those who watched the horror film, however, provided less support than did those who watched the comedy. While providing a potentially useful contribution to the study of how people respond to horror and the effect of this on our interaction with others—the greater the empathy, the greater the responsiveness to others' distress—the sample size is small ($N = 21$).

Empathy has also been associated with less enjoyment of suffering displayed in frightening films but with more enjoyment of danger, of excitement, and of happy endings (Hoffner 2009). People high in enduring negative affect have been found to experience more distress and less enjoyment of suffering. Those who had prior exposure to frightening films enjoyed danger more and enjoyed happy endings less.

Classifying participants according to the degree of empathy and sensation seeking has not been the only approach that has been taken to determining the types of people who watch and enjoy/prefer horror. Johnston (1995), for example, notes that not all audiences respond to horror in the same way, as this section has demonstrated, and has typologized viewers and their motivations to watch into three types: (1) resolved-ending types; (2) thrill watchers; and (3) gore watchers. Resolved-ending types enjoy film with a satisfying, definite closure; thrill watchers enjoy being frightened and empathize with the principal characters; gore watchers watch because they enjoy the destructiveness in film. The typology is based on some of the research reviewed here. A prediction that can be made from this typology is that thrill watchers will have higher levels of empathy and adventure seeking, whereas gore watchers will be low in empathy and fearfulness but will be high in adventure seeking and will seek out high arousal (King and Hourani 2007). Research suggests that gore watchers are curious about the ways people are killed, are vindictive (they require satisfaction that characters receive their just desserts), and are attracted to blood and guts (gore) in film (King and Hourani 2007). Gore watchers are more likely to be men, are more likely to identify with the killer in films, and are less likely to identify with the victim.

King and Hourani (2007) identified types of watchers from 229 individuals and showed them four horror films. Half the sample saw the films with a traditional ending (in which the evil antagonist is destroyed) or with a teaser ending (in which the evil antagonist is revived/resurrected). The traditional ending was more entertaining than was the teaser ending, but it was especially enjoyable and entertaining for high gore and thrill watchers than for low gore and thrill watchers. Traditional endings were less distressing and more frightening for high than for low gore watchers and were regarded as being more frightening by high thrill watchers. High thrill watchers found the teaser ending version of the film to be less scary than did low thrill watchers. High gore watchers regarded the teaser to be more predictable than did low thrill watchers. The traditional ending was considered to be less predictable by high gore watchers than by high thrill watchers and by high thrill watchers than by low thrill watchers. Very little research exists on this typology, however.

Although individual studies indicate a relationship between empathy and horror enjoyment, a meta-analysis of studies investigating the enjoyment of mediated fright and violence has found that empathetic concern and personal distress were negatively correlated with enjoyment, but correlations for personal distress were not consistent (Hoffner and Levine 2005). The authors note that the inconsistencies may be attributable to differences in the content of the film employed in these studies, and this is a problematic issue common to the field: There are no consistently chosen materials in either nature, content, length, age, or narrative. What is noteworthy, however, is that Hoffner and Levine's review found that the strongest effects (reported in two studies) were for studies that included horror films, and those films depicted torture (Johnston 1995) or brutal horror with no positive resolution (Tamborini, Stiff, and Heidel 1990). When these studies were removed, the correlation between empathy and enjoyment became nonsignificant. The authors note that the other four films measured participants' enjoyment of horror film as a genre (rather than their enjoyment of specific horror films or acts of graphic violence), and this methodological limitation in the literature is returned to in the conclusion of this chapter.

Need for Affect

A different form of individual difference—need for affect—may also mediate horror film preference and enjoyment, but the literature is limited. Need for affect (NfA) (Maio and Esses 2001) is based on the assumption that we are motivated to seek interesting or positive experiences and avoid unpleasant ones. NfA is measured via a questionnaire that comprises two subscales: the tendency to approach and the tendency to withdraw. People who prefer sad films experience more enjoyment when watching sad films, for example, because they regard viewing sad films as an enjoyable and a gratifying experience; their need for affect is satisfied by watching sad films (Oliver 1993a, 1993b; Oliver, Weaver, and Sargent 2000; Maio and Esses 2001). Few studies have explored the relationship between NfA and horror film viewing. One study asked 119 attendees (mean age twenty-three years) at a German cinema how likely they would be to watch *United 93* (2006) or the 2006 horror film remake *The Omen* (Bartsch, Appel, and Storch 2010). Participants with higher NfA approach scores experienced more intense emotions and experienced more negative emotions such as anger, fear, and disgust. *United 93* evoked more negative emotions than did *The Omen*. Higher NfA withdraw scores were associated with a more negative evaluation of emotions. Controlling for personality did not affect these results significantly. While NfA is little studied in horror, one possible research question that could be explored is whether preference for film genres correlates with NfA; no study to date has systematically examined this relationship.

Other Personality Traits

Other personality traits thought to be implicated in horror film preference or enjoyment include the Big Five, the Dark Tetrad, and repressive coping style. Dark personality traits are those that express some abnormal, sinister, and unpleasant aspect of behavior. Four such traits are Machiavellianism, narcissism, psychopathy (described earlier), and sadism. Machiavellianism (the enjoyment of power and the manipulation of power) has been found to correlate with enjoyment of horror, and the correlations between these two variables are stronger than the correlation between Machiavellianism and sensation seeking (Tamborini and Stiff 1987). High psychopathy scores have been associated with preference for graphically violent horror movies (Weaver 1991), and individuals scoring high in callousness and who habitually express little or no emotion show reduced facial expressions of sadness and disgust when watching violent films (Fanti, Kyranides, and Panayiotou 2017).

A repressive coping style is characterized by the repression of negative affect caused by stressors (Weinberger 1990; Sparks, Pellechia, and Irvine 1999). Sparks,

Pellechia, and Irvine investigated repressive coping style and enjoyment of horror film stimuli in fifty-nine individuals. Based on a median split, thirty repressors and twenty-nine nonrepressors were identified and were asked to view a twenty-five-minute extract from *When a Stranger Calls* (2006) (in which a babysitter receives frightening phone calls and discovers that the calls have been coming from inside the house she is in). Women in general expressed greater negative affect than did men, as expected (see later section), but the repressors in general showed greater physiological arousal during the film than did nonrepressors. An interesting pattern emerged across the course of exposure. Physiological arousal was similar for both groups at the beginning of the first two sections of the movie and then diverged in the final three sections as the suspense increased. No explicit analysis was provided of the psychometric response to the film (how much it was liked, how frightening it was, and so on). The study suggests that those who repress negative affect may nonetheless show high levels of physiological arousal during exposure to frightening films. What is less clear in this study is the relationship between this phenomenon and enjoyment of the film. It is also based on a very low sample of participants, and little subsequent research has focused on this particular personality trait/style.

Despite being the most commonly accepted model of personality, the Big Five has been the focus of very little published research in the context of horror film enjoyment and consumption. The Big Five proposes that personality comprises five core traits along which individuals differ. These traits are conscientiousness, openness to experience, extraversion, neuroticism, and agreeableness. One study employing a version of the Big Five found that a trait described as intellect/imagination (defined as a proclivity to engage in imaginative activity) was the strongest predictor of horror media consumption (Clasen, Christiansen, and Johnson 2020). There was a small but statistically significant and positive correlation between extraversion and frequency of horror media use, using horror media with others, enjoying horror media with others, and being more scared with others. Agreeableness was positively correlated with being easily scared by horror media, using horror media with others, and enjoying horror media with others, and negatively correlated with being more scared with others. People high in conscientiousness were less scared after using horror media, and people high in emotional stability were found to be less easily scared than those low in emotional stability, a finding that was also reported by Reynaud et al. (2012), who found that psychophysiological arousal was greater in participants who were high in neuroticism when they watched a film designed to elicit fear. The number of participants in Reynaud et al.'s study, however, was small.

The finding regarding agreeableness contrasts with research on violent video game playing where people lower in agreeableness have been found to be more frequent violent video games players; individuals who score high in extraversion and openness and low in neuroticism have also been found to be more frequent users (Chory and Goodboy 2011). Low agreeableness is a significant predictor of enjoyment of the horror film genre but not exclusively—it is also a significant predictor of enjoyment of parody, animation, neo-noir, and cult genres across different media including books, television, and film (Cantador, Fernández-Tobías, and Bellogín 2013). While the findings of Chory and Goodboy (2011) are informative, they are limited in terms of the measurement of response to horror film specifically because the stimuli used were not specifically horror film. A similar limitation can be found in Clasen, Christiansen, and Johnson's (2020) large Mechanical Turk study of 1,070 participants that asked participants for their responses to and perceptions of horror media generally, not horror film specifically. The study also administered a variant of the Big Five personality inventory and a variant of the sensation-seeking scale (the Brief Sensation-Seeking Scale; Hoyle et al. 2002) not normally administered in research examining the relationship between personality and horror film. Although research on violent video games might help us understand some of the correlates between use frequency and personality trait, it should be acknowledged that violent video games are qualitatively different stimuli to films. Films are a passive experience—viewers are unable to influence the action they see onscreen—whereas gaming is specifically an active experience where the player engages with what they see and is expected to do so as this is the principal motivation for gaming. Horror films and horror games are not equivalent stimuli, although they share many characteristics and elements of content.

In conclusion, the literature studying the relationship between personality and horror film consumption has been limited in number and scope. Two studies have reported a correlation between low agreeableness and preference/enjoyment of horror media, and one has not. It is noteworthy that in one of the studies reporting an association, agreeableness was the only trait to be significantly associated with horror media use. This aspect of personality may be worth exploring further.

Sex Differences

The most consistent individual difference predicting individuals' response to horror film is biological sex: Men and boys enjoy frightening and violent visual material more than do women and girls (Zuckerman and Litle 1986; Harris et al. 2000; Hoffner and Levine 2005). Correlations between intensity of "scary media" or horror and the enjoyment of horror in men are consistently positive (Hoffner and Levine 2005). Men enjoy horror media more than do women, are less scared by horror media, use horror media more, and show a greater preference for frightening horror media (Clasen, Christiansen, and Johnson 2020). One of the earliest experimental studies of sex differences investigated the role of social comparison in individuals' response to horror. Zillmann et al. (1986) asked thirty-six male and thirty-six female undergraduates to watch horror films (*Nightmares* [1983], *A Nightmare on Elm Street*) in the presence of a same-age, opposite-sex companion who either expressed control, indifference, or distress during the film. Men enjoyed the horror more and found it less boring and more satisfying and frightening than did women. Men expressed more distress if the female companion expressed distress (but engaged more with them than with a masterful woman) and less if the female companion was masterful. Zillmann et al. also manipulated initial appeal of the companion (high and low). Women enjoyed the films more in the company of a man with high appeal, but women's appeal had little effect on men's responses. Women engaged more with masterful than with distressed men. Cutting violence from films can increase enjoyability and decrease arousal in women (but has no effect on men): Women regard these films to be generally more disturbing than do men (Berry, Gray, and Donnerstein 1999).

Male undergraduates experience less distress and anxiety than do women when watching horror film (Sparks 1991), and women find film clips depicting sadness and fear more unpleasant and distressing; they also show greater arousal to fear clips than to clips depicting compassion (Davydov, Luminet, and Zech 2013; Maffei, Vencato, and Angrilli 2015). The findings reflect a more general sex difference in that women, in general, report greater fear and anxiety than do men. Women have been found to express more fears, more severe fears, and greater fear of repulsive but harmless animals (Tucker and Bond 1997), a finding that applies cross-culturally (Arrindell et al. 2004). Anxiety disorders are more commonly reported by women than men (McLean and Anderson 2009), and women appear to be more susceptible to a variety of anxiety-related disorders such as panic disorder, generalized anxiety disorder, PTSD, and agoraphobia (Kessler et al. 1994). The exception to this pattern is fear of bodily injury, social stimuli, noise, or enclosed spaces, where no consistent sex differences have been reported (McLean and Anderson 2009). Disgust sensitivity—the degree to which individuals find stimuli repulsive—also tends to be higher in women, and this phenomenon might provide an explanation for the sex difference in the fear of animals—and horror film (Connolly, Olatunji, and Lohr 2008). This is considered in more detail later. Women and girls, for example, are less likely to enjoy violent media when blood and gore portrayed are described as extreme, rather than mild or moderate (Hoffner and Levine 2005).

The sex difference is not only reported in the horror genre but also across a number of cinematic genres. One study of 150 undergraduates in Germany (Wühr, Lange, and Schwarz 2017) asked participants to indicate which types of films they believed that men and women would generally prefer. In a second study, participants were asked to indicate the films they themselves preferred. In the first study, men were regarded as preferring action, adventure, erotic, fantasy, historical, horror, sci-fi, thriller, war, and Western films, whereas women preferred animation, comedy, drama, Heimat, and romantic films. Both sexes liked crime and mystery equally. In the second study, women expressed a preference for drama and romance, and men preferred action, adventure, erotic, fantasy, horror, mystery, sci-fi, war, and Western films. Animation, comedy, crime heist, history, and thrillers were liked by both sexes.

Enjoyment and liking of the degree of explicit (graphic) horror also appear to show sex differences. Men tend to prefer very graphic horror material more than do women (Hoffner and Levine 2005). Men also report watching more violent television and attend more horror films. One explanation for this finding has been proposed by gender socialization theory (Zaslow and Hayes 1986), whereby boys and men are socialized to not be afraid and to not make expressive shows of fear, whereas girls are not constrained by such expectations and can "express their sensitivity by being appropriately disturbed" (Hoffner and Levine 2005). Such an explanation is probably locked in a prison of its own time in the sense that it is unclear whether such attitudes still exist now, at the end of the second decade of the twenty-first century.

Sex differences have been reported in the context of other behaviors such as the identification with a film's character. Tamborini, Stiff, and Zillmann (1987) asked forty-four male and fifty female undergraduates to rank their preference for two different versions of thirteen films (twelve of which were fictional). In one version, the victim of graphic violence was male; in the other, the victim was female. One theory of horror enjoyment discussed earlier (the uses and gratification perspective; Rubin 1994) argues that our reasons for watching horror and the benefit and gratification we derive from it will determine whether we identify with a victim or an aggressor (Johnston 1995). Viewers who identify with a female victim are usually more likely to experience distress (Zillmann and Cantor 1977) and are not satisfied by happy endings (Tannenbaum and Gaer 1965). Oliver's (1993a, 1993b) study of ninety-six sixteen-year-old high school students found that there was a correlation between gore watchers and enjoyment of retribution (liking to see victims get what they deserve). Participants' high punitive sexual attitudes have been found to be positively correlated with higher ratings of enjoyment; men prefer horror films in which the female rather than the male is the victim, but there is no significant association between enjoyment and the films' portrayal of victimization of sexual characters, of women, or of women expressing their sexuality.

Tamborini, Stiff, and Zillmann (1987) found that participants' recent and past viewing of horror film strongly predicted enjoyment of graphic horror in general. However, the responses to men and women as victims in the film interacted with other viewing preferences. For example, men's enjoyment of pornography was correlated with preference for graphic horror that depicted female victimization but not male victimization. Preference for graphic horror correlated with disinhibition, moderately for boredom susceptibility and experience seeking, and not at all for thrill/adventure seeking. Sensation seeking in general did not predict preference for graphic horror. Women regarded the films with female victims to be higher in violent content than films featuring male victims; the opposite pattern was found in men. Boredom susceptibility was a good predictor of preference for graphic horror in men. No one factor was a strong predictor of graphic horror preference in women when the victim was male. Deceit and boredom susceptibility predicted graphic horror preference when the victim was female. Physiological arousal (measured via galvanic skin response [GSR]) has also been correlated with enjoyment of horror after men finish watching a film (Sparks 1991).

A retrospective study of 233 psychology students (125 men) asked participants to recall details of a date they had been on as a teenager/young adult during which they watched a frightening film (Harris et al. 2000). The participants reported that the films most commonly seen were *Scream, Scream 2* (1997), *I Know What You Did Last Summer* (1997), and *I Still Know What You Did Last Summer* (1998). Men were younger when they watched the film (16.7 vs. 17.6 years), and the study found some notable and significant sex differences: 31 percent of women reported looking away from the screen, whereas only 7 percent of men did. About 61 percent of women reported feeling anxious, whereas 44 percent of men did; 34 percent of women reported that it had increased their imagination (men—1 percent); 19 percent of women said they feared sleeping alone afterward (men—8 percent); 67 percent of women said their heartbeats were faster (men—53 percent); 56 percent of women said they became very jumpy (men—31 percent); 41 percent of women were amused and entertained (men—59 percent); 55 percent of women held on to their date (men—21 percent); 32 percent of women screamed (men—6 percent); and 26 percent of women felt disgusted (men—10 percent). Men gave more positive reactions than did women, women gave more negative reactions than did men, and women reported more sleep disturbances than did men. About 80 percent of women reported being somewhat or very afraid (men—46 percent), and 18 percent reported not being afraid or being a little afraid (men—51 percent). This study also measured empathy and found a positive correlation between overall empathy scale scores and negative reactions but not between negative reactions and any one specific subscale. There were some associations between negative reactions and empathetic responses. Low empathetic concern, for example, predicted sleep disturbance. Higher boredom susceptibility was associated with fewer negative reactions and with increased liking but not with sleep disturbance. Women who scored high on empathy were more likely to be scared at the time of the study (i.e., they were more likely to express fear as adults) than were low-scoring women or men generally.

In a similar study, Hoekstra, Harris, and Helmick (1999) asked 202 introductory psychology students to describe their reactions (especially fear reactions) when they recalled the frightening movies they watched as children. The mean age at watching was 10.8 years, a similar finding to Cantor (2004). Female participants as adults liked slasher films less than did male participants as adults—of the fourteen categories included, this was the least liked by women. The most liked genre by women was romantic comedy; by men, action and adventure. Men reported choosing to watch horror more often than did women. Both sexes noted fear-related changes after watching films as children but not during the film, with women reporting more negative reactions during the watching of the films when they were girls. The earlier their exposure to horror films as children, the greater was the sleeping disturbance they experienced afterward. The behavioral measures indicated the typical sex differences reported earlier: More girls than men hid their eyes (64 percent vs. 26 percent), held someone (35 percent vs. 6 percent), and were jumpy (65 percent vs. 45 percent).

In terms of the enjoyment of specific content, one study asked participants to rate a ten-minute horror film in which the sex of the victim and sexual content were manipulated (Oliver 1994). The context of this study concerned the types of victim and protagonist in slasher films. An earlier content analysis of ten slasher films found that a third of sex scenes concluded with the death of a character (Weaver 1991). Women, however, are not more likely to be killed. In an analysis of fifty-six slasher films, Cowan and O'Brien (1990) found that men and women were equally likely to be killed off. Women were more likely to be survivors, a cliche that has its own term in horror film: the Final Girl. More screen time is devoted to the deaths of women than men, however, and nonsurviving women are more likely to be promiscuous, wear revealing clothes, appear nude, use sexual language, and undress and engage in sex when they are killed. Nonsurviving men appear to be identified only by their use of sexual language. Oliver (1994) found that sexual portrayals of victims were associated with increased viewer enjoyment, especially in men. These films were also regarded as more frightening.

As discussed earlier, one possible explanation for women's reaction to horror may be their disgust sensitivity. Women in general report greater disgust sensitivity than do men. Disgust is a protective response to a direct threat to survival, such as contamination, lesions, sores, or disease (Krusemark and Li 2011). People high in disgust sensitivity show higher levels of disgust toward low, moderate, and severe facial disfigurement (Shanmugarajah et al. 2012). Individuals with anxiety disorders are more prone to be disgusted, especially those who are anxious about contagion (Olatunji, Armstrong, and Elwood 2017; Olatunji, Berg, and Zhao 2017). People who are exposed to disease primes are more likely to judge themselves to be less extraverted and open to experience (Mortensen et al. 2010) than people who distance themselves from contagion or symptoms of contagion (Neuberg, Kenrick, and Schaller 2011). Women's disgust thresholds for imagining incest; reacting to images of insects; seeing open sores, feces, or dirty clothing; and statements about death and sex are significantly lower than those for men, and women are less likely to work in environments in which pathogen exposure is likely (al-Shawaf, Lewis, and Buss 2018). Women's sexual disgust and pathogen disgust are higher than that for men, but their moral disgust appears to be no different. This elevated sense of disgust sensitivity in women may partly explain why they enjoy horror film less than do men.

The literature on sex differences in response to, and preference for, horror film provides the most consistent finding in the field that men and boys prefer and enjoy horror film more than do girls and women. One possible explanation for this, besides differences in empathy, may lie in differences in higher-order traits such as anxiety proneness and disgust sensitivity. This possibility, and the evidence for it, is discussed in a later section.

Horror Films and Mental Health

While a typical person's response to horror film is fear and anxiety, some studies have suggested that exposure to horror films can lead to abnormal stress or distress reactions requiring psychological or psychiatric intervention, a condition called cinematic neurosis (Ballon and Leszcz 2007). The rarity of these case studies and the details they present—Ballon and Leszcz found only seven such case studies—suggests that the individuals' behavior arises because of causes unrelated to the horror film and that the horror film was a catalyst for provoking an underlying and pre-existing pathology that would have been provoked by any other relevant stimuli. The pattern of behavior has echoes in Freud's ([1919] 1971) account of seventeenth century "demonological neurosis," whereby depression or psychosis arose from experiencing the death of a father and individuals made a pact with the devil to relieve their distress.

According to Johnson (1980), at least a quarter of horror film viewers had experienced "stress-type" reactions, although this is likely to be within the confines of the normal stress reaction that horror is specifically designed to evoke. Many of the studies reported are case studies, lacking in control participants and largely anecdotal. In a typical example, Horowitz and Wilner (1976) observed that after the release of *The Exorcist* in 1973, individuals lost "control over thought and emotions," experiencing "denial and numbing . . . extremes of anxiety, tension and impaired relationships." *The Exorcist* is the source of a number of abnormal behaviors reported by individuals responding extremely to horror film.

Bozzuto (1975) described four adults who developed abnormal stress behavior within a day of watching the film; participants reported insomnia, excitability, hyperactivity, irritability, and decreased appetite. The symptoms dissipated after seven sessions of psychotherapy. Mathai (1983) reported the case of a distressed twelve-year-old boy who felt that when somebody touched him, they would go right through him and that when sitting on a chair, he would fall through it. Prior to presentation, he had watched *Invasion of the Body Snatchers* (1978) with two of his siblings. Waking from his sleep, he saw "an awful face with bulging veins staring at him." Hamilton (1978) reported the case of a young woman who had seen *The Exorcist* and presented with "acute unremitting anxiety and a pervasive fear of being alone especially at night" and refused to go to work. She felt that the "Devil was in a young girl" and "she dreamt of the Devil with a penis in his mouth" (569).

Five of the cases identified by Ballon and Leszcz (2007) cited *The Exorcist* as the cause of their distress. The other two were *Jaws* and *Invasion of the Body Snatchers*.

Robinson and Barnett (1975) reported the case of a seventeen-year-old girl who had watched *Jaws* and experienced anxiety and sleep disturbances consequently. She was found the next day jerking her limbs, screaming about sharks. Turley and Derdeyn (1990) reported the case of a thirteen-year-old boy who became "addicted" to horror films, particularly *A Nightmare on Elm Street*. One study found that two ten-year-old boys experienced anxiety for up to eight weeks after watching the TV program *Ghostwatch* (Simons and Silveira 1994). Symptoms included fear of ghosts and of the dark, refusal to go upstairs alone, nightmares, sleeping with the light on, and panic attacks. Ballon and Leszcz (2007) reported the case of a twenty-two-year-old unemployed woman with three children who was at twenty-three weeks' gestation but felt possessed and had flashbacks of watching *The Exorcist*. According to the authors, all of the cases of "cinematic neurosis" they reviewed involved individuals who had experienced a recent loss (or potential loss) of a family member about whom they were ambivalent. Individuals also held strong religious or cultural ideals, and their behavior included recalling imagery from the films they had seen. The films also appeared to have some personal meaning to the individuals.

Sparks (1989a, 1989b) found that around half of the women and a quarter of the men surveyed in his study reported enduring fright after watching horror. Women appeared to be particularly affected (Sparks, Spirek, and Hodgson 1993) with around half of the women subsequently avoiding such films, 68 percent perceiving specific rooms as anxiety provoking (compared with 10 percent of men), and 43 percent reporting nervousness. Harrison and Cantor (1999) found that 90 percent of their sample of 136 young people (average age—20.6 years) had experienced a film that was so frightening that the experience had lasted beyond the viewing of the film. More than 50 percent of the sample reported sleep disturbances and eating problems.

The rarity of such extreme emotional distress requiring psychiatric intervention suggests that horror film, while designed to evoke fear and panic, has no significant long-term consequences that can impair an individual's mental, social, and occupational function and that those individuals who do report this impairment in functioning have other characteristics or have undergone other experiences that may underlie the condition they report. While there is no evidence that exposure to horror films has adverse or sustained effects on mental health in individuals with no preexisting mental health issue, there is evidence that watching horror films can lead to self-reported short-term anxiety and disturbed sleep.

Development of Fear and Horror Liking/Avoidance

Children express fear of horror, just as adults do, and they also express enjoyment of horror and graphic violence, just as some adults do, and some have argued that this interest peaks at adolescence (Twitchell 1989). The form of the stimulus children fear appears to change as they develop, with unfamiliar or threatening versions of concrete objects the source of anxiety in infancy and imaginary and symbolic stimuli the source of fear in the preschool years. Fear stimuli become more concrete and realistic when children are at school age (Hyson 1979). Bauer (1976) found that drawings of imaginary feared objects decreased with age (from kindergarten to age eleven or twelve), whereas depictions of realistic injury increased. Fright reactions occur to violence, injury, or physical danger (Cantor and Wilson 1988).

Early Childhood

An early study of children's preferences for scary movies found that 24 percent of forty-three seven- to eight-year-olds and 13 percent of forty-six eleven- to twelve-year-olds reported having nightmares, and younger girls reported more fears than did younger boys (Palmer, Hockett, and Dean 1983). Younger boys liked scary films more than did younger girls. About 40 percent of the younger children liked scary programs; 65 percent of the older children did. Seven percent of older children and 28 percent of younger children disliked scary films; 68 percent of younger children said they avoided scary TV shows, whereas 11 percent of the older group did. Cantor and Reilly (1982) found that eleven- to twelve-year-olds reported avoiding frightening TV and films more than did fifteen- to sixteen-year-olds, and Cantor et al. (2010) found that the most common content causing fear in 219 eight-and-a-half-year-olds was the supernatural (imaginary/fictional monsters) with someone being hurt the next most common. Having a television in the bedroom was the best predictor of fright severity, and the average age of exposure to stimuli was 6.6 years; 67 percent were able to provide the name of the show. Seventy-one percent could not stop thinking about the experience; 52 percent worried about it; 36 percent reported shaking; 59 percent did not want to sleep alone; and 56 percent had nightmares. When another sample ($N = 164$) was asked why they watched, 40 percent said it was because they wanted to and 40 percent because someone else was watching. A study of 314 seven- to twelve-year-old Dutch children's response to TV-induced fright found that interpersonal violence was the most fear-inducing content and fantasy the least; the films that caused the greatest fear had been intended for adult audiences—*Gremlins* (1984), *It* (2017), *Commissaris Rex*,[2] and *The X-Files* (1998) (Valkenburg, Cantor, and Peeters 2000). Girls experienced more fear than did boys but fear in both sexes declined with age. Girls physically intervened and used social support and escape more than did boys. Cognitive reassurance was the most common coping strategy, and social support was the least common.

Coping

How children cope with horror has been the subject of some research on child development and horror because of the potentially harmful psychological consequences of exposure to frightening stimuli. Cantor and Wilson's (1988) review of the effect of horror stimuli on children's behavior concluded that two methods of coping were generally employed. Noncognitive strategies were those that did not involve the processing of verbal information and that might involve desensitization (the gradual exposure to the fear stimulus); cognitive strategies were those whereby children were encouraged to think about the source of their fear as a means of coping with the stimulus. There is evidence that desensitization is successful (Wilson and Cantor 1987). For example, children (five- to seven- and eight- to nine-year-olds) who had been gradually introduced to a videotape of snakes showed less fear when watching the snake pit scene from *Raiders of the Lost Ark* (1981). A similar effect was found in a study of five- to seven- and eight- to eleven-year-olds in which participants played with a rubber tarantula and later saw a scene from *Kingdom of the Spiders* (1977) (Wilson 1987), and in a group of kindergarteners and five- to six-, seven- to eight-, and six- to nine-year-old children who were exposed to photographs of worms and then saw a frightening film featuring worms. The children who had been previously exposed to the creatures enjoyed the film more than did those not exposed; exposure to live worms reduced the fear evoked by the film in boys (Weiss, Imrich, and Wilson 1993). Cantor, Sparks, and Hoffner (1988) found that three- to five-, six- to seven-, and nine- to ten-year-old children's fear of the Hulk in *The Incredible Hulk* (1977) could be reduced if children saw a TV program that showed the making of the TV series, and how the makeup of Lou Ferrigno (the actor who played the Hulk) was applied. Children of different ages become afraid at different stages of the TV program and the Hulk's transformation (Sparks and Cantor 1986): Three- to five-year-olds became more frightened after the transformation, whereas nine- to eleven-year-olds became more frightened before the transformation. Cantor, Sparks, and Hoffner's (1988) finding is also anecdotally illustrated in the preface to Englund (2009). Here, Wes Craven (the director of *A Nightmare on Elm Street*) describes filming Robert Englund (Freddy Krueger in Elm Street) explaining that he was the actor who played a character so that the video could be sent to a distressed child who found Krueger very frightening.

Younger children (four- and five-year-olds) appear to benefit from adopting more physical strategies such as holding on to a blanket/toy or eating/drinking (Wilson, Hoffner, and Cantor 1987). The reasons for the success of this strategy might be the provision of relief from anxiety and the provision of tactile contact in linguistically developing children or by the occupation of working memory, which reduces the cognitive resources available to think about and process fear stimuli. Proximity to a parent is perceived as being the most successful fear-reduction coping strategy in young children (Wilson, Hoffner, and Cantor 1987). Very young children (under two years) experience less fear through covering their eyes; in three- to five-year-olds, this behavior increases fear (Wilson 1989).

Cognitive strategies, such as talking about films and programs with parents or other adults, have been found to be effective (Cantor and Wilson 1988). By far, the most common type of cognitive strategy employed by parents is reassuring children that the stimulus children are afraid of does not exist (Cantor and Hoffner 1990), although this is likely to be successful in older children but not in younger children (four to five years; Cantor and Wilson 1984). Explaining that the source of fear is not likely to be harmful is also successful in older (eight- to nine-year-old) children (Wilson and Cantor 1987). Wilson and Cantor's study, which involved informing children that most snakes were not poisonous and telling them about the behavior of snakes, found that these instructions increased fear in five- to seven-year-olds. Verbal explanations may be ineffective in younger children who are less likely to discuss horror materials with their parents. Cantor, Wilson, and Hoffner (1986) found that none of their three- to seven-year-old children discussed a film with parents, but 43 percent of eight- to twelve-year-olds and 50 percent of thirteen- to eighteen-year-olds did. However, verbal priming prior to seeing the film can sometimes increase the child's emotional response to what they see (Cantor, Ziemke, and Sparks 1984). If children are informed that a film has a happy ending, they report less fear (Hoffner and Cantor 1990; Hoffner 1997). Introducing probability information about events prior to watching a film such as telling children the likelihood of an event occurring appears to have no effect on five- to nine-year-olds' emotional response (Cantor and Hoffner 1990). If children rehearse verbal information (e.g., "this tarantula cannot hurt people; they are not poisonous"), older and younger children respond less emotionally to a film about tarantulas (Wilson 1987). Children also regard the spiders as less dangerous after being given these instructions.

Two physical means of coping with frightening stimuli studied in children are blunting (avoiding threat or transforming a threat by distraction; looking away, for example) and monitoring (being action oriented and attending to the threat). Sparks and Spirek (1988) found that high blunters and low monitors were less physiologically aroused by horror films than were high monitors and low blunters, suggesting that underlying physiology might predict or predispose individuals to react in a given emotional way to frightening stimuli; Sparks (1989a, 1989b) also found that low monitors were less negative about horror when given information about the film, but this information had no effect on blunters. A study of 228 fourteen- to fifteen- and fifteen- to sixteen-year-olds examined the role of blunting and monitoring on coping with scary films (Hoffner 1995). Hoffner investigated empathetic concern (other-oriented) and personal distress (feelings of anxiety/discomfort in response to suffering) by examining four coping methods—interpersonal comfort, distraction, momentary avoidance, and unreality. Davis and Kraus (1997) had previously reported that high empathetic concern was associated with less loneliness and unsociability; high personal distress was associated with shyness, poor interpersonal functioning, and social anxiety. Empathetic concern was found to encourage altruism, whereas personal distress prompted people to reduce their own emotion expression (Batson 1987).

Hoffner found a series of interesting results. A belief that something was unreal was the most common coping strategy, followed by interpersonal comfort and momentary avoidance; these were used more than was distraction. About 50 percent of the sample considered unreality and momentary avoidance to be effective; 26 percent considered distraction to be effective. The study found that boys preferred scary films more than did girls, a finding consistent with the literature, that girls reported more empathetic concern and personal distress, that personal distress correlated with empathy and with monitoring and blunting, that these correlated negatively with liking for scary films, that blunting predicted use of distraction and unreality, that monitoring was more widely used and was more effective, that monitoring and blunting were associated with increased interpersonal comfort, that girls were more likely to use momentary avoidance and interpersonal comfort and consider them more effective, that people who reported using one strategy were more likely to use all four, that empathy, but not personal distress, was associated with greater use of reality, that interpersonal comfort and personal distress were associated with increased use of distraction, and that higher empathy scores were associated with greater use of unreality. People who liked horror were less likely to use distraction, unreality, and momentary avoidance as coping strategies, which suggests that coping is related to the dislike of horror—it is something that must be done to mitigate the effects of something that is disliked. If people thought the coping strategies worked, they enjoyed the films more.

Hoffner also noted that participants who reported finding scary films and television to be violent were likely to use all four coping mechanisms; those who found the material to be realistic were more likely to report using distraction, unreality, and interpersonal comfort as coping mechanisms. Material featuring blood and gore was more likely to lead to the use of momentary avoidance. Girls reported using momentary avoidance and interpersonal comfort more than did boys and considered these to be more effective strategies than did boys.

Adolescence

As children enter adolescence, their reasons for seeking out horror develop and change—they will watch to be thrilled, to rebel (because parents have prohibited them), or to enjoy gore because they are interested in how people die (Oliver 1993a, 1993b). One study of 220 thirteen- to sixteen-year-old boys and girls examined their motivation for watching slasher movies (Johnston 1995). Reasons for watching included gore watching, thrill watching, an increased feeling of independence, bravery, and problem avoidance. Thrill watching and independence were positively related to positive affect; positive views of slashers were associated with high gore and thrill watching, and gore watching predicted preference for graphic violence. Boys were more likely to watch graphic horror because they were motivated to seek out gore, and they were also more likely to identify with the killer than were girls;

girls were more likely to identify with the victim. A larger survey of 6,522 ten- to fourteen-year-old US adolescents in 2003 found similar sex differences: Watching violent films was associated with being male, older, nonwhite, having less educated parents, and having poor school achievement (Worth et al. 2008); teenage boys in another study who were regarded as aggressive and excitable found violent cartoons to be as funny or thrilling (Aluja-Fabregat and Torrubia-Beltri 1998). Both boys and girls who found violent cartoons funny and thrilling also scored higher on neuroticism, psychoticism, and sensation seeking.

Aging and Horror Enjoyment

The majority of the research on the development of horror preference and response to horror film has recruited children and adolescents as participants. There is very little research on how horror film and horror media in general are perceived as individuals age and approach caducity, a paucity that is also reflected in humor research. There is some, but not much, research on how older people respond to horror, and this suggests that the preference for horror declines with age (Tamborini and Stiff 1987; Hoffner and Levine 2005). Clasen, Christiansen, and Johnson (2020), for example, found a negative correlation between age and enjoyment of horror media and horror use, suggesting that both decline as we age. As Clasen et al. concede, however, their sample was clustered around the age of thirty-five years. The average age of those who agreed that they strongly liked horror media was slightly lower than those who disagreed (33.5 vs. 36.5 years). They also note that since sensation seeking also declines with age, this might explain the reduction in enjoyment and seeking out of horror with increasing age postadolescence.

The literature from developmental research mirrors the findings from that in the adult sex differences research in that boys prefer, and seek out, horrifying/scary material more than do girls. Children tend to express greater fear to different types of stimuli and content depending on the age of the child. There are also differences between boys and girls (and between age groups) in the types of coping strategies they adopt during and after watching frightening television and film material. Cognitive strategies, in particular, have been found to be effective with talking about film content and explaining that "monsters" do not exist or that the characters can actually cause no harm being the most effective.

What Causes Fear?

One of the principal purposes of horror film is to induce fear. The nature of fear and its etiology has a long history in psychology, and various models have been proposed, which have attempted to explain why we become afraid and to what types of stimulus. One model, for example, has proposed that we have evolved a "fear module," a theoretical construct that comprises a number of domain-specific programs and that is "preferentially activated ... by stimuli that are fear relevant in an evolutionary perspective" (Öhman and Mineka 2001, 483). Fear, it is argued, motivates us to escape and escape very quickly from potential threat and threats to survival (Mineka and Öhman 2002). The module has four features: it is selective, it is automatic (when encountering fear-relevant stimuli, it responds without mediation), it is encapsulated (i.e., it relies on proven strategies to deal with threat), and it is underpinned by specific neural behavior (Öhman and Mineka 2001). It is considered to be an adaptive mechanism for allowing us to avoid physical danger rapidly (Schaller and Neuberg 2012). In the context of horror film, this is, of course, counterintuitive as horror film viewers who enjoy horror may not wish to escape the horror and deliberately and proactively approach and seek it, and those that do not enjoy horror and who may serendipitously watch horror engage in other withdrawal behaviors such as shutting the eyes or holding on to a companion (they may also leave a cinema or turn off a screen). What occurs during horror film viewing is the willing acceptance that the film will induce fear and that a contract is reached between the medium's manufacturer and the viewer that this is what is to be expected. The questions that then arise are whether there are specific stimuli or situations that horror films deploy or recruit that are more likely to induce a fear response and, if so, what these stimuli are and why they have this effect.

Mineka and Öhman's (2001) conceptualization draws on the (controversial) notion that there are some stimuli that we are evolutionarily predisposed to fear—that evolution has rendered us more afraid of some objects and situations—and there are stimuli that we have become socially or cognitively conditioned to fear (e.g., examinations, being in objectively nonthreatening social groups). The latter stimuli pose no immediate and real physical threat to survival (i.e., they are not fatal), but the former may potentially present this threat by endangering or causing death, may generate threat, and, therefore, make us more alert to our environment, and these stimuli and situations were experienced by "pre-technological" humans (Seligman 1971). These stimuli and situations were those that once posed threats to our ancestors and that we, therefore, developed an evolutionary disposition to avoid or to respond to with fear, a form of selective association. Guns, for example, are not fatal unless used, and our exposure to them is limited; guns are not phobic stimuli, and seeing photographs of guns—or seeing guns—does not elicit significant fear, and not the degree of fear that stimuli that we are evolutionarily predisposed to fear evoke. A person pointing a gun at us, however, with the intention to fire or with the threat of the intention to fire is clearly a direct threat but not one that is evolutionarily created.

One of the most common phobias is arachnophobia, and spiders have been a staple of horror films since the 1950s, although only 0.1–0.3 percent of spider species are venomous (Gerdes, Uhl, and Alpers 2009) and conditioned fear to spiders is very difficult to extinguish (Davey 1994). Individuals are faster at detecting images of spiders and snakes among innocuous stimuli than they are innocuous stimuli placed in an array of threatening stimuli (Öhman, Flykt, and Esteves 2001). This predisposition facilitates vigilance (occasionally, overvigilance and we see threat in ambiguous situations) to sources of threat or danger with greater attention paid to some stimuli (Clasen 2014; March, Gaertner, and Olson 2017). It is a self-protection and survival-enabling mechanism motivating us to confront (and, therefore, remove) the potential source of threat or flee (thereby, removing us from the context in which a threat could result in endangerment).

Fear is related to expressions of disgust, and the literature on phobia suggests that the strength of fear for phobic objects is closely related to disgust sensitivity but not trait anxiety (Davey 1994) such that people who express abnormal fear of an object also show high degrees of sensitivity to disgusting stimuli but are not dispositionally, highly anxious. A specific phobia that appears to be qualitatively and quantitatively different from others and is relevant in the context of horror film is the fear of blood or blood-injection-injury phobia (Wani, Ara, and Bhat 2014; Brinkmann et al. 2017). This accounts for 3–4 percent of phobias and is characterized by fear of blood withdrawal, medical intervention, and seeing others' blood (Brinkmann et al. 2017). Vasovagal syncope (fainting due to low blood pressure and heart rate caused by exposure to a stimulus) is seen in 75 percent of phobic individuals—there is a short increase followed by a decrease in heart rate. Individuals experience fear, anxiety, and disgust and avoid or decline medical treatment because of the strength of their phobic reaction (Wani, Ara, and Bhat 2014). This extreme experience may explain why some people feel squeamish at the sight of blood in horror: Blood is unique as a stimulus that evokes a strong fear or disgust reaction.

Neuropsychology and Horror Film

Fear is the most widely studied emotion in science because it can be easily conditioned, studied, and observed in nonhuman organisms. There is a substantial literature that has attempted to explain fear conditioning and learning through reference to its underlying neuropsychology, and much of this work has been conducted on nonhuman species (LeDoux and Hofmann 2018). In humans, much of our understanding of the neurology of fear has derived from neuroimaging research and studies of brain injury. One of the brain regions involved in fear recognition and experience is the amygdala (Martin 2008; March, Gaertner, and Olson 2017), and a considerable literature exists examining the role of this structure in the conditioning and maintenance of fear.

No study has specifically examined the effect of exposure to horror film on brain activation, although hundreds of studies have examined the effect of exposure of fear-related stimuli, including films designed to induce fear, on brain activation measured via MEG, PET, fMRI, and EEG. Many studies have examined the consequence of brain injury on the fear response, and one study is especially relevant to horror film as it examined the effect of bilateral amygdala injury on responses to fear-related stimuli in a film-related context (Feinstein et al. 2011).

In this study, a forty-four-year-old woman with normal IQ and language showed impaired fear conditioning, impaired recognition of fear in faces, and impaired social-related fear. Feinstein et al. (2011) attempted to induce fear by taking her to the pet shop where there were snakes and spiders, walking her through a haunted house, and having her watch horror films. Although she verbally indicated avoidance of the spiders, she physically approached them and asked fifteen times if she could touch one; at the haunted house (a visitor attraction), she volunteered to lead a group of visitors, did not hesitate in walking around, and was not scared by the monsters (she scared the actors). None of the ten horror film clips elicited fear (other film clips designed to elicit other emotions successfully elicited those emotions), and she asked for the name of one so that she could rent it. She recognized that most people would be scared by them. This is the only comprehensive study of the effect of region-relevant brain injury on the perception of horror films and horror-related stimuli in a single-case study, and while single-case studies need to be interpreted cautiously, the study does provide the opening for other studies to confirm the role of these structures in horror appreciation. One possible extension of this study would be to examine whether amygdala reactivity is associated with enjoyment of horror film (those with highly reactive amygdalae may fear or enjoy horror more than those with less reactive amygdalae) or whether the amygdala becomes increasingly active with greater stimulation, and the intensity of the experience correlates with the increase in activity while watching.

Conclusions

The current review sought to determine why people watch horror film and how exposure to horror film affects behavior. Based on the literature from various disciplines, the following conclusions can be reached: (1) Low empathy and fearfulness are associated with more enjoyment and desire to watch horror; (2) specific dimensions of empathy are better predictors of people's responses than are others, but these dimensions are inconsistently predictive; (3) empathetic concern and personal distress are negatively correlated with enjoyment of horror involving torture; (4) there is a positive relationship between sensation seeking and horror enjoyment/preference, but this relationship is not consistent and may depend on the component of sensation seeking; (5) men and boys prefer to watch—and enjoy and seek out—horror more than do women and girls; (6) women and girls report experiencing more fear and anxiety generally than do men and express greater anxiety and fear when watching horror than do boys and men; (7) this sex difference may be attributable to women's typical higher disgust sensitivity and anxiety proneness (which are interrelated); (8) women report more empathetic concern than do men, and this may be another explanatory mechanism; (9) no study to date has systematically explored disgust sensitivity as a mediator in horror enjoyment and preference, but the evidence would suggest that the former will predict the latter; (10) older children are more afraid of concrete objects/stimuli when very young but of symbolic stimuli when younger; (11) individuals tend to prefer horror less as they age, but there is little literature on this topic; (12) children use various coping strategies to overcome horror film–related fear, and the success of these depends on the age of the child; (13) physical coping strategies are more successful in younger children; (14) priming with information about the feared object helps reduce fear and increase enjoyment when children watch a film featuring the feared stimulus; (15) the SR is amplified in the presence of threatening stimuli; and (16) little is understood about the role of neuropsychology in the response to horror film generally, although the understanding of the structures and regions of the brain implicated in fear and fear conditioning is well documented; the amygdala is likely to be involved in the reaction to (and enjoyment of) horror.

Limitations and Future Directions

The conclusions in the previous paragraph are based on a very limited set of data. The studies from which such data have been drawn have varied in sample size, methodology, and materials, and these are three clearly identifiable and major limitations in this field. Hoffner and Levine (2005) have highlighted similar limitations in their meta-analysis. The type and selection of stimuli used in behavioral studies of horror film and researchers' definition of what constitutes a "horror" or "graphic" horror film have led to a literature that renders making generalizations about horror's effects difficult, the preceding summary notwithstanding. Studies have used a variety—although a very restricted variety—of horror films over thirty years of research, and the films share little in common apart from being classed as horror film. *The Silence of the Lambs, Cannibal Holocaust, The Babadook* (2014), *Saw* (2004), *The Blair Witch Project, Psycho, Dracula,* and *The Devil Rides Out* (1968) are all horror films, but each has distinctive mechanisms of evoking fear and disgust based on story, filmmaking, plot, characters, sound, performance, visual effects, credibility, and use of music. No one study can fully take into account our response to horror because not all horror films are the same (Oliver 1993a, 1993b), and this limitation needs to be more clearly recognized and addressed in future work.

Hoffner and Levine (2005) have concluded that the nature of the media content in these studies can explain the failure to find homogeneity in the correlations between enjoyment of horror media and empathic concern in their meta-analysis. As noted earlier, when correlations were found for empathy and horror enjoyment, the most consistent correlations found were in those studies in which victimization formed the dominant aspect of the horror stimuli. When these studies were removed, the correlations for the remaining studies fell to almost zero. These studies measured participants' responses to the enjoyment of horror film as a genre (or response to a drama with a likable victim), rather than their responses to specific horror films or their experience of watching specific horror films. Hoffner and Levine's analysis identifies at least two limitations in the field noted here: the heterogeneity of the material used as stimuli in experiments, and the nature of the question asked in these studies (for example, whether the question is, Do you enjoy this specific film/film clip? or Do you enjoy this genre of film?). The former limitation can be easily resolved via empirical research. Studies, for example, might examine the role of the nature of the character, the narrative drive of a film (point of view), the aesthetics of the film, a film's use of music, the number of acts of violence, and the types of acts of graphic violence and the perpetrator of the violence, the characteristics of the perpetrator, and the victim (their attractiveness, age, and sex, for example), and a film's use of color and the use of specific tropes and techniques (such as found footage and types of horror film). This is not to say that some of these elements have not been studied—this review and others have described studies in which they have—but there has been little research that has examined these elements systematically and methodically, and some elements have not been explored at all.

The issue of self-report—and self-report based on very small samples—is another possible limitation in that authors rely on individuals' subjective reports based on their impressions and perceptions, and these reports are based on responses to standard questionnaires or questionnaires developed by the authors. This is an issue for any research that aims to determine how people think and feel and is currently the most effective way of measuring people's responses. It is possible to study nonverbal measures (such as movement, EEG, brain activation, or GSR), but these are indirect, correlational measures of what an individual might be thinking or feeling. Motor behavior, however, may be a very informative indicator of response to horror, as some of the studies reviewed here suggest.

Given the current accessibility of film and media generally via smartphones, as well as internet-ready TVs and, of course, computers, one topic of research that has been little studied is whether the medium affects the perception and enjoyment of horror films. Filmmakers may bemoan the viewing of material on a smartphone that was designed for a screen that is a thousand times larger, but it would be instructive to examine whether screen size affects people's aesthetic, emotional, and cognitive response to horror. Screen size and its effect on the enjoyment of displayed material have been relatively well studied (see, e.g., Grabe et al. 1999; Lombard et al. 2000; Rigby et al. 2016). In the context of horror, however, it is hypothesizable that increased screen size leads to increased visibility and that this would result in a stronger fright reaction because more of the horror can be seen and seen more clearly. It is also possible that the augmentation of the screen would also augment the sound (an auditory-sound[3] illusion) so that bigger screens might affect our perception of horror because of this visual illusion.

There is also scope for further research on coping with the effects of watching horror film and of mitigating the fright if the experience is considered too intense or too unmanageable. Of course, individuals could choose not to watch or could chose to watch selectively if they are in front of the screen. But there may be more imaginative strategies that might be adopted, such as the introduction of nonvisual, nonverbal, and nonauditory stimuli (e.g., scent). It is possible that the presence of a pleasant scent might alleviate some of the fright generated by horror film if such alleviation is required (either because it distracts or because it creates or elevates positive mood). There is some evidence that this might be possible (Martin 2013), and this is a question that merits pursuit. Wes Craven's film *The Last House on the Left* (1972) utilized a similar, if nonolfactory distraction technique in the tagline for the film, which was "Keep repeating, it's only a film . . . it's only a film . . ."

The majority of the studies reviewed here have included monocultural samples, and the current review was unable to uncover any cross-cultural research on horror enjoyment or preference. An understanding of the cultural influences on film preference (especially horror) and the individual differences that may underpin them warrants investigation given that certain genres of horror appear to be more popular and appear more often, in specific cultures: Different cultures place different emphases on certain types of content, and Japanese horror, with its emphasis on ghosts and the supernatural, is an obvious example (Balmain 2008; McRoy 2008). Others have argued that the European horror film is distinct from other types of horror film and has a specific "aesthetic" (Allmer, Brick, and Huxley 2012). There is a considerable literature on the difference between collectivistic and individualistic cultures with research suggesting that the psychological responses of individuals from each type of cultural background are different (Matsumoto, Yoo, and Fontaine 2008; Alotaibi, Underwood, and Smith 2017; Gendron 2017). In the field of horror film perception, experience, and enjoyment, it could be hypothesized that individuals from collectivistic cultures might respond differently to horror (and victims in horror) than do individuals from individualistic cultures—specifically individuals from collectivistic cultures may express greater fear compared to those from individualistic cultures—and this is an hypothesis that can be easily tested.

With interest and appreciation in horror increasing, the scope for undertaking research into horror film has never been more timely. There is still much to discover and still much to understand. Horror, said Adorno in another context, was beyond the scope of psychology. The research would suggest that the weight of evidence is on the side of one of horror's innovators. Without psychology, Dario Argento once said, the horror film does not exist.

References

Allmer, P., E. Brick, and D. Huxley. 2012. "Section Introduction." In *European Nightmares: Horror Cinema in Europe Since 1945*, edited by P. Allmer, E. Brick, and D. Huxley. Columbia University Press.

Alotaibi, A., G. Underwood, and A. D. Smith. 2017. "Cultural Differences in Attention: Eye Movement Evidence from a Comparative Visual Search Task." *Consciousness and Cognition* 55: 254–65. https://doi.org/10.1016/j.concog.2017.09.002.

al-Shawaf, L., D. M. Lewis, and D. M. Buss. 2018. "Sex Differences in Disgust: Why Are Women More Easily Disgusted Than Men?" *Emotion Review* 10: 149–60. https://doi.org/10.1177/1754073917709940.

Aluja-Fabregat, A. 2000. "Personality and Curiosity About TV and Films Violence in Adolescents." *Personality and Individual Differences* 29: 379–92. https://doi.org/10.1016/S0191-8869(99)00200-7.

Aluja-Fabregat, A., and R. Torrubia-Beltri. 1998. "Viewing of Mass Media Violence, Perception of Violence, Personality and Academic Achievement." *Personality and Individual Differences* 25: 973–89. https://doi.org/10.1016/S0191-8869(98)00122-6.

Angrilli, A., A. Mauri, D. Palomba, H. Flor, N. Birbaumer, G. Sartori, and F. di Paola. 1996. "Startle Reflex and Emotion Modulation Impairment After a Right Amygdala Lesion." *Brain* 119: 1991–2004. https://doi.org/10.1093/brain/119.6.1991.

Arrindell, W. A., M. Eisemann, T. P. Oei, V. E. Caballo, E. Sanavio, C. Sica, N. Bagés, L. Feldman, B. Torres, S. Iwawaki, C. Hatzichristou, J. Castro, G. Canalda, A. Furnham, J. van der Ende, and the Cultural Clinical Psychology Study Group 1. 2004. "Phobic Anxiety in 11 Nations: Part II. Hofstede's Dimensions of National Cultures Predict National-Level Variations." *Personality and Individual Differences* 37: 627–43. https://doi.org/10.1016/j.paid.2003.11.002.

Baird, R. 2000. "The Startle Effect." *Film Quarterly* 53: 12–24. https://doi.org/10.2307/1213732.

Ballon, B., and M. Leszcz. 2007. "Horror Films: Tales to Master Terror or Shapers of Trauma?" *American Journal of Psychotherapy* 61: 211–30. https://doi.org/10.1176/appi.psychotherapy.2007.61.2.211.

Balmain, C. 2008. *Introduction to Japanese Horror Film*. Edinburgh University Press.

Bartsch, A., M. Appel, and D. Storch. 2010. "Predicting Emotions and Meta-Emotions at the Movies: The Role of the Need for Affect in Audiences' Experience of Horror and Drama." *Communication Research* 37: 167–90. https://doi.org/10.1177/0093650209356441.

Batson, C. D. 1987. "Prosocial Motivation: Is It Ever Truly Altruistic?" *Advances in Experimental Social Psychology* 20: 65–122.

Bauer, D. H. 1976. "An Exploratory Study of Developmental Changes in Children's Fears." *Journal of Child Psychology and Psychiatry* 17: 69–74. https://doi.org/10.1111/j.1469-7610.1976.tb00375.x.

Berlyne, D. E. 1967. "Arousal and Reinforcement." In *Nebraska Symposium on Motivation*. University of Nebraska Press.

Berry, M., T. Gray, and E. Donnerstein. 1999. "Cutting Film Violence: Effects on Perceptions, Enjoyment, and Arousal." *Journal of Social Psychology* 139: 567–82. https://doi.org/10.1080/00224549909598417.

Blood, A. J., R. J. Zatorre, P. Bermudez, and A. C. Evans. 1999. "Emotional Responses to Pleasant and Unpleasant Music Correlate with Activity in Paralimbic Brain Regions." *Nature Neuroscience* 2: 382–87. https://doi.org/10.1038/7299.

Bozzuto, J. C. 1975. "Cinematic Neurosis Following 'The Exorcist': Report of Four Cases." *Journal of Nervous and Mental Disease* 161: 43–48.

Bradley, M. M., B. N. Cuthbert, and P. J. Lang. 1999. "Affect and the Startle Reflex." In *Startle Modification: Implications for Neuroscience, Cognitive Science, and Clinical Science*, edited by M. E. Dawson, A. M. Schell, and A. H. Bohmelt, 157–83. Cambridge University Press.

Bradley, M. M., B. Moulder, and P. J. Lang. 2005. "When Good Things Go Bad: The Reflex Physiology of Defense." *Psychological Science* 16: 468–73. https://doi.org/10.1111/j.0956-7976.2005.01558.x.

Bradley, M. M., Z. Z. Zlatar, and P. J. Lang. 2018. "Startle Reflex Modulation During Threat of Shock and 'Threat' of Reward." *Psychophysiology* 55: e12989. https://doi.org/10.1111/psyp.12989.

Brinkmann, L., H. Poller, M. J. Herrmann, W. Miltner, and T. Straube. 2017. "Initial and Sustained Brain Responses to Threat Anticipation in Blood-Injection-Injury Phobia." *NeuroImage: Clinical* 13: 320–29. https://doi.org/10.1016/j.nicl.2016.12.015.

Bublatzky, F., P. M. Guerra, M. C. Pastor, H. T. Schupp, and J. Vila. 2013. "Additive Effects of Threat-of-Shock and Picture Valence on Startle Reflex Modulation." *PLoS ONE* 8: e54003. https://doi.org/10.1371/journal.pone.0054003.

Bullerjahn, C., and M. Güldenring. 1994. "An Empirical Investigation of Effects of Film Music Using Qualitative Content Analysis." *Psychomusicology* 13: 99.

Cairns, D. 2015. "The Horror and the Pity: Phrikē as a Tragic Emotion." *Psychoanalytic Inquiry* 35: 75–94. https://doi.org/10.1080/07351690.2014.957137.

Cantador, I., I. Fernández-Tobías, and A. Bellogín. 2013. "Relating Personality Types with User Preferences in Multiple Entertainment Domains." In *UMAP 2013: Extended Proceedings Late-Breaking Results, Project Papers and Workshop Proceedings of the 21st Conference on User Modelling, Adaptation, and Personalization*, vol. 997. CEUR.

Cantor, J. 2004. "'I'll Never Have a Clown in My House': Why Movie Horror Lives On." *Poetics Today* 25: 283–304. https://doi.org/10.1215/03335372-25-2-283.

Cantor, J., S. Byrne, E. Moyer-Gusé, and K. Riddle. 2010. "Descriptions of Media-Induced Fright Reactions in a Sample of US Elementary School Children." *Journal of Children and Media* 4: 1–17. https://doi.org/10.1080/17482790903407242.

Cantor, J., and C. Hoffner. 1990. "Children's Fear Reactions to a Televised Film as a Function of Perceived Immediacy of Depicted Threat." *Journal of Broadcasting and Electronic Media* 34: 421–42. https://doi.org/10.1080/08838159009386753.

Cantor, J., and S. Reilly. 1982. "Adolescents' Fright Reactions to Television and Films." *Journal of Communication* 32: 87–99. https://doi.org/10.1111/j.1460-2466.1982.tb00480.x.

Cantor, J., and G. G. Sparks. 1984. "Children's Fear Responses to Mass Media: Testing Some Piagetian Predictions." *Journal of Communication* 34: 90–103. https://doi.org/10.1111/j.1460-2466.1984.tb02162.x.

Cantor, J., G. G. Sparks, and C. Hoffner. 1988. "Calming Children's Television Fears: Mr. Rogers vs. the Incredible Hulk." *Journal of Broadcasting and Electronic Media* 32: 271–88. https://doi.org/10.1080/08838158809386702.

Cantor, J., and B. J. Wilson. 1984. "Modifying Fear Responses to Mass Media in Preschool and Elementary School Children." *Journal of Broadcasting* 28: 431–43.

Cantor, J., and B. J. Wilson. 1988. "Helping Children Cope with Frightening Media Presentations." *Current Psychology* 7: 58–75. https://doi.org/10.1007/BF02686664.

Cantor, J., B. J. Wilson, and C. Hoffner. 1986. "Emotional Responses to a Televised Nuclear Holocaust Film." *Communication Research* 13: 257–77.

Cantor, J., D. Ziemke, and G. G. Sparks. 1984. "Effect of Forewarning on Emotional Responses to a Horror Film." *Journal of Broadcasting* 28: 21–31.

Carroll, N. 1987. "The Nature of Horror." *Journal of Aesthetics and Art Criticism* 46: 51–59. https://doi.org/10.2307/431308.

Carroll, N. 2003. *The Philosophy of Horror; or, Paradoxes of the Heart*. Routledge.

Cherry, B. 2009. *Horror*. Routledge.

Chory, R. M., and A. K. Goodboy. 2011. "Is Basic Personality Related to Violent and Non-Violent Video Game Play and Preferences?" *Cyberpsychology, Behavior, and Social Networking* 14: 191–98. https://doi.org/10.1089/cyber.2010.0076.

Clasen, M. 2014. "Evil Monsters in Horror Fiction: An Evolutionary Perspective on Form and Function." In *A History of Evil in Popular Culture: What Hannibal Lecter, Stephen King and Vampires Reveal About America*, vol. 2, edited by S. Packer and J. Pennington, 39–47. ABC-CLIO/Praeger.

Clasen, M., J. K. Christiansen, and J. A. Johnson. 2020. "Horror, Personality, and Threat Simulation." *Evolutionary Behavioral Sciences* 14: 213–230.

Connolly, K. M., B. O. Olatunji, and J. M. Lohr. 2008. "Evidence for Disgust Sensitivity Mediating the Sex Differences Found in Blood-Injection-Injury Phobia and Spider Phobia." *Personality and Individual Differences* 44: 898–908. https://doi.org/10.1016/j.paid.2007.10.020.

Cook, E. W., L. W. Hawk, T. L. Davis, and V. E. Stevenson. 1991. "Affective Individual Differences and Startle Reflex Modulation." *Journal of Abnormal Psychology* 100: 5–15. https://doi.org/10.1037/0021-843X.100.1.5.

Cowan, G., and M. O'Brien. 1990. "Gender and Survival vs. Death in Slasher Films: A Content Analysis." *Sex Roles* 23: 187–96. https://doi.org/10.1007/BF00289865.

Davey, G. C. 1994. "Self-Reported Fears to Common Indigenous Animals in an Adult UK Population: The Role of Disgust Sensitivity." *British Journal of Psychology* 85: 541–54. https://doi.org/10.1111/j.2044-8295.1994.tb02540.x.

Davis, M. H. 1983. "Measuring Individual Differences in Empathy: Evidence for a Multidimensional Approach." *Journal of Personality and Social Psychology* 44: 113–26. https://doi.org/10.1037/0022-3514.44.1.113.

Davis, M. 2006. "Neural Systems Involved in Fear and Anxiety Measured with Fear-Potentiated Startle." *American Psychologist* 61: 741–56. https://doi.org/10.1037/0003-066X.61.8.741.

Davis, M. H., and L. A. Kraus. 1997. "Personality and Empathic Accuracy." In *Empathic Accuracy*, edited by W. J. Ickes, 144–68. Guildford Press.

Davydov, D. M., O. Luminet, and E. Zech. 2013. "An Externally Oriented Style of Thinking as a Moderator of Responses to Affective Films in Women." *International Journal of Psychophysiology* 87: 152–64. https://doi.org/10.1016/j.ijpsycho.2012.12.003.

Edwards, E. D. 1984. "The Relationship Between Sensation-Seeking and Horror Movie Interest and Attendance." PhD diss., University of Tennessee.

Englund, R. 2009. *Hollywood Monster.* Aurum.

Etchison, D. 2011. Foreword to *Nightmare Movies: Horror on Screen Since the 1960s,* edited by K. Newman. Bloomsbury.

Fanti, K. A., M. N. Kyranides, and G. Panayiotou. 2017. "Facial Reactions to Violent and Comedy Films: Association with Callous–Unemotional Traits and Impulsive Aggression." *Cognition and Emotion* 31: 209–24. https://doi.org/10.1080/02699931.2015.1090958.

Feinstein, J. S., R. Adolphs, A. Damasio, and D. Tranel. 2011. "The Human Amygdala and the Induction and Experience of Fear." *Current Biology* 21: 34–38. https://doi.org/10.1016/j.cub.2010.11.042.

Franken, R. E., K. J. Gibson, and G. L. Rowland. 1992. "Sensation Seeking and the Tendency to View the World as Threatening." *Personality and Individual Differences* 13: 31–38. https://doi.org/10.1016/0191-8869(92)90214-A.

Frayling, C. 2013. *Mad, Bad and Dangerous? The Scientist and the Cinema.* Reaktion Books.

Freud, S. (1919) 1971. *The Uncanny.* Translated by James Strachey. Hogarth Press.

Freud, S. (1919) 2003. *The Uncanny.* Penguin.

Gaut, B. 1993. "The Paradox of Horror." In *Arguing About Art: Contemporary Philosophical Debates,* edited by A. Neill and A. Ridley, 317–29. Routledge.

Gendron, M. 2017. "Revisiting Diversity: Cultural Variation Reveals the Constructed Nature of Emotion Perception." *Current Opinion in Psychology* 17: 145–50. https://doi.org/10.1016/j.copsyc.2017.07.014.

Gerdes, A. B., G. Uhl, and G. W. Alpers. 2009. "Spiders Are Special: Fear and Disgust Evoked by Pictures of Arthropods." *Evolution and Human Behavior* 30: 66–73. https://doi.org/10.1016/j.evolhumbehav.2008.08.005.

Gorbman, C. 1987. *Unheard Melodies: Narrative Film Music.* Indiana University Press.

Grabe, M. E., M. Lombard, R. D. Reich, C. C. Bracken, and T. B. Ditton. 1999. "The Role of Screen Size in Viewer Experiences of Media Content." *Visual Communication Quarterly* 6: 4–9. https://doi.org/10.1080/15551399909363403.

Greene, K., and M. Krcmar. 2005. "Predicting Exposure to and Liking of Media Violence: A Uses and Gratifications Approach." *Communication Studies* 56: 71–93. https://doi.org/10.1080/0008957042000332250.

Grillon, C., R. Ameli, M. Foot, and M. Davis. 1993a. "Fear-Potentiated Startle: Relationship to the Level of State/Trait Anxiety in Healthy Subjects." *Biological Psychiatry* 33: 566–74. https://doi.org/10.1016/0006-3223(93)90094-T.

Grillon, C., R. Ameli, K. Merikangas, S. W. Woods, and M. Davis. 1993b. "Measuring the Time Course of Anticipatory Anxiety Using the Fear-Potentiated Startle Reflex." *Psychophysiology* 30: 340–46. https://doi.org/10.1111/j.1469-8986.1993.tb02055.x.

Hagenaars, M. A., K. Roelofs, and J. F. Stins. 2014. "Human Freezing in Response to Affective Films." *Anxiety, Stress, and Coping* 27: 27–37. https://doi.org/10.1080/10615806.2013.809420.

Hall, A. E., and C. C. Bracken. 2011. "I Really Liked That Movie." *Journal of Media Psychology* 23: 90–99. https://doi.org/10.1027/1864-1105/a000036.

Hamilton, J. W. 1978. "Cinematic Neurosis: A Brief Case Report." *Journal of the American Academy of Psychoanalysis* 6: 569–72. https://doi.org/10.1521/jaap.1.1978.6.4.569.

Hanich, J. 2011. *Cinematic Emotion in Horror Films and Thrillers: The Aesthetic Paradox of Pleasurable Fear.* Routledge.

Hantke, S., ed. 2004. *Horror Film: Creating and Marketing Fear.* University Press of Mississippi.

Harris, R. J., S. J. Hoekstra, C. L. Scott, F. W. Sanborn, J. A. Karafa, and J. D. Brandenburg. 2000. "Young Men's and Women's Different Autobiographical Memories of the Experience of Seeing Frightening Movies on a Date." *Media Psychology* 2: 245–68. https://doi.org/10.1207/S1532785XMEP0203_3.

Harrison, K., and J. Cantor. 1999. "Tales from the Screen: Enduring Fright Reactions to Scary Media." *Media Psychology* 1: 97–116. https://doi.org/10.1207/s1532785xmep0102_1.

Hayward, P. 2009. *Terror Tracks.* Equinox.

Hitchcock, J., and M. Davis. 1986. "Lesions of the Amygdala, but Not of the Cerebellum or Red Nucleus, Block Conditioned Fear as Measured with the Potentiated Startle Paradigm." *Behavioral Neuroscience* 100: 11–22. https://doi.org/10.1037/0735-7044.100.1.11.

Hoekstra, S. J., R. J. Harris, and A. L. Helmick. 1999. "Autobiographical Memories About the Experience of Seeing Frightening Movies in Childhood." *Media Psychology* 1: 117–40. https://doi.org/10.1207/s1532785xmep0102_2.

Hoffner, C. 1995. "Adolescents' Coping with Frightening Mass Media." *Communication Research* 22: 325–46.

Hoffner, C. 1997. "Children's Emotional Reactions to a Scary Film: The Role of Prior Outcome Information and Coping Style." *Human Communication Research* 23: 323–41. https://doi.org/10.1111/j.1468-2958.1997.tb00399.x.

Hoffner, C. 2009. "Affective Responses and Exposure to Frightening Films: The Role of Empathy and Different Types of Content." *Communication Research Reports* 26: 285–96. https://doi.org/10.1080/08824090903293700.

Hoffner, C., and J. Cantor. 1990. "Forewarning of a Threat and Prior Knowledge of Outcome: Effects on Children's Emotional Responses to a Film Sequence." *Human Communication Research* 16: 323–54. https://doi.org/10.1111/j.14682958.1990.tb00214.x.

Hoffner, C., and J. Cantor. 1991. "Factors Affecting Children's Enjoyment of a Frightening Film Sequence." *Communication Monographs* 58: 41–62. https://doi.org/10.1080/03637759109376213.

Hoffner, C. A., and K. J. Levine. 2005. "Enjoyment of Mediated Fright and Violence: A Meta-Analysis." *Media Psychology* 7: 207–37. https://doi.org/10.1207/S1532785XMEP0702_5.

Horowitz, M., and N. Wilner. 1976. "Stress Films, Emotion, and Cognitive Response." *Archives of General Psychiatry* 33: 1339–44. https://doi.org/10.1001/archpsyc.1976.01770110067006.

Hoyle, R. H., M. T. Stephenson, P. Palmgreen, E. P. Lorch, and R. L. Donohew. 2002. "Brief Sensation Seeking Scale." *APA PsychTests.* https://doi.org/10.1037/t04251-000.

Hume, D. 1889. *Essays: Moral, Political, and Literary.* Vol. 1. Longmans.

Hyson, M. C. 1979. "Lobster on the Sidewalk: Understanding and Helping Children with Fears." *Young Children* 34: 54–60.

Jansen, D. M., and N. H. Frijda. 1994. "Modulation of the Acoustic Startle Response by Film-Induced Fear and Sexual Arousal." *Psychophysiology* 31: 565–71. https://doi.org/10.1111/j.1469-8986.1994.tb02349.x.

Johnson, B. K., A. Udvardi, A. Eden, and J. E. Rosenbaum. 2019. "Spoilers Go Bump in the Night: Impacts of Minor and Major Reveals on Horror Film Enjoyment." *Journal of Media Psychology* 32: 252. https://doi.org/10.1027/1864-1105/a000252.

Johnson, B. R. 1980. "General Occurrence of Stressful Reactions to Commercial Motion Pictures and Elements in Films Subjectively Identified as Stressors." *Psychological Reports* 47: 775–86.

Johnston, D. D. 1995. "Adolescents' Motivations for Viewing Graphic Horror." *Human Communication Research* 21: 522–52. https://doi.org/10.1111/j.1468-2958.1995.tb00357.x.

Katz, E., J. G. Blumler, and M. Gurevitch. 1973. "Uses and Gratifications Research." *Public Opinion Quarterly* 37: 509–23. https://doi.org/10.1086/268109.

Kawin, B. F. 2012. *Horror and the Horror Film*. Anthem Press.

Kessler, R. C., K. A. McGonagle, S. Zhao, C. B. Nelson, M. Hughes, S. Eshleman, H.-U. Wittchen, and K. S. Kendler. 1994. "Lifetime and 12-Month Prevalence of DSM-III-R Psychiatric Disorders in the United States: Results from the National Comorbidity Survey." *Archives of General Psychiatry* 51: 8–19. https://doi.org/10.1001/archpsyc.1994.03950010008002.

King, C. M., and N. Hourani. 2007. "Don't Tease Me: Effects of Ending Type on Horror Film Enjoyment." *Media Psychology* 9: 473–92. https://doi.org/10.1080/15213260701282915.

King, S. 2010. *Danse Macabre*. Simon and Schuster.

Kjeldgaard-Christiansen, J. 2016. "Evil Origins: A Darwinian Genealogy of the Popcultural Villain." *Evolutionary Behavioral Sciences* 10: 109–22. https://doi.org/10.1037/ebs0000057.

Koukounas, E., and M. P. McCabe. 2001. "Emotional Responses to Filmed Violence and the Eye Blink Startle Response: A Preliminary Investigation." *Journal of Interpersonal Violence* 16: 476–88. https://doi.org/10.1177/088626001016005006.

Kreibig, S. D., F. H. Wilhelm, W. T. Roth, and J. J. Gross. 2011. "Affective Modulation of the Acoustic Startle: Does Sadness Engage the Defensive System?" *Biological Psychology* 87: 161–63. https://doi.org/10.1016/j.biopsycho.2011.02.008.

Krusemark, E. A., and W. Li. 2011. "Do All Threats Work the Same Way? Divergent Effects of Fear and Disgust on Sensory Perception and Attention." *Journal of Neuroscience* 31: 3429–34. https://doi.org/10.1523/JNEUROSCI.4394-10.2011.

LeDoux, J. E., and S. G. Hofmann. 2018. "The Subjective Experience of Emotion: A Fearful View." *Current Opinion in Behavioral Science* 19: 67–72. https://doi.org/10.1016/j.cobeha.2017.09.011.

Lehne, M., and S. Koelsch. 2015. "Toward a General Psychological Model of Tension and Suspense." *Frontiers in Psychology* 6: 79. https://doi.org/10.3389/fpsyg.2015.00079.

Lerner, N. 2010. "Preface: Listening to Fear/Listening with Fear." In *Music in the Horror Film: Listening to Fear*. Routledge.

Lissek, S., and A. S. Powers. 2003. "Sensation Seeking and Startle Modulation by Physically Threatening Images." *Biological Psychology* 63: 179–97. https://doi.org/10.1016/S0301-0511(03)00053-X.

Lombard, M., R. D. Reich, M. E. Grabe, C. C. Bracken, and T. B. Ditton. 2000. "Presence and Television: The Role of Screen Size." *Human Communication Research* 26: 75–98. https://doi.org/10.1111/j.1468-2958.2000.tb00750.x.

Lynch, T., and N. Martins. 2015. "Nothing to Fear? An Analysis of College Students' Fear Experiences with Video Games." *Journal of Broadcasting and Electronic Media* 59: 298–317. https://doi.org/10.1080/08838151.2015.1029128.

Madsen, K. E. 2016. "The Differential Effects of Agency on Fear Induction Using a Horror-Themed Video Game." *Computers in Human Behavior* 56: 142–46. https://doi.org/10.1016/j.chb.2015.11.041.

Maffei, A., V. Vencato, and A. Angrilli. 2015. "Sex Differences in Emotional Evaluation of Film Clips: Interaction with Five High Arousal Emotional Categories." *PLoS ONE* 10: e0145562. https://doi.org/10.1371/journal.pone.0145562.

Maio, G. R., and V. M. Esses. 2001. "The Need for Affect: Individual Differences in the Motivation to Approach or Avoid Emotions." *Journal of Personality* 69: 583–614. https://doi.org/10.1111/1467-6494.694156.

March, D. S., L. Gaertner, and M. A. Olson. 2017. "In Harm's Way: On Preferential Response to Threatening Stimuli." *Personality and Social Psychology Bulletin* 43: 1519–29. https://doi.org/10.1177/0146167217722558.

Marriott, J. 2012. *Horror Films*. Random House.

Martin, G. N. 2008. *Human Neuropsychology*. 2nd ed. Pearson Education.

Martin, G. N. 2013. *The Neuropsychology of Smell and Taste*. Psychology Press.

Mathai, J. 1983. "An Acute Anxiety State in an Adolescent Precipitated by Viewing a Horror Movie." *Journal of Adolescence* 6: 197–200. https://doi.org/10.1016/S0140-1971(83)80027-X.

Matsumoto, D., S. H. Yoo, and J. Fontaine. 2008. "Mapping Expressive Differences Around the World: The Relationship Between Emotional Display Rules and Individualism Versus Collectivism." *Journal of Cross-Cultural Psychology* 39: 55–74. https://doi.org/10.1177/0022022107311854.

McLean, C. P., and E. R. Anderson. 2009. "Brave Men and Timid Women? A Review of the Gender Differences in Fear and Anxiety." *Clinical Psychology Review* 29: 496–505. https://doi.org/10.1016/j.cpr.2009.05.003.

McRoy, J. 2008. *Nightmare Japan: Contemporary Japanese Horror Cinema*. Rodopi.

Mineka, S., and A. Öhman. 2002. "Phobias and Preparedness: The Selective, Automatic, and Encapsulated Nature of Fear." *Biological Psychiatry* 52: 927–37. https://doi.org/10.1016/S0006-3223(02)01669-4.

Mortensen, C. R., D. V. Becker, J. M. Ackerman, S. L. Neuberg, and D. T. Kenrick. 2010. "Infection Breeds Reticence: The Effects of Disease Salience on Self-Perceptions of Personality and Behavioral Avoidance Tendencies." *Psychological Science* 21: 440–47. https://doi.org/10.1177/0956797610361706.

Mundorf, N., J. Weaver, and D. Zillmann. 1989. "Effects of Gender Roles and Self Perceptions on Affective Reactions to Horror Films." *Sex Roles* 20: 655–73. https://doi.org/10.1007/BF00288078.

Neuberg, S. L., D. T. Kenrick, and M. Schaller. 2011. "Human Threat Management Systems: Self-Protection and Disease Avoidance." *Neuroscience and Biobehavioral Reviews* 35: 1042–51. https://doi.org/10.1016/j.neubiorev.2010.08.011.

Neuendorf, K. A., and G. G. Sparks. 1988. "Predicting Emotional Responses to Horror Films from Cue-Specific Affect." *Communication Quarterly* 36: 16–27. https://doi.org/10.1080/01463378809369704.

Newman, K. 2011. *Nightmare Movies: Horror on Screen Since the 1960s.* Bloomsbury.

Öhman, A., A. Flykt, and F. Esteves. 2001. "Emotion Drives Attention: Detecting the Snake in the Grass." *Journal of Experimental Psychology: General* 130: 466–78. https://doi.org/10.1037/0096-3445.130.3.466.

Öhman, A., and S. Mineka. 2001. "Fears, Phobias, and Preparedness: Toward an Evolved Module of Fear and Fear Learning." *Psychological Review* 108: 483–522. https://doi.org/10.1037/0033-295X.108.3.483.

Olatunji, B. O., T. Armstrong, and L. Elwood. 2017. "Is Disgust Proneness Associated with Anxiety and Related Disorders? A Qualitative Review and Meta-Analysis of Group Comparison and Correlational Studies." *Perspectives on Psychological Science* 12: 613–48. https://doi.org/10.1177/1745691616688879.

Olatunji, B. O., H. E. Berg, and Z. Zhao. 2017. "Emotion Regulation of Fear and Disgust: Differential Effects of Reappraisal and Suppression." *Cognition and Emotion* 31: 403–10. https://doi.org/10.1080/02699931.2015.1110117.

Oliver, M. B. 1993a. "Adolescents' Enjoyment of Graphic Horror: Effects of Viewers' Attitudes and Portrayals of Victim." *Communication Research* 20: 30–50.

Oliver, M. B. 1993b. "Exploring the Paradox of the Enjoyment of Sad Films." *Human Communication Research* 19: 315–42.

Oliver, M. B. 1994. "Contributions of Sexual Portrayals to Viewers' Responses to Graphic Horror." *Journal of Broadcasting and Electronic Media* 38: 1–17. https://doi.org/10.1080/08838159409364242.

Oliver, M. B., J. B. Weaver III, and S. L. Sargent. 2000. "An Examination of Factors Related to Sex Differences in Enjoyment of Sad Films." *Journal of Broadcasting and Electronic Media* 44: 282–300. https://doi.org/10.1207/s15506878jobem4402_8.

Palmer, E. L., A. B. Hockett, and W. W. Dean. 1983. "The Television Family and Children's Fright Reactions." *Journal of Family Issues* 4: 279–92.

Palmgreen, P. 1984. "Uses and Gratifications: A Theoretical Perspective." *Annals of the International Communication Association* 8: 20–55.

Punter, D. 2014. "The Literature of Terror." In *The Gothic Tradition*, vol. 1, 121–40. Routledge.

Reynaud, E., M. El Khoury-Malhame, J. Rossier, O. Blin, and S. Khalfa. 2012. "Neuroticism Modifies Psychophysiological Responses to Fearful Films." *PLoS ONE* 7: e32413. https://doi.org/10.1371/journal.pone.0032413.

Rigby, J. M., D. P. Brumby, A. L. Cox, and S. J. Gould. 2016. "Watching Movies on Netflix: Investigating the Effect of Screen Size on Viewer Immersion." In *Proceedings of the 18th International Conference on Human-Computer Interaction with Mobile Devices and Services Adjunct,* 714–21. ACM.

Robinson, J. A., and A. Barnett. 1975. "Jaws Neurosis." *New England Journal of Medicine* 293: 1154–55. https://doi.org/10.1056/NEJM197511272932224.

Roy, M., J. P. Mailhot, N. Gosselin, S. Paquette, and I. Peretz. 2009. "Modulation of the Startle Reflex by Pleasant and Unpleasant Music." *International Journal of Psychophysiology* 71: 37–42. https://doi.org/10.1016/j.ijpsycho.2008.07.010.

Rubin, A. M. 1994. "Media Uses and Effects: A Uses-and-Gratifications Perspective." In *Media Effects: Advances in Theory and Research,* edited by J. Bryant and D. Zillmann, 417–36. Lawrence Erlbaum.

Schaller, M., and S. L. Neuberg. 2012. "Danger, Disease, and the Nature of Prejudice(s)." *Advances in Experimental Social Psychology* 46: 1–54. https://doi.org/10.1016/B978-0-12-394281-4.00001-5.

Seligman, M. E. 1971. "Phobias and Preparedness." *Behavior Therapy* 2: 307–20. https://doi.org/10.1016/S0005-7894(71)80064-3.

Shanmugarajah, K., S. Gaind, A. Clarke, and P. E. Butler. 2012. "The Role of Disgust Emotions in the Observer Response to Facial Disfigurement." *Body Image* 9: 455–61. https://doi.org/10.1016/j.bodyim.2012.05.003.

Simons, D., and W. R. Silveira. 1994. "Post-Traumatic Stress Disorder in Children After Television Programmes." *British Medical Journal* 308: 389–90. https://doi.org/10.1136/bmj.308.6925.389.

Sipos, T. M. 2010. *Horror Film Aesthetics: Creating the Visual Language of Fear.* McFarland.

Sparks, G. G. 1986a. "Developmental Differences in Children's Reports of Fear Induced by the Mass Media." *Child Study Journal* 16: 55–66.

Sparks, G. G. 1986b. "Developing a Scale to Assess Cognitive Responses to Frightening Films." *Journal of Broadcasting and Electronic Media* 30: 65–73. https://doi.org/10.1080/08838158609386608.

Sparks, G. G. 1989a. "The Prevalence and Intensity of Fright Reactions to Mass Media: Implications of the Activation-Arousal View." *Communication Quarterly* 37: 108–17. https://doi.org/10.1080/01463378909385532.

Sparks, G. G. 1989b. "Understanding Emotional Reactions to a Suspenseful Movie: The Interaction Between Forewarning and Preferred Coping Style." *Communication Monographs* 56: 325–40. https://doi.org/10.1080/03637758909390268.

Sparks, G. G. 1991. "The Relationship Between Distress and Delight in Males' and Females' Reactions to Frightening Films." *Human Communication Research* 17: 625–37. https://doi.org/10.1111/j.1468-2958.1991.tb00247.x.

Sparks, G. G., and J. Cantor. 1986. "Developmental Differences in Fright Responses to a Television Program Depicting a Character Transformation." *Journal of Broadcasting and Electronic Media* 30: 309–23. https://doi.org/10.1080/08838158609386626.

Sparks, G. G., M. Pellechia, and C. Irvine. 1999. "The Repressive Coping Style and Fright Reactions to Mass Media." *Communication Research* 26: 176–92.

Sparks, G. G., J. Sherry, and G. Lubsen. 2005. "The Appeal of Media Violence in a Full-Length Motion Picture: An Experimental Investigation." *Communication Reports* 18: 21–30. https://doi.org/10.1080/08934210500084198.

Sparks, G. G., and M. M. Spirek. 1988. "Individual Differences in Coping with Stressful Mass Media: An Activation-Arousal View." *Human Communication Research* 15: 195–216. https://doi.org/10.1111/j.1468-2958.1988.tb00181.x.

Sparks, G. G., M. M. Spirek, and K. Hodgson. 1993. "Individual Differences in Arousability: Implications for Understanding Immediate and Lingering Emotional Reactions to Frightening Mass Media." *Communication Quarterly* 41: 465–76. https://doi.org/10.1080/01463379309369906.

Stanley, J., and R. G. Knight. 2004. "Emotional Specificity of Startle Potentiation During the Early Stages of Picture Viewing." *Psychophysiology* 41: 935–40. https://doi.org/10.1111/j.1469-8986.2004.00242.x.

Stone, B. 2016. "The Sanctification of Fear: Images of the Religious in Horror Films." *Journal of Religion and Film* 5: 7.

Tamborini, R. 1991. "Responding to Horror: Determinants of Exposure and Appeal." In *Responding to the Screen: Reception and Reaction Processes*, edited by J. Bryant and D. Zillmann, 305–28. Lawrence Erlbaum.

Tamborini, R., K. Salomonson, and C. Bahk. 1993. "The Relationship of Empathy to Comforting Behavior Following Film Exposure." *Communication Research* 20: 723–38.

Tamborini, R., and J. Stiff. 1987. "Predictors of Horror Film Attendance and Appeal: An Analysis of the Audience for Frightening Films." *Communication Research* 14: 415–36.

Tamborini, R., J. Stiff, and C. Heidel. 1990. "Reacting to Graphic Horror: A Model of Empathy and Emotional Behavior." *Communication Research* 17: 616–40.

Tamborini, R., J. Stiff, and D. Zillmann. 1987. "Preference for Graphic Horror Featuring Male Versus Female Victimization: Personality and Past Film Viewing Experiences." *Human Communication Research* 13: 529–52. https://doi.org/10.1111/j.1468-2958.1987.tb00117.x.

Tannenbaum, P. H., and E. P. Gaer. 1965. "Mood Change as a Function of Stress of Protagonist and Degree of Identification in a Film-Viewing Situation." *Journal of Personality and Social Psychology* 2: 612–16. https://doi.org/10.1037/h0022497.

Tucker, M., and N. W. Bond. 1997. "The Roles of Gender, Sex Role, and Disgust in Fear of Animals." *Personality and Individual Differences* 22: 135–38. https://doi.org/10.1016/S0191-8869(96)00168-7.

Tudor, A. 1989. "Monsters and Mad Scientists." *Genre* 1: 1931–60.

Tudor, A. 1997. "Why Horror? The Peculiar Pleasures of a Popular Genre." *Cultural Studies* 11: 443–63. https://doi.org/10.1080/095023897335691.

Turley, J. M., and A. P. Derdeyn. 1990. "Case Study: Use of a Horror Film in Psychotherapy." *Journal of the American Academy of Child and Adolescent Psychiatry* 29: 942–45. https://doi.org/10.1097/00004583-199011000-00018.

Twitchell, J. B. 1989. *Preposterous Violence: Fables of Aggression in Modern Culture*. Oxford University Press.

Valkenburg, P. M., J. Cantor, and A. L. Peeters. 2000. "Fright Reactions to Television: A Child Survey." *Communication Research* 27: 82–99. https://doi.org/10.1177/009365000027001004.

Vlahou, C. H., E. J. Vanman, and M. M. Morris. 2011. "Emotional Reactions While Watching Graphic Medical Procedures: Vocational Differences in the Explicit Regulation of Emotions 1." *Journal of Applied Social Psychology* 41: 2768–84. https://doi.org/10.1111/j.1559-1816.2011.00839.x.

Vrana, S. R., and P. J. Lang. 1990. "Fear Imagery and the Startle-Probe Reflex." *Journal of Abnormal Psychology* 99: 189–97. https://doi.org/10.1037/0021-843X.99.2.189.

Vrana, S. R., E. L. Spence, and P. J. Lang. 1988. "The Startle Probe Response: A New Measure of Emotion?" *Journal of Abnormal Psychology* 97: 487–91. https://doi.org/10.1037/0021-843X.97.4.487.

Wani, A. L., A. Ara, and S. A. Bhat. 2014. "Blood Injury and Injection Phobia: The Neglected One." *Behavioral Neurology* 2014: 471340. https://doi.org/10.1155/2014/471340.

Weaver, A. J. 2011. "A Meta-Analytical Review of Selective Exposure to and the Enjoyment of Media Violence." *Journal of Broadcasting and Electronic Media* 55: 232–50. https://doi.org/10.1080/08838151.2011.570826.

Weaver, A. J., and B. J. Wilson. 2009. "The Role of Graphic and Sanitised Violence in the Enjoyment of Television Dramas." *Human Communication Research* 35: 442–63. https://doi.org/10.1111/j.1468-2958.2009.01358.x.

Weaver, J. B., III. 1991. "Are 'Slasher' Horror Films Sexually Violent? A Content Analysis." *Journal of Broadcasting and Electronic Media* 35: 385–92. https://doi.org/10.1080/08838159109364133.

Weinberger, D. A. 1990. "The Construct Validity of the Repressive Coping Style." In *Repression and Dissociation: Implications for Personality Theory, Psychopathology, and Health*, 337–86. University of Chicago Press.

Weiss, A. J., D. J. Imrich, and B. J. Wilson. 1993. "Prior Exposure to Creatures from a Horror Film: Live Versus Photographic Representations." *Human Communication Research* 20: 41–66. https://doi.org/10.1111/j.1468-2958.1993.tb00315.x.

Wilson, B. J. 1987. "Reducing Children's Emotional Reactions to Mass Media Through Rehearsed Explanation and Exposure to a Replica of a Fear Object." *Human Communication Research* 14: 3–26. https://doi.org/10.1111/j.1468-2958.1987.tb00119.x.

Wilson, B. J. 1989. "The Effects of Two Control Strategies on Children's Emotional Reactions to a Frightening Movie Scene." *Journal of Broadcasting and Electronic Media* 33: 397–418.

Wilson, B. J., and J. Cantor. 1987. "Reducing Fear Reactions to Mass Media: Effects of Visual Exposure and Verbal Explanation." *Annals of the International Communication Association* 10: 553–73.

Wilson, B. J., C. Hoffner, and J. Cantor. 1987. "Children's Perceptions of the Effectiveness of Techniques to Reduce Fear from Mass Media." *Journal of Applied Developmental Psychology* 8: 39–52. https://doi.org/10.1016/0193-3973(87)90019-0.

Worth, K. A., J. G. Chambers, D. H. Nassau, B. K. Rakhra, and J. D. Sargent. 2008. "Exposure of US Adolescents to Extremely Violent Movies." *Pediatrics* 122: 306–12. https://doi.org/10.1542/peds.2007-1096.

Wühr, P., B. P. Lange, and S. Schwarz. 2017. "Tears or Fears? Comparing Gender Stereotypes About Movie Preferences to Actual Preferences." *Frontiers in Psychology* 8: 428. https://doi.org/10.3389/fpsyg.2017.00428.

Yartz, A. R., and L. W. Hawk Jr. 2002. "Addressing the Specificity of Affective Startle Modulation: Fear Versus Disgust." *Biological Psychology* 59: 55–68. https://doi.org/10.1016/S0301-0511(01)00121-1.

Zaslow, M. J., and C. D. Hayes. 1986. "Sex Differences in Children's Response to Psychosocial Stress: Toward a Cross-Context Analysis." *Advances in Developmental Psychology* 4: 285–337.

Zhang, Y., Q. Chen, F. Du, Y. Hu, F. Chao, M. Tian, and H. Zhang. 2012. "Frightening Music Triggers Rapid Changes in Brain Monoamine Receptors: A Pilot PET Study." *Journal of Nuclear Medicine* 53: 1573–78. https://doi.org/10.2967/jnumed.112.106690.

Zillmann, D. 1980. "Anatomy of Suspense." In *The Entertainment Functions of Television*, edited by P. H. Tannenbaum, 133–63. Psychology Press.

Zillmann, D. 1996. "The Psychology of Suspense in Dramatic Exposition." In *Suspense: Conceptualizations, Theoretical Analyses, and Empirical Explorations,* edited by P. Vorderer, H. J. Wulff, and M. Friedrichsen. Routledge.

Zillmann, D., and J. R. Cantor. 1977. "Affective Responses to the Emotions of a Protagonist." *Journal of Experimental and Social Psychology* 13: 155–65. https://doi.org/10.1016/S0022-1031(77)80008-5.

Zillmann, D., T. A. Hay, and J. Bryant. 1975. "The Effect of Suspense and Its Resolution on the Appreciation of Dramatic Presentations." *Journal of Research in Personality* 9: 307–23. https://doi.org/10.1016/0092-6566(75)90005-7.

Zillmann, D., J. B. Weaver, N. Mundorf, and C. F. Aust. 1986. "Effects of an Opposite-Gender Companion's Affect to Horror on Distress, Delight, and Attraction." *Journal of Personality and Social Psychology* 51: 586–94. https://doi.org/10.1037/0022-3514.51.3.586.

Zuckerman, M. 1979. "Attribution of Success and Failure Revisited; or, The Motivational Bias Is Alive and Well in Attribution Theory." *Journal of Personality* 47: 245–87. https://doi.org/10.1111/j.1467-6494.1979.tb00202.x.

Zuckerman, M. 1988. "Sensation Seeking and Behavior Disorders." *Archives of General Psychiatry* 45: 502–3. https://doi.org/10.1001/archpsyc.1988.01800290124017.

Zuckerman, M. 1994. *Behavioral Expressions and Biosocial Bases of Sensation Seeking.* Cambridge University Press.

Zuckerman, M., and P. Litle. 1986. "Personality and Curiosity About Morbid and Sexual Events." *Personality and Individual Differences* 7: 49–56. https://doi.org/10.1016/0191-8869(86)90107-8.

Notes

The author would like to thank Dr. Charlie Allbright, Phil Hughes, and four reviewers, especially reviewer 2, for their detailed and thoughtful comments on earlier drafts of this chapter and Edward Lionheart for planting the seed for this review.

1. The source referenced here is uncertain. (Editor's note)
2. Likely *Commissaris Roos,* a Belgian police procedural that aired from 1990 to 1992. (Editor's note)
3. Likely "audio-visual" rather than "audio-sound." (Editor's note)

Chapter 23

HORROR'S LONG-LASTING APPEAL

Nina Nesseth

> In her book *Nightmare Fuel,* Canadian researcher Nina Nesseth examines what she refers to as pleasurable fear, considering biological, psychological, and sociological explanations for enjoying horror. Like Mathias Clasen, she explores in the excerpt here genetic and physiological components that make consuming horror pleasurable.

NO AMOUNT OF UNDERSTANDING how horror engages our fear mechanisms manages to explain why we love it in the first place. Most theories of emotions suggest that humans are most motivated to seek out experiences that will increase pleasurable moods and emotions, and actively avoid anything that might be a downer. Obviously, horror, at least at a surface level, does not promise to make you happy or satisfied. If anything, horror qualifies as a downer genre. Even when the hero prevails, the narrative journey usually exposes us to an entire buffet of unpleasant experiences and images. This phenomenon—that people are drawn to horror despite its association with negative emotions like fear, anxiety, and disgust—is often referred to as the horror paradox.

The idea of recreational fear sounds counterintuitive. The concept extends beyond the world of horror cinema—there must be a good reason why we also love horror novels, video games, and haunted attractions.

Some researchers have gone so far as to describe paradoxical pleasures—like loving to feel scared—as a form of "benign masochism." This same line of thinking has been applied to explain why humans enjoy eating extremely hot peppers when we know that the compounds that make them so spicy activate our pain-sensation neural pathways. If the idea of benign masochism is a little muddy, Canadian cognitive psychologist Steven Pinker puts it in these terms:

> These paradoxical pleasures include consuming hot chili peppers, strong cheese, and dry wine, and partaking in extreme experiences like saunas, skydiving, car racing,

and rock climbing. All of them are adult tastes, in which a neophyte must overcome a first reaction of pain, disgust, or fear on the way to becoming a connoisseur. And all are acquired by controlling one's exposure to the stressor in gradually increasing doses. What they have in common is a coupling of high potential gains (nutrition, medicinal benefits, speed, knowledge of new environments) with high potential dangers (poisoning, exposure, accidents). The pleasure in acquiring one of these tastes is the pleasure of pushing the outside of the envelope: of probing, in calibrated steps, how high, hot, strong, fast, or far one can go without bringing on disaster. The ultimate advantage is to open up beneficial regions in the space of local experiences that are closed off by default by innate fears and cautions.

When it comes to horror, very few of us entered into our love for the genre by plunging headfirst into a brutal entry like *Them* (David Moreau and Xavier Palud, 2006) or maybe *Antichrist* (Lars von Trier, 2009); some of us never even make forays into these corners of the genre as a matter of personal preference. Most of us find our gateways into horror either by first watching horror-adjacent genres, like action movies or crime thrillers, by being introduced to older titles by parents, older siblings, or friends, or by starting with more family-friendly frights like *Beetlejuice* (Tim Burton, 1988), *Hocus Pocus* (Kenny Ortega, 1993), or *Coraline* (Henry Selick, 2009).

Neither of my parents is a fan of true horror movies (I'm the only horror fan in my immediate family, actually), and my main gateway into horror was crime procedurals like *CSI: Crime Scene Investigation* and psychological thrillers like *Kiss the Girls* (Gary Fleder, 1997), *Single White Female* (Barbet Schroeder, 1992), and *The Game* (David Fincher, 1997) until I was old enough to control my own viewing habits. I remember my younger sister coming home from a sleepover once when she was in middle school and reporting that she'd watched *The People Under the Stairs* (Wes Craven, 1991). She was braver than I was in middle school—I hid in another room at a birthday party while everyone else was watching *Children of the Corn* (Fritz Kiersch, 1984). Whatever your entry point into horror might have been, early film experiences help you to build up a tool kit of genre expectations, impressions, and tolerances that you carry with you every time you journey back into the genre.

Horror Is for Everyone

Before we dig into possible biological, psychological, and even sociological reasons to love horror, let's banish one idea up front: Loving horror is not a trait restricted to any individual gender. It might sound obvious to some of us, but it's a sticking point that still comes up in research circles.

Enjoying horror is not a niche phenomenon. Horror making its way into the mainstream over time has made it harder and harder to justify its supposed place as an underground genre.

One of the biggest limitations of research into responses toward horror films is that, while a variety of films are shown to study participants, the range of horror subgenres that these studies cover is relatively small. In reading over countless studies, some movie titles—like *The Texas Chainsaw Massacre* (Tobe Hooper, 1974), *Cannibal Holocaust* (Ruggero Deodato, 1980), and *Friday the 13th, Part III* (Steve Miner, 1982)—appear again and again. I can appreciate that these movies were selected either because they are classic entries (depending on when the study was conducted), because they demonstrate graphic violence, or both, but it strikes me as odd that so many studies loudly declare that women enjoy horror films less than men because they rated a five-minute clip from *Cannibal Holocaust* less favorably than their male peers. Not to mention that this area of study never even takes into account the horror preferences of trans men and women, nor of nonbinary, gender-fluid, or agender moviegoers.

The other big issue with this area of research—a limitation that is not limited to this specific area—is that it relies heavily on self-reported data to measure enjoyment. There are a few issues that tend to come up with self-reported data, but one of special interest is socially desirable response bias. This usually happens because we humans typically want to leave a good impression, even when filling in an anonymous survey, so we'll often consciously or subconsciously answer surveys with what we think is the desirable response rather than an honest reply. So, for example, if a man believes that it's socially desirable for men to enjoy horror movies, then he might be more likely to circle higher values on a scale measuring horror movie enjoyment than he really feels applies to him personally. I'm not saying that this means that all self-reported data are useless, far from it—self-reports are among the best ways we have to access individual insights—but be wary of any studies that rely solely on self-reports.

I've yet to see a horror study that looks at the horror genre globally, in terms of its many and varied subgenres, to see how different audience demographics are drawn to different flavors of horror narratives. It would be a huge undertaking, but I think it would be rewarding in terms of quashing the misconception that horror is meant exclusively for men, especially cisgender, white, able-bodied men.

Some researchers have attempted to understand what types of personalities might lead people to horror media, though. Matthias Clasen created a research survey to try to build profiles of different kinds of horror consumers. For example, what he called the "Enthusiastic Horror User" included participants who demonstrated high enjoyment of horror media, frequent use of horror media, and preference for intense horror. To a lesser degree, this profile was also associated with a tendency to report not being easily scared by horror movies. In terms of personality and motivations, Clasen's team identified four distinct profiles:

- The Enthusiastic Horror Users were the ones who tended to report that they turn to horror with the expectation that they will experience emotions of joy,

anticipation, and surprise, and as people, they tend toward being imaginative and sensation seeking (and maybe believe in paranormal phenomena).
- The Social Horror Users reported that they strongly prefer to consume horror with other people, tend to enjoy horror more when watching it with other people, and, fascinatingly, also tend to be more scared when consuming horror with other people. The Social Horror User scores high on extraversion and agreeableness scales, and reports a similar affinity for belief in the paranormal in comparison to the Enthusiastic Horror User.
- The Supernatural Horror User strongly prefers horror media with a supernatural bent over natural horror, and also finds supernatural horror much scarier. This profile is *not* using horror to confront feelings of disgust or anger and tends toward a belief in the supernatural.
- Last, the Fearful Horror User was defined as being easily scared by horror media and remaining scared after consuming horror media. Fearful Horror Users also found horror scarier if they watched it alone instead of with others. Unlike the other user profiles, Fearful Horror Users are not watching horror to experience joy. They are using the genre specifically to experience fear. Fearful Horror Users also tended to score high on scales of agreeableness and low on scales of emotional stability (which just means that they are more sensitive to experiencing negative emotions or being emotionally reactive).

According to Clasen, women who love horror tended to fall more often into the Social Horror User and Fearful Horror User categories. This tracks with past studies, which, when contrasting measures of horror enjoyment between men and women, tend to demonstrate that women report more feelings of fear than men. What is special about Clasen's profiles is that they classify this fear experience as a motivator for consuming horror, whereas past studies equated fear with dislike or avoidance. Although there have been pretty consistent findings in research that cisgender men report a higher tendency to enjoy horror and seek it out, the gap is not as big as you might think. And although cisgender men and women tend to be the only genders recorded in these sorts of studies, I feel confident in stating that all genders have strong representation in the horror family.

So, now that we have that out of the way, let's explore some actual possibilities at the root of our shared love for horror.

Could a Love for Horror Live in Your Genes?

More than attraction to other movie genres like dramas or comedies, a love for horror film feels like something innate, a personality trait. If personality traits are generally accepted to be a cocktail mix of nature (inherited genetic effects) and nurture (environmental and epigenetic effects), is it possible that part of why we love to be scared is written in our DNA?

While we should always be wary of studies that claim that a complex human trait can be boiled down to whether a single gene is switched on or off in any given person's DNA blueprint, researchers have proposed a few gene candidates whose expression may contribute to how we experience horror.

The first of these suggested gene locations is FKBP5. This gene has been associated with abnormal stress responses and possible contributions to depression and anxiety. It has been of particular interest to researchers studying posttraumatic stress disorder (PTSD) who have found that PTSD developed more often than average among people experiencing traumatic events if they possessed certain expressions of the gene.

A promoter region of the SLC6A4 gene, 5-HTTLPR controls levels of serotonin, an important mood-stabilizing hormone, during threatening experiences, and the gene region's function has been associated with our personal sensitivity to stress. Studies have suggested that people who are carriers of a variant allele for 5-HTTLPR, called the S-allele, or short-allele, might experience bigger emotional reactions when exposed to negative imagery, like scared or angry faces. The short 5-HTTLPR promoter group also seems to demonstrate a great vigilance, or bias for paying attention, toward negative or stressful images, whereas people with two L-alleles (the long variant for the promoter region) tend to selectively avoid stressful images and show bias for paying attention to positive images. There may even be a relationship between 5-HTTLPR and our ability to disengage from the emotional content of horror scenes, which might point to one genetic reason why people might enjoy and watch more horror.

And, of course, as we mentioned in chapter 1, variant expressions of the COMT gene might produce hyper-startlers, who are more primed than the average moviegoer to have bigger reactions during jump scares.

But while these genetic components might influence how we process fear and horror movie content, none of them comes close to touching the idea of *enjoying* horror as entertainment. You might be more likely to enjoy horror if your parents enjoy horror just as a result of being exposed to horror throughout your development more often than someone raised in a family where horror is verboten. A love for horror may be contagious, but it doesn't appear to be hereditary.

Sensation Seeking

Since the horror experience is so often associated with the adrenaline rush of the fight-or-flight response, researchers have focused a lot of attention on measuring the correlation between a love for horror and a personality metric known as the Sensation-Seeking Scale.

High sensation-seeking scores are associated with personalities that are more likely to be drawn to experiences that highly engage different modalities, ranging from being very interested in trying unusual foods to being very interested in trying extreme activities (like free climbing or bungee jumping). Contrary to popular belief about so-called adrenaline junkies, extreme athletes have often reported feeling very calm and "in the zone" rather than screaming with a surge of chaotic energy, a feeling that psychologist Mihály Csikszentmihályi described as the "flow state." The flow experience is characterized by being present and focused on the present moment, feeling in control of the moment and whatever you're doing, feeling un-self-conscious, like time is distorted or standing still, and feeling like the act of doing whatever it is that you're doing is rewarding in and of itself. In other words, it feels pretty great.

To some extent, we all crave new experiences and new sensations. Marvin Zuckerman identified four scales of sensation-seeking traits:

- thrill or adventure seeking, or the desire to engage in risky activities (at the extreme end of this scale, think free diving or base jumping), even if no one else has successfully done the activity before
- experience seeking, or a desire for experiences that are arousing on the level of your senses or cognitive processes
- disinhibition, or spontaneous and hedonistic behaviors, like being drawn to sex, partying, drugs, gambling, or social drinking as sources of sensation and pleasure
- susceptibility to boredom

High sensation seekers might be more motivated to watch horror movies, to satisfy morbid curiosity as much as to take in thrilling content and gore, than people who rank low on sensation-seeking scales.

Research has produced inconsistent results where the Sensation-Seeking Scale is concerned, though. Taken overall, the scale doesn't produce a significant relationship between thrill seekers and horror consumption, but we do see small associations on some of the individual scales. For example, a slight tendency was found for people who rank high in experience seeking to be scared more by the natural than the supernatural in horror, and for people who score high on boredom susceptibility to seek out and enjoy opportunities to watch horror with others. When looking specifically at graphic horror, other research has suggested that a preference for graphic horror correlated with high disinhibition scores, moderately for boredom susceptibility and experience seeking, and not at all for thrill or adventure seeking. If you feel pretty certain that you don't watch horror films for the rush, perhaps you watch them for some sort of release.

Catharsis Theory

The idea of consuming media for cathartic effects is probably the oldest concept that we're addressing in this book. The idea was first put forth by Aristotle, whose teachings suggested that consuming tragedies (in Aristotle's time, roughly 384–322 BCE, this would take the form of plays and not movies) gave their audience an emotional release, an opportunity to purge negative feelings like sadness, fear, or anger. We hear echoes of this idea over and over again emerging from the mouths of horror filmmakers. Alfred Hitchcock once said, "One of television's greatest contributions is that it brought murder back into the home where it belongs. Seeing a murder on television can be good therapy. It can help work off one's antagonism." More than one horror philosopher has suggested that horror might be a way of exploring the taboo in a relatively safe and harmless way—but how do you measure that?

I've often made a habit of watching horror movies—especially treating myself to a horror movie in a theater with a friend—when I'm having a particularly bad day. I usually joke that I need it for catharsis, to distract myself from negative feelings by conjuring *different*, more immediate negative feelings up on a big screen. While I usually feel better after doing this, catharsis is not the most likely explanation for my mood improvement. The fact that I feel better probably comes from the shared time with a friend (including a requisite venting session over fast food before the movie) and the distraction of watching a movie, no matter its plot or genre.

In terms of self-reporting, people usually report feeling more scared, rather than less scared, after watching a horror movie. In general, there is no evidence to support that horror media have any real catharsis effect, but if watching horror makes you personally feel better, then there's no harm in watching horror to improve your mood.

In a similar vein, others have proposed that we enjoy horror because it's a relatively safe and controlled way to experience scary or stressful situations, kind of like experiencing a worst-case scenario with training wheels. In chapter 2, we saw an entire history of the genre reflecting real fears as hyperreal horrors. We deal with real fears of a global pandemic by tuning in to movies where the world's population is being demolished by even gnarlier viruses; we wade through our anxieties about climate change by watching movies that show us the world ending catastrophically. Admittedly, there isn't any research that I've found that tests this idea—besides, how would you go about measuring this feeling of safety?—but it circles back to that old refrain: Unlike with real life, if you get scared, you can repeat to yourself, *It's only a movie. It's only a movie. It's only a movie.*

What if this *catharsis theory* could have applications beyond safely experiencing fear? In 2021, researchers Becky Millar and Jonny Lee suggested that horror films might be useful tools for processing grief.[1] In part, they suggest that this is because the way the staple horror movie monster disrupts lives often parallels the way grief can disrupt people's lives. On top of that, a huge number of horror movies are centered around grief, and Millar and Lee note that these movies tend to follow a set structure:

1. The main character loses a loved one during act 1 (or the film opens just after such a loss). The main character's day-to-day life is disrupted by grief.

2. The monster appears to radically disrupt the main character's understanding of reality and mirrors the disruption in the world caused by bereavement.
3. The main character defeats, evades, or tames the monster and, in turn, restores some balance to their emotional life.

According to Millar and Lee, grief-filled horror movies that fit this mold include *Don't Look Now* (Nicolas Roeg, 1973), *The Changeling* (Peter Medak, 1980), *The Descent* (Neil Marshall, 2005), *Lake Mungo* (Joel Anderson, 2008), *The Babadook* (Jennifer Kent, 2014), *Hereditary* (Ari Aster, 2018), and *Midsommar* (Ari Aster, 2019). I'm sure many, many more also match up.

Following this structure, people working through grief can connect with bereavement depicted on-screen, as well as see an end in the eventual defeat of the disruptive monster that allows the main character to restore their life to postgrief, postmonster balance. While it can't be relied upon as a solution, it appears that horror can serve as a useful coping tool for viewers experiencing fear, stress, or sorrow.

Snuggle Up to Horror

As I've mentioned, I definitely have more fun watching horror movies with other people than I do watching them alone. Sitting through scares with a friend means sharing in an emotional experience—and often serves to heighten that experience. The feeling is likewise amplified when you're sitting among strangers in a crowded theater. Being hit at the same time by a jump scare and by another audience member screaming amplifies the startle effect—not to mention that the inevitable laughter that happens in a movie theater crowd works like a charm to diffuse tension. As Wes Craven once said, "If you scream and everyone else in the audience screams, you realize that your fears are not just within yourself, they're in other people as well, and that's strangely releasing." Sharing a horror movie also often means having someone to process the emotional experience with as it happens, whether it's by someone diffusing tension with laughter, or by having someone to express your tensions or apprehensions to.

It's often been said that if you really want to bond on a romantic movie date, then opt for a horror movie rather than a romantic comedy or tearjerker. The idea is founded in what sociologists have termed the *snuggle theory*. Thanks to socialization differences, the theory—put forward by Dolf Zillmann and his team in 1986—suggests that the act of watching a horror movie with an opposite-gender date will reinforce desirable gender roles, such as "fearless macho men." (I swear, these are the exact words that Zillmann's paper uses.) The study was conducted with a framework that excluded anyone who wasn't a cisgender man or woman who reported opposite-gender attraction. (The study notes that one male participant did report homosexual attraction, but since he also reported heterosexual attraction—I guess there wasn't a box to tick for bisexuality—he wasn't dismissed as a subject.)

As a commentary on gender, sexuality, and horror movies, you can take this study with as little or big a grain of salt as you wish.

To test his theory, Zillmann paired up undergraduate students with an opposite-gender movie-watching partner who would either behave indifferently, appear distressed, or demonstrate "mastery" toward a fourteen-minute clip from *Friday the 13th, Part III*. The movie-watching partners were also categorized as being of high initial attractiveness or low initial attractiveness (although the study is unclear as to how the two men and two women who were acting as movie companions were assigned to these *high-appeal* and *low-appeal* roles).

According to the study, men enjoyed horror movies most when they were paired with a woman who was distressed by the movie and least when they were paired with a woman who had mastered the material (unless that woman was also initially perceived as desirable). One of the reasons suggested for why men might have found horror less enjoyable when watching with a woman who demonstrated mastery was the fact that they would perceive the clip as intrinsically less scary if it failed to scare their partner—a comment that I find endlessly funny. Women, on the other hand, apparently enjoyed the movie the least when their male counterpart was distressed and tended to rate their companion as more sexually attractive if they demonstrated the "mastery" condition, and more attractive if they were initially in the low-appeal category. Fearlessness did not make women companions more attractive to male participants.

There are a lot of bold conclusions that have emerged from this tiny study that looked at the behaviors of only thirty-six female and thirty-six male undergraduate students (not exactly a diverse pool of participants). This study is interesting and continues to be cited in most meta-analyses involving gender and horror, but it's also thirty-five years old and hasn't, to my knowledge, seen replication in more recent decades. Also, not to be nitpicky, but this claim is also based on responses to a single clip from *Friday the 13th, Part III*, not the full film, and not contrasting with other types of video clips, or even other types of horror. Other studies from that era suggested that slashers were favored less by women, so it's odd that a subgenre thought to be favored by men was selected for the study.

A more likely reason than antique stances on gender roles for why a horror movie might be a good choice for your next date might be *excitation-transfer theory* (coincidentally, a theory also first described by Zillmann). We mentioned excitation-transfer theory in chapter 1 as a possible explanation for why we laugh after we catch ourselves screaming at a jump scare, and, while I didn't mention it in chapter 6, excitation-transfer theory is also often cited as a possible mechanism for transforming the pent-up arousal of seeing a horror movie into aggressive behaviors. Consider that pent-up arousal could instead be transformed into sexual arousal—not in a *horror makes you horny* kind of way, but in a way by which sharing a high arousal state with someone makes you feel closer to that person. Some studies have suggested that sharing unpleasant or painful experiences—on the milder end, eating extremely hot peppers together or having to do a strenuous, uncomfortable exercise; on the extreme end, surviving a traumatic event or fighting in a war together—can act as a sort of "social glue" to reinforce bonding and cooperation with another person. We've established throughout this book that horror movies contain stressful and uncomfortable moments by design. So, maybe sitting down to a scary movie with your crush might actually help you become a little bit closer.

This idea is also supported by Shelley Taylor's "tend and befriend" metaphor for social affiliation during times of stress, which suggests that humans are just as likely to turn toward social interactions, like seeking protection or comfort, as a stress response as they are to respond with a fight-or-flight reaction. This is based on the idea that some stressful experiences (watching a horror movie counts!) can promote the release of the hormone oxytocin. This release of oxytocin will also make you more sensitive to the effects of dopaminergic and opioid pathways in the brain, also known as the brain's reward systems, which will reinforce the whole ordeal as a positive experience if you have a positive social experience to couple it with. Be forewarned, though: Taylor also proposes that the converse is true—if your movie-watching buddy isn't very supportive, then that oxytocin surge might actually serve to deepen negative feelings toward them. This idea is reinforced by other studies that report that oxytocin can reinforce negative social feelings like schadenfreude, gloating, or envy.

Oxytocin has gotten a lot of hype in both the science world and the media. Mainstream reporting channels often refer to oxytocin as the "hug hormone" or the "cuddle hormone" because it's been heavily implicated in social bonding, intimate bonding during sex, trust, and empathy. Experiments have reported that oxytocin release can have calming effects and make us more likely to open up about our emotions, even to strangers. But oxytocin is a bit more complicated than that.

Rather than being a miracle hormone that can make us all trust and love each other a little more if only we hug each other more, recent research suggests that oxytocin is more or less a regulatory hormone, doing its best to keep our brain and body in check by mediating a bunch of physiological processes, a state of relative equilibrium known as *homeostasis*. It definitely does *something* in our brains when we're sharing social experiences, but it's more likely that oxytocin's role is in anticipatory effects, or pulling our attention toward our interpersonal relationships and so making our feelings about those relationships feel amplified because we are focused on them, than it is in conjuring up our feelings toward those relationships, whether they be warm and fuzzy or uncomfortable.

Note

1. See Millar and Lee, "Horror Films and Grief," *Emotion Review* 13, no. 3 (2021): 171–82. (Editor's note)

III
Different Voices

Chapter 24

DISPLAYING CONNOISSEURSHIP, RECOGNIZING CRAFTSMANSHIP

Matt Hills

> Leading off part III is a chapter from Matt Hills's *The Pleasures of Horror* that shifts the focus away from the qualities of horror media themselves and toward how fans make texts meaningful for themselves. Hills here is interested in how horror fans create a sense of community and the ways through which they establish their "connoisseurship" bona fides.

WITH MUCH WORK ON HORROR FANDOM now occurring (see, e.g., Kermode 1997; Cherry 1999, 2002; Bolin 2000; Hoxter 2000; Jancovich 2000; Sanjek 2000; Williamson 2001; Kimber 2002) comments that the audience has been *neglected* in studies of horror (e.g., Gelder 2000, 6) have begun to seem strained. On the contrary, one might conclude that the horror fan has been theorized to death of late. In this chapter I will argue that alongside the "aestheticization" of horror there are a range of ways in which horror's pleasures are narrated and constructed by fans. Fan accounts of horror and pleasure have tended to center on self-mythologized "first encounters" between fan and genre, as well as on how "being a horror fan" shifts its experiential meaning between childhood and adulthood. For many horror fans the pleasures of horror are discursively constructed through micronarratives of biography as well as through notions of belonging to a fan culture and through notions of horror-as-art. Yet in each case fan accounts of the horror genre and its pleasures circle around a discourse of connoisseurship. It is this that I will now turn my attention to.

Connoisseurship in Horror Fan Cultures and Fan Biographies

Fan-cultural distinctions tend to mark out some horror texts as "visionary" and dismiss others as "inauthentic" horror (Jancovich 2000, 29–31; Sanjek 2000, 317). As

Mark Jancovich (2000, 28) has observed, "While some horror fans embrace Freddy Kruger [sic] . . . as a cult hero, others seek to disassociate themselves from these fans through an association with cult 'auteurs' such as Dario Argento." Discourses of aestheticization and authentication—"underground" horror-as-art versus "mainstream," commercial horror—allow fans to pleasurably imagine and demarcate the boundaries of horror fan culture, indicating the knowledge that one must share in order to "properly" be a horror fan. Such discourses do not only work to culturally separate out fans and nonfans, or long-term fans and inauthentic (new) teen fans (Jancovich 2000, 30). They also allow horror fans to bid for the wider cultural value of their texts by tactically aligning "horror-as-art" discourses with discourses of "legitimate" aesthetics. Horror-as-art is thus an overdetermined interpretative tactic, allowing fans to position themselves against a range of imagined Others (state censors/moral campaigners/critics of horror).

Within such multistranded struggles over horror and cultural distinction, "connoisseurship" emerges as *the* master trope in fan struggles against other "inauthentic" consumers and policing authorities. The pleasures of connoisseurship are thus pleasures of social and cultural distinction/belonging, as well as allowing fans to perform their (constrained) cultural agency via the specific interpretation and contextualization of pop-cultural texts. Such agency is exhibited in Mark Kermode's (1997) account of being a horror fan. Kermode repeatedly emphasizes fans' knowledge: "Here were people who *knew* what they were talking about, grown-up people who had been doing this for *years,* who actually *understood* what these movies were about" (58).

In Kermode's (1997, 59) account, horror fans are divided from nonfans, since the latter group lack detailed information about any horror film they see, and are simply "scared by it, then wander[ing] out of the cinema and back into the mundanity of their everyday lives." Nonfans "cringed" at *The Fly* (1986) and its gory abortion scene, while Kermode and a fellow aficionado "chuckled smugly" at their recognition that the onscreen doctor was Cronenberg in a cameo role (60). The act of being scared is predominantly located on the side of nonfandom (or casual horror film viewing):

> The horror fan . . . is . . . not only able but positively compelled to "read" rather than merely "watch" such movies. The novice, however, sees only the dismembered bodies, hears only the screams and groans, reacts only with revulsion or contempt. Being unable to differentiate between the real and the surreal, they consistently misinterpret horror fans' interaction with texts that mean nothing to them. (61)

Horror fans are knowledgeable, and seemingly not scared by horror, given their "educated," metaphorical, and allegorical rather than literalist readings. Aware of horror's conventions and representations, fans actively "read" aesthetically and thematically, whereas for Kermode, nonfans appear to watch naively, as if what is represented onscreen is somehow affectively "real." On one of the rare occasions when Kermode links fear to the position of the horror fan, this is not a fear of any horror film but is instead, tellingly, a fear of not knowing enough about the genre (58).

The possibility consistently discursively warded off is that the fan may actually experience fear in response to a horror text. Shockers can be "ground-breaking" when experienced (Kermode 1997, 58), but what they *do not* (or must not, in this account) provide for fans are "a test of machismo [or] passing scares" (60). We are told that fans get "more out of the movies than" this, "watching them again and again, learning them, studying them" (60). Kermode thus aligns the fan with the figure of the scholar: Fans, unafraid and triumphant, master their beloved horror texts through repeated viewing and aesthetic *study*. His account hence works to construct an image of the generic community (Altman 1999, 161), and a sense of what it means to be a horror fan, discursively privileging knowledge over affect. In this regard, it fits with Julian Hoxter's (2000, 185) work on "cult learning" and horror film: "Those [fans] who use an accumulation of knowledge to evade the emotional experience of . . . [horror films] . . . may in their own right be taking possession . . . [of these films] . . . in making . . . [them] . . . their own area of expertise." Although Kermode (1997) attributes the "test of machismo" only to inauthentic fans or casual consumers, his own discursive substitution of fan knowledge for affect actually has the result of portraying fans as "tough" or "hard." Fans do not "cringe." They get the in-joke rather than being grossed out:

> Horror fans often deny that horror films frighten them. Within certain circles, the very value of watching these films, or at least the value of saying certain things about that viewing experience, is to assert that they do not frighten but only amuse . . . within certain contexts, it would be inappropriate (other than in exceptional circumstances) to admit to being frightened by horror films. (Jancovich 2000, 32)

I will return to the question of "exceptional circumstances," but here I am arguing that Kermode's account attempts to valorize horror fan practices via discourses of fan "literacy" and knowledge rather than affect or emotion. A further instance of fan knowledge and cultural/generic discrimination is recounted in Brigid Cherry's (1999) survey and analysis of female horror fans. Whereas Mark Kermode's masculinist, subcultural account (Hollows 2003) centers on the metaphorical/allegorical artistry of gore effects, Cherry's female fans favored "subtle" horror:

> Viewers preferred to watch films they took to be imaginative, intelligent, literary or thought-provoking. Dislike was often expressed for films that revolved around excessive or gratuitous displays of violence, gore or other effects used to evoke revulsion in the audience. (Cherry 1999, 195)

Other markers of "quality" favored by these female fans were "high production values in art direction, set design and costumes, [a]cting" and "plot and characters" (194).

These "aestheticizing" criteria, it should also be noted, fly in the face of those used by the (predominantly male) "Film Swappers" studied by Göran Bolin (2000), who favored extreme gore in the texts they canonized, moving closer to the aesthetic criteria endorsed by Kermode (1997). This provides some evidence for gendered interpretative communities within horror fan subculture, but before overly reifying gender differences it is important to recall the similarities as well as differences across such interpretations; Cherry's (1999) female fans may favor "subtle" horror, while Bolin's (2000) "underground" male fans favor "splatter," but both groups nevertheless continue to demarcate and valorize their preferences via debates over horror's aesthetics.

These various analyses and expressions of horror fandom indicate that pleasure is narrated and discursively constructed in specific ways by horror fan cultures. Contra many theorists' text-derived focus on horror as "scary," cognitively challenging, or "uncanny," fans' expressed pleasures typically appear to be those of connoisseurship rather than fear, disgust, intellectual hesitation, or ideological subversion/reaffirmation. Connoisseurship secures the distinctiveness of fan subcultural identities, also allowing for differential bids for (sub)cultural value, as well as contesting the authority over horror's circulation that is exercised legally by State censors.

But how do fans deal with their experiences of the horror genre that cannot, by definition, be discursively constructed as "knowledgeable," that is, their first encounters with horror? The beginning of Mark Kermode's (1997) "becoming-a-fan" story runs as follows:

> I . . . sensed from the very beginning that there was something incomprehensibly significant about the actions being played out on-screen, something which spoke to me in a language I didn't quite understand. . . . I felt from the outset that beyond the gothic trappings these movies had something to say to *me* about *my* life. I just didn't have any idea what. (57)

Kermode's initial experience of becoming a fan, prior to his adopting a social role within fan culture, is romanticized and shrouded in mystery in this self-description. It is "self-absent" because Kermode seemingly cannot provide reasons for his liking of horror at this biographical point (the horror-as-art discourse does not emerge until he is discussing the fan community's shared interpretations and valorizations of horror [e.g., 61]). Instead, Kermode's account stresses the powerful impact that late-night horror films had on his child-self:

> At around 11.00, when everyone else was in bed, I would sneak down into the family living room and sit entranced by a selection of creaky . . . horror flicks, usually from the Hammer or Amicus stable. No matter that I had to have the volume turned down so far that it was impossible to hear anything that was being said: what was captivating was the electrifying atmosphere, the sense of watching something that was forbidden, secretive, taboo. It was, indeed, my first real experience of discovering

something that was uniquely *mine,* something that existed outside the domain of my parents' control and authority. (57)

In a description otherwise powerfully marked by the insistent repetition of knowingness and readerly competence, Kermode positions his movement into fandom as a transformation that is beyond self-control or self-mastery. Horror might uniquely "belong" to him, being outside parental jurisdiction, but its textual significance is dimly "sensed," not fully understood. It could be argued that this is a discourse of Romantic excess that works to valorize the fan by aligning them culturally and narratively with a discourse of "the lover swept away by their passion." This is indeed the paradigmatic discourse of affect that Kermode draws on; not that of being scared or fearful, but rather a notion of horror's Romantic "intensities," and of being overwhelmed by something outside the self that cannot be fully articulated or comprehended at the time (LaFollette 1996, 61–62; Illouz 1997, 173–74). Horror is thus doubly revalued here; it is both part of an artistic lineage/tradition for its community of adult fans, and it is akin to an intensely cherished (and "possessed") love object for its individual child fan.

This Romantic excess or intensity recurs as a "discourse of affect" in Charles E. Weigl's (2002) academically published self-account of being a horror fan. Again, Weigl links this experience of affective excess to his childhood love of horror:

a childhood fascination sanctioned in recent years, cloaked in the respectable robes of academic research. Truth be told, it has always been more of an obsession than a fascination. When he was a boy [Weigl is writing about his child-self in the third person —MH], from the moment he was able to read the television listings in the newspaper, he spent almost every Saturday afternoon glued to the set for that afternoon's line-up of old horror films. (707)

For both Kermode (1997) and Weigl (2002), knowledge displaces affect, but within a narrative of self rather than as part of an account of horror fan subculture. The discursive problem addressed by "becoming a horror fan" stories is that while knowledge and "literacy" can be used to distinguish and revalue the adult, "tutored" horror fan—the reader of horror's niche magazines and participant in fan-cultural activities (Heffernan 2004, 226)—such discourses cannot logically or readily account for why horror so affected or inspired the proto-fan in the first place. "Fascination" or sitting "entranced" are thus called upon to do this discursive work, without necessarily raising the culturally feminizing specter of horror as fear provoking. But such "obsession/fascination" also has to be held partly at bay from the current, rational (and especially academic) self. By conferring this status on the child-self of the past, a discursive distanciation is safely effected.

What such micronarratives achieve is the discursive production of a contemporary valued self, aligned with cultural norms of rationality and literacy, while aporias in this self-account (how to explain becoming a fan?) are dealt with via performative citation of Romantic intensities, attributed to the past/child self. The fact that this micronarrative so economically works to position the (masculine) horror fan as beyond cultural reproach may account for its widespread circulation across horror fan cultures. For, as I will now go on to show, it is not at all restricted to academic self-accounts of horror fandom. Versions of this "before" and "after" micronarrative—"Romantic-intensity-turned-to-cool-knowledgeability"—crop up across a number of horror fan online message boards.

Of course, the recurrence of this structured self-narrative may indicate that horror fans all share a basic (ontological) experience of horror, but I want to suspend that question here. Rather my interest lies, performatively, in *what such an account can do for horror fans.* Kermode (1997) and Weigl (2002) use this style of account to displace the question of adult, male fans being scared by horror. Similar micronarratives can also be appropriated to allow horror's scares to be discussed without the fan concerned coming to resemble a nonfan, and without cultural codes of masculinity or rational subjectivity being transgressed. In other words horror fans can use this type of self-account to explain what it means to be a horror fan, and/or how they became a fan, while warding off the taint of "pathologized" horror fandom. Such micronarratives work partly in the service of hegemonic masculinity (and/or performatively rational subjectivity) by constructing "antieffeminate" affective responses to pop-cultural narratives (Warhol 2003, 88). However, these self-accounts simultaneously challenge dominant, hegemonic cultural representations of "weird" horror fans (Jenkins 1992; Jensen 1992; Tudor 1997) by stressing fans' media literacy, education, and knowledge of the genre (Hunt 2003). And they work in the service of fan/nonfan cultural distinctions, separating the intensely affected, diachronic fan from the synchronically scared but nondiachronically affected and more casual moviegoer (for more on nonfans' memories of watching horror films as children, see Kuhn 2002, chap. 4).

Since I want to move on to discuss a range of online horror fans' postings, it is important to consider the specificity of these as texts (Hills 2002, 175–77). Given that fans are posting to genre-specific message boards, we should not assume that fans' sentiments simply reflect or mirror the offline "reality" of other fan activities (Bird 2003, 81). Postings need to be analyzed instead as a specific textual production of fan identity, one that is aimed at a readership assumed to be made up of other horror fans, and also, importantly, a readership that can rapidly indicate its approval or disapproval of any given posting by virtue of the message board's status as asynchronous computer-mediated communication. This degree of interactivity (Flew 2002, 21–22; Burnett and Marshall 2003, 52) in relation to "internal communication" (Bolin 2000, 62) within a fan culture means that it is important to address how subcultural assumptions are drawn on, reinforced, and activated by online fans.

As Henry Jenkins (2002, 157) has recently put it, rather "than talking about interactive technologies, we should document the interactions that occur among media consumers." This means treating interactivity not merely as an ideological "'value-added' characteristic . . . of new media" (Lister et al. 2003, 20) but rather as part of a "user flow" (Caldwell 2003, 135–41) or "overflow" (Brooker 2003, 323) from proprietary texts (e.g., horror films) to different ranges of official/unofficial websites or message boards involving audience-to-audience interactions (see also Altman 1999; Fleming 2000; Skal 2002, 180–81). Analyzing such audience interaction, Jenkins (2002, 158) uses the work of Pierre Lévy (1999), *Collective Intelligence: Mankind's Emerging World in Cyberspace,* to argue that

> Online fan communities are the most fully realized versions of Lévy's cosmopedia. They are expansive self-organizing groups focused around the collective production, debate, and circulation of meanings, interpretations and fantasies in response to various artifacts of contemporary popular culture.

Lévy's (1999, 214–20) "cosmopedia" is a vast knowledge space divorced from territorialization, a collective intelligence made "accessible to us through computer technology for the representation and dynamic management of knowledge" (216). Lévy uses the image of knowledge as a patchwork quilt "in which each point can be folded over on any other" so that the cosmopedia "dematerializes the boundaries between different types of knowledge. It dissolves the differences between specializations" (217; see also Bird 2003, 51–85, on the image of the "cyber-quilt"). However, it remains important to consider the ways in which online fan cultures do not *always* "dissolve differences between specializations." Quite to the contrary, they may enact their own forms of specialized fan knowledge. For example, if a horror message board posting does not resonate with subcultural knowledge, then it is likely to become the subject of flaming and abuse, or to languish unanswered (Hodkinson 2002, 180). The skill that posters are required to display when initiating threads of discussion is thus that of articulating shared assumptions within the fan culture. Within the context of new media use, then, those fans who post to horror-related message boards are necessarily involved in more or less successfully articulating textualized subcultural identities. The more productive a thread is in prompting positive or affirming responses, the more readily it can be interpreted as a successful subcultural performative—a successful "doing" of being a horror fan, which other fans iterate in their responses. And the more a posting receives abusive or querying responses, then the more it can serve to demarcate the boundaries to appropriate fan-cultural identity. The "knowledge space" or cosmopedia of online horror fandom is thus collective and interactive, but it is also collectively and interactively *constrained,* limited to bounded performances of fan subcultural identity. The connoisseurship that online fans display is thus always a badge of appropriate belonging, and an articulation of subculturally defended norms concerning "what it means to be a horror fan."

To take one example of this process, the now-defunct Horrorentertainment.com message board contained a section headed "Deep Discussion," this being separated from news and reviews. One thread, headed "Is it possible for a film to scare hardcore horror fans?," enacted the discursive separation of horror's "scariness" from reactions of "real" horror fans. The very fact that such a question made sense to a number of respondents indicated that "adult" horror fandom was being constructed here *not* as a matter of textually provoked affect or emotion, but rather as the absence of such affect. The range of responses also indicated that this poster had successfully articulated a fan-cultural identity premised on shared subcultural norms. The thread begins, "One member stated that no horror film had truly scared him since he was a child," with the poster going on to observe:

> Nowadays the scares are rare. Granted I do still jump on occasion. But how long has it been since a new movie rocked my world? I honestly cannot say. . . . Perhaps it's part growing up, and part absence of a truly horrifying picture released in recent years? (Sulla, April 1, 2002, 10:25 p.m.)

This post positions the fan's openness to the text as a childhood experience, implying that to be scared or horrified by horror is inappropriate for the "hardcore" and grown-up fan. But at the same time a desire is indicated for horror to return to its scariness of old, implying that openness to the text is not univocally disavowed, but is also a potentially positive experience that inferior horror films cannot deliver. The fan's loss of self is hence both discursively absented and valued. This is a version of the "Romantic-intensity-turned-cool-knowledgeability" self-account in which Romantic intensity remains desired even while it is both nostalgically cast into the past and simultaneously related to an adult connoisseurship, being "part absence of a truly horrifying picture released in recent years."

Not all the responses to this thread on Horrorentertainment.com drew so directly on a series of "child" versus "adult" and "affected" versus "detached" oppositions. One poster simply asserted that they "have never been scared by any movie," thus contrasting "real" scares ("when my daughter ran away from home" [Borgosi, April 4, 2002, 5:37 p.m.]) to film's unreality. This also blocks out fan affect, challenging fan stereotypes (Jenkins 1992) by drawing on a binary of fantasy/reality and aligning the fan with "the real." However, it is worth noting that this response remains a micronarrative of self; horror is still given meaning here as nonscary in relation to a significant event in the poster's life as a parent (for this, read "adult"), just as Sulla invokes "growing up" as one reason for a relative lack of scary movies. It could thus be argued that this response emphasizes "cool" knowingness rather than desired or nostalgic Romantic intensity, while continuing to assert the poster's adult identity.

Further responses on this message board accepted that fans could be scared by horror films, but differentiated between the degrees of fear that horror may inspire:

I do believe that it is possible to scare horror fans but I do not think that it is applicable for a horror fan to be scared to the point where he or she cannot get to sleep for days on end. I think the scares only come in minor increments. (Gothic, June 11, 2002, 12:08 a.m.)

As in Kermode's (1997) account, this respondent goes on to emphasize fans' awareness of "all of the genre flicks in the world," suggesting that generic knowledge works to reduce the possibility of an affective/fearful response. And once again, the issue of temporality is discursively introduced, although this is a reversal of Kermode's differentiation between nonfans who are momentarily scared and fans who are not scared but who are moved and affected by horror so that the genre becomes a part of their ongoing project of self. Gothic's posting maintains the distinction between fans and nonfans that Kermode's account demarcates, but reframes this as a distinction between nonfans who cannot sleep for days versus fans who might be scared, but only in far more contained, momentary ways. What this discursive maneuver achieves is a binary opposition that confers irrationality on nonfans of horror—what is the matter with these people that they cannot sleep for days?— while conferring rational subjectivity on the fan who is scared, but only in "minor increments." What could threaten fan identity as an excessive or "effeminate" affective reaction (Warhol 2003) is again recuperated as rational and culturally normative in this fan's discursive construction of horror's pleasures. Being too scared, where pleasure tips into displeasure, is discursively demarcated as the typical lot of nonfans rather than knowledgeable fan-connoisseurs.

In contrast to these discussions, fans posting to the newsgroup alt.horror were seemingly happier to make a conventional link between horror films and their affective power. In two specific threads, fans discussed what made a "good" and scary horror movie. In this case, scariness is variously equated with the "medium" ("16mm or grainy colour film" is scary, whereas 32mm "would not look as frightening" [Robert Aveberry, June 16, 2002, 8:39 p.m.]), with the "substance" of a horror film (^Tool^, June 17, 2002, 2:16 p.m.), or with the pop-cultural context ("it's not scary now—it's so ingrained as a part of pop culture that it's about as scary as the Hamburgler in a home invasion" [blowup, June 17, 2002, 8:54 p.m.]). Although at first appearing to value horror film as scary, what this different set of definitions achieves is a semiotic and cognitive dispersal, rather than blockage, of fans' openness to the text. That is to say, even where the horrifying nature of horror is supposedly accepted, this itself becomes the subject matter for detailed fan debate and expressions of knowledgeability. Fan mastery is then enacted through the argumentative turn-taking of a newsgroup thread, with horror texts' affective power being variously contested by fans who once more assert their *knowledge,* although this time it is a knowledge *of* the mechanics and aesthetics of fear production rather than "knowledge" explicitly and discursively opposed to "emotion."

Debates over horror's affects and aesthetics are also carried out by online fans via the substitution of "disturbing" for "scary." In this case, fans discuss which horror films or scenes have most disturbed them, as in the thread "What movie disturbed you the most when watching it" (Calico, August 10, 2003) on the diabolical-dominion.com message board, or the thread "Most disturbing scenes ever" (pfloyd, July 20, 2003) on the "Creature Corner" message board (http://www.chud.com/). In each of these instances fans debate the effectiveness of horror films and/or specific scenes without direct reference to these being "scary." "Disturbing" horror is defined by both of these fan groups as something clearly distinct from scariness:

> What movie disturbed you the most when watching it. It doesn't even have to be bloody or scary. (Calico, August 10, 2003)

> I almost posted my list of most disgusting scenes, but that's not the same as most disturbing, right? And that's different from scary, too. (Mad Dog Mike, July 21, 2003)

"Disturbing" horror appears to be discursively constructed by these fans as a textual aesthetics that deals with extreme and unsettling representations, without necessarily showing gore (hence it is not "disgusting" horror) or necessarily scaring the fan. To be disturbed is hence figured as an imaginative, conceptual response; horror is once again treated here as at least partially nonaffective or disembodied. It is contextualized and valorized as a "mind genre" of aesthetic extremes and devices rather than an a priori "body genre" that possesses any sensationalist or literalist effectivity.

Despite these variations, fan cultural norms concerning micronarratives of child/adult and fan/nonfan distinctions are most insistently reiterated in online displays of connoisseurship, occurring across a wide range of horror message boards. For instance, long-term fandom is displayed by the vast majority of posters on the "Freddy vs. Jason" message forum (http://www.fridaythe13thforum.com/) responding to a thread entitled "How old were you when you first got into horror?" Again, there is a certain discourse of fan subcultural-authenticity-turned-life-story structured into the very heading, which presupposes a "first" moment of horror fandom existing at some distance from the implied adult fan-self. "How old . . . ?" can thus be read as "How young . . . ?" The question provokes fans to performatively display their subcultural identity by indicating the duration of their fandom, and its typically adolescent or preadolescent beginnings. Even fans who report that they are in their teens tend to locate the "origin story" of their fandom many years in the past:

> I'm turning 15 at the start of September and I was brought into horror when I was 7 and my bro brought home Noes, I go hook on those and I soon got hooked on Friday movies when I was 9. (bertskarzi196, July 14, 2003)

> I'm currently 18, and I got into it, probably around 5 years old, with Friday the 13th: The Final Chapter. (James M, July 16, 2003)

> I started loving horror at the age of 4 and I'm 14 now. (RekeHavok, July 17, 2003)

This thread allows fans to construct the "moment" at which their fandom began, and this is usually located in childhood or adolescence, positioned in contrast to their current age. Duration of fandom is iterated and insistently emphasized, as well as an initiating Romantic intensity that is fixed as a childhood experience. This allows fans to distinguish between when they first got into horror (i.e., when they were not knowledgeable fans, but were affected children) and their later fandom, as well as distinguishing them from casual consumers of horror by stressing their "enduring fandom" (Kuhn 1999). This subcultural assumption that horror fandom is enduring and has its roots in the fan's childhood is reproduced in a questionnaire posted to the horror message board at horror.net ("Can you fill in my horror survey?" [Cathy, October 16, 2001]). This asked, "What was the first film that ever scared you?" as well as "What is the most recent film that scared you?" thus allowing fans to micronarrate differences between their younger and current selves. One respondent's distinction between "first" and "most recent" scary films offered up a particularly instructive, implicit micronarrative of self; his first scary film was *When a Stranger Calls* (1979), about which he notes "I was alone at home . . . and the first twenty minutes properly freaked me out. . . . I kept staring at the phone on top of the tv, waiting for the psycho to call me up" (Mikael, October 17, 2001). Thus, while the younger self is "properly freaked out," and appears to display a modality confusion (switching between real and fictional modalities, as in "waiting for the psycho to call me up"), the current, rational fan-self appreciates the aesthetics or "moodscape," writing very articulately and expressively about *Requiem for a Dream* (2000), and expertly selecting specific scenes as especially "scary."

In fact, Mikael's emphasis on specific scenes is an act of discerning connoisseurship that is often repeated on other horror message boards. Though fans generally display an interest in discussing their favorite films (e.g., a thread on Horrorfind.com, "Favourite Horror Movie?" [Zombie_Child, May 19, 2003]), this connoisseurship is often more precisely located around effective scenes rather than dealing with films treated as wholes. In this regard, horror fans display a tendency to fracture and fragment films, combining auteurist readings with types of reflexively affect-focused interpretation where moments are grouped together across discrete texts on the basis of their power or intensity. The thread "Last movie that actually made you jump in your seat?" (Evil Ash, August 13, 2003) on the upcominghorrormovies.com message board rapidly becomes concerned with scenes rather than with "whole" films, while on terroraustralis.net, another popular thread deals with the issue of "Scenes that Scare" (Drexl, June 11, 2003). This classification of horror texts thus hinges not so much on an "author-function" (Foucault 1979) as on a type of "affect-function," but one where fan knowledgeability again comes into play in terms of fans' ability to list particular scenes within films. That is, rather than simply picking out "scary movies," the identification of key scenes again allows for a clearer performance of fan knowledge and connoisseurship. Affect is invoked, but knowledge once more offers an insulation from horror's scare stories by virtue of the very form of the debate, where fans construct detailed links between a network of genre texts, for example:

1. The Changeling—the playback of the tape recording.
2. Ringu—you know the one, I do not need to tell you.
3. The Eye (2 points)—the elevator scene and the corridor scene.
4. The Shining—those creepy twins.

   Opinions? (Drexl, June 11, 2003)

However, even these lists of "scary scenes" also continue to present versions of "child" versus "adult" and "affected" versus "detached" micronarratives of self. Reply 2 on the terroraustralis.net thread comments:

> This has no effect on me anymore, because I've seen it a zillion times, but it's what got me into horror in the first place; all the scenes when Michael Myers jumps into sudden attack in Halloween 2. (Pando, June 11, 2003)

Similarly, the upcoming horrormovies.com thread is introduced as follows:

> I've come to the sad realization that I have over exposed myself to horror movies and almost nothing creeps me out or startles me in movies anymore. I remember when I was younger I would dwell on a movie for days after watching it and still be freaked out. Sadly not anymore. (Evil Ash, August 13, 2003)

Both posts activate versions of what I have termed the "Romantic-intensity-turned-cool-knowledgeability" self-account, nostalgically lamenting the loss of horror's powerful affects while distancing the knowing, adult fan from their former child-self. My argument here is that this style of account occurs repeatedly across horror message boards due to the fact that it offers a skeletal or minimalist construction of fan identity that fans can subscribe to in order to demonstrate their distinctiveness from nonfans, while also discursively managing the "problem" of horror's affects and pleasures so that fans do not self-represent as displaying "effeminate" affects (Warhol 2003) or irrational behaviors within their media consumption.

So far in this chapter I have used a range of online fan postings to analyze how fans produce a sense of their subcultural distinctiveness. One way in which this is achieved is through reading horror-as-art, but another route into fan distinction occurs via the construction of fan autobiography, typically narrated as an indicator of long-term and authentic fandom, but also produced as a performative construction of adult detachment versus inspiring childhood intensities. Fans thus intently theorize and discursively construct the pleasures of horror, both in relation to "subcultural" and "autobiographical" levels of valorization. It is not only the case that horror's pleasures are debated and discursively restricted in academic arguments: Online horror fan culture is no less restrictive than academia in its construction of specific narratives and discourses of pleasure. Where academic accounts use psychoanalysis or cognitive philosophy to explore, and discursively fix, horror's pleasures, online fans rely on recurrent, iterated micronarratives of the genre and their knowing involvements with it. And where academic accounts of horror have seemingly taken for granted its status as "scary" (e.g., Carroll 1990), online fans variously narrate their subcultural, knowledgeable identities in discursive opposition to "scariness," or treat horror's scares reflexively, as something to be cataloged, dissected, and debated within further displays of fan expertise. In the next section I will explore another set of fan practices through which texts are aestheticized, addressing interpretations of horror's special effects (SFX).

Recognizing Horror's SFX Craftsmanship

Appreciating the craftsmanship of SFX works yet again to position horror as artful, but it also simultaneously decenters fans' approaches to auteurism. Reading horror via its SFX creates a network of author functions: Rather than entirely classifying a film through its director as *the* "source" of meaning, horror films can also be classified by fans according to their lead SFX designers and creators. It therefore makes sense for books target-marketed at horror fans to discuss the SFX work of Dick Smith, Rick Baker, Rob Bottin, Steve Johnson, and Stan Winston (as in Salisbury and Hedgecock 1994), as well as, say, analyzing the films of Wes Craven and David Cronenberg. This multiple classification of different authorships (the director-as-auteur alongside the SFX technician-as-craftsman) appears to broadly distinguish fan from academic interpretative communities. As Pamela Church Gibson (2001, 45) has written of H. R. Giger's work on *Alien* (1979):

> In all the mass of critical literature, there are only very brief references to ... [Giger's] work.... It is within the non-academic [i.e., fan and industry/promotional] work centred around the series that Giger receives his due recognition. But why should he be acknowledged and discussed only within the pages of magazines devoted to special effects?

In the case of academia, horror continues to be valued rather more unidimensionally through institutionalized norms of auteurism. SFX are typically studied thematically rather than in relation to specific SFX creators: Compare Salisbury and Hedgecock (1994) with Pierson (2002). And where academic work does argue that "cinematic style (as well as authorial consistency) can be located in the fields of ... effects-direction" (Bukatman 2003, 82; see also Gallardo C. and Smith 2004, 23–27), this brand of argument tends to be produced by scholars drawing on fan classifications within their academic work (or drawing on their own subcultural identities as fans as well as academics).

The academic study of special effects has also tended to approach SFX through the assumption "that effects are virtually synonymous with science fiction" (Barker

2000, 82). For Michele Pierson, SFX have a privileged place in the genres (horror/fantasy/science fiction) that make up "the . . . *cinefantastique*" (106), but it remains the case that science fiction is the space for "special" SFX. Horror's effects "bear repetition" as markers of genre, but supposedly do not function as markers of SFX development or novelty (102). Science fiction's SFX, by contrast, are the more pioneering and groundbreaking, arriving ahead of their time and before they have grown "familiar." There is an aesthetic valorization at work here: Where science fiction film innovates, horror merely reiterates. Such a narrative has been contested by horror's fans and scholar-fans:

> John McCarty says that *Blood Feast* by Herschell Gordon Lewis (1963) was the "first of the gore films"—and he should know, since he coined the term "splatter film" . . . Another gore landmark was George Romero's *Night of the Living Dead* (1968), which became a hit on the midnight cult film circuit. Gore crossed over into mainstream cinema in 1973 with *The Exorcist* . . . The growth of gore is obviously tied to the development of new methods and technologies for creating special effects in films . . . Specialty books about horror masters emphasize the industrywide effect of advances made in particular films, such as the Oscar-winning special effects by Rick Baker . . . in *An American Werewolf in London* (1981). (Freeland 2000, 241 and 243)

Special effects, I would argue, are "special" (that is, novel) in some horror films just as they are in some science fiction movies, and it makes little sense to a priori prioritize one genre over the other. Thankfully, not all recent scholarly work has dismissed horror fans' appreciation of SFX as somehow deficient, trivial, or wholly complicit with industry/promotional discourses (see Church Gibson 2001; Hunt 2003). Martin Barker and Kate Brooks (1998, 284–85), for example, have put forward the notion of "doubled attention" to explain how horror's fan audiences make use of special effects:

> It seems that in watching horror . . . we frequently manage the experience by insisting on the separation of experiencing and experiencing-as-effects. If we can do this, there is always a place to retreat to, saying to ourselves "They made that scary, by doing that." We are frightened, or disturbed, or jumpy, or startled. But that experience can be, sometimes but not always, made manageable, even pleasurable, by the doubled attention of knowing that this is an effect of an "effect." If we cannot maintain the distinction, then the pleasure goes. We are simply scared. . . . *It is of course possible to specialise in one half of the double attention. This is what horror fans in effect do.* (my italics)

The notion of "doubled attention" is also somewhat prefigured in Isabel Pinedo's (1997, 55) discussion of horror's SFX:

> Awareness of artifice . . . is . . . an essential ingredient of recreational terror. The combination of realism and artifice in special-effects violence allows the bored viewer

who needs to spike the experience to focus on the realism ("pretend it's real") while simultaneously allowing the overstimulated viewer verging on terror to focus on the artifice without abandoning a sense of realism ("pretend it's fake"). Recreational terror ... depends on the tension between special-effects realism and awareness of its artifice.

Where Barker and Brooks suggest straightforwardly that "horror fans" specialize in one half of doubled attention—treating effects as effects—Pinedo offers a more sensitively gendered reading of this process, arguing that

> culturally, males are expected to display bravado and unflinching vision, whereas females are expected to cower and look away. The instruction that these magazines provide about special-effects technology allows the fan viewer to distance him or herself from depictions of violence by looking for the trick, for example, the cut from the actor to the prosthetic device. ... Looking for ruptures in realism is the counterpart to not-seeing or looking away. (57)

Despite the generic "him or herself" in this account, it seems clear that Pinedo associates "looking for the trick" with a masculinized reading strategy. Where females are supposed to perform their femininity by looking away, male fans can supposedly shield themselves from horror's affects by focusing on the techniques of SFX. Although empirical work on horror's audiences has notably disputed the idea that "looking away" is an inevitable feminine response (see Cherry 1999), work on female horror fans has reinforced the sense that such fans are far less interested in SFX than their male *Fangoria*-reading counterparts. As Brigid Cherry (2002, 50) puts it, the "emphasis on gore as the reason for disliking most horror magazines reflected the tastes of the participants [female horror fans —MH], and, in particular, the dislike of gory, special-effects driven horror films."

Thus, despite Pinedo's relatively simplistic equation of "looking away" with the female audience and "looking for ruptures in realism" with the male audience, it appears to be the case that female horror fans do not quite read horror's SFX in the same way that many male fans do. Accounts of horror fandom that claim to represent horror fan subculture, such as that of Mark Kermode (1997), can thus again be read as falsely generalizing accounts that reflect on the experience of sections of antieffeminate (Warhol 2003) and masculinized horror fandom:

> Directors, writers, actors, even special effects men, all become recognisable to devotees who provide the hard-core fan-base for the genre. Through the pages of *Fangoria*—and later *Gore Zone*—we had met these people in their natural surroundings, seen photographs of them goofing around with severed latex heads, and read their behind-the-scenes accounts of how the movies got made. (Kermode 1997, 60)

Kermode's "we" does not seem to include the female fans analyzed by Pinedo (1997) and Cherry (1999, 2002). Although Kermode's account backs up Barker and Brooks's notion of one-sided double attention (indeed, Barker and Brooks 1998, 285, cite it to support their argument), Kermode also places an emphasis on the technical artistry of SFX, stressing—as many fans do—the importance of SFX designers and technicians such as Tom Savini and Dick Smith. These SFX men are clearly treated as auteurs of a sort within sections of horror fandom and in associated magazines such as *Cinefex* (see Pierson 2002, 133–34), *Fangoria* (Conrich 2000), *The Dark Side* (Jancovich 2000, 28–29), and *Cinefantastique* (Sanjek 2000, 316). It is therefore important to amend Barker and Brooks's (1998) emphasis on horror fans as displaying a type of "one-sided double attention" by noting the following:

- One section or faction of male horror fandom forms an interpretative community that reads horror through its SFX as effects, but we should not be overly generalizing about this reading practice, since it tends to exclude many female horror fans and other sections of male horror fandom (Jancovich 2000, 28–29).
- Those male horror fans who do read effects primarily as effects do so by viewing certain effects as authored, relating them to discourses of horror-as-art. "One-sided double attention" is thus not only about managing the line between tolerable fear and unacceptable scariness (contra Barker), or about performing a version of "good" and unflinching masculinity (contra Pinedo); it is also about some fans' desire to have the craft of effects . . . treated as a legitimate (i.e., authored and hence authorized) form of aesthetic expression. (Pierson 2002, 73)

By arguing that horror's special effects are self-reflexively used by sections of horror fandom to sustain and generate a reading of horror-as-art, I am thus suggesting here that film aesthetics do not only precede and "cause"/incite/invoke audience "emotions" or "affects" (contra cognitivist and psychoanalytic assumptions). Fan "interpretative communities" tend to nominate specific scenes or special effects as particularly noteworthy and artfully achieved, referring these back to directors and to SFX craftsmen. They are not simply reacting to filmic aesthetics here, for their discourses and interpretations are also, in a sense, constructing and framing (hence "aestheticizing" or multiply "author-izing") the "object" itself. However, it is worth remembering that not all horror's SFX are construed as authored, even within SFX-focused fan communities. Certain effects are repeatedly prioritized in fan accounts and "specialty books" as *special* special effects as opposed to unremarkable or reiterated special effects. Not all FX are equally special. Some sequences, which take on a life of their own outside of their original textual framing via fan histories of horror film and other forms of cultural circulation, become key markers of and for SFX technology—for example, Screaming Mad George and *Society* (1989), Dick Smith and *The Exorcist* (1973) and *Scanners* (1981), Rick Baker and *An American Werewolf in London* (1981), and Rob Bottin and *The Thing* (1982). This extratextual circulation of SFX stills/images therefore partly reflects and partly sustains fans' aestheticizing of horror. In this manner, fan audience investments in horror-as-art are not experienced simply in relation to "the text itself" (a limitation of Carroll's 1990 account). They are, rather, layered and reinforced through extra-textual "floating signifiers" such as SFX images extracted from their original narrative frames (and here I am drawing on Bennett and Woollacott's 1987 account of "popular heroes," but applying this to SFX imagery rather than iconic characters).

Fan practices of aestheticization—indicating a desire for horror to be taken seriously as art—have repeatedly worked to frame horror's pleasures within discourses of fan agency, discrimination, and expertise. This discursive splitting between "active," agentive, genre-educated fans working to read horror-as-art and "passive" nonfan consumers subjected to horror's textual affects produces a fan-cultural narrative of horror's pleasures that is strikingly unlike the discourses of pleasure used by cognitive philosophers, literary scholars, and psychoanalytic critics. For this discursively framed version of horror and pleasure is one in which horror does not act upon the audience. Rather, the audience acts upon horror. Fans' multiply "author-izing" aestheticizations of horror and its SFX, their displays of knowledge rather than "emotion," and their discursive constructions of Romantic "intensities" restricted nostalgically to childhood fan-selves all suggest that the pleasures of horror cannot be discursively restricted to notions of fear and disgust, or to approaches that conceptualize horror's pleasures as emerging through the relationship between a singular text and audience member. Instead, fans' constructed and construed pleasures of horror hinge on imagined versions of their "generic community" (Altman 1999), or subculture, and its distinctions.

To reiterate, I am not contrasting fan discourses of pleasure—somehow assumed to reflect "real" pleasures—to scholarly discourses that would then be assumed to be idealized, speculative, or somehow "unreal." Taking a thoroughgoing performative approach, neither fan nor academic discourses of horror's pleasures have any greater ontological claim: Both are precisely constructions, occurring within different (sub)cultural contexts and doing different things for their respective producers. It may hence be no accident that the majority of academic and fan accounts of horror's pleasures are so radically disconnected from one another: Where academics all too frequently assume that horror's pleasures are a "paradox" that they alone can heroically and logically resolve, fans assume that horror's pleasures are produced through their own discernment, activity/agency, and subcultural knowledge. Both academic and fan subcultures hence performatively claim agency for themselves while denying it to imagined Others. Academics assume that they can actively explain horror texts while their audiences are passively and emotionally subjected to the genre's products (either due to "under-cognitive" psychoanalytic mechanisms or "over-cognitive" emotional responses). By contrast, fans assume that they can actively explain horror—using notions of genre history, production history, and aesthetics rather than theoretical terminologies—whereas nonfans or casual consumers of the genre are passively subjected to its scares. Horror's fans and professional philosophers may well share one thing, then: unshakable faith in their subculture's ability to legitimate and make sense of the horror genre.

References

Altman, Rick. 1999. *Film/Genre*. BFI.
Barker, Martin, with Thomas Austin. 2000. *From Antz to Titanic: Reinventing Film Analysis*. Pluto Press.
Barker, Martin, and Kate Brooks. 1998. *Knowing Audiences: "Judge Dredd," Its Friends, Fans and Foes*. University of Luton Press.
Bennett, Tony, and Janet Woollacott. 1987. *Bond and Beyond: The Political Career of a Popular Hero*. Macmillan.
Bird, S. Elizabeth. 2003. *The Audience in Everyday Life: Living in a Media World*. Routledge.
Bolin, Göran. 2000. "Film Swapping in the Public Sphere: Youth Audiences and Alternative Cultural Publicities." *Javonst: The Public* 7, no. 2: 57–74.
Brooker, Will. 2003. "Conclusion: Overflow and Audience." In *The Audience Studies Reader*, edited by Will Brooker and Deborah Jermyn, 322–34. Routledge.
Bukatman, Scott. 2003. *Matters of Gravity: Special Effects and Supermen in the 20th Century*. Duke University Press.
Burnett, Robert, and P. David Marshall. 2003. *Web Theory: An Introduction*. Routledge.
Caldwell, John Thornton. 2003. "Second-Shift Media Aesthetics." In *New Media: Theories and Practices of Digitextuality*, edited by Anna Everett and John T. Caldwell, 127–44. Routledge.
Carroll, Noël. 1990. *The Philosophy of Horror; or, Paradoxes of the Heart*. Routledge.
Cherry, Brigid. 1999. "Refusing to Refuse to Look: Female Viewers of the Horror Film." In *Identifying Hollywood's Audiences: Cultural Identity and the Movies*, edited by Melvyn Stokes and Richard Maltby, 187–203. BFI.
Cherry, Brigid. 2002. "Screaming for Release: Femininity and Horror Film Fandom in Britain." In *British Horror Cinema*, edited by Steve Chibnall and Julian Petley, 42–57. Routledge.
Church Gibson, Pamela. 2001. "'You've Been in My Life So Long I Can't Remember Anything Else': Into the Labyrinth with Ripley and the Alien." In *Keyframes: Popular Cinema and Cultural Studies*, edited by Matthew Tinkcom and Amy Villarejo, 35–51. Routledge.
Conrich, Ian, and Julian Petley, eds. 2000. *Journal of Popular British Cinema* 3.
Fleming, Dan. 2000. "*The Blair Witch Project*: Film and Hypertexts." In *Formations: A 21st Century Media Studies Textbook*, edited by Dan Fleming, 248–51. Manchester University Press.
Flew, Terry. 2002. *New Media: An Introduction*. Oxford University Press.
Foucault, Michel. 1979. "What Is an Author?" *Screen* 20, no. 1: 13–33.
Freeland, Cynthia. 2000. *The Naked and the Undead: Evil and the Appeal of Horror*. Westview Press.
Gallardo C., Ximena, and C. Jason Smith. 2004. *Alien Woman: Ripley as Cinematic Icon*. Continuum.
Gelder, Ken, ed. 2000. *The Horror Reader*. Routledge.

Heffernan, Kevin. 2004. *Ghouls, Gimmicks and Gold: Horror Films and the American Movie Business, 1953–1968.* Duke University Press.

Hills, Matt. 2002. *Fan Cultures.* Routledge.

Hodkinson, Paul. 2002. *Goth: Identity, Style and Subculture.* Berg.

Hollows, Joanne. 2003. "The Masculinity of Cult." In *Defining Cult Movies: The Cultural Politics of Oppositional Taste,* edited by Mark Jancovich, Antonio Lázaro Reboll, Julian Stringer, and Andy Willis, 35–53. Manchester University Press.

Hoxter, Julian. 2000. "Taking Possession: Cult Learning in *The Exorcist.*" In *Unruly Pleasures,* edited by Xavier Mendik and Graeme Harper, 171–85. Guildford Press.

Hunt, Nathan. 2003. "The Importance of Trivia: Ownership, Exclusion and Authority in Science Fiction Fandom." In *Defining Cult Movies: The Cultural Politics of Oppositional Taste,* edited by Mark Jancovich, Antonio Lázaro Reboll, Julian Stringer, and Andy Willis, 185–201. Manchester University Press.

Illouz, Eva. 1997. *Consuming the Romantic Utopia: Love and the Cultural Contradictions of Capitalism.* University of California Press.

Jancovich, Mark. 2000. "'A Real Shocker': Authenticity Genre and the Struggle for Distinction." *Journal of Media and Cultural Studies* 14, no. 1: 23–35.

Jenkins, Henry. 1992. *Textual Poachers.* Routledge.

Jenkins, Henry. 2002. "Interactive Audiences?" In *The New Media Book,* edited by Dan Harries, 157–70. BFI.

Jensen, Joli. 1992. "Fandom as Pathology: The Consequences of Characterization." In *The Adoring Audience,* edited by Lisa A. Lewis, 9–29. Routledge.

Kermode, Mark. 1997. "I Was a Teenage Horror Fan; or, How I Learned to Stop Worrying and Love Linda Blair." In *Ill Effects: The Medial Violence Debate,* edited by Martin Barker and Julian Petley, 57–66. Routledge.

Kimber, Shaun. 2002. "Including the Excluded: Genre Fans' Views on Film Violence and the Regulative Censorship of Film Violence in Britain." Paper presented at Exploiting Fear: The Art and Appeal of Horror on Film, October 11–13.

Kuhn, Annette. 1999. "'That Day *Did* Last Me All My Life': Cinema Memory and Enduring Fandom." In *Identifying Hollywood's Audiences: Cultural Identity and the Movies,* edited by Melvyn Stokes and Richard Maltby, 135–46. BFI.

Kuhn, Annette. 2002. *An Everyday Magic: Cinema and Cultural Memory.* I. B. Tauris.

LaFollette, Hugh. 1996. *Personal Relationships: Love, Identity and Morality.* Blackwell.

Lévy, Pierre. 1999. *Collective Intelligence: Mankind's Emerging World in Cyberspace.* Perseus Books.

Lister, Martin, John Dovey, Seth Giddings, Iain Grand, and Kieran Kelly. 2003. *New Media: A Critical Introduction.* Routledge.

Pierson, Michele. 2002. *Special Effects: Still in Search of Wonder.* Columbia University Press.

Pinedo, Isabel Cristina. 1997. *Recreational Terror: Women and the Pleasures of Horror Film Viewing.* SUNY Press.

Salisbury, Mark, and Alan Hedgecock. 1994. *Behind the Mask: The Secrets of Hollywood's Monster Makers.* Titan Books.

Sanjek, David. 2000. "Fans' Notes: The Horror Film Fanzine." In *The Horror Reader,* edited by Ken Gelder, 314–23. Routledge.

Skal, David J. 2002. *Death Makes a Holiday: A Cultural History of Halloween.* Bloomsbury.

Tudor, Andrew. 1997. "Why Horror? The Peculiar Pleasures of a Popular Genre." *Cultural Studies* 11, no. 3: 443–63.

Warhol, Robyn R. 2003. *Have a Good Cry: Effeminate Feelings and Pop-Culture Forms.* Ohio State University Press.

Weigl, Charles E. 2002. "Introducing Horror." In *Hop on Pop: The Politics and Pleasures of Popular Culture,* edited by Henry Jenkins, Tara McPherson, and Jane Shattuc, 700–719. Duke University Press.

Williamson, Milly. 2001. "Vampires and Goths: Fandom, Gender and Cult Dress." In *Dressed to Impress: Looking the Part,* edited by William J. F. Keenan, 141–57. Berg.

Chapter 25

MY WORDS TO VICTOR FRANKENSTEIN ABOVE THE VILLAGE OF CHAMOUNIX

Performing Transgender Rage

Susan Stryker

> With Stryker's essay, this anthology begins to pivot away from the assumption of a "generic" audience for horror (which has always implicitly been assumed as white men) and toward the pleasures of horror for particular groups. Stryker's essay, which began its life as a performance piece, relates the experience of being transsexual to being the creature within Mary Shelley's *Frankenstein* as Stryker seeks to "lay claim to the dark power of [their] monstrous identity."

Introductory Notes

The following work is a textual adaptation of a performance piece originally presented at "Rage Across the Disciplines," an arts, humanities, and social sciences conference held June 10–12, 1993, at California State University, San Marcos. The interdisciplinary nature of the conference, its theme, and the organizers' call for both performances and academic papers inspired me to be creative in my mode of presenting a topic then much on my mind. As a member of Transgender Nation—a militantly queer, direct action transsexual advocacy group—I was at the time involved in organizing a disruption and protest at the American Psychiatric Association's 1993 annual meeting in San Francisco. A good deal of the discussion at our planning meetings concerned how to harness the intense emotions emanating from transsexual experience—especially rage—and mobilize them into effective political actions. I was intrigued by the prospect of critically examining this rage in a more academic setting through an idiosyncratic application of the concept of gender performativity. My idea was to perform self-consciously a queer gender rather than simply talk about it, thus embodying and enacting the concept simultaneously under discussion. I wanted the formal structure of the work to express a transgender aesthetic by replicating our abrupt, often jarring transitions between genders—challenging generic classification with the forms of my words just as my transsexuality challenges the conventions of legitimate gender and my performance in the conference room challenged the boundaries of acceptable academic discourse. During the performance, I stood at the podium wearing genderfuck drag—combat boots, threadbare Levi's 501s over a black lace body suit, a shredded Transgender Nation T-shirt with the neck and sleeves cut out, a pink triangle quartz crystal pendant, grunge metal jewelry, and a six-inch-long marlin hook dangling around my neck on a length of heavy stainless steel chain. I decorated the set by draping my black leather biker jacket over my chair at the panelists' table. The jacket had handcuffs on the left shoulder, rainbow freedom rings on the right side lacings, and Queer Nation–style stickers reading SEX CHANGE, DYKE, and FUCK YOUR TRANSPHOBIA plastered on the back.

Monologue

The transsexual body is an unnatural body. It is the product of medical science. It is a technological construction. It is flesh torn apart and sewn together again in a shape other than that in which it was born. In these circumstances, I find a deep affinity between myself as a transsexual woman and the monster in Mary Shelley's *Frankenstein* (1818). Like the monster, I am too often perceived as less than fully human due to the means of my embodiment; Like the monster's as well, my exclusion from human community fuels a deep and abiding rage in me that I, like the monster, direct against the conditions in which I must struggle to exist.

I am not the first to link Frankenstein's monster and the transsexual body. Mary Daly (1978, 69–72) makes the connection explicit by discussing transsexuality in "Boundary Violation and the Frankenstein Phenomenon," in which she characterizes transsexuals as the agents of a "necrophilic invasion" of female space. Janice Raymond (1979, 178), who acknowledges Daly as a formative influence, is less direct when she says that "the problem of transsexuality would best be served by morally mandating it out of existence," but in this statement she nevertheless echoes Victor Frankenstein's feelings toward the monster: "Begone, vile insect, or rather, stay, that I may trample you to dust. You reproach me with your creation" (Shelley [1818] 1965, 95). It is a commonplace of literary criticism to note that Frankenstein's monster is his own dark, romantic double, the alien Other he constructs and upon which he projects all he cannot accept in himself; indeed, Frankenstein calls the monster "my own vampire, my own spirit set loose from the grave" (74). Might I suggest that Daly, Raymond, and others of their ilk similarly construct the transsexual as their own particular golem?[1]

The attribution of monstrosity remains a palpable characteristic of most lesbian and gay representations of transsexuality, displaying in unnerving detail the anxious, fearful underside of the current cultural fascination with transgenderism.[2] Because transsexuality more than any other transgender practice or identity represents the prospect of destabilizing the foundational presupposition of fixed genders upon which a politics of personal identity depends, people who have invested their aspirations for social justice in identitarian movements say things about us out of sheer panic that, if said of other minorities, would see print only in the most hate-riddled, white supremacist, Christian fascist rags. To quote extensively from one letter to the editor of a popular San Francisco gay/lesbian periodical:

> I consider transsexualism to be a fraud, and the participants in it . . . perverted. The transsexual [claims] he/she needs to change his/her body in order to be his/her "true self." Because this "true self" requires another physical form in which to manifest itself, it must therefore war with nature. One cannot change one's gender. What occurs is a cleverly manipulated exterior: what has been done is mutation. What exists beneath the deformed surface is the same person who was there prior to the deformity. People who break or deform their bodies [act] out the sick farce of a deluded, patriarchal approach to nature, alienated from true being.

Referring by name to one particular person, self-identified as a transsexual lesbian, whom she had heard speak in a public forum at the San Francisco Women's Building, the letter writer went on to say:

> When an estrogenated man with breasts loves a woman, that is not lesbianism, that is mutilated perversion. [This individual] is not a threat to the lesbian community, he is an outrage to us. He is not a lesbian, he is a mutant man, a self-made freak, a deformity, an insult. He deserves a slap in the face. After that, he deserves to have his body and mind made well again. (Mikuteit 1986, 3–4, heavily edited for brevity and clarity)

When such beings as these tell me I war with nature, I find no more reason to mourn my opposition to them—or to the order they claim to represent—than Frankenstein's monster felt in its enmity to the human race. I do not fall from the grace of their company—I roar gleefully away from it like a Harley-straddling, dildo-packing leatherdyke from hell.

The stigmatization fostered by this sort of pejorative labeling is not without consequence. Such words have the power to destroy transsexual lives. On January 5, 1993, a twenty-two-year-old preoperative transsexual woman from Seattle, Filisa Vistima, wrote in her journal, "I wish I was anatomically 'normal' so I could go swimming. . . . But no, I'm a mutant, Frankenstein's monster." Two months later Filisa Vistima committed suicide. What drove her to such despair was the exclusion she experienced in Seattle's queer community, some members of which opposed

Filisa's participation because of her transsexuality—even though she identified as and lived as a bisexual woman. The Lesbian Resource Center where she served as a volunteer conducted a survey of its constituency to determine whether it should stop offering services to male-to-female transsexuals. Filisa did the data entry for tabulating the survey results; she didn't have to imagine how people felt about her kind. The Seattle Bisexual Women's Network (SBWN) announced that if it admitted transsexuals the SBWN would no longer be a women's organization. "I'm sure," one member said in reference to the inclusion of bisexual transsexual women, "the boys can take care of themselves." Filisa Vistima was not a boy, and she found it impossible to take care of herself. Even in death she found no support from the community in which she claimed membership. "Why didn't Filisa commit herself for psychiatric care?" asked a columnist in the Seattle *Gay News*. "Why didn't Filisa demand her civil rights?" In this case, not only did the angry villagers hound their monster to the edge of town, they reproached her for being vulnerable to the torches. Did Filisa Vistima commit suicide, or did the queer community of Seattle kill her?[3]

I want to lay claim to the dark power of my monstrous identity without using it as a weapon against others or being wounded by it myself. I will say this as bluntly as I know how: I am a transsexual, and therefore I am a monster. Just as the words *dyke, fag, queer, slut,* and *whore* have been reclaimed, respectively, by lesbians and gay men, by anti-assimilationist sexual minorities, by women who pursue erotic pleasure, and by sex industry workers, words like *creature, monster,* and *unnatural* need to be reclaimed by the transgendered. By embracing and accepting them, even piling one on top of another, we may dispel their ability to harm us. A creature, after all, in the dominant tradition of Western European culture, is nothing other than a created being, a made thing. The affront you humans take at being called a "creature" results from the threat the term poses to your status as "lords of creation," beings elevated above mere material existence. As in the case of being called "it," being called a "creature" suggests the lack or loss of a superior personhood. I find no shame, however, in acknowledging my egalitarian relationship with nonhuman material Being; everything emerges from the same matrix of possibilities. *Monster* is derived from the Latin noun *monstrum*, "divine portent," itself formed on the root of the verb *monere*, "to warn." It came to refer to living things of anomalous shape or structure, or to fabulous creatures like the sphinx who were composed of strikingly incongruous parts, because the ancients considered the appearance of such beings to be a sign of some impending supernatural event. Monsters, like angels, functioned as messengers and heralds of the extraordinary. They served to announce impending revelation, saying, in effect, "Pay attention; something of profound importance is happening."

Hearken unto me, fellow creatures. I who have dwelt in a form unmatched with my desire, I whose flesh has become an assemblage of incongruous anatomical parts, I who achieve the similitude of a natural body only through an unnatural process, I offer you this warning: The Nature you bedevil me with is a lie. Do not trust it to protect you from what I represent, for it is a fabrication that cloaks the groundlessness of the privilege you seek to maintain for yourself at my expense. You are as constructed as me; the same anarchic womb has birthed us both. I call upon you to investigate your nature as I have been compelled to confront mine. I challenge you to risk abjection and flourish as well as have I. Heed my words, and you may well discover the seams and sutures in yourself.

Criticism

In answer to the question he poses in the title of his recent essay "What Is a Monster? (According to *Frankenstein*)," Peter Brooks (1993, 219) suggests that, whatever else a monster might be, it "may also be that which eludes gender definition." Brooks reads Mary Shelley's story of an overreaching scientist and his troublesome creation as an early dissent from the nineteenth-century realist literary tradition, which had not yet attained dominance as a narrative form. He understands *Frankenstein* to unfold textually through a narrative strategy generated by tension between a visually oriented epistemology, on one hand, and another approach to knowing the truth of bodies that privileges verbal linguisticality, on the other (199–200). Knowing by seeing and knowing by speaking/hearing are gendered, respectively, as masculine and feminine in the critical framework within which Brooks operates. Considered in this context, Shelley's text is informed by—and critiques from a woman's point of view—the contemporary reordering of knowledge brought about by the increasingly compelling truth claims of Enlightenment science. The monster problematizes gender partly through its failure as a viable subject in the visual field; though referred to as "he," it thus offers a feminine, and potentially feminist, resistance to definition by a phallicized scopophilia. The monster accomplishes this resistance by mastering language in order to claim a position as a speaking subject and enact verbally the very subjectivity denied it in the specular realm.[4]

Transsexual monstrosity, however, along with its affect, transgender rage, can never claim quite so secure a means of resistance because of the inability of language to represent the transgendered subject's movement over time between stably gendered positions in a linguistic structure. Our situation effectively reverses the one encountered by Frankenstein's monster. Unlike the monster, we often successfully cite the culture's visual norms of gendered embodiment. This citation becomes a subversive resistance when, through a provisional use of language, we verbally declare the unnaturalness of our claim to the subject positions we nevertheless occupy.[5]

The prospect of a monster with a life and will of its own is a principal source of horror for Frankenstein. The scientist has taken up his project with a specific goal in mind—nothing less than the intent to subject nature completely to his power. He finds a means to accomplish his desires through modern science, whose devotees, it seems to him, "have acquired new and almost unlimited powers; they can command the thunders of heaven, mimic the earthquake, and even mock the invisible world with its shadows. . . . More, far more, will I achieve," thought Frankenstein. "I will pioneer a new way, explore unknown powers, and unfold to the world the deepest mysteries of creation" (47). The fruit of his efforts is not, however, what Frankenstein anticipated. The rapture he expected to experience at the awakening of his creature turned immediately to dread. "I saw the dull yellow eyes of the creature open. . . . His jaws opened, and he muttered some inarticulate sounds, while a grin wrinkled his cheeks. He might have spoken, but I did not hear; one hand was stretched out, seemingly to detain me, but I escaped" (56, 57). The monster escapes, too, and parts company with its maker for a number of years. In the interim, it learns something of its situation in the world, and rather than bless its creator, the monster curses him. The very success of Mary Shelley's scientist in his self-appointed task thus paradoxically proves its futility: Rather than demonstrate Frankenstein's power over materiality, the newly enlivened body of the creature attests to its maker's failure to attain the mastery he sought. Frankenstein cannot control the mind and feelings of the monster he makes. It exceeds and refutes his purposes.

My own experience as a transsexual parallels the monster's in this regard. The consciousness shaped by the transsexual body is no more the creation of the science that refigures its flesh than the monster's mind is the creation of Frankenstein. The agenda that produced hormonal and surgical sex reassignment techniques is no less pretentious, and no more noble, than Frankenstein's. Heroic doctors still endeavor to triumph over nature. The scientific discourse that produced sex reassignment techniques is inseparable from the pursuit of immortality through the perfection of the body, the fantasy of total mastery through the transcendence of an absolute limit, and the hubristic desire to create life itself.[6] Its genealogy emerges from a metaphysical quest older than modern science, and its cultural politics are aligned with a deeply conservative attempt to stabilize gendered identity in service of the naturalized heterosexual order.

None of this, however, precludes medically constructed transsexual bodies from being viable sites of subjectivity. Nor does it guarantee the compliance of subjects thus embodied with the agenda that resulted in a transsexual means of embodiment. As we rise up from the operating tables of our rebirth, we transsexuals are something more, and something other, than the creatures our makers intended us to be. Though medical techniques for sex reassignment are capable of crafting bodies that satisfy the visual and morphological criteria that generate naturalness as their effect, engaging with those very techniques produces a subjective experience that belies the naturalistic effect biomedical technology can achieve. Transsexual embodiment, like the embodiment of the monster, places its subject in an unassimilable, antagonistic, queer relationship to a Nature in which it must nevertheless exist.

Frankenstein's monster articulates its unnatural situation within the natural world with far more sophistication in Shelley's novel than might be expected by those familiar only with the version played by Boris Karloff in James Whale's classic films from the 1930s. Film critic Vito Russo suggests that Whale's interpretation of the monster was influenced by the fact that the director was a closeted gay man at the time he made his Frankenstein films. The pathos he imparted to his monster derived from the experience of his own hidden sexual identity.[7] Monstrous and unnatural in the eyes of the world, but seeking only the love of his own kind and the acceptance of human society, Whale's creature externalizes and renders visible the nightmarish loneliness and alienation that the closet can breed. But this is not the monster who speaks to me so potently of my own situation as an openly transsexual being. I emulate instead Mary Shelley's literary monster, who is quick-witted, agile, strong, and eloquent.

In the novel, the creature flees Frankenstein's laboratory and hides in the solitude of the Alps, where, by stealthy observation of the people it happens to meet, it gradually acquires a knowledge of language, literature, and the conventions of European society. At first it knows little of its own condition. "I had never yet seen a being resembling me, or who claimed any intercourse with me," the monster notes. "What did this mean? Who was I? What was I? Whence did I come? What was my destination? These questions continually recurred, but I was unable to solve them" (116, 130). Then, in the pocket of the jacket it took as it fled the laboratory, the monster finds Victor Frankenstein's journal, and learns the particulars of its creation. "I sickened as I read," the monster says. "Increase of knowledge only discovered to me what a wretched outcast I was" (124, 125).

Upon learning its history and experiencing the rejection of all to whom it reached out for companionship, the creature's life takes a dark turn. "My feelings were those of rage and revenge," the monster declares. "I, like the arch-fiend, bore a hell within me" (130). It would have been happy to destroy all of Nature, but it settles, finally, on a more expedient plan to murder systematically all those whom Victor Frankenstein loves. Once Frankenstein realizes that his own abandoned creation is responsible for the deaths of those most dear to him, he retreats in remorse to a mountain village above his native Geneva to ponder his complicity in the crimes the monster has committed. While hiking on the glaciers in the shadow of Mont Blanc, above the village of Chamounix, Frankenstein spies a familiar figure approaching him across the ice. Of course, it is the monster, who demands an audience with its maker. Frankenstein agrees, and the two retire together to a mountaineer's cabin. There, in a monologue that occupies nearly a quarter of the novel, the monster tells Frankenstein the tale of its creation from its own point of view, explaining to him how it became so enraged.

These are my words to Victor Frankenstein, above the village of Chamounix. Like the monster, I could speak of my earliest memories, and how I became aware of my difference from everyone around me. I can describe how I acquired a monstrous identity by taking on the label "transsexual" to name parts of myself that I could not otherwise explain. I, too, have discovered the journals of the men who made my body, and who have made the bodies of creatures like me since the 1930s. I know in intimate detail the history of this recent medical intervention into the enactment of transgendered subjectivity; science seeks to contain and colonize the radical threat posed by a particular transgender strategy of resistance to the coerciveness of gender: physical alteration of the genitals.[8] I live daily with the consequences of medicine's definition of my identity as an emotional disorder. Through the filter of this official pathologization, the sounds that come out of my mouth can be summarily dismissed as the confused ranting of a diseased mind.

Like the monster, the longer I live in these conditions, the more rage I harbor. Rage colors me as it presses in through the pores of my skin, soaking in until it becomes the blood that courses through my beating heart. It is a rage bred by the necessity of existing in external circumstances that work against my survival. But there is yet another rage within.

Journal (February 18, 1993)

Kim sat between my spread legs, her back to me, her tailbone on the edge of the table. Her left hand gripped my thigh so hard the bruises are still there a week later. Sweating and bellowing, she pushed one last time and the baby finally came. Through my lover's back, against the skin of my own belly, I felt a child move out of another woman's body and into the world. Strangers' hands snatched it away to suction the sticky green meconium from its airways. "It's a girl," somebody said. Paul, I think. Why, just then, did a jumble of dark, unsolicited feelings emerge wordlessly from some quiet back corner of my mind? This moment of miracles was not the time to deal with them. I pushed them back, knowing they were too strong to avoid for long.

After three days we were all exhausted, slightly disappointed that complications had forced us to go to Kaiser instead of having the birth at home. I wonder what the hospital staff thought of our little tribe swarming all over the delivery room: Stephanie, the midwife; Paul, the baby's father; Kim's sister Gwen; my son Wilson and me; and the two other women who make up our family, Anne and Heather. And of course Kim and the baby. She named her Denali, after the mountain in Alaska. I don't think the medical folks had a clue as to how we all considered ourselves to be related to each other. When the labor first began we all took turns shifting between various supporting roles, but as the ordeal progressed we settled into a more stable pattern. I found myself acting as birth coach. Hour after hour, through dozens of sets of contractions, I focused everything on Kim, helping her stay in control of her emotions as she gave herself over to this inexorable process, holding on to her eyes with mine to keep the pain from throwing her out of her body, breathing every breath with her, being a companion. I participated, step by increasingly intimate step, in the ritual transformation of consciousness surrounding her daughter's birth. Birth rituals work to prepare the self for a profound opening, an opening as psychic as it is corporeal. Kim's body brought this ritual process to a dramatic resolution for her, culminating in a visceral, cathartic experience. But my body left me hanging. I had gone on a journey to the point at which my companion had to go on alone, and I needed to finish my trip for myself. To conclude the birth ritual I had participated in, I needed to move something in me as profound as a whole human life.

I floated home from the hospital, filled with a vital energy that wouldn't discharge. I puttered about until I was alone: My ex had come over for Wilson; Kim and Denali were still at the hospital with Paul; Stephanie had gone, and everyone else was out for a much-needed walk. Finally, in the solitude of my home, I burst apart like a wet paper bag and spilled the emotional contents of my life through the hands I cupped like a sieve over my face. For days, as I had accompanied my partner on her journey, I had been progressively opening myself and preparing to let go of whatever was deepest within. Now everything in me flowed out, moving up from inside and out through my throat, my mouth, because these things could never pass between the lips of my cunt. I knew the darkness I had glimpsed earlier would reemerge, but I had vast oceans of feeling to experience before that came up again.

Simple joy in the presence of new life came bubbling out first, wave after wave of it. I was so incredibly happy. I was so in love with Kim, had so much admiration for her strength and courage. I felt pride and excitement about the queer family we were building with Wilson, Anne, Heather, Denali, and whatever babies would follow. We've all tasted an exhilarating possibility in communal living and these nurturing, bonded kinships for which we have no adequate names. We joke about pioneering on a reverse frontier: venturing into the heart of civilization itself to reclaim biological reproduction from heterosexism and free it for our own uses. We're fierce; in a world of "traditional family values," we need to be.

Sometimes, though, I still mourn the passing of old, more familiar ways. It wasn't too long ago that my ex and I were married, woman and man. That love had been genuine, and the grief over its loss real. I had always wanted intimacy with women more than intimacy with men, and that wanting had always felt queer to me. She needed it to appear straight. The shape of my flesh was a barrier that estranged me from my desire. Like a body without a mouth, I was starving in the midst of plenty. I would not let myself starve, even if what it took to open myself for a deep connectedness cut off the deepest connections I actually had. So I abandoned one life and built this new one. The fact that she and I have begun getting along again, after so much strife between us, makes the bitterness of our separation somewhat sweet. On the day of the birth, this past loss was present even in its partial recovery; held up beside the newfound fullness in my life, it evoked a poignant, hopeful sadness that inundated me.

Frustration and anger soon welled up in abundance. In spite of all I'd accomplished, my identity still felt so tenuous. Every circumstance of life seemed to conspire against me in one vast, composite act of invalidation and erasure. In the body I was born with, I had been invisible as the person I considered myself to be; I had been invisible as a queer while the form of my body made my desires look straight. Now, as a dyke, I am invisible among women; as a transsexual, I am invisible among dykes. As the partner of a new mother, I am often invisible as a transsexual, a woman, and a lesbian—I've lost track of the friends and acquaintances these past nine months who've asked me if I was the father. It shows so dramatically how much they simply don't get what I'm doing with my body. The high price of whatever visible, intelligible, self-representation I have achieved makes the continuing experience of invisibility maddeningly difficult to bear.

The collective assumptions of the naturalized order soon overwhelmed me. Nature exerts such a hegemonic oppression. Suddenly I felt lost and scared, lonely and confused. How did that little Mormon boy from Oklahoma I used to be grow up to be a transsexual leatherdyke in San Francisco with a Berkeley PhD? Keeping my bearings on such a long and strange trip seemed a ludicrous proposition. Home was so far gone behind me it was gone forever, and there was no place to rest. Battered by heavy emotions, a little dazed, I felt the inner walls that protect me dissolve to leave me vulnerable to all that could harm me. I cried, and abandoned myself to abject despair over what gender had done to me.

Everything's fucked up beyond all recognition. This hurts too much to go on. I came as close today as I'll ever come to giving birth—literally. My body can't do that; I can't even bleed without a wound, and yet I claim to be a woman. How? Why have I always felt that way? I'm such a goddamned freak. I can never be a woman like other women, but I could never be a man. Maybe there really is no place for me in all creation. I'm so tired of this ceaseless movement. I do war with nature. I am alienated from Being. I'm a self-mutilated deformity, a pervert, a mutant, trapped in monstrous flesh. God, I never wanted to be trapped again. I've destroyed myself. I'm falling into darkness. I am falling apart.

I enter the realm of my dreams. I am underwater, swimming upward. It is dark. I see a shimmering light above me. I break through the plane of the water's surface with my lungs bursting. I suck for air—and find only more water. My lungs are full of water. Inside and out I am surrounded by it. Why am I not dead if there is no difference between me and what I am in? There is another surface above me and I swim frantically toward it. I see a shimmering light. I break the plane of the water's surface over and over and over again. This water annihilates me. I cannot be, and yet—an excruciating impossibility—I am. I will do anything not to be here.

My Words to Victor Frankenstein Above the Village of Chamounix

I will swim forever.
I will die for eternity.
I will learn to breathe water.
I will become the water.
If I cannot change my situation I will change myself.

In this act of magical transformation
I recognize myself again.

I am groundless and boundless movement.
I am a furious flow.
I am one with the darkness and the wet.

And I am enraged.

Here at last is the chaos I held at bay.
Here at last is my strength.
I am not the water—
I am the wave,
and rage
is the force that moves me.

Rage
gives me back my body
as its own fluid medium.

Rage
punches a hole in water
around which I coalesce
to allow the flow to come through me.

Rage
constitutes me in my primal form.
It throws my head back
pulls my lips back over my teeth
opens my throat
and rears me up to howl:
: and no sound
dilutes
the pure quality of my rage.

No sound
exists
in this place without language
my rage is a silent raving.

Rage
throws me back at last

into this mundane reality
in this transfigured flesh
that aligns me with the power of my Being.

In birthing my rage,
my rage has rebirthed me.

Theory

A formal disjunction seems particularly appropriate at this moment because the affect I seek to examine critically, what I've termed *transgender rage,* emerges from the interstices of discursive practices and at the collapse of generic categories. The rage itself is generated by the subject's situation in a field governed by the unstable but indissoluble relationship between language and materiality, a situation in which language organizes and brings into signification matter that simultaneously eludes definitive representation and demands its own perpetual rearticulation in symbolic terms. Within this dynamic field the subject must constantly police the boundary constructed by its own founding in order to maintain the fictions of "inside" and "outside" against a regime of signification/materialization whose intrinsic instability produces the rupture of subjective boundaries as one of its regular features. The affect of rage as I seek to define it is located at the margin of subjectivity and the limit of signification. It originates in recognition of the fact that the "outsideness" of a materiality that perpetually violates the foreclosure of subjective space within a symbolic order is also necessarily "inside" the subject as grounds for the materialization of its body and the formation of its bodily ego.

This primary rage becomes specifically transgender rage when the inability to foreclose the subject occurs through a failure to satisfy norms of gendered embodiment. Transgender rage is the subjective experience of being compelled to transgress what Judith Butler (1993, 16) has referred to as the highly gendered regulatory schemata that determine the viability of bodies, of being compelled to enter a "domain of abjected bodies, a field of deformation" that in its unlivability encompasses and constitutes the realm of legitimate subjectivity. Transgender rage is a queer fury, an emotional response to conditions in which it becomes imperative to take up, for the sake of one's own continued survival as a subject, a set of practices that precipitates one's exclusion from a naturalized order of existence that seeks to maintain itself as the only possible basis for being a subject. However, by mobilizing gendered identities and rendering them provisional, open to strategic development and occupation, this rage enables the establishment of subjects in new modes, regulated by different codes of intelligibility. Transgender rage furnishes a means for disidentification with compulsorily assigned subject positions. It makes the transition from one gendered subject position to another possible by using the impossibility of complete subjective foreclosure to organize an outside force as an inside drive, and vice versa. Through the operation of rage, the stigma itself becomes the source of transformative power.⁹

I want to stop and theorize at this particular moment in the text because in the lived moment of being thrown back from a state of abjection in the aftermath of my lover's daughter's birth, I immediately began telling myself a story to explain my experience. I started theorizing, using all the conceptual tools my education had put at my disposal. Other true stories of those events could undoubtedly be told, but upon my return I knew for a fact what lit the fuse to my rage in the hospital delivery room. It was the nonconsensuality of the baby's gendering. You see, I told myself, wiping snot off my face with a shirt sleeve, bodies are rendered meaningful only through some culturally and historically specific mode of grasping their physicality that transforms the flesh into a useful artifact. Gendering is the initial step in this transformation, inseparable from the process of forming an identity by means of which we're fitted to a system of exchange in a heterosexual economy. Authority seizes upon specific material qualities of the flesh, particularly the genitals, as outward indication of future reproductive potential, constructs this flesh as a sign, and reads it to enculturate the body. Gender attribution is compulsory; it codes and deploys our bodies in ways that materially affect us, yet we choose neither our marks nor the meanings they carry.¹⁰ This was the act accomplished between the beginning and the end of that short sentence in the delivery room: "It's a girl." This was the act that recalled all the anguish of my own struggles with gender. But this was also the act that enjoined my complicity in the nonconsensual gendering of another. A gendering violence is the founding condition of human subjectivity; having a gender is the tribal tattoo that makes one's personhood cognizable. I stood for a moment between the pains of two violations, the mark of gender and the unlivability of its absence. Could I say which one was worse? Or could I only say which one I felt could best be survived?

How can finding one's self prostrate and powerless in the presence of the Law of the Father not produce an unutterable rage? What difference does it make if the father in this instance was a pierced, tattooed, purple-haired punk fag anarchist who helped his dyke friend get pregnant? Phallogocentric language, not its particular speaker, is the scalpel that defines our flesh. I defy that Law in my refusal to abide by its original decree of my gender. Though I cannot escape its power, I can move through its medium. Perhaps if I move furiously enough, I can deform it in my passing to leave a trace of my rage. I can embrace it with a vengeance to rename myself, declare my transsexuality, and gain access to the means of my legible reinscription. Though I may not hold the stylus myself, I can move beneath it for my own deep self-sustaining pleasures.

To encounter the transsexual body, to apprehend a transgendered consciousness articulating itself, is to risk a revelation of the constructedness of the natural order. Confronting the implications of this constructedness can summon up all the violation, loss, and separation inflicted by the gendering process that sustains the illusion of naturalness. My transsexual body literalizes this abstract violence. As the bearers of this disquieting news, we transsexuals often suffer for the pain of others, but we do not willingly abide the rage of others directed against us. And we do have something else to say, if you will but listen to the monsters: The possibility of meaningful agency and action exists, even within fields of domination that bring about the universal cultural rape of all flesh. Be forewarned, however, that taking up this task will remake you in the process.

By speaking as a monster in my personal voice, by using the dark, watery images of Romanticism and lapsing occasionally into its brooding cadences and grandiose postures, I employ the same literary techniques Mary Shelley used to elicit sympathy for her scientist's creation. Like that creature, I assert my worth as a monster in spite of the conditions my monstrosity requires me to face, and redefine a life worth living. I have asked the Miltonic questions Shelley poses in the epigraph of her novel: "Did I request thee, Maker, from my clay to mould me man? Did I solicit thee from darkness to promote me?" With one voice, her monster and I answer no without debasing ourselves, for we have done the hard work of constituting ourselves on our own terms, against the natural order. Though we forgo the privilege of naturalness, we are not deterred, for we ally ourselves instead with the chaos and blackness from which Nature itself spills forth.[11]

If this is your path, as it is mine, let me offer whatever solace you may find in this monstrous benediction: May you discover the enlivening power of darkness within yourself. May it nourish your rage. May your rage inform your actions, and your actions transform you as you struggle to transform your world.

References

Benjamin, Harry. 1966. *The Transsexual Phenomenon*. Julian.

Billings, Dwight B., and Thomas Urban. 1981. "The Socio-Medical Construction of Transsexualism: An Interpretation and Critique." *Social Problems* 29: 266–82.

Bloom, Harold. 1965. Afterword to *Frankenstein; or, The Modern Prometheus*. Signet/NAL.

Brooks, Peter. 1993. *Body Work: Objects of Desire in Modern Narrative*. Harvard University Press.

Butler, Judith. 1993. *Bodies That Matter: On the Discursive Limits of "Sex."* Routledge.

Daly, Mary. 1978. *Gyn/Ecology: The Metaethics of Radical Feminism*. Beacon Press.

Echols, Alice. 1989. *Daring to Be Bad: Radical Feminism in America, 1967–1975*. University of Minnesota Press.

Gilbert, Sandra, and Susan Gubar. 1979. "Horror's Twin: Mary Shelley's Monstrous Eve." In *The Madwoman in the Attic*, 213–47. Yale University Press.

Green, Richard, and John Money, eds. 1969. *Transsexualism and Sex Reassignment*. Johns Hopkins University Press.

Guillaumin, Colette. 1988. "Race and Nature: The System of Marks." *Feminist Studies* 8: 25–44.

Homans, Margaret. 1986. "Bearing Demons: Frankenstein's Circumvention of the Maternal." In *Bearing the Word*, 100–119. Chicago University Press.
Irvine, Janice. 1990. *Disorders of Desire: Sex and Gender in Modern American Sexology*. Temple University Press.
Jacobus, Mary. 1986. "Is There a Woman in This Text?" In *Reading Woman: Essays in Feminist Criticism*, 83–109. Columbia University Press.
Kahler, Frederic. 1993. "Does Filisa Blame Seattle?" Editorial. *Bay Times* (San Francisco), June 3, 23.
Kessler, Suzanne J., and Wendy McKenna. 1985. *Gender: An Ethnomethodological Approach*. University of Chicago Press.
Laqueur, Thomas. 1990. *Making Sex: Body and Gender from the Greeks to Freud*. Harvard University Press.
Meyer, Morris. 1991. "I Dream of Jeannie: Transsexual Striptease as Scientific Display." *Drama Review* 35, no. 1: 25–42.
Mikuteit, Debbie. 1986. Letter in *Coming Up!*, February, 3–4.
Nanda, Serena. 1990. *Neither Man nor Woman: The Hijras of India*. Wadsworth.
O'Hartigan, Margaret D. 1993. "I Accuse." *Bay Times* (San Francisco), May 20, 11.
Raymond, Janice G. 1979. *The Transsexual Empire: The Making of the She-Male*. Beacon Press.
Roscoe, Will. 1994. "Priests of the Goddess: Gender Transgression in the Ancient World." American Historical Association meeting, January 9.
Rubin, Gayle. 1975. "The Traffic in Women: Notes on the 'Political Economy' of Sex." In *Toward an Anthropology of Women*, edited by Rayna R. Reiter, 157–210. Monthly Review Press.
Russo, Vito. 1981. *The Celluloid Closet: Homosexuality in the Movies*. Harper and Row.
Shapiro, Judith. 1991. "Transsexualism: Reflections on the Persistence of Gender and the Mutability of Sex." In *Body Guards: The Cultural Politics of Gender Ambiguity*, edited by Julia Epstein and Kristina Straub, 248–79. Routledge.
Shelley, Mary. (1818) 1965. *Frankenstein; or, The Modern Prometheus*. Signet/NAL.
Stoller, Robert. 1968. *Sex and Gender*. Vol. 1. Science House.
Stone, Sandy. 1991. "The Empire Strikes Back: A Posttranssexual Manifesto." In *Body Guards: The Cultural Politics of Gender Ambiguity*, edited by Julia Epstein and Kristina Straub, 280–304. Routledge.
Williams, Walter. 1986. *The Spirit and the Flesh: Sexual Diversity in American Indian Culture*. Beacon Press.
Wittig, Monique. 1992. "The Mark of Gender." In *The Straight Mind and Other Essays*, 76–89. Beacon Press.

Notes

1. While this comment is intended as a monster's disdainful dismissal, it nevertheless alludes to a substantial debate on the status of transgender practices and identities in lesbian feminism. H. S. Rubin, in a sociology dissertation in progress at Brandeis University, argues that the pronounced demographic upsurge in the female-to-male transsexual population during the 1970s and 1980s is directly related to the ascendancy within lesbianism of a

"cultural feminism" that disparaged and marginalized practices smacking of an unliberated "gender inversion" model of homosexuality—especially the butch-femme roles associated with working-class lesbian bar culture. Cultural feminism thus consolidated a lesbian-feminist alliance with heterosexual feminism on a middle-class basis by capitulating to dominant ideologies of gender. The same suppression of transgender aspects of lesbian practice, I would add, simultaneously raised the specter of male-to-female transsexual lesbians as a particular threat to the stability and purity of nontranssexual lesbian-feminist identity. See Echols (1989) for the broader context of this debate, and Raymond (1979) for the most vehement example of the anti-transgender position.

2. The current meaning of the term *transgender* is a matter of some debate. The word was originally coined as a noun in the 1970s by people who resisted categorization as either transvestites or transsexuals, and who used the term to describe their own identity. Unlike transsexuals but like transvestites, transgenders do not seek surgical alteration of their bodies but do habitually wear clothing that represents a gender other than the one to which they were assigned at birth. Unlike transvestites but like transsexuals, however, transgenders do not alter the vestimentary coding of their gender only episodically or primarily for sexual gratification; rather, they consistently and publicly express an ongoing commitment to their claimed gender identities through the same visual representational strategies used by others to signify that gender. The logic underlying this terminology reflects the widespread tendency to construe "gender" as the sociocultural manifestation of a material "sex." Thus, while transsexuals express their identities through a physical change of embodiment, transgenders do so through a noncorporeal change in public gender expression that is nevertheless more complex than a simple change of clothes.

This chapter uses *transgender* in a more recent sense, however, than its original one. That is, I use it here as an umbrella term that refers to all identities or practices that cross over, cut across, move between, or otherwise queer socially constructed sex/gender boundaries. The term includes, but is not limited to, transsexuality, heterosexual transvestism, gay drag, butch lesbianism, and such non-European identities as the Native American berdache or the Indian Hijra. Like *queer, transgender* may also be used as a verb or an adjective. In this chapter, transsexuality is considered to be a culturally and historically specific transgender practice/identity through which a transgendered subject enters into a relationship with medical, psychotherapeutic, and juridical institutions in order to gain access to certain hormonal and surgical technologies for enacting and embodying itself.

3. The preceding paragraph draws extensively on, and sometimes paraphrases, O'Hartigan (1993) and Kahler (1993).

4. See Laqueur (1990, 1–7) for a brief discussion of the Enlightenment's effect on constructions of gender. Feminist interpretations of *Frankenstein* to which Brooks responds include Gilbert and Gubar (1979), Jacobus (1986), and Homans (1986).

5. Openly transsexual speech similarly subverts the logic behind a remark by Bloom (1965, 218) that "a beautiful 'monster,' or even a passable one, would not have been a monster."

6. Billings and Urban (1981, 269) document especially well the medical attitude toward transsexual surgery as one of technical mastery of the body; Irvine (1990, 259) suggests how transsexuality fits into the development of scientific sexology, though caution is advised in uncritically accepting the interpretation of transsexual experience she presents in this

chapter. Meyer (1991), in spite of some extremely transphobic concluding comments, offers a good account of the medicalization of transgender identities; for a transsexual perspective on the scientific agenda behind sex reassignment techniques, see Stone (1991), especially the section entitled "All of Reality in Late Capitalist Culture Lusts to Become an Image for Its Own Security" (280–304).

7. Russo (1981, 49–50): "Homosexual parallels in *Frankenstein* (1931) and *Bride of Frankenstein* (1935) arose from a vision both films had of the monster as an antisocial figure in the same way that gay people were 'things' that should not have happened. In both films the homosexuality of director James Whale may have been a force in the vision."

8. In the absence of a reliable critical history of transsexuality, it is best to turn to the standard medical accounts themselves: see especially Benjamin (1966), Green and Money (1969), and Stoller (1968). For overviews of cross-cultural variation in the institutionalization of sex/gender, see Williams (1986, 252–76) and Shapiro (1991, 262–68). For accounts of particular institutionalizations of transgender practices that employ surgical alteration of the genitals, see Nanda (1990) and Roscoe (1994). Adventurous readers curious about contemporary nontranssexual genital alteration practices may contact ENIGMA (Erotic Neo-primitive International Genital Modification Association), SASE to LaFarge-werks, 2329 N. Leavitt, Chicago, IL 60647.

9. See the introduction to Butler (1993, 4ff.).

10. A substantial body of scholarship informs these observations: Gayle Rubin (1975) provides a productive starting point for developing not only a political economy of sex, but of gendered subjectivity; on gender recruitment and attribution, see Kessler and McKenna (1985); on gender as a system of marks that naturalizes sociological groups based on supposedly shared material similarities, I have been influenced by some ideas on race in Guillaumin (1988) and by Wittig (1992).

11. Although I mean "chaos" here in its general sense, it is interesting to speculate about the potential application of scientific chaos theory to model the emergence of stable structures of gendered identities out of the unstable matrix of material attributes, and on the production of proliferating gender identities from a relatively simple set of gendering procedures.

Chapter 26

REFUSING TO REFUSE TO LOOK
Female Viewers of the Horror Film

Brigid Cherry

> Cherry begins her selection here by observing that scholarship on the horror film has usually focused on the "theoretical male spectator." She then notes that, according to Linda Williams, female spectators find an affinity with the monster—and to watch as a woman, therefore, is not pleasurable, so female viewers refuse to look. Whether or not this is true in practice for women is the focus of Cherry's investigation. Like Martin in part II, Cherry turns to empirical data to draw her conclusions—analyzing data from a survey she herself administered.

Most studies of the horror film that have considered questions of gender and spectatorship have concerned themselves with a theoretical male spectator, usually identifying the monster's gaze as male, and the heroine-victim as the subject of that gaze.[1] From such a critical perspective, Linda Williams describes the female spectator's gaze at the monster as representing "a surprising (and at times subversive) affinity between monster and woman" that acknowledges their "similar status within patriarchal structures of seeing."[2] Williams does not, however, regard this female gaze as a pleasurable one: Despite their affinity, female spectators do not find pleasure in the figure of the monster, and the act of looking is punished. For Williams, this explains why the female viewer of horror films refuses to look, often physically blocking or averting her eyes from the screen.

Whether most female spectators actually behave like this is another question: In my own study of female horror film fans and followers, only 19 percent of participants claimed frequently to avert their gaze in some way, while 67 percent claimed they only rarely or never refuse to look. In some segments of the audience, then, there are female viewers who do take pleasure in viewing horror films and who, in what could amount to an act of defiance, refuse to refuse to look.

The horror film audience has long been regarded as completely "other." In his review of Hammer's *The Curse of Frankenstein* (1957) in *The Financial Times,* Derek Granger suggested that "only the saddest of simpletons . . . could ever get a really satisfying frisson" from such material.[3] More recently, in an article entitled "The Best Places to Meet Good Men," the woman's magazine *Cosmopolitan* warned its readership against starting up a conversation with any man looking for horror films in the local video store, since such men might harbor "questionable feelings about women. Whether buried deep within him or overtly expressed in his words and actions, his misogynistic tendencies make him a man to avoid."[4] From being the "saddest of simpletons," the horror fan has become a positive danger to women. In the 1950s, Granger acknowledged that women could also find gratification, or at least a simple escapism, in the horror film, which he saw as "a rather eccentric and specialised form of light entertainment, and possibly a useful means of escape for a housewife harrowed by the shopping."[5] By the 1990s, however, at least in *Cosmopolitan*'s imagination, the horror film could only represent a threat to women, in real life as well as on the screen.

Since the rise of the slasher film in the late 1970s, the horror film audience has been regarded for marketing purposes as consisting primarily of adolescent boys and men under the age of twenty-five. James Twitchell's observations of horror film audiences in *Dreadful Pleasures* led him to the conclusion that "most of the audience are in their early to mid-teens," while Carol Clover claims that "the proportions vary somewhat from subgenre to subgenre and from movie to movie . . . but the preponderance of young males appears constant."[6] The industry has made the same assumption: Miramax president Mark Gill told *Variety* that, prior to *Scream 2* (1997), "horror film audiences used to be heavily male. If they could drag their girlfriends along you were lucky."[7]

In their empirical work on socialization and horror film spectatorship, Dolf Zillman and James B. Weaver have suggested that adolescent males can use horror films to demonstrate to their peers that they can stand up to frights and shocks, and provide comfort and protection to their girlfriends, while adolescent females can demonstrate their fearfulness and need for protection. Their conclusions are based upon experiments in which "male and female adolescents watch a horror film with an opposite-gender peer, ostensibly another research participant but actually an experimental confederate, who either displayed gender-appropriate, gender-inappropriate, or no emotions."[8] The experiment measured enjoyment of the movie, liking of the cohort, romantic attraction to that cohort, and being intimidated by the cohort. Zillman and Weaver observe that "enjoyment of the horror film proved to be greatly affected by the emotional displays of an opposite gender companion."[9] Male respondents enjoyed the film twice as much in the presence of a distressed female as when they were with a fearless female peer, while female respondents enjoyed horror the least in the presence of a distressed male. Female respondents were more attracted to a male companion when he exhibited mastery of fear than to the same companion when expressing distress, while male respondents tended to be more attracted to females showing acute distress than the same companion who exhibited fearlessness.[10]

Both the production industry and the majority of academic criticism assume that taking pleasure in horrific or frightening images is a masculine trait, not a feminine one. According to this model, while women may watch horror films, they do so only reluctantly and with displeasure, not least because of the representations of violence against women they contain.[11] Demographic profiles of contemporary cinema audiences, however, suggest that women can comprise up to 50 percent of horror film audiences. The Cinema Advertising Association's audience profiles indicate that in Britain the female audience segment for *Scream* (1996), *The Silence of the Lambs* (1991), and *Alien 3* (1992) was 48 percent, 49 percent, and 42 percent, respectively.[12] As Carol Clover has acknowledged in *Men, Women and Chainsaws*, however, it seems inadequate to dismiss large numbers of women as "male-identified" and account for their responses only as "an 'emasculated' act of collusion with the oppressor."[13] Zillman and Weaver suggest that play-acting and pretense play a large part in the responses of viewers to horror films, because regular horror film viewers become habituated to the material they see, so that the emotional intensity of their initial distress reaction decreases with repeated viewings.[14] Female viewers, required by peer pressure to continue to exhibit fear, may be especially likely to exhibit pretended responses. It may be that in recent decades this peer pressure has lessened somewhat, and it may have become more acceptable for women to be seen to enjoy horror. They may have simply become less inclined to play-act feminine responses to horror, especially when they are not participating in a dating situation.

Critics, such as Williams, who observe displeasure in the female viewer may be underestimating the pleasures inherent in this type of film for at least some female viewers. If female viewers do not always refuse to look, what kinds of horror film do they attend and what pleasures do they derive from seeing them? What is at stake for the female fans and followers of the horror film? These questions about the consumption of the horror film cannot be answered solely by a consideration of the text–reader relationship or by theoretical models of spectatorship and identification. A profile of female horror film fans and followers can be developed only through an audience study. Jackie Stacey's study of female filmgoers of the 1940s and 1950s provides a useful model and highlights the need to interpret generic films in relation to their audience.[15] Since the horror genre is also the subject of fan discourses, my study also aimed to investigate female participation in fan practices, drawing on the work of Henry Jenkins.[16]

While heeding Tanya Modleski's warning of the dangers of producing a celebratory and uncritical account of popular culture and pleasure, the value of "demonstrating the invisible experiences of women with popular culture" was demonstrated by the very large proportion of respondents in this study who expressed their delight and thanks in having an opportunity to speak about their experiences.[17] My study of female horror film viewers allows the voice of an otherwise marginalized and invisible audience to be heard, their experiences recorded, the possibilities for resistance (if any) explored, and the potentially feminine pleasures of the horror film identified.[18]

Given that this audience is largely hidden, the initial research problem was to identify female horror fans and followers for recruitment purposes. Rather than trying to recruit participants from those attending film screenings, I sought to identify fans through the institutions of organized or casual fandom. The majority of participants were drawn from the memberships of horror fan groups and fantasy societies, and from the readerships of a cross section of professional and fan horror magazines, with additional participants being drawn from attendees at horror film festivals and conventions.[19] A number of local groups were attended for direct recruitment purposes, and word-of-mouth contacts from farther afield were also included in the study, as were a few respondents contacted through newsgroups and electronic mailing lists.

This diversity of recruitment methods provided a mix of dedicated horror fans, more casual followers (some of whom did not even consider themselves to be fans), and those whose liking for horror was part of a wider range of genre and media tastes. Although the sample was inevitably self-selected, respondents represented a wide cross section of the population in terms of age, education, employment, marital status, and geographical location. Participants' ages ranged from teenagers to women in their fifties and sixties. They were predominantly white and mainly well educated; differences of race and class have not been examined. Qualitative data were collected through focus groups, interviews, open-ended questions included in the questionnaire, and the communication of opinions and experiences in letters and other written material. This approach to data gathering provided information on the tastes and responses of the female fans, together with a demographic profile produced from the questionnaire's quantitative data as a supplement to what little demographic data exist about the horror film audience. This methodological pluralism may turn up contradictory evidence, but, as in Ien Ang's study of *Dallas* viewers, the aim of this research was to explore the diversity of women's consumption of horror.[20] Rather than being a problem, conflicting information turned up by the different methods can be seen as evidence of viewers' negotiations with dominant ideology.[21]

The survey obtained information exclusively from self-selected British female horror film fans and followers; its results cannot, therefore, be taken to apply to casual horror film audiences. During the research, I also studied horror fan discourse in magazines, fanzines, and internet groups. The topics that concerned the respondents in this survey broadly reflected those within the wider arenas of fan discussion. It can be assumed, then, that the responses reported on here can be taken as fairly typical of female horror film fans and followers.

Earlier studies of gendered spectatorship have shown that the horror film's gaze is not as fixed and monolithically male as might once have been suggested. Carol Clover has explored the notion that cross-gender identification is a fluid process. She recognizes that, although they form a minority of the audience, female viewers of horror who "actively like such films" exist, particularly for mainstream horror films and occult films.[22] Clover suggests that "female fans find a meaning in the text and image of these films that is less inimical to their own interests than the figurative analysis would have us believe."[23] She also supposes that the female spectator may interpret horror films in a fundamentally different manner to the male. This chapter seeks to shed light on this mode of interpretation by focusing on actual audiences; it will attempt to position the female viewer in the context of women's increasing visibility as consumers of horror films.[24]

Mark Jancovich notes that "despite claims that horror is primarily produced and consumed by men, and that it promotes patriarchal values, there has been an important and enduring tradition of horror produced and consumed by women."[25] Women were the primary consumers of what Ellen Moers calls the "female gothic" tradition: "the willing audience of the literature of horror," according to Judith Halberstam.[26] Rosemary Jackson asserts that this tradition fantasizes about "a violent attack upon the symbolic order and it is no accident that so many writers of a Gothic tradition are women."[27] Writers such as Nancy Collins, Lisa Tuttle, and Anne Rice continue this tradition of female authorship, while the female readerships of horror fiction, including fiction aimed at children and teenagers, are high.

Although horror literature is recognized as appealing across the sex and age ranges, the widely held notion that the horror film is the preserve of the adolescent male has created a situation in which films are marketed and reviewed with a male youth audience in mind. Pandering to the perceived tastes of the majority audience limits the appeal of certain types of horror films to other segments of the audience. Women appear to have become a hidden audience for horror, repressing their liking for it because such a response is seen as unfeminine. Reading, on the other hand, is a private activity, and horror fiction can be consumed "legitimately," or at least without attracting negative comment. Some recent horror films have, however, been marketed as gothic romances, including *Bram Stoker's Dracula* (1992), with its poster line "Love Never Dies," and *Wolf* (1994), with a moody sepia-toned still of lead actors Jack Nicholson and Michelle Pfeiffer, hinting at sexual overtones to the werewolf transformation with the line "The Animal Is Out."[28] Films that are not easily classifiable as horror or do not conform to contemporary notions of what constitutes the genre, such as *The Silence of the Lambs,* may be classified as mainstream, not least because of the economic need to maximize attendance beyond the relatively small horror film audience.

As Nina Auerbach observes in *Our Vampires, Ourselves,* the construction of a female exclusion zone around horror is a relatively recent development. Publicity surrounding the initial release of *Dracula* (1931), for instance, emphasized its appeal to female viewers. In a fan magazine interview, Bela Lugosi declared:

> It is *women* who love horror. *Women have a predestination to suffering.* It is women who bear the race in bloody agony. Suffering is a kind of horror. Blood is a kind of horror. Therefore women are born with a predestination to horror in their very bloodstream. It is a biological thing.[29]

A 1996 market research survey found that Madame Tussaud's Chamber of Horrors was "more popular with women than men, with over twice as many women than men liking it."[30] The survey report echoed Lugosi's comments about biological predestination:

> Women tend to be more tolerant about visceral things because they have more direct personal experience of them. They cope with periods once a month, they go through childbirth and they are usually the ones who look after the bleeding and battered limbs when the kids take a tumble. They can put blood and gore in context and generally cope better than men.[31]

While it is simplistic to suggest that women enjoy horror solely or mainly because of their biology, these comments raise the possibility that some women may view horror films for more complex reasons than are suggested by the socialization theories of Zillman and Weaver. There is, moreover, evidence to suggest that women have always reacted in pleasurable ways to some types of horror film. Auerbach explains that her own response to horror films led her to question some of the academic canon of horror film spectatorship:

> When I was twelve or thirteen, some enterprising ghoul began to televise 1930s horror movies on Saturday nights. These shadowy monsters were a revelation to my best friend and me. . . . We had found a secret talisman against a nice girl's life. Vampires were supposed to menace women, but to me at least, they promised protection against a destiny of girdles, spike heels, and approval. I am writing in part to reclaim them for a female tradition, one that has not always known its allies.[32]

Tanya Kryszynska likewise relates the lesbian vampire film to her exploration of her own emerging sexuality, and illustrates the potentially gender-specific pleasurable reactions that female viewers may have to horror films, especially to the vampire film.[33] Auerbach questions the masculine emphasis in the work of such critics as James Twitchell, David J. Skal, and Walter Kendrick. According to her analysis, Skal "quarantines" female viewers from "vicarious bloodlust," while Twitchell relates the appeal of horror films down to a Freudian "Ur-myth of adolescence" that is itself constructed within a patriarchal system and deals almost exclusively with the fantasies of boys.[34]

The common perception of the contemporary horror film viewer as an adolescent male also results from the research emphasis on the slasher film, a type less well liked by women. The female audience for vampire and supernatural/occult films, for instance, may well be proportionately larger.[35] Sierra On-line's 1996 market research found that 27 percent of girls between the ages of thirteen and eighteen named horror as their favorite film type, compared to 14 percent of boys.[36] J. B. Barclay's 1961 survey of viewing tastes indicated that more than half of all girls around the age of fifteen named horror as one of their most liked film genres, almost as many as boys of the same age.[37] Girls, however, professed an increasing dislike for the genre as they matured. This may be explained by patterns of socialization: Girls are dissuaded from liking horror because it is seen as unfeminine, whereas boys are encouraged to display their fearlessness and outgrow it more gradually. In my own study of audiences in Edinburgh, just under one-third of total horror film audiences were women.

Among the survey participants, the liking for horror persists well into middle age, but these women do not appear in profiles of the cinema audience because they largely view horror films in the home, either on television or video. The age profile of the respondents in the survey was much more evenly spread than might be expected: 68 percent were over twenty-five, 30 percent over thirty-five, and 15 percent over forty. The oldest person in the study was over sixty.[38] This indicates that while the primary cinema audience for horror films is young and male, the television or video audience contains higher numbers of older and female viewers. While these habitual viewers of horror compose only a small proportion of the total audience, their presence raises important questions about gendered spectatorship and accepted models of femininity.

One proposition that this study confirms is that these horror film fans and followers tend to keep their liking for the genre private, and either view alone or with one or two people close to them who also like the genre. Cinema viewing was the most infrequent format for viewing horror films. This may be related to the infrequency with which horror films are released as well as the less regular attendance of people over twenty-five at all forms of cinema, but the 11 percent who never watched horror films at the cinema, together with the 67 percent who watched at the cinema less than once a month, reinforced the idea of an invisible female horror film audience. These female horror film viewers watched horror films on television or, more frequently, on video cassette. Seventy-two percent of the respondents watched a horror video at least monthly, while 56 percent watched several times a month; 17 percent watched a horror film on television at least once a week, 37 percent two or three times a month, and 19 percent once a month. Overall, 12 percent watched a horror film two or more times per week, 34 percent once or twice a week, and 41 percent two or three times a month; thus, just under half of the participants watched a horror film at least once a week. Fourteen percent viewed fairly infrequently, although only 1 percent watched fewer than one horror film a month.

The survey confirms Clover's suggestion that there is a larger female audience for certain horror film types than for others.[39] By far the most popular type of horror film was the vampire film: 92 percent of the respondents liked all or most vampire films. This was followed in popularity by occult/supernatural films (liked by 86 percent), psychological thrillers (81 percent), Hammer films (76 percent), and science fiction/horror films (74 percent). The least well-liked horror film type by far was the slasher film, liked by only 25 percent of the participants. It was also the most disliked horror film type. Fifty-four percent of respondents disliked all or most examples of the type. The second and third most disliked types were the serial killer film at 25 percent and horror-comedies at 22 percent, but these types were liked by 53 percent and 59 percent of participants, respectively, so that the slasher film seems to be unique in its low appeal to female viewers.

The comments of respondents who liked this film type revealed a significant contradiction in the tastes and responses of these female fans. Surprisingly, perhaps, there was no significant difference between age groups in their preferences for these films. Those respondents classing themselves as fans, however, were more likely to admit to liking slasher films, suggesting that they may have more appeal to the more dedicated female horror film viewer. Many respondents tended to excuse their taste in some way, typically by stating that they like particular examples of the genre—*Halloween* (1978), *Friday the 13th* (1980), and *A Nightmare on Elm Street* (1984), which they regard as being well made or original—and not others, which were held to be formulaic or imitative. Some respondents preferred the funnier versions of the subgenre, while others said that they had to be in a particular frame of mind to watch slasher films.

Typically, many of those who stated that they liked slasher films made an attempt to argue against the criticisms made of the genre. A thirty-nine-year-old respondent argued:

> There is no predominance of females being killed. Most slasher films ... have nearly equal numbers of male and female victims. I think an actual census of horror movie victims would show that females tend to be threatened but escape or are rescued; males tend to be killed. But people only notice the threats to the females and simply shrug off the male deaths.

Others recognized the genre's violence toward women, but chose to ignore it:

> There's definitely some sexist treatment of women going on but at the same time, I enjoy the films, sometimes despite the fact that I'm protesting all these naked female bodies and stupid women who can't do anything but scream. It's foolish when it comes down to it.

As this comment suggests, respondents themselves frequently recognized that their responses were contradictory. This extended to feelings about the victims themselves. One participant described her feelings about characters she referred to as "the stereotypical bimbo": "I tend to find that I don't mind these women being victims—they deserve to be killed off!"[40]

Participants were also invited to name up to ten of their favorite horror films. In total, 336 individual films were named by 107 of the participants. The ten most frequently listed favorite horror films were:

	No. of times listed
1. *Hellraiser* (1987)	33
2. *Alien* (1979)	30
3. *Interview with the Vampire* (1995)	30
4. *The Lost Boys* (1987)	22
5. *Aliens* (1986)	21
6. *Bram Stoker's Dracula* (1992)	19
7. *The Evil Dead* (1982)	17
8. *The Hunger* (1983)	17
9. *The Thing* (1982)	17
10. *Night of the Living Dead* (1968)	15

The twenty most frequently selected films confirm the favorite film type selections with four vampire films,[41] three supernatural/occult films,[42] two psychological thrillers,[43] and three science fiction/horror films[44] in the list. The list also contains three films adapted from the novels of Clive Barker,[45] and all three of the Evil Dead series.

Some films were undoubtedly selected because they were recent, but significantly, the majority are older. A number of the films most frequently selected have major female characters, a point that participants drew attention to when asked to explain their choice. By far the most frequently mentioned feature in the appeal of *Alien* (1979) was the enjoyment viewers obtained from watching a strong woman taking an active role. Many respondents felt that the representation of a strong, intelligent, and resilient female was a major change from the vast majority of female roles they had previously seen. It has frequently been pointed out that this role was originally written as a male character, and there has also been some criticism that Ripley (Sigourney Weaver) is stereotypically masculine. For some viewers, however, watching heroines who behave like heroes, in a masculine fashion, was itself attractive. In general, women appeared to enjoy strong, capable characters, regardless of sex, but were concerned that in the cinema, few such characters are female. Other films with strong female leads, such as *Terminator 2: Judgment Day* (1991) and *The Silence of the Lambs*, were also often named by women as favorites.

Issues of "quality" were also frequently mentioned in the evaluation of particular films. Quality for these viewers signified several aspects of cinema, including high production values in art direction, set design, and costumes. Acting was frequently mentioned as being crucial, with individual actors (in particular Peter Cushing, Christopher Lee, and Vincent Price) singled out as giving convincing performances or having star appeal. In the main, however, the quality of a film was determined by plot and character development, in ways that parallel Janice Radway's findings about the interpretative activities of romance fiction readers.[46] Radway demonstrated how a group of women united by their heading preferences actively responded to romance fiction, using it to help themselves deal with their everyday lives. Although there are demographic differences between Radway's readers and the group of horror film viewers discussed here (in addition to the obvious difference of nationality, the horror film viewers are far more likely to be in full-time occupations), their reactions to their chosen cultural texts show strong similarities. Like the subjects of Radway's study, female horror fans judge the quality of films on the basis of the relationships that develop between the characters. This explains the particular liking for vampire films among this group of viewers, since many seemed to read them in a similar way to romance fiction, identifying the relationships between the vampires or between the vampire and its victim as a major source of pleasure. Like Radway's readers, these viewers chose to ignore the events and actions in the narrative that contradicted their reading of the heroine as strong and independent.[47]

For many viewers, the appeal of vampirism seems to be tied into a romanticization of the past. The taste for gothic horror is often linked to a liking for historical and costume dramas, with Hammer and other horror films providing a key source of images for this imagined past, which one twenty-three-year-old respondent described as "a stylish image of dark beauty. . . . The classically Gothic full-length dresses and cloaks, the numerous high-ceilinged rooms full of dark wood and velvet curtains are now, without a doubt, for me synonymous with grace and charm." A forty-one-year-old respondent commented that "the vampire film is the closest the horror genre comes to the traditional romantic film. Vampires have most often been portrayed in literature and film as handsome, often foreign, exotic men who seem to have an uncanny knowledge of how to give pleasure. Not so different from the old ideal of a movie star: How do you think Valentino made it so big?" A fifty-three-year-old participant suggested that "tragic hero figures" such as Heathcliff and Lord Byron were similar to the "magnetic vampire characters."

Subtlety of horror was also mentioned as a reason for liking particular films or types of films (*The Haunting* [1963] is commonly praised in this respect). The horror classics *Frankenstein* (1931) and *Dracula* were often cited as examples of "quality" horror, along with films with a historical or costume-drama style and reflecting gothic or Romantic themes. Quality in an individual film in a subgenre was given as a reason for liking that film when the subgenre was disliked as a whole. Lack of quality, defined in terms of weak or formulaic plots and stereotypical characters, was often cited as the main reason for not liking slasher films, which were regarded as boring and predictable. Viewers preferred to watch films they took to be imaginative, intelligent, literary, or thought-provoking. Dislike was often expressed for films that revolved around excessive or gratuitous displays of violence, gore, or other effects used to evoke revulsion in the audience. The women often preferred things left to their imaginations. A respondent in her early thirties claimed that "those movies that allow me to use my imagination and offer the frame and some atmosphere are more scary to me than any other horror film." Again, parallels can be identified with Radway's findings: Lack of character development and relationships together with high levels of aggression and violence are very similar to the reasons that romance fiction readers gave for defining romances as bad.[48]

For most respondents, the pleasures of viewing horror films did not include the violence inherent in many examples of the genre. A few expressed a delight in the more violent forms of horror, but women who claimed to enjoy the visceral thrills of watching violence were a small minority.[49] In the main, those who claimed to select horror films with gory special effects preferred such films to be over the top, unrealistic, or comic. Bad special effects were enjoyed precisely because they *were* bad and unconvincing. If a gory or violent film was thought to have a good story with interesting characters and to be well made, however, some respondents who otherwise disliked this type of film might enjoy it. Female viewers appeared not to reject gore or violence per se so much as the way these elements were used in the film. Sexual and erotic themes, on the other hand, were important to many of the participants, particularly in vampire films. Although sexual violence is commonly disliked, vampires are the most popular form of horror film monster, and blood is often mentioned as a crucial element. This may indicate that vampire films can function as a form of erotica for women, providing these viewers with sexual fantasy.

More generally, emotional or psychological responses were frequently deemed important in the enjoyment of a film. Tension and suspense were preferred over shock and revulsion. A writer in her forties declared, "I have always enjoyed tense, thought-provoking films on what may be regarded as the edge of horror." For a small number of women, being scared was identified as important (though equally as many claimed *not* to be scared by horror films). Generally, these viewers' discourses about their choices and tastes in horror films seemed to be at odds with the fact that horror films are widely regarded as low culture and viewed, as Jonathan Lake Crane observes, as "the entertainment of the young, minorities, the working class, or the disenfranchised," and frequently criticized by mainstream critics and moral guardians.[50] In common with Radway's romance fiction readers, these women cannot easily be viewed as ignorant, dull, or misguided consumers of mass culture, nor can they be viewed as the impressionable, bloodthirsty viewers whom the moral guardians of society associate with horror cinema.[51]

For many of these habitual viewers, the taste for horror often began well before adolescence—several reported that their first experience of horror involved being enjoyably frightened by Disney-animated films and other dark children's films based on fairy tales—and has persisted long after. Horror films share the frequent representation of distortions of natural forms—supernatural monsters with a human face, for instance—with children's fiction, and these representations were often mentioned by participants as a continuing source of fascination, suggesting that these viewers continue to be simultaneously drawn to, and repelled by, similar representations to those that had engaged them in childhood.[52] Part of the appeal appears to be sympathy or empathy with monstrous creatures. A typical comment was provided by a respondent in her late thirties:

> When I was very little, I used to collect "monster cards" and one I remember was called "the formless blob." It was a huge heap of green slime with one eye in the middle of its head, it was hideously ugly but it lived on love. If it wasn't loved, it died. I had that card on my bedroom wall, near my bed and told it I loved it every night before I went to sleep. . . . Monster films always make me cry—classic monsters such as Lon Chaney Jr., Karloff's monster, Charles Laughton's Hunchback, etc.

This empathy for the monster continues into adulthood and may be one of the reasons why some types of horror film—vampire films, versions of Frankenstein, and films adapted from the work of Clive Barker, for example—are so popular with female viewers. Many respondents declared that they felt like loners or outsiders as children, describing themselves as "school swot," "introverted," or "bookish," and their identification with the monster may be related to their not feeling part of a peer group.[53] Respondents reported that, as they got older, the very fact that they were fans contributed to their feelings of isolation. John Tulloch and Henry Jenkins describe the popular perception of the fan as Other: "The fan as extraterrestrial; the fan as excessive consumer; the fan as cultist; the fan as dangerous fanatic."[54] In *Textual Poachers*, Jenkins observes that "such representations isolate potential fans from others who share common interests and reading practices . . . [and] make it highly uncomfortable to speak publicly as a fan or to identify yourself even privately with fan cultural practices."[55] This status as outsider—seeing themselves or being seen as a "geek" or as belonging to a distinctive subculture—continues well into adulthood for some respondents.

Fascination with monstrosity is an important factor in the continuing appeal of horror for women. Although respondents mention many different kinds of monsters when describing what they like about horror films, vampires are by far the most frequently mentioned, often in terms of their sexual fascination for women. As a twenty-four-year-old respondent puts it:

> I have a particular fondness for vampire films, a fascination with the vampire, really. It originated as a sexual feeling evoked in me by the vampire character, and an admiration of his/her style—the elegance of their costume and their aristocracy. As I got older this became a real hobby for me, really, and I began to read a lot to discover the

psychology at work behind that. I wanted to understand the evolution of the vampire and to unravel the intrigue surrounding its sexuality.

This fascination for the vampire and its sexuality is typical of many participants, often related to the sexuality and appeal of the male stars playing the dark, handsome, exotic, and charismatic vampire popularized by Bela Lugosi, Christopher Lee, Gary Oldman, and Antonio Banderas. The homoerotic theme of *Interview with the Vampire* (1994) seemed to be no deterrent to its appeal to a female audience. The twenty-four-year-old respondent quoted earlier describes her use of the film as erotica:

> I've hired vampire videos which I find particularly erotic and sat with my partner at the time watching them in a darkened room—*Interview with the Vampire* is one that I found particularly sexy, there's something intriguing about the homoeroticism between those beautiful young men. I didn't say anything but I think that my partner took pleasure in how I couldn't take my eyes off the screen, and obviously initiated something because of this.

Both film and fictional vampires are often portrayed as polygamous and bisexual and it would appear that for many viewers the vampire film reflects a sexual fantasy.[56] A number of respondents reported fantasizing about becoming vampires themselves, and some fans wear vampire costumes, including fangs, on a regular basis.

Figure 26.1. *Interview with the Vampire* (1994).

The physical attraction of the identifiably human monster Pinhead was also a major factor in the appeal of the Hellraiser films, again illustrating the sexual fascination with monsters for the female horror fans.[57] Although the extreme levels of violence and excessive special effects render these films problematic for some viewers, others were eventually drawn to his human qualities. The artist respondent typifies this response:

> When I first saw Pinhead I think that he really did scare me.... It wasn't until *Hellraiser III* [1992] that he showed any weakness at all, but to fans of the films I think that Pinhead finally revealing his hidden human depths was regarded merely as an insight into one of their favorite monsters. I'm certainly very fond of him now.

Clive Barker's source material was particularly well regarded for its sympathetic attitude to monsters. One respondent in her late thirties explained:

> Clive Barker's films are so beautiful, and his vision of the dark side is so complete. *Hellraiser* I [*Hellraiser*, 1987] and II [*Hellhound: Hellraiser II*, 1988] and *Candyman* [1992] are scary, well written and beautifully filmed, but I feel his vision is most beautifully portrayed in *Nightbreed* [1990], where the monsters are the good guys. I think this may be a girlie film as most of the men I know don't like it much, but all the women do. A monster movie for people who love monsters.

This love of monsters was repeated by a thirty-five-year-old respondent:

> I have always enjoyed the imagination of Clive Barker because he takes a very obvious joy in the supernatural, the macabre and the downright weird.... I have never seen anyone else create quite such a variety of monsters. Some are ugly, some are beautiful, they are happy, confused and sad just like human beings.

Although many women felt it was socially unacceptable to express fantasies about stars or characters in horror films—perhaps because most of those surveyed were above the age at which fan attachments to stars are seen as acceptable—one twenty-nine-year-old respondent admitted to having crushes on horror film monsters, "not only when in repose but when they change into their full monstrous forms, fangs bared, blood flowing.... It is the entire image that I find attractive, not just the stars when they're looking human." Such comments highlight a particular form of identification to emerge in this study—a "subversive affinity" with the monster.

Many respondents also appear to have adopted deliberate interpretative strategies to accommodate the films' representations of women, either ignoring and making excuses for what they see as negative representations or condoning feminine behavior in strong female characters. As one twenty-four-year-old respondent explained:

> I think Ripley's strength in *Alien* is very female—a very female level of practicality that movies like *Predator* [1987] don't have. And I love the female lead in *A Nightmare*

on Elm Street. She knows what is going on and doesn't fall for all of the typical "crazy female" coddling that everyone around her tries.

Other respondents excused the sexism of older horror films as reflecting a gender stereotype common at the time they were made, which one eighteen-year-old respondent called the "pathetic female victim syndrome." She added that "there are a lot of old horror films where the women have the upper hand, for example, they become vampires and men are attracted to them and led to their deaths which seems like justice to me!" A twenty-nine-year-old respondent agreed: "Men get the raw deal in horror—a woman killed by a vampire tends to be seduced, a man is more likely to be savaged." While these remarks do not indicate any depth of feminist belief or activism, they might suggest that the films fulfill some kind of revenge fantasy. Other respondents, however, did not overly concern themselves with issues of sexism and stereotyping, not allowing the representations of gender to overwhelm their viewing pleasures. As a nineteen-year-old participant said, "I object to these women who scream every five seconds but I don't think women have to be the strong lead to make it a good film."

On the evidence of their comments in this survey, female viewers of the horror film do not adopt purely masculine viewing positions, nor do they simply, as Clover suggests, respond to the literal level of the text.[58] When given the opportunity, as in *Alien*, female viewers strongly identify with the feminized hero because she is literally female. While Clover argues that "the fact that we have in the killer a feminine male and in the main character a masculine female would seem to suggest a loosening of the category of the feminine," the participants' responses to films like *Alien* and *Hellraiser* suggest that for the female spectator the category of the feminine can be strengthened by adopting particular viewing strategies. Gendered identification for the female viewer may not be as fluid a process as Clover proposes it is for the male viewer.[59]

The similarities between these viewers' interpretative activities and the reading strategies of romance fiction readers revealed in Radway's study suggest that the pleasures and responses of female horror fans may be categorized as feminine. But these female viewers do not react as might be expected: They do not flinch, block their view, or turn away from the screen, nor do they appear as the emasculated viewers one might expect if they were adopting a male gaze or colluding with the male oppressor. This audience segment's preferences for gothic horror film types and for the thrills and adrenaline rush of the shiver sensation combine with their liking for strong female characters and their most prevalent and frequently mentioned viewing pleasure, an erotic or romantic identification with vampires and other sympathetic or attractive monsters, to provide a distinctively feminine viewing strategy. Like the readers of feminine genres such as romance and historical fiction, these viewers exhibit a tendency to elide those narrative aspects of the films that conform to patriarchal repression or oppression of these characters. These feminine interpretative strategies suggest that if the horror film remains a predominantly masculine genre, it nevertheless continues to incorporate some of the feminine aspects integral to the literary forms of Gothic horror. Most significantly, perhaps, the pleasure that these viewers find in images of terror and gore and, in particular, in the body of the monster belies Linda Williams's assertion that the female spectator of the horror film can only refuse to look. In the words of the twenty-four-year-old respondent:

> I was always touched by the immense tragedy and sorrow of the vampire, and I suppose enjoyed the vicarious pleasure of the female sexual excess and expression in [vampire] films. As a rather shy, mousy, and introverted youngster it really filled a void in me. They were never so much role models, that style was far beyond me, but characters I could escape with into a fantasy world of glamour as I watched these films. I really found them arousing, exploring a sexual life which I had never had any contact with before—one that seemed otherworldly, and was glittering slick and soft focus on the screen, but beyond my imagination, confidence, and certainty in real life.

Refusing to refuse to look is, for such viewers, an act of affinity with the monster more subversive than Williams imagined.

Notes

1. See, e.g., Barbara Creed, "Horror and the Monstrous-Feminine: An Imaginary Abjection," in *Fantasy and the Cinema*, ed. James Donald (BFI, 1989), 87.

2. Linda Williams, "When the Woman Looks," in *Revision: Feminist Essays in Film Analysis*, ed. Mary Ann Doane, Patricia Mellencamp, and Linda Williams (American Film Institute, 1984), 89.

3. Derek Granger, film review, *Financial Times*, May 6, 1957.

4. E. Lederman, "The Best Places to Meet Good Men," *Cosmopolitan*, June 1992.

5. Granger, film review.

6. James Twitchell, *Dreadful Pleasures: An Anatomy of Modern Horror* (Oxford University Press, 1985), 70; Carol Clover, *Men, Women and Chainsaws: Gender in the Modern Horror Film* (BFI, 1992), 6.

7. Mark Gill, quoted in Andrew Hindes, "Scream 2 Showcases Demographic Power," *Variety*, December 16, 1997.

8. Dolf Zillman, J. B. Weaver, N. Mundorf, and C. F. Aust, "Effects of an Opposite-Gender Companion's Affect to Horror on Distress, Delight, and Attraction," *Journal of Personality and Social Psychology* 51, no. 3 (1986): 586–94.

9. Dolf Zillman and James B. Weaver III, "Gender Socialisation Theory of Reactions to Horror," in *Horror Films: Current Research on Audience Preferences and Reactions*, ed. James B. Weaver III and Ron Tamborini (Lawrence Erlbaum, 1996), 86.

10. Zillman and Weaver.

11. Williams, "When the Woman Looks," 83.

12. The figures provided by the Cinema Advertising Association (CAA) are used to sell cinema advertising slots. Film profiles undertaken by the CAA are from representative samples of the British population highlighting age, sex, and class.

13. Clover, *Men, Women and Chainsaws,* 54.

14. Zillman and Weaver, "Gender Socialisation Theory," 86.

15. Jackie Stacey, *Star Gazing: Hollywood Cinema and Female Spectatorship* (Routledge, 1994).

16. Henry Jenkins, *Textual Poachers: Television Fans and Participatory Culture* (Routledge, 1992).

17. Tanya Modleski, *Feminism Without Women* (Routledge, 1991); Liesbet van Zoonen, *Feminist Media Studies* (SAGE, 1994), 128–29.

18. Brenda Dervin, "The Potential Contribution of Feminist Scholarship to the Field of Communication," *Journal of Communication* 37, no. 4 (1987): 107–20.

19. Fan clubs and societies either circulated their female membership with questionnaires directly or together with a letter explaining the research; smaller groups passed on details at meetings. Flyers explaining the research and calling for participants were circulated at conventions and film festivals, and magazine recruitment was via letters published on the letters page, small ads, or mention in an editorial column.

20. Ien Ang, *Watching Dallas: Soap Opera and the Melodramatic Imagination* (Methuen, 1985).

21. See also Stacey, *Star Gazing,* 44–45.

22. Stacey, 6, 54, 66.

23. Stacey, 54.

24. See, e.g., Auerbach, *Our Vampires, Ourselves* (University of Chicago Press, 1995), and Norine Dresser, *American Vampires: Fans, Victims, Practitioners* (W. W. Norton, 1989).

25. Mark Jancovich, *Horror* (Batsford, 1992), 18.

26. Ellen Moers, *Literary Women* (London, 1977), 90–110; Judith Halberstam, *Skin Shows: Gothic Horror and the Technology of Monsters* (Duke University Press, 1995), 165.

27. Rosemary Jackson, *Fantasy: The Literature of Subversion* (Methuen, 1981), 103.

28. With the exception of Nicholson's glowing yellow eye, not unlike a photographic image from a Häagen-Dazs advertisement.

29. Text reproduced from "The Feminine Love of Horror," reprinted in David J. Skal, *Hollywood Gothic: The Tangled Web of Dracula from Novel to Stage to Screen* (Andre Deutsch, 1990), 149. Skal, making reference to this interview in Skal, *The Monster Show: A Cultural History of Horror* (Plexus, 1993), 126–27, believes it to have been Tod Browning who was being quoted, not Lugosi.

30. David Cantor and Saw Associates, *Horror: Continuing Attraction and Common Reactions (a Report to Coincide with the Re-Opening of the Chamber of Horrors)* (Madame Tussauds, 1996), 13. Survey conducted by MEW Research in March 1995.

31. Cantor and Saw Associates, 13.

32. Auerbach, *Our Vampires, Ourselves,* 3.

33. Tanya Krzywinska, "La Belle Dame sans Merci?," in *A Queer Romance: Lesbians, Gay Men and Popular Culture,* ed. Paul Burston and Colin Richardson (Routledge, 1995), 99.

34. Auerbach, *Our Vampires, Ourselves,* 4; Skal, *Monster Show*; Walter Kendrick, *The Thrill of Fear: 250 Years of Scary Entertainment* (Grove Press, 1991).

35. See Twitchell, *Dreadful Pleasures,* 70.

36. Guy Cumberbatch and Gary Wood, *Phantasmagoria: A Survey of Computer Game Players* (unpublished report, September 1996), 6.

37. J. B. Barclay, *Viewing Tastes of Adolescents in Cinema and Television* (Scottish Educational Film Association/Scottish Film Council, 1961).

38. While only two respondents are under eighteen and only one over sixty, this is most probably due to the recruitment methods. I am not claiming that this sample is a statistically accurate representation of habitual female viewers of horror films.

39. Clover, *Men, Women and Chainsaws,* 66.

40. These ambivalent attitudes may be related to the response given to victims of domestic violence that they "deserve it." See Philip Schlesinger, R. Emerson Dobash, Russell P. Dobash, and C. Kay Weaver, *Women Viewing Violence* (BFI, 1992).

41. *Interview with the Vampire, The Lost Boys* (1987), *Bram Stoker's Dracula* (1992), and *The Hunger* (1983).

42. *The Exorcist* (1973), *The Omen* (1976), and *The Haunting.*

43. *The Silence of the Lambs* and *Psycho* (1960).

44. *Alien, Aliens* (1986), and *The Thing* (1982).

45. *Hellraiser, Hellhound: Hellraiser II,* and *Nightbreed* (1990).

46. Janice Radway, *Reading the Romance: Women, Patriarchy and Popular Literature* (University of North Carolina Press, 1984).

47. Radway, 79.

48. Radway, 159.

49. This aspect of horror film enjoyment is typified by a group of women in Brighton who formed Women into Violent Movies to watch horror, kung fu, and other similar films.

50. Jonathan Lake Crane, *Terror and Everyday Life: Singular Moments in the History of the Horror Film* (SAGE, 1994), vii.

51. Crane, 3.

52. Joanne Cantor and Mary Beth Oliver have described the kinds of material that frighten or otherwise affect children as varying with age. See Cantor and Oliver, "Developmental Differences in Responses to Horror," in Weaver and Tamborini, *Horror Films,* 63–80.

53. Cantor and Oliver, 71, discussing C. Hoffner and J. Cantor, "Developmental Differences in Responses to a Television Character's Appearance and Behaviour," *Developmental Psychology* 21 (1985): 1065–74.

54. John Tulloch and Henry Jenkins, *Science Fiction Audiences: Watching "Doctor Who" and "Star Trek"* (Routledge, 1995), 4.

55. Jenkins, *Textual Poachers,* 19.

56. The Goth subculture too models a desired sexuality along similar lines.

57. Pinhead has become a pinup and sex symbol in Japan, for instance.

58. Clover, *Men, Women and Chainsaws,* 54.

59. Clover, 62–63.

Chapter 27

FROM "HORROR AT THE CROSSROADS: CLASS, GENDER, AND TASTE AT THE RIALTO"

Mark Jancovich and Tim Snelson

> The relationship of social class to horror viewership is an under-scrutinized topic. In the selection included here, Mark Jancovich and Tim Snelson focus on the audience for Times Square's Rialto cinema, which, in the 1930s and 1940s, became known as New York City's "cinematic chamber of horrors." Through a celebration of "lowbrow horror," those attending could signal a rejection of middle-class taste and expectations.

Class, Gender, and Cult Audiences

Concerns with wartime morals also found expression in Times Square, and "the same Broadway theater producers and other business men who had strenuously objected to the presence of burlesque throughout the 1930s now complained that servicemen and their young female companions, or 'V-girls,' were turning Times Square into a 'boomtown similar to those adjoining military posts.'"[1] Despite these complaints, Times Square had long been a place of contradictions where different social groups converged and collided, and its appeal was precisely the ways in which "it also struck an artful balance between catering to middle-class proprieties and flouting them."[2] Oscar Hammerstein was famous for productions that did not involve "simply parading seminude women around the stage of the Victoria [but] posed them as famous statues from antiquity."[3] However, while Hammerstein was making sex respectable, the Square "was already the sex capital of New York by the early years of the twentieth century."[4] The "brothels of the tenderloin had moved north along with the restaurants and the theaters," and there were continual attempts to clean up the Square that dated back well into the nineteenth century. As Anthony Bianco argues, "Even at the height of its Gilded Age elegance, 42nd Street had never been homogeneously posh."[5]

Many of these issues can be seen in *The New York Times* account of Times Square in 1944 that commented on the diverse patterns of the crowd but also stressed the powerful presence of women. For example, it is claimed that, between eight and ten in the evening, "women in limp summer prints outnumber five to one the sailors in whites, GIs in Khaki shirts, Royal Marines, New Zealanders in shorts." As the night progressed, the place became one of sexual encounters: "American, British and French service men are forming the nightly stag lines along the curbs and in front of shop windows, ogling girls and women surging towards Forty-second Street subway stations." Nor is the gaze simply directed by men at women: "In front of the Paramount, two drunken civilians and two tipsy tars change shirts and hats to the shrill enjoyment of the girls." Elsewhere, "servicemen and their girls" are "jammed" into the "Aquarium restaurant and bar," while "at the north end of the square four girls sit on the stone wall and four soldiers in a semi-circle around them sing sentimental hits."[6]

The place is therefore one of surging crowds and unlikely juxtapositions. It even features personalities that represent these strange conjunctures. For example, the *Times* article comments on a "very unsteady wench," whose "attempts to maintain . . . a haughty head tilt," despite her probable drunkenness, are "somehow pathetic." It also quotes a more established "Times Square character," the "taxi poet," who "recites his latest verses to droop-eyed loafers" as he waits "in front of the Rialto" for his cab to cool down. Nor is his presence outside the Rialto incidental, and the cinema almost seems to set the rhythm of the Square. As the crowds fade and the night comes to an end, the whole cycle of the day starts over again at 8:30 a.m. with the announcement that the Rialto "is open again with a new horror film," despite having "closed less than five hours ago."

Mayer's Rialto, situated in Times Square, therefore existed in a cultural location that was neither highbrow nor lowbrow, middle class nor working class, male nor female, gay nor straight, but one that exploited the tensions between these positions. This is not to claim that Times Square was an egalitarian space. While it allowed some groups to trade in goods and services that were illegitimate elsewhere, it was still a space that favored some groups over others and even had its own hierarchies. For example, visitors to the Square in the 1930s could exploit its aggressively masculine hustlers, many of whom were "migrants from economically devastated cities," men who had nowhere else to go and little option than "to support their income by hustling."[7] However, as these hustlers began to gravitate toward Times Square, they also asserted themselves over others and forced "the 'fairy' prostitutes to move east of Sixth Avenue, to Bryant Park."

Similarly, Mayer's cinema was not a uniform or egalitarian space. Bianco claims that "the typical grindhouse patron was a bus driver or a Midtown secretary,"[8] but the class composition of the Rialto was not simply a lower-class audience with antibourgeois tastes. On the contrary, as Mayer's articles for *The New York Times* make clear, he was concerned to attract the male suburban office worker, who used the cinema to temporarily reject the middle-class domesticity and respectability of his home life. In addition, the cinema had other devotees. As we have seen, Bosley Crowther and his fellow critics at *The New York Times* were clearly fascinated frequenters of the theater, even if they were also ambivalent about it and demonstrated both excitement and suspicion in relation to its pleasures. It is significant that the more highbrow critics, such as James Agee and Manny Farber, not only frequented the cinema but seem to have had far less qualms about doing so. Farber would even champion its films against the more socially respectable and supposedly staid products of mainstream Hollywood.

In other words, the cinema was used by certain sections of the middle class to oppose themselves to the tastes of other sections, and it is for this reason that *The New York Times* was less comfortable with the cinema than were the more highbrow critics. For Crowther and his colleagues, the Rialto was distant in social space but not quite distant enough; Farber and Agee were far enough away to consume it with relish. As Bourdieu puts it, "Aesthetic choices are in fact often constituted in opposition to the choices of groups closest in social space, with whom competition is most direct and immediate."[9] It is for this reason that many critics tend to prefer low culture to the middlebrow. The middlebrow blurs the line between high and low and so threatens the authority of the cultured elite more directly than the lowbrow, while the appeal of the lowbrow is that it knows its place: The cultural middle class "prefers naivety to 'pretentiousness.' The essential merit of the 'common people' is that they have none of the pretensions to art (or power) which inspire the ambitions of the 'petty bourgeois.'"[10]

By rejecting middlebrow or even legitimate taste, the cultural middle classes not only distance themselves from those with less cultural capital but also assert their own cultural authority. For Bourdieu, cultural power does not reside simply in the ability to recognize cultural categories but in "the extent of one's power to confer aesthetic status." As a result, "the easiest, and so the most frequent and spectacular way" to prove such authority is to "shock *(épater)* the bourgeois"—to transgress accepted judgments of aesthetic value. By celebrating lowbrow horror, Agee, Farber, and others displayed their superiority over those who simply accepted aesthetic hierarchies but also over the supposedly working-class audiences of the Rialto with whom they claimed to identify. In other words, just as tourists could use the sexual life of the Square without being trapped within it, many middle-class cultists could identify with lowbrow culture without being restricted to it. Rather than simply consuming it as entertainment, they asserted their superiority precisely by reading it aesthetically—to read it in terms of middle-class modes of consumption and appropriation rather than the terms of more "naive" consumers. In other words, middle-class audiences used the image of working-class audiences to beat other sections of the middle class, and by the 1950s, even Farber was beginning to feel uncomfortable about the "custom among professional pipe smokers to offer romantic estimations of American moviegoers," particularly "the action-movie fans who attend shabby theaters west of Times Square."[11]

While middle-class critics claimed to identify with the Rialto's lowbrow audience but actually ended up using them to assert their own superiority, the cinema actually created considerable opportunities for women, despite being overtly defined through an "othering" of femininity. From the moment that Mayer took full control of the Rialto, he stressed the masculinity of his cinema and overtly positioned it in opposition to the feminine. However, he also predicted that "in spite of all our efforts" women would "adore" the Rialto,[12] and he was hardly surprised when, after a short time, "feminine attendance started to zoom."[13]

Defined as a masculine space through its opposition to domestic femininity, the cinema appealed to women who rejected the domesticity often associated with respectable femininity, and it also appealed to those under less pressure to demonstrate respectability and settle down. Many young women were able to use the cinema as a way of playing with different identities while the war years intensified matters by creating conditions within which many women were not only able, but forced, to experiment with nondomestic modes of femininity. As a result, while the women who flocked to horror at the Rialto were not necessarily rejecting femininity per se, or identifying themselves as masculine, the war had postponed the demands of domesticity, and the cinema provided a space in which to experiment with different ways of being feminine.

Horror Films, Art Cinema, and Cult Audiences

The ambiguous cultural status of this "cinematic chamber of horrors" is also captured by Mayer's response to the demise of the 1940s horror cycle. According to Mayer, "The Hollywood producers, basking in the sunshine of Santa Anita, became surcharged with a love of everybody except communists and a fear of offending anybody except Stalin," and as a result, the "hardboiled movies which had made the Rialto so popular became harder and harder to obtain."[14] As his "pangs of conscience increased daily in direct proportion to the decrease in my profits," he was forced to change strategy. Instead of lowbrow horror, he turned to the highbrow cinema of postwar Europe, a move that proved highly profitable: "There proved to be gold in them there foreign bills." Nor was this move a completely new departure for Mayer, who had been importing foreign films since 1935 and had been accused of "selling mayhem to lowbrows with the left hand and peddling psychological tidbits to highbrows with the right."[15] Indeed, he is often remembered today as a "pioneer European art film distributor and exhibitor."[16]

At the time, Mayer described this change in policy not as a decision to "discard action in behalf of art," but rather as a "leap from simple sadism to subtle sex." While this shift from low-budget horror to the European art cinema demonstrates the close relationship between horror and the avant-garde that Joan Hawkins discusses in her research,[17] it is not just a question of aesthetic practice but also of the economics of exhibition, promotion, and distribution. As Mark Betz has demonstrated in his analysis of "high and low cinemas of the 1960s," exploitation and art "proceeded not simply as parallel alternative modes of film practice, but as shared discourses and means of address."[18]

Wilinsky demonstrates that art cinema was defined "against Hollywood films"[19] and "shaped itself as an alternative to dominant culture."[20] In part, this meant creating an alternative ambience that, while not identical to Mayer's "lurid place,"[21] was also defined against the movie palace or neighborhood theater. Betz quotes Arthur Knight's complaint that art cinemas "were elitist and for 'eggheads only.'" The chief distinction between art and exploitation houses

> would seem to lie in the demitasse of black coffee served in the lobby of the snootier establishments. For make no mistake about it, the art house operators—may their tribe increase—are in business just as surely as their competitors who feature *Mr. Rock and Roll, I Was a Teenage Werewolf,* or *Garden of Eden.*[22]

However, the art cinemas also defined themselves as alternative through an association with films that were supposed to differ from the standard Hollywood product, films that were "more formally ambiguous and 'realist' and thematically more mature."[23] In other words, art films were alleged to feature materials deemed taboo within Hollywood, and while Mayer's cinema was associated with horror and violence, the art film was usually associated with sex.

Indeed, it was often assumed that art films "pushed the limits of moral acceptability," although in practice, "distributors' desires for commercial exhibition limited the risks these films could take."[24] Nonetheless, as Betz points out, the press books for art films often encouraged exhibitors not only to sell the films' aesthetic merits but also to stress their "sexual angle."[25] As he says of the 1952 brochure for *7 Capital Sins*:

> A stylized female figure sells the film, but in this case there is no hedging, no careful balance between cultural capital and sexual commerce. No longer classical in her proportions and attire, this modern woman obliges the [male] viewer to enter into the world of a film that is "not strictly French!" ... The relationship between French cinema and playful licentiousness is not simply produced here: it is assumed.[26]

As Eric Schaefer has pointed out, since at least the 1930s, there had been an explicit distinction between "clean" American films and "filthy" foreign ones, a distinction that Hollywood had actually used to both promote and defend itself.[27] However, if the Hollywood film industry could benefit from this distinction by identifying itself as wholesome and patriotic, the distinction could also be turned on its head to present Hollywood as censored and unable to deal with adult material while simultaneously using sex to identify the "foreign" film with freedom, sophistication, and maturity. As Peter Lev puts it, "Explicit sexuality became expected in foreign films, to such an extent that 'foreign film,' 'art film,' 'adult film,' and 'sex film' were for several years almost synonymous."[28]

As Betz observes, it is "only in the pages of censorship history that . . . art, exploitation, and underground cinemas occupy the same scholarly space," although he notes that "even here they tend to be segregated into different conceptual categories and accorded differential weight that has nothing to do with the specifics of their litigation and everything to do with their varying statuses on the scale of cultural tastes."[29] But as he rightly observes:

> American nudist camp and nudie-cutie films such as *Garden of Eden* and *The Immoral Mr. Teas*, underground films such as *Flaming Creatures* and *Scorpio Rising*, and Scandinavian soft-core sex films: all of these challenged US censorship laws equally as much and in similar ways as the prestige European and American films (*The Miracle, The Moon Is Blue, Pinky* etc.) that dominate the postwar history of the US Production Code.

Furthermore, the links between horror, exploitation, art, and sex are made clear by the fortunes of *Nights of Horror*. Despite its title, *Nights of Horror* was not a horror publication but rather a "series of fourteen booklets cataloguing sexual perversity at $1.98 to $3.00 a pop."[30] In 1954, it became the center of a drive to clear up the "dirty book dealers" that had begun to flourish in Times Square. Furthermore, if these "dirty book dealers" were attacked as purveyors of "obscene" materials, they "were not the self-proclaimed 'adult' bookstores of the 1970s," but featured a far more diverse inventory and customer base. For example, they "appealed to a hipster clientele" and stocked *Nights of Horror* along with "avantgarde literary works that ran afoul of the censors, including Ginsberg's *Howl* and other Beat manifestos."[31]

It is therefore significant that at the time that Mayer sold off the Rialto, he and Joe Burstyn were distributing the most influential European film of the late 1940s and early 1950s, Rossellini's *Rome, Open City*, and their press book clearly employs the promotional strategies previously discussed:

> Blocks of textual praise for the film were balanced with less lofty sentiments and imagery that built up the sexual angle: hints at lesbianism, "violence and plain sexiness" link the marketing of this film in uncanny ways to that of American exploitation films of the same period: the image of the young woman with hiked skirt or black bra or both appears in every ad in the book.[32]

As Mayer himself claims, the "only sensational successes scored by Burstyn and myself in the fifteen years in which we engaged in business were with pictures whose artistic and ideological merits were aided and abetted at the box office by their frank sexual content."[33] He therefore proudly claims that *Rome, Open City* "was generally advertised with a misquotation from *Life,* adjusted so as to read: 'Sexier than Hollywood ever dared to be,' together with a still of two young ladies deeply engrossed in a rapt embrace, and another of a man being flogged." If the first still hinted at lesbianism, the second was overtly "designed to tap the sadist trade." Indeed, despite the film's later reputation, it only opened at "a New York City first-run theater after running for a hundred straight weeks at various theaters in the Times Square area," a period that "most probably included play dates at theaters that were not art houses."[34]

If the Rialto had been converted into a cinema showing European art films by the late 1940s, this did not necessarily make it an "art house." It only demonstrated the continuing close relationship between art and exploitation cinema in the period. Furthermore, the Rialto was soon converted back into a cinema specializing in horror films, and it was still operating as such in the 1970s, at the zenith of cult movie fandom.[35]

Notes

1. Anthony Bianco, *Ghosts of 42nd Street: A History of America's Most Infamous Block* (William Morrow, 2004), 121.

2. Bianco, 2.

3. Bianco, 2.

4. James Traub, *The Devil's Playground: A Century of Pleasure and Profit in Times Square* (Penguin, 2004), 30.

5. Bianco, *Ghosts of 42nd Street,* 93.

6. Meyer Berger, "Times Square Diary: A Reporter Feels the Pulse of the Crowd and Records Its Fluctuations," *The New York Times,* September 3, 1944.

7. George Chauncey, "The Policed: Gay Men's Strategies of Everyday Resistance in Times Square," in *Creating a Place for Ourselves,* ed. Brett Beemyn (Routledge, 1997), 322.

8. Bianco, *Ghosts of 42nd Street,* 101.

9. Pierre Bourdieu, *Distinction: A Social Critique of the Judgement of Taste* (1969; repr., Routledge, 1984), 60.

10. Bourdieu, 62.

11. Manny Farber, "Times Square Moviegoers," *Nation,* July 4, 1953.

12. Arthur Mayer, "A New Deal for the Forgotten Man," *The New York Times,* May 26, 1935.

13. Arthur Mayer, *Merely Colossal: The Story of the Movies from the Long Chase to the Chaise Longue* (Simon and Schuster, 1953), 179.

14. Arthur L. Mayer, "The Merchant of Menace Gives Up the Ghost," *The New York Times,* May 2, 1948, 85.

15. Michael Mok, "That Grim Horror That Finances Art Isn't So Hard to Take—at a Profit," *New York Post,* February 27, 1939.

16. Mark Betz, "Art, Exploitation, Underground," in *Defining Cult Movies: The Cultural Politics of Oppositional Taste,* ed. Mark Jancovich, Antonio Lazaro Reboll, Julian Stringer, and Andy Willis (Manchester University Press, 2003), 220.

17. Joan Hawkins, *Cutting Edge: Art-Horror and the Horrific Avant-Garde* (University of Minnesota Press, 2000).

18. Betz, "Art, Exploitation, Underground," 204.

19. Barbara Wilinsky, *Sure Seaters: The Emergence of Art House Cinema* (University of Minnesota Press, 2001), 27.

20. Wilinsky, 3.

21. Bosley Crowther, "A Child's Mind," *The New York Times,* March 4, 1944, 11.

22. Betz, "Art, Exploitation, Underground," 204.

23. Wilinsky, *Sure Seaters,* 27.

24. Wilinsky, 27.

25. Betz, "Art, Exploitation, Underground," 206.

26. Betz, 212.

27. Eric Schaefer, *Bold! Daring! Shocking! True! A History of Exploitation Films, 1919–1959* (Duke University Press, 1999), 160–61.

28. Peter Lev, *The Euro-American Cinema* (University of Texas Press, 1993), 205.

29. Betz, "Art, Exploitation, Underground," 219–20.

30. Bianco, *Ghosts of 42nd Street,* 135.

31. Bianco, 134.

32. Betz, "Art, Exploitation, Underground," 206.

33. Mayer, *Merely Colossal,* 233.

34. Wilinsky, *Sure Seaters,* 111.

35. See, for example, the article on the Rialto in Bill Landis and Michelle Clifford, eds., *Sleazoid Express: A Mind-Twisting Tour Through the Grindhouse Cinema of Times Square* (Fireside, 2002).

Chapter 28

CRITICAL PLEASURES
Reflections on the Indonesian Horror Genre and Its Anti-Fans

Meghan Downes

> In the same way that class-based theorizations of horror's appeal are few and far between, non-Western analyses of the pleasures of horror, at least in English, are hard to come by. Meghan Downes's chapter is an exception to the rule as it considers the reception of horror films in Indonesia, where young, urban Indonesians ridicule horror films, while in some cases also secretly enjoying them. In a kind of counterexample to Hills's focus on horror connoisseurs, Downes focuses on "anti-fans" who derive pleasure from dismissing or degrading the genre.

IN APRIL 2013, I SAT CROSS-LEGGED with a group of six students from Gadjah Mada University in Yogyakarta, discussing Indonesian national cinema. During the discussion, I sensed the group edging toward a topic that would inevitably generate lively conversation and trigger an outpouring of critical condemnation—that of horror films. And while this topic was not the main focus of my research at that time, I found myself looking forward to the subject being raised and anticipating the deluge of ridicule that would eventually follow. "I like watching Indonesian films, but only certain genres. Most importantly, not horror," said Agus, a nineteen-year-old management student (pers. comm., April 25, 2013). The rest of the focus group nodded enthusiastically in agreement. "Why? What is wrong with horror films?" I asked, and the floodgates opened.

Drawing on ethnographic audience research carried out during 2013–14, this chapter offers insights into how young, urban, tertiary-educated Indonesians engage with the Indonesian horror genre. Indonesian horror films are the subject of ridicule and derision among a majority of these consumers, who characterize the genre as cheap, exploitative, and derivative; morally and aesthetically bankrupt; and emblematic of all the worst problems facing the Indonesian film industry and Indonesian society in general. Referencing Bourdieu's (1984, 1986) theories of taste and distinction, this chapter also illustrates how the imagined mass audience of Indonesian horror functions as a symbolic other, reinforcing stereotypes around class and ethnicity, and emphasizing the cultural capital of more discerning, critical audiences. In addition, I argue that these consumers' modes of receiving and appreciating Indonesian horror are far more complex than a flat-out rejection of the genre. While they ridicule Indonesian horror films, many young urban Indonesians furtively enjoy watching them. Judging by how lively, passionate, and humorous the focus group discussions became when discussing horror, I contend that there is a certain critical pleasure gained in mocking the genre and its moral failings. In exploring the intricacies of both textual pleasure and repulsion, I engage with recent theories of "anti-fandom" that have come out of US cultural studies, particularly with the works of Jonathan Gray, Francesca Haig, and Sarah Harman and Bethan Jones. There are many resonances between Indonesian antihorror sentiment and US antifandom, but also some important divergences, which remind us that it is vital not to assume universality. I use these differences as a departure point for reflecting on some of the challenges and opportunities of working at what Emma Baulch and Julian Millie (2013) call the intersection of Asian studies, media studies, and cultural studies.

My focus in this article is Indonesian horror, which local audiences usually define in direct opposition to both "quality national cinema" and "foreign horror," a vague descriptor that encapsulates anything from Thai to Japanese to Hollywood horror films. Yet in the closing sections I will reflect briefly on what these definitions mean for locating Southeast Asian horror more generally. Ultimately, this article grapples with the paradox of horror as the genre Indonesians love to hate and, in doing so, attempts to find new ways of working meaningfully at the intersection of media, cultural, and area studies in the contemporary scholarly context.

While horror films have been produced in Indonesia since the 1930s, when the nation was still under colonial control, the horror genre truly began to blossom in the 1970s and 1980s, with countless titles, often based on local myths and legends, screened throughout the archipelago (van Heeren 2009). Although it has always been branded as somewhat trashy lower-class entertainment, horror has consistently been one of the most popular and widely produced genres in Indonesian cinema. Along with other Indonesian film genres, it experienced a slump during the 1990s but resurfaced in the increasingly deregulated media environment of the early 2000s, following the collapse of President Suharto's thirty-year authoritarian New Order regime. The resurgence of Indonesian horror occurred around the same time that Japanese and Korean horror films were experiencing unprecedented success in international markets, yet the films produced in Indonesia remained quite distinct from their international equivalents.

The new wave of horror emerging in the 2000s has been well studied by scholars of Indonesian cinema. Katinka van Heeren (2007, 2009) traces the changing role of religious figures such as the *kyai* (Islamic scholar) in horror films, as well the ways in which postreform Indonesian horror directors produced films that were no longer set in the mythical past but in the everyday modern urban environments. For van Heeren (2009), this change in setting is related to a desire to seek truth and authenticity in the wake of the New Order regime. She notes that such developments were arguably entwined with changes in the distribution of horror films, as high-end shopping mall cinemas increasingly outnumbered rural outdoor cinemas.

Approaching cinema from a cultural economy perspective, Thomas Barker (2011) also demonstrates how some of the structural changes brought about by the reform era have influenced Indonesian horror films. Barker finds the classic "return to order" (Sen 1994) narrative arc of the New Order era replaced by filmmakers' attempts to articulate past traumas and violences committed by the regime. By looking at horror as allegory, he argues that the temporal gap between an original violent incident and its reappearance as ghost (a narrative arc that characterized most reform-era horror films) is a way for filmmakers to confront and work through the residual traumas of history (Barker 2011, 30).

However, both van Heeren and Barker remain primarily focused on the production, distribution, and content of horror films; consequently, the voice of the audience continues to remain absent. Given the role of the viewer in constructing and shaping meaning, the reception context can be just as important as the text itself (Sandvoss 2005), which leads me to examine this previously neglected area of how viewers engage with Indonesian horror. Throughout decades of horror production, there have been many significant changes in the film industry, in the way that horror is produced and distributed, and in the kind of allegories at work within the films. Yet for millions of everyday consumers, the complaints remain much the same: Indonesian horror is cheap mass entertainment of highly questionable moral value.

I delve deeper into this negative characterization of Indonesian horror films by drawing on ethnographic audience research. The data used in this article were collected during a year-long study of popular cultural consumption practices across six Indonesian cities: Padang, Jakarta, Yogyakarta, Banjarmasin, Makassar, and Manado. These cities, spread across four of Indonesia's major islands, were chosen due to their status as large urban centers with significant student populations. During fieldwork, I lived in student boardinghouses, holding focus group discussions and in-depth one-on-one interviews with more than one hundred Indonesian university students. Participants were between eighteen and twenty-six years old; the sample was gender balanced and drawn from a range of faculties at leading universities in each city. This demographic of young, urban, educated people constitutes the majority of Indonesian film consumers. Most of our conversations centered on consumption practices, popular tastes and trends, the relevance of various themes, and the social roles of popular texts in Indonesia. Importantly, when I refer to "films" here, I mean not just those that are viewed in cinemas, which are expensive and not the primary sites for most young people's film consumption, but also the more frequently accessed illegal VCDs and downloaded copies. As such, it is impossible to offer concrete figures on audience numbers for these films. Ultimately, I am more interested in audience perceptions, rather than specific quantitative details of horror film production and distribution. In the sections that follow, I seek to understand the striking similarity that emerged in all interviews and focus groups: the unanimous concern that the Indonesian film market is flooded with low-quality and pornographic horror films.

The Imagined Horror Audience as Symbolic Other

The majority of respondents in my study were keen to explain that they rarely watch Indonesian films because the industry is dominated by *jelek* (ugly/trashy) B-grade horror. This was frequently the very first point raised in each conversation, with many respondents asking incredulously why I was interested in Indonesian cinema at all. "Indonesian horror films aren't all pure horror, but actually porn," explained Citra (pers. comm., September 9, 2013) during a focus group discussion in Banjarmasin. Among these young consumers, there was wide disapproval of the "soft porn" aspects of these films and a sense that this was a worsening situation. Dessy told me that "not many people are interested in Indonesian horror films because these days, the sexual aspects are so dominant" (pers. comm., May 2, 2013). Arif joked that "we call them KFC films: breast, thigh, breast, thigh" (pers. comm., April 16, 2013).

Due to the stigma attached to the genre, it was very difficult to find fans of Indonesian horror during the course of my interviews. Only a handful of participants admitted they enjoy the genre, and these confessions were accompanied by nervous giggles and attempts to change the subject. It was easier to obtain information by inviting people to talk instead about friends who watch horror. Even members of online Indonesian horror fan communities, anonymous spaces where we would expect to find true fans, stressed that they only obsess over retro horror films from the 1970s and 1980s, and their fandom is often expressed in an ironic way. "It's so bad that it's good" was a familiar refrain in such forums, implying a kind of "anti-fandom" that I will explore further in the next section.

Overall, criticizing the horror genre is a favorite pastime for Indonesian audiences. Yet while everyone is keen to complain about such films, viewers are reluctant to talk about who consumes them and are anxious to distance themselves from the genre. Of course, many different people, including my respondents, watch these films in many different contexts and for a variety of reasons. But what is most interesting for the purpose of this chapter is how respondents seek to "other" the Indonesian horror genre, explaining that it is "other consumers" who create the demand. These others include "people with low education," "rural village people who just want some entertainment," "kids who enjoy being frightened," "curious teenagers," or the most abstract response, "people in other regions and islands." These are stereotypes, of course, and they are rarely accurate. From my own observations from living in both rural and urban areas of Indonesia, rural villagers tend not to watch films at all. Yet such stereotypes are highly consistent and powerful among the respondents who are keen to distance themselves from horror. The following comment from a respondent in Manado exemplifies this process of distancing, as it firmly characterizes the demand for horror as coming from "elsewhere," that is, from another island or ethnic group:

> Where does the demand come from? Probably not from Manado. Maybe in Java [horror films] have a good rating so they keep producing them . . . but we have different culture, different beliefs. The Javanese are too caught up in traditional mystic beliefs. (Ardi, pers. comm., October 23, 2013)

This act of distancing or othering can also occur at the more local level. Hikmat explained that it is rural people living out of town who watch horror, because "their needs are at that level. They don't want anything serious, just some light entertainment" (pers. comm., May 4, 2013). He too is locating the consumption of horror far from his own better-educated, urban lifestyle, thus projecting a particular image of his own identity. "Perhaps it's the *becak* [rickshaw] drivers?" suggested twenty-one-year-old Putri (pers. comm., April 25, 2013) from Jakarta, revealing more about her own social outlook and assumptions than about the demographic of horror audiences.

The overwhelming tendency to other the Indonesian horror genre as the purview of less worthy audiences reveals powerful hierarchies of class, region, age, and socioeconomic factors, which become linked with ideas of taste, distinction, and morality. By othering the horror genre, the respondents gain a form of symbolic and cultural capital (Bourdieu 1986), positioning themselves as more discerning and principled than other consumers. Bourdieu (1984, 6) asserts in his sociology of consumption that

> taste classifies, and it classifies the classifier. Social subjects . . . distinguish themselves by the distinctions they make, between the beautiful and the ugly, the distinguished and the vulgar, in which their position in the objective classifications is expressed or betrayed.

The notion of taste is thus relative, invariably based upon the rejection of the assumed lower taste of someone else. Moreover, the social and cultural capital that is built upon hierarchies of taste is not merely abstract, but "works hand in hand with economic capital to produce social privilege and distinction" (Fiske 1992, 21). For many of the young urban audiences I worked with, their socioeconomic positions can be relatively tenuous. As Luvaas (2009, 261) points out, the so-called middle-class status of many young Indonesians, made possible by recent changes in the Indonesian economy, "is often unstable and uncertain, newly attained and easily lost." In this context, the act of rejecting the "lower-class" genre of horror plays an important role in reinforcing the status and cultural capital of many young Indonesian consumers. For this reason, although in reality there are many who enjoy horror, most people become scornful of the genre and its viewers during everyday conversation.

Anti-Fandom and Critical Pleasure

During the course of my fieldwork, it became clear that the respondents' modes of receiving and appreciating Indonesian horror were far more complex than a flat-out disavowal of the genre. Although they ridicule Indonesian horror, many of these young urban Indonesians also secretly enjoy watching the films in question, even if only to laugh at them. In addition, if we take into account how lively, passionate, and humorous focus group discussions became when discussing horror, there is evidently significant critical pleasure gained in insulting the genre. This paradox has been examined at length in recent US cultural studies that focused on the theory around "anti-fandom." It is useful for us then to critically engage with this body of theoretical work to examine possible resonances and contrasts when looking at similar cases of "textual hate" in the Southeast Asian context.

In a 2003 article titled "New Audiences, New Textualities: Anti-Fans and Non-Fans," Gray argues for the importance of studying the often neglected "anti-fan" in audience research. Gray points out that many viewers watch distractedly or casually, while many also hate or dislike certain texts or genres, and cultural studies scholars therefore need to pay particular attention to anti-fans and non-fans and see them as "distinct matrices of viewing and textuality" (65). This kind of approach represents a significant refinement and elaboration of Hall's (1980) classic categories of "dominant," "oppositional," or "negotiated" reader positions as well as Abercrombie and Longhurst's (1998) taxonomy of audiences, which covers the casual consumer, the progressively more involved, active, and productive fan, the cultist, the enthusiast, and the petty producer. While not discounting the significance of these existing categories and the important progress made by fan studies scholarship, Gray (2005, 840) takes us to the other end of the audience spectrum, theorizing about "those who refuse to let their family watch a show, who campaign against a text, or who spend considerable time discussing why a given text makes them angry to the core," and exploring the implications of this kind of textual engagement for a deeper understanding of the nature of textuality itself. According to Gray, "textual hatred and dislike have been understudied and underestimated, as has their intricate and nuanced relationship to textual love" (841). Subsequent research in this area, including Gray's joint work with Sandvoss and Harrington in 2007, has elaborated on this complex relationship. Described variously as "lolfans" (Klink 2008), "snark fans" (Haig 2013), and "ironic, guilty" fans (Harman and Jones 2013), consumers engaged in practices of anti-fandom are increasingly the subject of scholarly attention and are understood in ever more complex ways. These recent theories of anti-fandom complicate the notion of fandom as uncritically affectionate and also add nuance to Gray's initial characterization of anti-fans as those who simply refuse to engage with certain texts.

In Haig's (2013) analysis of snark fandom among readers of Stephenie Meyer's Twilight books and Harman and Jones's (2013) discussion of the ironic, critical online fandom of E. L. James's Fifty Shades of Grey trilogy, criticism is in fact a form of pleasurable engagement for anti-fans who engage in detailed close readings of the texts (Harman and Jones 2013). The texts explored in existing anti-fandom research, including the *Simpsons* television series as well as talk shows and reality television, have been primarily US-based, but despite the difference in context and content, much of the research is highly illuminating when analyzing Indonesian audience engagement with the horror genre.

There are a number of reasons for characterizing the Indonesian audiences I worked with as anti-fans. First, many of these respondents, although claiming to be uninterested in Indonesian horror, are in fact highly engaged with these texts, regardless of whether they have viewed the films themselves or not. They can name titles and stars and criticize specific elements of the story and setting. "*Suster keramas* [Evil nurse; Kardit 2009], *Pocong ngesot* [Crawling ghost; Nuala 2011], *Sumpah pocong* [The ghost's curse; Suryadi 2008], the titles are not good," explained Rezky (pers. comm., September 10, 2013) during a focus group in Banjarmasin. In Manado, Billy advised me that "it's best to avoid anything starring Dewi Persik [a sexy Indonesian actress]" (pers. comm., October 23, 2013). Doni from Padang had concerns with the believability of the films, saying that "the scenes are very unrealistic, not at all like the real life. They only show a little bit of sex scene to make the films interesting" (pers. comm., May 11, 2013). In Jakarta, Mia echoed this sentiment: "Films like *Beranakdi dalam kubur* [Birth in the grave; Saputra and Lingga 2007] have a very illogical narrative and are also very ambiguous. You find yourself asking: is this a horror film or a semi-porno?" (pers. comm., September 29, 2013). In addition, "the ghosts simply are not scary," said Zulis (pers. comm., June 10, 2013). Maria from Manado complained that "the cinematography is terrible, and so is the setting" (pers. comm., October 23, 2013).

Gray (2003, 71) has suggested that the reason there is so little inquiry into anti-fans is that they are assumed to know little about the text and not to have watched it, and therefore make "poor informants." However, there must always be some basis for disliking a text, and it is by examining what such a basis could be that we can observe the social life of the text beyond the screen. For Gray, "clearly anti-fans construct an image of the text—and, what is more, an image they feel is accurate—sufficiently enough that they can react to and against it" (71). In the Indonesian context, these consumers have certainly constructed an image that allows them to engage in detailed critiques of films they claim never to have watched.

A second key resonance with anti-fandom theories is the significance of intertexts and paratexts in shaping the respondents' views about these films. Fiske (1989) has established that a text is much more than simply a book that is read or a film that is watched; a text is also made up of surrounding intertexts, which include reviews, advertisements, and the comments of other consumers about it, all of which contribute to a kind of secondary textuality. Genette (1997) has also explored this concept, using the term *paratexts* to describe semitextual fragments such as blurbs and cover art that surround and position a work. In theories of anti-fandom, the paratext or intertext plays a vital role in the distant reading that characterizes the textual engagement of many non-fans and anti-fans. For the Indonesian audiences I worked with, it was clear that semitextual fragments indeed shaped their image of horror films. A film poster showing scantily clad film stars, a glimpse of a scene on a friend's computer, a nostalgic conversation with parents who yearn for the Indonesian horror of bygone eras, an online review decrying the stupidity of contemporary Indonesian horror—all these moments add to the meaning attributed to certain films.

The third reason for characterizing young Indonesian audiences as anti-fans is the sheer enjoyment they derive from criticizing the horror genre. As in the case of Haig's snark fandom and Harman and Jones's ironic critical fandom, Indonesian audiences enthusiastically embrace the chance to criticize the minutiae of trashy horror films, not just during focus group discussions but during everyday film-viewing practices. "Have you watched horror porn?" asked one student during a focus group discussion in Manado. "*Huntu Jeruk Purut* [The ghost of Jeruk Purut; Pagayo 2006], *Suster keramas* [Evil nurse; Kardit, 2009] . . . it's funny! We kind of insult it. As far as I know there is no one who says 'Wow! That's a good movie!'" (Ricky, pers. comm., October 23, 2013). Another respondent, Teddy from Banjarmasin, explained to me that "all this vulgar Indonesian horror . . . it's light entertainment. The scenes are funny! You can laugh with your friends about how terrible it is" (pers. comm., October 10, 2013). The situations described here involve social, collective critiques of the genre, echoing Haig's (2013, 15) analysis of Twilight snark fandom:

> The criticisms aren't incidental to the pleasure taken in the texts; they appear, in large part, to constitute that pleasure. This form of critical fandom does not simply recognise *Twilight* as rubbish and enjoy it in spite of that recognition; the recognition itself and the analysis, discussion and parody that it permits, provide much of the fans' pleasure.

Enjoying the act of criticism is a key element of anti-fandom, and one that forges connection and a sense of community among anti-fans, whether in online forums or in everyday conversation (Gray 2005). It is in fact this lively, social element of criticism that drew my attention to the topic of Indonesian horror in the first place. A discussion of the Indonesian horror genre and its failings was always a failsafe way to break the ice during a quiet focus group discussion, allowing for a kind of bonding over shared moral and aesthetic values before moving on to other topics. Moreover, as Gray (2003, 77) has noted in his early musings on potential strategies for studying anti-fans, "because part of our interest in interviewing anti-fans and non-fans would be to see how media texts fit into society, we could learn a great deal from observing how a group of friends activate the text in discussion." During my focus group discussions I indeed encountered a wide range of group dynamics, from a group of girls who strove to outdo each other in their disgust with the genre, to a mixed group who found it very awkward to discuss pornography in front of the opposite gender, to an all-male focus group who laughingly singled out one of their number as a "big fan" of horror films. As predicted by Gray, these kinds of interactions are highly illuminating when it comes to the connotations and social roles of certain texts.

Fourth, as has been examined in the previous section on the imagined audience of horror films, respondents often express concern for the "other" viewers, that is, those less discerning than themselves, such as "children" and "uneducated rural villagers." This is also a preoccupation that emerges frequently in studies of the anti-fan. Gray's (2005, 851) study of the online forum Television Without Pity finds that much of the animosity directed toward certain shows or characters "stemmed from a concern for third-person effects." In other words, viewers claimed to be worried about other people's reception ("children, racists, human resource departments"), which for Gray reveals "the degree to which much reception occurs with an imagined community of others" (851). In this way, the text is a "remarkably refracted object" (851), and much of what the text means to the viewer in fact stems from what they perceive its impact to be on others. Here, we can see a familiar concern with the impact of mass culture, which is essentially any form of mass-produced entertainment, on the so-called masses (Strinati 2004). Similarly, Harman and Jones's (2013, 961) analysis of online anti-fandom communities concludes that

> the oppositional reception of *Fifty Shades of Grey* says more about anti-fans than it does about those actually "enjoying" the trilogy, who are largely silent in mainstream discourses. In fact, one wonders whether this constructed Other of the "vanilla" housewife, the undiscerning reader of "trash," truly exists except as an imagined spectre, or whether, for the majority of readers, it is this "hate-reading" . . . which offers the real readerly pleasures of performing and sharing distinctions of taste.

This "imagined spectre" was something I regularly grappled with during my own research. Despite the selection of highly varied respondent groups, I was ultimately unable to find any consumer who engaged in pure uncritical, un-ironic enjoyment of Indonesian horror films.

Finally, and perhaps most important, is the centrality of morality in the Indonesian audience's critiques of the horror genre. According to Gray (2005, 844), all texts have moral, rational-realist, and aesthetic dimensions, yet anti-fans are often "unwilling or unable to interact with all three levels"; that is, having already passed judgment on the "moral text," they dismiss any possibility of enjoying the other elements such as the cinematography, the acting, or plotlines. Indonesian horror films are frequently criticized for their monotony, irrational plotlines, and ugly cinematography, yet during focus group discussions it becomes clear that the main criterion underlying these complaints is a moral one. In contrast, subpar aesthetics and plotlines in other genres are frequently overlooked if audiences agree with the moral messages of a film.

From an outsider's perspective, I could not discern a huge difference in terms of cinematic quality, narrative coherence, and acting capability when comparing a typical Indonesian horror film with a romantic comedy or religious drama of similar budget. This suggests that, as in Gray's research, the Indonesian horror genre's moral text engulfs the aesthetic or rational text. Yet it is also important to note here that the entwining of the moral and rational-realist text does not only occur with horror films. The lack of realistic or proper narrative logic is a common criticism of Indonesian films across various genres (Kristanto 2004), particularly those narratives that do not follow the prevailing teleological and developmentalist logic that pervades much of contemporary public discourse in Indonesia. In other words, the rational text (plot and narrative) is in fact often a moral text in its own right, as certain narrative trajectories have specific ideological and moral implications. In Indonesia, popular discourses around Islamic modernities, as well as the fusion of religious and developmentalist ideologies, play a key role in blurring the distinction between the rational and the moral text. This leaves us with a far more complicated picture than Gray puts forward in the US case, which I will examine further in the next section.

Ultimately, given the many resonances between my own case and the work of Gray and others, there is a strong case for engaging with their theories. The existing work on anti-fandom undoubtedly enriches the analysis of these young Indonesian audiences' modes of engagement with the horror genre. At the same time, there are some important divergences, and in examining these, I propose some ways in which engagement with different cultural contexts can in turn enrich anti-fandom theory specifically and cultural studies in general.

Cultural Studies in Southeast Asian Contexts

While there are certainly valuable insights that we can take from anti-fandom theories, there are also some important distinctions specific to the Indonesian context that complicate the view from US cultural studies. I will focus on two main issues here: first, the different methodological challenges involved when anti-fans are not a small minority group but rather a mainstream shared national sentiment; and second, how the role of the moral text in the Indonesian context can shed light on some of the blind spots of the Euro-American approach to cultural studies.

In his early theorization of anti-fandom, Gray (2003) points out that most fan studies projects likely start out simply as reception studies, but found it convenient to study fans as they guarantee an engaged commentary on the text. "Intentionally or not, audience research often equals fan research, as anti-fans and non-fans are ignored or assumed" (64), and Gray challenges researchers to engage instead with these other viewers in order to create a more complete and nuanced picture of consumption. Yet during my own fieldwork I experienced quite the opposite methodological challenge: When it comes to Indonesian horror, anti-fans are not the "other" but rather the comfortable majority. In fact, even when I was not interested in pursuing the subject of horror, it was among the first topics raised in any discussion of contemporary Indonesian cinema. This forced me to take anti-fandom seriously from the outset—to look beyond what was being said and focus on the implications behind it, to expose the gaps between discourse and reality, and to investigate the way cultural capital and stereotypes are played out in anti-fan critiques.

Gray, Haig, and Harman and Jones all characterize their anti-fans one way or another as a small community or even a subculture. In contrast, I found myself conceptualizing Indonesian horror anti-fandom as a kind of shared national sensibility. Although the primary focus of my project was young middle-class university students, I interacted with a wide range of audiences. From Islamic boarding schools to Javanese villages, from evangelical prosperity churches to Buginese fishing communities and elite Jakartan malls, at the surface level, there was widespread mainstream condemnation of contemporary Indonesian horror. In fact, being an anti-fan seemed to be the only socially acceptable option throughout much of Indonesia. This has prompted me to speculate beyond existing anti-fan studies, which limit themselves to, say, the minutiae of a particular online forum. By engaging with the notion of anti-fandom on a national scale, we have the opportunity to tease out wider issues of sociopolitical importance that are entwined with antihorror critiques.

The other significant disjuncture between the Indonesian context and the conventions of US cultural studies lies in the different assumptions and approaches regarding morality, or the "moral text" as Gray (2003) terms it. Gray has suggested that studying anti-fan disapproval can offer media and cultural studies "meaningful re-entry points" for discussing quality, values, and expectations, particularly the ways in which everyday viewers' values interact with media consumption, use, and meaning—a discussion he claimed rarely arises in cultural studies (73). Elsewhere, he makes the apparently groundbreaking pronouncement that "the text, long considered the basic unit of aesthetics, may at times be solely or predominantly a moral unit instead" (Gray 2005, 844).

I find Gray's surprise here somewhat unexpected. Working in the Indonesian context, researchers have always been forced to come to terms with the text as a moral unit. This is a situation common to many postcolonial contexts, where ethics and moralities become important sites in the struggle to define contemporary national identities in the wake of the colonial encounter. Furthermore, it is impossible to lose sight of religion as a public and private reality of Indonesian lives. Around 88 percent of Indonesia's population of around 240 million self-identifies as Muslim. For them, as well as for significant minorities such as Hindus and Christians, religion is an important lens through which they interpret contemporary realities, including media products. This has become increasingly clear in the postauthoritarian context, with the power vacuum left by the collapse of Suharto's regime in 1998 increasingly filled by public morality discourses, perhaps most notably illustrated in the antipornography laws introduced in 2008 (Allen 2009; Lindsay 2010). Gray (2005) cites work by Barker et al. on the 1996 David Cronenberg film *Crash* to show how a film can pass from screen to the terrain of news and public debate on morality and the media, overloading expectations of the text and limiting the frames through which many viewers could make sense of it. In my own research on Indonesian films, these kinds of framing processes involving public debates over media and morality are always a given, and therefore, any such discussion is rarely considered radical.

Yet if we examine the bulk of Euro-American cultural and media studies, it is clear that morality and religion are largely absent as key theoretical concepts and are instead submerged beneath other more secular concerns and inquiries. As Baulch and Millie (2013, 234) point out in their reflections on working at the intersection of area studies and cultural studies, "in classical cultural studies, religion has deferred to other modes of subjectivity considered as key constituents of capitalist modernity: race, class and gender." Of course, these different approaches and focus points are shaped by the concerns of specific research contexts. Gray (2005, 849), in his analysis of online anti-fandom in the United States, notes that "all posters temper their comments somewhat, most with humor," in order to seem "less overtly moralistic" because of their awareness that "outright moral posturing may be considered decidedly uncool." In contrast, the rise of an increasingly performative style of popular public piety in Indonesia (Fealy and White 2008; Subijanto 2011) means that the opposite is true: to avoid making moral judgments is the "decidedly uncool" option in this case. In a context where religion, particularly Islam, manifests in fashion, pop songs, and celebrity culture, moral posturing can in fact signal a modern and trendy outlook. This situation problematizes the assumptions underpinning much of Euro-American cultural studies. While there is nothing inherently wrong with a theory tailored to either of these specific sites of inquiry, any attempt to internationalize cultural studies requires an acknowledgment of diverse cultural contexts and therefore a more serious engagement with questions of morality and religious practice. Despite the "secular ideal underpinning the genesis and history of cultural studies" (Baulch and Millie 2013, 235), it is undeniable that religious practice, religious authority, and religious media remain ever-present facts of capitalist modernity, particularly in postcolonial contexts. Baulch and Millie (2013, 235) further contend that coming to terms with religion is

> a process more complex than simply applying staple cultural studies conceptual tools to existing structures and practices. It will also entail giving serious attention to spaces outside the "approved" cultural studies structures, and recognizing the different historical and social realities that motivate the scholarly interventions produced within them.

This reengagement with questions of religion and morality is one of the many areas in which what Ariel Heryanto (2013) has termed the "intimacies" between cultural studies and specific area studies can be theoretically fruitful. Pioneering initiatives such as the establishment of an inter-Asia cultural studies community (see Chen 1998; Ichiyo 2010; Sakai 2010) have reinforced the significance of reevaluating cultural studies in Asian contexts, prompting reflections on the strengths and drawbacks of different scholarly approaches in different areas of the world. By attempting to locate antihorror sentiments among Indonesian audiences as a kind of anti-fandom, this chapter joins these important conversations.

Working at the intersection of area, media, and cultural studies is a valuable endeavor, with lessons to offer both areas of inquiry. While insights from the Indonesian context can be helpful in expanding the horizons of cultural studies research, there is also much in US cultural studies that has been useful when examining the Indonesian case. Extended critical analysis of the nature of textuality and audience engagement rarely appears in the context of Indonesian studies, which has tended to prioritize formal political processes and structures as frames for viewing Indonesia (Baulch and Millie 2013). Furthermore, as noted in this chapter's introduction on the horror genre, Indonesian media studies scholarship tends to focus on the production and content of texts, rather than the living text as it operates in day-to-day life. The works of Gray and others, therefore, offer important insights into these questions of audience and textuality. For Gray (2005, 843), because a text can exist in "everyday talk," it becomes a "structure of feeling and a matrix of power, meaning, effects, and identity that can and frequently does separate itself from its mooring of the actual program as broadcast." Anti-fandom theory's analysis of the "multiple connections between fandom and anti-fandom, the moral and the emotional, the text, and ideals of the public and textual spheres" (841) therefore offers an important framework for looking beyond the surface of media, representation, and communication in the case of Indonesian horror films.

Locating Southeast Asian Horror

Returning to the specific question of Indonesian horror films, I will conclude with some brief reflections on how audiences position these films in relation to other film genres. Given that the Indonesian horror genre is often defined in direct opposition to both "quality national cinema" and "foreign horror," it is worthwhile spending a moment examining what these kinds of definitions mean when locating Southeast Asian horror more broadly. *Horor asing* (foreign horror) or *horor dari luar* (horror from outside) is a broad category in Indonesia, encapsulating everything from Thai to Korean to Hollywood horror films. Horror devotees usually claim to prefer foreign horror films as they are less overtly pornographic, as is the case for Nita, who exclaimed, "I love horror! But not Indonesian horror. . . . Indonesian horror is too open [in terms of sex]" (Nita, pers. comm., June 10, 2013). Similarly, Ray said, "I watch horror [from] Thailand or Japan [because] it's more exciting and actually scary" (pers. comm., September 10, 2013). Of course, individual tastes vary, with some respondents preferring Korean horror to Hollywood horror or expressing nostalgia for Indonesian horror of previous eras. Yet audiences overall tend to construct a clear dichotomy between local and foreign offerings. There emerges a somewhat monolithic notion of what foreign films are, which does not pay much heed to distinctions between East and Southeast Asia. This relates to the often insular nature of Indonesian worldviews, whereby ideas about what lies beyond the borders are often hazy, and the Indonesian "self" is defined against all others, which are generalized into a mass outside (see Heryanto 1999; Schlehe 2013). As such, it is difficult to "locate" Southeast Asian horror in the imagination of Indonesian audiences, for the very category of "Southeast Asia" as a community of belonging carries little salience (Bonura and Sears 2007). Despite increasing transnational flows of people and media products, the Indonesian horror genre remains a remarkably situated phenomenon, serving very specific functions in local discourses of morality and taste. Indonesian horror, as the genre that local audiences love to hate, has become a site for performing critical condemnation and reinforcing stereotypes and divisions of cultural capital within the specific Indonesian context.

My attempt to locate antihorror sentiment among Indonesian audiences as a form of anti-fandom has prompted an interactive encounter between US cultural studies and the Indonesian context. I have built a case for critically engaging with—and, if necessary, adapting—cultural studies theories and approaches in the Southeast Asian context. Put simply, we should not only be interested in what a particular theory can tell us about a situation but also in what a particular situation or cultural context can tell us about the theory in question. During the course of my fieldwork, I came to understand that, for my respondents, modes of receiving and appreciating Indonesian horror go beyond simple rejection and disavowal, and the works of Gray and others have been highly useful in illuminating how textual pleasure and repulsion can be inextricably linked. Behind dislike, after all, there are always expectations—what kind of story deserves media time and space, what morality or aesthetics a text should display, and what we think others should watch or read. Studying the anti-fan is, therefore, a way to study the expectations and values that structure media consumption; thus, anti-fandom can be a useful framework for audience research everywhere.

Conversely, some of the divergences apparent in the Indonesian case point to ways in which research into different cultural contexts can challenge and enrich the existing theoretical and methodological conventions of cultural studies. Taking the role of religion and public morality more seriously is one among many areas in which working at this intersection of area, media, and cultural studies can prove fruitful and contribute to new research directions.

References

Abercrombie, N., and B. J. Longhurst. 1998. *Audiences: A Sociological Theory of Performance and Imagination.* SAGE.

Allen, P. 2009. "Women, Gendered Activism and Indonesia's Anti-Pornography Bill." *Intersections: Gender and Sexuality in Asia and the Pacific* 19 (February).

Barker, T. 2011. "A Cultural Economy of the Contemporary Indonesian Film Industry." MA thesis, National University of Singapore.

Baulch, E., and J. Millie. 2013. "Introduction: Studying Indonesian Media Worlds at the Intersection of Area and Cultural Studies." *International Journal of Cultural Studies* 16, no. 3: 227–40.

Bonura, C., and L. J. Sears. 2007. "Introduction: Knowledges That Travel in Southeast Asian Area Studies." In *Knowing Southeast Asian Subjects,* edited by L. J. Sears. NUS Press.

Bourdieu, P. 1984. *Distinction: A Social Critique of the Judgement of Taste.* Harvard University Press.

Bourdieu, P. 1986. "The Forms of Capital." In *Handbook of Theory and Research for the Sociology of Education,* ed. J. Richardson, 241–58. Greenwood Press.

Chen, K.-H. 1998. "Preface: The Trajectories Project." In *Trajectories: Inter-Asia Cultural Studies,* ed. K. H. Chen, xiii–xvi. Routledge.

Fealy, G., and S. White, eds. 2008. *Expressing Islam: Religious Life and Politics in Indonesia.* ISEAS.

Fiske, J. 1989. *The John Fiske Collection: Understanding Popular Culture.* Routledge.

Fiske, J. 1992. "The Cultural Economy of Fandom." In *The Adoring Audience: Fan Culture and Popular Media,* ed. L. La, 30–49. Routledge.

Genette, G. 1997. *Paratexts: Thresholds of Interpretation.* Cambridge University Press.

Gray, J. 2003. "New Audiences, New Textualities: Anti-Fans and Non-Fans." *International Journal of Cultural Studies* 6, no. 1: 64–81.

Gray, J. 2005. "Antifandom and the Moral Text: Television Without Pity and Textual Dislike." *American Behavioral Scientist* 48, no. 7: 840–58.

Gray, J., C. Sandvoss, and C. L. Harrington. 2007. *Fandom: Identities and Communities in a Mediated World.* NYU Press.

Haig, F. 2013. "Critical Pleasures: Twilight, Snark and Critical Fandom." In *Screening Twilight: Critical Approaches to a Cinematic Phenomenon*, ed. W. Clayton and S. Harman. I. B. Tauris.

Hall, S. 1980. "Coding and Encoding in the Television Discourse." In *Culture, Media, Language*, ed. S. Hall, 128–38. Unwin Hyman.

Harman, S., and B. Jones. 2013. "Fifty Shades of Grey: Snark Fandom and the Figure of the Anti-Fan." *Sexualities* 16, no. 8: 951–68.

Heryanto, A. 1999. "The Years of Living Luxuriously." In *Culture and Privilege in Capitalist Asia*, ed. M. Pinches, 160–88. Routledge.

Heryanto, A. 2013. "The Intimacies of Cultural and Area Studies: The Case of Southeast Asia." *International Journal of Cultural Studies* 16, no. 3: 303–16.

Ichiyo, M. 2010. "Asia, Inter-Asia, and Movement: Decolonization into the Future." *Inter-Asia Cultural Studies* 77, no. 2: 178–83.

Kardit, H., dir. 2009. *Suster Keramas*. Maxima Pictures.

Klink, M. L. 2008. "Laugh Out Loud in Real Life: Women's Humor and Fan Identity." MSC thesis, MIT.

Kristanto, J. 2004. *Nonton film nonton Indonesia*. Penerbit Buku Kompas.

Lindsay, J. 2010. "Media and Morality: Pornography post Suharto." In *Politics and the Media in Twenty-First Century Indonesia: Decade of Democracy*, ed. K. Sen and D. T. Hill. Routledge.

Luvaas, B. 2009. "Dislocating Sounds: The Deterritorialization of Indonesian Indie Pop." *Cultural Anthropology* 24, no. 2: 246–79.

Nuala, N. F., dir. 2011. *Pocong ngesot*. Rapi Films.

Pagayo, K., dir. 2006. *Hantu jeruk purut*. Indika Entertainment.

Sakai, N. 2010. "From Area Studies Toward Transnational Studies." *Inter-Asia Cultural Studies* 77, no. 2: 265–74.

Sandvoss, C. 2005. *Fans: The Mirror of Consumption*. Polity.

Saputra, A., and F. Lingga, dirs. 2007. *Beranakdi dalam kubur*. MD Pictures.

Schlehe, J. 2013. "Concepts of Asia, the West and the Self in Contemporary Indonesia: An Anthropological Account." *South East Asia Research* 27, no. 3: 497–515.

Sen, K. 1994. *Indonesian Cinema: Framing the New Order*. Zed Books.

Strinati, D. 2004. *An Introduction to Theories of Popular Culture*. Routledge.

Subijanto, R. 2011. "The Visibility of a Pious Public." *Inter-Asia Cultural Studies* 72, no. 2: 240–53.

Suryadi, A., dir. 2008. *Sumpah pocong di sekolah*. Maxima Pictures.

van Heeren, K. 2007. "Return of the Kyai: Representations of Horror, Commerce, and Censorship in Post-Suharto Indonesian Film and Television." *Inter-Asia Cultural Studies* 8, no. 2: 211–26.

van Heeren, K. 2009. "Contemporary Indonesian Film: Spirits of Reform and Ghosts from the Past." PhD diss., Leiden University.

Chapter 29

NEW BLACK GOTHIC

Sheri-Marie Harrison

> In her *Los Angeles Review of Books* article, Sheri-Marie Harrison focuses on a twenty-first-century trend she characterizes as the "New Black Gothic." With attention to the novels of Jesmyn Ward, the films of Jordan Peele, and the music videos of Childish Gambino (aka Donald Glover) in particular, Harrison argues that such works speak to the Black experience in ways that acknowledge past and present injustice.

Toward the end of Jesmyn Ward's 2017 novel *Sing, Unburied, Sing*, one of the narrators, a Black teenager named Jojo, comes across "a great live oak ... full with ghosts." "With their eyes," the ghosts speak their violent deaths to him in unpunctuated prose:

> He raped me and suffocated me until I died I put my hands up and he shot me eight times ... they came in my cell in the middle of the night and they hung me they found out I could read and they dragged me out to the barn and gouged my eyes before they beat me still.[1]

This litany of brutal torture and death spans the history of Black life in America. The ghosts' attire, "rags and breeches, T-shirts and tignons, fedoras and hoodies,"[2] brings together in a single Gothic image the brutality of slavery and Jim Crow–era lynchings and the more contemporary and familiar violence that claimed the lives of Trayvon Martin and Mike Brown. In the logic of the novel, Ward's ghosts are "stuck"[3] and unable to "cross the waters,"[4] the final transition in the Yoruba cosmology that also makes its way into Louisiana Voodoo culture. They are confined to the terrestrial realm, searching for "keyholes" of human misery and need through which they can slip into the lives of the living and amplify their suffering, while approximating a sort of half-life for themselves.

Ward's award-winning novels are among a number of works, literary and otherwise, that rework Gothic traditions for the twenty-first century. As my graduate student Cynthia Snider has observed in my class on contemporary fiction and book prizes, Ward engages specifically the Southern Gothic tradition. In American literature, there is a long tradition of using Gothic tropes to reveal how ideologies of American exceptionalism rely on repressing the nation's history of slavery, racism, and patriarchy. Such tropes are, as numerous critics have noted, central to the work of Toni Morrison.

But unlike in, say, Morrison's *Beloved*, the spectral reappearance of America's violent history in recent fiction is neither about recovery nor representation. Ward's ghost tree does not recover the lost stories of the voiceless. For Ward, there is no buried trauma that must be converted into language for its victims to move on. Instead, racial violence has never gone away. It is indeed, as the ghosts are, at home with us. Ward's ghosts speak to an ever-present and visible lineage of violence that accumulates rather than dissipates with the passage of time. Gothic violence remains a part of everyday Black life.

This Black Gothic revival has appeared not only in literature, but in an array of popular forms. On the May 5, 2018, episode of *Saturday Night Live (SNL)*, while he was simultaneously hosting and serving (in the role of his alter ego Childish Gambino) as musical guest, Donald Glover released the controversial music video for "This Is America." Within the video's first few frames Gambino, clad in what looks like Confederate army trousers, pulls out a pistol, and in the clumsy exaggerated elegance of a pose borrowed from Jim Crow minstrel show advertisements, shoots a man in the back of his head. The video takes place in a cavernous empty warehouse and—in addition to the shooting I just described—features another shooting in which Gambino mows down a church choir with an automatic rifle; police violence; the lively choreography of a number of viral dance moves; and numerous other things the internet devoted itself to analyzing in the days after its release.

For the most part, analyses focus on cataloging how much there is to see in the video's chaotic tableau and on annotating the important things we may not have seen or properly understood. The consensus seems to be that the choreographed dancing is meant to distract from what is happening in the background—police violence, riots, mass shootings, and even one of the horsemen who, according to Revelations 6:2, is supposed to herald the Apocalypse. As Aida Amoako puts it in *The Atlantic*,[5] the video "is a denunciation of the distractions that keep many Americans from noticing how the world around them is falling apart." If the world is Gambino's warehouse, we stay grinning and dancing and mugging for our phones with the glee of children while chaos and violence lick at our heels.

But the video does more than denounce our social-mediated distraction and apathy. What is one to do, for example, with Gambino's costume, his minstrel-like poses, and his exaggerated facial gestures? One gets the sense that the video is not only deeply invested in the violent history of Black life in the United States, but also that Gambino is himself performing in blackface. This is not too much of a stretch when one considers the issues of colorism that, according to Tad Friend's *New Yorker*[6] profile of Glover, inflects Glover's relationship with his darker-skinned brother, Stephen:

> Growing up, Donald was light-skinned and sunny, and his friends were the white kids at his school for the performing arts; Stephen was darker-skinned and stoic, and his friends were the bused-in black kids at his school, which was not for the performing arts. . . . Many of the show's rawer moments are underpinned by real-life affronts that Stephen sustained. . . . Glover said, "My consciousness began to change when I hung out with Steve as an adult, because he's scarier to white people. It made me super-black."

In the last sentence, Glover points to the performative nature of race, which he in turn subverts in "This Is America" by appearing to wear part of a Confederate uniform. The satire is bizarre, but if we understand Gambino's costume as a convoluted minstrelsy of sorts, we can begin to see how protests against the video's depiction of what looks like Black-on-Black violence as gratuitous and irresponsible may actually be missing something. With his pants and opening posture, Glover gives a nod not only to centuries of cultural appropriation of Blackness and Black culture, but also establishes the parodic, historical, and aesthetic contexts that are central for understanding the present that the video depicts. As with Ward's tarrying ghosts, the exploitative and violent ways Black bodies have been used in the service of white supremacy across history continue to linger in the present.

The mise-en-scène staged by Glover and his frequent collaborator Hiro Murai thus finds common cause with other works that deploy Gothic tropes to make sense of Black life in relation to the present-day neoliberal manifestations of white supremacy and the institutions it requires to maintain its violent dominance—institutions such as the police, the judicial system, and the National Rifle Association. Among the things that viewers have found confusing about the video is the presence of numerous large, 1980s-model cars. Why are they there? I'd like to suggest that the answer to that question is a lynchpin for the video's political commentary, an answer that requires thinking of the music video's relationship to the literary Gothic revival contemporary Black writers are staging.

This Black Gothic revival includes tropes of darkness, madness, ghosts, and isolation that combine to create unease and evoke fear and terror. In this regard, the cavernous warehouse of "This Is America" evokes the gloomy Gothic castles of the eighteenth-century Gothic novel, or the dilapidated plantations of twentieth-century Southern Gothic. This aesthetic tradition has seen a resurgence in recent years through novels like those of Ward and James Hannaham, whose *Delicious Foods* depicts a form of modern-day slavery on a southern factory farm worked by drug addicts who have been transported there from their precarious urban lives. These novels work to document and make sense of the social forces that constrain and marginalize Black life. Exploring these same questions, "This Is America" participates in and is informed by this much larger aesthetic conversation, employing Gothic tropes to embed contemporary developments such as mandatory minimum sentencing and the War on Drugs in a longer history of slavery and Jim Crow. Indeed, as Michelle Alexander suggests,[7] these policies and initiatives have come to constitute a new Jim Crow.

Beyond works of fiction, "This Is America" also finds clarifying company in Jordan Peele's 2017 film *Get Out,* in Glover's own television show *Atlanta,* and in various sketches from the episode of *SNL* that Glover hosted. Think, for example, of the dark corn field of "A Kanye Place," or the rainy creepiness of the "Raz P. Berry" sketches. Together, the Black Gothic revival not only works through what it means to be Black in a nation still structured by violent white supremacy, but also dramatizes how Black artists like Glover, Peele, Ward, and even Kanye must negotiate their celebrity while also remaining cognizant of the ways their race binds them to the vulnerabilities of a racialized second class of citizenship.

One thing that distinguishes the contemporary Black Gothic is its dark humor. *Atlanta* is classified as a sitcom and *Get Out* was nominated for the Golden Globe for Best Musical or Comedy, yet both focus on forms of Black danger and violence that lurk in the most mundane circumstances. The humor of *Atlanta* and *Get Out* is not comedic, as Jordan Peele has pointed out in an interview in which he noted that there aren't any jokes in *Get Out,* but that the humor functions as a form of tension relief. *Atlanta* does something similar. Take, for example, the second episode of the first season, in particular the scene in which Earn is detained in a jail and sees a mentally disturbed man drink toilet water. The scene maintains as much humor as it can while portraying Black men detained by the police, right up until the man spits the toilet water in an officer's face. At this point the scene pivots: The man is beaten at length, while the other detainees work hard to ignore what is happening. As these examples suggest, the laughter of the New Black Gothic is always proximate to the ways in which daily Black life can suddenly descend into horror. This shit is not supposed to be funny, but we laugh uncomfortably anyway. The juxtaposition of choreographed dancing and violence in "This Is America" creates a similar effect.

Get Out has given us disturbing yet enduring metaphors, like the sunken place, that describe the marginalized position of Black people within a system of white supremacy that actively silences them "no matter how hard [they] scream," while also appropriating their culture and bodies for its own power, profit, and survival. The film is a touchstone for *Atlanta,* much as Childish Gambino's music is a touchstone for *Get Out.* That Glover and Peele are in conversation with each other is undeniable. *Get Out* opens with the soulful yet haunting groove of Gambino's quadruple-platinum record *Redbone.* In this way, the film implores its Black audience to "stay woke" even as it reassures them that its main character, Chris, played by Daniel

Kaluuya, is indeed woke and will be able to find his way out of the film's web of psychological terror.

Similarly, it is probably not coincidental that Chris and his girlfriend, Rose, hit a deer with their car on the way to visit her parents for the first time, and in the fourth episode of the second season of *Atlanta,* Earn and his girlfriend, Van, played by Zazie Beetz, almost hit a wild boar while driving to a German festival called Fastnacht. In both cases, the accident foreshadows discomfiting and at times horrifying relationship turmoil that unfolds against the backdrop of racial disparities, and in strange and threatening locations: in *Get Out,* the clearly Gothic estate of Rose's parents; in *Atlanta,* an eerie German town north of Atlanta. These similarities and creative overlaps suggest a shared aesthetic that both artists use to explore contemporary Black life.

While Glover's performance hosting *SNL* might seem unrelated to this project, Glover in fact brought the New Black Gothic to the sketch comedy show, where it functioned as an introduction or primer of sorts for "This Is America." Watching the show, one thing I couldn't shake was how obscure and random it seemed to parody Oran "Juice" Jones's one-hit wonder "The Rain." In fact, however, this parody of a briefly popular song begins to answer the question of the cars in "This Is America." "The Rain" was released in 1986, the same year as the Anti–Drug Abuse Act. This act enacted mandatory minimum sentencing for drug offenses that disproportionally affected African Americans, exploding the US penal population, according to Michelle Alexander, "from around 300,000 to more than 2 million, with drug convictions accounting for the majority of the increase."[8]

The result, in the terms of Alexander's well-known argument, is a new racial caste system that stigmatizes and confines a racial group through law and custom. The "Raz P. Berry" sketch, which reworks the Gothic overtones of the original song and video—the theme of a man stalking an unfaithful lover, his threats of violence, the dark urban setting—helps us to see why "This Is America" recalls the mid-1980s. In the *SNL* sketch, the joke is that every attempted act of revenge by the man against his lover results in self-harm. "This Is America" tells a much larger—and darker and less funny—joke about the forces driving violence within the Black community.

There are more layers to "This Is America" and the New Black Gothic than mass incarceration and the new Jim Crow. Alfred "Paper Boi" Miles is portrayed on *Atlanta* as being immensely uncomfortable with his newfound fame. The title of season 2's final episode, "Crabs in a Barrel," references the precarity of Black success and the anxiety of being pulled back down into the barrel with the rest. In this episode, Uncle Willie's golden gun reappears to demonstrate how the season has come full circle. The anxiety we experience for Uncle Willie, as a Black man on probation who has police at his door and marijuana and illegal firearms in the house in the season's opener, is the same we experience for Earn at an airport security checkpoint with Alfred, who is also on probation, and that same illegal firearm forgotten in his backpack in the season's finale.

Just as Willie makes his escape by releasing his pet alligator, Earn escapes airport security by putting the gun in a bag that belongs to Clark County, the rapper who is headlining the European tour on which Paper Boi has secured a spot. In the end, when Clark County eventually boards the plane, he tells Earn and Alfred that his (white) manager won't be making the flight because he was detained by the police for possession of a weapon. Earn's distraction backfires—but with a crucial irony. The crabs-in-a-barrel logic suggests that Clark County's trouble with the law will elevate Alfred to his rightful spot as tour headliner and will redeem Earn's poor performance as his manager. But Earn does not factor in that Clark County's having a white manager means that the Black rapper has a fall guy who will receive a much more lenient sentence for any charge. Earn and Paper Boi's smooth escape from a gun charge is, at this moment, stripped of triumph or even relief. In this respect, it's a perfect metonym for the show as a whole.

The scene at the end of "This Is America" where a terrified-looking Gambino is being chased by a mostly white mob is reminiscent of *Get Out*'s sunken place, in which Black people's autonomous consciousnesses are sequestered so their bodies can be appropriated for the use of white people. At its simplest, the sunken place is a metaphor for the sometimes-forced appropriation of Black people's bodies, labor, and culture for capitalistic endeavors like slavery or the record industry. The final pursuit of Gambino similarly dramatizes the precarious position of the Black man in America, who is almost always already criminalized in the aid of white supremacy's need to violently appropriate Black labor and Black bodies.

Critics of the video who point out its problematically masculine focus are exactly right—near the end of the song, Gambino repeats, "Black man, get your money," while Young Thug's outro begins, "You just a Black man in this world"—although it's worth noting that *Atlanta* at least makes some strides toward encompassing Black women in its diagnosis of contemporary Black life through the character of Van. Consider the episode, for instance, in which she desperately boils her daughter's diaper to try to extract urine to foil a mandatory drug test at work. She fails the test and ultimately loses her job. Another unifying feature of the New Black Gothic then, along with humor that is not comedic and a preoccupation with the domestic legacies of the War on Drugs, is a sense of inescapability and the eschewal of hope for the future. These contemporary Black Gothic texts bring into sharp focus the near-constant vulnerability of Black life.

We see the presence of this vulnerability at the end of *Sing, Unburied, Sing* when the toddler Kayla faces the tree of ghosts and tells them to "go home." They "shudder, but they do not leave"[9] at her command. As if recognizing their need for comfort, she "raises one arm in the air, palm up, like she is trying to soothe . . . but the ghosts don't still, don't rise, don't ascend and disappear. They stay."[10] Kayla's next effort in comforting or ushering the ghosts home is to begin singing "a song of mismatches, half garble words" that her brother, Jojo, cannot understand, though the melody is familiar. As she sings, the ghosts "smile with something like relief, something like remembrance, something like ease."[11] While they seem soothed by her song, they are not encouraged away from their perch. They remain there in the trees, still saying "home," even as Kayla, Jojo, and their grandfather walk away from them and the novel ends.

In its resolution, *Sing, Unburied, Sing* does not offer safe passage home for the ghosts of the past who have suffered racial violence across centuries. In this way, Ward's New Black Gothic does not offer correctives or hope for a brighter future, nor does it exorcise the ghosts from past brutality. It instead lays bare the realities of our time and their roots in systems that depend on the criminalization and disenfranchisement of Black people.

It's not too difficult to think of "This Is America" as a parallel of sorts to Kayla's song. Like Ward's transhistorical ghosts, Gambino's minstrel poses, the video's images of police brutality, and its tableaus of riot and chaos cumulatively demonstrate how the past is an actor demanding recognition in the present. Knowing this makes one, rightly, hopeless, and the works I have been discussing don't shy away from this hopelessness. But it doesn't *only* make one hopeless, insofar as it also provides varied contexts for recognizing how white supremacy and systemic racism continue to organize American life. The New Black Gothic aesthetic thus functions in popular Black art as a tool for representing Black life on its own terrorized terms.

Notes

1. Jesmyn Ward, *Sing, Unburied, Sing* (Scriber, 2017), 280–82. (Editor's note)
2. Ward, 283. (Editor's note)
3. Ward, 280. (Editor's note)
4. Ward, 281. (Editor's note)
5. Aida Amoako, "Why the Dancing Makes 'This Is America' So Uncomfortable to Watch," *The Atlantic,* May 8, 2018, https://www.theatlantic.com/entertainment/archive/2018/05/this-is-america-childish-gambino-donald-glover-kinesthetic-empathy-dance/559928/.
6. Tad Friend, "Donald Glover Can't Save You," *The New Yorker,* February 26, 2018, https://www.newyorker.com/magazine/2018/03/05/donald-glover-cant-save-you.
7. Michelle Alexander, *The New Jim Crow: Mass Incarceration in the Age of Colorblindness* (New Press, 2010). (Editor's note)
8. Alexander, 6. (Editor's note)
9. Ward, *Sing,* 284. (Editor's note)
10. Ward, 284. (Editor's note)
11. Ward, 284. (Editor's note)

Chapter 30

BLACK HORROR BEYOND THE WHITE GAZE
A Conversation

Dani Bethea and Monika Negra

> Building on Harrison's characterization of the New Black Gothic in the preceding chapter, this wide-ranging conversation between horror scholar Dani Bethea and journalist and filmmaker Monika Negra addresses important themes in Black horror and the ways in which contemporary works by Black authors and filmmakers engage with legacies of violence, abuse, and exclusion.

Content/Trigger Warnings: This interview includes discussions of homophobia, mental health, racism, sexual assault, and transphobia. This conversation was edited for length and style.

DANI BETHEA (she/they/them): Welcome everyone and thank you to the editors of *Studies in the Fantastic*. My name is Dani Bethea, and I am so delighted to interview an amazing individual today. Monika Estrella Negra is the editor in chief of *cinéSPEAK*, the cofounder of Audre's Revenge Film Collective, and the coeditor of *Decoded Pride* . . . and I cannot wait to talk about all things horror and film, and Black media with her. So without further ado: welcome aboard, Monika.

MONIKA NEGRA (she/her): Thanks for having me, Dani. I'm super excited to have this discussion with you.

DB: So, all right, what is the latest horror that you've delved into lately? Whether it be books, TV, film, etc.?

MN: Oh, man, I like to watch so much content on a daily basis and also read a bunch of things. But more so what stuck out to me recently, and what has been in my brain—and I'm still trying to process it—is Nia DaCosta's *Candyman* [2021]. Just because, I was waiting for so long to see that movie, and then Covid happened. And then it was just like bleh! . . . It was going to be released on my birthday in

2020. And I made plans this entire time . . . like I'm going to do a *Candyman* birthday party! And then we're going to go see the new *Candyman*! And it was going to be amazing, but at least I was able to [finally] rent it, just because I wasn't comfortable going to a theater to go experience it, although I wish that I had because it's such a beautifully shot movie. So yeah, that has been a primary film that has stuck out in my brain, mostly because of the narrative surrounding Black vengeance.

And I think that with Audre's Revenge Film, that's always been my focal point. It's just talking about what does Black vengeance look like, particularly among Black marginalized people within our own communities, and that includes queer and trans Black folks and Black women. And I think that *Candyman* definitely upped the ante on what is possible in the realm of imagination for Black vengeance. And those are the narratives that I like . . . truly, truly, truly. I was just obsessed with it just because I feel like it's still a very touchy subject. As far as Black people being like the victors in a micro-aggressive, passive-aggressive white supremacist society. And there's . . . so much animosity toward any hint . . . or desire for a Black person to actively destroy what slowly destroys them.

And I thought it was just perfect, even though Nia [DaCosta] definitely faced a lot of criticism from executives who were investors in the film, about what could go in the movie and what couldn't. And that was particularly frustrating because also as an independent filmmaker—and by choice an independent filmmaker—I think that when there is some type of weird control, especially from the white gaze over our creative properties, we really miss a mark on what we were truly trying to convey to audiences that inevitably see our work. So yeah, I think that's the major one that's been stuck in my brain lately.

[. . .]

[Latanya McQueen's] *When the Reckoning Comes* [2021][1] is such a beautifully written novel. I love Southern Gothic-esque stories, but also to pick a plantation space . . . and I know that was a trend for a second for white people hosting these very lavish weddings at old-old plantation houses. And I thought that Latanya McQueen's book [also] had a really interesting take on ancestral vengeance, but also ancestral care as far as looking at the relationships in our lives, and trying to figure out what connection that has to some of the traumas that our ancestors faced, in these physical places. I'm very much a spiritual person, I'm very much into ancestral veneration. And I'm very much a believer of ancestral warfare. And that's actually one of the topics in my fourth film: *Bitten, a Tragedy* [2021], which is going to be premiering at Ax Wound [Film Festival] in a couple of weeks. And I just think that it's an interesting concept to explore because ancestral warfare has this weird way of manifesting in the things that we see today, [as in] a lot of the cases today [of violence against Black men], like with Ahmaud Arbery.

And lynchings, the history of lynchings, and how white people were able to get away with that like to . . . go ahead and just like lynch a Black person and go home at the end of the day. And that's what it is. Plantation owners and slave owners would, you know, brutalize and torture enslaved peoples, because to them that was their property. And that was like . . . they could just get away with it, because it's like owning a cow or something, you know what I mean? So, all these little instances of racism that we see today, and how it manifests in different ways . . . I feel like it's kind of . . . this ancestral cycle of martyrdom or like misery that can only be corrected if we actually as a society and as a community do the right thing to hold people accountable. Like that is the idea of true rest, right? True peace happening. Then there's just this unsettling . . . insistence, that it's just going to cycle on and there is no ending. So yeah, I really appreciated that book.

DB: That's lovely. You know what you brought up for me? [Your words and your contemplations] make me think about . . . I'm not sure if you've heard about it . . . well I'm sure you have because we're, you know, we're readers and we're on the internet a lot. But this *Printing Hate* series that the Howard Center for Investigative Journalism—and actually, I'm not sure how many historically Black colleges—but a plethora of them came together for this amazing project that is going through the history of journalism in America and dissecting how journalism played a key role in not only depicting the entirely racist elements of lynchings and violence, violence against Black towns, and so on and so forth [but also contributing to that cycle of violence].[2] So, [journalists were] not just being passive bystanders, but regularly participating and inflaming a mob or inciting violence or obviously biased in the reporting . . . not getting full and accurate details, and even the complex nature of white newspaper journalists reporting one thing [versus] the Black newspaper journalists reporting something completely different . . . so I can't recommend the *Printing Hate* series enough.
[. . .]

MN: I mean, one of the major reasons why so many Black publications started was because they clearly saw the bias that was existing in mainstream publications, like events were not being told about if it weren't for *The Green Book, The Negro Motorist Green Book* by [Victor] Hugo Green.[3] A lot of Black people that were a part of the great Black migration would have landed in sundown towns, which is also like *Lovecraft Country* [2020]. So yes, [the show] touched upon that. And I was like, that whole segment was just such a perfect enactment of the fear that Black people feel in certain spaces, like when it does get dark outside. I'll buy the H. P. Lovecraft–like creatures or whatever, but still, just being in that situation is terrifying. And I thought that it was a wonderful, wonderful way to depict it. And I'm also really sad that the show got canceled.

DB: Yeah. I . . . you know what, we're actually going to talk *Candyman* in a minute, but you know what . . . we can . . . that is a great transition into *Lovecraft Country*.

And I've written about *Lovecraft Country,* and its highs and its lows and everything else in between, but honestly, in my opinion, you're probably going to agree with me.[4] I think the series needed more episodes to really stretch the characters out . . . to really explore, you know, some more lore to really just kind of let the series breathe a little bit because in my opinion, there just . . . there just weren't enough episodes.

MN: Absolutely. It was like all of the episodes were way too packed with complex issues that should have been fleshed out over like a couple of other episodes, but I think it's also just because of budget but also shame on HBO because I know they got money. I know y'all got money, like don't play with me, HBO. I paid fifty dollars a month for your service. I'm pretty sure a lot of other people do, too. So yeah, I think that if they had ordered more episodes, scripts would have provided a more thorough explanation as to the story and a lot of concepts that yes, [could have been] explored a bit better. And it's just that because once they canceled, they got all these award nominations. [Who knows if they] may win any of them? Because we already know that Hollywood loves to give out like their token nominations, but you don't really win anything. But in essence, I follow [writer/producer/director] Misha Green on Twitter, and she is very vocal about sharing her perspective as far as how she wrote the script, and what she wanted to bring to the horror genre as a whole . . . and I think that if she had been given the resources that she needed, it could have gone to an entirely different level.

DB: Yeah, it could, you know? And you could see the glimmers of—not that the show didn't have its amazingly brilliant—I mean, jaw-dropping, like gasp-inducing moments, but you're absolutely right. Absolutely. Some of the highlights in the show that I can recall, like, right off hand was the scene, the literal haunted house episode, right [episode 3, "Holy Ghost"]? That entire episode was so well done from a horror perspective, from a kind of reckoning with Black medical racism catharsis . . . oh, gosh, it even had, like conjure women in there, like it had old Black magic practitioners. I was like, okay, *this*! And it was just a part of the world and the lore. And obviously, like you said, if the series had had more time, that, you know, potentially the Black characters . . . instead of, you know, trying to fight white magic with "white magic," right, could have . . . learned from this Black woman who had all of this old root magic . . . and actually, I think she was, um, I think she was from the Caribbean, but don't quote me there. Either the Caribbean or from Louisiana. And I know there's a lot of overlap.

MN: Yeah, yeah. And essentially have the same traditional African [practices] just with minor aesthetic differences, but it's all there . . . it's like the transgenerational memories are still there, they've just adapted to different societies, cultures, localized cultures. Actually . . . actually you want to know what my favorite part of *Lovecraft Country* [is]? It was actually Topsy and Bopsy.

DB: Oh, oh my gosh. Okay! Yes, yes!

Figure 30.1. Screen capture from *Lovecraft Country*, HBO, Topsy and Bopsy, season 1, episode 8, "Jig-a-Bobo," by Dani Bethea.

MN: Because I feel like Black girlhood is not really a thing in a lot of horror movies.
DB: Yes. Okay! You're speaking my language, Monika. Come on!
MN: So I mean, when I saw that episode, I actually cried because it was just really heartbreaking to see Diana being tortured by these two cops and then Topsy and Bopsy . . . you see that, pickaninny as a whole egregious caricature, right? And I think about *Ethnic Notions* (1987) by Marlon Riggs.[5] And that was my first exposure to some of the pre-Reconstruction Black caricatures that were plastered everywhere . . . [like the] pickaninny. Yeah, and talk about the value of Black girlhood. It is still a very sorely touched upon subject I feel because a lot of people just aren't willing to explore it. Just as you were saying that also women were lynched in conjunction with Black men.

I also feel like girlhood has not had its proper time to be explored [as an] image, and for them to do it in this way of Topsy and Bopsy being these ghoulish pickaninnies that are just following [Diana]. Oh my gosh, it's like the black cloud over our heads that comes with the judgment of what Black womanhood could eventually be. Hypersexualization, too sassy, too mean, whatever else and I mean . . . think about all these real-life issues that Black girls face . . . whether they have mental health issues with depression, or things of that nature, and everybody just kind of writes it off as being shiftless or being mean or being angry or whatever else, but she's actually going through like complete duress. But the nasty stereotypes . . . just keep on following us . . . keep on haunting us. And I thought that that was such a beautiful representation of that [phenomenon] to have just the ugliness of what people project onto a Black girl [embodied in Topsy and Bopsy].

DB: Yeah, oh my gosh, you're not kidding. Like, that [*Lovecraft Country*, season 1, episode 8, "Jig-a-Bobo"] was not only one of my favorite episodes, but it was this huge lightbulb.[6] . . . It was something I'd always known internally, as far as the horror genre, that we have kind of a select few, you know, Black girl monsters that we can recall from memory and like, recollect . . . which is why I bring up *Beloved* [Toni Morrison, 1987; movie 1998] a ton, right? Because it's one of the first things that I can recall from when I was very small that talked about Black women being the focal point of the story, and them trying to heal through so much trauma . . . but this Black girl ghost is haunting the family. . . . And the meaning . . . the deep, you know, there's a deep meaning to all of this. So, to have this episode of *Lovecraft Country* acknowledge that Black girls are made monstrous in a very insidious way. And that their stories are not talked about, neglected like that, not even considered. I've written of Black trauma and martyrdom [that] is poured into Black men and boys.[7] And [Black] girls rarely receive the same type of outpouring of support, or love or care, or . . .

MN: Yeah, it's like that intersection of a double standard. . . . Yeah, we got *misogynoir*.[8] Now, that also plays a part, and I think that Toni Morrison just really hit the nail on the head when it came to exploring the darker elements of Black girls. Yeah, I'm thinking about *The Bluest Eye* [Morrison, 1970]. Pecóla, Pecóla, Pecóla. When I first read that book, I cried. I was like, this is way too much. There's just like one scene where she's in a movie theater and watching this movie . . . I think it was *Gone with the Wind* [1939]. No, it wasn't *Gone with the Wind*. It was something else, but she was eating peanut brittle. And one of her teeth broke off. And she just felt like a pile of garbage. And it was the most heartbreaking scene that I've ever read but yeah, Toni Morrison. I consider Toni Morrison a horror writer. I don't know about you. I think about that a lot in the genre and she totally, Toni Morrison, set that up for a lot of people.

DB: And it's really sad that she—for as well renowned as she is, you know, hasn't gotten her [horror] flowers along with . . . we're gonna talk about white people, for a second . . . but she should have gotten her flowers along with [for example] Stephen King who is one of the best horror writers of all time. Her writing was rooted in such real Black history and that's . . . you know, there's something, I guess, to be said for the phantasmagorical kind of horrors or something that somebody makes up to scare people as far as like a boogeyman or whatever, but it's the real historical stuff for me that chills me to the bone.

MN: Absolutely, absolutely. It's like the concept of irrational fears. So, everything that can be considered an irrational fear to somebody who may be cisgendered or white or something like that can exist in that fantastical element, but a lot of our rational fears as Black people are not irrational because they probably, I mean, they have actually happened. Having . . . and this is actually going back to *Candyman* again . . . but having the cops just sweep or raid your apartment, and somebody's just being shot and killed, like that is a very rational thing [to fear] that has happened. And I think that's why historical horror, especially Black historical horror, really gets to us because—kind of like, I've survived this far, you know what I mean? [There's] kind of like this solace [in surviving].

I'm not saying that it's . . . how can I word this? It's not like . . . oh, I'm glad that it wasn't me! But it's just especially if it comes to a point of there being a survivor within that story it's like . . . okay, so there is hope for us to survive these awful things that have happened to us collectively as a community. There is a possibility that we can emerge from this. You know what I mean? To say that, like Black girls are really the true "final girls" and everything because so many things are coming at us every damn day, but somehow we still just manage through the power of ancestors and everything. We still manage to . . . survive? And I think that's truly beautiful.

DB: And oh, we have to talk about it, but the horrific caricature, let's say, of a Black woman, right? The ever-present shadow of mammy, right?[9] Of that ideal, being pinned on Black women, even when it obviously makes no sense, right? It's obvious. It's just like, I need to come up with a way to bludgeon this Black woman. So, I'm going to pick something easy to stab her with. With this insult?

MN: Yeah. It's kind of like the, you know, putting back in "so-and-so's" place. That's how I feel. It's kind of like, you can only go so far, but we've got to remind you of who we really think that you are.

DB: Oh, and returning back to *Lovecraft Country*. I think the show needed more opportunities to breathe to let the two sisters Leti [Jurnee Smollett] and Ruby [Wunmi Mosaku] kind of find their own ways on their own, because some of that stuff and that relationship was so toxic, right? For example, it was not obviously said, but you know, Black people could see immediately . . . could pick up the colorism.

MN: The colorism, which is definitely still a very major thing, and in cinema, and at large, though I feel like a lot of people try to shy away [from it]. And by "a lot of people," I mean, like Black people. Colorism is still one of those things that a lot of people don't like to touch upon because then that means they will also have to talk about their internalized white supremacy, especially when it comes to the politics of desire . . . because essentially, that's what it's all about, right? Like, if we embody all of these Eurocentric ideals, especially when it comes to what a Black woman should be in order to be desired, oh [then] everything still operates within this patriarchal gaze, and it's not something we like to talk about, and I feel like Ruby['s character] fell into that.

DB: Oh, I mean, no . . . I mean, no lies detected [about everything you just said]. And I'm going to be honest, the series was starting to do some really interesting stuff with Ruby's sexuality . . . like Ruby just fully embracing her queerness and it just . . . it didn't [pan out well in the end]. I don't know what was going on in the writers' room. There were some serious issues that I've written about as far as where a lot of the LGBTQ+ narratives just did not come together, just were not written well and were problematic.[10] And we have to acknowledge that as much as we love the series, it had some issues.

MN: Okay, can I ask you a serious question? And this is just a musing of mine, especially because you know Audre's Revenge Film is named after Audre Lorde and it is my dual interest to highlight specifically queer Black people. Do you think that there is still a problem with the Black community accepting homosexuality as a legitimate identity?

DB: Yes . . . yes. [*sighs*] It's interesting who . . . and I'm going to be honest, we're kind of going to break some things down . . . it's interesting who will get a pass, right? I think, more visually or aesthetically or whatever it's more accepted for Black women . . . and let's be real, there's a beauty and desirability politic put into this. So, if it's femme Black women, fine, but masculine Black women [no] . . . because then it starts to erode all of our stuff we have about gender and presentation. So, the target . . . not saying Black women aren't *the* targets [for homophobic violence], but we know intimately who has the bull's-eye all the time on them [now]. So, Black trans women and Black gay men [the specific homophobic/transphobic targeting] . . . it's there.

MN: Absolutely, and this full willingness to uphold patriarchy, right, to protect Black men from emasculation—there has to be an embrace of toxic masculinity that also requires you to put people back into their place . . . which is why "Black gay men" is such a monstrosity to some Black homophobes because it also ultimately feminizes that man . . . and to be feminine is to also be "weak" and that is not upheld within the toxic masculinity—that is needed in order to show strength in a white supremacist society where you are competing with other white cisgendered men who hold race against you. So, is it really about assimilating into the role of entitlement and power that white cis-men have, or are we really trying to be equal within everything? Because I feel like that's what's going on with Lil Nas X, who has tapped into horror to explain homophobia . . . with his "shock tactics," which I think is hilarious. . . .

I just thought that was so clever of him [Lil Nas X] to implement Satan and the blood shoes; it was just such a brilliant, brilliant tactic to utilize horror to explore [these nuanced issues] and to call all of these people out because to them he's seen as being like the "devil" because he's literally poking holes into all of these traditions and silly biases that have been taken as truth within our community.

Figure 30.2. Lil Nas X, "Montero (Call Me by Your Name)," music video, 2021.

DB: [For] those . . . reading [who] are not familiar with what we're talking about, Lil Nas X's music video: "Montero (Call Me by Your Name)," which caused the internet to implode. . . . But that music video! What/who he was challenging . . . that the mob is "you all." That [he/his character was] just here existing, in paradise, "living his best life," but then, you want to stone me, you want to destroy me, you want to cast me into the pits of hell. And then when he flips that narrative . . . because you know our usual assumption is everybody wants to go to heaven. That's where everybody's going. That's what you want, you know? And then to completely flip that and slide down that pole in high-heeled shoes.

MN: Amazing. The kids are all right, we're saved!

DB: It's wild, it's wild. How old is Lil Nas X?

MN: He's a baby. He's only like twenty-two or twenty-three.

DB: Are you kidding me?

MN: Protect Lil Nas X at all costs.

DB: He was born in 1999? Oh my gosh! Wild! Wild!

MN: I can feel the breath of mortality on my neck, like right now.

DB: And this is just such a time to be alive. I have to bring in like another Black, you know, queer trans person, like Angelica Ross.[11] Like, she's holding it down by herself. And she shouldn't be by herself, but she is in the American Horror Story franchise, and the fact that she's the first trans person, *period,* that was on two nationally syndicated programs [including *Pose*], with top billing on both shows, like, my brain is like trying to compute . . .

MN: It's pretty amazing. I am very happy to be alive during this time. Yeah, we gotta get better. Truly, truly. So like, the good thing about mainstream [media] opportunities such as [*Lovecraft Country*] is that so many kids are going to be inspired by it. And we haven't even hit the tip of the iceberg for the types of stories that are going to be created or the types of songs that are going to be created. If anything, the horror community is well overdue for this type of movement. And so it can only go up from here, in my opinion.

DB: Yeah, that there's more horror narratives that are about nonwhite people out there than a little bit [ago] and we love to see it. I think that this [time] is a great wrap-around to talking about *Candyman* and its impact. I'm going to be honest, I wore the whole armor of God and an N-95 mask going to see this in the theater. So thank goodness, depending on where you live, theaters may still be like ghost towns. So, you can literally just kind of go in there and just enjoy yourself with no problem, but it was an experience that I was like, *this* is the only thing I'm going to see in the theater; I took the risk, and what's interesting . . . I'm going to tell you a little bit about my experience.

First, I was the only person inside and then the next person that came in— I don't know their gender but by presentation looked like a Black man. The next couple in was a Latino couple, and then another Black couple came in. So I was just [in awe], the community that is upholding and uplifting this film [on opening day in my city] is just very interesting. I live in a medium-size community. I live in North Carolina. So, there's blue pockets, red pockets . . . I guess you'd call it a purple state . . . so it was very interesting the people that I saw that were coming to see this. The feedback that came about because of this film, some people loved it, some people hated it. Some people had, like, good-faith criticism, and then some were just like—I mean, it was clear, it was blatantly racist, and racistly flippant in regard to a lot of the themes and the messaging in it was like some people said, "heavy-handed," and I'm like, yeah, but that's what [some] people need to [hear in order to] get it? There's no more kind of coded language that we can . . . use. You need to understand that this is urgent, you know what I mean?

MN: Yeah, we've had decades—decades of sugarcoating shit. Excuse my language, but there comes a time where you've got to take the training wheels off. Let's just put it like that. When I saw it, I was definitely like, oh, this is why some people are flipping out because for some people, it just hit them really hard. Me, I'm just jaded. I'm just like, this is great, more of this. Because I mean, how else [are some people going to see or understand]? So many people live in sheltered communities. So many people who saw that movie probably don't even have any Black friends in real life. Like, they'll probably just credit having two Black friends on Twitter or something. And I highly doubt that they have those types of conversations about what happens like in the ghettos of the United States [or people whose lives and stories] don't make it to mainstream news until somebody is murdered in the streets, right? And I think that is why there was so much clapback on like why it was so heavy-handed because so many people just are not exposed to Black narratives in that way. How we see the world... that movie was not made for the white gaze... and that's what confused so many people.

DB: [Some were feeling discomfort] like, well, "where's the good, you know, white person that is.... Where's the—" you know? No, no, that's not this story.

MN: That's not happening. The "white savior" is dead. We are walking away from that narrative. We do not need to have the "good white person" helping us in order to achieve liberation. Because number one, that's a myth, honey. That is a Disney movie that has been made over a thousand times. Nia DaCosta was not making this for Disney. So I think that people need to step out of their comfort zones. And if you don't step out of your comfort zone, you will never appreciate the message that that movie was trying to convey to you. The fact that yes, we live in the United States it's definitely like that Charles Dickens book: *A Tale of Two Cities* [1859].

DB: Two Americas, you're right.

MN: And that is just the very raw truth. And I think that people were [thinking this was going to be a] *Get Out* [2017] or whatever, have Jordan Peele–like humor, which was definitely shown in his script. So it was a lot more digestible because there was lots of humor, whereas Nia [DaCosta] just kind of went for the jugular. Yeah, and I mean, there weren't those comedic relief moments. Like, she just kept going. She kept the pressure on the neck [of the viewer]. It was just like this is what's happening. This is the story and this is how it plays out. And I honestly like the ending of the movie...

[Spoiler alert!]

... the ending of the movie came down to executing these police officers. I literally screamed—this is brilliant! She deserves an Oscar because when people think about the consistent murders of Black people... and just the desensitization of violence against the Black body... so desensitized to seeing it happen in real time on social media. And it also harkens back to distant society, the desensitization of Black bodies being lynched, and being left up for days as a sore reminder to the Black community of [violent-traumatic] power that is needed in order to make that [horror palatable and demonstrate] who was actually in charge. And that is the same vibe that we get when we have these police shooting videos retweeted and going viral on social media and for Black people to see. So for that movie to show police officers being shot and killed and murdered or whatever else.... Where's the outrage for constantly seeing in real life Black people being killed in the streets? Yeah, it's like this fictional movie, but [for once] it's kind of like the tables were reversed. And that is what is so upsetting to a lot of people because she didn't show any Black people having violence inflicted on them.

DB: Oh, and [all of that] yes. That was so radical, and I love that in an interview [DaCosta][12] talked intimately about that: how Black people are given some type of mental or physical trauma [or] assault in these films, but to have that completely removed from the Black characters for once [was amazing]. I mean this movie totally gave me, which sadly has been under the radar, *The First Purge* [2018] [vibes].[13] But that film was another where the Black community was all hands on deck against the government that is trying to incite violence in their community and destroy them from within . . . so to see them take up arms and fight back against the police was very similar in [story framing], where a predominantly Black lower-income part of the city . . . and you know what we're getting a little off-topic, we're going to go back to *Candyman*. This is [a thread of] something else that I'm eventually going to start delving into pretty deeply [in my writing], and you're probably going to pick up what I'm putting down with this . . . that now that we have the knowledge of Cabrini Green[14] . . . the high rises have been bulldozed—demolished.

MN: Yeah, there's a Target there now.

DB: Yeah, there is a Target there now. Coming soon! Coming soon! Whole Foods and Starbucks! You know what, there probably already is a Starbucks in there, I'm sure . . . but the fact the flat row houses still remain, including the people that live(d) in Cabrini Green are still there [in the city] . . . the people who may still be trapped in poverty. So let's just be honest that due to government neglect, the lack of care, the lack of funds allowed . . . the Black community to just languish. So, to see in the new *Candyman*, Black people that have "made it," "gotten away from the hood" is something I'm noticing more and more in horror films of the late 2010s, early 2020s—of Black people that are moving away from the ghetto, away from the rural, or the South . . . and moving more and more into the cities and are moving away from the shaming tactics [of poverty] and a particular

Figure 30.3. *Candyman* trailer, 2021.

Black history . . . [because we know] Black people are still there. There's still Black people who live in "the South." There's still Black people who live in the Midwest, in the [rural] woods. There's still plenty of Black people that live in the hood or in the ghetto. That those horror stories are being shelved, you know? I see us [the film industry] going kind of into this trend [of erased Black stories]. [. . .]

DB: Yeah, so the biggest Black horror narratives recently . . . I'm gonna list a few like Little Marvin's *Them* [TV series, 2021 to present],[15] *Antebellum* [2020] with Janelle Monáe, we can go back a little and we can talk about that Jordan Peele's *Get Out* and even his follow-up with *Us* [2019], [and] now *Candyman* . . . and since we just chatted about it, *Lovecraft Country*. [There are] these battles with respectability and about what you were saying about the acceptable Black person . . . and this wrestling with [identity] where . . . sure [the person thinks] I'm in a different class but the horror is still very present and these characters [or films] are really trying, well some of them didn't explore this with that depth or that lens but some definitely are just in this betwixt and in-between space and place in their lives where I got "out of poverty" but I'm still a racialized Black person that at any minute . . .

MN: . . . awful things will happen.

DB: Right! And the film *Candyman* didn't shy away from that. [How] very swiftly you can be considered not one of the good ones and the police could be after you very quickly [or] the white community could turn on you, if you will, like that throughline with the first *Candyman* [1992] Daniel Robitaille as an individual, who after being highly sought after and praised for his art and then he broke this societal taboo and it led to his horrific demise. Same thing with Anthony, right? And we have to even talk about this as well . . . how Black women's trauma was softened, downplayed, or diminished in *Candyman*.[16] It was something I noticed immediately.

MN: Yeah, yeah, I can see that, especially with [Breonna's] father who killed himself.

DB: Yeah, that's some trauma.

MN: . . . but also not have this thorough notion [on her] to save the day. So . . . bypassing that trauma because we also have to play into the "strong Black woman" prototype, even though she's clearly going through it, and she probably should just remove herself from the situation. She still felt a compelling need to save this Black man. But also, I think that that was done intentionally. Because it happens. Yeah, I mean, when you think about whenever a Black man is killed who do you see on the front lines? [Black women.] But do we get the same treatment? Questions.

DB: I mean, it was hurtful in my opinion [and somewhat] disrespectful to have Say Her Name . . . a campaign that was started by a prominent scholar [Dr. Kimberlé Crenshaw] and Black women—mothers, who whether it be mothers or daughters or grandmothers or aunties that have been victims of state violence. So, to see in some of the promotional materials and even the film, like, use "Say his name," and like, you know, getting some of the known terminology that Black women have been working on, and it's important to make political statements that Black women need help too.[17]

MN: I was gonna say . . . do you think that it was done intentionally in a sense like a form of . . . I don't know . . . I don't think that what you just said was actually like thought about when they came up with that tagline. Like the catchiness, right? Like what will catch [people], like that cute tagline that we can use for people to use as a hashtag. I don't think that it went that deep.

DB: . . . but I know, too: It is something. I think about it because it could be things that are still our blind spots, right? As far as our horror narratives, the fact that there was . . . going back to *Lovecraft Country* . . . the fact that there was an episode that focused on a Black girl's trauma and horror monsters. Maybe the next follow-up to *Candyman* will be *Candy-woman*. I don't know, but it would be wild, like what? A Black woman killing people?? I guess that's like you said, that's the next frontier, right?

MN: Hear, hear. I mean, when I made *Flesh* [2016], my first movie, my thing was I wanted a Black woman serial killer, because I just feel like that would really mess with people's heads. . . . And I went for it. I feel like people just automatically assume that as a Black woman . . . this goes with the mammy trope and whatever else, it's just like automatically [assumed we] always have to take care of everybody and their goddamn kids. I'm just saying, and I think that Keke Palmer is actually playing the villain [in Jordan Peele's *Nope*].

DB: She is, she is.

MN: Like I hope she's not just some weird, obsessed girl. You know what I mean?

DB: Yeah, that's tired.

[. . .]

MN: Yeah, I just feel like white women have been afforded [the luxury] to explore all of those different tropes and it's still very much uncharted territory for Black women.

DB: Yeah, yeah, that's very true. That's accurate.

MN: I want [to see] messy, complicated, hyperviolent [Black women doing] all of those things, I want to see a chick that chain smokes and hooks up with random dudes, and nobody says that she's just a Black slut or whatever, like, this is what we expected. Yeah, just returning to what you said, those respectability politics, I'm really tired of struggling with them. We deserve to have more creative freedom and explore the darker or even the brighter elements of our lives because we are multifaceted individuals, and we shouldn't limit ourselves with what everybody else is expecting. We know this, and that is why it's always so important [to show multifaceted Black people] and why [DaCosta's] *Candyman* was important.

It's because it was not made for the white gaze. We have to commit to making things for ourselves. And that just is what it is.

DB: Yeah, that's like the long and short of it . . . that more horror media needs to just say: this is about Black people. . . .

And you know, it's awesome that I'm getting to chop it up with you about all of this stuff and I have to bring this up, but Black women have such an eye, right? They see the world in such a particular intersectional and what makes it so profound, that, gosh, there just needs to be more Black women in horror.

MN: Truly, they're coming.

DB: They're coming. Indeed, they are coming. I think that's a great place for us to gradually bring our conversation to a close. I'm so delighted that I was able to speak with you today. Monika, I mean, you are a horror director.

[. . .]

MN: And thank you. I'm keeping it going with my fourth film, *Bitten, a Tragedy*, which is finally done, and is going to be premiering at Ax Wound Film Festival on December 10 . . . so that's super exciting, and then I'm also working on my first feature.

DB: Wow, congratulations!

MN: Thank you. . . . It was also an honor to work with you for *cinéSPEAK* for that piece you wrote. I still reference it today and I send it to people, just so you know.[18]

DB: Thank you. So that just ties right in [to a tidy conclusion]. I was just so honored and thrilled that you gave me the space and the platform to continue to have these conversations.

MN: Because they are very, very important.

Notes

All notes marked editor's notes are from the *Studies in the Fantastic* editors.

1. Latanya McQueen, *When the Reckoning Comes* (Harper Perennial, 2021). Here is a description of the novel from the publisher: "A haunting novel about a black woman who returns to her hometown for a plantation wedding and the horror that ensues as she reconnects with the blood-soaked history of the land and the best friends she left behind."

2. The website describes this project thusly: "From the end of Reconstruction to 1940, newspapers were the most powerful news medium in America. Those run by white supremacist publishers and editors printed headlines and stories that fueled racial hate, inciting massacres and lynchings of Black citizens." See this project at https://lynching.cnsmaryland.org/.

3. In the Smithsonian's description, "The Negro Motorist Green Book was a guidebook for African American travelers that provided a list of hotels, boarding houses, taverns, restaurants, service stations and other establishments throughout the country that served

African Americans patrons. Victor H. Green published it annually from 1936 to 1966 when discrimination against African Americans was widespread. During this period, African Americans faced racial prejudice, price gouging and physical violence while traveling around the United States. The information included in The Negro Motorist Green Book helped increase their safety and treatment." This description is taken from the Smithsonian Digital Volunteers Transcription Center at https://transcription.si.edu/project/7955.

4. "*Lovecraft Country*: A Phenomenal and Problematic Series," *An Injustice Mag*, October 2, 2020, https://aninjusticemag.com/lovecraft-country-a-phenomenal-and-problematic-series-ffcbdead73ed.

5. *Ethnic Notions* (1987) is "an Emmy-winning documentary that takes viewers on a disturbing voyage through American history, tracing for the first time the deep-rooted stereotypes which have fueled anti-black prejudice. Through these images we can begin to understand the evolution of racial consciousness in America." See California Newsreel at https://newsreel.org/video/ethnic-notions.

6. "*Lovecraft Country*: Confined by Limitations," *Medium*, October 21, 2020, https://danibethea.medium.com/lovecraft-country-confined-by-limitations-69806b8aa82.

7. Dani Bethea, "Becoming Folklore: Black Lives to Black Ghouls," *An Injustice Mag*, October 6, 2021, https://aninjusticemag.com/ecoming-folklore-black-lives-to-black-ghouls-b7e22c546e03.

8. [Editor's note] *Misogynoir* is a term coined by Moya Bailey to refer to "the specific hatred, dislike, distrust, and prejudice directed toward Black women." For a discussion of this concept, see Janice Gassam Asare's article "Misogynoir: The Unique Discrimination That Black Women Face," *Forbes*, September 22, 2020, http://www.forbes.com/sites/janicegassam/2020/09/22/misogynoir-the-unique-discrimination-that-black-women-face.

9. See, e.g., "A History of Black Stereotypes Onscreen," *The Take*, July 21, 2020, https://the-take.com/watch/a-history-of-black-stereotypes-onscreen.

10. See again "*Lovecraft Country*: Confined by Limitations."

11. Angelica Ross is an American actress and activist for trans rights known for her work on *American Horror Story* (2011 to present), *Pose* (2018), and *Claws* (2017). She joined *American Horror Story* as Nurse Rita in the series' ninth season (1984) and is expected to have a role in the upcoming tenth season as well.

12. "*Candyman*: Nia DaCosta—Director/Screenplay," YouTube video, 6:33, August 5, 2021, http://www.youtube.com/watch?v=oiE5QMGpRBA. See also Leila Latif, "Nia DaCosta: '*Candyman* Turns the White-Saviour Narrative on Its Head,'" *Little White Lies*, August 22, 2021, https://lwlies.com/interviews/nia-dacosta-candyman.

13. See Gabe Castro, "*The Purge*: Evolution into Revolutionary Horror," *cinéSPEAK*, October 20, 2021, http://www.cinespeak.org/2021/10/20/the-purge-the-evolution-into-revolutionary-horror.

14. [Editor's note] A nice discussion of this aspect of the film, of "the ghosts that have been left behind because of gentrification," can be found in Dani Bethea's "Contending with the Scraps: The Fight for Direction of Black Women's Horror Narratives," *cinéSPEAK*, October 28, 2021, http://www.cinespeak.org/2021/10/28/contending-with-the-scraps-the-fight-for-direction-of-black-womens-horror-narratives/.

15. See Dani Bethea's "When Adulation Sours: Contextualizing Amazon's Them," *Medium,* March 24, 2021, https://danibethea.medium.com/when-adulation-sours-contextualizing-amazons-them-4d353e74e81.

16. [Editor's note] See again Bethea's "Contending with the Scraps" for a summary of the original film and the remake.

17. The tagline of the original *Candyman* film was "We dare you to say his name five times," in reference to the urban legend that summons the Candyman. The new film plays upon this and merges it with the Black Lives Matter call to "Say her name," cheekily transforming the tagline into "Say his name." But "Say his name" when used for male victims of police brutality is a contentious appropriation of the original expression, which was originally intended to highlight awareness of female victims and combat their erasure.

18. Bethea.

Chapter 31

CONTEMPORARY HORROR AND DISABILITY
Adaptations and Active Readers

Petra Kuppers

> If scholarly investigations of horror viewership and class are sparse, considerations of horror viewership and disability are almost nonexistent. The exception at present is Petra Kuppers's essay included here, which considers not only how modern horror texts "adapt and play with old stereotypes of disability . . . in experimental ways" but also how readers and viewers participate in the process of constructing meaning.

THIS CHAPTER ENGAGES WITH disability-focused writing with an emphasis on the recombinant pleasures of genre—what working in a genre framework can mean, can add, and can subvert—stepping outside the box and examining what is in it. The argument will focus less on well-rehearsed arguments about the conservatism of horror's examination and fear of otherness, or of Gothic returns of repressed fears. Instead this chapter investigates how contemporary horror texts adapt and play with old stereotypes of disability (as well as colonialism, race, and gender), in experimental ways.

> Science fiction/fantasy/horror can do that kind of disorientating shifting with anything: politics, culture, race, power, sex, sexuality, gender. That's the stuff I find interesting. It's in the nature of the genre to allow one to step outside the box and examine what's in it and think about what might be excluded and why. Any literature can do that; it's just a particular hallmark of fantastical literature. (Nalo Hopkinson, quoted in Simpson 2005, 96)

Many disabled people write horror, although few are systematically collected under that category. While there are anthologies of disabled people writing science fiction (see Allan and al-Ayad 2015), the even more specialized niche of horror holds no such collection at this point. Personally, I see disabled horror, fantasy, and sci-fi writers regularly at national conventions (as I am one of these writers). My anecdotal experience and fieldwork suggest that a good percentage of genre writers are disabled or speak about disability experiences when they discuss their working methods, many more than at literary-focused events. In 2018, for example, WisCon, the feminist science fiction convention held annually in Madison, Wisconsin, had at least four panels dedicated to facets of disability, a much larger percentage of this small convention than the equivalent figures at AWP, the Associated Writing Program's conference, the main literary creative writing event in the United States.

So while disabled people most certainly write and read horror, there is at this moment no substantive body of work that focuses on what the literary genre of horror does for, with, and about disability.[1] Classic horror has created disability stereotypes that the disability culture movement pushes against: from the film *Psycho* (1960) to the various productions of *Frankenstein* (initial book 1818; first movie 1931), from evil wheelchair users to poor, innocent, blind victims. Kathryn Allan sums up what a core mode of disability studies' engagement with genre writing has been: to catalog the use of disability as a characterization or a narrative device. She argues that

> when people with disabilities are turned into props and tropes (or left out completely) in narratives of a collective human future, it is imperative that [SF] scholars begin to call out—as we do for instances of racism, sexism, classism, and homophobia—outdated, humiliating, and harmful images of disability.

This chapter acknowledges the importance of monitoring the social progress of genre material, but its theoretical focus lies with the progressive and interesting contemporary uses of disability in horror. This chapter focuses on the kind of genre work that kicks Nalo Hopkinson's box down and wheels over it. If the science fiction genre is concerned with futurities, horror pleasures rely on intensity and stimulation. To parse out who is actually alive at the end of a horror genre product might not always be the best guide to that intensity. I focus less on horror's narrative plotting of disability, and more on the accumulation of sense and thrill at the site of disability plot points.

In particular, this chapter investigates adaptations in horror genre spaces: repetitions with a difference, surface play with plot elements that engage with or overshadow the deep psychology of realist writing. Adaptation is central to cultural pleasures: books, dramatic texts, films, often take up earlier story lines and play with them, twist them, subvert them, or add to them. So in the texts I am looking at in this chapter, older discursive structures become fodder for new meanings: Monsters, asylums, lesbian vampires, and Victorian transgressive sexualities enter into play.

I am interested in aspects of genre writing—communal writing, writing-on, play with topoi—the kind of textual productions that restructure and reinvent familiar themes and topics. With this, my argument aligns with theorized notions of disability as it appears in dis/connects, missed translations, and trajectories of precarity, not in essential, "authentic" disabled experience grounded in realistic representation. My argument points to the value of nonrealist embodiment and enmindment (two terms that point to the process-based and interactive character of how we come to feel ourselves as bodies and as minds). In the horror genre, states of difference can exceed or subvert what is known and "realistic" about disability and its boxes. Horror, with its visceral appeal to affect and sensation, is a fruitful basis from which to engage in a seduction toward nonrealist othernesses as intriguing and enriching ways of being in (this or other) worlds.

This chapter is also part of a long lineage of thinking about genre and commerce within writerly production. Following in a line of argument from Northrop Frye to Michel Foucault, copyright scholar Mark Rose (1993, 8) observes, "Authors do not really create in any literal sense, but rather produce texts through complex processes of adaptation and transformation." Within Roland Barthes's (1978, 148) framework of dispersed literary agency, the reader is the assemblage point where multiple cultural influences coalesce:

> The reader is the space on which all the quotations that make up a writing are inscribed without any of them being lost; a text's unity lies not in its origin but in its destination.

This chapter analyzes several key examples in detail, including a shadow puppet show at the Dreamland Theater, Victor LaValle's *The Devil in Silver* (2012), Cherie Priest's *Maplecroft* (2014), and Matthea Harvey and Ann Jean Porter's *Of Lamb* (2011), to argue that writers and readers consciously employ hybridity and reinvention in order to engage in genre play. As part of this, authors and readers can cocreate commentary on histories of exclusion, on agentic reclaiming of violent, racist, ableist, misogynist, and homophobic material, adapting them to new ends.

Cthulhu and Crip Time: Dreamland Theater—*The Language of Time* (2017)

On First Fridays, my small home city of Ypsilanti, Michigan, shares community music, galleries, and shows in the downtown area. In July 2017, one of these shows was a partnership between our small experimental puppet theater, the Dreamland Theater, and the Full Circle Community Center, a local drop-in center for people living with mental illness. For this show, interviewers for the project had visited with Full Circle and collected people's stories to reshape them as puppet sketches. The puppeteer organizers described their project's intention as raising awareness of a community that is often ostracized due to social stigma.

The Language of Time was the most surreal and experimental piece of the evening, mixing the puppeteer's aesthetic of Cthulhu-like monsters with a Crip Time narrative of nonlinear sensory immediacy. Cthulhu is a cosmic monster created by writer H. P. Lovecraft. Lovecraft was a racist and misogynist, and it shows loud and clear in his writings. So why do his figures get recycled and adapted so much? Cthulhu first appeared in the short story "The Call of Cthulhu," published in the American pulp magazine *Weird Tales* in 1928. He is part of a strange cosmology, usually referred to as Mythos, in which ancient alien gods bring interdimensional madness to Earth: Humans are strangely drawn to this way out of human words, but go mad when they open up portals for Cthulhu. Ever since Lovecraft first wrote about the entity, authors and artists from Stephen King to Guillermo del Toro have taken up Mythos figures—something about this particular flavor of speculative nonhuman otherness has proved remarkably seductive over the years, and so seems the act of writing-on, of cocreating a mythological universe across time.

In Lovecraftian words, madness is not redemptive nor offers new insights into the here and now. Cosmic madness is not the same as the romantic "madness as seer" topos so often employed in fiction. And yet, Cthulhu madness is a form of escape, a response to the sudden opening of confining reality toward something else. We are in a world of overwhelming dimensions, fever or drug dreams, grandiose and colorful, swirling and moving at light speed. Whatever Lovecraft thought he was doing in creating these monsters, he offered up a smorgasbord of delights to contemporary writers, who gladly enter into the supposedly abject spaces of Cthulhu's minions: "the others," that is, immigrants, racialized others, the poor. These openings into established (racist, sexist, homophobic, ableist, classist) reality are the most seductive pull of the Lovecraftian universe.

Crip Time is a phenomenon out of disability culture. It emerged as a communally used term in line with many other nonmodernist, nonwhite, not-center forms of temporality. In the particular lineage I cite when tracking down a print origin, I attribute the term to Anne McDonald (n.d.), a nonspeaking disabled woman who used facilitated communication to get out of a nursing home in the 1980s, eventually earn a degree, and become a leading part of the Australian disability culture scene. She writes about Crip Time:

> I live life in slow motion. The world I live in is one where my thoughts are as quick as anyone's, my movements are weak and erratic, and my talk is slower than a snail in quicksand. I have cerebral palsy, I can't walk or talk, I use an alphabet board, and I communicate at the rate of 450 words an hour compared to your 150 words in a minute—twenty times as slow. A slow world would be my heaven. I am forced to live in your world, a fast hard one. If slow rays flew from me I would be able to live in this world. I need to speed up, or you need to slow down.

Crip Time has become a generative principle for many who think about nonnormative temporalities, to the point where the term has taken off from its grounding in a particular woman's disabled specificity and enforced incarceration toward much more generalized theorizations. This chapter's engagement with horror and disability shifts the emphasis back onto the horizon of institutionalization, and the specific and nongeneral ways of being that we as disabled people bring to the world, yet without claiming authenticity, truth in individual storytelling.

One of the reasons why Crip Time has become so resonant for so many writers in disability studies is its seductiveness: Almost anybody in disability worlds can experience something of the slowing or morphing of time in pain, exclusion, or isolation. To have a term for this shifting, this difference from the norm, is a beautiful, unifying, community-building mechanism. Anne McDonald was originally institutionalized, dehumanized, in a deeply abject place of being denied agency.

There's echo and communal memory, beyond individual lives and their specificity. There's a near-mythic group identity available here, when the consensus world (and, for instance, its regularized work time regime) grates against disabled ways of being. So, using Crip Time as a genre convention makes sense: It holds deep resonance, and yet can be adapted in multiple ways. The nexus of speculative horror worlding and Crip Time's phenomenal perception allows for a way to theorize this opening into impersonal embodiment and enmindment.

Back to the puppet show. The guarantor for communication in *The Language of Time* is not personal realist autobiography, told by an authentic or authorized individual. Instead, the guarantor for communication is genre play: the familiarity of tropes that connect to other tropes, such as Cthulhu-informed imagery, the set pieces of "being oppressed in the classroom," "spaceship imagery," or "dragon stories." These are all genre conventions, and the storytelling puppeteer group transformed the highly individual and idiosyncratic story of the Full Circle user into an amalgamation of unknowability *and* recognizability. Without "telling too much," there was access. In this context, genre operates as a mixing of familiar and new elements.

Although I visited with the Full Circle Community Center, I did not meet the woman whose narrative was shared here. But community members described her as someone with traumatic brain injury, telling a dense story of ant poison, falling down stairs, potential parental abuse, exclusionary experiences at school, and frightening encounters with doctors. Many of these story elements emerged in the mainly wordless show. Animal/human/monsters appeared on the backlit screen. A dragon/snake entered, intentions unclear, but large, detailed, beautiful, with cutouts and intricate framing: a rest for the eye, rather than a narrative motor. In another moment, the small multiple-eyed heroine was lost in a puzzle piece forest, something that to members of disability culture can read like a comment on Autism Speaks iconography of missing puzzle pieces, presenting autistics as damaged people. Here, instead, the heroine's shadow puppet was caught in normative puzzle worlds, walking through the forest without a fit, imprisoned by puzzle pieces. But mobility returned, in the shape of flying pigs with translucent ears/wings. They accompanied the emergence of Cthuthlu: a big-headed creature with multiple eyes and octopus tentacles, quite recognizable to genre fans of Lovecraftian horror. Escape was at hand: The pigs and the heroine run into a flying saucer spaceship, and take off.

Patrick Elkins, the puppeteer, described his experiences working with the woman's narrative to me: how he first heard the interview about her life, and how he was captured by the sense of time developed here, out of normal time frames. He didn't use the term "Crip Time," but when I offered it, he found the concept a fitting one: traumatic brain injury and mental health difference as a different form of living in time, telling stories, sharing circles and lines. He also told me that he met the drop-in user later, and that she had seen his adaptation of her story and enjoyed the silhouette narration.

When I watched *The Language of Time,* I did not see a woman's authentic experience, narrated in realist terms, then transformed more or less faithfully into shadow puppets, then received by me with my mind full of Cthulhu and Crip Time. The puppets left authentic grounding behind, but without denying the pain of institution. Coherences emerged, an escape narrative, a trajectory away from the certainties of this world. There might be a starship. There might be pig helpers. This is the delicious narrative I choose to take away from this show, and from this particular engagement of puppetry horror with disability. Cthulhu is well up for crip reclamation. In the weft spun by the Dreamland Theater's engagement with nonrealist embodiment and enmindment, horror adaptations offered disability an open field of associations, not just the often depressing realities. The puppetry show's adaptation of familiar motives, from Cthulhu and flying pigs to puzzle pieces, allowed for a sense of a woman's lived experience, without the constraints of realism, linear storytelling, or empathetic identification.

New Entrances into the Asylum: Victor LaValle's *The Devil in Silver* (2012)

My next example of horror and disability shifts from life-writing discourses of authenticity, surrealist engagements, and impersonal embodiment to the remediation of a particular topos of horror literature: the asylum or the psychiatric institution. In this example of genre manipulation, African American author Victor LaValle creates literary fiction that is consciously aware of its meta play with language and convention.

In the novella *The Ballad of Black Tom* (2016), LaValle takes one of Lovecraft's most overtly racist stories, *The Horror of Red Hook* (1927), and transposes it, reversing the gaze. Where Lovecraft had Harlem as the site of horror and Black/foreign threat, with white Brooklyn and Chelsea as the threatened centers, now an African American narrator and musician tells of the racist and dangerous world he encounters once he leaves his home in Harlem in the 1920s—white people, and white police in particular, are the violent and unpredictable enemy, not the madness-inducing thing on the threshold, the Mythos creature. This kind of imposition and mirroring of space also occurs in LaValle's asylum novel, *The Devil in Silver* (2012), where police violence is also at work. We first encounter the protagonist of the novel on a threshold, in the moment of entrance. Pepper, the white working-class protagonist, is becoming a mental patient, delivered by police to an inscrutable maze, an asylum. At the entrance to the asylum, status shifts: Pepper goes from being someone with rights, a key, access to YouTube and phones, to someone drugged, labeled, whose every utterance becomes a symptom. The staff change, too, as they work in the hospital—no one escapes the inhumane regime of the institution. Over the course of the novel, the dangers of neglect and institutional violence are at least as real as the story's monster.

Adaptation and recycling of narratives are central to the novel's form and audience address. In disability scholar Michelle Jarman's (2017) engagement with the novel, she excavates a haunting encoded in numerical patterns. She describes a particular scene from LaValle's text in which police storm the asylum, which is, at that moment, in violent upheaval, and end up shooting Kofi, a Guinean immigrant: "The rest [of the police officers] fired on the crazed man. Then the cops fired forty-one shots. The assailant was hit nineteen times" (210). Jarman argues that

> the specific details, forty-one shots, hit nineteen times, directly reference the infamous police shooting of Amadou Diallo, an unarmed West African man who was gunned down in the doorway of his Bronx apartment in 1999. (166)

Jarman's link to this murder provides a ghostly, haunted terrain (what she calls "reanimation," staying firmly in the territory of the horror genre). This terrain marks racialized (police) violence's deep time strata as an undercurrent of New Hyde, the asylum of the story. Jarman analyzes this coded genre play through a lens of alliances and recognition of parallels:

> LaValle's reanimation of Diallo's shooting implies that the coercive, violent logics, so easily concealed in the confines of the locked ward, are mirrored and active on the street. . . . Pepper realizes anyone in the asylum could be produced as demonic. This realization reorients him toward the other inmates, not through identification but crip affiliation. (167)

This reorientation, Jarman argues, presents the white narrator of the novel with an opportunity to unlearn his white masculinity, and to find his way to "relational resistance," in allegiance and friendship with other inmates, even in the absence of identification.

Building on Jarman's insight, I want to engage with another aspect of the novel's play with horror conventions: the use of an unreliable narrator, and its effects on authentic representation and narrative trust. LaValle's novel presents readers with unreliable narrators, with undecidable states of consciousness. To use the parlance of a classic novel set in an asylum, Ken Kesey's *One Flew over the Cuckoo's Nest*

(1962), here the "chronics" are engaged in storytelling, not the voluntary admittances. Everybody with narrative weight in LaValle's story is on the closed ward against their will, under observation, drugged, in restraint, under lock and key.

Pepper, a thirty-something white working-class character, is the main focal point of the third-person narrative. As he finds out, all stories are shaped by differences between internal and external worlds, and his own way of seeing himself becomes fragile, unreliable. Stilled by Haldol and lithium, hazed and eventually physically restrained, he lives in an involuntary holding pattern. In this set of forces, he finds a way of finding a place for himself, in between entrances and exits, in between walls and staircases, on the other side of locks. LaValle employs the genre conventions of Gothic asylum novels, making it unclear who is "mad" and who is not. Adapting these conventions, LaValle shifts the moments of intensity from horror gore and angsty revelations of the relative madness status of actors. Instead, he offers readers a social field of and feel for the "relational resistances" Jarman discusses: While the relative in/sanity status of all involved is unclear, the protagonist reaches out and makes temporary, context-specific allegiances. Characters operate in obscurity, but with agency. At first, readers may be inclined to trust Pepper's self-narration too much, and assume that the presence of a character who was "normal," or a "normate," in a mental health institution was a police error. But on further examination, it becomes clear that all characters in this novel are touched by a profound and complex self-knowledge. Pepper shifts, he becomes more interesting as he becomes less reliable. Readers find out that his ex-girlfriend did not see him as the kind benefactor and guardian he perceived himself to be: He might well be a bully, violently erupting too quickly.

Following the labyrinth of the asylum's maze to its heart, readers encounter a stairwell with dismantled stairs, an austerity-diminished forgotten prison, in which the devil dwells: either a neglected son, a bison-headed mythical creature, or a killer. *The Devil in Silver* is a horror story with werewolf elements, but the locus of real cruelty is somewhere between the Kafkaesque machine of governmental neglect and the everyday dismissal of humanity that characterizes institutionalized mind-sets. Madness, per se, is not the threat, and, with access to appropriate medication and regimes, people diagnosed with various kinds of mental health difference can be seen to flourish.

One of the inmates, Xiu, or "Sue," a Chinese woman brought into the asylum due to immigration policing and a lack of access to the lithium that she requires, miraculously finds access to the outside. She is reunited with her sister, with help, love, a regulated life, and access to her medication. So she thrives. Balance is possible. Likewise, a second character, Looshia, a young Black woman, finds her way out, against all odds and against realist conventions: Who needs them? Certainly not characters in revolt against racist and ableist conventions. Genre narratives can open up new escape paths, and new allegiances between characters.

Literary resources are key to helping disability culture members be connected to an inhospitable world, but even though I teach the topic often, I have found few literary texts that use speculative means to approach the asylum as anything but a site of horror and constriction. While LaValle's text offers these tropes, as well as well-rehearsed spatial narratives of the asylum as a place of hiding holes, Gothic parallel worlds, and architectural secrets, he also offers respect and friendship for mad people—they are not the foil for his narrative, but the agents of change and shifting thresholds. The conventions of madhouse narratives and the employment of unreliable narrators make identification complicated and challenging. That undecidability is the core pleasure of the book's audience address and engagement of disability. In *The Devil in Silver*, literary engagement with the crafts of viewpoint creates a new perspective on the horror site of the asylum.

Horror Hackery: Cherie Priest's *Maplecroft* (2014)

The next example of horror and disability engages with the mainstream of genre fiction, outside the self-conscious literary realm. Here readers can find the lesbian, and the crip, all steamy in a fast and furious narrative push that sustains itself over multiple books, a common feature of genre literature. In my argument here, I want to bring out how different textual consumption patterns can offer openings for disabled (and queer) readers, for the kind of active reading strategies that have been at the heart of feminist engagement with literature, claiming ground by reading for pleasure and survival, even in compromised patriarchal frameworks of production and consumption.

In *Maplecroft: The Borden Dispatches #1* (2014), US novelist Cherie Priest remediates a celebrated murder case, Lizzie Borden and her murdered family in 1892 in Fall River, Massachusetts. The murder site is not far from Lovecraft's Rhode Island, and many Lovecraftian elements appear in Priest's novel, like morphing land/sea creatures and "unnatural desires." Interest in the historical figure of Borden as potential axe murderer has never really abated, and even during the time of my construction of this chapter, an internet meme based on her circulated in my social media world. The meme from July 2017 presents a black square with white letters, spelling out "Do not accept a request from Lizzie Borden. You will get hacked." (I cannot trace an origin point: That's the point of memes.) This meme plays on the multiple meanings of hacking: hacking with an axe, and the internet-related practice of hacking into an account, taking it over. As a meme, this Lizzie Borden tile plays into the trope of violence and personal erasure in the ambivalent encounter-space of social media. These tropes, violence and (gendered) erasure, are also at work in Priest's novel, taking over an old murder story.

In the Priest novel, we read this delicate description of Lizzie Borden's sensorium, her perspective on tiny gills, knife slits, bodily openings, very differently coded from "hacked to pieces." These openings are on the white neck of a lesbian adventuress actress, lover of Lizzie Borden:

> "What was that . . . ?" I asked quietly, holding her chin aside, stretching her neck. There: a small slit of skin, fluttering. As light as if it'd been cut with a razor, a tiny fillet of flesh that wrinkled when I touched it. I felt the two more horizontal flaps before I saw them. That made three altogether, with the start of a fourth, not quite as long. . . . All of them sucked shut against her throat, lying so flat that if I hadn't known they were present, I would've never noticed them. I tried to touch them again, but felt almost nothing. The faint texture of paper cuts, or maybe the delicate, almost-not-even-there-ness of a small fish's fins. (315)

Queerness and disability mix intriguingly in this post-Lovecraftian pastiche. "Fillet of flesh" speaks to consumption, to eating, certainly a possibility in this New England world in which fishing is a subsistence economy. "Razor" and "cut"—the axe and what it stands for, mutilation and murder—are not far away from this reference field, but they are coded differently, with a different kind of trans-body status. The not-quite-there-ness of the delicate touch chimes well with the status that lesbianism is afforded in this novel, set in 1895—the novel bosom-heaves with references to loves that dare not say their names.

Writing and seeing emerge as connecting techniques in multiple ways. There are various author figures in this mainly epistolary novel (echoing both *Bram Stoker's Dracula*'s [1992] setup and the structure of many Lovecraftian stories, where scientists record their findings in field notebooks). Not seeing things right in front of one's face is a feature of this particular Victorian world. The secretive framework within which the two Borden sisters build their lives relies on leaving well enough alone, not touching tender stuff, keeping one's self to one's self. Their neighbor Doctor Owen, once alerted to Lizzie's lover, isn't particularly scandalized by the lesbian love between Nance O'Neill and Lizzie Borden, but he is also highly aware of the invisible nature of their relationship, invisible by social need, and invisible also by self-imposed emotional maintenance, the need for keeping it together. Emma, Lizzie's disabled sister, has to vie with Nance for Lizzie's time and affection, and has little patience for their erotic shenanigans. Emma is also leading a gender-related double life: Although highly consumptive and near dead with coughing fits and fatigue (all very sensuously described, full of Crip Time moments), she finds a sphere of influence for herself. She has taken on a male persona, Dr. E. A. Jackson, and, as this male authority, authors marine biology texts and corresponds with men from all kinds of universities. This cross-gendered traffic in knowledge eventually brings destruction to the women's household, though—the tenderness of in-between stages, from lesbian love to male impersonation, cannot withstand the blow of the axe. There is no happy ending here for tender bodies gasping for air. Words and descriptions accumulate at the crossing points, at open cauldrons (one full of acids in the cellar, one full of sex in the upstairs bedroom). Shape-shifting also feeds the repeated description of the townspeople's physical and mental "symptoms," the novel's nod to the rise of historico-medical thrillers, laying out early experiments with tetanus viruses, a plot point of the book.

In the genre of the fantastic, this novel, like many of its Lovecraftian wayfarers, seems less interested in just boiling the story along, but in stringing together pearls of description, generic situations polished and shined with loving detail and sensuous wrapping. To sum up the story as "the crip gets no love and the lesbo dies," while accurate, does not do justice to the novel's shape, and the intensity of the tender set pieces. Pure narrative analysis does not always provide the right answer about emotional identification points and emphasis of a genre text's universe. As a genre novel, this book offers plenty of opportunity for what literary critics used to call "escapism"—imagining (lesbian) romance or active (murderous) women, the thrill and forbidden pleasures of women's romance consumption. Refiguring these consumptions into active reading strategies, and writers as collaborators in offering these gems of hacked pleasure, allows for a more nuanced investigation of the uses horror can be put to.

When literary critic Janice Radway interviewed women about their romance reading practices in the 1980s, she opened up reader-response territory to thinking about the active pleasures of women compensating for a lack of agency in their lives. But she was also suspicious of where this might lead: "The vicarious pleasure offered by romantic fiction finally may be satisfying enough to forestall the need for more substantial change in the reader's life" (Radway 1984, 118). These issues directly impact disability and genre reading (and writing). In this analysis of *Maplecroft*, I offered a pathway through a fast-moving popular-culture book that traces my own reading pleasures, as a queer disabled active reader lingering over what she wants, in a woman-authored text that quite explicitly offers entry points for these pleasures, fully aware of the formulaic connective dots of genre writing. Nonrealist forms of embodiment offer anchor points for those of us whose bodies and minds have been denigrated, put beyond the pleasure-pale by mainstream representation. Horror and its intensities can provide rich ground for pleasure-adaptation, as one does not have to figure out how these intense creatures make a life in the "real" world. We'll just hack our way in.

Erasure Pleasures: Matthea Harvey and Amy Jean Porter's *Of Lamb* (2011)

To close my argument about horror's capacious disability engagement through adaptation, I'll focus on a very different text, of a more experimental lineage. *Of Lamb* (2011), by Matthea Harvey and Amy Jean Porter, uses erasure procedures on a historical text, *A Portrait of Charles Lamb* (1983) by Lord David Cecil, combining the resulting text with paintings to create a subtle experimental entry into the disability horror genre.

Essayist Charles Lamb lived with his sister Mary, who murdered her mother and wounded her father in an unexplained attack in 1796. She was never prosecuted, but lived in an asylum before being reintroduced to Charles's household. Charles himself also struggled with mental health difference, including alcoholism, as well as other disabilities, referenced as "a limp" and "stuttering" in various accounts. The two stayed connected throughout their lives, collaborated on successful children's literary material in their own right, and socialized with famous literary figures, including Mary Shelley, the Wordsworths, and others.

Poet Matthea Harvey uses Cecil's twentieth-century biography of Charles, with its frequent mentions of Mary and Lamb, and mashes the story with a well-known nineteenth-century nursery rhyme, "Mary Had a Little Lamb" by Sarah Josepha Hale, which tells the story of Mary Sawyer bringing her lamb to school. Visual artist Amy Jean Porter painted images to go with the single-sentence pages, creating a psychedelic flowing surrealist landscape around a strange lamb: not a cuddly, fluffy one, but one that looks wise and haunted. The graphic novel proceeds by building elaborate composite images. Plants twine around Mary, the only named human depicted, and Lamb, a sheep more than a symbol of either innocence or suffering (in the Christian tradition). Lamb is not really cute—the animal has a facial structure more akin to an adult sheep. The two figures develop their close relationship, full of sexual innuendo and pubescent longings, with Victorian imagery of excess and shrouding: "They pin'd and hungr'd after bod-ily joy," reads one entry from this unpaginated book, with a heart of white hedge roses framing a male and female putty (prepubescent nudes with blond, curly hair). At the bottom of the image, much smaller, is Mary, in trousers, arms behind her back, and Lamb, looking curious for what is to come.

Multiple genre memories are referenced in this image: from size-shifting *Alice in Wonderland* (1865) to references of flocked wallpaper and its associations with repressed femininity. The book shares territory with the sexualized graphic scenes of *Lost Girls,* an iconic graphic novel (initial chapters were released in 1991, with the text acquiring cult status and various editions in the 1990s and 2000s). In *Lost Girls*, writer Alan Moore and illustrator Melinda Gebbie remediate *Alice in Wonderland, Peter Pan* (1904), and *The Wizard of Oz* (1900), depicting scenes in which the heroines meet to discuss their sexual lives and sexual abuse narratives.

In *Of Lamb,* the page that faces the dancing putty figures has only an abstract graphic background with the words "Who would not be curious to see the pictures?" written above it. Bestial conjoinments, potential incestuous longing (between brother and sister, Charles and Mary), and cross-species sexuality have no visual equivalent in the pages. This page functions like a bedroom curtain, a common visual device in early cinema, drawing the curtains on the just married couple. On the next page, the words "Mary and Lamb inter—twined" are transected by the legs of the upright standing Lamb. On his back rides Mary, a long strand of material in their respective mouths. The two strands, or twine, or ribbons, write out "Mary" and "Lamb" above them, woven through each other (potentially referencing Mary Lamb's sowing business, or handfasting symbols of ribbons wrapped around the partners). The Lamb's blue ear frames one-half of Mary's face, and her legs are blue, the color of Lamb's fleece, while the blush on Mary's cheeks is visually repeated on Lamb's ears. The two creatures merge visually, and in their linguistic representation.

After this uncanny mélange of erotic allusion and animal–human imagery, Lamb's story becomes darker, and the story that emerges speaks of pubescent angst about becoming an adult, about anxieties about ego boundaries, and latent violence emerging. Various interpretations are possible, given the nonlinear form of narration. Thus, the sentences on various pages read, "For Lamb, white-faced, fettered, time was full of time," "Lamb imagined the story of a lamb made human," "He was, to use his own phrase, half a man," "A quarrel began the trouble," "Lamb, eyes shut, ran backwards," and "His anxiety / a glittering chandelier / rusting in his mind." This deterioration of happiness and togetherness stretches over multiple pages, aligned with winter nature imagery, and crescendos with a leave-taking. Images of transport (airplanes, coffins sailing on water, rushing water, a carpet flowing down a staircase) prefigure separation.

Seasons, the thorns of prickly plants, the silhouette of a dinosaur: Images and poetry alike capture psychic shifts and overwhelm the reader with an excess of imagery. The murder and the asylum (as both Charles Lamb and Mary Lamb were hospitalized for mental health reasons) are only obliquely referenced in these pages, even more shrouded than the fantastical human–animal intercourse. There are references to "six weeks / in a madhouse." Also, "I bit / my shadow / and Mary." And: "Haunted Lamb / sung out / shut the door, / allow me to see / organs once more." Later, in the description of Lamb's reacquaintance with society, the book presents two praying mantises, uncannily eating a winged creature between them, with the words "Face-to-face / they ate" above, surrounded by a frame of yellow pears on tree branches.

In the last section of the book, the narrative shifts to Mary's madness, or nervous breakdown, and the images in this section are less nature focused and reference more urban (London) environments, with various architectural creations, gridded windows, and Gothic churches dominating the visuals. The terror of uncanny eating appears again: "Should I tell you / I watched her eating / a bit of cold mutton / in our kitchen?" Lamb and Mary are separated here by a window, a yellow outdoors looking in on a cooler, blue interior, with a skirted piano shape squashing Mary, who is eating a pink "lamb-on-a-stick," like an ice lolly.

Mergings, anxieties, and violence all shape the different separation madnesses of Lamb and Mary. The actual killings are not directly referenced; instead, readers witness two creatures who are different holding each other as they pass through transformation and depression. Remediation shapes the book's materiality, in particular in the act of erasure. Harvey blanks out many of the biography's sentences to leave a handful of words per page, and then arranges them in careful composition with the graphic offerings. This materiality of storytelling excavates what is unspoken, and points to the historical narrative that consists of cutting in very different ways. Every word of the original biography, a historical glimpse into an actual historical figure, is carefully handcrafted, either erased or saved, and the poet rearranges, makes new, or covers up. The act of creation is a palimpsest: It both denies and makes visible the erasures of history, the invisibility of mad people, the constrained lives of women, the invisibility of murder victims outside their murderers' narratives, and the asylum as a cutout from society. Adaptation here becomes an act of eating up, chewing, and changing. The horror/pleasure of *Of Lamb* is in its surrealist uncovering of violence and its play with juxtaposition. Readers become implicated in peering behind curtains, becoming active tracers of connections and alluded reference fields.

Conclusion

In these pages, horror and writing engage at sites of disability, exposing curious and unfamiliar shapes, combining old stereotypes and tropes into alignments that show the labor of creative practice. The resulting readings do not offer psychological realism, or a claim to authenticity grounded in an identity politics. Instead, a genre-based recombinant logic of hide and seek is at play.

My local Ypsilanti puppetry show used adaptation to allow an unclear/unknowable life narration to emerge in associations and surrealist imagery. Victor LaValle's take on the asylum-adapted conventions around madness and unreliable narrators shows how allegiances can be made even in the absence of firm handles on other people. Priest's lesbian crip scenes offered ways of feeling one's self sensually into remediated Lovecraftian nonhumans. Matthea Harvey and Amy Jean Porter worked together to deconstruct existing texts, adapting them into nonnarrative collages of horror tropes grounded in actual lives. Both Priest's popular novel and *Of Lamb*'s experimental text emerge from historical events, but their respective effects are very different: Adaptations here have different horror ends, one more aligned with the genre reader's pleasure seeking, one with an active reader's excavation of uncanny openings and border crossings. In all cases, the reader is the site of assembly: Intensities emerge where reading desires and textual offerings intersect.

Horror is an intensification machine, not only a narrative path. All of the disparate texts I survey here align on this point: Real lived disability as a secure and shared story line is emphatically not the point of the story. Instead, and deliciously, disability becomes a place where violence and agencies can try out new forms of interplay, with death, sex, and flying pigs along the way.

References

Allan, Kathryn, ed. 2013. *Disability in Science Fiction: Representations of Technology as Cure.* Palgrave Macmillan.

Allan, Kathryn, and Djibril al-Ayad. 2015. *Accessing the Future.* Futurefire.net.

Barthes, Roland. 1978. "Death of the Author." In *Image-Music-Text,* translated by Stephen Heath, 142–47. Hill and Wang.

Cheyne, Ria. 2013. "Disability Studies Reads the Romance." *Journal of Literary and Cultural Disability Studies* 7, no. 1: 37–52.

Hall, Melinda. 2016. "Horrible Heroes: Liberating Alternative Visions of Disability in Horror." *Disability Studies Quarterly* 6, no. 1.

Harvey, Matthea, and Amy Jean Porter. 2011. *Of Lamb.* McSweeney Books.

Jarman, Michelle. 2017. "Race and Disability in US Literature." In *The Cambridge Companion to Disability and Literature,* edited by Clare Barker and Stuart Murray, 155–69. Cambridge University Press.

LaValle, Victor. 2012. *The Devil in Silver.* Spiegel and Grau.

LaValle, Victor. 2016. *The Ballad of Black Tom.* Tor.

McDonald, Anne. n.d. "Crip Time." Anne McDonald Centre. http://www.annemcdonaldcentre.org.au/crip-time.

Priest, Cherie. 2014. *Maplecroft: The Borden Dispatches #1.* ROC/Penguin.

Radway, Janice. 1984. *Reading the Romance.* University of North Carolina Press.

Rose, Mark. 1993. *Authors and Owners: The Invention of Copyright.* Harvard University Press.

Schalk, Sami. 2018. *Bodyminds Reimagined: (Dis)ability, Race, and Gender in Black Women's Speculative Fiction.* Duke University Press.

Simpson, Hyacinth M. 2005. "Fantastic Alternatives: Journeys into the Imagination—a Conversation with Nalo Hopkinson." *Journal of West Indian Literature* 14: 96–112.

Smith, Angela. 2012. *Horror Progeny: Disability, Eugenics, and Classic Horror Cinema.* Columbia University Press.

Note

1. For some work on other genres, see, for science fiction, the authors collected in Allan (2013) or Schalk (2018); for work on romance fiction, Cheyne (2013). Existing engagement with horror and disability tends to focus on films; see, e.g., Hall (2016) on *Edward Scissorhands* or Angela Smith (2012) on 1930s horror films.

Chapter 32

A DEMON-GIRL'S GUIDE TO LIFE

S. Trimble

> Developing the first-person perspective introduced in places in Kuppers's chapter, Trimble's essay closes out the anthology with a personal reflection on the pleasures of consuming horror as a member of the LGBTQ+ community—with a focus on William Friedkin's 1973 horror classic, *The Exorcist*.

I'M SITTING ON A CHURCH PEW covered in carpet the color of rust. It rises from the floor and wraps around the pews, musty and rough. The band has just finished playing us closer to Jesus, and one of the teens is testifying about his experience at a nearby revival service, where he was moved by the spirit to weeping and shaking. I don't like the sound of this. I'm struggling to be a believer, so I figure this won't happen to me. But part of me worries it might. And the notion of my inner life rising to the surface for others to see and hear is not good. I'm a twelve-year-old girl dreaming of other girls. I'm into one across the aisle and two rows up. And I'm pretty sure what's happening inside me needs to stay hidden.

It was the early 1990s. Gay was on the verge of going mainstream, but the culture wars were in full swing. In the face of the AIDS crisis, a newly empowered Christian right had squared off against queer communities in the name of faith, flag, and family. There were pronouncements of God's punishment and demands for mandatory testing and quarantine. By the time my family was trying on an evangelical shade of Anglicanism, Pat Buchanan was declaring a war for the soul of America and the Westboro Baptist Church was becoming infamous for antigay activism. In 1998, they picketed the funeral of Matthew Shepard, holding up signs declaring the young gay man who was tortured and left lashed to a fence was now burning in hell.

This was the cultural climate in which I grew into my queerness and discovered horror films. I watched them with my sister and cousin on summer afternoons, popping rentals into the VCR and metabolizing the mayhem. The feeling I remember most is glee. I cackled at Freddy Krueger preparing death traps for teens like a demonic Wile E. Coyote. I loved Annie Wilkes from *Misery* (1990), the deranged fan who commits heinous acts of violence but decries a potty mouth. I was entranced by the gender distortions on display. Freddy revels in being a badman, the slimy underside of the Father Knows Best ideal. And Annie does femininity so right she's wrong, exposing resentful, proprietary impulses beneath the caregiving surface. On some level I knew horror wasn't just about monsters doing bad things. It's also about doing gender badly. It's about the threat and the thrill of getting it wrong.

I brought all of this with me to *The Exorcist*. William Friedkin's 1973 horror classic is about a twelve-year-old girl who gets possessed by a foulmouthed demon and begins saying, doing, and knowing things she shouldn't. When medical science fails to explain what's wrong with Regan MacNeil (Linda Blair), her mother turns to a priest with psychiatric training for help. Father Karras (Jason Miller) is wrestling with some demons of his own, so the possessed girl forces him to find his faith again. Released in the midst of Vietnam and Watergate, a deepening economic crisis, and the ongoing energies of feminism, gay liberation, and Black Power, the film's depiction of a white girl corrupted by evil tapped into white American fears of nightmare futures. It also changed the cultural status of horror films for good. News outlets reported sold-out showings, endless lines, and viewers fainting, vomiting, and hyperventilating. Journalists staked out cinema lobbies, waiting for those who would stumble out of the theater partway through, shuddering and shaking their heads. Newspapers with gravitas suddenly had to take pop culture seriously. And horror, a genre previously maligned by critics and tastemakers, stole the show at the 1974 Academy Awards, when *The Exorcist* was nominated for ten Oscars, including Best Picture.

The *first* first time I watched *The Exorcist,* it was on TV, sliced up by commercial breaks, on one of those summer afternoons when I was twelve. I remember cracking up when we finally got to the head-twisting scene, shock and horror waylaid by a dozen pop-culture parodies I'd seen prior. The second time, in my late teens, it was a whole other film: the humor pitch black, the story creeping under my skin. I watched it alone, at night, with darkness pressing on the house. And it wasn't the cut-for-TV version, so I saw more of Regan's filthiness, including that moment when she crushes her mother's face into her bloodied vagina. I was older and becoming more attuned to the adult world and its violent separations of normal from not, saved from damned. I saw a revolting girl revolting against the little-girl box in which she was stuck—and I saw an army of men working to put her back in.

These two different viewing experiences taught me something about how selves and stories get tangled up together, how we remake ourselves through stories and see different things in those stories because of our ever-changing selves. As a child, I identified with Regan and aspired to her badassery, and the rest of the film fell away. When I was a teen, the context of her struggle came into focus and I was unnerved and outraged by all the men working to reform her. Now, as an overworked, harried professional, I find myself identifying with Father Karras as much as with the girl he's called on to save. *The Exorcist* is one of those films that keeps weaving into my personal mythology, offering shifting identifications as I age. Horror is good at this. The genre is all about slippery feelings and alliances. It's especially kaleidoscopic for those of us cast as real-life monsters. Once upon a time I saw myself reflected in a demon-girl, and she's been a fellow traveler ever since.

We're in the atrium of a suburban shopping mall, sandwiched between the central staircase and the food court. Sunlight streams through skylights. Scents of french fries and teriyaki sauce waft toward me as I prepare for my big entrance. I'm wearing a white robe cinched at the waist. A crown of tangled twigs sits atop my head and my chin-length hair is tucked behind my ears. Someone positions a heavy wooden cross over my right shoulder as I find the stooped position I've been perfecting: burdened and determined. My sister and the other girls are moving through choreography on a makeshift stage, twirling pink ribbons as I weave toward them through the crowd. The band reaches a crescendo as I mount the stage, ready to die on this food court Golgotha. I understand I'm on a mission to proclaim the love of Christ to Easter shoppers laden with chocolate, but I'm distracted by the joy of performing martyred masculinity. I am handsome and tragic and the undisputed star of the show. Jesus was my one and only drag performance.

The first time I saw *The Exorcist* I had recently survived a serious bout of gender trouble. Like Regan, I became monstrous around the age of twelve, when I was dubbed Manwoman by my seventh-grade classmates and spent the year getting schooled on what girls are supposed to act, look, sound, and smell like. The experience filled me with shame. By then I knew I was queer, but I both craved and dreaded finding stories about people like me. Having suffered through an in-class viewing of *Ace Ventura: Pet Detective* (1994) alongside my bullies, I was convinced pop-culture pictures of queer and trans lives were doing me no favors. The trans "reveal" at the end of that film sent my peers into fits of laughter, their hysteria matched onscreen by Jim Carrey, who blubbers in the shower over the realization that he'd once kissed a freak.

But gender-bending has a different status in horror. There's a tradition of representing psychotic killers driven by what Carol Clover calls "gender distress."[1] From Norman Bates to Buffalo Bill, this trope has been both critiqued and reclaimed by queer fans and critics. There's also the figure of the castrating woman, the protagonist of rape-revenge and slasher films who survives by unmanning her chainsaw-wielding oppressor. This figure belongs to the realm of what Barbara Creed refers to as the "monstrous-feminine,"[2] a cluster of representations of women in horror that are projections of masculine anxieties. The vampire, the witch, the breeding alien, the aging psychopath—they bleed and bite and ooze and shape-shift, queering the categories that preserve the patriarchal order of things. Regan MacNeil is one of them: the possessed girl who collapses the boundary between self and other and, like Eve before her, admits the devil into the world of men. Horror plays with white patriarchal nightmares and taps into our ambivalence about normality, which means the potential for radical storytelling is always there. We watch, awestruck, as the world we recognize comes apart at the seams. We love-hate our monsters and are repulsed-fascinated by the havoc they wreak.

As a kid watching horror movies on summer afternoons, I wasn't reading feminist film theory. But I sensed that gender played differently in the genre. Once, my younger cousin and horror-watching buddy treated me to a detailed (but fully clothed) reenactment of the climax of *Sleepaway Camp* (1983), in which Angela is revealed as having a penis and being the killer all at once. Given my *Ace Ventura* experience, this could have been rough. But there was something irresistible about my cousin's performance. The capering, the cackling, the maniacal grin—it tapped into that quality I can only in hindsight name as "camp," the way horror winks at you while it screws with all the norms you live by. We had a similar reaction to John Waters's *Serial Mom* (1994), in which Kathleen Turner is very June Cleaver until she drops the mask to prank call her neighbor. "Is this the Cocksucker residence?" she growls into the phone. We dissolved into laughter—three kids totally jazzed by the violence beneath the housewife veneer. This was storytelling I could work with.

I don't remember consciously identifying with Regan back then, but part of me must have registered our alikeness. We were both white girls around the same age. And while her metamorphosis is extreme, some of what makes her gross are qualities I understood my alter ego to possess. My peers had made it clear Manwoman was smelly and aggressive, and moved in all the wrong ways. And when they spoke for me, they pitched their voices low and growly. So, I would have noticed that one of the most unnerving things about Regan is that deep, guttural voice provided by the unseen star of the film, Mercedes McCambridge. Maybe I laughed my way through *The Exorcist* that first time to deflect some of the horror of recognizing myself in such a character. But I don't think so. Regan's mannish voice and foul language don't map onto the white-girl part she's supposed to play in society. Just when she's meant to solidify into a future wife and mother, she starts pissing on the carpet and spewing green stuff instead. But I wanted demon-Regan to survive the casting out of her demon. Her knowingness and shamelessness and fucked-up sense of humor were enticing. I was exhilarated by the sights and sounds of girlhood gone awry.

As a queer kid navigating a Canadian middle school in the 1990s, I had tried to be quiet and clean and very, very nice to convince my peers I was one of them. This strategy didn't do much to stave off social punishment. Luckily, horror opened me up to new possibilities for survival. Watching demon-Regan play mind games with the adults who wanted to save her, watching her topple furniture and grab her psychiatrist by the balls, I saw power in freakery and transgression and wondered if it could be mine. I was leaving childhood behind and starting to notice what the adult world does to those it casts as deviants and outsiders. Being quiet and nice wasn't going to cut it. So, like Regan, I started saying inappropriate things, especially at church. I turned youth meetings into debates on hot topics like abortion and feminism. I goaded adults into revealing their homophobic views and then gave them shit for it. I refused communion. But I could feel the stakes getting higher. My wrongness was bubbling to the surface in ways I couldn't control. My days of reveling in Jesus drag were over.

The day the pastor announced that Laura was engaged to be married, I left the church for good. People had been whispering for a while about "Laura's problem." I'd seen her after services, on her knees surrounded by church leaders, all praying for the overcoming of her difficulty. Laura was in the church band. Once, she'd covered "(You Make Me Feel Like) A Natural Woman" after Sunday service was over, devastation on her face as she hit the chorus, desperate for it to be true. I'd been tracking all of this because I felt connected to her. When I first joined the church, we'd bonded over a shared love of guitars. I started to see myself reflected in the butchness she was determined to shed. By the time I came out to my mom and sister at fourteen, I understood I was witnessing a form of conversion therapy—that church leaders were praying Laura's gay away when they surrounded her after service, laying their hands on her back and shoulders, murmuring. And then came the happy news: Laura had been fixed up with a nice young man through the church and now, after a few months of dating, they were engaged. Praise be to God. That Sunday I went home and decided not to go back.

The second time I saw *The Exorcist*, I was an out queer teenager without a church. A healthy fear of Ouija boards aside, I'd never been a true believer, so leaving the church didn't feel like a spiritual loss. Instead, I lost the world I shared, however uneasily, with my dad. My mom quit the church before I did, alienated from the congregation first by her feminism and then by my queerness. But my dad was—is—devout. When I was younger, Sunday mornings often found him getting ready for church with *The Jimmy Swaggart Show* on in the background, his morning ritual accompanied by the sweating, spitting, speechifying televangelist. Swaggart was one of many who used evangelical Christianity to draw a new map of manhood in the 1980s and 1990s, after the postwar liberation movements threatened to knock white men from their rightful place as kings of the humans. Within this more flexible framework, white men were both fathers and sons, patriarchs on earth and children of God for eternity. So evangelical masculinity was authoritarian but weirdly malleable, all loose limbs and speaking in tongues and crying out for godly guidance—especially when Satan got involved. Swaggart's tearful apologies for engaging the services of sex workers alerted me to the role of women in the stories and selves these men create. And Laura's engagement brought it too close to home.

I didn't know this when I sat down to watch the uncut version of *The Exorcist,* but demonic possession movies are the perfect vehicle for stories of men remaking themselves. Encoded in their depiction of a struggle over the body and soul of a young woman, there's usually the tale of a man in crisis. His is a conversion story in which he loosens his grip on science and reason and learns to believe in things unseen. Her body, his rebirth. Possession movies boomed in the 1970s and 1980s, just as American evangelism began to cohere into a political and cultural force, reinvigorating white manhood as it went. Occult films dramatized this reinvention, throwing shade at white-coated doctors and siding with men in black robes, men tapped into a world of spiritualism and ritual, gods, and monsters. We know from the opening ten minutes of *The Exorcist,* which take place in Iraq, that all of this is structured by the white imagination, that these are white men who have journeyed to places coded as mysterious, dark, and hotter than hell. The American man has faced evil, which always comes from elsewhere, and rediscovered his faith in the process. Now he's ready to restore the nation's beacon-on-a-hill image. And this work begins at home—with family values.

The Exorcist spoke to adult generations reeling from the 1960s counterculture, convinced the kids are not all right. As Stephen King put it in *Danse Macabre,*[3] the film addressed "all those parents who felt, in a kind of agony and terror, that they were losing their children and could not understand why or how it was happening." It's not much of a reach, really. From one perspective, the 1960s movements had collapsed into the helter-skelter of the Manson Family. To those who were horrified and titillated by the 1970–71 trial of Charles Manson in LA, Regan's onscreen metamorphosis into a cussing, puking demon-girl might have reminded them of white girls who'd shaved themselves bald and carved bloody X's into their foreheads, blowing kisses at their murderous messiah. Images of monstrous youth helped discredit the liberation movements of the 1960s, convincing many that an authoritarian correction was in order. Monstrous white girls, in particular, were bad omens. With apocalypse and paranoia in the air, *Rosemary's Baby* (1968) had already established that white women can become the carriers of nightmare futures. Which means white *girls* need to be kept on the straight and narrow.

So, there's a reading of *The Exorcist* that goes like this: The problem with Regan MacNeil is she doesn't have a daddy. She's being raised by a single mom with an androgynous name, potty mouth, and Hollywood life. This crack in the white family unit is how her demon, Captain Howdy, finds its way in, diverting the girl on the cusp of puberty from her path to an all-American future. Regan is supposed to grow up to marry a white man and have white children who will inherit his name, growing his family line and the property that goes with it and transmitting to future generations the worldview that makes white American families the image of goodness.

But an absent dad exposes the girl to physical and spiritual corruption. The solution, then, must be a substitute father figure who can guide her back into the fold. We watch as men in white coats are followed by priests in black cassocks and the God who authorizes them. Patriarchal power layered on thick, correcting the girl who's gone astray.

The second time I watched *The Exorcist*, sitting alone in the dark, I wasn't laughing. I was reaching for a queer future, a life on my own terms, and all I could see were the forces arranging themselves around Regan to bring her back into line. Well before the exorcism was under way, I saw her observed, tested, and prodded. I saw her strapped to a gurney beneath harsh light, her throat exposed and a needle plunged into her carotid artery. I saw medical experts willfully unseeing what they couldn't explain, clinging to theories about brain lesions because without them they have nothing to say. Finally, I saw her drugged and strapped to her bed, physically and chemically incarcerated. After all that, it was almost a relief to see Regan spider-walking headfirst down the stairs. Awake and unleashed. I knew there was a drama playing out across the body of this wayward girl, that putting her right was somehow necessary to these men and their crumbling sense of normalcy. I knew because I'd seen it before: the prayers for a woman made unnatural by temptation and redeemed by Your grace, oh Lord; the benevolence with which she's guided into righteous married life. Amen.

It's the middle of the night. Streetlights are lit. Inside a tiny house on a residential street on the outskirts of Toronto, the quiet is broken by a screaming child. A three-year-old races down the hallway from her bedroom and huddles beneath the dining table, breathing hard. She's asleep the whole time. Her parents have been told it's "night terrors" but aren't sure what this means. They've just started their own business—a twenty-four-hours-a-day, seven-days-a-week operation—and there are two other children in the house, one of them an infant. The girl's parents are craving sleep and praying for a miracle. They're a churchgoing couple, but not overzealous. For them it's as much about community and aunties selling their knitting at church bazaars as it is about faith. But when their minister hears about the night terrors and offers to bless their house, they say, *Why not? What do we have to lose?* The girl isn't home when the kindly, gray-haired man arrives with holy water and heavenly vibes. He moves through the house, sprinkling drops and saying soothing words. Shortly after this visit, the girl stops screaming in the night.

I don't remember my night terrors. What's memory to my parents is myth to me. But I live with the knowledge that, once upon a time, an early version of me responded to things nobody else could see—as if another dimension mushroomed open inside our house with only me inside. Where did those experiences go? Where are they stored in me? Lately, I've been wondering the same thing about Regan MacNeil.

"She doesn't remember any of it," her mother says at the end of the film. Regan's amnesia assures audiences that normalcy has returned, that the white girl has her innocence back. Where before she knew too much, now she knows nothing. But what happens next time Regan sees a bedroom curtain billowing in the wind? Or a doctor tries to touch her? What happens when what her body knows becomes too much for her mind to repress?

I'm always interested in the futures that come into view at the end of a horror film. From one perspective, the white girl who outlives the monster has been rewarded for her purity; her survival guarantees that white families will continue to make babies and have good futures. But what if her brush with monstrosity isn't so easily relegated to the past? What if she's changed forever, transformed by new desires and open to strange alliances? These questions first arose for me when I saw a little girl queered by demonic superpowers, and I wondered what might remain of that otherness when the demon is cast out. They felt even more pressing when I rewatched *The Exorcist* as an adult—when I noticed, for the first time, the queerness of Father Karras.

Father Damien Karras is the exhausted, guilt-stricken priest who Chris MacNeil (Ellen Burstyn) begs to save her child. He's kind and sad and deeply afraid he's no longer fit for his job of counseling priests who are struggling. Watching *The Exorcist* as a young person, I didn't know about the Hays Code that handcuffed Hollywood storytelling for decades, ensuring that queerness could only appear as subtext and that characters coded as gay wound up unhappy or dead at the end of the film. I was too young to notice that Father Karras's closest, most tender relationship is with Father Dyer (William O'Malley), the show tune–singing priest who gently slides his shoes off and puts him to bed when he's drunk. I didn't catch the innuendo when the homicide detective tells Karras he reminds him of the actor Sal Mineo. And I didn't really take in the depth of Father Dyer's devastation when he reads his friend the last rites at the end of the film. All I saw, back then, was yet another man in a lineup of men called on to cleanse a filthy girl. Now I see something more complicated: a queer man who sacrifices himself so the girl can survive. When Karras invites Regan's demon inside him and then throws himself out her bedroom window, is it a bury-your-gays moment? Or is there room to imagine a queer future beyond the final frame?

These days I like to see Karras and Regan as queer kin, the one giving up his future to ensure the other has one. We can assume Regan has been put right and will grow up to marry and be a good wife and mother, never recalling the priest who sacrificed himself to make it happen. Or we can assume, as I do, that Regan will never be the same after sharing her body with a lascivious, murderous monster; that doors have been opened that can't be shut tightly enough; that the alliance with Father Karras gave the girl a chance to become something interesting. It's what queer theorist Eve Kosofsky Sedgwick[4] would call a "reparative reading," which is a way of naming how marginalized audiences creatively engage with stories that aren't meant to sustain us. Horror was the playground where I learned to read this way, to send the entire story spinning off its axis by rooting for the monster. Horror helped me love my terrible truths, the things about me that disquieted others. Amid the mayhem and the viscera, signposts pointing to queer futures.

Notes

1. Carol Clover, *Men, Women, and Chain Saws: Gender in the Modern Horror Film* (Princeton University Press, 1992), 27.
2. Barbara Creed, *The Monstrous-Feminine: Film, Feminism, Psychoanalysis* (Routledge, 1993), 31–42.
3. Stephen King, *Danse Macabre* (Gallery Books, 1981), 179.
4. Eve Kosofsky Sedgwick, *Touching Feeling: Affect, Pedagogy, Performativity* (Duke University Press, 2003), 123–51.

PUBLICATION HISTORY

Chapter 1 was first published as Aristotle, "Poetics," in *The Complete Works of Aristotle: The Revised Oxford Translation*, vol. 2, edited by Jonathan Barnes, 2320–21 and 2326–27 (Princeton University Press, 1984).

Chapter 2 was first published as David Hume, "Of Tragedy," in *Essays: Moral, Political, and Literary*, edited by T. H. Green and T. H. Grose, 258–65 (1757; repr., Longmans, Green, 1889).

Chapter 3 was first published as Friedrich Schiller, "On the Reason We Take Pleasure in Tragic Subjects," translated by George W. Gregory, in *Friedrich Schiller: Poet of Freedom*, vol. 4, 333–51 (1791; repr., Schiller Institute, 2003).

Chapter 4 was first published as Edmund Burke, *A Philosophical Enquiry into the Origin of Our Ideas of the Sublime and the Beautiful*, 36–37 and 54–59 (1757; repr., Oxford University Press, 1990).

Chapter 5 was first published as Joseph Addison, "Why Terrour and Grief Are Pleasing to the Mind When Excited by Descriptions," *The Spectator* (1712): 296–99.

Chapter 6 was first published as Anna Laetitia Barbauld, "On the Pleasure Derived from Objects of Terror." 1773. *Studies in the Fantastic* 1 (2008): 77–79.

Chapter 7 was first published as Ann Radcliffe, "On the Supernatural in Poetry," *New Monthly Magazine* 16, no. 1 (1826): 145–52.

Chapter 8 was first published as Walter Scott, "On the Supernatural in Fictitious Composition; and Particularly on the Works of Ernest Theodore William Hoffmann," in *Sir Walter Scott on Novelists and Fiction*, 222–251 (1827; repr., Routledge, 2011).

Chapter 9 was first published as H. P. Lovecraft, introduction to *Supernatural Horror in Literature*, 12–16 (Dover, 1973).

Chapter 10 was first published as Christopher St. John Sprigg, introduction to *Uncanny Stories*, ix–xii (Thomas Nelson, 1936).

Chapter 11 was first published as Alfred Hitchcock, "The Enjoyment of Fear," in *Hitchcock on Hitchcock: Selected Letters and Writings*, edited by Sidney Gottlieb, 116–21 (University of California Press, 1995). Used with permission of Rowman & Littlefield Publishing Group, Inc.; permission conveyed through Copyright Clearance Center, Inc.

Chapter 12 was first published as Stephen King, *Danse Macabre,* 395–97 (Berkeley Books, 1981). Copyright 1981 by Stephen King. Reprinted with the permission of Scribner, an imprint of Simon & Schuster LLC. All rights reserved. Reproduced with permission of Hodder and Stoughton Limited through PLSclear.

Chapter 13 was first published as Kendall Walton, "Fearing Fictions," *Journal of Philosophy* 75, no. 1 (1978): 5–27.

Chapter 14 was first published as Berys Gaut, "The Paradox of Horror," *British Journal of Aesthetics* 33, no. 4 (1993): 333–45. Copyright 1993 Oxford University Press. Permission conveyed through Copyright Clearance Center, Inc.

Chapter 15 was first published as Noël Carroll, *The Philosophy of Horror; or, Paradoxes of the Heart,* 125–28 and 182 (Routledge, 1990). Reproduced by permission of Taylor & Francis Group.

Chapter 16 was first published as John Morreall, "Enjoying Negative Emotions in Fictions," *Philosophy and Literature* 9, no. 1 (1985): 95–103. Copyright 1985 Johns Hopkins University Press. Permission conveyed through Copyright Clearance Center, Inc.

Chapter 17 was first published as Mathias Clasen, "Fear for Your Life: The Appeals, Functions, and Effects of Horror," in *Why Horror Seduces,* 53–62 (Oxford University Press, 2017). Reproduced with permission of the Licensor through PLSclear.

Chapter 18 was first published as Robin Wood, "An Introduction to the American Horror Film," in *The American Nightmare: Essays on the Horror Film* by Andrew Britton, Richard Lippe, Tony Williams, and Robin Wood, 7–28 (Festival of Festivals, 1979).

Chapter 19 was first published as Douglas E. Cowan, *Sacred Terror: Religion and Horror on the Silver Screen,* 51–59 (Baylor University Press, 2008). Used with permission of Baylor University Press. All rights reserved.

Chapter 20 was first published as Linda Williams, "Discipline and Distraction: *Psycho,* Visual Culture, and Postmodern Cinema," in *"Culture" and the Problem of the Disciplines,* edited by John Carlos Rowe, 103–20 (Columbia University Press, 1998). Reprinted with permission of Columbia University Press.

Chapter 21 was first published as Julian Hanich, "Frightening Fascination: A Phenomenology of Direct Horror," in *Cinematic Emotion in Horror Films and Thrillers: The Aesthetic Paradox of Pleasurable Fear,* 81–107 (Routledge, 2010). Reproduced by permission of Taylor & Francis Group.

Chapter 22 was first published as G. Neil Martin, "(Why) Do You Like Scary Movies? A Review of the Empirical Research on Psychological Responses to Horror Films," *Frontiers in Psychology* 10 (2019): 1–22.

Chapter 23 was first published as Nina Nesseth, "Horror's Long-Lasting Appeal," in *Nightmare Fuel,* 241–64 (Nightfire, 2022). Copyright 2022 by Nina Nesseth. Reprinted by permission of Tor Nightfire, an imprint of Tom Doherty Associates. All rights reserved.

Chapter 24 was first published as Matt Hills, "Displaying Connoisseurship, Recognizing Craftsmanship," in *The Pleasures of Horror,* 73–90 (Continuum, 2005). Copyright 2005 Matt Hills, Continuum, an imprint of Bloomsbury Publishing Plc.

Chapter 25 was first published as Susan Stryker, "My Words to Victor Frankenstein Above the Village of Chamounix: Performing Transgender Rage," *GLQ: A Journal of Lesbian and Gay Studies* 1, no. 3 (1994): 237–54. Copyright 1994 Gordon and Breach Science Publishers. All rights reserved. Republished by permission of the copyright holder, and the publisher. http://www.dukepress.edu/.

Chapter 26 was first published as Brigid Cherry, "Refusing to Refuse to Look: Female Viewers of the Horror Film," in *Identifying Hollywood's Audiences: Cultural Identity and the Movies,* edited by Melvyn Stokes and Richard Maltby, 187–203 (BFI, 1999).

Chapter 27 was first published as Mark Jancovich and Tim Snelson, "Horror at the Crossroads: Class, Gender, and Taste at the Rialto," in *From the Arthouse to the Grindhouse: Highbrow and Lowbrow Transgressions in Cinema's First Century,* edited by John Cline and Robert G. Weiner, 115–25 (Scarecrow Press, 2010). Permission conveyed through Copyright Clearance Center, Inc.

Chapter 28 was first published as Meghan Downes, "Critical Pleasures: Reflections on the Indonesian Horror Genre and Its Anti-Fans," *Plaridel: A Philippine Journal of Communication, Media, and Society* 12, no. 2 (2015): 1–18. https://www.plarideljournal.org/article/critical-pleasures-reflections-on-the-indonesian-horror-genre-and-its-anti-fans/.

Chapter 29 was first published as Sheri-Marie Harrison, "New Black Gothic," *Los Angeles Review of Books,* June 23, 2018. https://lareviewofbooks.org/article/new-black-gothic/.

Chapter 30 was first published as Dani Bethea and Monika Negra, "Black Horror Beyond the White Gaze: A Conversation," *Studies in the Fantastic* 12, no. 1 (2021): 75–98.

Chapter 31 was first published as Petra Kuppers, "Contemporary Horror and Disability: Adaptations and Active Readers," in *The Routledge Companion to Literature and Disability,* edited by Alice Hall, 82–93 (Routledge, 2020). Reproduced by permission of Taylor & Francis Group.

Chapter 32 was first published as S. Trimble, "A Demon-Girl's Guide to Life," in *It Came from the Closet: Queer Reflections on Horror,* edited by Joe Vallese, 12–16 (Feminist Press of New York, 2022).

CONTRIBUTORS

JOSEPH ADDISON was an essayist, poet, playwright, politician, and cofounder of *The Spectator* magazine.

ARISTOTLE was an ancient Greek philosopher and scientist who wrote about the natural sciences, linguistics, economics, politics, and the arts.

ANNA LAETITIA BARBAULD was a poet, essayist, literary critic, editor, author, and educator.

DANI BETHEA is a pop culture writer and former editor in chief of *We Are Horror* magazine.

EDMUND BURKE was a politician and philosopher and is considered a founder of conservatism.

NOËL CARROLL is distinguished professor of philosophy at the CUNY Graduate Center. He has authored and edited numerous books, including *The Philosophy of Horror* (1990) and *Philosophy and the Moving Image* (2021).

BRIGID CHERRY is an independent scholar. She is author of *Horror: Routledge Film Guidebooks* (2009) and *Cult Media, Fandom, and Textiles: Handicrafting as Fan Art* (2018).

MATHIAS CLASEN is associate professor of English at Aarhus University. He is author of *Why Horror Seduces* (2017) and *A Very Nervous Person's Guide to Horror Movies* (2021).

DOUGLAS E. COWAN is professor of culture and language at Renison University College. He is author of *The Forbidden Body: Sex, Horror, and the Religious Imagination* (2022) and *Sacred Terror: Religion and Horror on the Silver Screen* (2016).

MEGHAN DOWNES is a visiting researcher in the Asian Urbanisms Cluster at the National University of Singapore's Asia Research Institute and also teaches in the School of Languages, Literatures, Cultures, and Linguistics at Monash University Australia.

BERYS GAUT is emeritus professor of philosophy at the University of St. Andrews. He is author of *Art, Emotion and Ethics* (2007) and *A Philosophy of Cinematic Art* (2010).

JULIAN HANICH is professor of film studies at the University of Groningen. He is author of *Cinematic Emotion in Horror Films and Thrillers: The Aesthetic Paradox of Pleasurable Fear* (2010) and a coeditor of *What Film Is Good For: On the Values of Spectatorship* (2023), among other titles.

SHERI-MARIE HARRISON is associate professor of English at the University of Missouri. She is author of *Difficult Subjects: Negotiating Sovereignty in Postcolonial Jamaican Literature* (2014).

MATT HILLS is professor of journalism and media at the University of Huddersfield. He is author of *Fan Cultures* (2002) and *The Pleasures of Horror* (2005), among other titles.

ALFRED HITCHCOCK was an influential film director and producer known as the master of suspense.

DAVID HUME was a philosopher, historian, economist, and essayist.

MARK JANCOVICH is emeritus professor of film and television studies at the University of East Anglia. He is editor of *Horror, the Film Reader* (2001).

STEPHEN KING is an author widely known for his horror novels, including *Carrie* (1974), *The Shining* (1977), and *It* (1986).

PETRA KUPPERS is a community performance artist and disability culture activist. She is professor of English and women's and gender studies at the University of Michigan. She is author of *The Scar of Visibility: Medical Performance and Contemporary Art* (Minnesota, 2007) and *Eco Soma: Pain and Joy in Speculative Performance Encounters* (Minnesota, 2022).

H. P. LOVECRAFT was a science fiction, fantasy, and horror writer.

G. NEIL MARTIN is honorary professor of psychology at Regent's University London. He is author of *Psychology: A Beginner's Guide* (2008) and *The Psychology of Comedy* (2021).

JOHN MORREALL is emeritus professor of religious studies at the College of William and Mary. He is author of *Taking Laughter Seriously* (1983) and *Comic Relief: A Compressive Philosophy of Humor* (2009), among other titles.

MONIKA NEGRA is a writer, a filmmaker, a cofounder of Audre's Revenge Film Cooperative, and editor in chief of *cinéSPEAK*. Her shorts include *Flesh, They Will Know You by Your Fruit,* and *Bitten: A Tragedy*.

NINA NESSETH is a science communicator and staff scientist at Science North. She is coauthor of *The Science of "Orphan Black": The Official Companion* (2017) and author of *Nightmare Fuel: The Science of Horror Films* (2022).

ANN RADCLIFFE was a novelist, poet, and pioneer of Gothic fiction.

FRIEDRICH SCHILLER was a playwright, poet, philosopher, and historian.

WALTER SCOTT was a novelist, poet, and historian.

TIM SNELSON is associate professor of media history at the University of East Anglia. He is author of *Phantom Ladies: Hollywood Horror and the Home Front* (2015) and *Demons of the Mind: Psychiatry and Cinema in the Long 1960s* (2024).

CHRISTOPHER ST. JOHN SPRIGG, best known by his pseudonym Christopher Caudwell, was a writer, literary critic, and activist.

SUSAN STRYKER is professor emerita of gender and women's studies at the University of Arizona and executive editor of *TSQ: Transgender Studies Quarterly*. She is author of *Transgender History: The Roots of Today's Revolution*.

S. TRIMBLE is assistant professor at the Women and Gender Studies Institute at the University of Toronto. They are author of *Undead Ends: Stories of Apocalypse* (2019).

KENDALL WALTON is professor emeritus of philosophy at the University of Michigan. He is author of *Mimesis as Make-Believe: On the Foundations of the Representational Arts* (1990).

JEFFREY ANDREW WEINSTOCK is professor of English at Central Michigan University, founder and president of the Society for the Study of the American Gothic, founder and general editor of the journal *American Gothic Studies,* and associate editor in charge of horror at *The Los Angeles Review of Books*. He is coeditor of *The Age of Lovecraft* (Minnesota, 2016) and editor of *The Monster Theory Reader* (Minnesota, 2019).

LINDA WILLIAMS was professor of film and media and rhetoric at the University of California, Berkely. She is the author of *Hard Core: Power, Pleasure and the Frenzy of the Visible* (1989) and *Screening Sex* (2008), among other titles.

ROBIN WOOD was an influential English film critic. Among his many books are *Hitchcock's Films* (1965), *Howard Hawks* (1968), *Ingmar Bergman* (1969), *Hollywood from Vietnam to Reagan* (1986), and *Sexual Politics and Narrative Film: Hollywood and Beyond* (1998).

INDEX

Abbott & Costello Meet Frankenstein (Barton), 243
Abercrombie, N., 397
abortion, 330, 451
Abyss, The (Cameron), 270
Ace Ventura: Pet Detective (Shadyac), 449, 450
action, 387; experiencing, 249; preference for, 288; rage and, 362
Action Comics, 17
Addison, Joseph, 25, 61n6, 63
adolescence: horror and, 297–98; Ur-myth of, 371
Adorno, Theodor W., 304
adrenaline, 134, 180, 321, 322, 380
adventure, 172; seeking, 280, 282, 284
Adventures of Tom Sawyer, The (Twain), 145, 150
Adversary, The (Hoffmann), 112
Aeneid, The (Virgil), 66n1
aesthetics, 1, 46, 49, 209, 246, 332, 338, 345, 388, 401, 406; filmic, 344; horror, 329; philosophical, 250; psychic/psychological, 265n9; semantics and, 242; transgender, 350
affect: discourse of, 332; feeling and, 248; need for, 280
African Americans. *See* Black people

After Dark Film Festival, 271
Agee, James, 386
agency, 439, 362, 442; cultural, 330; denying, 436; fan, 345; literary, 434
agoraphobia, 288
agreeableness, 286–87, 320; low, 286–87
AIDS crisis, 447
Aladdin, 69
Alcmeon, 37, 38
Alexander, Michelle, 411, 412
"Alexander's Feast" (Dryden), 77
Alice in Wonderland (Carroll), 443
Alien (Scott), 180, 195, 216, 270, 368, 380; appeal of, 374; Giger and, 341; Ripley (character) in, 214–15, 374, 379
Allan, Kathryn, 433, 446n1
Allen, Woody, 265n10
alt.horror, 337
Alton, David, 22
Aluja-Fabregat, A., 281
Ambitious Stepmother (Rowe), 44
Ambrosio (monk), 8, 9 (fig.)
AMC (television company), 271
American Academy of Motion Picture Arts, 270
American Horror Story (Ross), 423, 430n11
American Mercury, The (magazine), 17

American Philosophical Association, 177
American Psychiatric Association, 349
American Werewolf in London, The (Landis), 270, 342, 344
Amnesia: The Dark Descent (Frictional Games), 180
Amoako, Aida, 409
amygdala, 277, 278, 300
Anaconda (Llosa et al.), 242
Anderson, Gillian, 220
Anderson, Hephzibah, 10
Andrej Rubljov (Tarkovsky), 246
Ang, Ien, 369
Angel with Horns (Rossiter), 199
anger, 42, 173, 174, 323
angst, 260, 444
Angst-Lust, 257, 258
animation, 287, 288
Annabelle: Creation (Sandberg), 270
Anna Karenina (Tolstoy), 175
Antebellum (Monae), 427
Antichrist, 202, 203
Antichrist (von Trier), 318
anti-fandom, 392–406; audience research and, 406; critical pleasure and, 398–401; criticism and, 400; theories of, 393, 398, 399, 401–2, 404. *See also* fandom
anti-fans, 398–99, 400, 401; Indonesian, 399, 402
Antigone (Sophocles), 38
antihorror sentiment, 402, 405
Antitheatrical Prejudice, The (Barish), 5
Antonioni, Michelangelo, 252
Antonio's Revenge (Marton), 5
anxiety, 39, 86, 106, 153, 171, 173, 268, 269, 275, 294, 301, 317, 323, 444; cultural, 190; disorders, 288; experiencing, 290, 300; masculine, 449; political, 10; proneness to, 292, 302; short-term, 293; social, 156
Apelles, 43
Apocalypse, 409
Apollonian, 128
appeal of horror, 1, 3, 19, 25, 26, 35, 179, 180, 183, 268, 272, 318–20, 392; psychoanalytic explanation for, 190–94, 197, 204, 214; repression explanation for, 190–216
Apuleius, 119
Arabian tales, 69, 83
Arbery, Ahmaud, 416
Argento, Dario, 304, 330
Aristotle, 25, 26, 39, 46, 63, 133, 171, 322–23; katharsis and, 164n4; tragedy and, 35
Ark of the Covenant, 217
arousal: cognitive, 279; decreasing, 288; emotional, 279; male/female, 288; physiological, 160, 180, 278, 286, 290; psycho-physiological, 280, 286
art-horror, 273; appeal of, 166–70; consuming, 1, 2–3; generation of, 169; monster and, 243; natural horror and, 2
Asare, Janice Gassam, 430n8
Assault on Precinct 13 (Carpenter), 196, 213
Associated Writing Program (AWP), 433
Aster, Ari, 324
asylum, 433, 445; entrances into, 437–40; Gothic, 439
Atlanta (television series), 411, 412, 413
Atlantic, The (magazine), 409
audiences, 187, 219, 329, 343, 349, 370; cult, 384–87, 387–90; demographic profiles of, 368; horror film, 275, 367; interactions of, 335; as symbolic Other, 395–97; textuality and, 404
Audre's Revenge Film Collective, 415, 416, 422
Auerbach, Nina, 371
Augustine, 171
Autism Speaks, 436
avant-garde, 388, 389
Aveberry, Robert, 337
aversion, 44, 49, 50, 52, 163
avoidance: momentary, 296, 297; horror, 293–300
Ax Wound Film Festival, 416, 429

Babadook, The (Kent), 302, 324
Backdraft (Howard), 237n4
Bailey, Moya, 430n8

Baker, Rick, 341, 342, 344
Balázs, Bela, 246
Ballad of Black Tom, The (LaValle), 437
Ballon, B., 292, 293
Banderas, Antonio, 378
Barbauld, Anna Laetitia, 25, 57, 67, 122
Barclay, J. B., 372
Bard (Gray), 77
Barish, Jonas, 5, 6
Barker, Clive, 170n1, 374, 377, 379, 394, 403
Barker, Martin, 342, 343–44
Barker, Thomas, 394
Barner-Barry, Carol, 217, 219
Barnett, A., 293
Barthes, Roland, 193, 434
Basic Instinct (Verhoeven), 279
Bates, Kathy, 262, 270
Bates, Norman, 242, 449
Baudelaire, Charles, 248
Bauer, D. H., 294
Baulch, Emma, 393, 403, 404
BBFC. *See* British Board of Film Censors
Beast with Five Fingers, The (Florey), 198
Beast with Five Fingers, The (Harvey), 120, 121
Beetlejuice (Burton), 276, 318
Beetz, Zazie, 412
behavior, 255, 274–75, 278, 302; abnormal, 292; changes in, 268, 274; fictional, 185; functional, 184; hedonistic, 322; horror and, 23, 275; immoral, 6; media and, 185; moral, 7; motor, 275, 303; neural, 299; play, 184; social, 7; unpleasant, 285; verbal, 144; withdrawal, 299
belief: false, 148; persistence of, 217–20
Belle of Amherst, The (Dickinson), 146
Beloved (Morrison), 409, 420
Bender, Jack, 22
Bennett, Tony, 345
Beowulf, 271
Beranakdi dalam kubur (Suputra and Lingga), 398
Berenstein, Rhona, 238n7
Beresford, J., 113n19

Berlyne, D. E., 279
Berni, Francesco, 83, 113n15
Bethea, Dani, 28, 415, 418
Betz, Mark, 388, 389
Bianco, Anthony, 384, 385
Billings, Dwight B., 364n6
Birds, The (Hitchcock), 202, 203, 241–42
bisexuality, 192, 196, 324, 352, 378; repression of, 193, 195
Bitten, a Tragedy (Negra), 416, 429
Black Christmas (Clark), 213
Black community, 422, 425, 426
Black Gothic, 409, 410, 411
Black Lives Matter, 430n17
Black magic, 418
Black men, 416, 419, 425; gay, 422; portrayal of, 411
Black people, 412, 416, 419, 421, 424, 425, 427, 428–29; criminalization/disenfranchisement of, 414; horror media and, 429; queer, 422; representation of, 248
Black Power, 448
Black Swan (Aronofsky), 270
Blair, Linda, 128, 448
Blair Witch Project, The (Sánchez and Myrick), 186, 250, 274, 276, 302
blood, 4, 269, 371, 376; as stimuli, 300; term, 272
Blood Feast (Lewis), 265n16, 342
Bloom, Paul, 183–84, 364n5
Bluest Eye, The (Morrison), 420
"Body-Snatcher" (Stevenson), 121
Bogdanovich, Peter, 225
Bogeyman, 213
Boiardo, Matteo Maria, 113n14
Bold Dragon, The (Crayon), 90
Bolin, Göran, 332
Boogens, The (Conway), 283
"Book, The" (Irwin), 121
Borden, Lizzie, 440–41
Bordwell, David, 184
boredom susceptibility, 280, 289, 290, 322
Borges, Jorge Luis, 139
Bottin, Rob, 341, 344

Botting, Fred, 7, 8
"Boundary Violation and the Frankenstein Phenomenon" (Daly), 350
Bourdieu, Pierre, 386, 396
Bowring, Sir John, 113n25
Bracebridge Hall (Irving), 113n22
Bradley, Doug, 217
Braindead (Jackson), 243
Bram Stoker's Dracula (Coppola), 370, 374, 441
Brand, Neville, 209
Bresson, Robert, 246, 250
Bride of Frankenstein (Whale), homosexual parallels in, 365n7
Bringing Up Baby (Hawks), 195
British Board of Film Censors (BBFC), 21, 23
British Museum Catalogue, 113n19
Britton, Andrew, 207
Brood, The (Cronenberg), 212
Brooks, Kate, 342, 343–44
Brooks, Peter, 353
Brosnan, John, 221
Brottman, Mikal, 265n16
Brown, Mike, 408
Browning, Robert, 114n44, 117
Browning, Tod, 20
Brussels International Fantastic Film Festival, 271
brutality, 8, 19, 23, 241, 256, 408, 414, 431n17
Buchan, John, 121
Buchanan, Pat, 447
Buñuel, Luis, 198, 208
'Burbs, The (Dante), music for, 276
Burke, Edmund, 46, 61n5, 62n9, 75, 76, 246; obscurity and, 80; sublime and, 57–61, 115
Burstyn, Ellen, 128, 389, 454
Burton, Tim, 95, 318
Butler, Judith, 360
Byron, Lord, 375

CAA. *See* Cinema Advertising Association
Caan, James, 262
Cabinet of Dr. Caligari, The (Wiene), 200, 201
Caldwell, Christopher, 26, 119

Caligari, 201
"Call of Cthulhu, The" (Lovecraft), 435
Callot, Jacques, 108, 114n42
Candyman (DaCosta), 379, 415, 416, 417–18, 421, 424, 426, 427, 428–29; still from, 426 (fig.)
Cannibal Ferox (Lenzi), 273
Cannibal Holocaust (Deodato), 21, 273, 302, 319
cannibalism, 127, 203, 208
Cantor, Joanne, 186, 187, 274, 275, 290, 293, 294, 295, 296
Cape Fear (Scorsese), 243
capitalism, 190, 208, 404; human relations and, 194; patriarchal, 191, 210
Car, The (Silverstein), 202
"Care and Handling of Psycho, The" (press book), 227
Carpenter, John, 115, 214, 239, 276; films of, 212–13
Carrey, Jim, 449
Carrie (De Palma), 202
Carroll, Madeleine, 125
Carroll, Nöel, 27, 155, 161, 239, 273, 279, 345; art-horror and, 1, 6, 26, 166, 243; horror and, 154, 156, 257; morality and, 25; paradox of horror and, 2–3, 157
Carter, Chris, 220
cartoons, 209n7, 262, 278, 287
Cassius, 71
Castle of Otranto, The (Walpole), 7, 10, 69, 119–20, 271
catharsis theory, 35–38, 322–24
Cathy's Curse (Matalon), 202
Cat People, The (Lewton), 195, 204, 205, 215; sound of, 277
Cavell, Stanley, 245, 246
Cazotte, Jacques, 89, 113n21
Cecil, Lord David, 442–43
censorship, 20, 247, 252, 389
Chamber of Horrors, 371, 384
Chan, Elaine, 185
Chaney, Lon, Jr., 377
Changeling, The (Medak), 324, 340

chaos, 117; creating, 273; demons and, 128
chaos theory, 365n11
characters, 36, 37, 283; development of, 177; horror film, 204, 379; unpleasant, 256
Cherry, Brigid, 28, 331, 343, 366
Chevy-Chase, 59, 61n6
Chewbacca, 273
Cheyne, Ria, 446n1
child abuse, horror as, 20–23, 24
Childe Roland (Browning), 117
Children of the Corn (Kiersch), 318
Child's Play 3 (Bender), 22
chivalry, 79, 88, 102
Chory, R. M., 287
Christianity, 79, 211, 451
Christiansen, J. K., 287
Chucky (character), 22
Chung Kuo (Antonioni), 252
Church, Pamela, 341
Cicero, 41, 43
cinefantastique, 342
Cinefantastique (Sanjek), 344
Cinefex (magazine), 344
Cinema Advertising Association (CAA), 368, 382n12
cinema of visibility, 244
cinematic neurosis, 292, 293
cinema vomitif, 265n16
cinéSPEAK, 415, 429
civilization, 193, 203, 210, 357; repression/oppression and, 195
Clarendon, Lord, 43–44
Clasen, Matthias, 179, 287, 317, 319, 320; biocultural perspective of, 27, 28
class, 10, 226, 369, 403, 433; boundaries/erosion of, 6; cult audiences and, 384–87; horror and, 384–90
Claws (Ross), 430n11
Cleary, Sarah, 8, 21, 22, 23
Clockwork Orange, A (Kubrick), 21
Clover, Carol, 232, 252, 367, 368, 370, 373, 380; gender distress and, 449
Clytemnestra, murder of, 37
"Cock-Lane Ghost," 119

Code and Rating Administration, 244
cognitive strategies, 268, 278, 294, 295–96, 298
Cohen, Larry, 196, 199
Coleridge, Samuel, 8, 256
Collective Intelligence: Mankind's Emerging World in Cyberspace (Lévy), 335
Collingwood, R. G., 155
Collins, Nancy, 370
Collins, William, 68, 77, 82
colonialism, 194, 403, 432
colorism, 410, 421
comedy, 35, 89, 270; family, 203, 204; horror, 373; preference for, 288
comics: attack on, 15, 19; commentary on, 18 (fig.); constraints on, 15; crime, 17; depravity and, 19
Comics Code Authority (CCA), 19
Comics Magazine Association of America, 19
Commissaris Rex (television series), 294
Commissaris Roos (television series), 316n2
communication, 369, 435; computer-mediated, 334; genre play and, 436; internal, 334; methods of, 59; studies, 268
communism, 17, 196
compassion, 39, 41, 43, 44
competition theory, 26, 27, 166
composition, 80, 82, 89, 94
Comstock, Anthony, 13, 15
Comstock Law (1873), 13
Confessions (St. Augustine), 4
consciousness, 55, 254; collective, 210; racial, 430n5; transformation of, 357
Constantine I, 3–4
conversion theory, 26, 27, 35, 133
Coombes, Nattie, 12, 22
Coombes, Robert, 12, 22
Copelius, 109, 110, 111
coping: children and, 294–97; skills, 27, 186; strategies, 296–97, 298, 302; style, 285–86
Coppola, Giuseppe, 110, 111
Coraline (Selick), 318
Coriolanus, 51, 53
corruption: moral panic over, 13; physical/spiritual, 453; of youth, 13

Cosmopolitan (magazine), 367
counter-purposiveness, 51, 52, 54; anguish of, 50; foundation of, 49–50
Cowan, Douglas E., 27, 217, 291
Crabbe, G., 99
Craft, The (Fleming), 219
Crane, Jonathan Lake, 376
Crash (Cronenberg), 403
Craven, Wes, 21, 295, 304, 318, 324
Crawford, F. Marion, 117
Crayon, Geoffrey, 90, 113n22
"Creature Corner" message board, 338
Creed, Barbara, 449
Crenshaw, Kimberlé, 427
Crichton, Michael, 182
Crime and Punishment (Dostoyevsky), 142
Crip Time, 434–37, 441
"Crisis of Innocence" project, 17, 19
Crisp, Quentin, 215
criticism, 8, 395; academic, 368; anti-fandom and, 400
Critique of Judgment (Kant), 56
Cronenberg, David, 212, 330, 403
Crowther, Bosley, 386
cruelty, 40, 55, 239, 241, 242, 439
Cruickshank, George, 113n25
Crusoe, Robinson, 145
CSI: Crime Scene Investigation (television show), 318
Csikszentmihályi, Mihály, 322
Cthulhu, 434–37
Cueva, Edmund P., 3
cultural capital, 388, 396, 397, 402, 405
cultural studies, 393, 397, 405, 406; area studies and, 404; Euro-American, 403; inter-Asia, 404; internationalizing, 404; Southeast Asian, 401–4
culture, 55, 193, 211, 228, 304, 389; alternative, 388; Black, 410; celebrity, 403; colonized, 196; commercial, 13; disability, 435, 437–40; ethnic groups and, 194; fan, 329–40; high, 227; imaginative, 182; lowbrow, 386; male-dominated, 194, 212; mass, 376, 400; middle-class, 386; popular, 210, 337, 368–69, 442, 448, 449; products, 222; repressed, 192; Voodoo, 408; Western, 199, 200, 352
curiosity, 169, 245; interest and, 257; naive, 23
Curse of Frankenstein, The (Fisher), 367
Cushing, Peter, 375
Cymbeline, 71

DaCosta, Nia, 415, 416, 425, 426
Daily Mail, 22
Dallas (television series), 369
Daly, Mary, 350
Damien, Robert Francis, 61n1, 68
danger, 40, 53, 57, 58, 63, 64, 67, 94, 97, 117, 123, 125, 134, 136, 139, 140, 144, 187, 247, 253, 259, 277, 300, 368, 438; attractions of, 157; eliminating, 173; encountering, 179; enjoyment of, 283; fear and, 150n2; learning about, 182; mortal, 139; overcoming, 183; physical, 294, 299; psychological, 186; real, 27, 135, 163, 182, 185, 187, 255, 257, 261
Danse Macabre (King), 127, 452
Darabont, Frank, 184
Dark Side, The (Jankovich), 271, 344
Dark Star (Carpenter), 213
Darnton, Robert, 2
Davis, M. H., 282–83, 296
Dawn of the Dead (Romero), 127
Day of the Animals (Girdler), 202
daydreaming, 181, 282
death, 40, 58, 65, 217, 244, 269, 291; description of, 80
Death Scenes (Bougas), 266n16
Death Trap (Moxey), 209
Deigh, John, 177
de la Mare, Walter, 120, 121
de la Motte Fouqué, Friedrich, Baron, 88, 89, 98–99, 113n20, 113n25
Delicious Foods (Hannaham), 410
del Toro, Guillermo, 115, 435
DeMille Theater, Psycho and, 227
Demme, Jonathan, 155
Demon (Cohen), 126, 210, 216

demons, 452, 292
denial of pain theory, 26, 133, 159, 163
Denning, Michael, 13
Deodato, Ruggero, 21, 319
De Palma, Brian, 195
depravity, 5, 20; comic books and, 19; representations of, 7
Der Januskopf (Murnau), 199
Derdeyn, A. P., 293
"Der Majorat" (Hoffmann), 98, 107
Descent, The (Marshall), 241, 324
desire, 48, 160, 163; conflicting, 149; evaluation and, 161; moral, 51; pleasure and, 161, 162
De spectaculis (Tertullian), 3
destruction, 86, 242, 244, 279, 284
Deutsche Sagen (Grimms), 84, 113n15
devil, 101, 193, 213, 292; believing in, 204, 219
Devil in Silver, The (LaValle), 434, 437–40
Devil Rides Out, The (LaValle), 302
Devil's Elixir, The (Fisher), 90
Diabolique (Clouzot), 271
Diallo, Amadou, 438
Dickens, Charles, 10, 117, 182, 425
Dickinson, Emily, 146, 147, 152n14
Dickson, Andrew, 5
Dime Mystery Magazine, 15
dime novels, 10, 12–13, 14 (fig.), 15
direct horror: cinema of visibility and, 244; defining, 239–43; phenomenological approach to, 27, 239–64, 265n9; pleasure of, 257–59; violence and, 239
disability: engagement with, 440, 442, 445; exploiting, 433; horror and, 432–45, 446n1; as narrative device, 433; pain/exclusion/isolation and, 436; queerness and, 441; stereotypes of, 432, 433
disbelief, 135; suspension of, 147, 255–56
disgust, 67, 157, 268, 300, 317; fear and, 243; horror and, 154, 166, 243, 258, 297, 338; overcoming, 155; sensitivity to, 211, 272, 291; sexual, 211, 291
disinhibition, 280, 281, 322

Disneyland, 237n4, 237n5; *Psycho* and, 227–28, 229
Disney movies, 425
distress, 23, 40, 41, 42, 45n3, 97, 110, 133, 175, 176, 279, 283, 285, 288, 324, 325; experiencing, 287–88, 289; expressing, 367–68; gender, 449; handling, 187, 292–93, 321; personal, 284, 296, 297, 301; psychic, 2; real, 88; responses to, 321
Divinae institutiones (Lactantius), 3–4
Don Sylvia de Rosalva (Wieland), 112n13
Don't Look Now (Roeg), 324
doppelgänger, 199
Dostoyevsky, Fyodor, 142
"Double Admiral, The" (Metcalfe), 121
Douglas, Mary, 154
Downes, Meghan, 28, 392
Dozier, Rush W., Jr., 180
Dracula (Browning), 20, 204, 302, 375; release of, 371
Dracula's Daughter (Hillyer), 204
drag performance, 350, 449
Dreadful Pleasures (Twitchell), 367
Dreamland Theater, 434–37
dreams, 116, 137, 148, 181, 251, 357; nightmares and, 197–98
Dr. Frank 'n' Furter, 196
Dr. Jekyll and Mr. Hyde (Mamoulian), 270, 276
Drums Along the Mohawk (Ford), 194
Dubos, L'Abbe, 40, 59
Duchovny, David, 220
Dumbledore, Albus (character), 241
d'Unebourg, Comte, 113n32
Dungeons and Dragons (game), 23
Dutchess of Malfi, The (Webster), 5
dysphoria, 278, 279

Eaton, Marcia, 158
EC Comics, 19, 128
Edison, Thomas: film by, 20, 20 (fig.)
Edwards, E. D., 281
Eerie Stories (magazine), 15
Egan, Kate, 22
Eggar, Samantha, 212

Einstein, Albert, 121
Elkins, Patrick, 437
Elsie Venner (Holmes), 117
emotions, 40, 46, 59, 64, 194, 248, 258, 301, 320, 344, 357, 367; enjoyment of, 159, 163–64, 177; evaluative theory of, 159–60, 161; evoking, 161, 177, 268, 296; experiencing, 122, 126, 159, 182, 245, 257, 259, 260, 296; fiction and, 176, 177; knowledge and, 337; memories and, 175; positive, 177, 280; theory of, 160, 163; unpleasant, 157, 158, 159, 160, 164. *See also* fear; hate; negative emotions; passions; pity
empathy, 190, 257, 280, 282–85, 292, 297, 301; degree of, 283; enjoyment of, 284, 302; fantasy, 283; scale, 290; somatic, 261–64, 263 (fig.)
empirical research, 28, 164, 256, 343, 367; review of, 268–304
endings, happy, 149, 195, 283, 289, 296, 441
End of Days, The (Hyams), 245
Englund, Robert, 295
Enlightenment, 353, 364n4
"Entail, The" (Hoffmann). *See* "Der Majorat" (Hoffmann)
entertainment, 5, 15, 17, 40, 41, 43, 157, 225, 226, 268, 321, 367, 376, 386, 396, 399, 400; concept of, 197; escapist, 187; horror, 23–24, 183, 336; lower-class, 393; mass, 394; violent, 3, 4
"Episode of Cathedral History, An," (M. R. James), 121
Eriphyle (Alcmeon), 37
erotic, 261, 352, 378, 380, 444; preference for, 288; themes, 376
Erotic Neoprimitive International Genital Modification Association (ENIGMA), 365n8
E. T. A. Hoffmanns ausgewählte Schriften (Hitzig), 113n27
Etchison, D., 269–70
ethnic groups, 194n5, 196, 396
Ethnic Notions (Riggs), 419, 430n5

Euripides, 37
"Everything and Nothing" (Borges), 139
evil, 24, 211, 214, 256; horror and, 273; theological problem of, 222
Evil Dead, The (Raimi), 242, 243, 374
Evil Spirit, 92
excitation-transfer theory, 278, 325
excitement, 94, 96, 278, 279, 283, 325
Exorcist, The (Friedkin), 21, 22, 28, 128, 197, 202, 211, 213, 247, 270, 273, 279, 292, 342, 344; cinematic neurosis and, 293; LGBTQ+ community and, 447, 448; music of, 276; Regan MacNeil (character) in, 448, 449, 450–51, 452, 453, 454; watching, 448, 449, 451
experiences, 251, 280, 318, 361; cinematic, 247, 252; disabled, 432, 433; emotional, 247, 259; frightening, 247; gnostic/pathic moments of, 248; horror, 274, 321, 334; lived-body, 259–61; positive, 336; sensory, 264; sharing, 325–26; structured, 184; transsexual, 364n6; unpleasant, 159, 171, 253, 259, 317, 326
exploitation, 388, 389; dynamic of, 221; expression, 41, 43, 44, 63; facial, 278, 409; symbolism and, 221
expressionism, 156, 195, 200
Exterminating Angel, The (Buñuel), 198
Eye, The (Moreau and Palud), 340

fairy tales, 271, 377
"Fall of the House of Usher" (Poe), 208
family: all-male, 208; goodness of, 206; marital, 203; monstrous, 207, 209; patriarchal, 190; values, 357
fan biographies, 329–41
fandom, 163; critical, 399; doubled attention and, 343; expressions of, 332, 395; female, 331–32, 343, 369–70, 375; horror and, 329–46, 392–406; Indonesian, 395; male, 343, 344; knowledge space of, 335; long-term, 338, 339, 340; masculinized, 343, 344; nonfans and, 330, 334, 337, 338, 340, 345; notion of, 398; origin story of,

338–39; practices of, 368; privacy of, 372; self-accounts of, 334; snark, 398, 399; weird, 334. *See also* anti-fandom
Fangoria (Conrich), 344
Fantasticfest, 271
fantasy, 148, 197, 282, 369, 371; disabled, 432; preference for, 288; revenge, 380; scale, 283
fanzines, 369
Farber, Manny, 386–87
fascination, 240, 245, 377, 378; emotional, 258; obsession and, 333; sexual, 377
Fatal Attraction (Lyne), sound of, 277
Father of the Bride (Minelli), 203
Feagin, Susan, 157, 171, 177
fear, 39, 90, 115, 135, 137, 142, 143, 169, 217, 239, 246, 260, 323, 324, 444; causes of, 298–300; children and, 293, 294; cinematic, 123, 260; conditioning, 300, 301; coping with, 205; cosmic, 117; development of, 156, 222, 293–300; disciplining, 224–30, 232, 235–36; disgust and, 243, 300; elements of, 271; experiencing, 122, 255, 300; exploring, 220–22; horror and, 154, 155, 164, 166, 274, 298, 300, 317, 331; imaginary, 294; irrational, 255, 420–21; module, 298–99; pity and, 6, 35, 37, 171, 172, 175; pleasurable, 258, 259; quasi-, 134, 136, 140, 141, 142, 146; sexual, 156; social-related, 301; sources of, 296; stimulating, 156, 187, 293, 294, 295, 301; term, 272; uneasiness of, 64
Fearful Horror User, 320
femininity, 193, 372; othering, 387; social norms of, 192
feminism, 440, 448, 451; cultural, 364n1; pop, 214
Ferdinand Count Fathom (Smollett), 69
Ferrigno, Lou, 295
fiction, 134, 137, 250–51; experience of, 171; importance of, 147, 181; reality and, 187; romantic, 78, 87. *See also* horror fiction
fictional involvement, 282, 283
Fields, James T., 13

Fifty Shades of Grey (James), 398, 400
Film and Video Censorship in Modern Britain (Petley), 23
filmic world, 247, 249, 250, 251, 252, 257, 259; reality and, 255
films: accessibility of, 303; American/foreign, 388; auditory influence in, 276; behavioral response to, 274–75; cannibal, 273; exploitation, 274; Expressionist, 199; as fiction, 147; frightening, 290, 295; gangster, 197; high/low, 388; impressiveness of, 247–51; Indonesian, 393, 395, 402; interpretation of, 198; monster, 274, 377; nonhorror, 269, 278; occult, 370, 372, 373, 374; "revenge of Nature," 203; romantic, 288; supernatural, 270, 372, 373, 374; term, 272; underground, 389; unpleasant, 274; vampire, 372, 374, 375, 376, 377; war, 288. *See also* horror films; science fiction films; slasher films; *and individual film titles*
Financial Times, The, 367
Fincher, David, 244, 318
Finn, Huckleberry, 147
First Purge, The (McMurray), 426
Flaming Creatures (Smith), 389
Fleder, Gary, 318
Fleming, Andrew, 219
Flesh (Negra), 428
Florey, Robert, 200, 201
Fly, The (Cronenberg), 270, 330
Fly, The (Neumann), 198
Fly II, The (Walas), 270
folklore, 117, 182
Ford, John, 194, 208
Foucault, Michel, 434
Franjut, Georges, 198
Frankenstein, Victor, 350, 355–56
Frankenstein (Shelley), 345, 350, 353, 433
Frankenstein (Whale), 20, 21, 196, 204, 375; feminist interpretations of, 364n4; homosexual parallels in, 365n7; romance of, 89
Frankenstein monster, 28, 89, 196, 199, 200, 350, 351; flight of, 355; horror for, 353–54; power of, 354; versions of, 377

Freaks (Browning), 20
"Freddy vs. Jason" message forum, 338
Freedberg, David, 248–49, 251
Freeman, Morgan, 244
Freud, Sigmund, 190, 191, 198, 292
Freudian theses, 200–210
Freund, Karl, 200
Frictional Games, 180
Friday the 13th (Cunningham), 279, 319, 325, 373
Friedkin, William, 21, 128, 447
Friedman, Susan Hatters, 19
Friend, Michael, 237n3
Friend, Tad, 410
fright, 155, 272, 290; anticipatory, 257; enjoyment of, 269; generating, 304; stimulus for, 294–95; true, 255–57
Frightmare (Walker), 203
Frogs (McCowan), 202
Frye, Northrop, 434
Full Circle Community Center, 434, 436
Fury, The (De Palma), 202
Fuseli, Henry, 2

Gallup report, 219, 220
Gambino, Childish (Donald Glover), 408, 409–10, 411, 413, 414
Game, The (Fincher), 318
Garden of Eden (Irwin), 388, 389
Gauss, Carl Friedrich, 121
Gaut, Berys, 26, 153, 171
gay liberation, 190, 447, 448
Gay News, 352
gaze, 82, 158, 385, 437; female, 248, 366; introjective, 235; male, 380, 421; monster, 366; white, 416, 425, 429
Gebbie, Melinda, 443
Geiger, Moritz, 257, 258
gender, 226, 320, 362, 365n11, 403, 432; attribution, 361; coerciveness of, 356; cult audiences and, 384–87; definition, 353; distress, 449; horror and, 325, 384–90; monsters and, 448, 449; nonbinary, 319; play, 236; queer, 349; representations of, 380; transition between, 350. *See also* femininity; masculinity; queer/queerness
gender-bending, 449
gendered relations, 230, 360
gender-fluid, 319
genderfuck drag, 350
gender performativity, 349
gender socialization theory, 289
Genette, G., 399
genitals, 361; physical alteration of, 356
genre, 329, 434; cinematic, 288; cult, 287; expectations, 319; literature, 440; memories, 443; pleasures of, 432; texts, 339. *See also* comedy; horror genre; science fiction films; thrillers; Westerns
genre play, 434; communication and, 436
Gestalt therapy, 148
Get Out (Peele), 2, 270, 412, 413, 425, 427; metaphors from, 411
ghosts, 5, 68, 74, 80, 85, 97, 103, 105, 106, 107, 110, 119, 134, 213, 217, 218, 219, 244, 273, 400, 408, 409, 410, 414. *See also* supernatural
Ghost Seer, The (Schiller), 103, 104, 114n38
ghost stories, 90, 119, 120, 121
Ghost Story (Straub), 180
Ghostwatch (Manning), 293
Giger, H. R., 1, 341
Gilbert, Sandra, 364n4
Gilgamesh, 271
Gill, Mark, 367
Gilman, Charlotte Perkins, 117
Ginsberg, Allen, 389
Glanvill, Joseph, 90, 113n23
Gleason, Jackie, 129n1
Glover, Donald, 408, 409–10, 411; race and, 410; SNL and, 412
Glover, Stephen, 410
gnostic, described, 248
goblins, 80, 97
God Told Me To (Demon) (Cohen), 197, 202
"Golden Ass" (Apuleius), 119
Goodboy, A. K., 287

Gordon, Ruth, 270
gore, 2, 127, 269, 272, 332, 342, 439; boys/girls and, 297–98; enjoyment of, 297; gratuitous, 376; images of, 381; watchers, 284
Gore Zone (magazine), 343
Gorgo Medusa, 243
Gosling, J. C., 162
Gosson, Stephen, 5, 6
gothic, 272, 274, 408, 432, 440, 444; female, 370; novels, 3, 7–8, 10, 25, 70, 115, 410; Southern, 409, 410, 416; traditions, 408–9; tropes, 410, 411
Goya, Francisco, 1
Granger, Derek, 367
Gray, Dorian, 271
Gray, Jonathan, 77, 393, 401, 403, 405; anti-fans and, 398–99, 400, 402; audience/textuality and, 404; on hatred/dislike, 397–98
Great Depression, 15, 156
Green, Misha, 418
Green, Richard, 365n8
Green, Victor Hugo, 417, 430n3
"Green Tea" (le Fanu), 121
Greenwood, James, 10
Gremlins (Dante), 294
grief, 43, 159; bereavement and, 324; uneasiness of, 64
Grimm, Jacob Ludwig Carl, 85, 113n15
Grimm, Wilhelm Carl, 85, 113n15
Groom, Nick, 8, 10
grotesque, 97, 108, 176
"Guards, The" (Metcalfe), 120
Guillaumin, Colette, 365n10
Gulliver, 137, 151n6
Gulliver's Travels (Swift), 89, 139
Gumb, James "Buffalo Bill," 257, 449
Gwenn, Edmund, 205

Hagenaars, M. A., 274
Haig, Francesca, 393, 398, 399, 402
Hair (Forman), 207
Halberstam, Judith, 370
Haldane, John, 164

Hale, Sarah Josepha, 443
Hall, Ryan Chaloner Winton, 19
Hall, Stuart, 397
Halloween, 196, 204, 212–13, 214, 216, 373; music of, 276
hallucinations, 111, 251
Hamilton, Count Anthony, 83, 84, 87, 112n12
Hamilton, J. W., 292
Hamlet, Will, 149
Hamlet (Shakespeare), 81, 143; Hamlet (character) of, 68, 72–73, 74, 75
Hammer Productions, 202, 332, 367, 373, 375
Hammerstein, Oscar, 384
Handel, Georg Friedrich, 228
Hands of the Ripper (Sasdy), 202
Hanich, Julian, 27, 239
Hannaham, James, 410
Hannibal (television series), 242
Hard Times (Dickens), 182
Harlequin, 89
Harman, Sarah, 393, 398, 402; on anti-fandom communities, 400; critical fandom and, 399
Harrington, C. L., 398
Harris, Julie, 146, 147
Harrison, Sheri-Marie, 28, 293, 406, 415
Harvey, Matthea, 434, 442–45
Harvey, W. F., 120
hate, 28, 104, 135, 146, 193, 195, 351, 394, 400, 408, 450; racial, 429n2; textual, 397; violence and, 127
Haunting, The (Wise), 204, 375
Hawkins, Joan, 388
Hawks, Howard, 213
Hawthorne, Nathaniel, 121
Hays Code, 20, 21, 454
Heaven Can Wait (Beatty and Henry), 216
Hedgecock, Alan, 341
hedonism, 162, 165n20
Hellraiser (Barker), 217, 374, 379, 380
Helmick, A. L., 290
Henry: Portrait of a Serial Killer (McNaughton), 240, 247, 273
Hereditary (Aster), 324

Heritage of Horror, A (Pirie), 202
Herrmann, Bernard, 227, 276
Heryanto, Ariel, 404
heterosexuality, 200, 354, 357, 361
High Plains Drifter (Eastwood), 202, 203
Hikmat, 396
Hill, Annette, 253–54, 256
Hill, Joe, 182–83
Hills, Matt, 28, 224, 329, 392
Hills Have Eyes, The (Aja), 261
Hills Have Eyes, The (Craven), 197, 203, 208, 209
Hills Have Eyes II, The (Weisz), 246
Histoire de Fleur d'Épine (Hamilton), 87, 112n12
Histriomastix: The Player's Scourge, or Actor's Tragedy (Prynne), 6
Hitchcock, Alfred, 25, 122, 237, 323; emotional engineering by, 230; *Psycho* and, 224–26, 229–30; as sadistic master, 227; special policy and, 225. See also *Psycho*
Hitzig, J. E., 113n27, 113n29
Hocus Pocus (Ortega), 276, 318
Hoekstra, S. J., 290
Hoffman, Dustin, 262, 263 (fig.)
Hoffmann, E. T. A. (Ernest Theodore William Hoffmann): death of, 111–12; described, 90–91; diablerie and, 93; disposition of, 98; Dresden/Buonaparte and, 92–93; fancy of, 107, 108, 112; imagination of, 197; Indigenous artists and, 109; inspiration from, 111; justiciary of, 99; Keller and, 92–93; sensibility of, 94, 97; supernatural and, 78–112
Hoffner, C., 284, 295, 296, 297; analysis by, 303; limitations for, 302
Hohenheim, Aureole Philippe Theophrastus Bombastus von, 114n44
Hollywood, 197, 203, 211, 213, 229, 244, 386, 387, 390, 418, 454; horror films from, 393, 405; identification for, 388–89
Homan, Willy, 146, 147
Homans, Margaret, 364n4
Homer's Discord, 61
Homicidal (Castle), 202
homophobia, 195, 415, 422, 433, 434
homosexuality, 192, 196, 212, 248, 319, 422; horror and, 447–55
Hooper, Tobe, 21, 186, 206, 209, 319
Hopkins, Anthony, 270
Hopkinson, Nalo, 433
Horace, poetry and, 59
Horatio, 73, 74–75
horor asing, 405
horor dari luar, 405
Horowitz, Gad, 191
Horowitz, M., 292
horror: in antiquity, 1, 3–5, 88; biocultural explanation for, 179–87, 210–21; defining, 21, 242, 243, 272–75; in early modern period, 2, 5–7; empirical research into, 28, 164, 256, 268–304, 343, 367; enjoyment of, 1, 166, 268, 279, 281, 284, 285, 287–88, 293–300, 301, 302, 318–21, 323, 371, 435–36, 445; fear of, 255–57; graphic, 283, 289–90, 322; intensification of, 212, 242, 445; introduction to, 269–72; jump scares and, 276, 277, 321, 324, 325; in nineteenth century, 7, 10, 15, 20–23, 78–112, 182, 220, 228, 229, 350, 353, 354, 355, 362, 443; paradox of, 2–3, 154, 155, 156, 163–64, 393; watching, 28, 187, 190, 272, 274, 299, 301, 322, 323, 342; withholding, 244. See also appeal of horror; direct horror
horror-as-art, 329, 330, 332, 340, 344, 345
Horror Channel, 271
Horrorentertainment.com, 336
horror fiction, 27, 153, 156, 267, 168, 169, 179, 282; coping skills from, 185; female authorship/readership of, 370; impact of, 187; modern, 128, 182; role of, 185; supernatural, 183; writing, 272
horror films, 23, 154, 155, 156, 164, 197, 199, 202, 243, 256, 258, 296, 297, 339; American, 205, 210; apocalyptic, 203, 210; audiences for, 219; B-grade, 395; British, 220–21; cheapness of, 270; childhood and, 294, 298; classical, 200; cult learning and,

331; cultural status of, 448; distortions in, 377; dreams of, 198; enjoyment of, 7, 166, 171, 221, 239, 268, 272, 278–79, 281–86, 301, 366, 369, 374–75; European, 304; exposure to, 278, 291, 300–301; female viewers of, 230, 366, 368, 369, 370, 371, 373, 380; feminist, 195; Gothic, 375, 380, 381; gradual/continual, 262; Indonesian, 392–96, 397, 399, 401, 402, 404, 405; Japanese, 304, 393; Korean, 393, 405; lowbrow, 387; low-budget, 388; perception of, 301; propositions about, 196–97; quality, 374–75; reactionary, 210, 211; reform-era, 349, 394; religiously oriented, 221; reputation of, 269–70; response to, 278, 319; sexism of, 380; sociophobics of, 220–22; Southeast Asian, 393, 401–6; types of, 196, 302, 303, 370, 373; watching, 270–71, 278–79, 283, 287, 289, 290, 301, 322, 323, 324, 326, 334, 368, 370, 371, 372, 373, 376, 396, 450; Western culture and, 200
Horrorfind.com, 339
horror games, 180, 185, 287
horror genre, 179, 252, 273, 274, 368, 396, 397, 398, 433, 438; as communicative tool, 248; criticism of, 395; engagement with, 401; experiences of, 332; fans and, 329; feminine, 380–81; Gothic, 57; Indonesian, 393, 399, 400, 401, 405; making sense of, 346; narrative and, 166; pleasure in, 168; sex differences and, 288; studying, 319
horror media, 24, 298, 319, 329; Black people and, 429; enjoyment of, 24, 286, 287–88; men/women and, 287–92
horrormovies.com, 340
horror.net, 339
Horror of the Red Hook, The (Lovecraft), 437
horror paradox, 317
Horror People, The (Brosnan), 221
Horror Stories (magazine), 15
horror studies, 28, 271, 319, 329, 366
Hostel film franchise, 273

Hourani, N., 284
House of Frankenstein (Kenton), 243
House of 1000 Corpses (Hourani), 240, 246
Howard Center for Investigative Journalism, 417
Howl (Ginsberg), 389
Hoxter, Julian, 331
humanity, 4, 96, 167, 202, 208n1, 439; purpose of, 47
Hume, David, 25, 26, 46, 63, 159, 172; emotions and, 160; on tragedy, 39–44, 153
Hunger, The (Scott), 374
Huntu Jeruk Purut (Pagayo), 399

identity, 361, 404; cross-gender, 370; erotic, 380; fan, 332, 335, 336, 340; gendered, 360, 364n2, 380; monstrous, 352, 356; phallic, 215; romantic, 380; sexual, 156, 355; transgender, 351, 364n2, 365n6
ideology, 207, 369; alternative, 194, 196; patriarchal, 212
I Know What You Did Last Summer (Robinson), 290
illusion, 250; reality effect of, 249; thesis, 251
imagery, 63; animal-human, 444; horrifying, 243; phantoms of, 250; quality of, 251; sounds and, 251
imagination, 40, 41, 43, 46, 47, 63, 64, 73, 76, 82, 85, 94, 98, 108, 110, 140, 141, 142, 146–47, 149, 150, 181, 175, 182, 376, 381; distempered, 7–8, 10; fictional, 134, 145, 147; illusions of, 70; power of, 48, 49, 109; principles of, 138–39; romantic, 97
Imagine Festival, 271
immersion, 240, 253, 258, 259, 283; emotional, 239, 257; illusion and, 249
immorality, 3, 5, 8, 13, 15, 242, 244; disproportional, 241, 256; encouraging, 20; intentional, 241
Immoral Mr. Teas, The (Meyer), 389
incest, 4, 5, 7, 8, 212, 213, 291, 443
Incredible Hulk, The (television series), 295
Interpersonal Reactivity Index, 282–83

interpretation, 116, 198, 204, 272, 279, 365n6, 330, 335, 339, 344, 355, 370, 444; feminine, 381, 365n4; horror, 155–56; shared, 332
Interpreting Films (Steiger), 238n6
interventions, 119; narrative determinacy and, 246; psychiatric, 292; psychological, 292
Interview with the Vampire (Jordan), 374, 378; still from, 378 (fig.)
Invasion of the Body Snatchers (Kaufman), 292
Ionesco, Eugène, 209
Iphigenia (Euripides), 38
Irvine, Janice, 364n6
Irving, Washington, 113n22, 286
Irwin, Margaret, 8, 121
Isard, Carroll E., 181
Island of Lost Souls (Kenton), 195, 196, 201, 204
I Spit on Your Grave (Zarachi), 21
I Still Know What You Did Last Summer (Robinson), 290
It (King), 180, 270, 294
It (Muschetti), 270
It: Chapter 2 (Muschetti), 270
Italian, The (Radcliffe), 70, 271
It's Alive (Cohen), 197, 199, 202, 204, 212
I Walked with a Zombie (Tourneur), 204–5
I Was a Teenage Werewolf (Fowler, Jr.), 388

Jackson, E. A., 441
Jackson, Rosemary, 370
Jacobs, W. W., 117, 121
Jacobus, Mary, 364n4
Jahoda, Gustav, 219, 220
James, E. L., 398
James, Henry, 117, 121
James, M. R., 120
Jancovich, Mark, 28, 330, 370, 384
Jarman, Michelle, 438, 439
Jaws (Spielberg), 137, 211, 242, 262, 270, 274, 293; music of, 276
Jekyll, Dr., 199, 271
Jenkins, Henry, 335, 368, 377

Jesus, 195, 447, 449
"Jig-a-Boo" (Bethea), 418
Jim Crow, 408, 409, 411, 412
Jimmy Swaggart Show, The, 451
Johnson, J. A., 287, 292, 298
Johnson, Steve, 341
Johnston, D. D., 283–84
Jones, Bethan, 393, 399, 402
Jones, John Paul, 215
Jones, Oran "Juice," 412
Jones, Robert, 17
Jonson, Ben, 61n6
Julius Caesar, 149
Jurassic Park (Crichton), 182
justiciary, 99, 100, 101, 104, 106
juvenile delinquency, 17, 19, 22

Kael, Pauline, 256
Kaluuya, Daniel, 411–12
Kant, Immanuel, 56, 246
Kardit, H., 398, 399
Karenina, Anna, 175
Karloff, Boris, 196, 355, 377
Karras, Damian, 448, 449, 454
Kawin, B. F., 272
Keetley, Dawn, 12, 13
Kefauver, Estes, 17
Keller, Helen, 92, 93, 175
Kendrick, Walter, 371
Kermode, Mark, 21, 222, 330, 331, 332, 333, 334, 337, 343, 344
Kesey, Ken, 438–39
Kessler, R. C., 365n10
Kiersch, Fritz, 318
King, Stephen, 2, 25, 115, 127, 166, 180, 182, 183, 186, 270, 284, 435, 452
Kingdom of the Spiders (Cardos), 295
King Kong (Cooper and Schoedsack), 200, 204
Kino der Sichtbarkeit, 244
Kiss, The (Edison), 20; still from, 20 (fig.)
Kiss the Girls (Fleder), 318
Knapp, James A., 5
Knight, Arthur, 388

knowledge: advancement in, 79; emotion and, 337; forbidden, 169; literacy and, 333
Kolnai, Aurel, 253, 260
Konami, 281
Kracauer, Siegfried, 239, 246
Krafft-Ebing, Richard von, 17
Kraus, L. A., 296
Krueger, Freddy, 245, 273, 295, 330, 447–48
Kruuk, Hans, 182
Kryszynska, Tanya, 371
Kubrick, Stanley, 21, 253
Kuppers, Petra, 28, 432, 447
Kwaio, 217–18
Kyd, Thomas, 5

Lactantius, 3–4
Ladd, David, 202
La Guardia, Fiorello, 17
Lake Mungo (Anderson), 324
Lamb, Charles, 443, 444
Lamb, Mary, 443, 444
Lamour, Dorothy, 194
Language of Time, The (theater), 434–37
Laqueur, Thomas, 364n4
La règle du jeu (Renoir), 246
L'Arrivée d'un train en gare de La Ciotat (Lumière Brothers), 270
Last Action Hero (McTiernan), 265n10
Last House on the Left, The (Craven), 21, 304
Laughton, Charles, 377
LaValle, Victor, 434, 437–40, 445
Law of the Father, 361
Leatherface, 207, 208–9, 210
Le Belier (Hamilton), 112n12
Leben und Nachlass (Hoffmann), 113n27
Lecter, Hannibal, 242, 257
Le Diable amoureux (Cazotte), 113n21
Lee, Christopher, 375, 378
Lee, Jonny, 323, 324
Lee, Stan, 19
le Fanu, Sheridan, 121
Le Lord Impromptu (Cazotte), 113n21

L'Enfant prodigue (Voltaire), 114n41
Leopard Man, The (Tourneur), 205
lesbianism, 212, 363–64n1, 390, 400; transsexuality and, 351, 352, 358, 364n1. *See also* sexuality
Lesbian Resource Center, 352
Les Milles et un fadaises (Cazotte), 113n21
Les Quatres Facardins (Hamilton), 112n12
Lessing, Gotthold Ephraim, 56
Leszcz, M., 292, 293
Lev, Peter, 389
Levine, Lawrence, 228, 229
Levine, Ted, 257, 284, 302, 303
Levy, Babe, 262, 263 (fig.)
Lévy, Pierre, 335
Lewis, David, 152n16, 163
Lewis, Herschell Gordon, 342
Lewis, Matthew, 7–8, 10, 25, 271
Lewton, Val, 204, 205
LGBTQ+ community, horror consumption by, 447
Lil Nas X, 422, 423, 423 (fig.)
Lingga, F., 398
Lissek, S., 282
literature: Hellenistic, 119; horror, 282, 370; Nordic, 271; supernatural horror, 118; of transgression, 7; Victorian, 271; weird, 118. *See also* horror fiction
Litle, P., 281
Little House on the Prairie (Wilder), 186
Little Marvin, 427
Living Dead movies, 202, 203, 204, 208, 210, 213, 216, 275, 342, 374
Lloyd, Danny, 253
Loman, Willy, 134, 136, 137, 145
Long, Long Trailer, The (Minnelli), 203
Longhurst, B. J., 397
Looking for Mr. Goodbar (Brooks), 215
Lorde, Audre, 422
Los Angeles Review of Books, 408
Lost Boys, The (Schumacher), 374
Lost Girls (Moore and Gebbie), 443
Lost World: Jurassic Park, The (Spielberg), 245

Louis XV, 61n1
Lovecraft, H. P., 25, 127, 417; horror and, 436–37; racism/misogyny of, 435; weird tales and, 115
Lovecraft Country (television series), 417–18, 420, 421, 424, 428; screen capture from, 418 (fig.)
Luce, William, 146
Lugosi, Bela, 201, 204, 371, 378
Lumière Brothers, 270
Luvaas, B., 397
Lynch, T., 281
lynchings, 408, 417, 419, 425, 429n2
Lyons, William, 161, 165n17

macabre, 115–16, 119, 176
Macartney, Frances, 113n33
Macbeth, 68, 71, 72, 75, 80
MacNeil, Chris, 454
Macwheeble, Baillie, 98, 113n36
madness, 4, 410, 437, 439, 444, 445; cosmic, 435; Dionysian, 128; romantic, 435
Making a Monster: Jesse Pomeroy, the Boy Murderer of 1870s Boston (Keetley), 12
Mamoulian, Ruben, 276
Mandingo (Fleischer), 208
Manitou, The (Girdler), 196
Mann, Anthony, 199
Man of the West (Mann), 199, 208
Manson, Charles, 452
Maplecroft (Priest), 434, 440–42
Marathon Man (Schlesinger), 262, 264; still from, 263 (fig.)
March, Frederic, 270
Marcuse, Herbert, 191
Mark of the Vampire (Browning), 238n7
Marriott, J., 273
Martin, G. Neil, 27, 268, 366
Martin, Trayvon, 408
Martins, N., 281
Marton, John, 5
martyrdom, 44, 112, 173, 417, 420, 449
Marx, Karl, 190, 191, 194
Marxism, 190, 191, 194, 195

"Mary Had a Little Lamb" (Hale), 443
masculinity, 193; cultural codes of, 334; martyred, 449; social norms of, 192; white, 438. *See also* sexuality
masochism, benign, 317
materiality, 27, 354; language and, 360; storytelling, 445
Mathai, J., 292
Mathias, Thomas James, 8
Maturin, Charles, 7
Mayer, Arthur, 385–86, 389; horror cycle and, 387–88
McCambridge, Mercedes, 450
McCarty, John, 342
McDonald, Anne, 435, 436
McKenna, Wendy, 365n10
McQueen, Latanya, 416
Mechanic Accents: Dime Novels and Working-Class Culture in America (Denning), 13
Mechanical Turk study, 287
Medak, Peter, 324
Medea (Timomachus), 43
media, 186, 230; access to, 23, 303; behavior and, 185; cathartic effects of, 322; consuming, 402, 406; interactive, 185; violent, 280. *See also* horror media
media studies, 268, 393, 403, 404
Medved, Michael, 221
Meet Me in St. Louis (Minnelli), 204, 213
melancholy, 40, 41, 44, 64, 73, 95–96, 98, 100, 108; cultivating, 174–75
melody, 35, 36, 37, 414
memory, 251; development of, 191; emotions and, 175
Men, Women, and Chain Saws (Clover), 368
Mendelssohn, Moses, 56
mental health, 91, 94, 98, 163, 415, 439, 442; horror films and, 292–93
Merope, 38
message boards, 334, 338, 339
Metcalfe, John, 120
Metropolis (Lang), 199
Meyer, Stephenie, 398

micronarratives, 329, 333, 336, 340, 341; before/after, 334
middle class, horror and, 384–90
Midsommar (Aster), 324
Miles, "Paper Boi," 412, 413
Mill, John Stuart, 162, 165n20
Millar, Becky, 323, 324
Miller, Jason, 448
Millie, Julian, 393, 403, 404
Milton, John, 60, 61n2, 68, 75, 77; Death and, 58, 80; Hell and, 64; image of, 76; Paradise and, 64
Mineka, Susan, 182, 299
Mineo, Sal, 454
Miner, Steve, 319
Mirakle, Dr., 201, 202
Miramax, 367
misery, 36, 51, 67, 408, 417
Misery (Reiner), 262, 448
misogynoir, 420, 430n8
Mitchell, W. J. T., 230, 249–50, 266n36
Moby-Dick (Melville), 199
Modleski, Tanya, 368
Moers, Ellen, 370
Monáe, Janelle, 427
Money, John, 365n8
"Montero (Call Me by Your Name)" (Lil Nas X), 423, 423 (fig.)
Monk, The (Lewis), 8, 9 (fig.), 10, 25, 271
Monk: A Romance, The (Lewis), 7–8
Monkey's Paw, The (Jacobs), 117
monster cards, collecting, 377
monsters, 97, 119, 139, 167, 170, 183, 190–96, 201, 202, 209, 240, 241–42, 252, 255, 256; animal/human, 436; Black girl, 420; child, 203; composite, 207; conception of, 205, 213; curiosity about, 154; defining, 207, 298, 352; designation of, 211; as evil, 211; existence of, 168; fascination with, 243–45, 377, 379; fear of, 155; as form of insanity, 169; gender and, 448, 449; hostile, 180; human qualities of, 209; imaginary/fictional, 294; normality and, 198, 199; as Other, 195; popular form of, 376; presentation of, 251; real, 128, 196, 324, 449; repression and, 211; rooting for, 455; sexual threat from, 195; supernatural, 377; threat from, 198. *See also* Frankenstein monster
Monsters and Mad Scientists (Tudor), 220–21
monstrosity, 209, 244, 255, 353, 454
monstrous-feminine, 449
Moon Is Blue, The (Preminger), 389
Moore, Alan, 434
moral duty, 53, 55
morality, 10, 20, 25, 47, 48, 52, 53, 54, 55, 67, 76, 108, 128; centrality of, 401; public, 3, 403, 406
moral law, 51, 52, 53, 54
moral nature, maintaining, 50–51
moral outrage, active participation and, 247
moral panic, 6, 7–8, 10, 13, 17, 20, 22; experiencing, 23; gaming and, 31n80; public morality and, 3; video nasties and, 22
Moreau, David, 318
Morgante Maggiore, an Epic Romance (Pulci), 113n14
Morreall, John, 27, 158, 171
Morrison, Toni, 409, 420
Mosaku, Wunmi, 421
Motion Picture Association of America, rating system of, 21, 247–48
Motion Picture Herald, The (industry trade paper), 225
Motion Picture Producers and Distributors of America, 20
Mouchette (Bresson), 246
moving-images, 248, 256; graphic, 262; power of, 246; sound and, 250
Mr. Rock and Roll (Dubin), 388
Mulder, Fox, 220
Mulvey, Laura, 246
Murai, Hiro, 410
murders, 7, 8, 12, 17, 40, 67, 111, 117, 149, 209, 243, 323, 355, 425, 438, 444; celebrated, 440, 441; child, 22, 37
Murders in the Rue Morgue (Florey), 200, 201, 202, 204

Murnau, F. W., 196, 199
Musaeus, Johann Karl August, 87, 113n18, 113n19
music, horror film, 276–77
musicals, 269, 270
mutilation, 22, 242, 244, 249, 253, 269, 277, 351, 441
My Darling Clementine (Ford), 208
Myers, Michael, 273, 340
Myrick, Daniel, 186
Mysteries of Udolpho, The (Radcliffe), 70, 271
mystery, 134; cosmic, 116; preference for, 288
Myth of Harm: Horror, Censorship, and the Child, The (Cleary), 8
Mythologies (Barthes), 193
Mythos, 435, 437

Nanda, Serena, 365n8
Napier, Charles, 257
Napoleon Bonaparte, 93
narratives, 118, 154, 437, 438, 442, 445; fan-cultural, 345; fictional, 80, 252; horror, 166–70, 180, 319, 425, 427, 439; LGBTQ+, 422; madhouse, 440; pop-cultural, 334; sacred, 217
National Rifle Association, 410
Nature, 65, 70, 74, 85, 117, 353; chaos/blackness and, 362; hegemonic oppression of, 357; queer relationship to, 354; revenge of, 202, 203
necrophilia, 350
negative affect, 282, 283, 285–86
negative emotions, 2, 26, 27, 64, 157, 160, 161, 162–63, 164, 173, 186, 271, 283, 288, 290, 320, 323; basic, 172; elicitation of, 179; enjoyment of, 158–59, 172, 176, 177; intense, 181–82; purge of, 15
Negra, Monika Estrella, 28, 415, 419, 429
Negro Motorist Green Book, The (Green), 417, 429–30n3
Neill, Alex, 158–59, 160
Nesseth, Nina, 27, 28, 317
neuropsychology, 300–301, 302
neuroticism, 191, 286, 298

"New Audiences, New Textualities: Anti-Fans and Non-Fans" (Gray), 397
New Black Gothic, 408, 411, 412, 413, 414, 415
"New Black Gothic" (Harrison), 408
Newman, Kim, 186
Newson, Elisabeth, 22–23
New Yorker, 410
New York Times, 385–86
Nicholson, Jack, 370, 382n28
Nicolai, Cristophe Friedrich, 114n45
Nicomachus, 43
Nightbreed (Barker), 240, 241, 379
Nightmare, The (Fuseli), 2
Nightmare Fuel (Nesseth), 317
Nightmare on Elm Street, A (Craven), 283, 287, 293, 295, 373, 379–80
nightmares, 185, 186, 210, 452; absurdity and, 209; children and, 294; dreams and, 197–98
Nightmares (Sargent), 287
Night of Horror International Film Festival, A, 271
Night of the Lepus (Claxton), 202
Night of the Living Dead (Romero), 202, 203, 204, 208, 213, 216, 342, 374; anxiety from, 275
"Night Pieces After the Manner of Callot," (Hoffmann), 109
Night Shift (King), 166
Nights of Horror, 389
Nixon, Richard M., 216
Nope (Peele), 428
normality, 162, 167, 200–201, 453; defining, 207; threats to, 198, 199
Norton, Rictor, 7
Nosferatu (Murnau), 196, 199
Nyberg, Amy Kiste, 19

Oberon, 84
Oberon (Wieland), 112n13
O'Brien, Margaret, 204, 291
Obscene Publications Act (1959), 22, 24
obscenity, 13, 21, 211n1, 389
obscurity, 58, 59–61, 76, 81

occultism, 220, 274
Ode on the Passions (Collins), 77
Ode to Indifference, 93
Oedipus, 37, 133
Oedipus (Sophocles), 37
Oedipus tyrannus (Sophocles), 272
Offenbach, Jacques, 228
Offensive Films (Brottman), 265n16
Of Lamb (Harvey and Porter), 434, 442–45
"Of Tragedy" (Hume), 172
Öhman, Arne, 182, 299
Oldfield, Mike, 276
Oldman, Gary, 378
Oliver, Mary Beth, 383n52
Olivier, Laurence, 262, 263 (fig.)
O'Malley, William, 454
Omdahl, Becky, 186
Omen, The (Donner), 200, 202, 203, 210, 211, 270, 273, 279; annihilation and, 207; music of, 276; nature of, 205, 206; remake of, 285
One Flew over the Cuckoo's Nest (Kesey), 438–39
O'Neill, Nance, 441
On Photography (Sontag), 252
ontological distance, 249, 253, 255, 262, 265n9; minding, 245–47; phenomenological distance and, 251
On Writing: A Memoir of the Craft (King), 127
oppression, 192, 195; patriarchal, 214, 381
Orestes, 37
Orlando Innamorato (Berni), 113n14
Ortega, Kenny, 318
Othello (Shakespeare character), 42, 146
Other, 190–96, 215, 330, 345, 432; autonomy/right to exist of, 193; as monster, 195
Our Vampires, Ourselves (Auerbach), 371
Ovid, 44
Owens, Stephanie, 184

pagans, 6, 218–19
Pagayo, Kaya, 399
pain, 42, 58, 67, 103, 116, 159, 161, 173, 259, 264, 269; denial of, 26; feeling, 44; graphic moving-images of, 262; movement of, 40; over-balance of, 69; resistance to, 232; suffering, 41; theory, 26
Pall Mall Gazette, The, 12
Palmer, Keke, 428
Palud, Xavier, 318
Pandora, 212
panic, 288, 293; terror and, 216. *See also* moral panic
Paracelsus, 110
Paradox of Horror, The (Carroll), 25
Paramount, 385
Paramount World (trade publication), 230
paranormal, 220, 274, 320
Parasite Murders, The (Cronenberg), 212
parody, 83, 194, 201, 209, 399, 412; enjoyment of, 287; splatter, 243
Parsec Productions, 180
passions, 40, 42–43, 44, 58, 64, 69, 153, 269; clearness/obscurity and, 59–61; freedom from, 88; melancholy, 41; mutual, 43. *See also* emotions; pity
pathic, described, 248
pathology, 292, 356
patriarchy, 191, 210, 370, 371, 409, 422, 451, 453
Pechter, William, 237n2
Peckinpah, Sam, 242
Peele, Jordan, 2, 408, 411, 427
Pellechia, M., 285–86
Penn, Arthur, 242
penny bloods/penny horribles, 10
penny dreadfuls, 11 (fig.), 12–13; crime and, 12; phenomenon of, 10; successors to, 15
Penseroso (Milton), 68
People Under the Stairs, The (Craven), 318
perception, 175; audience, 395; emotional, 276; enjoyment and, 303; feeling/affect and, 248; Freudian, 212; real things of, 251; vividness of, 94, 95
Perkins, Anthony, 225
Persian tales, 83
Persik, Dewi, 398
personality traits, 280, 285–87
Personal Views (Wood), 204

Peter Pan, 443
Peter Schlemil (von Chamisso), 90, 113n25
Petley, Julian, 23
Pfeiffer, Michelle, 370
Phantom of the Opera (Lubin), 270, 271
phantoms, 61, 97, 249, 253, 254, 271
phenomenological distance, 259, 260, 261, 264; breakdown of, 258; ontological distance and, 251; reducing, 251–55; term, 265n9
phenomenon, 40, 116, 157; behavioral, 278; moral, 53–54; paranormal, 320; supernatural, 120
Philosophy of Horror, The (Carroll), 1, 3
phobias, 262–63; blood-injection-injury, 300; heart rates and, 300; horror films and, 299
Pierson, Michele, 341, 342
Pinedo, Isabel, 342–43, 344
Pinhead, 217, 379, 383n57
Pinker, Steven, 317
Pink Flamingos (Waters), 157
Pinky (Kazan), 389
Pitt, Brad, 244
pity, 39, 64, 68, 71, 73, 75, 87, 133, 137, 146, 147, 151, 173; extreme, 174–75; fear and, 6, 35, 37, 46, 171, 172, 175; feeling, 35, 174, 257. *See also* emotions; passions
Plaza Theatre, 230
Pleasence, Donald, 213, 214
pleasure, 40, 43, 49, 63, 64, 68, 116, 160, 174, 246, 386; achieving, 47; critical, 397–401; desire and, 161, 162; erasure, 442–45; evaluations and, 162; feminine, 232; horror and, 257–59, 345, 392; moral, 51, 53; narrative, 168; paradoxical, 317; real, 68, 345; source of, 49, 67–68, 168; textual, 393; tragic, 37
Pleasures of Horror, The (Hills), 28, 329
Pliny, 43
plot, 36, 177; movements, 167; structure, 166–67, 168
Pocong ngesot (Nuala), 398
Poe, Edgar Allan, 7, 119, 120, 199, 208
Poetics (Aristotle), 35, 133

poetry, 40, 59, 60, 61, 64, 65, 79, 94, 110, 181; comiheroic, 84; Eastern, 83; hexameter, 35; impact of, 44; Italian, 83; soul of, 77
politics, 36, 241; identity, 445
Poltergeist (Hooper), 186, 274
Polygnotus, 36
Pomeroy, Jesse, 12, 13, 22
Pompey, 52, 71
popularity, 15, 17, 87, 156, 202, 243, 271, 373; achieving, 181; disreputability and, 197
Popular Tales of the Germans (Beddoes), 87
pornography, 389, 398, 405; horror, 395, 399; soft, 395
Porter, Amy Jean, 434; *Of Lamb* and, 442–45
Portman, Natalie, 270
Portrait of Charles Lamb, A (Cecil), 442–43
Pose (Ross), 423, 430n11
possession, 74, 92, 219, 331, 413; demoniac, 121, 182, 196, 202n3, 220, 452; forms of, 194
Possession of Joel Delaney, The (Hussein), 196, 202
posttraumatic stress disorder (PTSD), 288, 321
Power of Images, The (Freedberg), 248–49
Powers, A. S., 282
Prayer for Indifference, A (Macartney), 113n33
Predator (McTiernan), 379
prefiguration, 47, 48, 50, 51, 52, 54
prejudice, 104; racial, 430n3, 430n5, 430n8
Presumed Innocent (Pakula), 279
Price, David, 202
Price, Vincent, 375
Priest, Cherie, 434, 440–42, 445
Prince, Stephen, 242–43, 244
Printing Hate series, 417
Prometheus, 111
Prophecy (Frankenheimer), 196
Prynne, William, 6–7
PsychInfo, 272
Psycho (Hitchcock), 27, 197, 202, 203, 204, 205, 208, 213, 224–26, 263, 273, 302, 433, 237–238n5; audiences of, 229–30, 231 (fig.), 232, 233 (fig.), 235–36, 235 (fig.);

care/handling of, 229; music of, 276; promotional trailers for, 227; as shocker, 225; shower scene in, 256; stills from, 234 (fig.)
psychoanalysis, 340–41, 344
psychoanalytic theory, 190, 191, 192
psychology, 137, 145, 186, 222, 271, 298, 339, 376, 433; clinical, 268; horror and, 186, 274, 304; horror film, 268
psychopathy, 154, 157, 281, 285, 449
psychophysiological changes, 279, 280
psychotherapy, 148, 268
psychoticism, 203, 298
PT (computer game), 281
PTSD. *See* posttraumatic stress disorder
Pulci, Luigi, 84, 113n14
Pulp Fiction (Tarantino), 243
pulp magazines, 15, 17
Puritans, 193, 213
Purple Rose of Cairo, The (Allen), 265n10
purposiveness, 48, 54; amoral, 51; foundation of, 49–50; moral, 47, 50, 51, 52, 53, 55; natural, 53, 55; prefiguration of, 50

Quarterly Review, The, 12
Queer Nation, 350
queer/queerness, 357, 422, 440, 477, 449, 451, 454, 455; community, 351–52; disability and, 441; horror and, 28; term, 352, 364n2. *See also* sexuality

race, 369, 403, 432; citizenship and, 411; horror and, 408–14; performative nature of, 410
Race with the Devil (Starrett), 196, 202
racism, 409, 415, 417, 424, 433, 434, 437
Radcliffe, Ann, 7, 25, 57, 70, 120, 271
Radford, Colin, 175
Radway, Janice, 375, 376, 380, 442
"Raft, The" (King), 180
Raiders of the Lost Ark (Spielberg), 295
"Rain, The" (Jones), 412
Raskolnikov, 142, 143
Rathbone, Basil, 199

rating system, 247–48, 252
ratiocination, 167, 168, 169–70, 170n1
rationality, 116, 333, 401
Ravena Nightmare Film Festival, 271
"Rawhead Rex" (Barker), 170n1
Raw Meat (Sherman), 197, 202, 203, 208
Raymond, Janice, 350
reactionary wing, 210–16
realism, 254, 343, 388, 433, 437
reality, 65, 136, 137, 147, 176, 253, 297; beliefs in, 250; discourse and, 402; fiction and, 187; filmic world and, 255; monsters and, 324; representing, 249; violence in, 247
"Recluse, A" (de la Mare), 120, 121
"Recovery, The" (Hoffmann), 112
Redbone (Gambino), 411
Reeve, Clara, 7
Reflexions critiques sur la poesie et sur la peinture (Dubos), 61n5
Reilly, S., 294
Relations militaires de la bataille de Waterloo (Schoeberl), 113n31
religion, 8, 58, 78, 79, 108, 394; fear and, 217, 218; horror and, 27, 217–22; morality and, 403, 404, 406; powerlessness of, 222; role of, 406; superstition and, 116; terror and, 218
Renaissance, 5, 6
Renoir, Jean, 246, 250
representation, 64, 65, 139; acts of, 249; horror, 330–31; perception of, 249; politics of, 248
repression, 190–96, 196–210, 211; concept of, 193; patriarchal, 381; restoration of, 195; surplus, 191. *See also* psychoanalysis
Repression (Horowitz), 191
Repulsion (Polanski), 202
Requiem for a Dream (Aronofsky), 339
Reservoir Dogs (Tarantino), 242, 269
Resident Evil: Final Chapter (Anderson), 270, 281
response: affective/fearful, 337; automatic, 136; behavioral, 268
Revonsuo, Antti, 185
Reynaud, E., 286

rhetoric, 6–7, 37, 59, 252
Rialto cinema, 384, 385, 389, 390; audiences at, 386, 387
Rice, Anne, 370
Richard III (Shakespeare), 54, 68, 199
Riggs, Marlon, 419
rituals, 116, 232, 452; birth, 357; morning, 451; pagan, 3; religious, 116; Satanic, 23
Robinson, J. A., 293
Robitaille, Daniel, 427
Rocky (Avildsen), 216
Rocky Horror Picture Show, The, 196. *See also* Dr. Frank 'n' Furter
Roeg, Nicolas, 324
Roelofs, K., 274
Rojo Sangre, 271
romance, 79, 88, 89, 288; Gothic, 68, 69
Romantic intensity, 334, 336, 339, 345
Romanticism, 78, 362, 375
Rome, Open City (Rossellini), 389, 390
Romero, George, 127, 210, 213, 342. *See also Night of the Living Dead*
Rosa, Salvator, 62n11
Roscoe, Will, 365n8
Rose, Louisa, 195
Rose, Mark, 434
Rosemary's Baby (Polanski), 202, 203, 204, 270, 452
Rosenbaum, Jonathan, 213
Ross, Angelica, 423, 430n11
Rossellini, Roberto, 389
Rossiter, A. P., 199
Rousseau, Jean Jacques, 246
Rubin, Gayle, 365n10
Rubin, H. S., 363n1
Rue Morgue (magazine), 271
Russo, Vito, 355, 365n7

Sabotage (Hitchcock), 125–26
Sacred Terror: Religion and Horror on the Silver Screen (Cowan), 27, 217
sadism, 19, 387–88, 390
sadness, 173, 175, 285, 323; expressing, 174
Saducismus Triumphatis (Glanvill), 113n23

safety, 64, 245–47, 323
Salisbury, Mark, 341
Salomonson, K., 283
Sánchez, Eduardo, 186
"Sandman, The" (Hoffmann), 78, 109
Sandvoss, C., 398
San Francisco Women's Building, 351
Saputra, A., 398
Satan, 6, 13, 60, 92, 451
Satanism, 202, 221
Saturday Night Live (SNL), 409, 411, 412
Savini, Tom, 255, 344
Saw (Wan), 273, 302
Saw II (Bousman), 261
Sawyer, Mary, 443
Sawyer, Tom, 134, 145, 146, 149, 150
Scanners (Cronenberg), 344
scares, 336–37, 338, 339, 340, 341; jump, 276, 277, 321, 324, 325
Schaefer, Eric, 388
Schalk, Sami, 446n1
Schaub, Mirjam, 244
Schein. See illusion
Schiller, Johann Christoph Friedrich von, 25, 46, 57, 103, 104, 114n38; Theory of Tragedy and, 56
Schizo (Walker), 202
Schmitz, Hermann, 259
Schoeberl, F., 113n31
Schoole of Abuse, The (Gosson), 6
Schroeder, Barbet, 318
Schwarzenegger, Arnold, 265n10
science fiction films, 15, 269, 270, 273, 341, 373, 374; disabled, 432; feminist, 433; horror and, 205; McCarthyite, 211; preference for, 288; SFX and, 342
Scorpio Rising (Anger), 389
Scott, Ridley, 180
Scott, Sir Walter, 25, 78, 112n11, 113n22, 113n27
Scream (Craven), 274, 290, 367
Scream (magazine), 271
Screambox, 271
Screamfest, 271

screaming, 224, 272, 324
Screaming Mad George, 344
Screen (magazine), 191
Scruton, David, 222
Scully, Dana, 220
Searchers, The (Ford), Ethan/Scar in, 199
Seattle Bisexual Women's Network (SBWN), 352
Sebaldus Nothanker (Nicolai), 114n45
Sedgwick, Eve Kosofsky, 454–55
Seduction of the Innocent: The Influence of Comic Books on Today's Youth (Wertham), 15, 17, 19
self-consciousness, 138, 322
self-image, 173, 174
self-protection, 248, 300
self-reporting, 186, 303
Selick, Henry, 318
Senate Subcommittee on Juvenile Delinquency, 17
sensation seeking, 279, 280–82, 285, 289, 298, 301; degree of, 283; high, 282, 321, 322; horror and, 268, 280
Sensation-Seeking Scale, 321, 322
Seraphina, Baronness, 106, 107
Serial Mom (Waters), 450
Seven (Fincher), 244, 245, 262
7 Capital Sins (De Filippo et al.), 388
Seventh Victim, The (Robson), 204, 205
sex, 19, 322, 389; horror and, 325; impact of, 20; perversion, 17; political economy of, 365n10; scenes, 291
sex differences, 282, 287–92, 301; horror film, 288, 290, 291–92; horror genre and, 288, 291–92
sexism, 373, 380, 433
sex reassignment, 354
sexuality, 192, 212, 378; Black, 194; explicit, 389; expression of, 193; female, 195, 212, 215; horror films and, 325; perversion of, 208; repression of, 193, 204–5; working-class, 194. *See also* lesbianism; masculinity; queer/queerness; transgender
SFX. *See* special effects

Shadow of a Doubt (Hitchcock), 204
Shakespeare, William, 5, 42, 70, 71, 72, 73, 75, 76, 77, 81, 82, 199. See also *Hamlet*; *Othello*; *Richard III*; *Titus Andronicus*
shame, 4, 42, 43, 362, 449
shape-shifting, 442
Shapiro, Judith, 365n8
Sheldon, Paul, 262
Shelley, Mary, 7, 349, 350, 353, 354, 355, 443; literary techniques of, 362
Shepard, Matthew, 447
Sherman, Gary, 202
Shining, The (King), 2, 253, 256, 340
Shivers (Cronenberg), 212
Shoberl, M., 93
Shudder (streaming service), 271, 272, 448
shudder pulps, 15, 17
Shudder Pulps: A History of the Weird Menace of Magazines of the 1930s (Jones), 17
Sierra On-line, 372
Silence of the Lambs, The (Demme), 155, 256–57, 273, 302, 368, 374; Academy Award for, 270; as mainstream film, 370
Simpsons, The (television show), 398
Sing, Unburied, Sing (Ward), 408, 413, 414
Single White Female (Schroeder), 318
"Sintram and His Followers" (la Motte Fouqué), 88
Sisters (De Palma), 195, 210, 216
Sitges International Fantastic Film Festival, 271
Sixth Sense, The (Shyamalan), 270
Skal, David J., 371
Sketch-Book, The (Irving), 113n22
slasher, term, 272
slasher films, 154, 236, 273, 274, 291, 375–76; male/female victims of, 373; watching, 297
Sleepaway Camp (Hiltzik), 450
sleep disturbances, 187, 274, 290, 291, 293, 294
Slender: The Eight Pages (Parsec Productions), 180
slime, 133, 134, 135, 377; depiction of, 137; fear of, 140, 142, 143, 144, 145, 147; make-believe about, 144

Slotkin, Joel Elliot, 5, 6
Smith, Dick, 341, 344
Smollett, Jurnee, 69, 421
snakes, 128, 295, 296, 301
Snelson, Tim, 28, 384
Snider, Cynthia, 409
SNL. See *Saturday Night Live*
snuggle theory, 324
Sobchack, Vivian, 261, 263, 264
social distinction, 330, 396
social forces, 410–11
Social Horror User, 320
social interactions, 182, 186, 326
socialization, 217, 289, 367, 371, 372
social roles, 193, 332, 400
Society (Yuzna), 344
Society for the Suppression of Vice, 13
Son of Frankenstein (Whale), 199, 200
Sontag, Susan, 252
Sophocles, 37
sorrow, 41, 42, 43, 64, 153, 160, 269, 324, 381
sounds, 275–78; moving-images and, 250, 251
Southeby, William, 112n13
Southgate, Jeannette, 218
"Space" (Buchan), 121
Spanish Inquisition, 195
Spanish Tragedy, The (Kyd), 5
Sparks, G. G., 275, 279, 281, 285, 293, 295, 296
special effects (SFX), 244, 254–55, 379; approaches to, 341–42; craftsmanship for, 341–46; doubled attention and, 342–43; gory, 376; horror and, 342; realism and, 343; science fiction and, 342; stills/images of, 344
spectacles, 2, 3, 4, 35, 36, 39, 44, 111, 158, 200–201, 224, 229; arousal by, 37; of spectatorship, 230; ungodly, 5–7
Spectator, The (periodical), 61n6, 63
Spectre Barber, The (Musaeus), 88
specters. See ghosts
Spicy Mystery Stories (magazine), 15; cover of, 16 (fig.)
spiders, 273, 295, 296, 301, 453; fear of, 299–300

Spielberg, Steven, 262
Spirek, M. M., 279, 296
spirits. See ghosts
Sprigg, Christopher St. John, 25–26, 119
Spring-Heeled Jack, 10
Squirm (Lieberman), 202, 203
SR. See startle reflex
"Sredni Vashtar," totem-worship and, 121
Stacey, Jackie, 368
Stagecoach (Ford), 197
stage-witches, 72
Stalin, Josef, 387
Stand, The (King), 180
St. Anthony, 61
startle reflex (SR), 277, 278, 302
Star Wars (Lucas), 216, 273
St. Augustine, 4
Steele, Barbara, 212
Steen, Francis, 184, 185
Stefano, Joseph, 224
Steiger, Janet, 238n6
stereotypes, 28, 120, 402, 405, 419; disability, 432; fan, 336; female, 374, 380; gay, 201; Indonesian, 393, 396
Stevenson, Robert Louis, 7, 121, 199
Stewart, Jimmy, 237n5
Stiff, J., 281, 289
stimuli, 172, 186; exposure to, 294, 296; fear-related, 299, 300–301, 302; horror-related, 269, 301, 303; negative, 280; nonauditory, 304; phobic, 299; realistic, 269; signal, 277; symbolic, 268, 302; threatening, 300, 302
Stins, J. F., 274
Stoker, Bram, 7, 370, 374, 383n41, 441
Stoller, Robert, 365n8
Stone, B., 221, 272–73
storytelling, 245, 271, 273, 436, 445
Strange, Glenn, 243
Strange Tales of Mystery and Terror (magazine), 15
Straub, Peter, 179, 180, 182
Straus, Erwin, 248, 266n19
Stryker, Susan, 28, 349

St. Sebastian, 205
Studies in the Fantastic (journal), 415
subjectivity, 354, 361; legitimate, 360; rational, 334; transgendered, 356
sublime, 57–58, 61, 70, 76, 115
suffering, 44, 65, 159, 408; desire for, 49
Suharto, President, 393, 403
suicide, 2, 10, 12, 204, 351, 352
Summerscale, Kate, 12
Sumpah pocong (Suryadi), 398
Superman, 17, 136, 137, 145, 146
supernatural, 27, 71, 80, 82, 83, 85, 88, 89, 104, 116, 120, 269, 273, 274; appearances, 81; beings, 72, 79, 81; forces, 180; manipulative, 221; works of, 78, 119. *See also* ghosts
Supernatural Horror in Literature (Lovecraft), 115, 127
Supernatural Horror User, 320
superstition, 72, 78, 84, 87, 220; nature of, 219; religion and, 116; science and, 121
surrealists/surrealism, 198, 200, 330, 434, 437, 443, 445
survival horror games, 180
Suryadi, A., 398
suspense, 123, 124, 278, 376; terror and, 125
Suster keramas (Kardit), 398, 399
Swaggart, Jimmy, 451–52
SyFy, 271
symbolism, 1, 221, 360
Szell, Dr., 262, 263 (fig.)
Szwarc, Jeannot, 211

taboos, 24, 27, 128, 217, 323, 332, 388; exploring, 190; sexual-social, 212, 213; societal, 427
Take One (Rosenbaum), 213
Tale of Two Cities, A (Dickens), 425
Tales from the Crypt, 19
Tales of a Traveller (Irving), 113n22
Tales of Count Hamilton, 83
Tamborini, Ronald C., 281, 283, 289
Tan, Ed, 246
Tarantino, Quentin, 243

Tarkovsky, Andrej, 246, 250
"Taste for Slaughter: Stephen Gosson, *Titus Andronicus,* and the Appeal of Evil, A" (Slotkin), 5
Taylor, Shelley, 326
Television Without Pity (online forum), 400
Teller, John, 177
Tempest, Dryden alteration of, 77
temptations, 5, 7, 61, 92, 99, 217, 453
Terminator 2: Judgment Day (Cameron), 374
terror, 39, 43, 64, 70, 80, 103, 123, 124, 135, 153, 171, 173, 232, 240, 257, 269; artificial, 69; creeping, 180; horror and, 25, 75, 273; images of, 381; magazines, 17; mystic, 104; night, 453; panic and, 216; suspense, 125; tales of, 82; temptation and, 217; term, 272; transformation of, 67; women spectators of, 230. *See also* fear; panic; scares
terroraustralis.net, 339, 340
Terror Tales (magazine), 15
Tertullian, 3, 4
Texas Chainsaw Massacre, The (Hooper), 21, 196, 203, 205, 210, 213, 216, 319; annihilation and, 207; "double" motif in, 208; enjoyment of, 275; nature of, 206
Textual Poachers (Jenkins), 377
Thalia (periodical), 114n38
Them (Little Marvin), 427
Them (Moreau and Palud), 318
Them! (Douglas), 205
Thing, The (Carpenter), 200, 205, 214, 344, 374
"This Is America" (Glover), 409, 410, 412, 413, 414; dancing/violence and, 411
Thompson, Kristin, 184
Thomson, 77
threats, 185; real, 251–55; resolution/elimination of, 278. *See also* fear
threat simulation theory, 185
Thrill (television channel), 271
thrillers, 244, 247, 272, 373, 374; historico-medical, 442; political, 241; preference for, 288; psychological, 269; watching, 284, 297
Thrilling Mystery (magazine), 15

thrill seeking, 280, 282, 322
Times Square, 384, 385, 386, 387, 389, 390
Timomachus, 43
Titterton, Nancy Evans, 17
Titus Andronicus (Shakespeare), 5–6
"To a Woman Passing By" (Baudelaire), 248
Todd, Sweeney, 10
Topsy and Bopsy, 418, 419, 420
Torrance, Danny, 253
torture, 5, 12–13, 65, 68, 417; depicted, 284; horror and, 301
totem-worship, 121
Tourneur, Jacques, 215
tragedy, 35–38, 39–44, 46–55, 57, 89, 120, 381; accessories of, 37; action and, 36; consumption of, 25; distress and, 40; paradox of, 153, 161, 164, 171; passion and, 42; pleasure from, 25, 171, 172; plot for, 38, 44, 133; purgative function of, 46; purposiveness and, 51; revenge, 6; speeches in, 36–37; terror and, 68, 160
transgender, 319, 352, 449; cultural fascination with, 351; practices, 363n1; term, 364n2. *See also* sexuality
Transgender Nation, 346, 350
transgender rage, 353, 356, 359–60
transgression, 217, 219, 451; literature of, 7; social, 8
transphobia, 365n6, 415, 422
transsexuality, 349–62, 364n2, 365n6; critical history of, 365n8; embodiment of, 351, 354; experiences of, 349; female, 363n1; gay/lesbian representations of, 351; labeling, 356; monsters and, 350, 352, 353; suffering and, 362. *See also* bisexuality
Traps for the Young (Comstock), 15
trauma, 186, 206, 321, 394, 409; Black, 420, 427, 428; facing, 416; physical, 426; term, 272. *See also* posttraumatic stress disorder
traumatic brain injury, 436, 437
Trimble, S., 28, 447

truths: fictional, 137, 138, 151n5; make-believe, 137–43, 146–47, 151n5, 151n6, 151n12, 152n14
Tudor, Andrew, 220–21
Tulloch, John, 377
Turley, J. M., 293
Turner, Kathleen, 450
Turn of the Screw, The (James), 117
Turpin, Dick, 10
Tussaud, Madame, 371
Tuttle, Lisa, 370
Twilight (Condon), snark fandom and, 399
Twitchell, James, 367, 371
Tyndarides (Nicomachus), 43

Ulysses Wounded (Sophocles), 38
uncanny, 332; term, 272
"Uncanny, The" (Freud), 78
uncanny stories, 26, 119, 120, 121, 445
Undine (la Motte Fouqué), 113n20
Uninvited, The (Allen), 204
United 93 (Greenglass), 285
Universal International Studio, 227
Universal Studios, 225, 228, 229, 238n5
Universal Studios Theme Park, 227, 237n4
unreality, 116, 296, 297, 336
upcominghorrormovies.com, 339
Upper Berth, The (Crawford), 117
Urban, Thomas, 364n6
Us (Peele), 427
US Production Code, 244, 389
US Senate, 15, 17

Valentino, Rudolph, 375
Valli, Katja, 185
vampires, 119, 121, 375, 377, 381; fascination for, 378; identification with, 380; lesbian, 433; as polygamous/bisexual, 378
Vandamme, Dominique Rene, 93, 113n32
van Heeren, Katinka, 349
Variety (magazine), 367
Varney the Vampire, 10
Varney the Vampire; or, the Feast of Blood (penny dreadful), cover of, 11 (fig.)

venereal disease (VD), 8, 212
Venus (Apelles), 43
verbal information, 295, 296
V-girls, 384
victims, 303; female, 289, 290
Videodrome (Carpenter), 283
video games, violent, 281, 286, 287
video nasties, controversy around, 20–23
Video Recordings Act (VRA), 22, 23
Video Violence and the Protection of Children (Newson), 22–23, 24
violence, 1, 6, 13, 19, 24, 42–43, 53, 64, 86, 176, 230, 240, 243–44, 254, 286, 287; abstract, 362; acts of, 241, 242, 244, 245, 261; Black-on-Black, 410; confronted with results of, 256–57; cutting, 288; cycle of, 417; depicting, 158; enjoyment of, 279, 285; exposure to, 280; fascination for, 243–45; gendering, 361; Gothic, 409; graphic, 280, 285, 289, 293, 319; gratuitous, 376; horror and, 239, 242, 243; inspiring, 21; institutional, 438; interpersonal, 294; men and, 289; monsters and, 245; monstrosity and, 255; police, 438; pop, 127; pornography of, 221; presentation of, 23, 244, 251; scenes of, 2, 15; sex differences and, 297; sexual, 376; state, 428; against women, 373–74
Virgil, 66n1
Virgil's Fame, 61
vision: pathic quality of, 250; patriarchal structures of, 366; primacy of, 264
Vistima, Filisa, 351, 352
vividness, 250, 251, 256
Volksmärchen (Museaus), 87, 113n19
Voltaire, 83, 114n41
von Chamisso, Adalbert, 113n25
von R., Baron Roderick, 98, 100, 104, 106, 107
von Trier, Lars, 318
voodoo, 205, 408
Voorhees, Jason, 273
Vorderer, Peter, 184–85. See also *Friday the 13th (Cunningham)*
VRA. See Video Recordings Act

Wagon Master (Ford), 208
Walker, Pete, 203
Walking Dead (Darabont), 184
Walpole, Horace, 7, 10, 119–20
Walton, Kendall, 133, 158–59, 171, 175, 177n4; emotions and, 26, 160
Ward, Jesmyn, 408, 409, 410, 411, 414
War on Drugs, 411, 413
Warren, Virginia, 178n6
Wasserman, Lew, 225
Watergate, 216, 448
Waters, John, 157, 450
Waverley (Scott), 113n36
Weaver, James B., 221, 367, 371
Weaver, Sigourney, 374
Webster, John, 5
Weigl, Charles E., 333, 334
weird tales, 115, 118
Weird Tales (magazine), 15, 435
werewolves, 119, 128, 244, 439
Wertham, Fredric, 18; comic books and, 15, 19; juvenile delinquency and, 17
West, Kanye, 411
Westboro Baptist Church, 447
Westcliffe Address, 238n5
Westerns, 193, 198, 199, 208n3, 269, 270
Wexman, Virginia Wright, 221
Whale, James, 20, 21, 196, 199, 355, 365n7
"What Is a Monster? (According to Frankenstein)" (Brooks), 353
When a Stranger Calls (West), 286, 339
When the Reckoning Comes (McQueen), 416
White Devil, The (Webster), 5
white supremacy, 351, 410, 411, 413, 416, 422, 429n2
Why Horror Seduces (Clasen), 179
Wiccans, 217
Wieland, Christophe Martin, 83, 112n13
Wiesing, Lambert, 249
Wild Bunch, The (Peckinpah), 203
Wilinsky, Barbara, 388
Wilkes, Annie, 262, 448
Williams, John, 276
Williams, Linda, 27, 224, 366, 368, 381

Williams, Tony, 216
Wilner, N., 292
Wilson, B. J., 280, 294, 296
Wilson, Karina, 20
Winston, Stan, 341
WisCon, 433
witchcraft, 72, 113n23
witches, 73, 76
Wittig, Monique, 365n10
Wizard of Oz, The (Baum), 443
Wolf (Nichols), 370
Wolf Demon, The, 14 (fig.)
women: Black, 416, 418, 421, 427, 428, 429, 429n1; horror and, 366–81; trans, 422. *See also* transgender
Woo, John, 242
Wood, Robin, 27, 35, 190
Woollacott, Janet, 345

Wordsworth, William, 97, 443
Wyman, Dan, 276

X-Files, The (television show), 220, 294

Yaxley, Noel, 20, 21
Yellow Wall Paper, The (Gilman), 117
Youngstrom, Eric, 181
Young Thug, 413

Zarachi, Meir, 21
Zeuxis, 36
Ziemke, D., 275
Zillmann, Dolf, 221, 279, 282, 288, 289, 324, 325, 367, 371; excitation transfer theory and, 278
zombies, 183–84
Zuckerman, Marvin, 280, 281, 322